T0330303

Electricity Markets

Electricity Markets

Pricing, Structures and Economics

Chris Harris

John Wiley & Sons, Ltd

Other Wiley Editorial Offices

John Wiley & Sons Inc., 111 River Street, Hoboken, NJ 07030, USA

Jossey-Bass, 989 Market Street, San Francisco, CA 94103-1741, USA

Wiley-VCH Verlag GmbH, Boschstr. 12, D-69469 Weinheim, Germany

John Wiley & Sons Australia Ltd, 42 McDougall Street, Milton, Queensland 4064, Australia

John Wiley & Sons (Asia) Pte Ltd, 2 Clementi Loop #02-01, Jin Xing Distripark, Singapore 129809

John Wiley & Sons Canada Ltd, 22 Worcester Road, Etobicoke, Ontario, Canada M9W 1L1

Wiley also publishes its books in a variety of electronic formats. Some content that appears in print may not
be available in electronic books.

British Library Cataloguing in Publication Data

A catalogue record for this book is available from the British Library

ISBN-13 978-0-470-01158-4 (HB)
ISBN-10 0-470-01158-0 (HB)

Typeset in 10/12pt Times by Integra Software Services Pvt. Ltd, Pondicherry, India
Printed and bound in Great Britain by Antony Rowe Ltd, Chippenham, Wiltshire
This book is printed on acid-free paper responsibly manufactured from sustainable forestry in which at least
two trees are planted for each one used for paper production.

To Sally, for patience, and everything else

Contents

Preface

I have had much assistance from my friends and colleagues, who are experts in the many fields covered in this book. I have consistently found a disapproval at the inevitable over-simplification of their disciplines, coupled with an appreciation of accessible explanations of other disciplines. Whilst I believe that I am justified in my obstinacy in maintaining this compromise in order to pursue the multidisciplinary approach that I believe to be essential in constructing a market design, I do apologise for the compromises to depth and purity, and request that the reader views the descriptions as introductory and explanative, rather than definitive, and invite her and him, when requiring further knowledge, to read the excellent textbooks available, some of which are included in the references.

December 2005

Acknowledgements

Warm thanks to Lynton Mogridge, Ian Rodgers, Alan Joslin, Frank Prashad, Danny Hann, John Putney, Haydyn Brown, John Millar, Richard Hotchkiss, John McCaul, Anita Longley, Tony Dicicco, Jonathan Aitken and Adrian Winnett for assistance with enquiries about facts and methods, and comments and useful hints.

I would like to take this opportunity to express my thanks for inspiration and support over the last few years to David Bramley and Hélyette Geman.

Finally, I would like to express particular thanks to Derek Bunn for support in embarking on this project and for such useful guidance. Any views expressed in this book are mine alone.

Introduction

In the last part of the twentieth century, electricity had moved backstage after its supporting role in the 'white heat[1] of the technological revolution'. With the technology apparently solved and delivered, the Electricity Age[2] was a forgotten age, surpassed by the Information Age.

It has been suggested that the age we are entering now is the age of Natural Capital, in which resource depletion and environmental impact become key drivers. Given that electricity delivers almost all energy that is not muscle power or used directly by combustion of organic and fossil material, electricity may again play centre stage. The Electricity Supply Industry (ESI) market solutions must match the big picture policy solutions and contend with complex and interactive issues.

Buchanan, in 'the Power of the Machine', published in 1991, stated that 'One way or other, it is probable that the comparative stability of power technology enjoyed in the present century cannot be maintained much longer', citing the energy crisis which begins to loom, and the insufficiency of pace of technological change (particularly in this case in relation to nuclear fusion power and renewable technology). Indeed it is a common, if not universal, view, that in the interval between the fossil world and the new renewable (and possibly nuclear) world, the economics of providing fossil fuel fired generation at a similar price to today, will not stack up in the 21st century in the circumstances of source depletion and increasing costs of environmental impact abatement. The question is the extent to which the industry can bridge this gap without substantial and sustained state intervention in consumption.

Perhaps the most universal change in the ESI in the ten years either side of the millennium, has been, and will be, the increase in market orientation, caused by the general increase in market activity in other commodities and products, the pressure on the industry, and the organisational response of the ESI in facing new challenges. Whilst the overall paradigm to which the ESI is evolving, in response to policy change is broadly similar in almost all countries, the pace and stages of development differ widely, and ideal ESI structures are highly dependent on local factors such as political ideology, climate, and indigenous energy endowment.

This book is about markets, and how the structure of markets and behaviour of participants can and do cause prices to respond to drivers such as consumer needs, energy endowment, capabilities of physical installations, regulatory impositions and policy objectives. It is intended to inform, rather than promote, attack, defend or apologise for markets, but undoubtedly any textbook is coloured by the background and opinion of the author. I believe in the *potential* of competitive markets to deliver an industry performance that is aligned to energy policy with a socially determined trade-off between costs/disbenefits and

---

[1] Speech by Harold Wilson, Prime Minister of the UK. Labour Party Conference. 1 Oct 1963.

[2] Wilson (1994) defines the period to be 1875 to 1945, preceded by the copper age, bronze age, iron age, coal age, steam age (coal, iron and steam), and oil age, and followed by the atomic age. Brennan *et al.* define the beginning of the electricity age as being 1882, the date of the opening of the Pearl Street power station in the USA.

benefits. I believe that the challenge, albeit a great challenge, is essentially a technical one, which can be achieved by better communication to stakeholders of the interdependencies of issues and better design of the whole marketplace of which electricity is a part.

There are three reasons for this belief in the potential of competitive markets to deliver a policy solution;

Firstly, markets are efficient vehicles for clearing quantitative information concerning preferences of diverse and interdependent issues for a multitude of participants, at least at the margin. Where whole markets fail, it is largely because the market structure is such that specific important information, such as impact of production on society, is absent, and therefore the market is incomplete. The challenge is to make the market complete enough to capture all of the important signals (such as environmental costs) without making it too complicated to understand and administer. Whilst the inter-relationship between produced goods (electricity) and simultaneously produced bads (e.g. emissions) has added a whole new layer of complexity, the gradual increase in commoditisation is making these tractable. In addition to this we will show that the increasing use of traded options can overcome some of the greatest problems of market incompleteness for single commodities, namely the capture of preferences not just for certain conditions at the margin, but for a variety of scenarios, with different probabilities.

Secondly, through the profit motive, markets create the incentive for efficiency, particularly if the market signals (which become manifest as prices) are clear, strong, stable, and visible in the long term. Where market power occasionally causes 'excess' rent to some participants, it is largely because the long term signals have been ineffective and therefore that a market scarcity could not be addressed by timely new entrance. When this occurs, it is a result of poor market structure, poor communication, unstable policy, or poor regulation.

These two reasons are well known, and much discussed. It is the third reason that has excited me so much during my years in the industry. A proper functioning market, with efficient signals, has a third benefit, and that is to reward innovation, and specifically 'routinised[3] innovation' at a day-to-day operational level. This is, in my view, a feature that is more important in the ESI than in any other industry, and the reason arises from the physical nature of electricity.

This naturally begs three questions;

(i)   What is special about electricity in a market context?
(ii) Can unbridled competitive free markets work for electricity?
(iii) If not, how can the commercial arrangements for electricity be organised and regulated, and how can market-like techniques be used to realise some of the potential of competitive free markets?

On the first question, the delivery of electricity is instantaneous and at long distance, and the nature of electricity causes the microeconomics of power generation to change at an extraordinary frequency – around 48 times per day. The result is that the 'command and control' method of planning and management is inefficient, because it cannot effectively capture the complex interdependencies and does not effectively address the constant stream of opportunities that arise. This can only be captured by the response of operators who are sufficiently capable and empowered to contend with a set of external value signals and

---

[3] See Baumol in 'the Free Market Innovation Machine' for an exposition of this.

a set of internal capabilities and constraints. These value judgements require the signals such as energy price, capacity price, and emission cost, to be monetised and efficiently communicated so that the net of cost and revenue can be quickly maximised.

On the second question, experience to date is mixed, and we are forced to remind ourselves that 'For all their power and vitality, markets are only tools. They make a good servant but a bad master and a worse religion'.[4] The benefits of markets have been tempered by the problems of local market power, and of constructing markets that are simple enough to use and complex enough to satisfy complex requirements. An efficient market will efficiently deliver a performance that optimises cost for a set of policy signals. If the signals are absent or mispriced, or if market intervention creates alternative or unstable signals then the market will efficiently deliver the wrong solution. Proper market design can harness the capability of markets whilst reining in the potential for excess and abuse. A dilemma in designing markets is that the potential for abuse increases with the detail, accuracy, sensitivity and complexity of market signals. It is an act of faith to assume that contrary to the mantra of 'greed is good',[5] that participants act in a manner that is mindful of their civic responsibilities. To quote Ormerod,[6] 'The enlightened pursuit of self-interest is seen as the driving force of a successful economy, but in the context of a shared view of what constitutes reasonable behaviour'. I follow Rousseau in believing that we must assume that people are essentially good, but only behave badly when the institutional arrangements force or encourage them to do so. Indeed, whilst moral and social responsibility is often forgotten in making the assumptions of the behaviour of economic man in guiding the Invisible Hand[7] of Adam Smith,[8] it is important to remember that the theoretical heritage of economics runs through with such responsibility. Hence to understand the impact of responsibility in economics, we do not need to add it in, we just need to stop taking it out.

Whilst fully efficient markets work efficiently, it is sensible to question whether, given the effective policy signals and an overall framework, a partly inefficient market can deliver part of the objective, or whether it is actually worse than no market at all. In particular, is the issue of market power in such a complex market as electricity both too large to ignore and too intractable to solve? This question is much discussed, and in reality is too big a question to answer in one bite. In any one circumstance, it must be answered in a well defined context (for example, socio-political environment, indigenous energy mix, patterns of power usage, institutional framework of government and private enterprise, legacy organisational structures and arrangements for the flow of money in return for electricity and services, and absolute and relative levels of poverty).

Whilst the competitive markets have generally worked, they have not worked perfectly, and the California example has shown that the transition towards market structure can go badly wrong if regulatory and political intervention is incompatible with the market operation. Nevertheless there have been more successes and fewer failures than might be indicated by observing the media. Market failures make better media headlines than market successes. So 'world gripped by power blackout'[9] is a better candidate for attention than

---

[4] Hawken *et al.* (1999) in 'Natural Capitalism'.

[5] This phrase was caricaturised by the character Gordon Gekko in the film 'Wall Street', but the origins were in a speech by Ivan Boesky (who later went to prison), in which he said to an audience at University of California in Berkeley 'greed is healthy', to rapturous applause.

[6] Ormerod (1994).

[7] Smith (1776). The view that markets operate to the optimisation of the common good, as if guided by an invisible hand.

[8] Adam Smith is regarded as the founding father of economics in its modern sense.

[9] BBC online 15 August 2003. Referring to the blackout in New York.

'electricity delivered cheaply and effectively again' Similarly 'disaster from new regulation' makes better headlines than 'service remains poor and price high due to absence of reform'.

The development of electricity markets has been very much on the back of the development of modern commodity markets, which themselves have been underpinned by the development of modern financial markets. Though they appear to have been with us for as long as we remember, it was only in 1971 that the collapse of the Bretton Woods[10] agreement of fixed foreign exchange rates effectively opened the way to the foreign exchange markets, and now quantitative finance is a mainstream activity and a popular postgraduate course. Whilst cost of risk, and correlation remain two major problems that are essentially unsolved, there has arisen a common currency of quantitative techniques that allows for definition and solution of many microeconomic issues.

To the third question, what does seem essential to me that in a modern world where markets play an increasing role domestically and internationally, and in an increasing array of products and services from labour to computer chips to cars to money to carbon dioxide allowances, that in addressing local issues, whether to optimise within a system, or to design a system, that a knowledge of the relevant market disciplines and dynamics is essential. In doing so, we reiterate that whilst a fully free market is not the right solution at all times and places, that it is rare indeed for market disciplines not to be appropriate for valuation, prioritisation and optimisation decisions.

To make markets work, we must address the challenges that they give us, which appear to be fourfold:

(i)   Capture, rationalise, prioritise and assign values to policy issues, and articulate them in a form that the industry can engage with.
(ii) Ensure that the market structure can efficiently deliver all of the required signals through market prices, taxes, obligations and other economic signals.
(iii) Inform industry participants, stakeholders, and opinion formers about the workings of the ESI and of the interdependencies, and how to effectively construct and use signals.
(iv) Where the market cannot directly deliver the signal, enable policy makers and regulators to provide economic and prescriptive adjustments in an incremental, measured and intelligent manner, that takes account of interdependencies, so that market failure does not occur.

This must be done in such a way that the industry can plan far enough ahead to adjust its physical make-up by invention, build, modification, and closure of installations. This will allow the ESI to face the enormous challenge of delivering a sustainable environmental solution, at a cost that is acceptable in terms of domestic welfare and industry factor costs. I will not present solutions, and certainly not a standard solution, as the differing nature of the drivers in different countries means that there is not a one-size-fits all solution. Indeed, I hope that it will become apparent that national variations in the local physicalities of energy source and associated generation technology, the topology and connectivity of the infrastructure and the socio-political culture, require the modifications of the 'best basic' market model to be complex and extensive.

The market solution to the ESI is treated here as a solvable problem. There is a great body of thoughtful insight on low and high level problems faced by the ESI, both in the

---

[10] The Bretton Woods agreement was signed in 1944 to aid post war reconstruction, was fully in place in 1959 and collapsed in 1971 with the exit of the USA. Scammell (1975).

general sense and for particular countries and particular circumstances. However, such are the complexities, that a relatively high level of technical and/or local knowledge is assumed, and hence much of this insight is practically inaccessible. This book aims to equip the reader with sufficient broad knowledge of the ESI and technical knowledge of the key disciplines, both to address practical situations with the basic tools, and to understand the thoughtful insights already available in learned journals, books and elsewhere. Perhaps a little knowledge is a dangerous thing, but many policy decisions have been made with violations of some very basic scientific, economic or technological principles. It is to the discredit of the ESI that opinion has often been prioritised over education.

All stages of market development are equally important and in this book greatest attention will be paid to the design and structure of mature markets, and the role of regulation in implementing policy in a competitive marketplace. This is where the leading edge is, and developing markets will set much store from the experiences learned in the more mature markets. 'Markets' are interpreted in a wide sense, to include charging mechanisms, incentives and policy instruments such as taxes.

The book is structured so that the chapters can be read in any order, according to the particular interest of the reader.

Chapters 1 to 4 set the scene and introduces all of the facts and context that will allow us to examine market models in detail without getting bogged down in minutiae, or omitting facts and explanation that are essential to the examination.

(i)   Chapter 1 introduces the nature and basics of electricity with a brief history of electricity supply and the functions of the sectors under the 'unbundled' model.
(ii)   Chapter 2 describes in more detail each of the key functions of energy sourcing, generation, transmission, distribution, metering and supply.
(iii)   Chapter 3 views the industry from the perspective of its stakeholders and examine their drivers and issues, the way that stakeholders influence and interact with the industry, and how policy is formed.
(iv)   Chapter 4 introduces the concept of industry liberalisation, what is driving it, and the high level structural response of the industry.

Chapters 5 to 8 build on our understanding of electricity markets by layering on increasing degrees of sophistication.

(v)   Chapter 5 temporarily puts aside the complications of capacity, location and environment and focuses on the core principles of the different forms of market that can be used, from the monopoly model, through the 'pool' models, to a bilateral market in keeping with modern markets in other commodities.
(vi)   Chapter 6 then concentrates on the management of planned and unplanned variation in supply and demand rates, the different models that can be used, and how the system physically operates. This is under the general banner 'Capacity'. Capacity management is then integrated into the market model.
(vii)   Chapter 7 then considers the practical realities of moving electricity through a network that is costly to build, maintain and operate and which experiences physical limitations such as thermal losses and line congestion. This is under the general banner 'Location' and the various ways of managing location signals in a market structure are examined.

(viii) Chapter 8 then introduces the third main complication to market structures (after capacity and location) which is the environment. The environmental issues are introduced and discussed at high level and in a global context, and then the various market and regulatory mechanisms to optimise the total environmentally adjusted outcome of the industry are considered.

Chapters 9 and 10 deal with the principles and application of pricing and economics of the industry, in the context of the attributes of the industry described in Chapters 1 to 4, and the market structures for energy, capacity, location and the environment described in Chapters 5 to 8.

(ix) Chapter 9 concerns pricing with particular attention to wholesale derivative prices
(x) Chapter 10 introduces and discusses those aspects of economics that pertain directly to the ESI, which are referred to in the rest of the book.

Chapters 11 and 12 then examine two specific themes.

(xi) Chapter 11 deals with power plant economics from a financial perspective, with particular reference to the mapping of physical characteristics to financial characteristics.
(xii) Chapter 12 examines security of supply. This issue is perhaps the most important issue for the electricity supply industry and is the subject of much confused and uninformed debate. The issues are highly complex and hence, while elements of security of supply are dealt with in almost all of the other chapters, the threads are drawn together in the end of the book.

If this book succeeds, then the reader will have a greater technical understanding of the industry and of the interaction between policy issues, between technical issues, and between technical and policy issues, and how the application of market disciplines is essential throughout. It is better knowledge of these interactions and disciplines that we need to help us all to move forward into an uncertain world.

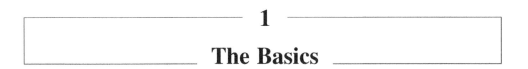

1

The Basics

1.1 HOW ELECTRICITY WORKS

To understand how electricity can behave as a commodity, we must understand its physical characteristics. We must offer a caution at this point; this is not an engineering text and a full description of alternating current is beyond the scope in hand. The purpose here is to understand electricity sufficiently to understand electricity markets, and to do so we resort to 'folk' definitions, and simplified analogies. Such methods can only go so far without excessive inaccuracy, and hence some aspects of locational market models in particular cannot be covered without a proper engineering description of alternating current (AC). The reader is referred to engineering texts for these. To quote Stoft,[1] 'Most of the basic properties of AC power flows that are needed to design markets can be understood in terms of this essentially DC model, but some important phenomenon are purely AC in nature'.

Electric current involves the movement of an electromagnetic field that is visualised as the collective movement of electrons through an electric conductor, driven by differential concentrations of electrons that repel each other.

Direct current (DC) is driven by voltage differentials between two points on a wire, as we see in Figure 1.1. So if voltage is applied to a line at the point on the left, it will 'push' current to the right. If the current flowing down the line is direct then there will be a consistent voltage differential between the two points.

This movement can then create *heat*, as the electrons give up their energy by repeated collision with the electrons in the atoms in the conductor, or *movement* through the electromagnetic action described below.

The current I is related to the voltage V and the electrical resistance R of the wire by Ohm's law, $V = IR$. The power P (rate of delivery of energy, in this case from a resistor in the form of heat) imparted is the multiple of the voltage applied and the current flowing. So, $P = IV$.

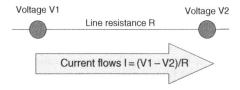

Figure 1.1   The relationship between current, voltage and resistance by Ohm's law

Equipment such as kettles and conventional electric light bulbs work through the resistance of the conductor creating heat, and they are termed resistive load.

---

[1] Stoft (2002).

Fleming's rule tells us that electric current can be produced by the movement of a conductor in the presence of a magnetic field, or the movement of a magnetic field across a conductor. The passage of electric current itself creates a magnetic field, and changes in electric current cause changes in the magnetic field. Magnetic fields can be visualised as field lines which are crossed by a conductor. Fleming's rule also works in reverse, so the movement of a magnetic field across a static conductor, or the movement of a conductor across a static field, also causes the conductor to move.

Changes in electric field across the current in the coils of a motor containing a magnet causes the motor to move. The movement of the motor then pushes current in the opposite direction and 'impedes' it. If the power source stopped instantaneously, then the motor would gradually slow as the current created by the motor is converted to heat due to the resistance of the wires. If there is no electrical or mechanical resistance or any inductance anywhere in the circuit, then the motor will turn in perpetual motion as it receives kinetic energy from the current it creates, at the same pace as the kinetic energy creates electrical energy.

A transformer works by the changing currents in the input coil creating a magnetic field in the iron core, which then creates currents in the output coil. Note that it is the change in the current that causes the field. With direct current in the input coil, no current would flow in the output coil. The ratio of numbers of coils determines the current and voltage entering and leaving the transformer.

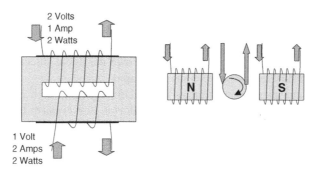

Figure 1.2   Actions of a transformer and a motor

A voltage that is applied in a cyclic manner by a power generator will cause a cyclic, or alternating, current which has a 'phase' that is measured by the timing of the peaks. Figure 1.3 shows alternating current in three circuits. Circuits A and B are out of phase, and circuits B and C are in phase. If the phase differential is constant,[2] or at least moving very slowly, then the circuits are said to be synchronous.

Electric motors, that use current through coils to drive the motor are said to have an inductive load. A coil, or solenoid has the same impedance effect. The current passing through the coil sets up a magnetic field which then varies as the current varies and then opposes the voltage. Large diameter conductors (such as in high voltage transmission line that are large to reduce resistance) also have an impedance due to the effect of eddy currents behaving like small solenoids. Fluorescent light bulbs also have an inductive load.

---

[2] For example, positions on the same wire, separated by a long distance.

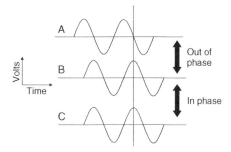

Figure 1.3   The phase of Alternating Current (AC). C can be connected to B, but A cannot

With direct current, applied by a battery of cells, there will be a consistent voltage differential between the two points. For alternating current (AC) whilst the differential changes, the peak voltage can be the same at both points. Whilst at any instant it is the voltage differential that drives the current, it is more convenient to understand it in terms of the phase differential between the points. To draw power, either for resistive or inductive load, it does not matter which way the current is flowing.

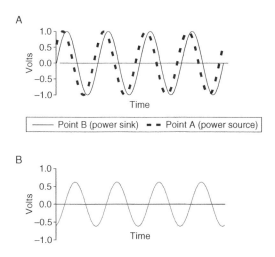

Figure 1.4   Pictorial representation of how voltage difference between points can result from a phase difference in alternating current between the points without a differential of peak-to-peak voltage

This visualisation of alternating current is in reality a 'DC-like' visualisation that is only correct if the frequency is very low. At high frequencies, the current is not simply related to the voltage differential.

Impedance affects the relative phase, or 'phase angle' between the current and the voltage. The result of this in long transmission line is that the phase angle increases, and to stabilise the power, a reactive source is required. Reactive power is described in the appendix. For a purely inductive load, current lags voltage by 90°, and for a purely capacitive load, current leads voltage by 90°.

1.2   EARLY DEVELOPMENT OF THE ELECTRICITY SUPPLY INDUSTRY (ESI)

'As far as domestic applications are concerned, electricity has wrought a revolution that is so complete that it is virtually taken for granted in most homes in the advanced industrial societies' – Buchanan in 'the Power of the Machine'.

Electricity providers are commonly grouped in the category of 'utilities', along with providers of services such as clean water, waste water removal, gas and telecommunication. While electricity provision is commonly regarded as a basic utility that is noticeable in the most developed economies only when it fails, in developing countries electricity provision remains a core aspiration and development indicator.

The electricity industry is a young one, post dating the industrial revolution. Whilst electricity was known by the ancient Greeks in the form of static electricity, it was not until the 'second electrical revolution'[3] of the 1880's that power for lighting and motors was used to any degree, while still over a quarter of the world's population does not have access to electricity.

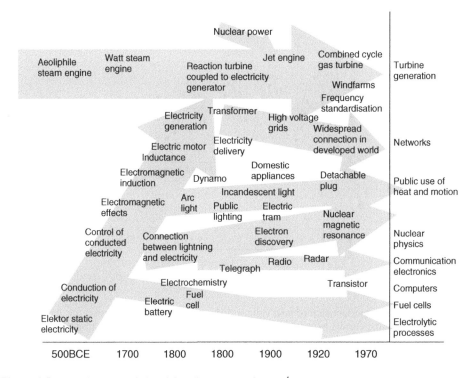

Figure 1.5   Development of electricity discovery and usage[4]

---

[3] Term used by Hall (1998). The 'first electrical revolution' was the use of weak current electricity *'schwachstrom'* for telegraph and telephone. Strong electricity for light and power is there termed *'starkstrom'*. The book also contains an excellent account of the impact of the electrical industry on the city of Berlin.

[4] See Kuhn (1962) for a commentary on the discovery of electricity. See Hyman for history in the USA.

The early days of the Electricity Supply Industry (ESI) were driven by discovery and private enterprise. Whilst experimental usage grew during the 19th century, for example the lighting of an opera in Paris in 1844[5] with arc lights, it was the growth of public incandescent lighting using power stations as a source that marks the beginning of the ESI. Development during the first 15 years was rapid as we can see from the chronology[6] below.

1878 Creation of incandescent light bulb by Swan in the UK[7]

1878 Street (arc) lighting in Paris[8]

1879 Creation of long lasting incandescent light bulb by Edison and Jehl in the USA[9]

1881 Opening of Godalming power station in the UK[10]

1882 Opening of Pearl Street power station in the USA[11]

1882 First transmission lines in Germany (2400v DC, 59 km)[12]

1883 Holborn viaduct power station in the UK

1885 Commercially practical transformer (William Stanley)

1885 Hydro power station and 56km transmission in France

1885 Public electricity supply in Norway[13]

1887 Interior lighting in Lloyds Bank, London UK

1887–9 High voltage alternating current transmission in Deptford, UK

1887 Public electricity supply in Japan[14]

1889 Single phase alternating current transmission (4 kV, 21 km) Portland Oregon, USA

1893 Three phase AC transmission (12 kV, 179 km) Germany

1894 generators used to supply motor pumps in mines in Malaysia[15]

1895 Public electricity supply in Australia

In Great Britain, for example, by 1909 there were already laws denying new entry without licence and by 1914 there were 70 power stations in London.

---

[5] Munson (1985).

[6] History books differ by the odd year, perhaps due to national pride!

[7] Ensor. Swan and Edison joined to avoid conflict over patents and the company used the Edison patent.

[8] Hall (1998).

[9] Jehl (1937), in which is described how all manner of materials were used as trial filaments, including the beards of the researchers!

[10] Landes (1965).

[11] The moment of the throw of the switch was witnessed by the lighting of 106 light bulbs in the offices of the Morgan bank, winning a bet of $100 for Thomas Edison. The offices of the New York Times were also lit. Source Munson (1985).

[12] Rustebakke *et al.* (1983).

[13] CIGRE (2001).

[14] CIGRE (2001).

[15] CIGRE (2001).

Soon after this burst of development were attempts to standardise. For example, the first attempt to standardise frequency to 60 Hz in the USA was in 1891, although Southern California Edison did not convert from 50 Hz to 60 Hz until 1949.

1.3   THE LIFECYCLE OF ELECTRIC POWER

Central to almost all aspects of electricity is the issue of storage. Whilst most commodities can absorb production and demand variations by delivering to stock and withdrawing from stock, this cannot be done for electricity. While we shall see that there are various methods that amount to storage, for the moment we can assume that electricity must be consumed as it is produced.

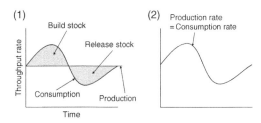

Figure 1.6   (1) The use of storage to maintain even production through a consumption cycle for storable commodities, (2) The necessity to consume electricity as it is produced, and vice versa

The essential stages in the lifecycle in electric power are:

(i)   energy sourcing;
(ii)   power generation;
(iii) network transportation, divided into high and low voltage;
(iv)   supply management;
(v)   consumption.

There are in addition three essential activities that can be considered as part of the supply chain, since every megawatt (MW) of electricity that passes through the network passes through them. They are:

(vi)   system operation;
(vii) market operation;
(viii) metering.

And finally, something which cannot be ignored, which is:

(ix)   disposal and environmental impact.

Energy Sourcing – Starting with the energy source, a natural asset under (initially) common ownership must be exploited to create electricity. This source might be underground (e.g. nuclear or fossil fuel), renewably harvested (e.g. energy crops), or arriving naturally (e.g. wind and water). The sourcing activity may require several activities after initial gathering, such as processing and refining, and then delivery to the power station. The political economics of natural resource extraction have been worked out over the last five thousand years, with the prevailing answer in the late 20th century following the same prevailing political ideology[16] that is driving the ESI. This is the ideology of free markets, as opposed to state run stewardship of national assets. Hence, there is limited opposition to a natural asset being extracted by foreign companies, and then exported, provided that there is sufficient national benefit along the way in the form of royalties, taxes, infrastructure, employment and development. However, the debate over security of supply recognises the fact that national attitudes may change when these resources become scarce in the country of 'ownership'.

Power generation – Power generation is the process by which an *in situ* energy supply is converted to electricity and delivered into the electricity transportation infrastructure or directly to a 'host' load. To deliver into the infrastructure requires a high degree of control of the electrical product (for example, synchronisation, ability to vary load to provide and not consume reserve, voltage stability). To generate power, requires not only a source of energy, but fair physical and economic access to the full energy source infrastructure which may include pipeline or rail, road, and ports. Similarly, the generator requires fair physical and economic access to the consuming customer. This requirement may be limited, in the form of adjacent host load, or extensive in terms of geographical distance, and barriers in the forms of regulation, laws and local factors.

Transportation – To transmit and distribute power entails extensive and possibly intrusive access requirement to the physical equipment of pylons, transmission and distribution lines, transformers and other equipment and their presence may have a substantial amenity impact in terms of the disruption of views. This requires property rights that would be quite impossible without the support of local and national governments. Transportation is a natural monopoly and hence is subject to regulated prices.

Supply management – While consumers require all of the upstream activities, such as generation and transportation, to occur, electricity is delivered to most consumers as a 'bundled' retail product. Consumers pay a price to the suppliers for the delivered product, and the suppliers arrange everything else.

System operation – System operation is electrical management of the system, particularly in the short term (less than one day). Because of the need for production and demand to match perfectly and continuously (to a resolution of fractions of a second), then in the short term there is no time for multilateral interactions, and a single system operator must coordinate.

Market trading – In the more mature markets, electricity is traded several times from the first producer sale to ultimate consumer delivery.

Market operation – Market operation involves the commercial arrangements for energy and capacity trading between participants and the system operator, and coordination of such commercial arrangements between participants.

---

[16] The mining industry was not changed so much by the imposition of free market political ideology, but by the lessening of rejection to it, in response to an inability to extract using internal funding, expertise, equipment and technology, while treating the resources as national assets to be extracted only by national companies.

Metering – While cost is incurred at all points of the supply chain, there is only one source of revenue – the consumer. To pay for electricity, the consumer must have a definitive price and amount to pay for. The meter is clearly the source of information, but in practice the processes are highly complicated. Hence we regard metering as an important and distinct part of the supply chain.

Disposal and environmental impact – This can variously be regarded as the last stage of the life cycle of electricity, a by-product of electricity production, or an input factor. Whilst the impact is predominantly incurred in the generation sector, it is rendered inevitable by the act of consumption.

1.4   DEVELOPMENT, STRUCTURE, COORDINATION, LEGISLATION OF THE ESI

The organisational development of the ESI responded to the technological capabilities and the sources of funds, and the legislature responded to the organisational development. The variety of structural forms of ownership, operation and control is a result of the technical complexity of the industry and the variety of physical and socio-economic legacy and contexts in which it resides. Electricity in developed countries is regarded as a necessary utility that cannot reasonably be withheld and which must be provided at an affordable price to all consumers. The provision to all customers including the poor, remote, and rural, is called universal service.

In the late 19th century, in which electricity supply could be said to have become an industry, the economic model in the industrial nations for new infrastructure development such as railways and canals was a mixture of private and municipal development, with a series of laws and rulings that first increased the standardisation and coordination and then increased the degree of public ownership and control where national interests dictated that it should do. Then, as much as now, the organisational structure of the ESI was strongly shaped by the prevailing political paradigm.

Closely following attempts to standardise were attempts to regulate. For example, in 1898 Samuel Insull[17] in the USA who tried to impose regulation over 'debilitating competition' and New York and Wisconsin initiated state regulation of utilities in 1907, while England took a more liberal view and allowed a 'rabble of small inefficient electrical undertakings with which parliament had unwisely saddled the country'.[18]

In the early days, electricity usage was largely for municipal installations such as light-houses[19] and street lighting. In fact, the product sold was light, rather than electricity. The provision of the service used a levy and the municipality contracted directly with the utilities with names such as 'Illinois power and light' which raised debt and equity from private investors. The earliest installations were a matter of civic pride.

With the rapid arrival of new utilities providing light and power and light to an increasing number of buildings, the need for greater coordination became apparent, and legislation[20] was set up to systematise the procedure for setting up public supplies. Then national grids

---

[17] An Englishman in charge of the Chicago Edison company. Chicago became the 'Electric City'. See Platt (1991).

[18] Ensor (1936).

[19] The discussion of the economics of lighthouses forms part of economic history with legacy that remains relevant to the ESI. See Coase (1974).

[20] For example the 1882 Electricity Act.

began being set up by statute. For example, in the UK, in the 1926 Electricity (Supply) Act. the General Electricity Board was created and the National Grid began development and construction. Between 1920 and 1950, most houses in Europe and America became connected to the networks.

1.5 NEW OWNERSHIP STRUCTURE

Whilst nationalisation was the solution in the 1940's to mass provision of standardised public services, the 1980's development was to reduce costs and increase innovation through competition.

The motivations, scope and timescales of the industry players are strongly influenced by their ownership and finance, and there are four key categories of ownership, namely;

(i)   investor owned corporations;
(ii)   public sector (towns, municipalities, states, nations,[21] public corporations, federal agencies);
(iii) cooperatives (in practice, a very small percentage);
(iv)   individuals or privately owned companies (in practice, a very small percentage of large infrastructure and large companies).

Without doubt, the current trend in each sector is towards investor owned corporations, and this destination has been, and is being, arrived at by distinct routes, as shown in Figure 1.7.

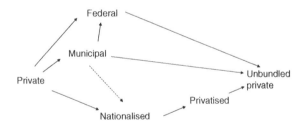

Figure 1.7 Representation of the different journeys taken in different countries en route to unbundled private companies

Nationalisation (acquisition of private companies by the state) of the ESI was a significant event in each country where it has occurred, and left its legacy on the industry. While the ESI in most countries came under public ownership in some form, there was a significant difference between the national model, in which the ESI concerned electricity alone and the municipal model, in which the municipality has wider responsibilities and was more responsive to local issues than national ones. Intermediate between the two models was the Federal model, which was like nationalisation on a smaller scale.

---

[21] These may be in the form of public bonds with an actual financial guarantee from government, a de facto guarantee from government, or an actual or implicit government commitment to guarantee revenue. For example the Moyle interconnector from Scotland to Northern Ireland.

The public interest and (notwithstanding privatisation), inherent public ownership of the ESI is apparent in each part of the industry, with the possible exception of the physical process of power generation.

1.6 SELECTED COUNTRY EXAMPLES

The development in different countries was different,[22] and strongly influenced by the national political model, whether it be centralised (such as Great Britain or France), federal (such as the USA, Australia and Argentina), or with a strong municipal element (such as in central and northern Europe). A short section cannot do justice to all the countries of the world, and the following is a selection of countries that are of particular importance in the understanding of electricity markets.

1.6.1 Europe

Great Britain – early development from 1880 was rapid, but the coordination of electricity supply took some time. For example, prior to nationalisation in England and Wales in 1947–8, there were 600[23] separate electricity undertakings based on over 400 generating stations. The Central Electricity Board was initially set up as a statutory corporation like the British Broadcasting Corporation, rather than a nationalised industry, but even just before privatisation, only two fifths of the 569 distribution undertakings were supplied directly by the grid. On nationalisation in 1947, the British Electricity Authority comprised 14 independent area boards, effectively responsible for everything except transmission. Acts of Parliament were passed to facilitate new entrants, but the reality in most cases was that a small new entrant could not surmount the entry barriers or gain fair access to paying customers. For example, the 1983 Energy Act in UK to promote competition to the Central Electricity Generating Board, had, to quote Margaret Thatcher, the Prime Minister at the time, 'no practical effect'.[24] Only the creation of large new players from the national monopoly could achieve change at the desired pace. The industry commenced privatisation in 1990[25] and has since experienced fragmentation in generation, followed by some consolidation, and vertical integration of the unbundled supply businesses with generation businesses. The frontiers of deregulation continued to be rolled back in all areas, including metering, connections, site services and distribution networks.

France – The ESI grew from hydropower in the Alps, and was used for electrochemistry and public transport and lighting. The hydro sources were nationalised in the 1920's, the national grid was formed in 1936, and nationalisation in 1946 formed Electricité de France (EDF). EDF, the 'national champion' began the French nuclear programme in the 1970's, culminating in substantial exports of power[26] and a programme of international acquisition.[27] EDF has been an innovator in tariff structures. In France, as in virtually all systems, there is private

---

[22] For a summary of several nations as of 1994, See IEA (1994). For current status with respect to degree of competition and degree of public ownership see Rufín (2003).

[23] Weir Committee (1925).

[24] Thatcher (1993).

[25] For a commentary on privatisation and the results, see Henney (1994).

[26] 11% net export as a percentage of domestic production in 2004. Compiled from IEA (June 2005).

[27] For further information on mergers and acquisitions in Europe during the key period of 1998 to 2002 see CERNA (2002).

generation as well as state owned generation. The political model in France is the 'social contract' in which EDF signs a commitment to technical and financial performance. The privatisation of EDF began in November 2005 with a share offering of 15 % of the shares.

Germany – The early development in Germany[28] was quite different to that in Great Britain and France. Soon after the birth of the ESI in 1878 in Britain and America, Germany took the lead[29] and led the world until 1913. Indeed Berlin was called the *Elektropolis*[30] by some. Utilities grew from the shareholder owned manufacturers and had detailed contracts with the cities for the supply of light and power, executed by the *Magistrat* of civil government. Partial universal service was mandated, prices were set by regulation, and compulsory purchase by the state was protected against for set periods. Electricity demand in the First World War, and then coal export requirements under reparations agreements from the treaty of Versailles, stimulated the growth of lignite mining for power, and the government entered into what we now call power purchase agreements with the private utilities. Regional utilities with both private and public/private ownerships grew in strength. Nationalisation was envisaged to make a single transmission grid and a pool, and indeed a nationalisation Act was passed in 1919. However, this was never implemented. The extent of public share ownership increased, and the system today is divided into five interconnected control areas, with four dominant vertically integrated utilities. The two largest utilities, RWE and E.ON embarked on a programme of international acquisition.

Scandinavia – The well known Nordpool power exchange began in 1991 as Statnett Marked AS in Norway, and was joined successively by Sweden (1996), Finland (1997), Western Denmark (1999) and Eastern Denmark (1999). In Norway, the largely hydro based system is mainly municipal with some state ownership, and most but not all of the grid being state owned. In Denmark, the two major transmission companies are owned by the major generators, Elsam and Elkraft. In Finland, grids are owned by state and private consortium and also market power. There are many distribution companies in each country and consolidation is occurring gradually.

Greece remains a state owned vertically integrated monopoly.

Spain has a mixture of public and private ownership, with the state being the major shareholder of the national champion ENDESA and the grid RED ELECTRICA. The largest Spanish companies engaged in international acquisition, particularly in South America.

Italy – The state owned vertically integrated monopoly Enel was fully privatised in 1999 after nationalisation in 1963 and later transformed to a joint stock company with the state as major shareholder. Transmission was unbundled and smaller generating companies were formed in the 2000's from specified plant and then divested. Independent CCGT power production in the 2000's has been facilitated by market reform, divestment from Enel and production shortfall from the ending of nuclear power, the lack of coal and the high price of oil for oil fired stations.

---

[28] Then Prussia. For a fuller account, see Hughes (1983).

[29] Hall (1998); Hughes (1983).

[30] von Weiher, 'Berlins Weg zur Elektropolis' taken from Hughes (1983).

1.6.2 Development in the Americas

USA – In the USA,[31] whilst there were many investor owned utilities, the Public Utility Commissions had a high degree of control, and could regulate the utilities and set prices. However, the extensive geographical holdings (three utilities controlled over half of the generation in the USA), meant that it was hard to identify value chain costs and therefore hard to regulate them. Accordingly, the Public Utility Holding Company Act (PUHCA)[32] of 1935 forced the breakup of the large utilities into regional vertically integrated utilities. In the same year, the Federal Power Act was passed, which gave the Federal Power Commission (which became the Federal Electricity Regulatory Commission in 1978), the authority to grant licenses for generation and transmission, which gave them the control to ensure fair and non discriminatory access. These two Acts kept power in the hands of the state.

Regional cooperation continued between control areas. In 1927 three utilities signed the PA-NJ agreement to form the first integrated power pool, which became PJM after two more utilities joined in 1956. PJM has developed on a more or less continuous basis since its formation and remains an industry pioneer. There were agreements before that such as the Connecticut Valley Power Exchange which interconnected two utilities, and many utilities still in existence were born, such as the Tennessee Valley Authority (1933) and the Bonneville Power Authority (1935).

Technical management grew through self regulation in the form of Reliability Councils, ten of which merged in the late 1960's to form the North American Electricity Reliability Council NERC.

Policy decisions are often driven by events, and a seminal moment in the history of the ESI in the USA was the 'great Northeast blackout' in the USA in 1965. Like most blackouts in developed economies, this was due to the knock on consequences[33] of a fault, affected 30 million consumers, and spread hundreds of miles from Buffalo to all corners of the Northeast.

In 1973, after the first oil shock, Nixon launched Project Independence with a legal deterrent to generation from imported fossil fuel in the form of oil and natural gas.

In 1978, under the Carter administration, the Public Utilities Regulatory Policy Act (PURPA) was passed, which forced the incumbents to accept power generation from independent 'qualifying facilities' at the avoided cost of incumbent. The qualification condition was generally for power to be generated from renewable sources. In practice, although by 1992, albeit a lean year for construction, 60 % of new entrants were independent power producers, predominantly fossil fired.

The Energy Policy Act 1992 created the capability for the independent generators to sell power directly to the local distribution-and-supply companies, rather than having to sell to power generators. This paved the way for deregulation. The Act also extended the power of the FERC to order utilities to provide transportation on a non discriminatory basis. The implementation of the Act was in FERC Orders 888 and 889 in 1996. FERC 888 in fact

---

[31] For further information, see Brennan, Palmer and Martinez (2002). For an account of the development of the ESI in the USA from the early days to the 1980's, see Munson (1985).

[32] In order to support competition, the Senate voted in July 2005 to repeal PUHCA.

[33] This is called a transient stability event. Transient stability is described in 2.3.1.2. One of the reasons that Consolidated Edison took a long term to return is that they did not have 'black start' capability (see section 2.2.21) and needed power from the grid to start.

interpreted transmission in a wide sense and in addition to simply making the wires available to access, specified reserve, balancing and ancillary services.[34]

The standard market design (SMD) was a bold experiment which potentially had far reaching effects beyond open access. It specified:

(i)   independent transmission provider;
(ii)   flexible transmission service with tradable congestion[35] revenue rights;
(iii)   transmission pricing reforms;
(iv)   open and transparent energy spot markets; day ahead and real time markets for energy and ancillary services;
(v)   congestion management through location marginal pricing;
(vi)   market monitoring;
(vii)   regional planning process along with a resource adequacy requirement;
(viii) creation of regional state committees to address planning, siting, and other issues.

However, it proved to be a step too far at a time when debate about markets and liberalisation in the post-Enron post-California crisis environment is rife and agreement insufficient. Accordingly the notice of proposed rule making for SMD was terminated in July 2005.[36] The Enron experience and the knock on effect on power marketing firms, both on the way up and the way down, had a significant influence, with the result being that at present, 'At the very least, the pace of wholesale and retail competition and the supporting restructuring and regulatory reforms has slowed considerably since 2000' Joskow (2003).

Canada – The Canadian model is quite different to that of the USA, with most utilities being vertically integrated and owned by the provinces, with varying degrees of competition.

South and Central America – South America was an early leader in electricity deregulation, with Chile in 1982, followed by Argentina (1992), Peru (1993), Bolivia and Columbia (1993), Central American Countries (1997), and Brazil, Mexico, Ecuador in late 1990's. As of 2002,[37] the degree of private ownership in generation was Chile 90 %, Argentina 60 %, Peru 60 %, El Salvador 40 %, Brazil 30 %, Ecuador 20 %, Costa Rica 10 % and Mexico 10 %.

1.6.3   Australasia

Australia – Australia is a very large country with six states, two territories and large distances between population centres. Constitutional responsibility for electricity resides with the state governments. State interconnection began in 1959 and continues. The National Electricity Market (NEM) has membership of five states and one territory. Ownership is substantially unbundled and private, with state ownership being highly corporatised.

New Zealand – New Zealand is one of the pioneer countries for wholesale markets, beginning in 1996. The generation and transmission sectors were state owned with unbundling of distribution and supply, formation and divestment of small hydro stations and one generator, and deregulation, from 1995 to 1998.

---

[34] The transmission companies in question generally owned generation assets.
[35] Congestion means exceedance of the limits of the transmission lines.
[36] FERC docket No. RM01-12-000.
[37] Source InterAmerican Development Bank.

1.6.4   Asia

China – China has the fastest growing ESI in the world. Responsibility for the energy sector is shared between ministries. The semi-autonomous State Power Corporation (SP) was formed in 1997, assuming control after the Ministry of Electric Power. Funding has been a mixture of grants, subsidised loans from central government with some funding from provincial and local utilities. SP plans to unbundle and create full competition in generation in the years to 2010. Organisational of SP is regional.[38]

India – India is the world's sixth[39] largest energy consumer. State Electricity Boards run the distribution sector and own most generation. Liberalisation in the 1990's was designed to encourage investment in independent power producers, but third party access through the grid and complex cross subsidies have created commercial challenges, and foreign investment has been limited and with mixed experiences.

Japan – The ESI was monopolised by the state during the Second World War, and converted to state owned regional vertically integrated monopolies in 1951. Reform began in 1995 with little change in ownership.

Russia – The joint stock company RAO UES, initially a monopoly arising from the Soviet system and still with state ownership of the majority, maintains control of the grid, has divested vertically integrated regional 'Energo's' but retains extensive share ownership of them. Planned reforms are extensive, to encourage foreign investment capital and provide the requisite third party access. Gas is particularly important in Russia due to the large volume produced there.

1.6.5   Africa and the Middle East

Ownership remains almost entirely in the hands of states, while independent power production exists to varying degrees. Privatisation is planned in several states, but is commonly delayed or with no particular deadlines.

---

[38] For a diagram of the 27 companies, see Loi Lei Lai (2001).
[39] Source EIA (2003).

2

Structure, Operation and Management of the Electricity Supply Chain

The ability of the ESI to deliver the policy objectives is influenced by its structure and its physicalities, such as technology and energy sources.

The electricity supply chain can be conveniently divided into energy sourcing, power generation, high voltage transmission, low voltage distribution, metering and supply. We cover the organisational structure and development of the ESI in Chapters 3 and 4 and in this chapter we establish the physical, technical and mechanical aspects of the electricity supply chain, with particular emphasis on those aspects that influence, and are influenced by, market development.

2.1 ENERGY SOURCES

There are seven forms of energy that can interchange between each other as part of the power production process. These are: nuclear, thermodynamic, potential, kinetic, mechanical[1] elastic, electrical/electromagnetic and chemical. These are shown schematically below.

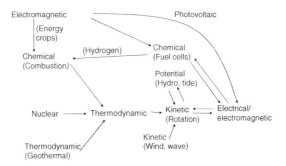

Figure 2.1 Interchange between energy types

The power generation mix in different countries varies markedly, and the biggest factors influencing the mix are:

(i) historic **legacy of energy imports** from long term trade partners;
(ii) natural **endowment** of fossil fuel or renewable energy in a form amenable to power generation;
(iii) **politics and social/cultural** opinion in relation to coal mining subsidies, nuclear power, emissions, renewable energy and related matters;
(iv) **effectiveness** of the ESI in coordinating, managing commercial relationships, and efficiently and reliably delivering energy and capacity;

---

[1] This form of conversion is called piezo electric. It is not used for provision of heat or motion.

(v)   general **transportation** infrastructure to, from and in the country in question;
(vi) **climate**, which affects heating demand in winter and air conditioning in the summer;
(vii) legacy of **district heating,** which uses steam rather than power and gas for space heating.

2.1.1   Fossil fuel

Fossil fuel accounts for 24.4 %[2] of total primary energy source (TPES) in the world and 20.5 % in OECD countries and is burnt in power stations in solid, liquid and gaseous form. The ESI accounts for 16.1 % and 19.4 % respectively of world and OECD energy usage respectively. Opinions differ with respect to the future role of fossil fuel. What is in doubt is whether the rate of increase of efficiency in the whole value chain for fossil fuel from exploration to usage will over a long period[3] outweigh the rate of depletion. For the purposes of examining the ESI, it is enough to know is that there is a will and a financial pressure to reduce our dependence on fossil fuel.

Fossil fuel fired power generation, uniquely, covers the whole spectrum of 'load factor'[4] from 'baseload' plant to 'peaking' generation, as a direct result of the combination of fuel prices and generation technologies. The fuel determines the technology and the technology determines the operation. Similarly, emissions are determined by the fuel, technology and the operation.

Fossil fuel is commonly associated with emissions, particularly carbon dioxide, sulphur dioxide ('SOx'), and nitrogen oxides ('NOx').

The transportation involved in fossil fuel generation is extensive, and the concentration of sources creates a price gradient and a security of supply gradient. We will examine these later when we consider location in Chapter 7 and security of supply in Chapter 12.

2.1.1.1   Solid fuel

Solid fuel has forms dependent on age. The youngest is peat,[5] which is still burnt in places such as Ireland.

Brown coal or 'lignite' is a young coal that is commonly surface mined in places such as, in volume order,[6] Germany (21 %), Russia (9 %), USA, Greece, China, Australia and Poland. The low calorific value and high moisture content dictates combustion of the lignite near where it is extracted. The low calorific value per dry tonne, and the high moisture content makes the cost of transporting the fuel significantly higher than transporting the power that can be made from the fuel on site and so in practice lignite does not travel internationally as hard coal does.

'Hard coal', 'steam[7] coal', or simply 'coal' looks more like what we use on barbecues and is divided into sub bituminous coal at the youngest end, through to bituminous coal, and eventually anthracite. Coal has been used extensively since the steam age over 200 years ago,[8] and resulting depletion of surface coal means that the costs of hard coal extraction are relatively high in Europe.

---

[2] 2003 – Source IEA Key World Energy Statistics 2005 for all similar data in section 2.1 unless otherwise noted.
[3] For discussion on price growth see sections 9.5.2 and 10.1.27.
[4] Described in section 2.2.
[5] Still younger is biomass, but this is not classified as fossil fuel, as it is renewable in normal timeframes.
[6] Source EIA (2003).
[7] So called because it is used to make steam from water. Coking coal is used for steelmaking.
[8] Sea coal, initially mainly exposed by the action of the sea, was used extensively enough in the 16th century in England for Queen Elizabeth to complain about the effect of its burning on the atmosphere of London. (Ackroyd 2001).

Production volumes of steam coal are[9] in, in order, China (37%), USA (25%), India, Australia, South Africa, Russia, Indonesia, Poland, Kazakhstan and the Czech Republic and export volumes are from, in order, Australia, Indonesia, China, South Africa, Russia, Colombia, USA, Canada, Kazakhstan and Poland.

The technology of coal boilers and combustion is quite specific, and power station boilers were commonly designed to burn local coals. The increasing trend to burn a range of coals, including imported coal, commonly requires changes to the configuration and operation of the plant.

The driver for coal mining subsidies is protection of the direct and indirect labour associated with coal mines. Coal is intimately connected to the industrial, economic, political and social heritage of many nations. While state subsidies are generally outlawed in the EU, coal (along with steel) has a special position that arises from the legacy of the EU. Of the three treaties that formed the basis of the original European Economic Community, the European Coal and Steel Committee of 1951 was one. This enshrined the rights of the state to subsidise[10] coal production.[11] For example, in some countries the government makes up the difference between the price of international coal delivered to power stations and the cost of mining and delivering domestic coal.

Coal mining is a good example of how ESI changes that have long term socio-economic impact (in this case the displacement of labour) must themselves happen at a pace that can accommodate such changes without excessive interruptions. While self sufficiency in energy was as much a driver for coal production as labour protection, the argument has shifted to the balance between managing gradual change of industry and the management of depleting resources and pressure on the environment.

Two economies particularly important in the consideration of coal and coal fired generation are India and China. Over 50% of energy and over 70% of power generation in India is fuelled by coal. In China, over two thirds of energy and between 70% and 80% of power generation are by coal.

As environmental limits tighten and internationalisation of the coal market increases, specification becomes more and more important, and the different characteristics of coal are developing 'factor' or 'basis' costs.

Text Box 2.1 – The physical characteristics of coal

Coal is not a simple homogeneous commodity, and has many features that affect its use in power station in terms of cost, damage, operation, and emissions. Each of the factors listed below, and several others can vary greatly from coal to coal:

(i) **Sulphur** – While 1% sulphur by weight is a rough average for international coal, sulphur coal can vary from about 0.1% up to around 2%.

(ii) **Nitrogen** – Although coal does contain some nitrogen that contributes to the formation of nitrogen oxides, collectively called NOx. NOx is mainly produced from

---

[9] Source EIA (2003).

[10] For example in the UK, coal has been in decline since 1913, and increased its reliance for offtake by the ESI from 14% in 1947 to 79% by 1992. Henney (1994).

[11] For example in the mid 1990's the 'kohlepfennig' (coal penny) consumer levy in Germany, or the coal backed contracts to regional electricity companies with regulated consumer prices in Great Britain.

Text Box 2.1 – Continued

    nitrogen in the air as a result of a hot flame. Different coals have different flame characteristics or restrictions on changing the flame characteristic in the boiler

(iii)   **Chlorine** – Chlorine is highly corrosive and can reduce boiler life substantially.

(iv)   **Slagging and fouling** – Elements in coal other than carbon, hydrogen, nitrogen and oxygen ideally leave the boiler as ash, but some coals are more susceptible to the formation of slag, which reduces boiler efficiency and can cause damage.

(v)   **Heavy metals** – Especially mercury. Leave as ash or in the flue gas.

(vi)   **Moisture** – Impacts efficiency since the water is heated and leaves as steam. Also increases transportation and handling costs.

(vii)   **Ash** – Must be disposed of in dedicated lagoons.

(viii) **Hardness** – Coal entering the boiler is pulverised to fine consistency in mills. Hardness affects mill wear and efficiency.

(ix)   **Calorific value (CV)** – Coal throughout to the boiler is limited by the mills. Low CV coals can reduce output and efficiency.

(x)   **Carbon dioxide** – The greater the carbon/hydrogen ratio in the coal, the greater the CO_2 emitted per unit of energy delivered.

(xi)   **Volatile organic compounds (VOC's)** – Leave in the flue gas.

(xii)   **Volatiles** – Which can cause loss of energy of the stockpile, fires in the mills that pulverise the fuel, and flame effects.

Each of these factors affects the production cost, requires investment and maintenance cost, and affects the reliability and availability of the plant. They can be treated as factor costs. In general there are engineering solutions to each issue but each costs money. The physical make up of coal is particularly important in the evaluation and monetisation of the environmental impact of its combustion.

Petroleum coke – called 'pet coke' for short, is a by-product of the refining process and can be co-fired in some coal fired power stations. Sulphur content is high (in excess of 5 %) and hence it is only suitable for plants with flue gas desulphurisation. At around 50 million tonnes per year, global output is less than 1 % of that of coal.

2.1.1.2   Liquid[12] fuel

The use of **heavy fuel oil**[13] accounts for 6.9 % of power generation but is decreasing in power stations, because the fuel is too expensive for 'conventional' generation and not suitable for the efficient 'combined cycle' generation.

Diesel generation is widely used from domestic size to industrial. Although the efficiency is low, the generation is highly portable and the fuel is widely available.[14] In many countries,

---

[12] Liquid when burnt. They often have to be heated to liquefy them.

[13] Heavy fuel oil is a relatively low value product of crude oil refineries that is a viscous solid at room temperature. The price is dictated by the demand for the product and the cost of 'cracking' it in the refinery to make higher value products.

[14] The diesel is the same as is used in cars, plus and minus different additives. It is commonly dyed due to the different taxation status accorded to diesel for domestic consumption.

diesel generation is a mainstream backup for failure of the ESI to deliver reliable (or any) power.

Orimulsion (an oil/water mix mainly from Venezuela), oil residue (from well bottoms and from crude oil cracking) and other forms of fossil fuel are used in different plants in different parts of the world. The total percentage production is very small, supply is limited at any one time by production capacity, and combustion is commonly complicated with high emissions.[15] At present, this form of power does not play a significant physical or economic role in power generation.

The cracking process converts high molecular weight hydrocarbons to low molecular weight hydrocarbons and hence there is a degree to which fossil fuel can be converted to more attractive and useful forms. Some forms of fossil fuel under the ground are expensive to extract but the application of technology and/or higher prices is increasing output. Currently, **tar sands**, which have been extracted in Canada since 1978[16] are continually decreasing the output cost, and **oil shale**, should it become economic to extract is the subject of vast[17] resources.

2.1.1.3   Gas

'Natural gas' is predominantly composed of methane (CH4), and is commonly called simply 'gas'. Variations in composition (mainly CO2/CH4 ratio) require separate pipeline systems in many instances. It accounts for 19.4 % of ESI production.

Gas fired generation covers a very wide range of sizes and extent to which steam is used directly, and this creates a degree of flexibility for fuelling. Some plants are designed specifically to accommodate alternative fuels such as blast furnace gas, refinery gas, distillate, naphtha and other gases. Due to the direct hot gas exposure of turbine blades,[18] that are built to operate very fine tolerances, to very high temperatures and gas velocities, they must be specifically designed to operate with a particular fuel diet. The most advanced combined cycle gas turbines are highly sensitive to even small changes in calorific value and moisture content. For example, the widening of specification of gas in the UK in 2005 to accommodate a wider range of fields during depletion of some, and the associated change in gas initially caused technical issues in some power stations.

The stoichiometric equation for the combustion of hydrocarbons is $4C_xH_y + (4x+y)O_2 = 4xCO_2 + 2yH_2O$. For the same amount of thermal energy, coal involves around 50 % more production of carbon dioxide than gas does. From a carbon dioxide perspective, a major uncertainty for gas is the methane losses involved in the extraction. Methane has 20 times the greenhouse effect of carbon dioxide and hence a loss rate from exploration[19] to combustion exhaust of 5 % would double the estimate of greenhouse gas effect of gas utilisation.

---

[15] While these are commonly captured at the end-of-pipe in the power plant, the unit cost of capture is high.

[16] Lomborg (1998).

[17] According to one source (Craig *et al.* 1996) the oil shale resources (as distinct from reserves) are eight times more than all other fossil fuel resources combined.

[18] The turbine blades experience the harshest treatment, but the full 'hot gas path' from combustion silo to exhaust, experiences damage.

[19] An executive from one of the Russian oil giants was recently asked what the loss rate was, to which he replied 'I don't know. It is unimportant'.

2.1.2   Nuclear

Nuclear power accounts for 15.8 % of electricity production. There are two types of nuclear reaction – fission, in which uranium 235[20] splits into smaller atoms, and fusion in which the hydrogen isotopes of deuterium (sourced from water) and tritium (sourced from lithium) atoms combine to form inert helium. Fusion has only functioned practically so far in the form of a bomb. Research into the technological possibility for nuclear fusion continues.

As of 2004, the main sources of uranium are[21] in, order, Canada (29 %), Australia (21 %), Kazakhstan, Niger, Russia (estimated), Namibia, Uzbekistan, USA, Ukraine and South Africa.

Nuclear power has been a significant source of electricity since it began[22] in the UK in 1956, and nuclear generators continue to be built in, for example Finland, Czech Republic and Slovakia. Along with coal, nuclear power was the subject of two of the treaties that formed the basis of the original European Economic Community. The Euratom Treaty fostered the international cooperation for the development of civil nuclear power in 1957.

Nuclear power has an uncertain future, due to widely varying ideology and definition of the potential damage of nuclear power. For the enthusiasts it represents a long term solution (now rejuvenated by the carbon dioxide agenda), for others it is considered a stopgap technology, and for others it has no future place in the energy solution.

2.1.3   Renewable combustible matter

There are essentially four categories:

(i)   Waste and by-products still **homogenous** and in natural or near-natural form (such as woodchips, palm oil and chicken litter).
(ii) Other **waste from manufacture**.
(iii) **'Post-use'** waste (such as domestic refuse or methane from the dump).
(iv) **Energy crops** grown specifically for combustion, commonly on land which for reasons of agricultural subsidy was set aside and no producing crops. This kind of energy can be co-fired with fossil fuel in conventional plant or burnt in dedicated plant. Transport of these is expensive due to the limited sources, low ratio of energy to weight and size, and small sizes of the dedicated power generators or long distance to co-firing generators.

The primary combustion process is that of hydrocarbons, and hence renewable combustible matter produces CO2. Power plants consuming methane that would have been released to the atmosphere have a reduction on net greenhouse gas release.

2.1.4   'Hot' natural energy

Since nuclear and fossil fuel energy is converted into power via the production of heat, then it is apparent that a direct heat source such as geothermal energy or thermal energy from solar power can do the same. Being of low temperature, the energy 'quality' is low

---

[20] The predominant natural form of uranium is U238. It has to be enriched to approximately 3 % concentration for nuclear reactors. For further information see WANO (2005).

[21] Source: WANO (2005).

[22] The first controlled chain reaction was by Enrico Fermi from a 'pile' of uranium in an abandoned squash court in Chicago in 1942.

(see thermodynamics text box in section 2.2.18) and heat does not travel efficiently. Hence the power generation must be near the source (which often may not be an ideal place to operate a power station), and the sources are commonly not near demand. Iceland has a substantial proportion of power from geothermal sources, and as a result has attracted energy intensive industries.

2.1.5 'Cold' natural energy

The sources are essentially water (lakes and rivers, waves, and tides), wind (offshore and onshore), and sun[23] (photovoltaic). The issues are source, capture, installation scale, amenity, variability of primary energy source and the usability of the product that is created by the technology. The energy source is large and sustainable and hence growth in power generation technology in developed nations is focussed on this area. Hydro power accounts for 15.9 % of electricity supply overall, but in many countries this percentage exceeds 50 %.

2.1.6 Hydrogen

The need to maintain a mix of generation types means that combustion is likely to remain the dominant form of power generation for the next few decades, and there is a strong incentive to use a fuel that does not cause substantial emissions. Hydrogen can be burnt in combined cycle gas turbines[24] after some adaptations.

Hydrogen is not captured directly as an indigenous source of energy in its own right and must be made from other chemicals by thermal, chemical or biological methods. Currently 95 %[25] of production of hydrogen is produced chemically from methane, and in fact around 5 %[26] of US natural gas is used to make hydrogen, mainly in refineries and petrochemical plants. Hydrogen capture at the wellhead could also capture the carbon dioxide at the same time, and use the existing gas infrastructure for hydrogen transportation and combustion. Production from water (by solar action) and biomass (from bacteria and sunlight) is expected to increase, and this may eventually happen on an industrial scale.

Whilst hydrogen power is not economic using current technology, it is likely to become economic over the next 50 years as fossil fuel becomes more expensive due to depletion, and the cost of the associated environmental load from its combustion rises. Since the production of hydrogen can be remote from the combustion its economics, once produced, are very similar to those of primary fuels.

2.1.7 Stored

While it is an oversimplification to say that electricity can't be stored, it is correct that it cannot be practically stored in the form of current.

Electricity in the form of current can be used to make energy forms that can then be converted back to current. The dominant form of power generation that is designed specifically to store energy produced by alternating current (AC) is pumped storage, in

---

[23] The sun is used for heating, and there are technologies to use the heat to generate power. Archimedes is reported to have enabled the Roman fleet to be set on fire with focussing mirrors in 212 BC (Foley 1976).

[24] For example the Peterhead plant in the UK plans to make hydrogen and carbon dioxide from oil, burn the hydrogen in a (repowered) combined cycle gas turbine, and inject the carbon dioxide back into the oil field. Source BP.

[25] National Hydrogen Association.

[26] 1997. President's Council of Advisors on Science and Technology.

which motors drive water up to a lake at one time, and then hydro power is made at a later time. Typically efficiencies of large plant are 96 % for motor and generator, 77 % pump and turbine, 97 % pipeline and tunnel and 95 % line losses, giving an overall 67 %.[27]

Another method of potential significance is industrial scale fuel cells, which convert electrical energy to chemical energy and back using a form of fuel cell with tanks of electrolytes separated by a semi permeable membrane. The technology is potentially scalable to industrial size.

There are other storage methods such as compressed air storage, heat storage, secondary batteries, superconducting magnetic energy, flywheels and supercapacitors. Currently, these have application only for specialised use.

Despite high capital costs and low efficiencies, electricity storage has high potential economic significance because of the need to maintain a continuous electricity balance in the system and the increasing generation from sources with high unintentional variations in load, such as from wind power. As power prices rise, storage becomes more attractive because the absolute differential between peak and off peak prices rise.

2.1.8   Consumables

Power stations have a number of consumables such as hydrogen for cooling, sulphur trioxide for improved precipitator performance, purified water, carbon dioxide for purging and propane for firing. Whilst the cost of these is small in relation to primary fuel, they can be important in the consideration of short term security of supply.

2.1.9   Integration of energy sourcing and power generation

Energy sourcing and fuel production should be regarded as an integral part of the electricity life cycle.

In gas, 'Take or pay'[28] contracts between generators and fuel suppliers have volume arrangements to suit the shared economics of production and consumption by having a minimum take (thereby ensuing investment payback on the production asset) a maximum take (recognising the maximum productive capacity and providing a bonus for accelerated production) and a consumer volume flexibility within the year (recognising the effect of breakdowns and natural variation in demand). These take or pay contracts create a high degree of mutual dependency between producer and consumer on one another's economics. For example, the take or pay clauses, and the interruptibility clauses are commonly 'non ruthless', meaning that they may not be exercised in response to market conditions for the fuel. 'Burner tip' supply contracts for gas to power stations, require the gas to be physically burnt, and may not be opportunistically sold in the open market for gas. Similarly, since the volume option is held by the consumer, supply cannot be withheld to make opportunist sales to the open wholesale market, and interruptions must be for genuine physical reasons. The contracts contain a high degree of indexation to transparent and tradable indices (for example oil prices and retail price indices) and non transparent indices (such as indices that are related to specific elements to which producer or consumer are exposed). This mutual

---

[27] Weedy and Cory (2001).

[28] These contracts have designated maximum and minimum quantities and are described in section 6.4.1. The name 'take or pay' arose since the minimum payment corresponds to the minimum take, even if the fuel is not consumed.

exposure to long and short term economics, and the mutual dependency for source and for demand creates a vertical integration of sorts between much fuel production and power generation.

In lignite, the cost of transporting lignite means that the mine and the power station are local monopoly and monopsonies, and require extensive coordination, and hence are usually under common ownership.

In hard coal, the historic proximity of the power station to the mines creates a strong mutual dependence and in addition, the power stations are commonly designed to suit local coals. However, this relationship is more decoupled than it was previously due to the internationalisation of the coal market.

In nuclear power, the specific requirements for safety in transportation and the rest of the supply chain restrict the wholesale trading of nuclear fuel. There is therefore a high degree of mutual dependence between miners, processors and generators. Similarly there is high mutual dependence between nuclear generators and of downstream operators such as spent fuel reprocessors and decommissioning agents.

In renewable energy there is a close link between sourcing/capture and renewable electricity generation. The generation of renewable power requires (i) energy 'delivered' to site, (ii) the technology to convert the energy source to usable power, (iii) consents and permits for construction of plant and infrastructure, and for continued activity. The generation activity concerns the activity once the energy has 'arrived' on site. This is driven by the available technology. The sourcing is a distinct activity. The number of suitable sites is commonly limited, and the construction and utilisation of plant and infrastructure will inevitably have some (positive and negative) effect on local environment and amenity. The permitting process intimately binds together the impact on the sourcing area and the benefit provided by the power. Similarly, the generation technology is driven by the specifics of energy sources and the nature of the power produced.

2.2   POWER GENERATION

From a system and economic perspective, the energy provided by the power generator is best categorised in terms of load factor. Load factor is variously described as; (i) the number of hours generated over the year divided by the number of hours in the year, or (ii) the amount of generation, in megawatt hours, produced over the year divided by the theoretical maximum (flat out at nameplate[29] capacity all year round with no planned or unplanned reduction or cessation).

Baseload[30] plant, ideally runs continuously all year round with a steady load, some of which can contend with load variations to add to system stability and reserve capability. In Europe this is generally lignite fired conventional plant and gas fired combined cycle generation and in the USA it is hard coal plant. Nuclear generation tends to run baseload wherever it is installed. Baseload plant has the lowest marginal cost of production, and is said to be 'high merit'.

---

[29] Thermodynamics determine that power output capacity and efficiency depend on 'ambient' conditions such as air temperature, water body temperature, pressure and humidity. Nameplate capacity tends to be 'ambient adjusted' to an international benchmark.

[30] Baseload is also called 'round the clock' (RTC).

Peaking plant operates at a load factor below about 15 % and down even below 0.1 %. The spectrum is from 'peak lopping' in which the plant is expected to run at certain times of day in certain seasons, to more of a reserve function to cover events such as demand spikes or sudden outages of large generation units that can occur quite suddenly.

Between peaking and baseload is '**mid merit**', or 'cyclic' generation, that generally operates between about 15 % and 70 % load factors. It is the dispatch and economics of mid merit plant that is the most interesting in terms of market operation.

Due to the absence of storage capability for alternating current, and the very low level of dynamic response of consumer demand to signals such as instantaneous price, the amount of power produced must at every instant equal the amount of power consumed, plus electrical losses. The high degree of natural variation in demand and the high degree of typical variation in generator breakdowns, means that an extremely high level of flexibility must be built into the power generation complex. To provide a wide array of forms of flexibility (response time, volume, sustainability and cost, long or short term) requires a mix of power generation energy source and source-to-power conversion technology. In addition, power generators are required to provide 'ancillary services'.

In designing markets, we need to characterise plant in the simplest terms possible. These are;

(i)   **Energy conversion** – Fuel diet, efficiency, and availability (the amount of the time that the required service can be provided).
(ii) **Environment and amenity** – Impact on air, ground and water and other impacts.
(iii) **Flexibility** – Capacity, reserve, and other forms of flexibility.
(iv) **Reliability** – The probability of being able to deliver the planned service. This is quite distinct from availability (hours per year for which the plant is expected to be available) although closely related to it.
(v)   **Cost** – The cost of providing each of the above on a fixed and variable basis.
(vi) **Ancillary services** – These can be categorised as flexibility services such as frequency response and black start capability, and other services such as the provision of reactive power.

As we model in a more sophisticated manner, we will need to model in more detail (for example maximum loading rate and sustainability of flexible power, or different kinds of emissions), and add more elements such as location and size.

To understand how these can (and cannot) be delivered, it is useful to understand the technology behind them.

2.2.1   Turbine generation

Section 1.1 describes how the rotation of a magnet/electromagnet inside a magnetic field can create alternating current. The great majority of power generation is caused by this rotation, and of this the great majority of rotation is driven by a turbine. A turbine is essentially a fan in reverse. Liquid or gas is projected at the turbine blades which causes a pressure differential from one side of the blades to the other. The twist on the blades causes the pressure to turn the turbine on its axis. The turbines rotate synchronously[31] with the grid and the copper windings in the (rotating) generator rotor transfer energy electromagnetically to the copper windings in the (static) stator. The voltage is then stepped up in the unit transformer, commonly from 11–22 kV to 275–400 kV and out to the switchyard and to the network.

The power and efficiency of turbines are calculated using the pressure differentials and flow across them, which are in turn calculated using thermodynamics and computational fluid dynamics.

2.2.2 Open cycle

In open cycle generation, the combustion of gas creates heat which creates pressure. In the very simplest design, the gas would simply blow at the turbine after combustion, but to maximise efficiency the gas and air are pressurised in a compressor (which is like a turbine in reverse) prior to combustion. The high pressure gas strikes the turbine, which has a number of rows of blades.

Open cycle turbines do get built, especially for peaking plant, and are relatively quick and cheap to install. However, the low economic efficiency of burning an expensive fuel means that open cycle gas turbines ideally run at very low load factor (less than 1 %) or are 'retrofitted' with a combined cycle. In mature markets in mature economies, open cycle gas turbines (OCGT's) play a less and less important role. In immature markets in developing economies, they represent an expedient manner to provide power, particularly if there is a nearby demand 'host' for the generation, and dependency on the national system is required to be limited. OCGT's have a wide range of efficiencies from around 25 % to above 40 % for modern aeroderivative engines, and can be designed to run with oil as well as gas.

The local atmosphere at the front row of the gas turbine is extremely aggressive, principally due to the high temperature, and this limits the form of the fuel that can be used to fire gas turbines. For example, it is not practical to drive a gas turbine from a coal burner, as the fuel does not have time to combust before it hits the blade, has excessive particulate matter in the form of non combustible products that become ash, and is excessively corrosive from matter such as chlorine and metal salts.

The absence of large volumes of hot gas either on the hot gas path or in a steam section means that energy storage capability is very low. The provision of energy balancing by load variation could be done by varying the rate of fuel inflow. However, since metallurgical damage on turbine blades from turbine inlet temperatures, and the high consequential damage from fragments passing through many expensive rows of blades are the primary limiting factor to efficiency, then it is clear that this method of energy balancing is damaging to the plant. In addition to this, open cycle gas turbines are generally not required for energy balancing. They are either not connected to the grid, or if they are connected to the grid, then they are used for reserve and would run either infrequently and at full capacity or not at all.

2.2.3 Conventional thermal generation

In conventional thermal generation, the turbine is driven not by hot gas, but by purified water in the form of steam.

---

[31] Power with variable influx of energy, such as wind and wave, tends to be asynchronous.

Fuel combusts in a boiler with a large surface area composed of water and/or steam pipes. The water/steam is heated on contact with the hot metal tubes and, before and after various recirculations, the steam strikes the turbines. The exhaust steam then passes through the condenser to cool. The condenser is like a boiler in reverse, and the heat is carried away by thermal contact (across the heat exchanger tubes) with water from a nearby water body and by evaporation through a cooling tower.

The fuel combustion itself happens by the projection of the fuel into[32] the boiler through a series of burner nozzles. To do this with coal, it must first be pulverised in the mills[33] to the consistency of face powder.

Efficiency of well run conventional generation is commonly around 35 %[34] for plant built in the 1970's, with efficiency rises of around 0.25 % per year of build date.

While most coal is delivered directly to the bunker that feeds the mills, much can be delivered to the coal stock, and the ability to store and segregate stock and to blend means that not only can the fuel be stored generally, but there is some control on the planned variations in characteristics such as emissions and flexibility.

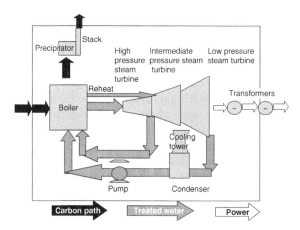

Figure 2.2   Schematic depiction of a conventional fossil fuel plant, showing the path of treated water

Operating cost is minimised by having large units and large numbers of units per site. Very large units do exist (for example the $6 \times 660\,MW$ Drax coal plant in England, and the 950 MW Niederaussem nuclear plant in Germany). However, very large units increase the vulnerability of systems, as a single unit breakdown has a significant effect on the system. Hence, small systems have largest units that are correspondingly small.

While the large components and large infrastructure associated with coal fired power stations means that they have a relatively high footprint on the landscape per installation,

---

[32] Fuel can instead be fed in on a chain grate or in a fluidised bed.

[33] The mills are essentially large grinding machines. The coal is blown into the pulverised fuel pipes through a classifier, which rejects the larger particles.

[34] Measures of power station efficiency that are practically useful must be defined carefully. The definition used here assumes that the calorific value of the coal already compensates for loss of latent heat as the water leaves as steam (i.e. the lower heating value) and is then 'gross net net', meaning that the efficiency includes power used by the power station.

this footprint is actually very low per MW of production compared to the various forms of distributed generation.

Conventional generation plant has a high degree of interdependence between the parts. At each stage there is diversion of energy, for example the diversion of steam for reheat, or drawing electricity from the unit transformer to drive the auxiliary motors. Similarly, a loss of function at one stage can be made up by another stage, albeit at a loss of efficiency. For example not all mills will run simultaneously, so a mill can be brought into service if one fails. Similarly a heat or pressure loss in one part of the system can be made up at various other parts of the system. All this adds up to complex loose system which cannot be readily modelled. The idiosyncrasies of each particular plant are well known and managed by the operators.

The amount of energy generally present in conventional plant, with the potential for short term release, is large relative to other plant except for hydro plant. The tolerance to release/store some energy in the form of temperature and pressure to temporarily produce more/less power is high. The energy storage capability is higher in the older subcritical[35] plants that have a large steam water interface. The volume of hot gas inside the boiler is also large (typically $20,000\,m^3$) and therefore there is also some energy storage in the combustion products. The high surface area of metal also represents a large thermal mass. Energy flow is adjusted by valves at many stages of the process.

The dominant types of conventional plant are hard coal, lignite, oil and nuclear. The fuel and combustion/fission characteristics are quite distinct, and this drives the plant design. The design then affects the performance due to, for example, inherent flexibility, safety limits, knock on impact of component failure and materials performance limits. For example, varying the heat output from a nuclear reactor requires raising and lowering the control rods. The water circulating is at very high temperature and the high safety design factors require thick metal, particularly for high pressure technologies such as the Pressurised Water Reactor. Thick metal undergoing thermal change endures internal high stresses which could conceivably cause cracking, and this limits the rate of thermal change, and hence the rate of load change in nuclear power stations.

Due to the transport inefficiency of lignite, the lignite power generators are commonly situated next to the mines (although the area of extraction will move by many kilometres over the mine life).

Coal fired generators can commonly be converted to allow the additional burning of gas, or renewable matter (either through the mills or directly fed). In the case of gas, usually only the burners need to be modified. In the case of renewables, a number of changes need to be made at all points from fuel arrival, through the whole combustion path, to emission capture and ash disposal.

Blending of other combustible material such as waste or organic matter is dependent on the boiler technology (particularly boiler geometry and fuel delivery mechanism). Depending on fuel and technology, the other material can be fed in on a chain grate, pulverised in a mill (pre-blended or not), form part of a circulating fluidised bed, or fed in adapted burners.

---

[35] In subcritical plant, the steam turns back to water in the cycle. In supercritical plant (which is newer), the temperature is above the supercritical point so there is no water/steam transition in the boiler.

2.2.4 Combined cycle

In a combined cycle gas turbine (CCGT), the hot gas from an open cycle gas turbine exhausts into a boiler called a heat recovery steam generator (HRSG) and the resulting steam drives the steam turbine. Gross efficiency of gas plant is around 45 % for plant built around 1980, with around 0.5 % extra per year of build, although there appears currently to be a technology limit at around 60 %, due principally to the limitation in making a turbine blade material that can operate at a higher turbine inlet temperature. The construction time for gas turbines is short relative to coal fired power stations, partly due to the small footprint (total space occupied, visual impact, road and rail delivery infrastructure, local environmental impact) which results in shorter consenting, and partly because there is less on site installation required than in conventional plant.

2.2.5 Combined heat and power (CHP)

Steam is commonly used for heating living and working spaces and for industrial instal-lations. However to use fuel to create low grade (low temperature) heat is wasteful of its thermodynamic potential and rather than raising the steam directly for use as heat, it is most efficient[36] to use the fuel first to generate power and then to use the exhaust (or at least intermediate steam) as heat. This is the principle of combined heat and power.

Combined heat and power can operate at a large scale (over 100 MW, with the limit generally being the local demand for heat) and on a very small scale. At the smallest scale, CHP 'microgeneration' (generating electricity at home from domestic gas) has been installed in hundreds of thousands of households. The economics of mass microgeneration in the form of domestic CHP is still in question.

Combined heat and power, also called co-generation, or simply 'cogen' is favoured by governments due to its high efficiency, and there has been a consistent effort to support it through mechanisms such as tax breaks, inclusion of CHP as valid for certificates that can be redeemed for feed-in tariff or similar, and relaxed status on moratoria.[37]

Since the amount of steam produced can vary widely, from 100 % power generation to 100 % steam generation, a definition is used to determine whether a specific CHP installation qualifies for tax and other benefits. The definition of 'good quality CHP' is X * power efficiency + Y * heat efficiency, where X and Y depend on specifications such as plant size.

Desalination plants have high requirements for heat and pressure and are commonly sited near demand for power, and hence these are ideally suited by building combined heat and power.

Trigeneration is a development of combined heat and power and simultaneously produces heat, cooling and electricity.

2.2.6 Turbines driven by water

Hydro turbines convert the potential energy of water into electricity by using the water pressure to drive turbines. The water sources are lakes (filled naturally or by pumps) and

---

[36] The reasons are thermodynamic. Combustion of fuel produces 'high quality' heat that should be spent wisely. Waste heat is low quality but still useful.

[37] In the UK, there was a moratorium on the build of combined cycle gas turbines after the 1998 White Paper on energy sources, to smooth the transition to lower coal demand. The moratorium did not apply to CHP and there was no specification on the percentage of power output that had to be steam. Partly for this reason, gas fired power stations continued to be built.

rivers. Hydro power is highly scaleable, with current installations ranging from 18,000 MW (Three Gorges[38] in China) down to domestic scale generation. Hydro power is generally classified as 'large' or 'small' with quite different treatment due to the completely different scale of their ecological and safety[39] impact.

For a lake driven hydro plant, the energy input is in the form of the potential energy from the rainfall in the catchment area. The output is determined by the efficiency of the turbines and water transportation, and limits of minimum and maximum reservoir levels and maximum rate of change of water height.

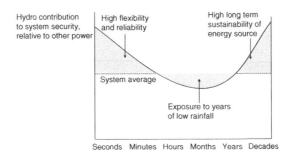

Figure 2.3 The contribution of hydro power relative to other forms of power, to system security, over different timeframes

The most efficient economic use of the water energy is to use it for peak generation and hence the turbine capacity is generally large relative to the volume of water in reserve. Some lakes could empty in a matter of hours, but the very large lakes experience a volume variation over several years.

Hydro power can be 'run of river', in which there is no storage mechanism, or 'reservoir' (generally classified as low head or high head) in which the output can be varied. Reservoir base hydro generation has the following characteristics that are of enormous importance in market design.

(i)   very highly reliability;
(ii)   very fast response;
(iii)   very high ramp rates;
(iv)   energy source driven by nature not economics (once plant/catchment are built);
(v)   energy source highly variable in all timescales;
(vi)   large turbine size compared to water volume means that energy source is limited in terms of continuity of generation;
(vii)   low marginal costs;
(viii) very low quasi fixed costs;
(ix)   high capital costs.

---

[38] Chinese Embassy. The Itaipu dam in Brazil and Paraguay has 12,600 MW capacity.

[39] Major failures of dams are extremely rare but can be disastrous if sudden. 2,200 died in the Johnstown flood of 1889 in the US.

Tidal power is essentially similar as run-of-river hydro power, but with much greater technical difficulties, fewer suitable sites, and common requirement to work for incoming and outgoing tide. The largest (240 MW) by far was built on the Rance estuary in France over 30 years ago. The next largest (18 MW) is in Annapolis in Canada. A 2,200 MW tidal fence, using a Davis turbine is being planned for the San Bernadino Strait in the Philippines, and an 8,640 MW barrage has been proposed in the Severn Estuary in the UK. In common with dams, tidal power has a significant impact on the local ecology and environment.

Wave power can work in a number of ways on or below the water surface.

2.2.7 Wind

Wind power is highly complementary to both hydro power and thermal generation. Wind is generated on wind farms with up to hundreds of wind turbines of up to 2–3 MW. The overall failure of wind farms has low variability[40] due to the low interdependence (this is in stark contrast to nuclear power for example), but the overall unintended variation in wind power output is high because wind (in a very similar way to electricity, and quite unlike coal or nuclear fuel), cannot be stored.

The method of generation from a wind turbine is essentially the same as in conventional generation and hydro generation, in that the turbine is driven by pressure on the blades, but the nature of the source is quite different. In conventional generation, the steam that drives the turbine is enclosed, pure and at high pressure. The temperature and pressure are highly controlled. For wind turbines, the wind is highly variable in speed and direction, and there is considerable airborne matter to damage the blades through impact and corrosion. The power is not generally synchronised and usually the turbines have to stop in very high winds.

2.2.8 Non turbine generation

The amount of electricity produced other than by rotation of turbines is very small (the sum total of power not generated by nuclear, hydro, gas/coal/oil is only 1.9 % and of this the majority is turbines powered by wind and combustible renewable matter) and the influence of non turbine generation on the power complex is correspondingly small. Non turbine generation is, and will in all likelihood continue to be, highly distributed.

Opinions differ widely on the extent to which photovoltaic power (PV) will provide a significant component of networked energy supply. Here solar PV can be bracketed with hydrogen power – it may and perhaps must be part of a future solution, but plays a relatively minor role in the solutions required for the gap years.

Magnetohydrodynamic, or MHD[41] generation can generate electricity without a turbine or other form of 'prime mover' but this, and other forms of non-turbine generation are not economically viable at present.

2.2.9 Distributed power generation

Since electricity was first harnessed, the continuous trend has been concentration of power generation into larger and larger units and for these units to feed into the high voltage

---

[40] The exception is 'type faults', that apply to a whole fleet of plant of one type. At this point, a type fault that causes a fleet of turbines to be taken out of services has not been experienced in wind power.

[41] In the film, the 'Hunt for Red October', the Soviet submarine is driven by MHD.

transmission grid. In the 21st century this trend is partly reversing in the most developed countries, due to the increase in the extent of renewable generation and, to a lesser extent, the increase in small scale combined heat and power. The generation that feeds into the distribution network is said to be distributed, or 'embedded'.

The size limitation is due to energy source availability, concentration and transportation. For example, a plant burning chicken litter, or methane from a waste dump has a rate of energy inflow that cannot be altered simply. While biomass can be transported, it has low calorific value per unit of weight, low density (making in bulky), and costly. The transportation also reduces the green credentials of the generation. Renewable energy is commonly in a form that cannot be concentrated to the same degree as fossil fired generation. Wind power is a good example, in which, rather than concentrating the wind, the turbines must cover a large geographical area.

Whilst the number of sites for small unit renewable generation is generally increasing, wind power is a special case and the coordination of these sites to form a concentrated output is also increasing. So, for example, wind farms are now being designed and built that are several hundred MW in size, equivalent to a large fossil fired unit. The trend in hydro power is ambiguous at present, since concentration of sourcing is quite possible with giant dams, but the politics of dams is in a state of flux. For this reason, hydro power is classified in terms of large and small, with quite distinct treatment.

Distributed generation is also cited as a solution to security of supply in relation to network failure. The argument goes that if the generation is near the demand, then there is less exposure to network risk, and lower geographic and electrical concentration reduces exposure to terrorism, weather events and electrical events. On the other hand, plant not connected to the grid and able to receive instructions from the system operator is less capable of supporting the network with reserve and capacity. Similarly, there are arguments and counter arguments for the effect of distributed generation on efficiency. On the one hand, concentration of power to a high voltage network maximises the efficiency of electrical flow in one direction. On the other hand, embedding of power can reduce the total flow of power.

2.2.10   The production of environmental and amenity impact factors

We can view the environment impact factors conceptually as shown in Figure 2.4.

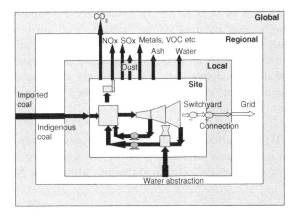

Figure 2.4   Depiction of relationship between plant and environment at site, local, regional and global level

In Chapter 8, the environmental and amenity impact of power generation and the categorisation of the wider impact of power generation are described. Using that categorisation, the most significant impact of power generation is in the form of emission to air, ground and water. Of those emissions, the most significant in terms of impact are emission to air of carbon dioxide (CO_2), nitrogen oxides (NOx), sulphur dioxide (SOx) and particulates. The impact on water is more complicated, involving heat, volume and emissions.

The natures of these are actually quite different and they have different solutions.

Carbon dioxide – The combustion of fossil fuel involves the oxidation of carbon and hydrogen to carbon dioxide and water. Given that coal contains only about 5 % hydrogen, it is clear that the production of carbon dioxide is an inevitable and necessary consequence of producing power by combustion. Usually, the only way to reduce CO_2 production from a particular fuel is to reduce fuel consumption, either by producing less power, or by producing the power more efficiently. In brief 'carbon in – carbon dioxide out'. It is possible to sequester the carbon after combustion.

Particulates and Dust[42] – Fossil fuel is formed from the decay of organic matter and then the compression and transformation over geological time. Just as organic matter is not purely composed of carbon, then fossil fuel is also not purely composed of carbon. Similarly, air is not purely oxygen, and contains gaseous and other matter. Other than carbon dioxide, and water, what would leave the power station, if there were no collection, would be (i) unburnt carbon, (ii) gaseous substances derived from the fossil fuel, transformed (such as NOx) or untransformed, (such as mercury vapour), (iii) gases derived from air, transformed (such as nitrogen oxides), or untransformed (such as nitrogen) and (iv) solid substances, untransformed (e.g. silicates) and transformed (e.g. oxidation products of the non carbon elements of the fossil fuel). These solid substances form ash, some of which exists as very fine particles of less than 10 microns[43] in size, called PM10's. Particulates include dust, and also include the subsequent formation of particulates from other emissions. For example the formation of droplets from sulphur dioxide emission.

Sulphur dioxide is formed by the combustion of the sulphur that is an inherent content of the coal (and oil and, to a lesser extent, gas). The oxidation of sulphur is not necessary to gain the energy from the fossil fuel, but it is inevitable unless the sulphur is removed prior to combustion. The amount of sulphur dioxide produced on combustion can be reduced by selecting a fuel with lower inherent sulphur content. Since all producers who have a economic or regulatory incentive to reduce sulphur consumption (which may be distinct from sulphur production after abatement techniques) will look to source low sulphur fuel, then it is apparent that low sulphur coal will commonly in some way be problematic (for example expensive, scarce, distant, unreliably supplied or associated with technical difficulties).

Nitrogen oxides (NOx) production is divided into three types: 'prompt NOx' produced by oxidation of nitrogen in the air at the flame front, by nitrogen in the air in the hot region beyond the flame front, and from the nitrogen in the fuel. Most of the NOx produced comes

---

[42] Dust and particulates are distinct. Particulates are designated by size in microns, and can be formed after emission.
[43] A micron is one millionth of a metre.

from the combustion air rather than from the fuel and some of this is naturally reduced back to gaseous nitrogen in the hot part of the furnace. Hence net production of NOx is dependent on the characteristics of the flame, the temperature and chemical composition of the gases in the different parts of the boiler.

Water – Power stations do have other impacts on the environment and the abatement of these impacts has relevant economics. For example, water abstraction affects levels of water bodies and water tables as well as occasionally unintentionally capturing some fish. Water outflow heats[44] the water body as well as having the potential to pollute it with oils, biocides, chemicals or other pollutants. Steam from cooling towers occasionally affects road visibility and surface condition. Each of these can be reduced at a cost, and there is a trade-off between cheap power and environment and amenity.

Volatile Organic Compounds (VOC's) – These are associated with coal and oil fired production.

Mercury and other heavy metals – These are present in coal and oil and partially escape in flue gases.

Ash – Ash is collected from the boiler and the flue and represents a disposal problem, since more is produced than can be consumed in road building and similar uses. Whilst ash is generally non reactive, the action of water trickling through ash 'lagoons' over long periods can leach out metals. Where this is the case, the lagoons are lined with durable impermeable material such as clay or high density polyethylene to protect ground water.

Nuclear – The potential incidence of impact factors from nuclear power is treated in an entirely different manner to, for example, CO2. For CO2, the fact of production of CO2 is not debated, only the impact. For accidental release of nucleotides the damage is not questioned (although the amount of damage is). What is questioned is the likelihood of production of the impact factor. The other environmental aspect of nuclear power is the accumulation of waste.

Health and safety – In addition to environment and amenity impact by power stations, there is the (positive and negative) impact of working at power stations and in the energy life cycle including energy sourcing, transportation and waste disposal. The power generation industry has good[45] safety statistics relative to other industries with similar physical characteristics, and the majority of accidents are 'everyday' ones, such as slips and trips, and driving to work.

Measurement – Many emissions and other impact factors can be measured on a continuous basis. The techniques vary from fairly primitive (e.g. the attenuation of light shone through flue gases) to sophisticated. Instantaneous measurement commonly has a high degree of uncertainty.

---

[44] This commonly increases fish population and size, thereby attracting fishermen.

[45] In Great Britain: Office of National Statistics – Statistics of Fatalities in Industries 2004/5. Mesothelioma, that is epidemiologically associated with contact with asbestos, which was commonly used in construction before 1975 and present in power station lagging affects current figures due to the long lead time from exposure to experienced health effect.

2.2.11   Abating the production of environmental impact factors

Most of the environmental pressure from the ESI comes from power generation. In a sense, consumption is the cause of this environmental pressure, but it is hard for a government to find effective mechanisms to encourage consumers to reduce consumption, and it is relatively practical for government to reduce the production of environmental impact per MWh of electricity.

The environmental and amenity performance of power generation has improved on a continuous basis over the last 100 years, and hence it is not easy to assign an absolute cost to performance improvement relative to no[46] abatement. It is however, possible to assign a cost of improvement relative to current performance. Environmental impact abatement has been driven by relative impact, abatement cost and abatement capability.

There are many environmental factors, but in keeping with the intention to understand and explain market structures, and to focus on the priority issues, we will consider in particular the emissions of CO_2, SO_x and NO_x, and will mention in passing dust/particulates and water, since their different behaviour introduces us to some interesting market concepts, particularly in terms of the 'translation' of regulatory limits to commercial signals.

In focussing on markets, we should be mindful not to pay insufficient attention to local impact and the trade-off between impacts at different geographical scales from local to global. An obvious historic example of trade-off was in the building of tall stacks so that the flue gas was removed from the local area and diluted[47] before returning to earth. Trade-offs remain in the modern era. For example, the delivery and removal of the by-products from environmental abatement (such as the delivery of lime/limestone and the gypsum that is produced in sulphur abatement), incurs extra road traffic, which can have an impact on local amenity to the affected population.

In addition to the obvious method of reducing consumption, there are six generic methods of reducing environmental impact:

(i)   **Displace** one form of generation by another with less impact (e.g. new plant for old plant, gas for coal), on a temporary or permanent basis.
(ii)   **Consume less fuel** for the same amount of power by raising efficiency.
(iii) **Source fuel** which has less inherent impact.
(iv)   **Reduce the inherent production** of factors causing impact (e.g. NO_x, heat to water bodies, visual amenity).
(v)   **Capture** the factors on site or prior to environmental release (so called 'end of pipe' solution).
(vi)   Reduce factors or impact **downstream** (displacing the output to less sensitive areas, diluting, or capture).

The economic alternative must also be considered, which is the Willingness to Accept. The saved money could be spent on leisure or alternatively on an environmental solution for a different impact, or healthcare funding with benefits that outweigh the health cost of the emission.

---

[46] Setting the benchmark, such that environmental schemes can be reviewed, and compensated relative to the benchmark, proves to be problematic, and many schemes submitted to the various carbon funding bodies, have been rejected.

[47] 'Dilution is the solution to pollution' was a commonly used phrase.

Some technologies reduce more than one impact factor, and some reduce one impact factor at the expense of another. For example flue gas desulphurisation captures other substances than SOx, but increases CO2 production.

2.2.11.1 SOx reduction

Sulphur dioxide production per MWh of electricity can be reduced. Using the categorisation described above, the methods are:

(i)   Reduce the **load factor**[48] of the plant, or (ultimately) close the plant.
(ii) Increase **efficiency**.
(iii) Source **fuel** with less inherent content of sulphur, or which has had sulphur removed[49] prior to arrival at the power station. This can be done at the refinery or gas processing plant. Calcium in coal also reduces the emission of SOx by capturing it as calcium sulphate.
(iv) Inherent production of SOx from sulphur containing fuel cannot be changed. The sulphur coming out of the power station is the sulphur that comes into the power station.
(v)   **Capture** the sulphur dioxide. The principle method is Flue Gas Desulphurisation (FGD). This method has been used at least since 1930[50] and involves passing the flue gas through a spray of sea water, lime or limestone. Lime/limestone requires quarrying, physical transportation of raw material, and gypsum output, decrease in efficiency from the power requirements of the plant, and direct production of carbon dioxide. Another method of sulphur capture are scavenging the sulphur prior to combustion or circulating fluidised beds which retain the sulphur in the bed.
(vi) Reduce the **local** SOx concentration, by the use of tall chimney stacks. Local Air Quality studies are usually standard procedure when building power stations.

2.2.11.2 NOx reduction

(i)   Reduce the **load factor** of the plant, or (ultimately) close the plant. Note that NOx is not related to fuel burn as closely as sulphur is, and start ups can create more NOx that is indicated from the energy of start.
(ii) Increase **efficiency**. This is only a weak effect for NOx. In addition, conditions for low NOx (a reducing atmosphere and a cooler flame front) can be low efficiency conditions if they increase unburnt fuel levels.
(iii) Source **fuel** with less inherent production of NOx. Some NOx is produced directly from nitrogen in organic compounds in the fuel, but this is relatively slight. Different fuels do have different inherent NOx production due to the inherent flame character-istics. For example, dense anthracite coals burn slowly and the boilers are designed to accommodate a long flame, and this can cause high NOx production. However, since the boiler is commonly designed around the coal, then change in fuel can have limited NOx impact and in practice NOx is not a primary motivator for fuel change.

---

[48] Note that this does not necessarily reduce total environmental impact, or even SOx production, as it depends on the form of generation increased by the withdrawal of the SOx producer. In addition, the possible increase in market price may cause negative welfare effects that are worse than the willingness to accept SOx.

[49] This can be done for oil, by 'scavenging' the sulphur with elements such as manganese, and for gas (by amine scrubbers). Sulphur can be removed from coal by magnetic filtration but this is not economically viable at industrial scale.

[50] Battersea Power Station in central London. Twidell (1995).

(iv) Reduce **inherent production** of NOx. This is a key method for NOx reduction. This is done by flame characteristics, stoichiometric environment (principally the amount of oxygen present) at the flame edges, and temperature and stoichiometric environment in the region after the flame. The technologies can be applied in sequence, for example by addition of air above the flame. The arrangement of burners in coal fired power stations can be optimised to reduce NOx. The amount of air intake can be adjusted. Low NOx burners which alter the flame characteristics can be retrofitted. Finally, NOx can be optimised by minimising load changes and by operating the plant at levels which have minimum NOx (this is generally somewhat below full load but there can be high NOx bands).

(v) **Capture** the NOx. There are two principal methods: Selective catalytic reduction and selective non catalytic reduction. Ammonia is consumed and water and harmless nitrogen gas are produced.

(vi) Reduce the **local** NOx concentration, by the use of tall chimney stacks. Local Air Quality studies are usually standard procedure when building power stations.

2.2.11.3 Carbon dioxide reduction

(i) Reduce the **load factor** of the plant, or (ultimately) close the plant.

(ii) Increase **efficiency**.

(iii) Source fuel with less inherent production of CO_2. Within a generic fuel type (coal types, gas, oil, etc.) there are variations of ratio of carbon to calorific value, but these are relatively slight and in practice not a key motivator for changing fuel diet for specific installations.

(iv) Reduce inherent production of CO_2. The production of carbon dioxide is an inevitable consequence of the combustion of hydrocarbons.

(v) **Capture** the CO_2. It is possible to capture carbon dioxide from the flue gas, or prior to combustion. The carbon dioxide is then stored in liquid form and eventually sequestered under the ground in places such as depleted oil wells. Some technologies and established and operational and some are under development.

(vi) Reduce the local CO_2 concentration. Carbon dioxide, apart from its greenhouse gas effect, does not present a direct risk to health,[51] amenity or environment.

2.2.11.4 Water impact reduction

Given that conventional plant efficiency is commonly below 40 % and that all of the waste energy turns to heat, then it is obvious that the heat production by power stations exceeds the electrical energy production by at least 50 %. The heat transport is generally provided by water, either directly by intake from and outflow to a water body and/or water from a water body passing through a cooling tower and being partly lost as steam.

(i) Reduce the **load factor** of the plant, or change the **running pattern**. Thermal plume is a cumulative effect over a period of hours. The temperature in the plume of the water body (and therefore the ability to receive the heat without damage) depends on ambient temperature, industrial activity upstream of the power station, current and water

---

[51] Carbon dioxide is a heavy gas and causes asphyxiation if inhaled at high concentrations in an enclosed space. Power stations have safety procedures to prevent this.

management in the form of locks and dams, depth and prevailing height of the water body. Reduction of load factor for water impact reasons is a relatively rare event in most plant and normally affects sustained generation more than instantaneous generation.

(ii) Increase **efficiency**. An efficiency gain at the plant has a corresponding impact on the thermal output.

(iii) Source fuel with less inherent impact on water. This is not a significant motivator for fuel diet.

(iv) Reduce **inherent impact** on water. The initial plant design will take into account the trade-off between efficiency and water impact. For example, air cooled condensers reduce the heating of water bodies. Once built, the design changes for water impact are limited and uncommon.

(v) Capture of emissions to water. Emissions to water are strictly limited by regulation. With the exception of accidental release, the emissions are not considered to be of the form that causes concentration in the biosphere.

(vi) Reduce the **local** water impact. Water impact is essentially a local/regional one and hence for thermal generation there is little trade-off between local and long distance impact.

2.2.11.5 Dust and particulate reduction

(i) Reduce the load factor of the plant, or (ultimately) close the plant. Although clearly if the plant is not running there is no dust emission, load factor reduction does not unequivocally reduce dust output, and in particular may not reduce the dust output relative to the regulatory measure. Dust output is minimised by optimisation of generation at constant load, and is at its maximum during start up as dust has settled and the combustion is less efficient as the boiler warms.

(ii) Increase efficiency. If boiler efficiency is reduced due to leaks, etc. then the harder firing of the boiler can create more dust. Hence better boiler efficiency can have the effect of reducing dust.

(iii) Source **fuel** with less inherent dust production. Different fuels can vary quite substantially in terms of ash and the form of ash that creates dust, and by combustion characteristics that cause different levels of retained carbon in the ash (making it dark in appearance). This can be a limiting factor to fuel diet, although commonly there are operational changes and minor retrofits that can accommodate a regular diet of new fuels.

(iv) Reduce **inherent impact** on health and amenity. The dispersion and the health impact is dependent on the particle size (small is worse).

(v) **Capture** of emissions. Dust is reduced by electrostatic filters that are placed prior to the flue stack. They are large steel plates that are electrically charged. The electric field polarises the dust particles, which are then attracted to the nearer of the plates, and then drop to the floor after banging ('rapping') the plates. The particles in some coals have low dielectric properties and hence poor capture levels in the precipitators. This can be partly solved by injecting the gas with particular chemicals. For example, with some irony, low sulphur coals often require the injection of sulphur trioxide. Dust performance can be moderately altered in the short term by operational changes (for example start up pace and procedure), configurational changes (e.g. adding precipitator passes, adding bag filters, altering mill classifiers), or fuel input changes. We will in section 8.4.3 briefly consider the common application of dust limits and how trans-lators can convert them to plant operation incentives.

(vi)   Reduce the local impact. Dust is essentially an inert material but can be a risk to health in high concentrations. Like water, airborne dust is mainly a local impact.

(vii) Reduce NOx production.

2.2.11.6   Ash reduction

(i)   **Reduce load factor** – Ash production is a direct function of fuel burnt, so 'coal in, ash out'.

(ii)   **Increase efficiency** – See above. Increased efficiency also reduces carbon wasted in ash and thereby reduces ash production per MWh produced.

(iii) **Source fuel with different ash content** – This is a key limiter for fuel diet. Ash is a consequence of non carbon coal content in coal (silicon, aluminium, iron, calcium respectively).

(iv)   **Reduce inherent impact** – Ash lagoons are lined as described in section 2.2.10. Carbon in ash makes it black and thereby unsuitable for use in road construction. Reduction of carbon in ash thereby reduces the amount of ash that must be disposed of.

(v)   **Capture** – Ash is captured and placed in special lagoons in most industrialised countries. This requires procurement or lease of the land and the lagoon preparation, as well as the transport cost to the lagoon.

(vi)   **Reduce local impact** – Local impact can be caused by wind picking up fly ash. This can be reduced by a number of means such as water spraying.

2.2.12   Constructing the emission abatement stacks

Many of the regulatory methods of reducing emissions are optimised by economic optimisation of emission abatement, and this is best done by the construction of abatement stacks, that rank the reduction schemes according to cost and then choose the cheapest.

2.2.12.1   Stack of emission abatement by load factor reduction

The first and most obvious way to reduce emission is to stop generating. To the generator we can calculate the value of not generating for a particular hour by the lost opportunity cost. We initially ignore complications such as start energy and emission and cost, power station failure, demand uncertainty, price uncertainty, definitions of marginal cost, volume reduction to maintain price in an orderly market and other emissions, each of which is dealt with throughout this book.

The price duration curve represents how many hours there are expected to be in the year ahead above each particular price. The optimal generation for the power station is to run for all the hours in which the market clearing price exceeds the marginal cost of generation. Now if the least valuable hour is foregone in order to reduce SOx emission, we know the lost revenue and the decrease in SOx output, and hence the marginal cost of SOx reduction. We can then reduce production further and further until there is no production at all. This is shown in Figure 2.5. This applies to SOx, NOx and CO2. Note that this is highly sensitive to the level and shape of the price duration[52] curve.

---

[52] Figure 5.8 is an example of a load duration curve. Figure 4.9 is an example of a price duration curve.

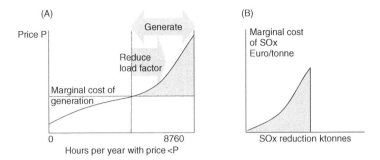

Figure 2.5 (1) The price duration curve for a single unit. The shaded area shows the generation ignoring emission limits, (2) The marginal cost stack for reducing annual emission for this unit by reducing load factor. The shaded area corresponds to that in (1)

To include the effect of start up and shutdown, the principle is similar. When we ignore starts, the sequence of generation of hours in the price duration curve is unimportant, when we consider starts, the generation hours must be in chronological order. This is described in more detail in section 5.1.5.4 and we arrive at an output diagram of similar form, with marginal cost of abatement changing with the amount of emission reduction. In this case however, the marginal cost of reduction does not necessarily increase in a monotonic[53] fashion with increasing reduction, although in practice this is approximately the case.

2.2.12.2 Stack of emission abatement by efficiency increase

Having examined the simplest method of emission abatement we examine the second generic method – efficiency increase. To the extent that emission is tied directly to the fuel input (such as SOx and CO2) then emission reduction in relation to operational, configurational, or technological change can be modelled. To the extent that emissions can be decreased by efficiency change, they can be treated as an input factor cost with the fuel.

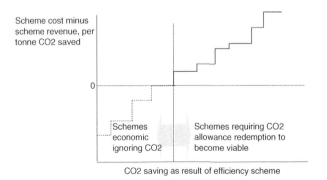

Figure 2.6 Power station schemes. Cost minus revenue with market price of CO2 set at zero

---

[53] Monotonic means that any load factor reduction leads to a reduction in emissions.

Additionality[54] can be hard to prove, as many efficiency schemes would have been enacted even without the CO2 benefit. In practice; (i) positive net present value (NPV) is a necessary but not sufficient criterion, and cash payback period, internal rate of return, return on risk adjusted capital and other criteria are also required and (ii) project hurdle rates for net present value exceed the rates implied from the capital asset pricing model (sections 10.1.24.1 and 11.6.4) due to the higher believed risks (the corporation as a whole diversifies its project risks).

Some methods of increasing efficiency are listed in section 2.2.18.

2.2.12.3   Stack of emission abatement by fuel change

Fuel input change is particularly important for SOx. As described in section 2.2.11.1 and Text Box 2.1 in section 2.1.1.1, whilst it is quite possible to source lower sulphur fuel, this comes with various difficulties. As a general rule, it is possible to make operational and configurational changes to solve the difficulty[55] of burning 'difficult' coals, including the potential safety impact. Therefore we can build a cost stack for SOx reduction from fuel sourcing. There is in fact a wide variation in sulphur content (around 0.1 % to 2 %) and hence substantial SOx reduction potential.

Figure 2.7 shows an example of the cost stack for SOx. When considering schemes, the full cost must be taken in to account. For example, a long term sourcing contract for specific low sulphur coal reduces the optionality of the power station to close earlier or later than initially scheduled and also limits load factor variations. Since the options can be sold, lost optionality becomes loss of revenue. Consistent capture of the low sulphur fuel market exposes the generator to security of supply issues since the plant may become non viable with other fuels, and therefore exposed to fuel supply problems or fuel specific issues.

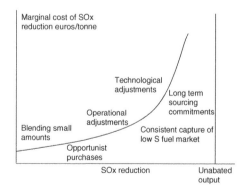

Figure 2.7   Schematic representation of the cost of different methods of SOx reduction

---

[54] The additionality principle is that funding is not provided for CO2 if they were going to happen anyway regardless of CO2.

[55] For example, mill inertion to reduce fire risk of volatile coals, mill classifier adjustment to reduce dust, decreased burner redundancy to accommodate coals with low caloric value.

2.2.12.4   Stack of emission abatement by capture

Capture of SOx through the construction of flue gas desulphurisation is a major undertaking and is an all or nothing activity. Similarly with carbon dioxide sequestration. Capture of other items such as NOx and dust, or reduction of water impact, is a much more incremental activity.

2.2.12.5   Combining abatement schemes

Combining the three stacks from load factor reduction, fuel change, and end-of-pipe capture is not an easy matter, even for a single emission. To do so requires a specific ordering. One method is as follows:

(i)   Construct the load factor abatement stack.
(ii)   Construct the whole fuel sourcing stack for each increment of the load factor abatement stack.
(iii)   Join the two stacks in self consistent manner. The possibility of double counting schemes is shown in Figure 2.8, for displacement of an increasing volume of coal with a new coal of a particular sulphur content. The same must be done for displacement by coal with varying sulphur content.
(iv)   Evaluate investment schemes. For deterministic schedules, this is shown by the criterion of the area of A is less than the area of B in Figure 2.10.

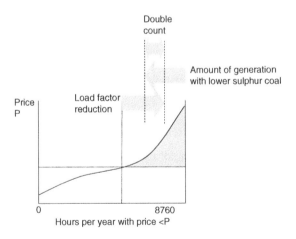

Figure 2.8   Avoiding double counting of emission abatement by two simultaneous methods. Load factor reduction limits the abatement from switching fuel by limiting the amount to fuel

If the fuel change schemes are incremental and do not involve capital cost, then the two stacks can be joined together as shown in Figure 2.9.

If the scheme involves a capital cost then it appears as a block. The economics are shown in Figure 2.10.

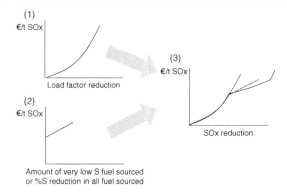

Figure 2.9   Joining the stacks from two methods of emission abatement

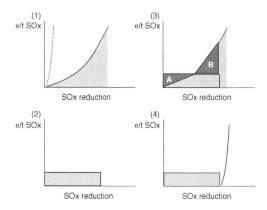

Figure 2.10   Stacks of load factor reduction and major investment in capture. (1) Load factor reduction schemes with and without the major capture, (2) major capture with no load factor reduction, (3) evaluation of major investment (A < B), (4) both schemes coincident

2.2.12.6   Abatement of two emissions from one scheme

Load factor reduction generally reduces all emissions, but because of the effect of starts, the effects are not quite coincident. The load factor reduction stack can be optimised for one emission and then the effect of the other estimated, or the stack can be optimised by taking a fixed damage ratio between the two emissions. The latter method effectively creates a price of one emission using the currency of the other emission. Figure 2.11 shows the impact on SOx and NOx emissions by load factor reduction. Note that the NOx curve is bumpier because whilst SOx is associated purely with the energy consumption, NOx output is increased on starts, and hence schedule changes which change the starts/hours ratio experience a greater change in NOx than SOx.

Load factor reduction generally reduces all emissions for the particular unit, and hence some form of aggregate value must be assigned to the total emission. One method would be to weight the emission abatement values so that the total emission is expressed in terms of a benchmark emission. This might be, for example, reflective of the market values of allowances, or the relative environmental damage, and is discussed in section 10.1.12.

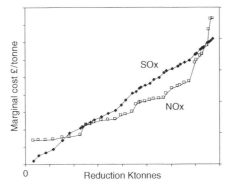

Figure 2.11   Effect of load factor reduction on annual SOx and NOx emissions for coal plant. Source National Power

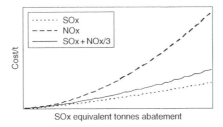

Figure 2.12   Emission abatement stacks for individual emissions, and of aggregate emission as measured by applying a weighting factor to one of the emissions

The same method can be developed to include the common situation where reduction of one factor is associated by increase in another. We can draw a graph of changes in the level of one emission relative to impact on the other emission for a base case optimised with a particular rule, or we can use the same method as shown in Figure 2.12, with the sign changed where emissions are increased.

The treatment is the same as for schemes that reduce both emissions, except the sign of one of the emission changes is reversed.

2.2.13   Stock management

Stock management is important for coal fired power stations.

Coal is weighed[56] on arrival at the plant and assay samples are taken. Periodically the coal stock volume is checked by aerial survey, and by sampling the compacted density the stock weight is estimated. From the assays, the calorific value of the coal stock is measured (the 'heat account') and the sulphur content (the sulphur account[57]).

---

[56] By weighing the goods vehicles before and after unloading.

[57] 'Heat account' is an established term. 'Sulphur account' is not. It is harder to calculate than the heat account because coal density, sulphur percentage by weight, and calorific value by weight are all required for each area of the coal stock.

2.2.14 Flexibility

We have seen that energy must be produced at the instant it is consumed, and we will see that demand variation, and generator and network failures are such that the production complex must be highly flexible. Flexibility covers a very wide spectrum in time, so much so that the nature of flexibility is different for each timeframe. In this book, we regard the ability to produce more or less electricity for the period in question, relative to central plan, to be expressed as positive and negative capacity.

The limitation on capacity is different at different times. For example, in the long term, the limitation on fossil fuel is really on energy rather than capacity, as it is energy consumption rather than capacity maintenance that both depletes the fuel and limits the allowable combustion due to environmental impact. In a slightly shorter term, the limit is more on the dependency on generation capacity and this is discussed in more detail in Chapter 12 on security of supply.

In this book, primary attention is paid to the structured management of flexibility at an hourly resolution, and the interaction of the appropriate mechanisms with shorter term effects on system operation and annual term effects on security of supply. The mechanisms that will be described in Chapter 11 will be shown to marry plant operation in market circumstances to long term valuation and optimisation of environmental consequences. Flexibility provision below a resolution of about hourly is commonly termed 'reserve' and 'ancillary services'. The flexibility that is called for only a small percentage of the time is commonly termed 'capacity'. Here, they are all included in the same family.

Flexibility has many dimensions. The principal dimensions are:

(i)   Physical capability to deliver;
(ii)   response time;
(iii) delivery rate in MW/minute;
(iv)   sustainability of provision once called;
(v)   amount in MW.

Both system and plant operators take a strong interest in:

(i)   cost structure of capacity capability, lost opportunity, energy delivery and of delivery rate;
(ii)   likelihood of uptake.

From a market design perspective, there are four key elements:

(i)   reserve and flexibility within the half hour period, and short term plant warmth;
(ii)   the cost structure of three plant states – full load, minimum stable generation, and standby (off and ready), and of the changing between states;
(iii) the annual fixed cost of plant, including investment cost and capacity costs;
(iv)   long term capacity.

The issues of capacity and environment have much commonality to other industries. The special challenges of flexibility are particular to the ESI.

The figure below shows an approximate mapping of the capacity requirements of the ESI.

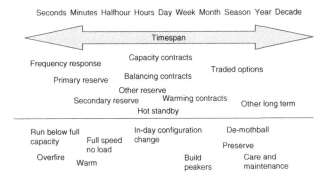

Figure 2.13   Depiction of response and capacity mechanisms, commercial and physical

Starting with the shortest term flexibility, there is frequency response, commonly termed primary response. To provide frequency response, governors[58] on the plant[59] control steam and fuel flow.

The older subcritical coal plant can release energy quickly since, as described in section 2.2.3 the thermal energy stored in the plant is considerable. While an instant release of energy by, for example, the opening of steam valves into the turbine, delivers energy immediately, this energy is 'borrowed' and must be replaced in the plant. This is picked up early in the plant and ultimately by more fuel. The pick up of energy from one mechanism to another is shown in Figure 2.14.

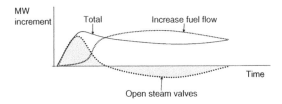

Figure 2.14   The individual and total energy delivery profiles for an example of the delivery of primary and secondary response

To keep the plant in a condition to provide this response requires it to be (i) running below full capacity and (ii) maintaining higher pressures than are optimal for efficiency and plant life usage (see appendix). The former incurs lost opportunity cost and efficiency cost (see section 2.2.18). The latter incurs plant damage cost. In addition to this, the load variation from the provision of frequency response incurs plant damage due principally to the increase in transient temperature effects.

Plants with low storage, such as CCGT rely more directly on fuel intake adjustment to adjust short term energy flow. While the provision of frequency response is often mandatory in the grid code, plant operators try to limit the load variation in order to protect the

---

[58] Governors are mechanical or (more commonly) electrical devices that sense changes to frequency and automatically change some feature of the plant such as steam valves.

[59] Since the phase of the plant can only vary very slightly from that of the nearby grid, then it is obvious that the frequency at the plant will be almost identical to that of the grid.

blades of the gas turbine. For maximum efficiency, turbine blades operate close to their metallurgical limits, and load variation increases the effective operating temperature as shown in Figure 2.15.

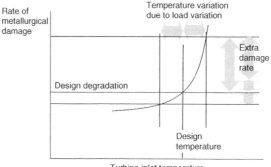

Figure 2.15 Because of the strong curvature of the damage vs. temperature curve, temperature variations cause an increase in the rate of damage without altering average efficiency

Within the day, upward and downward flexibility is maintained by plants changing load between full load and minimum stable generation.[60] Operating at minimum stable generation is generally benign to plant due to the lower temperatures, but the cycling of the plant can be damaging, particularly for plant with thick metal such as nuclear plant and some older thermal plant, particularly in the USA. In addition, operating at minimum stable generation is inefficient for thermodynamic reasons, and wasteful of fixed heat (see section 2.2.18) and because plant configurations are optimised for full load, not minimum stable generation.

Frequency response is measured in (i) time to start delivering energy, (ii) rate of energy delivery increase/decrease in MW/minute, (iii) sustainability of response and (iv) frequency sensitivity (at what deviation from standard system frequency does the response begin), (v) maximum MW provided.

More than one form of flexibility can be offered at the same time, but there is a degree of mutual exclusivity.

We can simplify flexibility in commercial terms by categorising it into three:

(i)   **Reserve** – Positive and negative energy delivered between seconds and minutes of request, and called under a medium commercial framework agreement which is not tied to specific periods.
(ii) **Balancing** – Positive and negative energy delivered over five minute to half-hour periods between half an hour and a few hours after instruction. Generally voluntary participation and no forward commitment.
(iii) **Options and other capacity mechanisms** – Generally positive energy delivered over a halfhour to few hour period. Generally called between a week and a day in advance of delivery. Sometimes committed up to months or years in advance, sometimes sold up to about a week prior to delivery.

---

[60] The load level below which the plant is incapable of operating effectively, for example due to insufficient steam temperatures, excessive vibrations, excessive NOx production, etc. As with most plant factors, minimum stable generation can be reduced by operational and configurational measures.

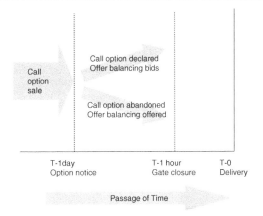

Figure 2.16   Depiction of voluntary flexibility in terms of options

There is not a high correlation between the requirements of the system operator for the different kinds of flexibility. Hence, although plant cannot commit to provide mutually exclusive services in advance (for example, frequency response and balancing that could take the plant above maximum capacity[61]), there are some circumstances in which one form of capacity can be offered after the drawdown of the other form has become certain. For example, if a bilateral call option has been declared or abandoned, then balancing can be offered (positive capacity if the call was abandoned and negative capacity if the call was declared). This can be resolved by comparing the commitment period and the notice and delivery period. Frequency response is commonly committed for a whole year, with notice that is virtually instantaneous and redeclarable. This form of response therefore has a high degree of mutual exclusivity with other forms. An option, however, will be committed to up to some months in advance, but the delivery for a period of hours will commonly be certain a day or days in advance. If a call option (the call on more power) is declared, then negative balancing can subsequently be offered. If the call option is abandoned, then positive balancing can subsequently be offered.

Since commitments must be honoured, the plant must decide in advance (i) what energy to sell forward, (ii) what options to sell and (iii) what reserve commitments to agree to. Some examples are shown in Figure 2.17. It is assumed here that the plant can be off or viably run at all levels between minimum stable generation and nameplate capacity. We ignore the necessary time for state changes.

The unit operator must decide what contracts to sell. They have different expected total values, degrees of financial certainty, degrees of schedule and ramp rate uncertainty, and degrade the plant in different ways.

Much plant was designed for the efficient production of energy, with relatively little design attention paid to short term flexibility. The result is that plant has commonly been run beyond design specification and some problems have been experienced in service.

---

[61] Capacity in this sense is economic capacity. While as we can see, plants can often run beyond normal capacity, because use of system charge is commonly related to the maximum generated capacity, then it is not economic to run for a very short period above normal capacity.

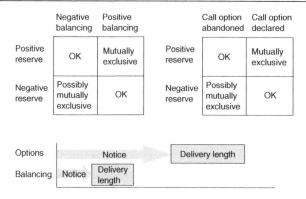

Figure 2.17   Interaction of options, balancing bids and offers and reserve commitments

Short term flexibility requirements have increased for a number of reasons, including:

(i)   In a competitive supply market, the demand information that suppliers have is less than for a monopoly supplier. Hence demand forecasting is less accurate, and hence there is less notice period for required load changes, and corresponding higher ramp rates.

(ii)   In a market supplied by a monopoly generator, smooth load following can be centrally coordinated. In a competitive free market, it is not possible to coordinate so closely and hence some units are required to have faster ramp rates to ensure sufficient ramp rate for aggregate generation.

(iii) In order to reduce total fixed costs, the capacity margin has decreased in many countries. Therefore each plant has to provide greater flexibility as a proportion of unit capacity.

(iv)   The increase of renewable must-run plant, and wind power in particular, combined with a general decrease of flexibility of thermal plant as the CCGT + nuclear/coal (i.e. relatively inflexible to relatively flexible) ratio decreases.

The result of all this is that conventional coal plant plays a significant role in energy balancing.

Some plant, particularly conventional plant, can provide load above the normal capacity. The first method is simply to run the plant closer to the operating limits of the materials. This can be done, but, as shown in Figure 2.15, is very damaging to the plant. Other methods including injecting water or steam in front of a gas turbine, in order to increase the mass flow at the turbine. This decreases blade life in a measured manner. Another method is to reduce the extent of recirculation of heat in conventional plant. The effect on efficiency is shown in Figure 2.19. This can generally be done on a sustained basis, although this is rare due to the high fuel costs. It is an important source of reserve for a one-in-twenty cold winter if capacity margins are low.

Water injection is a way to increase power output at the expense of efficiency. By injecting water in front of the turbines, the mass flow is increased, and thereby the power output. The efficiency loss is caused by the conversion of warm water to hot steam. Steam injection is similar but with less efficiency loss. Injection also increases the damage rate of the turbine blades.

2.2.15 Reliability and availability

It is the nature of conventional generation that outage rates are high compared to installations in other industries. There are a number of reasons for this, including the operation of materials at close to their limits in aggressive conditions, the age and complexity of power plants, and the limited redundancy of the process.

A 20 year old coal plant would typically have planned outages for around 8 % of the time and unplanned outages for a further 8 % of the time. Planned and unplanned outage rates and timing can be altered, at a cost, by a mix of operational, configurational, and maintenance measures.

Plant outage rate is closely related to:

(i)   Quality of operating procedures.
(ii) Operating regime. Between overhauls and inspections, plant will accumulate damage continuously and become more susceptible to failure. Plant starts are believed to substantially increase the rate of major failure. Different regimes have different windows for opportunity maintenance (plant repair without having to schedule an outage).
(iii) Plant condition. As described in the appendix, plant condition can be approximately modelled by the accumulation of damage for hours-and-starts and the cumulative spend on the plant. Plant failure rate is closely related to plant condition.

From the market design perspective, what is important is the ability to model planned and unplanned outages, to accommodate for the reliability aspect of the marginal cost of generation, and, to a lesser extent to make an efficiency adjustment for the average impact that partial outages have on operating efficiencies.

2.2.16 Reactive power

Reactive power is described in the appendix. To produce reactive power, the generator must advance the phase of the voltage. This changes the *power factor* of the unit. This is done either by executing a 'tap change' which changes the number of turns on the generator transformer, or by increasing the 'excitation' of the rotor. This increases the current in the rotor, which causes the wires to heat, which in turn increases the degradation on the inter-turn insulation.

While a plant must be synchronised to the grid to produce reactive power, it does not need to be producing active power.

Some wind power designs consume reactive power. The wind turbine is coupled through the gearbox to a rotor, and the generator is driven inductively[62] rather than synchronously.

2.2.17 Three phase

If the stator has a single winding around its circumference, then the electromotive forces in different elements of the winding are not in phase and hence the total voltage across the stator is less than the sum of the individual turns. By having three sets of wires, this problem is avoided and hence the maximum power available from a machine of particular capacity is increased. These three wires connect to the three wires in the transmission grid.

---

[62] The mechanism is as in Figure 2.18, but the rotor and generator are not synchronised, and the phase slips. To generate synchronous power, the turbine itself must be synchronised and pole slip does not and must not occur.

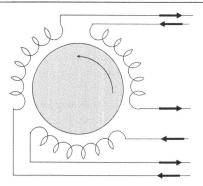

Figure 2.18   Three phases of stator around the generator rotor of a power station unit

2.2.18   Efficiency

We can simply model the efficiency of a power station in relation to load by considering the 'fixed heat', that is required to drive the turbines at full speed and maintain synchronisation with the grid but not actually produce power, and the variable heat, that is required to produce load. It is immediately obvious that there is a strong efficiency benefit from running at the highest load possible.[63]

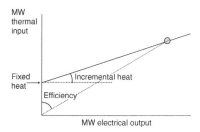

Figure 2.19   Turbine efficiency in relation to load

To run a plant below capacity in order to provide reserve alters material damage (better in some areas and worse in others) and entails a loss of efficiency.

Efficiency can be enhanced by, for example:

(i)   Reduced percentage of fixed heat, by running at **higher load**.
(ii)   **Reduced rate of partial outage**, or other de-rating which causes running at low load.
(iii) Increased input **temperature** and decreased output temperature.
(iv)   Optimal **configuration** of pressure and temperature at each stage.
(v)   **Cycle alteration** such as regeneration (using turbine exhaust to heat the gas exiting the compressor), intercooling (cooling between compression stages) and reheat (heating turbine stages).

---

[63] The limitation is generally the physical performance and degradation of metal in pressure parts and gas turbine blades at high temperature.
[64] This shows the graph for a single valve steam turbine. For various reasons due to the way that output is controlled, some plants have convex (upward curving) efficiency curves, and some have concave curves. For a convex curve, see Wood and Wollenberg (1996).

(vi)   More efficient **circulation of heat**, heat transfer and use of waste heat (for example air heaters, cooling tower repack).

(vii)   Improved **heat exchange efficiency**.

(viii) **Energy consumption** (auxiliary system of pumps, fans, heat and light for buildings, other energy consumption such as fuel delivery).

(ix)   Reduce energy of start (for example by reducing start time).

(x)   General measures, such as leak reduction and reduction of clearances.

(xi)   **Turbine efficiency** (replant with new blades, or maintenance and washing of existing blades).

(xii)   Fuel **combustion improvement** by mill enhancements, burners, air ratio, fuel/air distribution, etc.

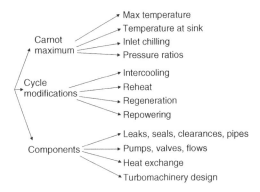

Figure 2.20   Some methods of efficiency enhancement for thermal plant

Because atmospheric conditions of air pressure and temperature and (more importantly) water temperature change, output and efficiency (particularly for CCGT's) is sensitive to ambient conditions, with best performance in cold weather.

Text Box 2.2 – Thermodynamics

The most efficient thermodynamic cycle that uses a heat source and a heat sink to generate work, is the Carnot cycle. The Carnot cycle has four (reversible) stages: (i) isothermal (constant temperature) heat addition and (ii) isentropic (constant entropy) expansion, (iii) isothermal heat rejection, (iv) isentropic compression. The efficiency of this, and all reversible cycles is $\eta_{thermal,reversible} = 1 - T_L/T_H$, where T_H is the temperature at the beginning of the cycle, (equivalent to the gas turbine blade and the boiler) and the end of the cycle (the exhaust). The three key cycles for power generation are the Brayton (open cycle gas turbines), Rankine (steam plant), and Brayton-Rankine (CCGT). These are less efficient than the Carnot cycle but can be made more efficient by making them more like the Carnot cycle (for example reheat, intercooling and regeneration). It is clear why materials are designed for high input temperature. For further information see Çengel and Boles.

2.2.19   Cost

Apart from the factor costs such as fuel and emission permits, there are a number of factors that alter the fixed and marginal cost of production

(i)   **Technology**.

(ii)   **MW/unit** – Operating costs per unit do not increase in direct proportion with unit size and hence operating cost per MW decreases with unit size. This has caused a gradual increase in unit size over the years to around 500 MW.

(iii)   **Units/site** – Similarly to MW/unit, operating cost per MW decreases with total size of plant.

(iv)   **Environmental effects** – in terms of abatement cost and allowances and taxes.

(v)   **Plant value** – In section 10.1.24, we will show that, in a competitive free market, in which customers switch supplier, and assets change hands, that the financial holding cost of the plant (that forms part of fixed costs and which must be recovered) is dependent on the prevailing market value of the plant. This in turn depends on the revenue available from the plant.[65]

(vi)   **Depreciation status** – The depreciation of accounting value should not in theory affect the operation of the plant, since the plant should always be revalued at market. However, in practice, depreciation below market value causes a lowering of the financial element of fixed costs. The sale of plant also changes its accounting value. When fair returns are examined by regulators, they pay particular attention to depreciated value.

(vii)   **Obsolescence**. Advances in plant technology, particularly in efficiency, make older plant obsolescent over time, even if in perfect condition. This becomes manifest in the lowering of market prices. This reduces the plant value, and therefore the financial fixed costs, which encourages old plant to run more.

(viii) **Residual life**. The residual life of the plant, described in the appendix, affects the marginal cost of the plant in the manner described in section 6.4.5.

(ix)   **Plant life usage** – This is an approximation of the future maintenance cost incurred by operation, and depends on plant design, age, condition and other factors. This is described in more detail in the appendix.

(x)   **Failure rate** – Failure causes repair cost and lost opportunity cost to the generator. It also causes cost in making good the committed power sold by purchasing it in the market.

(xi)   **Operating regime** – This affects the plant damage costs, as the equivalent operating hour cost calibration applies to an established operating envelope. These marginal costs can change outside the envelope. For example, the interval between running periods affects the capability to do opportunity maintenance. Staffing costs are also dependent on regime, since any regime that is incompatible with domestic life requires incentivisation and often the use of contract labour. The operating regime also affects efficiency through starts, part loading and other effects.

(xii)   **Provision of ancillary services** – This is similar to plant life usage and refers specifically to the provision of ancillary services, such as frequency response and reactive power while on load. This increases the damage rate to the plant by, for example, overfiring, transient steam temperatures, higher pressures and heating of rotor wires.

---

[65] The problem of the circular argument here is discussed in section 10.1.24.

(xiii) **Position on the network** – Depending on the position on the transmission or distribution networks, the plant experience different fixed and variable charges, and these are also dependent on generation profile.

2.2.20 Generation mix

Demand is highly heterogeneous with respect to location, periodicity, variability, inductive/resistive characteristics and voltage sensitivity. No single kind of power can effectively serve the demand, and a power generation mix is required. The key items in the mix are:

(i)   location;
(ii)   network position (grid connected or distribution embedded);
(iii)   fuel source and fuel logistics;
(iv)   short term unplanned variation in natural source (e.g. wind, run of river hydro);
(v)   short term planned variation in natural source (e.g. tidal);
(vi)   medium term variation in natural source (e.g. hydro);
(vii)   availability;
(viii)   reliability;
(ix)   flexibility (planned and unplanned);
(x)   reactive power provision or requirement;
(xi)   provision of the family of reserve and black start;
(xii)   fixed/marginal cost ratio;
(xiii)   capacity (MW)/energy capability (MWh/year) ratio;
(xiv)   actual load factor;
(xv)   fuel cost periodicity and variability;
(xvi)   outage phasing;
(xvii)   outage characteristics (trips, de-ratings, fleet wide type faults, etc.);
(xviii) environmental load of each type;
(xix)   size.

Although some power generation is built for peaking generation, it is most common for units to be built for baseload operation. This is for:

(i)   technological reasons (new units with new technology have best efficiencies);
(ii)   risk and finance reasons (cash generation is important in early years of financing, and baseload revenue risk is easier to predict and quantify);
(iii) gaming reasons.

The result is that older units fall down the merit order until either; (i) the marginal net revenue from running at low load factor is less than the fixed costs,[66] (ii) the reliable flexibility that is required for low load factor running cannot be sustained and (iii) the environmental performance degrades so that marginal abatement costs become prohibitive, or they cannot comply with tightening regulations.

---

[66] Older power stations tend to be small, thereby incurring high fixed costs per MW installed.

2.2.21   Requirements for ancillary services

Ancillary services that are provided by generators to the grid to maintain the electrical stability of the system. There are three main services that are provided:

(i) **Reserve** – This is the most important and concerns the ability to change load quickly and is a family of response, reserve, balancing, flexibility and capacity.
(ii) **Reactive power** – The need for reactive power is described in the transmission section and the provision is described in the generation section. To provide reactive power, the plant must be synchronised.
(iii) **Black start** – Power plant commonly uses electricity imported from the grid to run the auxiliary motors and other general electrical requirements to start the plant. To maintain stability after possible network failures, there are a number of plants that can start up with no imported power.

In the USA, the Federal Electricity Regulatory Commission (FERC) specifies six ancillary services, namely:

(i) regulation and frequency response service;
(ii) energy imbalance service;
(iii) operating reserve – spinning reserve service;
(iv) operating reserve – supplemental reserve service;
(v) scheduling, system control, and dispatch services;
(vi) reactive supply and voltage control from generation sources service.

The first five are in the same family that encompasses reserve. Each entails variation in energy output over different timeframes and for different amounts.

2.2.22   Plant dynamics

Information about plant dynamics accompany the simple hours-MW-cost provided to the system operator. They can run into pages of information but can be summarised:

(i) **Notice to synchronisation** – This is the time take from notice to the first capability to deliver load. It is highly dependent on the warmth of the plant (up to around 36 hours since last running) and on the plant configuration maintained in readiness.
(ii) **Ramp up** – The maximum ramp rate in MW/minute is dependent partly on the exposure of the plant to damage from differential expansion, partly due to working practices by which the various parts of the plant are warmed, and partly a commercial decision on limitation on plant life usage during start and fuel expenditure during warm up.
(iii) **Ramp down** – Ramp down generally puts less stress on the plant than ramp up, but there are limits, particularly in relation to differential contraction.
(iv) **Minimum on time**.
(v) **Minimum off time** (various sequencing effects require the minimum on and off times).

2.2.23   The relative value of the different forms of plant service

There are many dimensions to the delivery of power stations, and to the variability of the commercial value of the different aspects. Figure 2.21 shows examples.

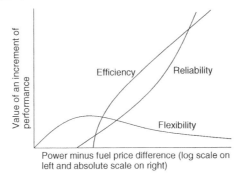

Figure 2.21   Value of three core power station features with respect to variations in the market price for power-minus-fuel at a set conversion rate

2.2.24 Generator hedging

We show in Chapter 11 how we can build up a financial model for a power station by first imagining that it is a fuel-to-power converter that is free of non fuel marginal costs, emissions, or failure, and then relaxing these assumptions by taking these factors into account.

Power generators have a 'delta'[67] exposure to all factor costs. We can calculate the deltas by defining the plant in derivative terms by using the plant model in Chapter 11 and the derivative techniques of Chapter 9. The cost factors and their characteristics are set out in this chapter.

There are two particular features to note for power generator hedging:

(i)   High merit power plant has high fixed costs in relation to quasi fixed and marginal costs. This increases the delta to market prices, and for a plant with zero marginal costs, is equal to the plant capacity in all tenors.

(ii) As is described in section 10.1.24, fixed costs are closely related to plant value. For mid and low merit plant, a relatively large percentage of plant value is in 'time value' (the vanilla option and extra flexibility contracts described in Chapter 11). For this reason, hedging the plant delta is insufficient to capture plant risks, and the option value should also be hedged if the market liquidity is available.

When executing the hedges, the following factors should be taken into account:

(i)   The cost of risk for the particular risks for the generating company, in relation to other risks carried by the holding company (such as those carried by a supply division[68]).

(ii) The cost of risk drift contained within the forward price of the market.

(iii) The cost of risk of other risk transfer companies, such as insurers.

(iv) The estimated risk preference profile of the shareholder.

(v) All variable cost and revenue elements should be taken into account, as well as their correlation to each other. For example, labour costs and equipment costs are positively correlated with plant margin. Direct environmental costs in the form of emission permits should be included in the hedge decision, as should shadow costs.

---

[67] The delta here is the change in annual or through life net present value of the plant, according to a unit change in one of the factors.

[68] One division should hedge with the other.

Figure 2.22 illustrates the fundamental difficulty of using demand signals to drive new build. The optimum hedge for supply companies barely overlaps the optimum hedge for a producer once the funding has been committed.

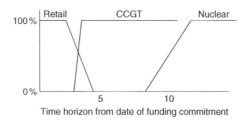

Figure 2.22   Hedging periods for a retail business, a combined cycle gas turbine and a nuclear plant, just after funding is committed

2.3   HIGH VOLTAGE TRANSMISSION, NETWORK OPERATION, SYSTEM OPERATION

2.3.1   Electrical networks

We have seen that electricity is instantaneously delivered; with small delivery costs, over very long distances, and that the storage difficulty means that the rate of delivery (and therefore the value) changes at an exceptionally fast pace (as fast as seconds). It is the time-space characteristic of electricity, more than any other, that drives the ESI.

However, we cannot leap to the modelling assumptions that the electricity grid; (i) has zero resistance, reactance and (as a result), constraint, (ii) that the grid is so extensive that power can always be routed along a contract path, without having to worry about its actual physical path and (iii) that no part of the network ever fails. Therefore network considerations are essential in the design of electricity markets.

2.3.1.1   The basics

Networks can be described as high voltage transmission or 'grid' networks, low voltage distribution networks sometimes called 'wires', and interconnectors between grids. The exit voltage at which distribution picks up electricity from the transmission grids is commonly around 110 kV.

The electrical losses in the conducting wires are inversely proportional to the voltage (see section 2.3.1.5) and hence power is transmitted at the highest voltage that is safe, practical and has acceptable risk to flashover.[69] Hence voltage from the power generator is typically 'stepped up' to around 400,000[70] volts (400 kV) for transmission before stepping down through a series of transformers as far as domestic voltages of 230[71] or 110 volts in most

---

[69] The clearance required is upward curving with respect to line voltage, thereby having a substantial effect on required tower height for high voltage lines. Flashover is the main cause of fault in electrical interruption, usually caused by natural or man made accident, or unchecked growth of trees.

[70] The highest used in practice is 765 kV.

[71] Domestic equipment is built to accommodate different voltages within 10 % tolerance, as some countries have slightly different domestic voltage standards.

countries. To transform voltage, the current must be alternating current (AC), and this is the main reason that modern power systems use alternating current. Direct current (DC) is used in special situations such as very long lines at very high voltage (lines losses are lower for DC), and interconnection between AC systems which are out of phase, such as France and England, or Texas and neighbouring states.

The standard[72] for AC frequency is 50 Herz (cycles per second) in most places except for the USA, the Western part of Japan, much of South America and a few other places where it is 60 Herz. Higher frequency has the advantage of requiring smaller generators and the disadvantage of causing higher line impedance and, to a lesser extent, resistance. Neighbouring control areas with different frequencies, such as Brazil and Argentina use frequency converters.

Electrical energy in the form of current can travel through thousands of kilometres of wires at $\frac{2}{3}$ the speed of light,[73] and hence any electrical load anywhere on the system will simultaneously affect all generators everywhere,[74] and also means that the AC is synchronised across the whole system. The synchronisation of the grid means that the inertia of the system is enormous. Note that while the inertia is treated as electrical inertia, it is in practice the kinetic energy in the rotating parts of the power stations. Most generators have automatic governors that detect the tiny falls in frequency that arise from load variations, and respond by providing more energy, for example by opening valves for the steam that drives the turbines.

Coordination between network operators allows synchronous operation over very large areas, and it is the management of reserve that enables this to happen.

To be synchronous, the system does not have to be in phase across the whole system. Indeed in very long systems, the phase may vary by more than one cycle from one end to the other, as long as there are no loops that allow a connection between out of phase sections.

Current is transmitted on the grid using 'three[75] phase', which requires three wires, as described in section 2.2.17.

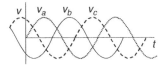

Figure 2.23   Three phase (power cycles)

2.3.1.2   Limits

There are four kinds of limits that affect large power lines, namely thermal limits, stability limits, security limits and reactive power limits.

Thermal limits – The passage of electric current through wires of finite resistance causes the wires to heat up. Excessive heat causes the wires to sag by thermal expansion, and to

---

[72] In the early days, frequency was primarily driven up by the need to reduce flicker in light bulbs.

[73] Electromagnetic waves travel about two thirds as fast in metal as they do in a vacuum.

[74] This is the case for resistive load. Inductive load is more localised but still over a range of tens to hundreds of kilometres.

[75] Higher phases, particularly six or twelve, have advantages in thermal loading of lines and transmission efficiency but are not standard. See Weedy and Cory (2001).

permanently lengthen and lose strength by annealing.[76] In addition, thermal overload can damage ancillary equipment such as transformers (for example breakdown of the insulating oil, and of the interwire packing), insulators, breakers, relays and other equipment.

Stability limits – To remain stable, the system must remain synchronous, with stable phase differences. There are three kinds of stability, steady state, transient and dynamic. The phase of the voltage leads and lags slightly in different parts of the system, but the system must overall remain synchronised. Synchronising forces keep generator rotors (and motors) close to the phase of the voltage in the lines, but if the rotor moves too far ahead of the field then the synchronising force weakens and a 'pole slip' and desychronisation can occur. For steady state stability, the steady angle between rotors and wire voltage must be within certain limits. Transient stability refers to the ability of the system to respond to major disturbance in such a manner that steady state stability is regained. This is affected by the interconnectivity of elements that can cause disturbance, such as line outages. System response to disturbance is usually evident within about one second. Line impedance, and therefore line length between generation and load affects power angle and therefore steady state stability. Load changes affect stability since they cause and require changes in generation. Dynamic stability refers to system response to small oscillations in the system. If the oscillations are damped, then the system is stable. If they are amplified then the system is unstable. To prevent this, a number of technical measures are required, each of which has an impact on power generators.

Security limit – Security limits, also called transfer limits, are a result of needing to maintain a particular level of redundancy on the whole system, given particular levels of thermal limits and stability limits. These limits apply to groups of lines.

Reactive limits – Transmission lines have an impedance that causes the current to lag. This causes stability issues. Without reactive power injection at the generating units or on the transmission lines, this would limit the power flow as described in the appendix.

2.3.1.3 Kirchhoff's laws

Kirchhoff's laws, written in 1845, enable us to understand the basics of electrical flows in networks. They apply for both DC and AC. It is common in market design to simplify locational signalling by using 'DC-like' modelling, in which the system is modelled as if it were DC, with impedance playing the role of resistance.

Kirchhoff's current law (KCL) is that the total current flowing in and out of any point must be zero.

Kirchhoff's voltage law (KVL) is that the total voltage change around a loop must be zero.

These can be described simply. We cannot 'lose' current, and there can be only one voltage at a particular point.

---

[76] Metals are made of tiny crystals called grains and faults called dislocations. Dislocations and grain boundaries can move faster when metal warms and the rearrangement weakens the metal.

2.3.1.4   Use of Kirchhoff's current law to plan line voltage

Consider a resistive load at the end of a transmission line. Figure 2.24 shows Ohms law for the line and for the load. From Kirchhoff's first law we know that $I_{AB} = I_{BC}$. The power lost/extracted in the line and the load are $I_{AB} V_{AB}$ and $I_{AB} V_{BC}$ respectively, or $I_{AB}^2 R_{AB}$ and $I_{BC}^2 R_{BC}$ respectively. Substituting in, we get $P_{BC} = (V_A - V_B)^2 \frac{R_{BC}}{R_{AB}^2}$ so we can clearly see that to deliver maximum power for minimum loss, we want low line resistance and high line voltage.

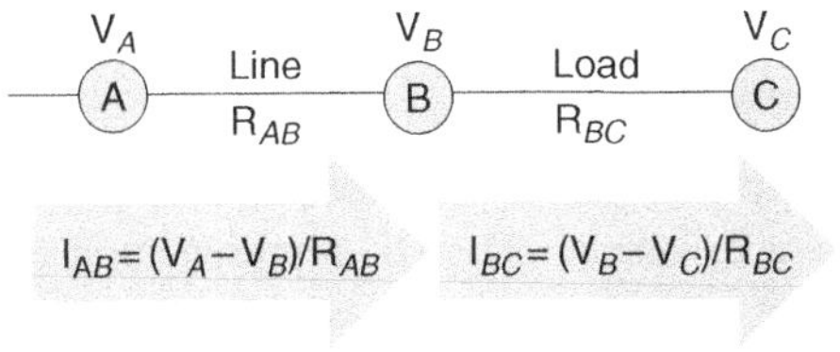

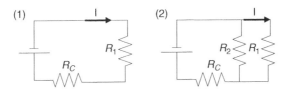

Figure 2.24   Application of Kirchhoff's law to a transmission line and resistive electrical load

Whilst most energy loss on transmission is due to resistance, some is due to insulator leakage, corona for overhead lines, and dielectric losses in cables.

2.3.1.5   Losses in relation to power flow

We can see the relation between losses and load in a simple DC model.[77]

Figure 2.25   Simple DC model to show losses. (1) Circuit with one load, (2) with additional load

The power drawn in the first circuit is $P_1 = I^2 R_1$ and the losses in the first circuit are $L_1 = I^2 R_C$ where R_C is the resistance of the circuit.

In the second circuit, the current through the initial load is unchanged, and the current through the second load is (from KVL) $I \frac{R_1}{R_2}$

The power drawn in the second circuit is $P_2 = I^2 R_1 + I^2 \left(\frac{R_1}{R_2}\right)^2 R_2$ and the losses in the second circuit are $L_2 = \left(I + I \frac{R_1}{R_2}\right)^2 R_C$

With a little substitution and rearrangement we have:

$$\frac{L_2/P_2}{L_1/P_1} = 1 + R_1/R_2 = \frac{P_2}{P_1}$$

So the losses, expressed as a percentage of useful load, increase with the load. For example, if load doubles, the loss percentage doubles, and the absolute amount of losses quadruples.

---

[77] For more formal treatment, see Wood and Wollenberg (1996).

This is important in the consideration of market mechanisms for losses. For example, a standard loss factor adjustment for a particular node will only approximately reflect the average losses incurred as a result of flow into or out from the node.

In a networked power system, incremental losses from generation cannot be definitively assigned, since an extra MW of generation could be divided amongst the load in different ways according to convention, for example, *pro rata* or according to local demand stacks. On the demand side, incremental losses could be assigned from the least cost generation solution before and after a 1 MW in demand at a node.

2.3.1.6   Loop flow in a simple loop

When doing market design, it is sufficient for most purposes to use a 'DC-like' method and model as if impedance were resistance. The DC representation of the system is sufficient for an intuitive understanding of the key concepts such as constraint, loop flow and location marginal pricing.

We can use Kirchhoff's laws to help us with DC load flow. Figure 2.26 shows the simplest loop, with three nodes. This loop is part of a bigger network. To properly represent a small network with three nodes, we would show nodes A and C connected up via an electromotive force, and an earth point at which voltage is notionally zero. In Figure 2.26 and subsequent figures, we have transformed the voltage source to a current source.

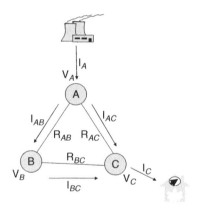

Figure 2.26   Representation of Kirchhoff's Current and Voltage Laws to determine loop flows

In Figure 2.26, we see from KCL that $I_A = -I_{AB} - I_{AC} = -I_C = -I_{BC} - I_{AC}$ where the sign convention here is positive for current flowing to the node.[78]

We see from KVL and Ohms law that

$$V_C = V_A - I_{AB}R_{AB} - I_{BC}R_{BC} = V_A - I_{AC}R_{AC}$$

$$I_{AB}R_{AB} + I_{BC}R_{BC} = I_{AC}R_{AC}$$

$$I_{AB} = \frac{R_{AC}}{R_{AB} + R_{BC}}$$

---

[78] In transmission networks, nodes are called buses. The terms are used interchangeably here.

Taking the simple case for equal resistance on all lines, then we can see by inspection that two thirds of the current will flow along route AC and one third will flow along route ABC.

KCL and KVL can be applied to AC systems, by replacing resistance R by the reactance Z.

2.3.1.7 Location marginal pricing in constrained networks

Understanding loop flow is critical in the understanding of the location element of electricity markets.

Consider an electrical system with three buses, two are connected to generation units and one of which is connected to demand load. One unit is more expensive than the other in terms of marginal cost, there is no connection between the buses A and B, and there is no line constraint.

To minimise the generation cost, the system operator dispatches the cheaper plant to its maximum capacity and dispatches the more expensive plant for the remainder of the energy.

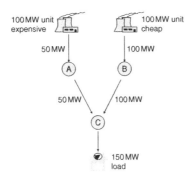

Figure 2.27 Least cost dispatch in system with no loop

Now consider a connection between buses A and B so the system now has a loop. The system operator can control flow by (i) dispatching units, (ii) instructing alteration of load, (iii) connecting and breaking circuits and (iv) altering the impedance (and capacitance which offsets the impedance) and resistance of the lines and associated equipment.

If the system operator can break the connection between A and B, then the situation is as before. However, suppose that this cannot happen for other reasons such as small load on the line, system security, or other reasons.

Firstly consider what happens to the power from unit A. Kirchhoff's laws tell us that while we might wish for electricity from B to flow straight to C, that some will flow first to A.

We can represent the total flow by superposing the flow from each generation unit to each load. In the case of equal impedance, then the power flow from each unit will be as shown in Figure 2.28.

Now suppose that line BC has a thermal limit of 83.3 MW, i.e. it is at its limit. Here we must note that the line limit will not actually prevent the current flowing, it is just harmed by the flow. Therefore the flows must be adjusted (if not by reactance changes) by redispatch of units. It is clear that any increase in load at bus C must be met by an increase in flow on line AC. Elementary algebra tells us that, using the same impedances as before, that this

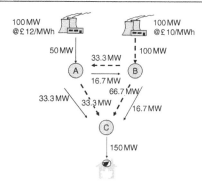

Figure 2.28 Power flow, expressed by the superposition of individual flows from units to load

must be done by increasing the generation at unit A and *decreasing* the generation at unit B. This is shown in Figure 2.29.

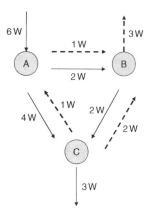

Figure 2.29 Satisfaction of increment in demand at node C, given a constraint on line BC, by increasing generation at A and decreasing generation at B

We can see by inspection, that if the marginal costs of generation at A and B are £ 12/MWh and £ 10/MWh respectively, then the marginal cost of power at node C is formed from the marginal cost of generation at A (£ 12/MWh) plus the cost of redispatch (£ 12/MWh − £ 10/MWh), or a total of £ 14/MWh. The location marginal cost at node C is therefore greater than the most expensive plant on the system.

By extending the network slightly, we can show that by adding a bus D with an associated load, that under certain conditions, it is advantageous from a system perspective to 'dump' load at bus D and pay load D to take the power away. This example is worked through in the appendix.

Extending still further, we can see that the effect of constraints can be far reaching. In the appendix we show an unconstrained network that is tied by unconstrained tie lines to a constrained system. The constraint on one system is felt on the other.

2.3.1.8   Joining of control areas

Consider two simple systems with one generator and one consumer each, which then interconnect to each other. The mutual impact can be seen with a simple diagram. By connecting the 200 MW system to the 50 MW system we cause a 37.5 MW flow from C to A and B to D and in doing so increases the flow from A to D by 37.5 MW. This may exceed the line constraints and therefore drive new transmission build in one control area to accommodate flow through it. Whilst total losses fall from interconnection, the losses through AB increase.

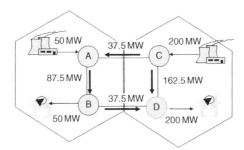

Figure 2.30   Issues of compensation from connecting control areas. For details see text

2.3.1.9   Security and redundancy

In developed countries, a high premium is allowed for to provide system security from blackouts, at a very high probability confidence level. To ensure a particular level of system security requires the system to have inbuilt redundancy so that the failure of one piece of equipment allows the load to be diverted without system failure. If the system can still deliver the load with one failure but not a second failure in the affected area, then the system is said to have 'n minus one' redundancy. Similarly 'n minus two' redundancy allows for two failures.

The need to protect system security at any one instant means that the system operator will control the plant dispatch in order to limit the line loadings such that a particular confidence level of system security is maintained. This limit acts over and above the thermal limit of individual lines.

Figure 2.31 shows a simple network with three buses, two units and one load. The system operator can choose to dispatch only A or only B, or to dispatch both below full load (for

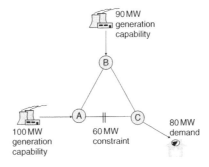

Figure 2.31   Three node system with line constraint, for calculation of network failure effects

a greater marginal cost) to reduce the probability and extent of lost load. The probabilities are shown in the table.

Let us assume that the generators do not fail, but that the lines have failure probabilities as follows: AB = 5 %, AC = 5 %, BC = 2 %. Very high fail rates are used for the purposes of illustration.

Supposing that only generator A is hot. We can then calculate our probabilities of various levels of lost load according to the probabilities of the different combinations of failures.

Table 2.1   Probabilities and lost loads arising from all possible line failure combinations, with only generator A on load

ab	ac	bc	lost load	probability
fail	OK	OK	20	4.7 %
OK	fail	OK	0	4.7 %
OK	OK	fail	20	1.8 %
fail	fail	OK	80	0.2 %
fail	OK	fail	20	0.1 %
OK	fail	fail	80	0.1 %
fail	fail	fail	80	0.01 %
OK	OK	OK	0	88.4 %

We can do the same for B on load only, and for both A and B on load, and express this in terms of confidence:

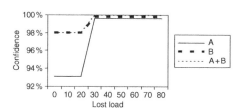

Figure 2.32   Confidence levels for different levels of lost load, with only unit A available, only B available, and both available. Assumes no generator failure

Here we see that having A in readiness in addition to B, gives us only a relatively small increase in confidence for lost load.

However, we must also take into account the probability of generator failure, which is in practice far higher than the probability of line failure. Here we assume failure probabilities as follows: A = 10 %, B = 20 %.

The number of failure combinations is now far higher. The confidence diagram is shown below. Now the order of importance of the generators is reversed.

The system security choice must be made across the whole probability spectrum, so the dispatch that optimises[79] reliability at one level of confidence or lost load, is different to one at a different confidence or lost load.

---

[79] If line failure is incorporated into the market model, then line failure probability is sometimes ignored for market pricing. See section 5.1.5.1.

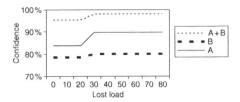

Figure 2.33   Confidence levels for different levels of lost load. Generator failures included

2.3.1.10   Reactive power

Reactive power must be provided to the grid in order to maintain stability. Whilst active power can travel from any part of the system to any other at the speed of light, subject only to losses and dispatch restrictions due to constraints, reactive power (which is explained in the appendix) does not travel in the same way and it must be supplied near (within ten's of km) the requirement.

As well as producing active power, generators can produce or consume reactive power as described in section 2.2.16. In addition to the production of reactive power by generators, the transmission grid can produce reactive power by capacitors or synchronous compensators. There is a limited capability at the point of consumption to alter reactive power requirements by altering the mix of resistive (e.g. heating and incandescent lighting) and inductive (e.g. motors and fluorescent lights) load.

2.3.1.11   Synchronous interconnection

The inertia of the synchronous network and therefore its stability (provided that there are not sources of instability) increases with its size. Inter control area transfer is also more efficient if using synchronous AC, without any conversion, rather than rectifying to DC and then converting back to AC. Figure 2.34 shows the main UCTE synchronous regions in Europe. The other synchronous regions are all Ireland, Great Britain and Nordel.

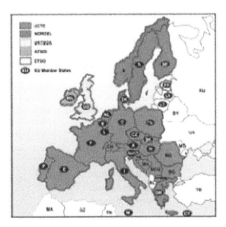

Figure 2.34   Synchronous regions in the European area. Source UCTE system adequacy forecast 2005–2015. Reproduced with permission. The UCTE region is divided as shown. Western Ukraine is also synchronous with UCTE

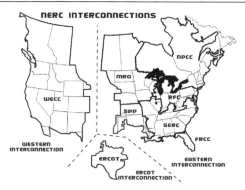

Figure 2.35 Synchronous regions in the USA. Source NERC – reproduced with permission

2.3.2 Functions associated with network operation

Energy networks are natural monopolies since it is inefficient to duplicate the physical network, and the balancing requirements for energy management mean that many short term decisions must be unilateral.

Whereas the power generation sector generally has a single function (provision of energy, capacity and ancillary services), the networks are regulated because they are monopolies,[80] and because they are regulated they are subject to more influence. The position of the high voltage networks (commonly called 'grids') , means that they take on a number of functions.

Because of the national reach and monopoly position of the network operators, the management of the ESI is closely associated with the transmission sector. There are in fact many functions, many of which can be deregulated, or outsourced. There is no single model for the functions variously described as independent system operator, system operator, transmission system operator, market operator, and the various other functions such as managing the physical grid, planning, authorisation, etc.

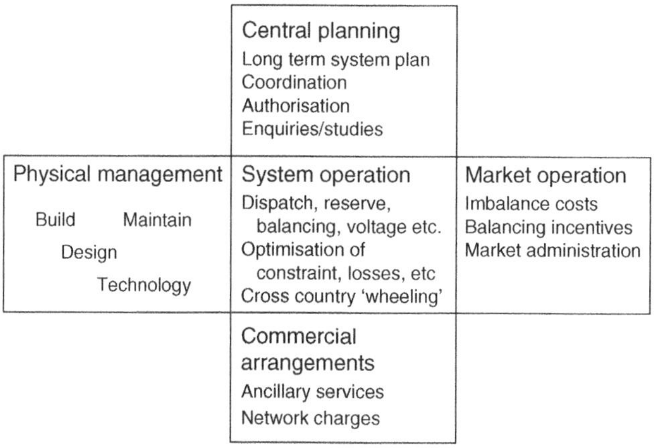

Central planning Long term system plan Coordination Authorisation Enquiries/studies		

Physical management
 	
Build   Maintain
 	
Design
 	
Technology
	System operation
	Dispatch, reserve,
	  balancing, voltage etc.
	Optimisation of
	  constraint, losses, etc
	Cross country 'wheeling'
		Market operation
		Imbalance costs
		Balancing incentives
		Market administration

	Commercial arrangements Ancillary services Network charges	

Figure 2.36 One representation of the functions associated with transmission and system operation

---

[80] Parallel networks are not efficient, but the continuous evolution of neighbouring networks under different owners does erode the monopoly to some extent. There are many examples of parallel networks in the gas system.

2.3.2.1   Physical management of the transmission grid

The grid involves a number of physical components such as towers, civil structures, lines, bushing insulators, breakers and busbars, relays, capacitors, transformers, meters, rectifiers and frequency converters and static var compensators. These require regular testing and maintenance in normal service, and repair from electrical, man made, or weather events. Technological innovation and implementation can be the province of either the owner or operator of the grid.

2.3.2.2   Asset management owning (financing)

Being monopolies, privately owned or corporatised transmission owner operators have regulated revenues. The regulatory intention is that the return on investment is sufficient to attract debt and equity capital without paying an excess return. The return on equity capital is dependent on the amount (variance) and type (correlation to other types) of risks faced, and the amount is in turn affected by the financial gearing (debt/equity ratio) of the firm.

In order to calculate the fair return, the regulator considers three main costs that must be recovered

(i)   Return on Regulated Asset Value (RAV) of installed assets;
(ii) capital expenditure proposals;
(iii) operating costs.

These costs are not recovered directly from consumers, but by the supply companies that have the data and the billing infrastructure to do so. On the same bill that recovers other non transmission related costs (such as energy, distribution costs, value added tax, levies, cross subsidies, rebates and other costs), are also included other costs related to transmission but which are not intended for the asset owner. These can include, for example, losses, constraint costs, balancing costs, ancillary service costs and others.

The asset owner takes the risk that the operating and capital costs exceed those estimated and provided to the regulator, unplanned capital expenditure due to repair (some recoverable from charges and some not), incentives and penalties.

2.3.2.3   System operation

Even where there is specific recognition of the term 'system operator' and designated roles and responsibilities, these responsibilities vary greatly from country to country and control area to control area.

For our current purposes, we define the role of the system operator to be short term (less than about one day) energy management with the given installed infrastructure after the market operator or power exchange has played her part. This therefore includes:

(i)   **Optimisation** with respect to constraint costs, losses, system security and (for pool markets, unconstrained cost).
(ii)   **Dispatch** (for pool markets) and redispatch (for pool and multilateral markets).
(iii) Dispatch of **feed-in** plant.
(iv)   Dispatch of **centrally managed plant** (e.g. large hydro and nuclear).
(v)   **Balancing** (real time balancing of energy flows).
(vi)   All forms of energy **reserve** that are called under grid code or ancillary service contracts.

(vii) Other **ancillary services** (reactive power).
(viii) Medium term **framework arrangements** for ancillary services, including black start.
(ix)   Medium term bilateral arrangements for **energy and capacity**, either through the multilateral wholesale market or privately, engaged to maintain system security.
(x)   **Cross control area** arrangements, including energy contracts, wheeling contracts, interconnector capacity, reserve and other ancillary service contracts.
(xi)   Short term **demand forecasting**.
(xii) **Estimation of generator fail events** on load or future, energy shortfall and failed start or return to service.
(xiii) *Ex ante* and *ex post* **cost allocation** to generation and supply companies.
(xiv) Participation in **market design**.

Even if the supply sector is separate from the generation and transmission sectors, the system operator generally still estimates expected demand. This is for several reasons:

(i)   There is no clear incentive for monopoly supply companies to submit accurate estimates.
(ii) There is some incentive for private supply companies to bias their estimates.
(iii) Aggregate demand is driven by factors common to all regions and hence analytic resource need not be excessively duplicated.
(iv) The need for rapid analysis and short communication chain encourages the analysis to be close to the point of despatch decision.
(v)   Generation failure must also be estimated. The grid operator also estimates the likelihood of generator failure, although since there are more company specific factors, the grid also requests failure expectation estimates from the generators.
(vi) When a customer switches from one supplier to another, the new supplier may only have generic information about the customer based on the type of premises, whereas from the perspective of the grid, consumption is not changed by change of supplier.

2.3.2.4 Market operator

The function of the market operator is separate to that of the system operator, although it can be performed by the same entity (or at least by groups under the same entity).

The function of the market operator in the pool does include optimal dispatch from submitted offers, and hence must, at the very minimum, be done in close coordination with the transmission grid.

The function of the market operator in a multilateral market is not to manage energy flows, but to ensure that the commercial arrangements between supply companies, the system operator and producers are robust, and that the system is not commercially abused (for example by inappropriate use of market power).

The way that the market operator operates for pool markets, bilateral markets, the balancing mechanism, and imbalance is described in section 5.6.

2.3.3 Coordinated planning of generation and transmission build

Network infrastructure is built incrementally, and once installed, is virtually immobile. Networks evolve gradually: (i) to increase connectivity between existing demand and existing generation sites, (ii) to respond to demand movement driven by growth, decline and demographic change and (iii) to connect new generation sites which differ from old sites according to changing fuel proximity and other reasons.

Because they evolve and production and demand centres evolve, the networks are never perfectly suited to the current situation.[81] The very existence of high voltage networks, and flow along the networks, is some proof of the dislocation between the generation and the consumption.

There is generally no licence obligation of non-monopoly generators to generate electricity, only a regulatory requirement not to use discretionary withdrawal of generation to elevate prices for the withdrawn generating units or for other generating units. Generating units can change hands with little restriction. This limits the role that generators have in planning the system overall, although the need to gain the various permissions to build and connect to the infrastructure does naturally involve generators in the planning process.

Consumers have no role in the planning process. Although there are usually economic signals to encourage the gradual relocation of demand towards areas of net generation, the signal is in practice very weak compared to all of the other reasons for choosing location. The exception is the most intensive energy users, such as aluminium smelters, who do actively seek out the cheapest locations for electricity.

From a planning perspective, it is clear that the network must be built in some kind of coordination between generation build/close and consumption changes. However the planning roles of the transmission grid owner, the generators, and the consumers are very distinct.

The grid owner has no role in generation build, close, siting or authorisation (excepting the permissions required for the associated transmission build and strengthening). Clearly however, there is a need to play some form of coordinating role. This commonly happens in four stages:

(i)   The grid owner collects the generator plans going forward about seven years.
(ii) The grid owner reports to government on the evolving electricity map with particular attention to security of supply.
(iii) The grid owner assesses what the optimum build of transmission assets would be to match the generator plans.
(vi) Consideration is given to the economic signals to generation and demand to encourage siting in electrically optimal locations.

Text Box 2.3 – Information used in planning grid construction

In constructing the energy map, the grid owner updates a large amount of information, including:

(i) **Demand**. Current demand location, demographic trends, where it is shifting to and from, what the ratio of consumption to gross domestic consumption (GDP), called the energy intensity is, what the GDP growth forecast is, daily/weekly/seasonal profile trends, trends in demand management, temperature trends.

---

[81] We note that in both planning of infrastructure build, and of on the day dispatch, that simultaneous optimisation of generation and transmission is preferred.

Text Box 2.3 – Continued

(ii)   **Embedded generation**. Current, planned, expected, load profile.

(iii) Current level of **losses, constraints**, reactive power, stability, redundancy.

(vi)   Chosen level of system **exposure to local/regional failure**.

(v)   **Generation**. Installed capacity, planned capacity, expected capacity, rebuild, fail rate, fuel types and expected load factors, location, flexibility, intermittency, reactive power effects, black start capability.

(vi)   **Fuel logistics** and logistical redundancy, energy source diversity.

(vii) Prevailing **political and media climate** (relative pressure on cost or on security).

(viii) **Interconnector flows** and very long range flows.

(ix)   **International change** factors – ability of system to contend with increased or reduced imports of power and/or fuel.

(x)   Current and future compliance of physical installations with current and future **laws and regulations**.

(xi)   **National emissions**.

As a general rule, prevailing constraints and new generation build are the primary driver for investment in new transmission lines. We see in section 2.3.1.7 and the appendix the substantial effects that constraints can have on location marginal pricing. In theory, the transmission operator can establish the 'congestion rent' (the change in the total cost of demand before and after a build of transmission infrastructure) to calculate the optimum build. In practice, it is not quite so simple. For example: (i) the grid owner cannot actually collect the rent and then spend it, because there is limited incentive, and indeed mechanism, to pay it years in advance (ii) the congestion rent calculated with economic and engineering principles, does not precisely match the congestion rent indicated by changes in transmission tariffs and market prices and (iii) rent is collected at the average whereas incentive is at the margin.

The visual amenity impact of power towers and transmission lines is high. This requires consideration of the amenity impact and thence (if on balance the construction is still required) an extensive process of consultation.[82] It is in fact common for distributors to have few limitations on erection rights for poles on public land, wires over public and private land, and strong rights for erecting poles on private land. Erection of transmission infrastructure is much more restricted.

2.3.4   Signals to build

In order for investment to be reflective of the benefit imparted, and for the respective build of transmission and generation to be economically optimal, then the build of transmission infrastructure should be funded by charges to the ESI, at a fair risk adjusted rate of return.

Ideally, signals to build can be created by creating a commercial mechanism that allows the capture by the builder of the 'congestion rent' described in Chapter 7. There have been very significant improvements in methodology, agreement and practical agreements over the last ten years, but there remain many issues with this.

---

[82] Typically this period exceeds the corresponding period for power generators. A power station on a new site requires transmission infrastructure of course.

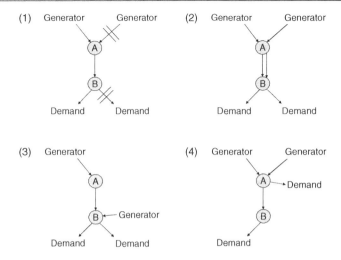

Figure 2.37   Alleviating constraint on line AB (1) Inability for generation to serve demand due to constrained line, (2) Solving by strengthening the line, (3) Solving by moving generation, (4) Solving by moving demand

There is not, in most instances, an explicit connection between discretionary build of transmission and of committed generation build or of demand growth.[83] A generator will in general have either one site in mind, or a limited range that is often largely dependent on legacy such as existing infrastructure, permits, or fuel logistics. The location decision within one company, to the extent that it exists at all, commonly does not have the economic importance that it deserves. Whilst the generator may take an economic view of where it is 'best' to build generation from the perspective of maximising consumer and producer surplus, it is in practice highly dependent on the actual operation of the rules for transmission connection and utilisation. These can be highly variable, due to: (i) the general flux of trialling of new methods for charging and (ii) long range effects due to the physical and market connection of neighbouring control areas/markets. In addition to this, changes in the ratio of charging to generation and demand, alters the amount, geographical gradient[84] and general structure of transmission charging to generators. Currently the extent to which electrical location alters the geographical placement of demand (for example, the building of factors) is to all intents and purposes non existent.

The problem from a signal to build perspective is that the lowest frequency practical is reset tariff and market mechanisms is about five years, so at a random time, there are only $2\frac{1}{2}$ years of known tariff structure. This exceeds the time interval from consent to commercial operation even for combined cycle gas turbines, which have the shortest time from plan to build of all main generation types. Hence a single price control review provides little signal to build. More important is the precedent set for methodological principles and stakeholder compromises.

Figure 2.38 shows schematically how transmission lines can grow between nodes according to different criteria. In the figure, LMP stands for location marginal pricing, and the LMP figure depicts schematically the ability to alter electrical flow at the nodes.

---

[83] Argentina is an unusual example in which users propose and vote for major expansions in a Public Contest.

[84] In theory, altering the generation/demand split does not affect the geographical gradient, but in practice, practical and political considerations limit the maximum or minimum charge, and this can be altered by adjusting the gradient.

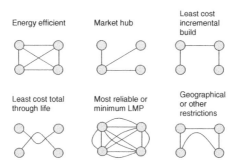

Figure 2.38 Schematic representation of the result of incremental line build, according to different criteria

Note that under many market models, generators can be incentivised[85] to produce on the 'wrong' side of constrained lines, since they can gain the clearing price under 'postage stamp' pricing[86] and then gain 'constrained off' balancing revenue.

There are in practice a number of modelling issues relating to location signalling;

(i)   System modelling is complicated enough even in a regulated monopoly in a closed system, limited by country borders. In an international setting the problems increase.

(ii)   National plans make assumptions about interconnector flows.

(iii)   The incremental cost within country A of an increase in long term interconnector flow to, from, or to and from, country B is not easy to determine.

(iv)   For several build projects, the congestion rent available to each interacts, and hence is dependent on the order of calculation of build increment.

(v)   Countries and country borders commonly have a long term list of essential schemes, with approximate prioritisation and timing. The driver is the trade-off between disamenity and cost of transmission lines and towers and the saving in electrical losses, cost of constraint and system security.

(vi)   Initial planning of networks involves the use of electrical topology, which views the system as a set of demand nodes, generation nodes and lines which have electrical rather than geographical characteristics. This establishes the need to connect nodes to each other, using new transmission lines.

(vii)   Equity in the distribution of benefits arising from transmission build.

The result is that the connection between recoverable congestion rent and incremental build cost is approximate, and transmission build signals are therefore approximate.

2.3.5 Interconnection

Interconnectors refer to transmission lines between control areas. As the coordination of control area management increases, then synchronous interconnectors are regarded as just

---

[85] Whilst there can be a balancing or capacity incentive to build in the 'wrong' place, this is almost always overwhelmed by the regional signals in, for example, connection charges and use of system charges.

[86] See section 7.4.1.

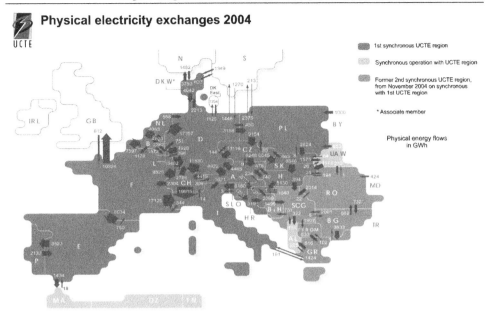

Figure 2.39   Cross border flows in the European area. Source UCTE. Reprinted with permission

part of the network. Where the networks are at different frequencies, out of phase, or physically far apart, then DC interconnectors are used.

For a given level of installed generation, then interconnection increases total system security, and the alleviation of constraint makes inter control area trading and wheeling more effective.

The interconnectivity of networks has been increasing on a more or less continuous basis for the last 100 years. Figure 2.40 shows the percentage of cross border flow as a percentage of the total flow in the UCTE (Europe) area over the last 30 years.

2.3.5.1   Physical boundaries of the high voltage network

Transmission networks are predominantly natural monopolies and where there is competition, it is at the boundaries of the network, principally the entry and exit points. This is shown schematically in Figure 2.41.

2.3.6   Charging mechanisms available to the grid and system operators

The operation of the mechanisms is considered in more detail in Chapter 7 on location. The principal charging mechanisms map to the principal costs of the various functions involved with transmission, and are often allocated accordingly:

(i)   **Connection** – This is a one off cost for connecting the production or consumption to the electrical infrastructure. Since electrical flows are changed, then there can be

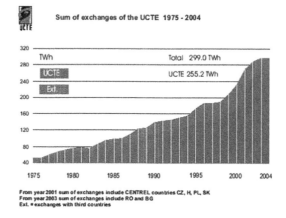

Figure 2.40   Growth of interconnector flow in the UCTE region. Source UCTE. Reprinted with permission

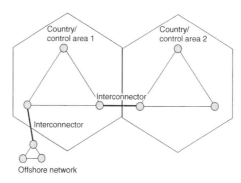

Figure 2.41   Physical boundaries of the transmission system

long range effects and requirements for build of transmission infrastructure (see for example of long range effects). These 'deep entry' costs can be included in the initial connection costs for new entrants, or smeared across all participants in the use of system charge. The deep entry cost needs to consider future as well as current electricity flows.

(ii) **Use of system** – This is an annual charge for access to the electrical infrastructure. This generally varies according to location and is generally charged according to maximum capacity utilisation or some proxy measure for it.

(iii) **System balancing** – This charge is related to the cost of the system operator for balancing the system between five minutes and a few hours ahead. This can alternatively be collected through imbalance charges. Under many regimes, the charges for system balancing exceed the costs, and the surplus revenue can be smeared back to the industry in a number of ways.

(iv) **Reserve** – This is related to the cost that the system operator incurs in securing capacity for the provision of the family of reserve, as well as that for delivery over and above the cost of the energy.

(v)   **Cross subsidies** – Just as supply companies can act as collection agent for taxes, the transmission system operator can act as collection agent for any cross subsidies that are best collected according to capacity requirements and therefore conveniently collected with use of system charges.

(vi) **Losses** – Since the electrical energy taken out of the system is less than that put in, then the losses must be accounted for.

(vii) **System operator incentives** – Since transmission provision and system operation are regulated monopolies, many costs are 'passed through' to the ESI participants. In order to incentivise the system operator to minimise losses, minimise costs of constraints, maximise system security, and other factors, system operators commonly operate an incentive scheme under the jurisdiction of the regulator.

(viii) **Reactive power charges** – Reactive power consumption can be specifically charged for.

(ix) **Wheeling** – Participants who 'wheel' power into the control area, or all the way through, must pay wheeling fees.

2.4   DISTRIBUTION

The distribution system currently forms a very passive role in energy management and the design of the ESI in general. This is despite the fact that in terms of consumer bills, the high cost of losses,[87] high extent and low accessibility of physical infrastructure means that the costs are comparable with that of generation for the residential sector. Indeed if 'commercial losses' (e.g. theft) of electricity are included, then distribution costs can exceed generation costs.

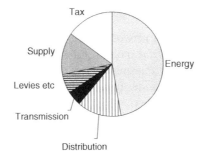

Figure 2.42   Typical constitution of cost elements of residential electricity provision

The distribution sector picks up the energy from the grid, commonly at around 110 kV and delivers it to virtually all[88] electricity consumers. The asset and customer base is highly distributed and the tasks and challenges to the distribution system are quite distinct to that of the grid.

Historic legacy and changing practice means that the definition of distribution varies. The widest definition is for distribution to include all ESI activities downstream of the

---

[87] Compared to transmission there are lower voltages, higher leakages, longer lines per unit of power delivered, thinner wires with higher resistance, and more transformers. In addition, commercial losses do not exist in transmission.

[88] A very small number of users, such as steelworks, draw power directly from the high voltage grid.

transmission grid with the exception of that part of the distributed generation sector that is privately owned. The narrowest definition, that we shall use here, is from transmission exit at low voltage up to, but not including, the electrical infrastructure at the site of consumption.

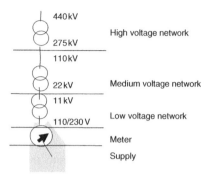

Figure 2.43   Extent of definition of distribution. Widest definition includes medium voltage network and supply. Narrowest definition includes only low voltage network. Voltage definitions vary

The customer interface, particularly in relation to connections, metering and disconnections, means that there is a close relationship between distribution and supply. Ownership is often common or vertically integrated. The rules of the EU directive and of market reform generally, are clear however[89]; distribution should be unbundled from supply.

As with transmission, there can be competition at the system boundaries with independent distribution network operators.

2.4.1   The roles of the distribution network operator

The management of the distribution network is quite different to that of the transmission network. The infrastructure is itself far more distributed and real time management of the systems are more 'passive' than for transmission.

The increase of embedded generation, particularly of generation that is intermittent, or causing the requirement of reactive power, can substantially change the flow and the requirement to manage distribution networks 'actively' in real time.

Distribution network operators offer services such as connections, although this can be deregulated to allow competition. Emergency services tend to be retained as monopoly functions.

Although the distribution sector has the lowest profile in the ESI, there is the highest interaction with the consumer, particularly if metering activities are retained. Not only is connection and disconnection usually managed by the distribution network operator, but the most significant customer experience, that of blackout is almost invariably due to distribution faults.

Because of the local nature, distribution network failures have low media profile, but it is salutary to note that the well publicised failure in California was only for an average of 1.7 %[90] of peak and on only six days. Crudely speaking, over a year, this represented a

---

[89] See Jones (2004).

[90] Calculated from figures in Sweeney (2002).

0.03 % loss rate over the year. This is broadly comparable to a residential loss rate from distribution network failure.

2.4.1.1 Charging

Charging for distribution is similar to charging for transmission, with a capacity and energy charge. Network charging is commonly designed on the assumption that electricity flows into the transmission grid from the generators, and out of the distribution grid from the consumers. Therefore more grid connected generation or distribution connected demand increases the requirement for infrastructure build. The connection of demand to the grid or generation to the distribution network can therefore actually reduce infrastructure requirements. Charging arrangements are increasingly designed to accommodate the cost reflectivity of the connection and have been made more complicated by the growth of embedded generation. For example, in Great Britain, embedded generation installed prior to April 2005 currently does not pay distribution use of system charges. The relative effect of embedded generation capacity on 'shallow' and 'deep' entry is shown in Figures 2.44 and 2.45.

2.4.1.2 Distribution price regulation

Distribution networks are local monopolies and therefore have their revenues controlled by regulation. The charges are closely connected to the regulated asset value, operating costs, and capital expenditure plans. Various functions that can be provided by distribution companies, with or without competition, such as metering and connections, can be included in the price regulation, have separate price regulation, or be fully deregulated.

Broadly speaking, distribution revenues are reviewed about every five years and within the price control period, prices tend to rise on an index of RPI minus X, where RPI is the retail price index and X is a mixture of relative total factor productivity[91] of the distribution sector and imposed 'stretch' on company performance.

Three aspects of distribution networks are important from a price risk perspective. These are; (i) the inflation indexing commonly used, which clearly places inflation risk with the suppliers and consumers, (ii) the energy costs associated with the network (for example losses) and (iii) temperature (warm winters cause revenue losses to the distribution companies, which can cause charge recovery in the ensuing years).

2.4.2 Entry connection cost

There is a high one off cost of connection for a house to the distribution network. The line to the house and the associated equipment such as local transformer and consumer unit (the box with the fuses) commonly have a capacity of around 100–500 Amps which is more than common peak requirement. Hence, this aspect of capacity charge is not closely associated with peak or average demand.

The situation is more complicated for production. A small producer embedded in the distribution system incurs a cost similar in nature to that of consumption and its costs can be considered on a standalone basis. If the producer is slightly larger, but still embedded in the distribution system, it may be that the power input alleviates an electrical constraint upstream in the distribution network and hence the production asset actually reduces the

---

[91] Improvement in techniques, etc. The total factor productivity of industry as a whole is implicit in RPI.

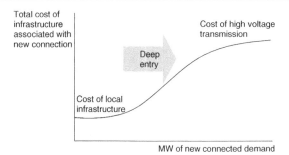

Figure 2.44   Cost of connection of consumption assets in relation to consumption

total investment requirement in the network. As the generator gets bigger, then not only must it input at a higher voltage (causing a higher cost for shallow connection), but it may start creating constraints and infrastructure requirements at high voltage. A conceivable connection cost profile to the network operator is then as shown in Figure 2.45. Negative connection charges do not occur in practice.

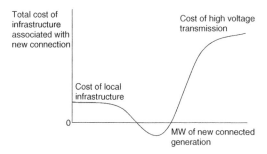

Figure 2.45   Possible cost of connection of production asset in relation to output

This will not only depend on the relative timing of growth of the production and local and near local demand, but on other aspects such as loop flow effects, whether the producer produces or consumes reactive power, system security and stability and other effects.

2.5   METERING

Metering has an unduly low profile in the ESI. It is not usually regarded as a sector in its own right when considering the standard unbundling designation described in section 1.3, and is commonly viewed as part of the distribution sector. However, the physical aspects of metering and the data management arising from the meter reading accounts for a total cost that commonly exceeds the cost of transmission and is comparable with the costs of distribution and of power generation.

The disciplines required for solving the problem of metering are quite different to those of power generation and network management, and hence metering is described here, albeit briefly. However it is important to stress the emphasis of the role of metering in the most durable solution for the increasing issues of sustainability and the environment, the solution of simply consuming less.

When undertaking detailed analysis of industry solutions, in the short and long term, in developed and developing countries, it turns out that metering is commonly at the heart of the problem, and on the critical path. The problem is commonly that when the solution is described at a high enough level to get onto a small number of pages, or to a non technical audience, that metering somehow drops out of the dialogue.

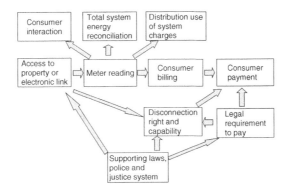

Figure 2.46   The central position of metering in the financial cycle for energy

2.5.1   Metering and the consumer experience

Over the long term, demand reduction is a major or most significant element in solving energy and environmental issues, and in order to do so, the meter must play a key role in the 'consumer experience' of electricity, since electricity is so invisible in its own right. The invisibility is increased by billing through direct debit in bank accounts.

The reason that metering is so critical is that the meter is the key interaction point between consumer and the market. Only through physical technology, information technology, and highly efficient business process in the supply sector can this interaction point be managed to manage energy demand.

2.5.2   The metering lifecycle

The stages in the metering lifecycle are:

(i)   **Research and development**.
(ii)   **Manufacture**.
(iii)   **Installation** and connection to the site infrastructure and distribution network.
(iv)   **Energisation** (allowing the energy to flow through the fuse, and the meter to run).
(v)   **Registration** (with the central administrator for meters).
(vi)   **Safety** inspection.
(vii)   **Theft management**, at and upstream of the meter.
(viii) **Emergency services**.
(ix)   **Repair**.
(x)   **Reading** (arranging, visiting, physical read, customer read, automatic read).

(xi)   **Reporting the reading** or estimate into a supplier, agent or central system.
(xii)   **Validation** of the meter reading (use of an algorithm and past data to check that reading is not likely to be in error).
(xiii) **Data management** (aggregation of meter read information, submission in data flows).
(xiv)   **Replacement**.
(xv)   **Disconnection** (de-energisation, de-registration, complete removal, etc.).

Each of these can be unbundled, and is, to various degrees in different countries.

As part of this life cycle, the cost of the simplest meter is very small and is far outweighed by the other costs, the most expensive of which, is the time and expense of arrival of the meter reader to the premises and the associated costs of arranging the visit, and repeating visits when access is not gained.

2.5.3   Meter types

Considering the advances in information and physical technology and the criticality of demand management in long term energy solutions, the lack of development in technological implementation in metering over the last 50 years is extraordinary.

The key classification features of meters are:

(i)   **Communication medium** (e.g. physical inspection, limited/medium/long range radio wave, through static telephone line, to mobile telephone network, to personal computer, through electric cable, mixed[92]).
(ii)   **Communication protocol** (specific or standard).
(iii)   **Temporal collection resolution** (minute, halfhour, two period clock[93]).
(iv)   **Storage capacity** (past data of energy and non energy).
(v)   **Non energy data** held (e.g. address, consumer name, meter serial num, other meter technical data, supplier, billing and payment history).
(vi)   **Inward communication** (live or historic prices, tariff information, consumption history and profile, device information, bills sent, bills paid).
(vii)   **Display vehicle** (simple dial, through personal computer, flat screen, touch screen, other output device, mobile telephone).
(viii) **User interaction for payment** (receipt of billing history, insertion of proprietary card, insertion of money, insertion of credit card, acceptance of keyed payment instruction).
(ix)   **Device sensing** by consumer unit[94] (circuits or devices).
(x)   **Local device management** (turn devices down/off[95] by manual command at meter, accept instruction through the meter and automatically direct to specific devices, automatic timing of device supply).
(xi)   **Remote meter and device management**. This could be supplier driven and executed, for example by radio or telephone signal, or through the electrical wires.

From an electricity market perspective, three features are particularly important, in approximate order:

---

[92] The Telegestore system with 30 million installations in Italy communicates firstly from the meter through the electrical wires to the substation, and the aggregate signal is sent by mobile telephone network to the data communication centre.

[93] Twice yearly clock change must be taken into account if applicable.

[94] In almost all situations currently, the meter and the consumer unit are separate. If the degree of external interaction, for example live pricing, increases, then the interaction between the meter and the consumer unit has to increase.

[95] It should be noted that there are safety considerations with turning devices off and on, particularly if unattended.

(i)   Temporal collection resolution.
(ii) Standardisation of data protocol.
(iii) Inward receipt of live price information.

The meter owner requires an investment return over the meter life (which is the lower of physical life and obsolescence replacement life) and charges the supply company a rent that is amortised over this life. If the consumer changes supplier and the new supply company requires (and has a right to demand) a different meter for compatibility or functionality reasons, then the meter owner loses the rent since neither the old nor new supply company will pay the rent on the old meter. There are several solutions, for example:

(i)   The meter company could accept the loss and charges a higher general rate to compensate for such losses.
(ii)   The supplier could pay a connection fee equivalent to buying the meter, that is rebated on supplier switch according to the revised meter value, which may be zero.
(iii) The new supplier could pay a meter termination fee if, and only if, the meter is changed at his request.
(iv)   Consumer could pay directly for metering.
(v)   Meter asset provision could be a regulated business and hence protected from loss of revenue.

It is clear that metering issues (for example[96] by installation of meters incompatible with change of supplier) can impact competition in supply. Indeed, while deregulation of the metering industry should in theory enhance innovation, it has historically done so, and competition in metering and competition in supply appear to be mutually exclusive[97] in the absence of more satisfactory arrangements to protect the asset value.

2.6   SUPPLY

The supply sector, also called the retail sector in competitive markets, does not produce or deliver energy but purchases it from generators, pays the networks for transportation, pays various other charges (such as metering and levies) and charges the consumers. The presence of the supply sector means that the generation, transmission and distribution sectors can concentrate on core business. Supply sectors vary in nature. For example they can be driven by brand and outsource the billing and energy management, or driven by need to find a route to market for generated power. Three key activities for suppliers are:

(i)   **Customer relationship** – brand, inbound call centre management, outbound call centre management, cross selling, energy services.
(ii)   **Risk management** – wholesale energy, network costs, environmental costs, credit[98] management.
(iii) **Physical and data process** – Metering, information management, connections, service delivery.

---

[96] A more subtle entry barrier is the refusal of a meter reading agent to read meters for a new entrant. The incumbent, with a high density of meters then has lower reading costs than a new entrant.

[97] See, for example, Littlechild (2005 II).

[98] Note that although network costs are regulated on behalf of consumers, that consumer default incurs loss to the supplier and not to the network operators.

The last stage of the ESI in terms of the physical path of electricity is the consumer, but it is the first stage in terms of finance. To collect from consumers requires the issue and delivery of bills followed by payment. This requires such apparently basic features such as customer address, meter readings, and the rights associated with disconnection. These are by no means easy (even in developed ESI's in developed economies) and to collect the bill requires each and every step has to be fulfilled. It is obvious that the upstream electricity sectors cannot function without state aid if money is not arriving at the consumer end.

2.6.1   Billing

The collection of bills from the customers is an expensive and critical item in the most developed economies, and it is the first and most important step on the critical path in developing economies. It is apparent that a highly effective coordination is required between primary legislation, secondary legislation, legislature, police, local authorities, tax authority and collection, welfare and other agencies.

Even in developed countries where requirement to pay bills is clear, and enforcement and disconnection is supported by law, then billing is a problem area in the ESI.

At first glance, the billing activity would appear to be very simple. The consumer bill is determined by a wholesale and network charging structure, and the difference between two meter readings. These are then applied to energy, transmission, distribution, supplier costs, levies, taxes and other costs. If the rules are constant and everything works perfectly then the activity would indeed be simple. In practice, change events and the complexities of error handling for millions of meter readings and customers make the process highly complex.

We have already noted that lack of development in meter technology is probably the greatest barrier to demand management. Problems in gathering and handling meter readings are the single greatest problem in both driving competition in the retail sector, and in enhancing the customer experience to create a closer connection to environmental aspects of the product and consumer choice.

Some problems in the relation between metering and billing are shown in Figure 2.47.

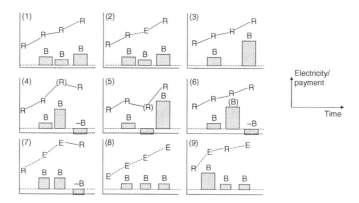

Figure 2.47   A few examples of billing/reading problems. (1) Correct, (2) Estimated but correct, (3) Correct high bill after missing bill, (4) Incorrect high bill from incorrect read, (5) Correct high bill from incorrect prior read, (6) Incorrect high bill, (7) Likely validation failure of correct read, (8) All bills estimated, (9) Incorrect estimate from penultimate read error. R = read. E = estimate. B = bill

These problems cause multiple errors, for example in:

(i)   **Change of supplier** – uncertain allocation of consumption between suppliers.
(ii) **Change of tariff** – uncertain allocation of periods to different tariffs.
(iii) **Non supplier direct costs, such as distribution costs** – Uncertain allocation between different charging periods.
(iv) **Total energy reconciliation** – Total energy flow is not fully reconciled,[99] but allocated by market share, and meter errors cause market share errors.
(v)   **Costs collected by suppliers** or incurred by them by regulation according to volume, for example value added taxes, energy efficiency commitments, and renewable obligations.

2.6.2   Consumer segmentation

In Chapter 9 we examine the drivers of demand in order to establish the movement of price. To understand the drivers of demand, it is useful to segment consumption. For example, industrial and commercial consumers have less temperature sensitivity to demand than residential consumers.

(i)   **High level** consumer classification – Industrial and Commercial, Small and Medium Enterprises, Residential.
(ii)   Consumer **sub classification** – type of installation, number of sites per customer.
(iii)   **Geographical region** – For network costs.
(iv)   **Local region** – For demographic modelling.
(v)   **Voltage** – For network and other costs.
(vi)   **Meter resolution** – High resolution (e.g. halfhourly) or no resolution.
(vii)   **Demand management** – Interruptibility, price responsiveness.
(viii) **Periodicity of demand** – in day, weekly, seasonal.
(ix)   **Capacity/energy mix** – For network and customer service costs.
(x)   **Universal service** – mandatory requirement to supply even if unprofitable.
(xi)   **Subsidy status** – benefit or cost.
(xii)   **Welfare status** – fuel poverty, cross subsidy, disconnection protection.
(xiii) **Economic buyer** – procurement activity, strategic activity, outsourced to agents, etc.
(xiv)   **Fuel labelling appetite** – particularly green.
(xv)   **Price management** – Standard tariff, indexed price, fixed price, price options.
(xvi)   **Regulatory status** – eligible for competition or not.

2.6.3   Regulatory requirements

Where the supply sector is not a monopoly, it does not have regulated returns. In addition it does not have a substantial physical asset value and for merger and acquisition companies, supply companies are usually valued by multiplying the number of customers of each type by the value per customer of each type.

Nevertheless since consumer price, particularly in the residential sector, and particularly for the fuel poor in the residential sector, is a key indicator for regulators, regulators take a

---

[99] Whereas for gas, meters can be reconciled over the medium term because leakage losses are so small, power losses cannot be accurately estimated. Short term gas metering accuracy is limited by variations in 'linepack' gas in the pipes.

strong interest in consumer prices. Regulators in particular look for signs of collusion and of excess returns. In practice both are very difficult since all suppliers have similar cost bases and make similar price responses to external changes, and *ex ante* returns are highly dependent on *ex post* decisions such as energy hedging decisions.

2.6.4   Consumer agreements

2.6.4.1   Standard agreements

There are essentially two kinds of standard consumer agreement, 'tariff' and 'fixed contract' (usually simply called 'contract').

In a tariff agreement, the consumer may pay a standing charge and has a fixed rate for consumption that applies at all times and for all volumes. The consumer is said to have a volume option. This option is said to be exercised 'non ruthlessly' – that it is that consumption will depend only on the 'natural' (i.e. exogenously determined) demand and is not responsive to market prices. The tariff price takes into account an assumed profile of consumption.

In a contract agreement, the consumer may pay a standing charge, and has a fixed halfhourly profile for energy consumption. While there is a single contract price, it is calculated using the profile of consumption and prices through the peaks and off peaks. In the most rigid contracts, the consumer must sell back (or 'spill' if there is no notice) power if consumption falls, and buy more when consumption rises. Most contracts allow a variation of demand around the agreed profile. This is identical to the take-or-pay, or swing contracts described in section 2.1.9.

2.6.4.2   Contracts for demand management and interruption

Consumers can enter contracts for demand management (reduction of consumption by a designated amount), interruption (complete curtailment of supply). There is also an intermediate contract in which consumption is reduced to a certain level.

For tariff agreements, none of these methods are practical at large scale because

(i)   The fixed tariff means that the only way to get a price response is to have an 'interruption rate' (which would be impractically high, since domestic electricity prices are already much higher than wholesale prices, and hence the supplier would be paying extremely high prices).
(ii)   There is no simple mechanism to curtail electricity supply to single houses, and curtailment is generally to be avoided for safety reasons as well as inconvenience.
(iii) Most metering and billing arrangements do not currently support residential demand management.

For industrial and commercial fixed volume contracts, demand management is more straightforward. If the metering is halfhourly (as it is for almost all industrial and commercial sites), then there is the potential to reduce demand at halfhourly resolution, and to sell the energy to the supplier at a pre-agreed or market rate. Pre agreed is much more practical to administer.

For industrial and commercial swing contracts, the situation is less easy. On having a demand reduction request, the consumer would naturally declare a requirement for the maximum volume allowed by the swing contract. This represents a 'ruthless' exercise of the swing contract (which are generally priced non ruthlessly). One contract with less moral hazard is an agreement to reduce load, not by a certain amount, but to a certain amount. While the optionality granted to the supplier is somewhat indeterminate, the supplier does have the advantage of limiting the maximum load as needs. This reduces capacity costs.

Demand management is very difficult to price. Whilst the wholesale energy option can be calculated using the techniques described in Chapter 9, the network element is much harder. Suppose that a customer has a 50 MW baseload demand and offers demand reduction options for 10 MW, then he may reasonably request to pay an infrastructure capacity charge for only 40 MW for the whole year. However, unless the network company is party to the transaction, then the *ex ante* capacity charge for that consumer levied to the supply company is unchanged. This issue is illustrated in Figure 2.48.

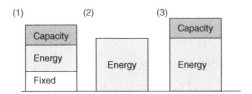

Figure 2.48   Demand management rebate to consumer. (1) Consumption tariff, (2) Wholesale energy price doubles. 'Energy only' rebate for demand management, (3) Rebate for energy and infrastructure

2.6.4.3   Contracts for increased demand

As is apparent from sections 2.6.5 and 9.4, the provision of swing is costly to suppliers and inevitable under the current status of metering and billing arrangements. Consumers can reduce the costs for flexibility by purchasing options with less flexibility than swing contracts but which are still sufficient for the particular requirements.

It is obvious from this, that while it is practically complicated to have sensible signals for demand management without high resolution smart meters, the provision of theoretically infinite capacity to the consumers with flat tariffs is costly in terms of infrastructure.

2.6.4.4   Unbundled contracts

The approximate cost breakdown of suppliers was shown in Figure 2.42. We can see that supply companies pay for items such as network services. Since this adds to the marginal cost structure of the suppliers, then they factor these costs into the consumer agreements.

A consumer could, if he wished to, enter into an unbundled contract, in which the different elements are visible. For example:

Contract price per month =

Wholesale electricity prices times energy volumes, at halfhourly resolution
+ Network costs (which can be further unbundled into their elements)
+ Renewable obligations costs
+ Supplier standing charge

+ Supplier variable charge (including value added tax, cross subsidies, volume dependent supplier obligations and other volume dependent elements)
+ Other charges

Consider the comparison between a fully bundled contract and a partially unbundled contract in which the wholesale electricity is paid for on a floating basis. For the sake of argument, let us assume that this is the pool price PPP.

For a single halfhour, ignoring the standing charge, the amount due is PPP*MW consumption.

The expectation of this cost goes up and down with forward prices. This gives the consumer freedom of action (although a far higher degree of work and responsibility), since he can hedge in the wholesale market to lock in his cost.

Non energy costs which are specifically unbundled are termed 'pass through'. Over time, all costs are passed through.

2.6.4.5 Green contracts and fuel labelling

Managing more than one fuel label is difficult as described in section 8.6, but it is possible, and is beginning in some countries. Consumer interest in fuel labelling has grown considerably from a low level a few years ago.

2.6.4.6 Product development

Different consumer segments demand different products. The figures below broadly represent how the product development journeys interact with each other. Product development in electricity is essentially similar to that in other commodities in the industrial market, and in fixed income and financial services to the domestic market. Larger customers pressurise the industry to unbundle costs in order to facilitate cost comparison and increase access to the wholesale market, and large customer products get taken up by customers of smaller and smaller size.

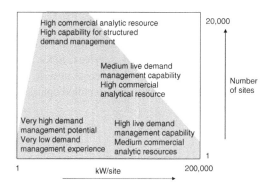

Figure 2.49 Demand management capability by consumer segment. Total energy bill and number of firm's employees is highest on the top right

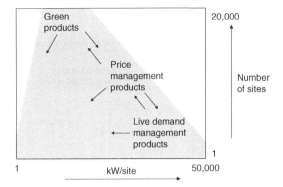

Figure 2.50   Main origins of key products, with growth into other segments

2.6.4.7   Limitations to residential consumer agreements

In Great Britain consumers are protected by an item of regulation borrowed from other retail sectors, to prevent them from being locked in to a particular supplier. This so called 28 day rule means that agreements must allow the residential consumer to exit the agreement with 28 days' notice.[100] This rule has a significant effect in, for example, innovation in metering, offering of tariffs protected from price rise, and supplier hedging.

2.6.5   Supplier profit and loss profile in relation to wholesale price

Two key features drive this relationship, and thereby the hedging strategy:

(i)   The price/demand relationship is convex as shown in Figure 9.64.
(ii) Supplier fixed costs are finite.

A good example is the relationship between profit and temperature. For expected temperatures, the supplier makes the expected profit, and the tariff margin covers the suppliers fixed costs. If autumn[101] temperature falls, the supplier initially makes more money because volumes increase, and the marginal tariff revenue exceeds the marginal element of energy and network costs. As temperature continues to fall, the supplier has to go to market to buy the electricity, just as the electricity price rises to bring on more generation. The result is a profile looking like Figure 2.51.

2.6.6   Retail pricing

In common with other commodities, the retail price is less volatile than the wholesale price. The effect is called 'stickiness' and arises because it is more practical for suppliers and more helpful for consumers to minimise the frequency and level of price change. Over a period of time, stickiness should not change the average retail price in relation to the average wholesale price, apart from the effect that it has on cost of risk.

One way of reducing retail price volatility is by implicitly indexing it against a weighted average of current and past wholesale prices. So, for example, the retail price for electricity

---

[100] The author of the rule, introduced when the market first opened recently said that 'in retrospect, the rule seems to have distorted and restricted retail competition for UK domestic customers'. Littlechild (2005I).

[101] In mid winter, the tariff (which is non seasonal, the tariff can be below the wholesale price and direct marginal costs).

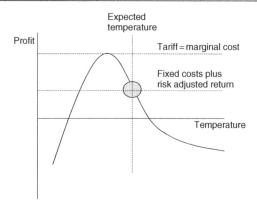

Figure 2.51 Profit and loss profile for a supplier to the residential sector in relation to ambient temperature

delivered in 2008 could weight 30 % and 70 % of the out-turn of wholesale prices in 2006 and 2007 respectively. This is a purely lagged index.

Assuming that the indices only refer to two years either side of the delivery year, then we can represent our retail price indexation as follows:

$$P_{R,i} = uplift + \sum_{i=j+2,j=n}^{i=j,j=n-2} P_{W,ij} W_{ij}$$

Where uplift here is the full non-energy cost of supply, which here is assumed to be known and constant.

$P_{R,n}$ is the retail price for delivery year n

$P_{W,ij}$ is the wholesale price for delivery year i, in observation[102] year j

W_{ij} is the weighting applied to $P_{W,ij}$

Uplift is the supplier cost premium, network costs and all other non energy costs. We initially assume that all 'basis' risks are zero.

Using this format, we can illustrate our first example, in which we used a lagged index, as shown in Table 2.2.

Table 2.2 Lagging indexation of consumer price contract

	2006	2007	2008	2009	2010
2006	30 %				
2007	–	70 %			
2008	–	–			

Wholesale index delivery date

Observation date

---

[102] i and j correspond to T and t in Chapter 9.

We can further decrease the volatility of our retail price, by using forward as well as spot prices for our index. So, for the delivery year 2008, we may partially index our retail price to the forward price for the year 2009 as observed in 2008. Table 2.3 shows a purely leading index. This also decreases the lag (which reduces the ability of consumers to arbitrage the lagged prices).

A purely leading index would look like

Table 2.3 Leading indexation of consumer supply contract

	2006	2007	2008	2009	2010
2006					
2007	–				
2008	–	–		70 %	30 %

Finally of course, we have the simultaneous index:

Table 2.4 Simultaneous indexation of consumer supply contract

	2006	2007	2008	2009	2010
2006					
2007	–				
2008	–	–	100 %		

So, overall, we might expect for delivery year 2008 something like

Table 2.5 Mixed indexation of consumer supply contract

	2006	2007	2008	2009	2010
2006	20 %	15 %	5 %	0 %	0 %
2007	–	25 %	10 %	5 %	0 %
2008	–	–	10 %	5 %	5 %

Table 2.6 Numbering of hedge programmes in Table 2.4. The table is divided into lagged (1–5), mixed (6), simultaneous (7) and leading (8 9) indices

	2006	2007	2008	2009	2010
2006	1	2	3		
2007		4	5	6	
2008			7	8	9

2.6.7 Hedging

We discuss hedging in this section because price risk and hedging is at the core of a supply business, and because the economics of discriminatory pricing are as important as the development of prices. The subject is rather involved, and the reader[103] may wish first to read Chapter 9 on pricing and derivatives.

---

[103] Some readers may recognise the techniques described here as 'quotational period' indexing and hedging. Some commodities early in the life cycle (such as concentrate for refining) are sold on a quotational index basis to the terminal market commodity, with a lagged index.

To consider hedging, let us initially ignore customer switching, changes in volume per customer, and risk to uplift (e.g. network charges).

2.6.7.1 Hedging a lagged index

Consider first a purely lagged index. We sell power for delivery in 2008 indexed at the average price out-turn of 2006. We assume for simplicity a baseload demand.

In 2005 (and all prior years), then our risk position is long for the year 2006 (since we receive more money if the price out-turn for 2006 is high), and short for the year 2008 (since we source and deliver the power physically in 2008). It is clear at this point that we have a long position in the 2006/2008 spread and make/lose money if the market moves more to backwardation[104]/contango.

The appropriate hedge position in (and before) 2005 is then to 'buy versus average'[105] for 2008 physical or financial (buy all the days of 2008 at fixed price, and sell all the days of 2008 at floating index) for 2008, and 'sell versus average' for 2006. If average contracts do not trade, then the hedge is to buy the forward contract for 2008 baseload, and sell the forward contract for 2006 baseload.

As January 1st 2006 arrives, it is clear that our 2006 hedge starts to unwind (if we sold physical rather than financial then we need to buy daily in the spot market). By the end of the year we have a long position in 2008 that will cover our physical commitments at a known contract price, a certain cash flow from the closure of the 2006 hedges, and a certain cash flow of the 2008 deliveries to consumers.

2.6.7.2 Hedging a simultaneous index

If we have committed to sell in 2008 indexed at the average price for 2008, then we engage in no hedges in advance, and we buy 'hand to mouth' in the prompt market at the index price and sell on at the same price.

2.6.7.3 Hedging a leading index

Suppose that we have sold for delivery in 2008 indexed at the average forward price for 2010 as observed during the year 2008. In this situation our risk position is short 2008 and long 2010. As before we have zero nominal aggregate exposure in 2005 but this time we make/lose money if the market moves more to contango/backwardation (i.e. the opposite for a lagged index).

Hence our hedge in 2005 (and earlier) is to buy versus financial average of 2008 (or buy the baseload forward contract) and sell versus forward average of 2010, observed in 2006. Note that this average rate contract is slightly different to the previous (standard) average rate contract, as now we have 365 observations of the forward price of a whole year, not 365 spot contracts. This is not a standard traded contract in the electricity market. We can instead sell the 2010 baseload contract and buy back 1/365 of it each day in 2006.

---

[104] Contango is upward slope of price curve. Backwardation is downward slope.

[105] The terminology used in the markets is both confusing and inconsistent. Here 'buy versus average' is equivalent to the standard terminology 'buy fixed, sell average' and creates a long risk position.

2.6.7.4   Hedging a mixture of leads and lags

Once we have worked out how to hedge pure leads and pure lags, the rest is easy. We simply divide the contract into its index portions, calculate the hedge requirement for each, and then hedge the aggregate. So for the example in Figure 2.52, we have nine separate hedge programmes for the delivery year 2008 (numbered in Table 2.6), each with a designated percentage of the 2008 throughput. We add this hedge programme to the hedge programmes for all the other delivery years.

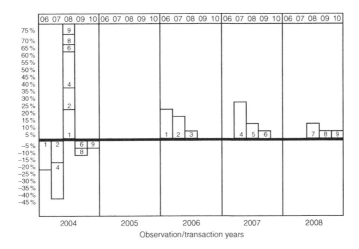

Figure 2.52   Hedge development for the price index profile shown in Table 2.5 for each of the contract years 2006 to 2010

Note that whilst in the first year, the hedge is purely a spread position, that when the first index observation year arrives then a long hedge position develops. The development of the long position is as shown in Figure 2.53.

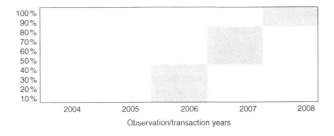

Figure 2.53   Development of net long hedge position in Figure 2.52

Note that whilst a short position in one year and a long position in a different year would appear to be a risk to the slope and not the height of the forward curve, the strong attenuation of forward volatility with tenor does in fact give a disproportionate weighting to the nearer contract. We can see that this element of price risk is actually long rather than short.

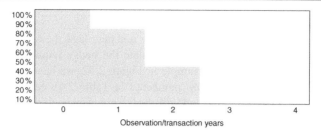

Figure 2.54   Risk position implied from Figure 2.52

The presence of a leading component of the index means that short selling does not occur in practice.

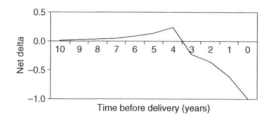

Figure 2.55   Net delta (in spot equivalent) of a two year lagged index

2.6.7.5   Customer switching

Let us suppose that suppliers have a degree of product differentiation and that customer switching is determined by variations in customer preference, and by consumer events such as moving house. We assume for a moment that there is no price led switching and no consumer marketing campaigns. Let us also assume that the tariff is the same for all customers in each supply company, and that the total volume consumed is deterministic, inelastic and known.

In this instance, customer 'churn' (arrival and departure of customers with no net change) has no impact on hedging.

However, customer switching exposes supply companies to net volume change as well as churn. Consider a market with three suppliers of approximately equal size. Suppose now that supplier A hedges 100 % of his anticipated volume (one third of the total), B hedges 50 %, and C does not hedge at all.

If the wholesale market prices rise, then A has a lower cost base. With a cash flow advantage, A can lower prices and gain market share. C cannot respond because this would incur negative cash flow (assuming that uplift = 0 for the sake of argument). A may feel that he can take advantage of C's vulnerable cash flow position by lowering price and increasing market share. A can migrate price back to the market average and therefore maintain the increase in market share. For this strategy to make sense, the net present value of the market share must exceed the saving that was voluntarily handed to consumers. In general, retail prices are indeed affected by hedge positions (note that this effect is not included in the price index matrices shown).

If prices fall, then C can afford to drop prices below the level indicated by the pricing matrix. A, however has a problem, since he has purchased electricity at high prices and can only sell at low prices. Whilst in the situation of rising prices, C could at least cede consumer volume and minimise losses (theoretically) to zero, A must sell the power, and may as well maintain consumer volume and sell in the retail market at a lower price, than maintain prices, cede volume and sell the power in the wholesale market.

There are some technical points to note:

(i)   Taking an implicit indexation as the pricing basis, then deviation from that pricing behaviour is explicitly related to (i) liquidity and (ii) use of competitive advantage in liquidity. If liquidity were infinite,[106] then pricing is unaffected by hedge position.

(ii) There is an asymmetry of positions in market rises and market falls. In a market rise, the unhedged supplier can shed tariff customers to reduce losses by raising tariffs. In a market fall, the hedged supplier has a crystallised market loss that cannot be mitigated. This asymmetry (that we have over-simplified somewhat), has some resonance with the kinked demand curve, described in section 10.1.5.2. It is causes a short bias to the supplier risk position (i.e. less need to buy).

(iii) A supplier who consistently hedges significantly differently to the market average will eventually get into trouble.[107] In gaming terminology, this effect is called 'gamblers' ruin'.

(iv) The aversion to hedging differently to the market average is 'loss aversion' rather than 'risk aversion'. The distinction is mentioned in section 9.1.22.

(v)   It is clear that not only does the consumer indexation influence the hedge but that the hedge influences the consumer price. Therefore in practice, hedging is more complicated than is shown here.

2.6.7.6   *Market share uncertainty*

The prior expectation of aggregate demand, before the effect of short term changes such as temperature, is relatively constant in electricity. Hence the prior volume uncertainty of a supplier is essentially the uncertainty of market share. The market share uncertainty reduces the hedge buying requirement.

Figure 2.56   Hedge adjustment from the uncertainty in market share arising purely from hedge policy differences

---

[106] Of course, infinite liquidity implies zero cost of risk.

[107] Equity value can be enhanced by an incorrect hedge since equity value cannot fall below zero. However, this involves a moral hazard by treating bond repayments as an externality.

2.6.7.7 The effect of customer switching and discriminatory pricing on risk position

We have noted to this point that all 'joiners, stayers and leavers' have the same tariff prices and hence that customer churn with no volume change has no effect on market risk position. Suppose instead that joiners have different implicit price indexation to stayers (and therefore leavers). This price discrimination[108] can happen in a variety of ways, for example a price campaign may give a particular deal to new customers, whether it be up front incentives, different degrees of service, greenness, price capping, flooring, exit costs, etc. In this case, the joiners will have a stronger lead element to prices than the stayers. As joiners become stayers, the proportion of lead in the index mix falls.

Now customer churn becomes important, because the percentage of lead changes. As stayers leave, the energy purchased on their behalf is not required and cannot be passed to the joiners if 'out of the money' and need not be passed to the joiner if 'in the money'.

Hence the total hedge is equal to the hedge calculated for all stayers (with an array of implicit index formulae) plus the index formulae on all customers churning with the same terms, plus the index formulae for the leavers modified by the attrition rate, plus the hedge for joiners not yet arrived, and zero in the case for joiners with pure lead.

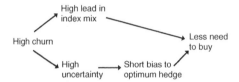

Figure 2.57   Impact of churn on hedge position in the presence of discriminatory pricing

2.6.7.8 The hedge effect of fragmentation in the supply market

We have seen that variation in supplier hedge policy reduces the overall supplier hedge. It is worth considering what happens at the extremes of monopoly and highly fragmented market.

In a fully fragmented market, then no individual supplier has the power to force a market share reduction of those suppliers who find themselves with an out of the money hedge position. At first sight then, there appears to be no gaming response. However, in this world, suppliers will pursue all business that has a marginal benefit. This drives the indexation to simultaneous (since a simultaneous indexer can beat either leaders or laggers on price), and hence drives hedging to zero.

In a monopoly market the situation is the opposite. Let us initially continue to assume the demand is inelastic. Therefore the monopolist is effectively providing a service to consumers by price smoothing. This can be done by increasing the leads and lags. This in turn increases the hedge requirement. Note however, that this still does not cause the supplier to hedge 100 % for far forward years.

Price elasticity is important for two particular reasons here.

---

[108] Here we use the term 'discrimination' in a formal sense, see section 10.1.15.

(i) **Demand management** – Sustained high prices do eventually cause structural (i.e. sustained even after price fall) consumer response.

(ii) **Electricity is an input factor rather than a consumed commodity.** Therefore international comparison of electricity prices is important for export competitiveness. So a national monopoly on electricity is not an international monopoly on electricity as input factor. This causes the monopolist in a country with open borders to index and hedge in a manner that is closer to a fragmented market than a monopolist in an autarky (closed economy).

2.6.7.9   The nature of consumption

Some customers consume electricity as an input factor to an industrial or commercial process. Others consume it only for private purposes. However, even for private consumers, they derive no benefit from the electricity, but the goods that it produces, such as heat, light, motion and communication. Consumption is then 'roundabout'[109] rather than direct. For industrial and commercial consumers, the issues are essentially the same as for suppliers, although much diluted since electricity is a lower percentage of factor costs. For those who consume electricity for purely private purposes, it is theoretically optimal to hedge for the short term, but to take into account the ability to adjust demand in response to prices (reducing the hedge) and varying personal circumstances, currency inflation and income inflation.

2.6.7.10   Hedging the price/demand relationship

We see in Figures 2.51 and 9.63 that the combination of the strong relationship between wholesale price and demand, and the fixed[110] price variable volume tariff agreements, means that the supplier has a concave (negatively convex) portfolio value with respect to price. What we must note here is that if the supplier does not buy options, then to the simple forward 'delta' hedge position must be added an additional delta arising from (i) the (even[111] and odd) higher order derivatives of price, particularly $\partial^3 \pi / \partial P^3$ where π is the portfolio value and P the relevant wholesale price and (ii) higher orders of risk/loss aversion.

2.6.8   Supplier risk and supplier charges

We have seen that from a cost of loss perspective, that it is optimal for suppliers to bias their hedge positions to the market average. The problem is that this average is not known in the public domain. Even if the aggregate hedges of all suppliers for all years were known, the range of explicit and implicit indexations and fixed prices that suppliers have with their customers is unknown.

The result is that suppliers carry substantial risk. Since suppliers are low fixed cost, high marginal cost businesses,[112] due to the very high proportion of external costs which are

---

[109] Readers may notice some similarity with the roundabout visualisation of production described in section 10.1.3.

[110] By out-turn most of the index has been fixed.

[111] Since cost of risk is asymmetric, the even orders are important, although the odd orders dominate.

[112] We see in section 10.5.15 the advantage of a high fixed/marginal cost ratio for new entrance.

common to the industry, and hence are very exposed to loss of liquidity[113] due to loss of cash flow.

Suppliers can take a number of mitigating actions for their hedge risk, including:

(i)   **Revealing sufficient information about hedge programmes for the industry average to be estimated.** Although the uncertainty 'unfairly' transfers money from the supply to the consumer sector, this is eventually passed through in terms of cost of risk. However, price diversity does stimulate competition and price and hedge related communication can be viewed as (and indeed could conceivably be) collusion. The problem is compounded by the increasing requirements of investors and credit rating agencies to have sight of hedge positions.

(ii) **Vertically integrating** – At first sight this would appear to offer no advantage in a liquid market other than transaction cost saving. However, generation businesses have a high fixed/marginal cost ratio and hence can withstand poor cash flow years better than retail businesses, and hence represent a liquidity hedge. Generators have a liquidity risk to competitor hedging that is similar to that of retailers although less pronounced. Whilst there is no consistent offset between the two risks, the risk diversification saves the group over all.

(iii) **Explicit indexation and fixed price contracts with customers.** If customers engage in consumer contracts that are hedgeable, then the reduction in retailer risk enables the product to be offered at a lower expectation margin.

2.6.9   Swing in industrial and commercial contracts

Whilst the normal contracts described in section 2.6.4 are intended to be fundamentally fixed price fixed volume contracts, a fixed price fixed volume contract is in practice hard for consumers to manage since (i) demand volumes are not precisely determinable in advance, and (ii) supply companies are better placed to estimate systemic variations in demand (due to temperature for example) than the consumers.

Accordingly, it is common to specify a volume range which may be daily or even halfhourly as well as annual. This is described as 'swing' in Chapter 9.

2.6.10   Demand side management

Under the pool system, the grid estimates demand, and end consumers simply draw power, and the supply companies pay the pool selling price PSP regardless of volume drawn. Note that the grid had previously estimated the demand, the relationship between demand changes and known factors such as weather, and that price elasticity of demand is low.

Under the bilateral model, most consumers still draw power in a price insensitive manner, but the supply company must either buy the power in advance from other market participants or risk paying a high imbalance cost.

The supply companies then directly experience the price elasticity of generation, since demand drawn above the amount expected and contracted will be subject to a punitive price. There is clearly an incentive for the supply company to estimate accurately and to send

---

[113] The bankruptcy of TXU Europe in the UK in 2002 was due to liquidity problems from a long hedge position in a falling market. The price in Great Britain is now over double the prices at which TXU Europe was long but they had insufficient liquidity to hold on to or 'roll forward' the position.

some kind of economic signal to its customers to minimise variations (fall of demand below expected and contracted amount causes the supply company to 'spill' power back to the grid at very poor prices).

There are a number of ways of signalling, most of which use price as incentive. One problem that we have in demand management is that in using economic signals to reduce demand, we may be efficient in neoclassical terms, but not in welfare terms. By increasing electricity prices to reduce demand, the reduction may be more to budget constraint than willingness to accept curtailment. This is discussed in more detail in Chapter 10.

2.6.10.1   Demand management in the residential sector

The residential sector has the greatest potential to manage average demand and instantaneous demand, but it has been more than the ESI has been capable of to date to actually create the information, mechanism and the incentive to do so. To do this requires changing consumer attitudes, regulation, metering, consumer agreements, welfare intervention and industry processes.

2.6.10.2   Demand management in the industrial and commercial sector

This sector has the greatest practical commercial capability to manage short term demand, but in general the least flexibility to change demand without major disruption to processes. Consumer contracts with swing are not suitable for demand reduction since the reduction can be measured, although full interruption can be measured by agreeing a benchmark demand such as the average demand.

Fixed price fixed volume contracts are very amenable to short term demand management and the consumer can either sell options in advance or sell forward contracts as electricity prices rise. Fixed price fixed volume contracts require a contractual structure that deals with imbalance. Variable volume contracts with simultaneous indexed prices are amenable to short term demand management.

3

Policy – Issues, Priorities, Stakeholders, Influencers

'Communism is Soviet Power plus the electrification of the whole nation' – Lenin (1920)

It is not too much to expect that our children will enjoy in their homes electrical energy too cheap to meter, will know of great periodic regional famines in the world only as matters of history, will travel effortlessly over the seas and under them and through the air with a minimum of danger and at great speeds, and will experience a lifespan far longer than ours as disease yields and man comes to understand what causes him to age. – Lewis L. Strauss, chairman of the US Atomic Energy Commission. Speech to the National Association of Science Writers, New York City September 16, 1954

What we need is an energy policy that encourages consumption – George Bush – address delivered in Trenton, New Jersey, September 23 2002

The task now . . . is to invent an energy policy designed to address the new problems of the environment and gas import dependency. It has yet to be delivered. – Helm (2003) – concluding statement in 'Energy, the State and the Market'.

Access to electricity is not a luxury for poor communities. Global poverty will not be reduced without energy to increase production, income and education, create jobs and reduce the daily grind involved in just having to survive. Over 1.6 billion people do not have access to electricity (27 % of the world's population). In South Asia only 40 % of the population have electricity, and in sub-Saharan Africa the electrification rate is only 22.6 %. Four out of five people without electricity live in rural areas. Private utilities will not extend networks to areas where it is unprofitable to do so, unless the governments provide subsidies to pay the costs. – Intermediate Technology Development Group[1] (2004)

The truth is, no country is going to cut its growth or consumption substantially in the light of a long-term environmental problem. – Tony Blair, Prime Minister of the UK. New York. September 2005

These quotes exemplify the diversity of approaches and degrees of optimism of different participants and observers at different times in different places, and thereby the challenge in constructing regional ESI's that interact in a global context through issues such as emissions and global energy sustainability.

---

[1] On website. Now renamed Practical Action (www.itdg.org).

In this short chapter we shall find that energy policy[2] is commonly a mixture of issues, wishes, ideologies, practical measures, policy instruments and structural solutions. In order to understand, define, respond to, or even make policy, we need to make sense of it.

The policy profile of energy has increased on a more or less continuous basis since the oil crises of the 1970's, and the relative profile of electricity in the energy complex has increased rapidly since the late 1990's. The challenge is to establish a common framework for the articulation of policy issues and policy solutions.

3.1   AGENDAS AND POLICY FORMATION

To begin with, policy, whether formally articulated or not, results from agendas, which themselves result from experience, observation and opinion. A convenient representation of the influences on the policy agenda is shown in Figure 3.1.

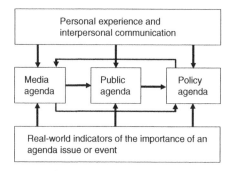

Figure 3.1   Influences on the policy agenda[3]

This representation is useful to us because, whilst recognising that significant change arising from policy objectives may take 20 years to form and deliver, the formation of public opinion can be virtually instantaneous in response to events that are directly experienced, or represented through the media.

Security of supply is a good example of an issue that can be subject to instantaneous events and response. The blackout of a major city, which may be due to a transient instability that may be just as likely under all market regimes and ownership structures, hits the headlines, and stimulates debate on nuclear power, market liberalisation, industry structure, and the geopolitical exposure to import of fuel from concentrated sources. For example the 'Great Northeast Blackout' in the USA in 1965 was a stimulus for a raft of reforms.

We can be more specific in the context of the restructuring of the ESI. The restructuring is driven in part by the need to respond to a series of issues which are either new or of increasing importance, and in part by the application of political ideology consistent with application in other industries. Whilst the high level agenda does not necessarily require rationalisation, the practical implementation of policy, and the structures that support and

---

[2] Hogwood and Gunn (1984) specified ten uses of the term 'policy' – a label for a field of activity, expression of purpose or desired state of affairs, specific proposals, decisions, authorisation, a programme, an output, an outcome, a theory or model, or a process.
[3] Parsons (1995) adaptation of McQuail and Windahl (1993).

enable the delivery of policy objectives, requires a degree of formality, a testing of ideas and facts, and a recognition of social and political context.

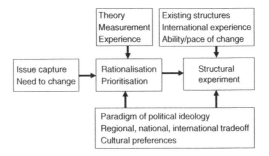

Figure 3.2   The formation of the restructure of the ESI

The free market political ideology applied to the ESI across the world is remarkably consistent. This is in some part due to the fact that change takes some decades to fully implement, and because the implementation lags the ideology, the practical ramification of the ideology does not get fully tested. In other words, we await the results of the global experiment!

The prevailing ideology for the solution is free market liberalisation. Liberalisation must create local and international solutions for all of the energy themes mentioned, as well as ensuring proper control, risk management, and embed into the political, monetary and fiscal structures of national and international economies.

3.2   POLICY ISSUES AND DRIVERS

Having established the major role that the media and public agenda play in the formation of policy and on the requirement to articulate and defend the policy, we need to find a way to gather and organise the media and public issues that have no inherent organisation or structure in their own right.

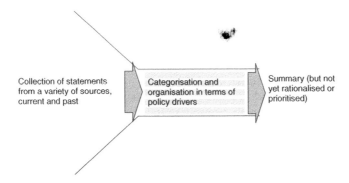

Figure 3.3   Organisation of issue statements in terms of policy drivers

The high level policy drivers in the ESI can be categorised as social, political, international, commercial and economic/financial. The ability to deliver these using the available energy endowments is determined by the technological and organisational capability of the industry.

(i)   **Social drivers** – These involve attitude to the environment and amenity, long term sustainability and universal affordability of domestic services. Social Drivers are highly differentiated between countries and within countries. They are long term and national in focus, and are influenced by such factors as culture, history, climate, topology and indigenous energy sources.[4] National environmental policy in particular is closely related to social drivers.

(ii) **Political drivers** – These involve media, party politics, election timing and manifestos, and the prevailing political ideology. They are strongly affected by international political climate, and the prevailing ideology of free markets is driving the ESI in most countries of the world. Where this is not the case, it is commonly a reaction to events with high enough media attention or on a large enough scale to become political drivers.

(iii) **International drivers** – These involve supranational bodies and regional barriers. The influence of supranational bodies and agreements such as the EU, World Trade Organisation, United Nations, World Bank and the Kyoto protocol that have a high degree of independent actual or *de facto* authority by virtue of the commitments of the members to the body or agreement to abide by their edicts. Whilst the tariff barriers to regional and world trade are decreasing, the non tariff barriers remain significant, and the ease of transport of electricity could create drivers where the regulatory regime in one economic zone gives rise to lower costs than in an adjacent zone, due to what may be perceived as lower standards for health, safety, general welfare, environment[5] and amenity, governance and control, or other factors. The EU has addressed this issue, since the pace of liberalisation has varied widely within the 15 member states of the EU in 2003, and more so with the accession of ten further states in 2004. Processes were set up to minimise the competitive advantage of a neighbouring country with a laxer regulatory system, and a new vocabulary with words such as comitology (committee procedure using advisory committees of experts) and *acquis* (shared rights and obligations).

(iv) **Commercial drivers** – These involve the ability and requirement of industry to compete internationally. Whilst public service obligation and the provision of universal service[6] were associated with franchise protection, it was fairly easy for government to communicate with the ESI (which generally had domestic rather than foreign ownership) with respect to long term planning, and have long term relationships with it. However with industry fragmentation, foreign ownership and cost pressure from competition, the ESI itself has no direct interest in the health of the nation, and policy and regulatory signals have to be constructed so that ESI incentives are aligned to the public good.

(v)   **Economic/financial drivers** – Electricity costs have a direct effect on household economics and the competitive capability in the export market. Electricity forms part of the monetary and fiscal structure of nations since all households and industries use it. A tariff uplift (for example to pass through an environmental cost, stranded cost, or cost of policy change) can be discretely applied as an indirect tax. Privatisation

---

[4] Indigenous landscape and resource have a strong impact on culture (see, for example Schama 1995), and the employment from resource extraction has a strong impact on social structures and attitudes.

[5] The pollution haven theory is examined in section 10.2.2.

[6] Universal service is the provision of service to all sectors, including the poor and remote, which have higher costs to serve, and which therefore require cross subsidy to maintain provision.

represents borrowing by the government, since the government gains cash in return for the future earnings that the investors will receive.

The list of issues is gathered from a variety of sources including parliamentary debate, media, pressure groups, industry communication, government ministries, civil service and other institutions. The list below is a sample, grouped into the categories mentioned.

(i) Social

- environmental, amenity, social drivers;
- the nuclear question;
- environmental taxes and the cost of environmental impact mitigation;
- fuel poverty;
- cross subsidy.

(ii) Political

- energy and national fiscal structure;
- the role of the regulator;
- drive from international organisations and treaties (e.g. Brussels, Kyoto);
- new prominence of security of supply;
- geopolitics and sustainability of fossil fuel;
- growth of free market ideology;
- fossil fuel energy pathways and fossil fuel depletion;
- evolution of political ideology;
- welfare and universal service in a competitive marketplace
- the currency problems associated with the international trading of carbon dioxide allowances.

(iii) International

- harmonisation of coherent energy policies;
- globalisation;
- developing and transition economies;
- trade across borders with different environmental rules.

(iv) Commercial

- experimentation with fragmentation and consolidation;
- commoditisation of energy, capacity, emissions, transmission;
- credit and liquidity in generation and trading;
- the hydrogen economy;
- renewable technology;
- distributed generation, microgeneration;
- restructure of the electricity supply industry and horizontal integration;
- demand management and demand reduction;
- infrastructure and stability challenges of renewable energy.

(v) Economic

- subsidy;
- tax;
- universal service;

- price discrimination;
- gaming.

3.3 POLICY OUTCOMES AND INSTRUMENTS

In response to the policy agenda, energy policies emerge both through expressions of intent (for example the percentage of electricity that will be from renewable sources by a particular date), the setup of initiatives (such as the various carbon trusts) and the imposition of laws and regulations.

To make sense of the 'action' part of energy policies, as distinct from the ideology part, they can be conveniently broken down in terms of policy outcomes, structural outcomes and instruments. Here are some examples:

(i) **Policy outcomes** – For example, cost, productivity, environment, consumer choice, maximisation of asset value, universal service, affordability, security of supply, reduction of government debt.

(ii) **Structural outcomes** – For example, privatisation, competition, vertical de-integration, break up of monopolies, attraction of private investment, universal service obligations, affect on indigenous coal industry, setup of wholesale market, third party access, presence of regulator.

(iii) **Instruments** – For example, competition, grid integration, open access, tax, subsidy and cross subsidy, laws, legislature/police/penal system, regulations, regulatory arbitration, regulatory enforcement, technological prescription, details of market structure, market intervention.

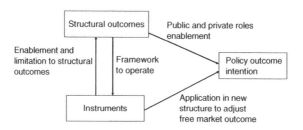

Figure 3.4   Interaction of policy elements to form policy outcomes

For example, Sally Hunt[7] lists five major structural changes that are required for the policy outcomes. These are: (i) demand side management, (ii) wholesale trading arrangements, (iii) transmission business model, (iv) reduction of supply side entry barriers and (v) retail access.

So, demand reduction is a policy outcome with impact on strategic policy objectives such as security of supply, environmental enhancement and resource conservation. Demand side participation, defined as reduction in consumption in response to price, is a structural outcome, made possible by other structural outcomes by, for example: (i) consumers having visibility of real time consumption rate (through the meter) and real time prices, (ii) consumers having a commercial mechanism for benefiting from temporary demand reduction

---

[7] Hunt (2002).

and (iii) system operators having an *ex ante* method of contracting or anticipating such response. Instruments are, for example, (i) real time meters, (ii) option contracts that give the consumer a defined medium term benefit for the provision of flexibility and short term benefit for the actual demand reduction and (iii) contracts with the system operator that secure capacity, call on flexibility, or provide flexibility. Alternatively, a structural outcome could be no encouragement or facilitation of demand side participation, followed by the application of instruments such as rolling blackouts, legal requirements of consumption reduction relative to specified benchmarks, or interruptions in reverse order of priority.

The presence of a wholesale market is a policy outcome with impact on strategic policy objectives such as access to competition which should lead to increased efficiency and lower prices. Structural outcomes are more specific, for example, a pool market, a bilateral market, or an exchange. Instruments are, for example, single period or average price caps, government or system operator direct participation in the market, contracts for difference, traded options and more complex contracts such as 'swing' contracts.

International trading or fair access through transmission grids are policy objectives that are facilitated by the structural outcome of having workable arrangements for accessing grids, paying for access, paying for use, and for 'wheeling'[8] short and long distances. The instruments are, for example, capacity auctions, financial transmission rights, forward contracts in nodal market prices, or physical transmission rights.

Sally Hunt specifies three key prerequisites for the ESI to function effectively from a policy perspective. These are:

(i)   adoption of a coherent national model;
(ii) restructure of privately owned companies;
(iii) revision of the line between federal and state jurisdiction.

These are structural outcomes of some substance and clearly require coordination, vision and imposition both within and without the ESI.

It is essential that the ESI structure and market structure in particular are aligned to, or at least not in conflict with policy objectives. If not, the market will fail because instruments will be sporadically applied by government to address specific perceived shortcomings, and the application in a non aligned market creates unintended as well as intended consequences. Examples are a patchwork of windfall taxes, taxes with differential impacts on different sectors, moratoria, new laws, differential approval of consents, different levels of policing of international regulations, concessions and tax breaks. In the neoclassical model, the market, the industry and the consumers self align to an optimum, and the policy challenge is to establish a framework for valuation and execution of externality charges. In the classical model policy intervention is more focussed on aggregate ESI outcome scenarios (including externalities) without specific valuations and prescriptive adjustment to the production mix.

Here, we must recognise the tension between two approaches to the exactness of policy definition. At one extreme, in keeping with the 'six-sigma'[9] approach in manufacturing, strategic outcomes are closely tied to milestones which are measurable, detailed and low level. At other extreme, the timescales are very long, the milestones flexible or not defined,

---

[8] Wheeling is the term generally for transporting power from a producer to a consumer across an area that is inhabited by neither or only one of them.

[9] The six-sigma approach is a data driven approach pioneered in General Electric and used in many of the world's major firms. Great store is set by strong definitions.

and the outcome subject to interpretation. The former creates a higher level of accountability but may cause a focus on outcomes according to measurability rather than importance. The latter gives a greater degree of flexibility to place energy policy in a wider social context, but can also allow too much elasticity for success to be declarable without actually being attained.

3.4   ENERGY POLICIES

3.4.1   Policy trends

Energy policies have been quite different in developed, transition and developing countries.

From the early 1950's to the 1990's, the idea of a Common Energy Policy for the EU was on and off the agenda several times. The evolution of the main themes is instructive.[10] The heritage of the EU in Euratom and the European Coal and Steel Committee was quite apparent in the early periods.

Objectives set in 1960[11] for realisation by 1985 were:

(i)   increase in nuclear power and oil and natural gas production and maintain coal production;
(ii)   limit import dependence;
(iii) reduce projected demand;
(iv)   increase ratio of electricity consumption to total consumption.

Objectives set in 1979 for realisation by 1990 were:

(i)   reduce energy intensity (ratio of energy consumption to gross domestic product);
(ii)   reduce ratio of oil consumption to total consumption;
(iii) increase ratio of nuclear and solid fuel to total energy sourcing for power generation;
(iv)   encourage renewable energy;
(v)   Pursue pricing policy to attaining energy objectives.

Objectives set in 1986 for realisation by 1995 were:

(i)   improve efficiency of demand;
(ii)   maintain oil consumption and limit oil import dependency;
(iii)   maintain natural gas consumption as a part of the energy mix;
(iv)   increase ratio of solid fuel consumption to total energy sourcing and promote solid fuel consumption;
(v)   reduce ratio of hydrocarbon sourced power generation to total generation (to less than 15 %!);
(vi)   increase renewable energy;
(vii)   improve conditions for security of supply;
(viii) reduce risks of energy price fluctuations;
(ix)   apply European Community price formation principles to all energy sectors;
(x)   balance energy and environment through the use of best available technology;
(xi)   improve energy balance in less developed areas of the EU;
(xii)   develop a single energy market;
(xiii) coordinate external relations in the energy sector.

---

[10] Precis from table in McGowan (1990).
[11] COM (74) 1960.

We can summarise the trends:

(i)   Continuous encouragement of **nuclear power** from 1956 to the 1980's, followed by country led policies with no particular steer from the EU (for example, cessation in Italy after a 1987 referendum, an open minded and incremental approach in the UK in the 2003 energy white paper, active debate in Germany, new build authorised in Finland in 2005, and agreed in 2004 to plan in Poland), and a nuclear programme in France from the 1970's resulting in 78 %[12] of domestic production being nuclear.

(ii)   Continuous encouragement of **domestic coal production** up to around 1990, followed by disparate country led policies and coupled with a commitment to improvement in power generation technology for efficiency and environmental impact abatement.

(iii)   Continuous encouragement of **renewable energy** from the late 1970's but with few active measures until the 1990's.

(iv)   Belief in **commodity price control**, later migrated to a belief in a single energy market with price control, and later migrated to a belief in an internal energy market subject to constraints rather than control.

(v)   Growing belief in the importance of a coherent **EU-wide energy policy**.

(vi)   **Security of supply**, supported principally by limiting imports of energy.

(vii)   **International coordination**.

Up to the end of the century, these trends continued, with increased attention on market evolution and liberalisation.

During the 21st century, energy policies in the most developed countries have become more specific and more strategic. While the policies of different countries and supranational organisations differ in emphasis, they can commonly be expressed under seven themes, which are set out below in approximate priority order:

(i)   **Security and sustainability of supply** – This turns out to be very difficult to define, and is discussed in detail in Chapter 12.

(ii)   **Price** – partly as demand signal, partly for welfare, partly for industrial competitiveness.

(iii)   **Environment** (particularly CO_2, renewable energy, nuclear power).

(iv)   **Demand management**, industry efficiency.

(v)   **Foreign policy and trade, harmonisation with supranational institutions**.

(vi)   **Open access**.

(vii)   **Industry governance and discipline**.

In Europe in 2005, the key themes are efficiency, the European internal market, renewables, safety and security of nuclear energy, external policy relationships and environmental research. Indeed the emphasis on research and development has become an increasingly common theme in the most developed economies since 2004, and carbon dioxide increasingly dominates the environmental agenda. Whether the economic scale of such research bears comparison with the economic scale of other measures such as carbon dioxide limits, renewables obligations, feed-in tariffs, universal service requirements and various taxes and subsidies, remains to be seen.

---

[12] 2004. Compiled from IEA figures (June 2005).

In transition economies, the ordering of policy objectives is approximately as set out below;

(i)   Facilitation and encouragement of **inward investment**.
(ii)   Leverage of **energy resources** or access to energy resources.
(iii) International **alignment** – including liberalisation, audit and benchmarking, driven in large part by conditions for aid and by requirements for membership of institutions.
(iv)   Long distance **energy logistics**.
(v)   Stronger **regional electricity markets** as an essential component of regional economic zones.
(vi)   **Collection** of amounts owed by consumers.
(vii) **Pragmatic approach to international environmental agreements and rules**.

These are more oriented to international alignment. Liberalisation is commonly seen as the rule for inward investment and aid. Membership of associations such as the EU further requires harmonisation as does the requirement for strong regional markets and access to international energy markets. Such harmonisation includes, for example, a commitment to environmental regulation. In addition to international alignment, transition economies commonly look to use reform to strengthen their energy resource position, whether this be better access to import, or better leverage for exports of energy or of control of energy logistics.

In developing economies, the different priority of the policy objectives makes them appear to be quite different:

(i)   **Electrification** (construction of networks and connection to them).
(ii)   Legal, fiscal, monetary and regulatory **stability** for generators.
(iii) Strengthening of **transportation** infrastructure.
(iv)   Solving the problem of **funding** the build of infrastructure.
(v)   **Rationalisation** of legacy system of subsidy and cross subsidy.
(vi)   Control of **corruption** and enablement of new entrants to operate.
(vii) Reduction of **regular blackouts**.
(viii) Solving the **vicious circles** – poor service increases payment default which causes service deterioration. Similarly, poor industry impairs ability to pay taxes which impairs ability to fund national infrastructure.

These are much more concerned with the basics of providing a service and creating financial stability to encourage participants. The primary activity is 'electrification', the connection of industry and households to the network which is not excessively overloaded, the generation of power into the network for most of the time. For the industry to be self standing without government subsidies for the majority of costs, then metering and collection supported by government is seen as essential. Whilst price is important, particularly since the percentage of domestic bills accounted for by electricity are high, price is secondary to actually delivering the electricity, and becomes a priority only when this is happening.

Opinions are not in short supply, and a variety of organisations and agencies provide (often unsolicited) recommendations from their own perspective. One of the better sets is the World Energy Council on sustainability in 2005:

(i)   Keep all energy options open.
(ii)   Invest in infrastructure.
(iii) Adopt a pragmatic approach to reform.
(iv)   Prioritise reliability.

(v)   Promote regional integration.
(vi)   Exploit 'win-win' climate change opportunities.
(vii) Ensure technical innovation.
(viii) Foster and sustain public understanding and trust.

Electricity policies form part of over-arching policies. The 'Washington Consensus' is a good example of 'the lowest common denominator of policy advice by the Washington-based institutions to Latin American countries as of 1989'[13] At the time, the policies were:

(i)   Fiscal discipline.
(ii)   Redirection of public spending to drive economic returns and improve income distribution.
(iii) Tax reform (flatten the tax curve, by lower tax threshold and lower top rates).
(iv)   Interest rate liberalisation.
(v)   Liberalisation of currency markets.
(vi)   Trade liberalisation.
(vii) Privatisation and openness to foreign direct investment.
(viii) Deregulation.
(ix)   Secure property rights.

The liberal (called 'neoliberal') flavour of these policies are quite apparent.

3.4.2 Formation of policy

Being so deeply entrenched in national characteristics, it is hard to specify a timeline for the growth of individual elements of policy before adoption, but the adoption of policy changes, and associated paradigm changes can be tracked and planned. We have already noted that policy outcomes are uncertain, and therefore the trial-and-error process naturally encourages us to make steps that are small and reversible. Figure 3.5 is a representation of how policy can evolve.

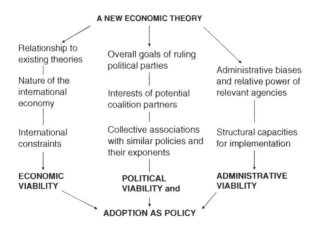

Figure 3.5   From Parsons (2003), adapted from Hall (1989)

---

[13] John Williamson, who originated the phrase.

The effect of shocks is described in section 10.8, and therefore policy transitions require careful management.

3.5 FRAMEWORK

'I do not see the government's task as being to try to plan the future shape of energy production and consumption. . . Our task is rather to set a framework which will ensure that the market operates in the energy sector with a minimum of distortion and energy is produced and consumed efficiently'. Nigel Lawson, Chancellor of the Exchequer, UK government, 1982.[14]

In order to direct the policy and regulatory agencies to encourage the industry to deliver a prioritised set of objectives over an acceptable timeframe and at an acceptable cost a framework is required to cover everything from capturing issues to measuring outcomes.

We can conveniently construct the framework from four elements:

(i)   **Communication framework** – To understand the issues and organise them in the form of drivers – e.g. to understand the production and impact of NOx and the importance of security of supply. This is shown in Figure 3.6.

(ii) **Valuation framework** – To make informed judgements of priority and relative value between environmental and amenity damage, and competing demands.

(iii) **Welfare and the redistribution of wealth** – The combination of incomplete markets and increasing fragmentation of delivery under the competitive model threatens the aggregate welfare of society. Policy makers need to communicate the proper trade-off between equity and surplus, the placement of responsibility to deliver welfare, and facilitate the delivery if required, through mechanisms such as cross subsidy and discriminatory pricing.

(iv) **Political and organisational framework** – To democratise the relative importance of issues, create an accountable regulatory framework, and allow the market to work.

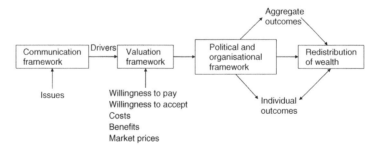

Figure 3.6 Representation of the elements of policy framework

---

[14] Abbreviated from quote in Helm (2003).

The most challenging of these from a policy perspective, is the valuation framework.[15] Policy makers must take all the issues captured in the communication framework and make decisions based on ethics, politics, utility, the relative importance of current and future generations, as well as making judgements on the accuracy of the highly imperfect data from the communication framework.

It is questioned whether, given the great difficulty in assigning values, and the ethical consequences in assuming the validity of the neoclassical model described in section 10.1.3, that it is appropriate at all to take a valuation approach to social matters such as the environment. Here we remember that market disciplines are highly effective even when there is no market, and attend to the economic principles in Chapter 10. If the prioritisation is not done then the system may break down. Excessive prescriptive regulation leads to economically inefficient delivery of policy objectives and high prices. Expensive power variously leads to protest, non payment, fuel poverty and impact on the national economy.

3.6   DOMESTIC INSTITUTIONAL PLAYERS

The ESI is governed through a cascade of arrangements of increasing level of detail. The approximate structure is as follows:

(i)   International laws and regulations.
(ii)   National primary legislation (Acts of Parliament).
(iii)   National secondary legislation (the detailed drafting of acts of Parliament and subsequent formation of statutory instruments[16] noted in primary legislation).
(iv)   Licence conditions arising from primary and secondary legislation.
(v)   Industry codes managed by governance bodies (these bodies often arise from legislation and licence conditions, and are semi-autonomous to the industry.
(vi)   Direct regulation, interpretation of rules and laws, and determination (arbitration) by the regulator.
(vii)   Direct action, guided by primary legislation (energy specific, or general laws such as competition law), by government bodies.
(viii) Bilateral and multilateral agreements between entities, both regulated and unregulated.
(ix)   Additional self regulation – generally through industry codes, signed on to voluntarily and multilaterally agreed.

The nature of the construction and operation of the rules is that most powerful (international laws and primary legislation) are the least detailed, and hence the latitude for interpretation can be wide. As we descend through the cascade, the potential for influence becomes greater.

ESI participants are very mindful of all influencers and stakeholders of policy, partly because these may be expected to reflect some of the views of the shareholders, partly because opinions inform companies on the issues and tradeoffs, and partly because the taking of an opposing position can be highly distracting of corporate attention.

---

[15] Readers may note that the use of a valuation framework is an implicitly neoclassical approach. The key problems of neoclassical application in this context are described in Chapter 10.

[16] For example the details and structure of an obligation such as a renewable supply obligation, or the formation of a governance body.

The domestic institutional players are numerous, and each has a different form of influence:

(i)   Parliament and election manifesto promises from the ruling party.
(ii)   Government ministries, legislature and civil service – local, regional, national, author-
        ities and inspectorates for example for health and safety and environment.
(iii)   Government sponsored watchdogs.
(iv)   Economic regulators.
(v)   Service quality regulators.
(vi)   Issue based pressure groups and charities – e.g. Greenpeace, Friends of the Earth,
        Help the Aged.
(vii)   Local interest pressure groups.
(viii) Local organisations.
(ix)   Government initiatives – e.g. carbon trusts, technology funds, grants.
(x)   Regulatory and self-regulatory bodies.
(xi)   Local implementation of international initiatives – e.g. Kyoto limits for CO2 emissions.
(xii)   Think tanks, universities, prominent individuals and other opinion formers.
(xiii) Industry bodies – producer associations, network associations, consumer associations,
        industry groups.

These players have requirements that are in tension, for example between local and national
issues, or between the economy and the environment. It is difficult to arrive at a consistent
approach. In addition to this, there is the tension of timing. Political actions are closed
synchronised with election cycles which are short term in nature, and long term political
commitments made by one government may not be adhered to by a subsequent government
ascending from opposition.

3.7   THE ROLE AND INFLUENCE OF INTERNATIONAL PLAYERS

Consider this extract from the EU:

> . . . an integrated European internal market, not a market simply limited to European
> Union Member States . . . .
>   . . . a wider European internal market, properly implemented, will lead to increased
> competition and lower prices, will permit increased environmental protection over
> a wider area, and will enhance security of supply throughout Europe. EU directive
> 96/92/EC

This policy statement typify (i) the 'hands on' role that supranational institutions typically
take in the ESI, in this case in ensuring that competition policy is obeyed and (ii) the
expansive view that supranational institutions typically take beyond the borders of the remit
of the institution.

Supranational institutions have considerable power. They do not simply represent aggregate country views and lobbying points on policy issues, but assume an independent[17] role

---

[17] We can interpret this as forcing agreement of non Pareto optimal (i.e. non unanimous) decisions by having the requirement
to abide by majority decisions as a membership condition of the club. To some extent this avoids the problem of the Arrow's
impossibility theorem described in section 10.1.11.2 by achieving consensus, but the dilution of the financial signal is still problematic
in Pareto terms.

in taking a long term and international view. The tradeoffs are therefore different. Whilst country by country tradeoffs are well managed, issue by issue tradeoffs are not necessarily. So, for example, the cost of environmental measures is more distant from overall economic planning than it is for member states.

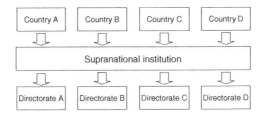

Figure 3.7 Conversion of national interest trade-offs to policy driven agendas

For example, the power of the EU has enabled it to drive through a number of directives that have substantial impact on the ESI. To be enforceable, directives must be transposed to national law, although the regulations are enforceable. There are varying degrees of latitude by which they are policed. In general the EU approach is to continue a fast paced agenda of directives that not all participants can/do initially adhere to or keep up with, and then pressurise non compliant participants through benchmarking and direct pressure. Some of the directives that have substantial effect on the ESI are shown in Text Box 3.1.

Text Box 3.1 – Some EU Directives affecting the ESI

(i)   Electricity
(ii)   Gas
(iii)   Security of Supply
(iv)   Freshwater Fish
(v)   Energy Products Tax
(vi)   Air Quality Framework
(vii)   Waste
(viii) Emission Trading
(ix)   Large Combustion Plant
(x)   Water Framework
(xi)   National Emission Ceiling
(xii)   Integrated Pollution Prevention Control
(xiii) Habitats

4

Liberalisation, Deregulation and Regulation

The current reform in the global ESI is often presented as being a sudden change. Whilst it is certainly true that there are, in any one country, step changes of rules, regulations, laws and structures, that are commonly associated with a timetable of deadlines, they are in practice part of a continuum in which major structural changes take about ten years to agree, and ten years to implement and settle down. Similarly, whilst there have been changes and even reversals of direction, such as in parts of the USA, the global direction has been consistent for the last 30 years.

At high level, the reasons for reform are the growing belief, based partly on experiences to date, that by market orientation, the industry can more efficiently deliver the policy objectives outlined in Chapter 3. Current reform is very much along the lines of the political ideology that has prevailed since the 1980's – that of competitive free market.

Having begun as liberalised free enterprise in the 1880's, and fallen into municipal, federal hands over the next few decades, the liberalisation experiment began in 1970's with a partial opening of the generation sector to new entrants from whom the utilities were required to buy, and continued in the 1980's with the beginning of consumer choice. The 1990's saw the beginnings of competitive electricity markets with the growth of pool models, and the year 2000 saw the first bilateral physical[1] market with the New Electricity Trading Arrangements (NETA) in England and Wales. Change was then rapid with the proliferation of market opening and power exchanges across the world, and development of the market models for capacity, location and environmental factors.

The journey has been broadly consistent in most countries and has been characterised by many elements, such as reform, liberalisation, deregulation, re-regulation, third party access, privatisation and unbundling. Many of these elements are now complete in many countries and at this point, the countries are considering the virtues and drawbacks of the new model, and in some places such as Pennsylvania-New Jersey-Maryland (PJM) in the USA, taking the market model to new levels of technical complexity.

The challenge has been to open the market to competition in a measured and controlled manner such that each stage can be viewed in retrospect with regard to intended and unintended impacts. In doing so, there is the recognition that networks have a strong tendency to being natural monopolies, and hence that liberalisation and deregulation must begin with power generation and supply. It is quite apparent that both are dependent on use of the networks. If there is common ownership of networks and generation, or networks and supply, or both (as there is in a national monopoly), there is conflict of interest, so that the incumbent is incentivised to raise the entry barrier and excessively charge the new entrants. Hence, new entrants need to be guaranteed free and fair access to power generation or consumption. This is by no means simple, even with the best will of the incumbents because

---

[1] Whether the arrangement is truly physical is a moot point. The contracts are described in Chapter 5.

the operation of power generation and of the transmission grid is optimised as a single entity. Hence to allow competition, it is first necessary to restructure the national monopolies into vertically deintegrated (unbundled) form, and for there to be some form of commercial arrangement between the unbundled tiers so that this arrangement can be followed by the new entrants.

4.1 THE LIBERALISATION PARADIGM

Whilst 'deregulation' has a specific meaning (stepwise opening of the monopoly sectors with regulated prices to competition), liberalisation has a more informal use.

There are essentially three components to liberalisation in the ESI:

(i)   Reduction of the role of the state, in terms of ownership, command and control, prescriptive solutions and direct cross subsidy.
(ii) Creation and enhancement of competition by deregulation, vertical de-integration (unbundling), horizontal de-integration (divestment) and regulated third party access.
(iii) Increasing choice for consumers and participation in short and long term demand management and responsibility to secure their energy.

We have already noted that the reform of the ESI in virtually every country in the world is bringing it closer to the free market paradigm. Since this journey takes a very long time, the development in all countries but Great Britain[2] falls far short of the point at which the issues of an unbridled free market become apparent.[3]

From an industry perspective, some liberalisation objectives, are, in approximate order:[4]

(i)   Introduce competition in generation.
(ii)   Introduce customer choice.
(iii) Deal with independent power producer and stranded cost issues.
(iv)   Attract private investment.
(v)   Entrench universal service obligations.
(vi)   Promote integration of the grid.
(vii) Reduce debt.

4.2 STEPS

We have noted that (i) the ESI is highly complex due to the special nature of electricity and (ii) that there is a very wide variation in key factors such as energy endowment and social model. There is no 'one size fits all', and since no policy maker can unilaterally impose a new model and design by committee is difficult. Therefore the ESI takes incremental steps. This is shown in Figure 4.1.

---

[2] The 'Great Britain' in the United Kingdom of Great Britain and Northern Ireland comprises of England, Scotland, and Wales. The New Electricity Trading Arrangements initially applied to England and Wales and then were extended to Scotland in 2005 to cover the whole of Great Britain. Northern Ireland is connected to Scotland by an undersea interconnector. International comment on the ESI in the 'UK' prior to 2005 generally refers to England and Wales, and includes Scotland from 2005.

[3] California was not an unbridled free market. Far from it.

[4] Steering committee from the World Energy Council Asia Pacific Members WEC (2001).

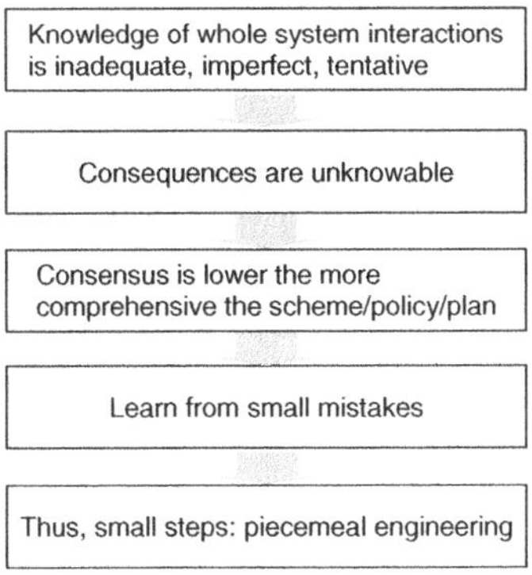

Knowledge of whole system interactions
is inadequate, imperfect, tentative

Consequences are unknowable

Consensus is lower the more
comprehensive the scheme/policy/plan

Learn from small mistakes

Thus, small steps: piecemeal engineering

Figure 4.1 Planning small changes in a complex market[5]

Most countries are undertaking liberalisation in some form, and the starting point, pace and scope varies in each country. There are several steps. The list below is in approximate order, but this has been different in different places.[6]

(i)   corporatisation;
(ii)   unbundling;
(iii)   ring fence chosen sectors. For example, nuclear, hydro, grid;
(iv)   privatisation;
(v)   forced divestment and fragmentation of the incumbent utilities;
(vi)   deregulate;
(vii)   reregulate;
(viii)   further fragmentation;
(ix)   further unbundling and opening to competition;
(x)   re-integration of some sectors and cross sectoral integration;
(xi)   re-consolidation;
(xii)   horizontal integration with other industries;
(xiii)   entry of financial institutions into the wholesale markets;
(xiv)   pressure on retail deregulation;
(xv)   further deregulation of networks and metering;
(xvi)   revise model.

These changes are described below, ordered by logical sequence of explanation, rather than chronology.

4.2.1   Unbundling (and de-integration)

Unbundling is one of the foundations of ESI reform. It is the separation of the vertically integrated industry sectors in such as manner as to facilitate competitive and non discriminatory access of participants to means of operation and route to market for the products or services. It is clear, for example, that if a generator wishes to access the consumer market

---

[5] After Popper (1945). Adapted from Parsons (1995).
[6] For a useful chronology in 20 developing/transition countries, see Jamasb (2002).

that without unbundling, a vertically integrated participant could easily deny access to the delivery of electricity.

At the highest level, the industry divides neatly into the four sectors described in Chapter 2 – generation, high voltage transmission, low voltage distribution and supply. We have also considered fuel contracting as a closely related upstream tier, and metering as a distinct tier lying between (and partly in) distribution and supply. Each unbundled stage can undergo extensive unbundling, by initially creating internal entities with service level agreements between them, and then outsourcing non strategic activities.

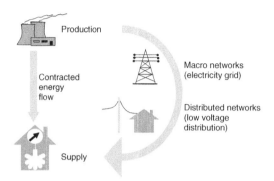

Figure 4.2   The unbundled ESI model, showing the four main industry sectors

There are different degrees of separation in the unbundling processes that should be considered as stages.[7]

(i)   **Functional separation** – This involves the separation of the day to day business and operation of the divisions. Whilst resources should be clearly allocated between the divisions, there is no specific requirement for the interbusiness arrangements to be on a commercial basis. For example, one could be a cost centre. However, the path is clearly laid open for full separation, since cost centres can optimise and prioritise effectively only if the services provided have clear monetary signals, thereby forcing the profit motive, a profit centre approach and then standalone businesses.

(ii) **Operational separation** – This involves separation of long term decisions, capital expenditure and operation of the businesses. This is a natural progression from functional separation, and the natural separation of board level decisions makes the path for board level separation.

(iii) **Accounting separation** – This involves the formal production of separate accounts for the different parts of the business. Whilst this requirement may at first sight appear a relatively straightforward one, involving capital expenditure, depreciation, core operating budgets and some form of financial arrangement between the respective divisions, the construction of full statutory accounts for each division actually sets a clear path for full separation of the businesses since all resources must be accounted for in one business or other, and all flows of commodity or service from one to another should be treated as 'arms' length' arrangements on commercial terms. In practice, the journey

---

[7] Slightly different terminology is used for the stages of unbundling. For definition in the context of EU energy law, see Jones (2004).

from informal interbusiness arrangements to formal commercial arrangements is a long one and hence there are many degrees of accounting separation.

(iv) **Legal separation** – The component companies are completely separate from a legal perspective, although they could be ultimately owned, in whole or part, by the same entity.

(v) **Ownership separation** – This means no significant common ownership.

As a general rule, partial unbundling of generation is the first step, by allowing and encouraging private new entrants. This can be regarded as stepwise deregulation. The next major step is the separation of the high voltage grid from the other sectors. The unbundling of supply from distribution is generally a late stage, and gradual deregulation of metering, and networks at their boundaries and various support services continues after the main unbundling is complete.

4.2.2 Corporatisation

Corporatisation is a necessary precursor to unbundling because the unbundled sectors cannot operate independently without being corporatised.

Corporatisation[8] is the process by which a publicly owned company with a public service franchise and purpose starts to behave like an investor owned company. This itself has many elements:

(i) The requirement of each entity not to lose money, with no cross subsidy from one entity to another. (Pareto optimality, applied within the firm).

(ii) Migration of some long term and high level responsibilities back to governments. For example nuclear decommissioning.

(iii) Public service becoming a requirement rather than a purpose.

(iv) Preparation for unbundling by internal transfer pricing, and service level agreements.

(v) Increased independence from the fiscal and monetary structure of the nation. For example, payment of taxes, payment for fuel.

(vi) End of requirement to create labour.

Consider initially a centrally managed economy. This is depicted in Figure 4.3. In the extreme case for a closed economy with no money, then labour and natural resource replaces the tax required to buy equipment.

Whilst the model may look excessively communist, it does effectively illustrate real world situations in which there is little or no measurement of commodity flow, cost/price, or quality. It is also quite obvious that there is no framework for competitive generation to be compensated for power provision because there is no internal valuation for access requirements through the networks, services such as metering, and revenues for the electricity.

One of the first stages of corporatisation is by introducing formal arrangements between the sectors that will be unbundling. This includes payments for goods and services. The arrangement is shown in Figure 4.4. Each sector has cash inflow and goods and/or service outflow.

---

[8] There is no unique definition of this. For example, Hunt and Shuttleworth describe the behavioural change as 'commercialisation' and the organisational change as 'corporatisation'.

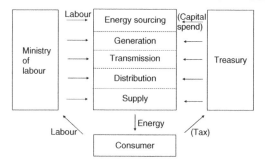

Figure 4.3   Arrangement for a centrally planned economy with no corporatisation or unbundling

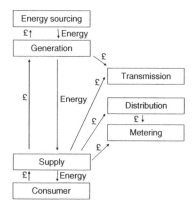

Figure 4.4   Internal commercial arrangements between the divisions to be unbundled in a corporatising central electricity company

4.2.3   Ring fence some activities under state control

Regardless of ownership, the state is the ultimate guarantor of ESI performance. Accordingly, governments have been reluctant to relinquish control in some areas. The main three areas are described below.

Nuclear power – This has commonly remained under national control because it has been considered that governments should be able to determine the amount of nuclear power generation in the future, that nuclear decommissioning funds can only be assured[9] by public sector retention, that consolidation of nuclear power maximises safety, and that overall public interest with respect to such a long term issue as nuclear power can only be served by having national ownership and accountability through the electorate.

Hydro power – The case for public sector retention for existing large hydro plant for the protection of public ownership of natural resources is not particularly compelling in countries which have been happy to privatise fuel and mineral extraction. However, the construction

---

[9] We see in section 11.6.1 the respective positions of creditors and shareholders. Employees are also key stakeholders in the firm. None have an explicit vested interest in the obligations of the firm if and when it becomes bankrupt.

of large dams requires such significant tradeoffs between national and local environment that sometimes the public interest can only be best served by public ownership. The control of hydro dispatch is also highly useful for the system operator. In addition, international aid, commercial loans and 'soft loans' in relation to large hydro schemes and the sheer size of the schemes often calls for a high degree of state involvement.

National grids – National grids are commonly retained because it was felt, with some justification, that the grids form the focal point through which the industry is managed in the short and long term. By maintaining control of the grid, there was *de facto* control on every other sector, and by maintaining control of the grid, it was possible to form a coordinated view of security of supply, and then facilitation of whatever construction is required to alleviate this.

In each case, there is now an increasing level of private ownership.

4.2.4 Forced divestment and fragmentation of the incumbents

Competition is enhanced by increasing the number of participants. If the number of participants is one or few, then the number of participants can be increased by dividing up the incumbents into approximately equal or unequal sizes, or by forcing the incumbents to sell pieces of their business, such as power stations.

4.2.5 Privatisation

When the state monopoly has been corporatised, vertically unbundled and horizontally fragmented, then the component parts can be privatised, one at a time, or all together.[10]

There are essentially three types of privatisation – (i) widely distributed, in which the share price is set low and there is a *per capita* allocation to the population, (ii) public offerings, in which investors (both strategic and institutional) buy the stock and (iii) trade sale, in which the whole organisation is sold to a single company.

The privatisation process is a very sensitive one, since the ESI is seen as a national asset and there is often a risk (perceived or actual) that the stock is sold at low prices to individuals and companies with political connections. There is less sensitivity about nationalisation to widely disseminated domestic shareholders.

4.2.6 Deregulation

The regulated sector is comprised of privately owned local monopolies, but has prices, revenues and/or profits regulated by government through the regulator. Deregulation is the process by which parts of the regulated sector are opened to competition.

We have seen how the generation sector has generally been open to competition for a long time, and even when the dominant incumbent generator is regulated, generation competition is not usually classed as deregulation.

Almost always, deregulation begins by a gradual opening of the supply sector to competition, starting with the very largest consumers, with a phased opening of the market to smaller and smaller consumers, and eventually residential consumers.

---

[10] Since the ESI is so capital intensive, extensive privatisations can exceed the short term capability of the stock markets to absorb the stock at full value.

4.2.7   Reregulation

The deregulation process leads to the existence of two distinct sectors – the deregulated sector which is open to competition, and the regulated sector which has regulated prices or revenues.

Regulation is applied to both sectors, but is more of a monitoring, guiding and policing role in the deregulated sector than a price setting one.

4.2.8   Further fragmentation

The opening of the market, and the divestment of incumbents creates opportunities for strategic investors. It is commonly considered that access to the market is best found, not by building a company from scratch but by buying a company and using that as a base for expansion. The divestment from incumbents also created the ability (the money from the sales) and the desire (to expand when domestic expansion was not possible) for foreign strategic investments by the incumbents. Historically, this caused the prices of investments to rise so much that many incumbents continued to sell assets voluntarily after the forced divestments were complete.

4.2.9   Cross industry horizontal integration

The opening to competition also facilitates strategic entry into the market from large companies with relevant skills, such as oil majors, construction companies, banks and super-markets.

4.2.10   Re-consolidation

In some cases, the fragmentation of generation was so much that market prices fell to marginal costs, leaving many generators to lose money via their fixed costs. This caused a degree of reconsolidation. In addition to this, there has been extensive international consolidation, particularly in Europe. In 2006 Europe has six dominant transnational electricity companies. In the USA, the consolidation has been more a result of the failure of companies or deregulated arms of companies in the wake of the Enron saga,[11] than of transnational mergers and takeovers that occurred in Europe.

4.2.11   Entry of financial institutions

The presence of financial institutions should be regarded as a measure of success, of market reform. Financial institutions can enter the industry in a number of ways including strategic investment, loans, wholesale market trading and electricity supply. There have been several circumstances in which creditors have acquired the assets of power companies as collateral on default.

4.2.12   Pressure on retail deregulation

From a regulatory perspective, the retail sector is the most important sector, since this is the interface between ESI and consumer.

---

[11] Enron began in 1985 as a gas pipeline company, starting trading electricity in 1994, peaked in share price in August 2000, and filed for Chapter 11 creditor protection in December 2001 in the middle of financial scandal. See Fox (2002).

4.2.13   Further deregulation of networks and metering

As described in Chapter 2, networks contain many functions. Any function that can be outsourced can be deregulated. So, for example, transmission construction need not be the sole province of transmission network owners or operators. In addition, networks can be deregulated at their boundaries, for example by allowing independent network operators from the end of the network to the consumer, offshore networks and interconnectors. Further deregulation can be in connections, siteworks, meter ownership, meter management, meter reading and meter data processing.

4.2.14   Revise model

There are a number of measures of success for ESI reform. In the light of these we must decide: (i) if there has been sufficient market reform to achieve success and (ii) if the market has reformed substantially, then how should we adjust the model to improve ESI performance in delivering welfare, (iii) how to deliver further economic and environmental efficiency.

For example, the more fragmented the market, the harder it is to enforce, and indeed deliver, universal service, due to the commercial impact of the required cross subsidy. This is discussed in more detail in Chapter 10 on the welfare aspects of pricing.

There are a number of areas to examine, including:

(i)   **Prices** – what has been the effect of reform on prices, and what can be done?
(ii)   **Consolidation** – how much is too much?
(iii)   **Demand management** – will market mechanisms eventually deliver this, or must a prescriptive solution be applied?
(iv)   **Data** – is the electricity meter flow data structure robust enough to recover from errors and to handle events such as change of supplier, occupier, or meter?
(v)   **Metering** – to facilitate demand management, should parts of the metering sector be regulated or deregulated?
(vi)   The **macroeconomy** – how much do increasing prices resulting from environmental limitations affect the economy?
(vii)   The **environment** – taxing externalities, or command and control.
(viii) **Security of Supply** – assignation of responsibility or mechanisms for security of supply.
(ix)   **Universal service**.
(x)   **Cross subsidy**.

4.3   CONDITIONS FOR REFORM

Early stage reform, such as corporatisation, and high level administrative unbundling, provides quite different challenges to late stage reform, such as exposing elements of transportation to competition and the development of wholesale derivative markets. To enter each stage of reform, there are prerequisites in terms of will and capability.

(i)   **Generation capacity** – The implementation model depends greatly on the current generation capacity in relation to demand. If capacity is insufficient, then priority is fair market access rather than competition in generation. If capacity is excessive, then the divestment of ownership must provide current stability (possibly including vesting arrangements for stranded assets), both for the dominant incumbent and the new players, as well as a road map for both retirement and new build.

(ii) **Investment environment** – This is enhanced by stability of laws and taxes, mature local financial markets, freely traded currency, absence of hyperinflation and low country risk.

(iii) **Rationalised cross subsidies** – The cost of low consumer prices arising from industry subsidy must be recovered by taxes, either from the subsidised consumers, or other consumers. In this circumstance, new entrance is not possible, and the cross subsidy system has to gradually unravelled.

(iv) The will to **disaggregate the ESI from the national economy** to some degree. The ESI can be a haven for employment in both the ESI and in the fuel sector.

(v)   A **high voltage grid** that is sufficiently present and reliable.

(vi) The ability to collect tariffs for electricity, supported by the laws, police and courts, property access rights and disconnection rights.

(vii) **Supportable universal service** requirements.

4.4   THE ROLE OF THE STATE

The problem facing investors and consumers is to devise an institution that will balance these interests and powers. The tension between the investor and the consumer can be side-stepped by state ownership, which has the coercive power to finance the sunk capital without requiring the assurance of a future return from the utility. Alternatively, it can attempt to reconcile private ownership with consumers' political power through regulation. Either way, network utilities operate under terms set by the state – Newbery (1999)

Even in a fully privatised industry, the ESI is a collection of assets, existing property rights, right to build, franchises and obligations that has an inbuilt legacy relationship between private and public sectors that is *de facto* and informal as much as it is formal. These relationships built up incrementally as the industry developed, with a few step changes such as nationalisation and deregulation that in fact made relatively slight differences to this collection.

The state therefore retains an intimate connection with the running of the ESI. The various aspects of state involvement are examined later.

(i)   The state is the ultimate guarantor even if companies in the industry fail. In developed economies, this is particularly important in the consideration of security of supply. The state has a remit to monitor the current and likely achievement of national and international policy objectives that are affected by the ESI, and to intervene where the delivery falls short or can be enhanced.

(ii) Electrification (connection of the population to the electrical infrastructure) is seen as an essential development for welfare and economic growth.

(iii) In the absence of a complete market for 'bads' such as emissions, the state must manage aggregate welfare by economic or prescriptive instruments.

(iv) Since the market does recognise fuel poverty, government intervention is required to alleviate it by mechanisms such as subsidy, cross subsidy and discriminatory pricing.

(v) The ESI is a significant component of the fiscal macroeconomy of nations.

The state performs numerous roles, for example:

(i)   The participation of the ESI in the fiscal structure of the macroeconomy.
(ii)   The setting of policy.
(iii)   Primary legislation (Acts of Parliament) to drive and control policy.
(iv)   The conversion of direct taxes to indirect taxes (see section 10.2.3.1).
(v)   The management of those parts of the ESI that remain under state control.
(vi)   Consumer subsidy if the requirement for cross subsidy within the ESI is reduced.
(vii)   Corporate cross subsidy by taxation and concessions.

4.4.1 The national macroeconomy

Regarding Europe, the consequences of deregulation are puzzling at the present time: the two countries with the lowest cost of producing electricity in April 2004 were:

The most deregulated one, in the UK, with a cost of production of 0.048 euros per kilowatt hour.

The most centralised one, France, with a cost of production of 0.051 euros per kilowatt hour. H. Geman, in 'Commodities and Commodity Derivatives'

This quote provides a good example of how prices are not the only measure of the success of liberalisation, and that prices are but one outcome of political model and industry structure. We can see in Figure 4.5 that there can be a wide variety of electricity prices, depending on the degree of state subsidy, which itself is dependent on the tax revenue (and welfare saving if unemployment is reduced) from the ESI. Indeed either the fully managed model or the open market model can in theory achieve low prices when pursued to its logical conclusion.

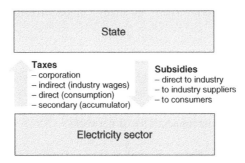

Figure 4.5   The role of the ESI in the fiscal structure of the macroeconomy

4.4.2 Mechanisms of government influence

Regardless of ownership, the government has ultimate right of control. To the industry, this represents a 'moral hazard' as described in section 10.5.16, as well as a potential lifeline for ailing companies as well as protection for consumers. The government is the *de facto* ultimate guarantor of the industry performance in terms of the delivery of electricity to consumers.

Governments can and do retain substantial influence of nationalised and other private companies. Such mechanisms include:

(i)   **Shares** – Full or partial ownership, golden shares (a share with significant voting rights but no significant economic value).
(ii)   **Legislation** – Primary legislation (Acts of Parliament), secondary legislation (the detailed drafting of the Acts).
(iii)   **Taxes** – New taxes, windfall taxes, change in tax rates, tax breaks, categorisation of tax liability.
(iv)   **Licences** – Generally determined by legislation, moratoria, as 'soft' mechanisms such as slowing down the ongoing series of permissions.
(v)   **Rules and regulations**.
(vi)   **Arbitrating and determining**[12] On disputes between different parties, and on interpretation of laws and regulations.
(vii)   **Administration** – Slowing the operation of the company by means of enquiry and general administration.
(viii) **Retained ownership** – Of key sectors, such as those mentioned in Section 4.2.3.
(ix)   **Discretionary enforcement** of laws and regulations, and implicit connection between ESI implementation of one policy and enforcement of a completely separate law or regulation.

Each of these can have differential effects on different sectors and different players within the same sector.

4.5   MEASURES OF LIBERALISATION AND DEREGULATION

Since liberalisation and deregulation is a global experiment, it is natural to wish to compare the experiences across the world. There are many comparative indicators, some of which are listed here.

European Commission – Directorate General, Transport and Energy – Energy liberalisation indicators in Europe (2001) – This considers the regulated and deregulated sectors separately. In the deregulated sectors it considers matters such as development of competition and development of the wholesale markets. In the regulated sectors it considers matters such as access and interconnectivity of networks.

EU benchmarking studies – These are published specifically in relation to the EU Directives, but are quite general in nature, and include non EU countries such as Norway. The first, second and third benchmarking reports were produced in 2001, 2003 and 2004, and focus on matters such as liberalisation timetables, roles of regulators, market monitoring, network

---

[12] The main rules are set by primary legislation (Acts of Parliament) and secondary legislation (detailed drafting of the Acts) and regulators commonly have limited statutory powers. However, regulatory decrees enjoy strong government support and hence appeal to higher powers (such as competition commissions, supranational laws and interpretation under primary and secondary legislature is prohibitively expensive and time consuming for all but the most material disagreements).

access and tariffs, as well as other issues such as treatment of congestion, transmission investment, interconnection, cross border tariffs and balancing services.

Center for the advancements of energy markets (CAEM) Retail Energy Deregulation Indicator (2001) – This considers specifically the retail sector. It has 22 criteria, each with a score of 1 to 100. Examples are:

(i)   Is there a detailed plan for customer choice?
(ii)   How many customers can currently make a choice and how many have switched to competitive suppliers?
(iii) Are there standard business practices and is competition in metering and billing allowed?
(iv)   Is generation deregulated and is there a vibrant wholesale market?
(v)   How are customers integrated into the programme? Are they informed about their options? Is customer information disseminated to promote competition? Are customers encouraged to shop in the competitive market?
(vi)   Are utilities encouraged to offer new services and to cut costs for the transportation services they provide?
(vii) Has the state commission adopted internal reforms to accommodate their new responsibilities?

Objective indices – The Herfindahl index, also called the Herfindahl-Hirschman (HH) index, is a measure of market concentration that is used in many industries. The HH index is the sum of the squares of the percentage market shares. So, a market with two equal participants would have an HH index of $50^2 + 50^2 = 5\,000$. Not only is the index a simple and effective indicator, but it has a foundation in economics[13]. There are various other indices such as the Lerner index and the entropy index, but the HH index is by far the most commonly applied. An index number of around 1 800 is commonly considered[14] satisfactory by regulators. This can be achieved by having six firms of equal size.

Aid agencies – The aid agencies, such as USAID, in order to ensure gainful use of their investment, frequently apply conditions for the granting of aid, and these are frequently related to liberalisation. They create internal or published benchmarks. These include:

(i)   **Degree of market opening (domestic)** – percentage open, pace of opening, extent of export-import, reciprocity of international commercial arrangements, third party access.
(ii)   **Market Monitoring** – Competition, publication of information, unbundling, market rules and grid code.
(iii) **Tariffs** – Separate tariffs for energy and transportation, clarity of cross-subsidies, targets and incentives for regulated entities, fair cross-border tariffs, sensible tariff pass through arrangements for stranded costs.
(iv)   **Regulation** – Existence of regulatory body, powers, independence from ruling party.

---

[13] If consumers spend a fixed income on a good, then the HH index yields an exact measure (up to the proportional constant) of industry surplus. For further information, see Tirole (1988).

[14] Day and Bunn (2001).

There are also a number of studies[15] by consulting organisations, academic institutions and international bodies, and best practice guides.[16]

4.6 REGULATION

> Neither the soft method of government by exhortation nor the tough method of government instruction meets the requirements of the case. What is required is something in between, a middle axiom, an order from above which is not quite an order –
> E.E. Schumacher, from 'Small is Beautiful. A study of economics as if people mattered'

This quote exemplifies the challenge of regulation. In theory, the regulator is provided with a clear remit, clear policies to deliver, and strong guidance on prioritisation, the approximate trade-off between prices and environmental benefits, and the proper level of cross subsidies. In practice the guidance is more general, with the exception of targeted interventions in issues of high political sensitivity.

In practice, the great difficulty in *ex ante* assessment and quantification of effects means that it is common for none of these to be in place. The regulator is therefore given an order that is not quite an order, must do the same to the ESI, and has to interpret the gaps in the rules of engagement.[17] The range of country specific issues and existing political structures and stages of development of markets generally means that the regulatory model of the ESI is quite different in different places.

Figure 4.6 Ideal link between policy and regulation

In regulating the industry, the regulator is mindful that the ESI is a domestic industry which is a source of national pride, and that transient loss of power at national level receives international attention out of proportion to its economic consequence.

We can view the development of regulation in terms of a series of arrangements between the industry, the regulator and the government. Here we describe some models that evolve. No particular significance should be assigned to the labels assigned to them, which are used for convenience here and are not in common usage.

---

[15] Examples of studies are CERA (2004), Jamasb (2002), Jamasb, Newbery and Pollitt (2004), Jamasb, Mota, Newbery, Pollitt (2004), CIGRE (2001). The ERRA website contains country profiles for all member countries. The EIA website contains many country profiles. Neither are particularly intended for benchmarking but are useful in this context.

[16] Regulatory Assistance Project, HERA (2002).

[17] A good example is security of supply, in which secondary legislation may specify responsibility to a ministry to deliver security of supply, and yet no individual component of the ESI to have obligations in this regard.

4.6.1 *Quid pro quo* model for regulatory change

The incumbent agrees to support market change in return for: (i) the present sustenance of a climate in which he can make a level of return that is judged fair and (ii) the time required to make the preparation for a competitive market. The incumbent provides both the expertise and the resource for constructing the codes, market rules, as well as significant contribution to the details within the license conditions.

In this model, the incumbent is commonly subject to a greater degree of restraint, both voluntary[18] and imposed, than the new entrants, and commonly benefits from a sustenance of an 'orderly market', and hence tolerates the more aggressive market behaviour of some new entrants.[19]

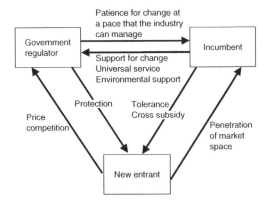

Figure 4.7 *Quid pro quo* model for agreement to change

4.6.2 Prescriptive model for regulation

The incumbents themselves, with detailed knowledge of the rules, often work to their advantage within the regulatory envelope (see Figure 4.9). The policing often occurs not on a case by case examination of events, but with regard to the overall annual profits of the firm.

As the deregulation takes hold and either the new entrants grow or become more numerous or the incumbents become fragmented, the incumbents begin to lose service obligation as the primary objective and become more commercially focussed.

If the engagement between government, industry and the regulator is ineffective the regulator then resorts to a model that is prescriptive and enforcing. Since the imposed rules are so complicated and market power so easy to exert locally, regulatory arbitrage occurs.

In this circumstance the ESI has neither the design and consistency of a controlling mind or the benign influence of the invisible hand. The debate is fragmented, and dominated by special interests and short term response to *ex post* occurrences, and results in limited stability, costing, or outcome of policy. The result is disenfranchised stakeholders and lack

---

[18] Whilst voluntary restraint would appear to be counter to the objective of private firms, the ESI commonly exhibits a strong sense of purpose in staff, and ruthless exploitation of regulatory loopholes is not possible.

[19] See section 10.5.

Figure 4.8   The half way house between centrally managing the ESI and having a market solution without agreement with government and prescriptions from government and the regulator

of new entrance to the market. This problem exists in all kinds of economies, for example the California Crisis,[20] the failure of the Enron Dabhol project in India,[21] and in Colombia.[22] This approach has been called iatrogenic[23] failure by several observers.

The interactions in the ESI are highly complex, and the retrieval of unbiased and accurate data requires a high degree of closeness to the industry. Accordingly, for prescriptive solutions determined by the regulator to be effective, the regulator would have to actually run the industry with experts from the industry. With such closeness, this would in practice mean that the industry runs the regulator!

Regulators can exert price controls, but this is more difficult than is apparent. If the regulator imposes an annual average price cap, it also becomes *de facto* a price floor[24] by the combined recognition of the role of the incumbent in setting prices and in indication a level at which regulatory action is triggered (and thereby below which it is not triggered). The incumbent has scope to alter profit within the rules, for example to disproportionately increase prices in periods of high generation (and correspondingly high demand) and decrease prices in periods of low generation. This preserves the regulated time weighted average price. Each level of regulatory sophistication that is added to reduce/prevent exploitation, leads to an increase in the commercial sophistication for extracting rent within the adjusted rules.

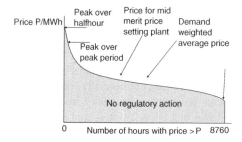

Figure 4.9   The regulatory price envelope, above which there is regulatory action or attention

---

[20] Sweeney (2002).

[21] Fox (2002). This was widely covered in the Indian Press.

[22] Ayala and Millán (2003).

[23] Literally, (illness) caused by the doctor.

[24] This is enhanced by the role of the cap as a focal point. For more on focal points, section 10.5.18.

4.6.3 Regulatory engagement

A more positive relationship is one of regulatory engagement. Broad policy objectives are developed as described in section 3.2, and the impositions on the ESI are economic rather than prescriptive. There is a far more cooperative relationship between the ESI and regulators and policy makers. The ESI can plan in advance what the cost of the energy policy would be, and it can then be adjusted before implementation.

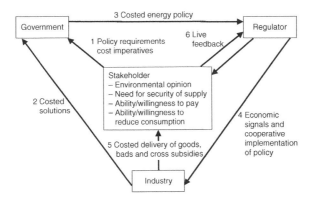

Figure 4.10   Engagement between the interested parties

In particular, environment impact change is so essential and the cost so high to deliver that an inefficient solution cannot be afforded. In this mode, the industry gains by the ability to deliver solution at least cost, and the consumer gains from the cost limitation.

4.6.4 Economic regulation

Economic regulation can be usefully defined as 'The explicit public or governmental intervention into a market to achieve a public policy or social objective that the market fails to accomplish on its own'.[25] In this sense it lies alongside the rest of regulation and is itself limited to the application of purely economic tools such as trades, taxes, fixed or limited prices.

4.7 REGULATORS

There is an essential place for regulators in the full spectrum of ESI structures from fully integrated and centrally managed to fully unbundled and deregulated with mature wholesale markets.

Whilst the varying natures of ESI's and of political structures and of legacy arrangements in different countries mean that functions of regulators differ, they have the same general purpose which is to monitor competition and market power, to assist in the implementation of national and international energy policy and to assist in the commercial development in the ESI, particularly with regard to deregulation and wholesale markets. They can also act as policy implementer, policeman, watchdog, instrument of industry accountability, communicator and international policy integrator.

---

[25] Regulatory Assistance Project.

Some characteristics of good regulators were described by Jorge Vasconcelos.[26] These are:

(i)   independence – from industry and party politics.
(ii)   'reasons-giving' – justification and explanation.
(iii) transparency.
(iv)   stability and predictability.
(v)   promotion and facilitation of general interest objectives.
(vi)   efficient allocation of natural resources and capital.
(vii) fairness.

There are a number of different regulatory models[27]:

Fully independent – Regulators are civil servants, and independent of any specific ministry. As a result, they can find themselves in conflict with ministries, as indeed the ministries can find themselves in conflict with each other.[28] The independence gives the regulator a substantial *de facto* role in policy formulation. Examples are – UK (Ofgem), Italy (autorita energia), Belgium (CREG), Ireland (CER), Austria (e-control), Portugal (ERSE), Turkey (EMRA), Hungary (HEO).

Regulator as Ministerial Adviser – Here the regulator is attached to a ministry, and advises on, rather than formulates policy solutions. Examples are France (CRE), Spain, (CNE), Luxembourg, Greece (RAE), Croatia (CERC), Czech Republic (ERU), Slovakia (URSO), Latvia (PUC), Lithuania (NCC), Malaysia (EC).

Light handed regulation – Here the industry substantially self governs, and market intervention tends to be *ex post*, enquiring after specific events. Examples are Sweden (STEM), Denmark (energitilsynet), Finland (electricity market authority).

Competition authority as regulator – Not being attached to a ministry, the regulator is very similar to an independent regulator, although with a greater emphasis on competition and market development, relative to policy implementation. An example is the Netherlands (DTE).

Self regulation – The presence of a regulator independent of the industry is generally regarded as essential, and hence pure self regulation is becoming less common. Germany appointed a regulator (BNetzA) as recently as 2004.

The examples should be treated with caution, as the roles and role requirements can change rapidly.[29]

Regulators can be funded by taxes, or by levies to the ESI, mainly through price regulated entities such as distribution.

---

[26] Head of Council of European Energy Regulators (CEER) at the Energy Regulation and Investment Conference in Budapest in 2002.

[27] The categorisation, and the examples, is broadly based on a presentation by Source Pedro de Sampas Nunes. Director: conventional energy, DG TREN, at the ERRA Conference Budapest 2002. It should be noted that regulators do change their function over time and hence the classification should be viewed as illustrative.

[28] A common example is the ministry of the environment, and the ministry for trade and economy.

[29] See, for example, Bower (2003).

Regulators do not have exclusive control over the industry. For example, the competition authority, international competition law, international agreements and directives, ministry for trade and industry, and ministry of the environment all have authority of one form or other. It is natural for there to be some tensions between the objectives of the regulator and that of the other bodies.

4.7.1 Regulatory indicators

Due to the wide variation in stages of liberalisation development in different countries, and the widely varying functions of regulators, benchmarking is not straightforward. Examples of features examined are:

(i)   **Resources and autonomy** – Budget amount, source, approval and schedule.
(ii)   **Commissioners** – Numbers, term lengths, positions, experience, salaries.
(iii)   **Scope of authority** – Electricity, gas, district heat, other.
(iv)   **Disputes** – Dispute resolution power, scope of power, mechanism for appeal, effectiveness of decision pending panel, scope of review.
(v)   **Licensing** – Issuance, number, types.
(vi)   **Monitoring** – Information collection, verification of information, audits, enforcement mechanism, violations.
(vii)   **Transparency** – Annual reporting requirements, publications of reports, independent audit, code of ethics, conflict of interest.
(viii) **Accountability** – Open hearings on tariffs and licenses, publication of decisions, explanation of decision, timeframe, confidentiality.

4.7.2 Market monitoring by the regulator

It should be clear from the discussions in this book about gaming, behaviour, market power, risk and fixed cost recovery, that market equilibrium is tenuous. The regulator then has a difficult job in monitoring the market. Participant behaviour that may use a degree of market power but still result in rent below fair value is hard to criticise, but it is also apparent that for low load factor plant, the actual through life (*ex post* and *ex ante*) rent is extremely hard to calculate.

4.7.3 Price regulation

The sectors for which the regulator directly sets prices or revenues is commonly termed the regulated sector. The baseline for regulated prices is commonly the same price as the previous year, plus inflation, minus an 'X' percentage to drive efficiency improvements, plus an allowance for designated capital expenditure for new or improved provision.

It is very common for the regulator to allow companies to increase returns over that implied from the regulatory regime, either by decreasing costs, or by a performance based incentive regime.[30]

---

[30] For a review on incentive regulation, see Vogelsgang (2002).

4.7.4 Rate of return regulation

Rate of return regulation specifies an upper limit to the rate of return on capital. This actually creates an incentive to increase[31] capital above the optimum level and therefore causes an upward bias on prices.

Price regulation and revenue regulation are very similar to rate of return regulation in practice since both are driven by the fair return on capital.

4.8 INDUSTRY KEY PERFORMANCE INDICATORS

The liberalisation journey must be intended to enhance the performance of the ESI. The key performance indicators are listed here:

(i)   **Electrical** – Stability of voltage, frequency, phase, harmonics, etc.
(ii)   **Interruption** – Lost hours per year in fuel, generation, transmission and distribution.
(iii)   **Sustainable** – Medium term economic sustainability, long term energy source sustainability.
(iv)   **Environmental** – Absolute degree of local, regional and global impact, and local and regional amenity.
(v)   **Price** – Low prices in the wholesale market and for residential, small and medium enterprise, industrial and commercial sectors.
(vi)   **Welfare** – Degree of fuel poverty, universal service.
(vii)   **Stability** – Legal, regulatory, financial.
(viii)   **Electrification** – Percentage of population supplied.
(ix)   **Risks** – Exposure to single events (e.g. hurricane, cold winter, drought, terrorism, fuel supply interruption) and systemic events (type faults, geopolitics, oil prices, emission permit prices).
(x)   **Competition** – Not a goal in its own right, but a measure of capability for the other measures.

---

[31] The Averch Johnson Effect.

5

Market Structures for Electricity

Good coordination cannot overcome bad market design. Markets in power, more than most markets, are made, they don't just happen – William H. Hogan. Federal Energy Regulatory Commission Technical Conference on Interregional Coordination. Washington, DC. June 19, 2001

It is no exaggeration to say that if we had had to rely on conscious central planning for the growth of our industrial system, it would never have reached the degree of differentiation, complexity, and flexibility that it has attained – Hayek. F. (1945) From 'The Road to Serfdom'

These two views may appear at first sight to be divergent, and indeed Hogan points out that 'coordination for competition' is apparently an oxymoron. However, without an effective forum in which to engage, with clear mechanisms, rules and procedures, electricity is simply too fast, fluid and complex a commodity to harness in a market that has no rules, governance or structure. Just as we require rules on which side of the road to drive our cars, to stop at traffic lights, and to prevent us from speeding, we require market rules to create uniform contract specification, coordinate our real time schedules and prevent abuse of the system.

The time/space characteristic of electricity causes particular challenges, and a well designed market structure is essential to engender the motivation and innovation on which the free market relies. This is particularly the case, for example, for concentration of liquidity and management of clearing prices above marginal costs.

In this chapter we describe the main market models of the ESI, namely central management, pool, bilateral and exchanges.

In this book, we define the electricity market in terms of four building blocks, namely Energy, Capacity, Location and Environment. We will express each in tradable form so that for each industry activity there is, for each element of the building blocks, a buyer, a seller, a volume, a time, and a price.[1] Whilst not all of the markets are mature, and some currently exist in certain places, there is no theoretical or practical reason why markets cannot evolve in each of the elements.

The definitions used will be as follows:

(i) **Energy** – The planned production and consumption of energy with specific attention to halfhourly dispatch.
(ii) **Power capacity** – In most cases, this is the maintenance of the capability to increase or reduce generation or demand, relative to plan or commitment, for specified periods[2] and in all timeframes from one second to fifty years. In several instances, capacity means the maximum generation or transportation capacity of power generation units and networks.

---

[1] A useful shorthand for this is 'buy, sell, weight, rate, date'.

[2] There are three dimensions of time period – the period of the commitment, the period of each individual run, and the notice period for engagement of the short term commitment.

(iii) **Location** – All aspects of the ESI that are dependent on location. This includes in particular; (i) transmission losses, constraints, voltage and system security, (ii) physical and political geography of the environment, (iii) different laws and taxes across borders, (iv) different monetary values.

(iv) **Environment** – All aspects of impact on environment (air, ground, water), amenity, social matters and employment allowances and regulations that are caused by the installation and operation of the ESI.

To the greatest extent possible, this chapter focuses on 'Energy' as defined above. The workings of the details of models for capacity, location and energy are described at high level in this chapter and with detail and discussion in the chapters dedicated to these subjects.

The choice of building blocks is deliberate, and specifically raises the priority of two key elements of policy design, namely environment and security of supply. In doing so, many features that are local to the industry are initially ignored.[3] Just as the final market design must be tested bottom up and top down against policy objectives, the same must be done for operational pre-requisites. These pre-requisites must then be patched into the overall design.

The description will focus on the wholesale part of the market since the wholesale market is the medium in which the industry participants communicate directly with one another. The retail sector, where consumers actually buy energy, is described in section 2.6.

In the top down, or 'normative' view, we work directly from energy policy and map the policy elements into a high level market structure. We then construct a high level method of joining the elements together. We then attend to some details, and attempt to add patches to market design to fix the problems. In the bottom up, or 'positive' view, we attend to the specifics of the electricity market as it is, and then adjust the market in order to render the market more capable of adjusting to new policy objectives. Both must be done in parallel, as there is a limit to which high level design can be envisioned in abstract and a limit to which incremental changes to current market structure can achieve a specific objective.

In using these building blocks, we begin with a macro view of the ESI in the wider context, designing it at high level, and then attend to what might outside the ESI be regarded as 'technical details' such as reserve energy balancing. Perhaps this does little justice to the technical marvel that somehow manages to keep hundreds of thousands of tonnes of machinery, spread across thousands of kilometres, in synchronous rotation at fifty or sixty cycles per second, but this marvel is well addressed in the many textbooks on the subject.[4]

A good example of building block design that operates at the middle level between technical detail and the macro view, concentrating on system operation, can be found in Sally Hunt's 'Making Competition Work in Electricity'. The building blocks, in the order she presents, are; (i) imbalances, (ii) congestion management, (iii) ancillary services and (iv) scheduling and dispatch. Here, the operation of the system is prioritised, and then wider factors such as environment, long term capacity, demand management and others must be incorporated later into the overall design.

We start with the basics of dispatch and merit order in the centrally managed system. We separate the mechanisms of dispatch and trading of energy from the mechanisms for

---

[3] We might term this approach a 'details to follow' approach. For the view that market design should begin with real time dispatch and balancing, see Hogan (1995).

[4] e.g. Weedy and Cory, Wood and Wallenburg.

capacity. In doing so, we will find that the changes at each stage of market maturity are actually very slight. It is the behavioural changes, industry restructure and regulatory changes that accompany the mechanistic changes that make the market changes appear so great.

The development of markets can be represented as shown in Figure 5.1.

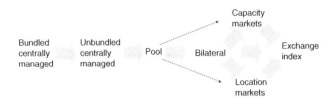

Figure 5.1   Stages of market development from the centrally managed model

The bundled centrally managed system, as shown in Figure 4.3, is not examined here, since any recognition of costs makes the model behave as an unbundled centrally managed system. A system with no recognition of costs is possible, since dispatch will match input to output, but is of no particular interest in a market context.

5.1   THE BASICS OF PLANT DISPATCH

The system operator already has the information on the network, and begins with maintaining and analysing this information. There are five further basic activities in the optimisation of plant dispatch. These are:

(i)   acquisition of the information on demand;
(ii)   acquisition of the information on the available generation cost stack;
(iii) construction of the trial schedule and then a series of adjusted schedules;
(iv)   dispatch notification and instruction;
(v)   post dispatch management such as ancillary services, and balancing.

It will become obvious that the use of detailed plant cost structures for efficient system management is so extensive, that 'cost' becomes almost indistinguishable from 'price', even if the whole ESI is centrally managed by a single owner. Hence the change from public to private ownership (involving the explicit change from cost to price) is not a momentous event in system modelling terms. In fact it is almost a non event. It is the associated changes in the market behaviour and competitive dynamics that make the change to private ownership significant. Gaming and behaviour are described in section 10.5.

5.1.1   Acquiring the information on demand

In the centrally managed system, the system operator estimates the grid connected demand profile for the following day and days. Demand is aggregated at Grid Supply Points. The system operator has the real time information 'top down' from the grid supply point meter history. The distribution companies (and supply companies after unbundling) have the historic information at consumer[5] meter level (i.e. bottom up). The transition from top down information to bottom up information is important in capacity management in highly deregulated markets. In the centrally managed system and in the first stages of liberalisation, there is only one supplier – called the single buyer, and therefore the single buyer has access to all available consumption records. The same is effectively true if distribution and supply are integrated with no 'out of area' supply activity other than to distribution areas, as the distributor has the consumption history for the demand at the grid supply points.

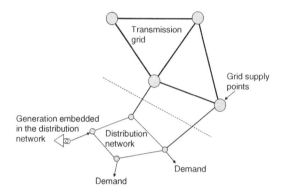

Figure 5.2   The exit from the transmission system and entry into the distribution system

The demand profile uses the following key pieces of information:

(i)   Last year's and previous[6] years' profile.
(ii)   Demand trend based on gross domestic product (GDP) growth and trends in energy intensity.[7]
(iii)   Weather forecast, particularly temperature, wind chill and cloud cover, and trends such as global warming and urbanisation. Also special events such as hurricanes and solar eclipse.
(iv)   Time of dawn and dusk.
(v)   Bank holidays, television schedules and other consumer diary events.
(vi)   Trends in domestic equipment such as air conditioners and equipment with clocks.
(vii)   Changes in financial incentives to alter consumption such as off peak rates supported by meter clocks.
(viii) Installation, trends, prevailing conditions and other factors for embedded generation.
(ix)   Changes to the transmission and distribution infrastructure, particularly constraints and losses.
(x)   Economic incentives for reducing losses and constraints, and the impact on participant behaviour.

---

[5] This information is highly imperfect. The majority of meters do not have half hourly resolution, but a resolution determined by the reading frequency of the meter. As a result, consumer meters are not used for short term prediction of aggregate demand. However, they are very necessary in predicting trends in segmental demand.

[6] Note that it is not correct to take an average consumption of previous years for the period in question, as the averaging process reduces the amplitude of peaks which are not on a set time/date. To capture the peakiness, it is necessary to average the previous year's load duration curves for the season.

[7] The ratio of demand to GDP.

In addition, in developing and some transition countries, there are extra measures such as

(xi) Recent blackout history which causes a demand spike from reconnecting appliances with intermittent power consumption, such as refrigerators.

(xii) Change in electricity theft, installations, repairs and breakdowns of distribution equipment.

Finally, the system operator considers the potential for voluntary and involuntary interruption of supply. Some large installations that are connected directly to the grid, and particularly aluminium smelters can accommodate short term interruption without great difficulty, and such structured interruption capability is treated as power generation capacity. The system operator (actually the distribution sector for sites connected to the distribution system) has a priority order for involuntary interruption, with places such as hospitals being the highest.

The factors mentioned above can also be used to construct a full probability distribution for demand in each halfhour in each grid supply point. In theory this can be used for the construction of the full probability distribution for aggregate demand. In practice, this would require a full correlation matrix which would be impossible to construct with available data, matrix algebra of prohibitive computation requirement, and context adjustment to correlations that would be virtually impossible. The system operator therefore regards most variation to demand in aggregate for the whole system. The distinction between distribution network area and aggregate area becomes more important when we consider the problem of decentralised management of capacity in Chapter 6.

The stack is a supply-demand curve that every economist will recognise and which assumes that price elasticity of demand is zero. Where large consumers agree to make a planned drop in planned consumption (called demand side participation), the 'negative demand' is treated as generation in this model.

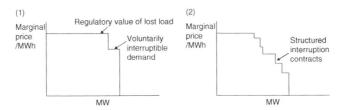

Figure 5.3 Demand function. (1) Centrally managed system with a small number of interruption arrangements, (2) Bilateral system with widespread consumer led management

5.1.2 Management of variation in demand in the centrally managed system

Even if the prior estimation of demand is as good[8] as it can be, there is still a probability variation associated with it, as the main drivers of short term demand change relative to prediction.

---

[8] Commonly, the mean absolute percentage error in demand forecasting with a two hour horizon is around 2–3 %.

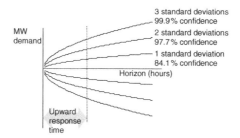

Figure 5.4   The profile of potential variation in demand

The result is that about half of the time, some units will either be redispatched higher than initially instructed load, or run when there was initially no load instruction, and similarly about half the time, units will be turned down or have their starts cancelled.

5.1.3   Acquiring the basic information on generation capability

The system operator begins with a list of all generation units that are connected to the grid. For each one of these, he requires three basic items of information:

(i)   **Availability** – The daily profile of availability of the unit.
(ii)   **Cost** – This is the marginal cost per MWh as presented to the system operator. The definition of 'cost' varies widely. In the fully liberalised bilateral market, the cost is simply the price at which the generator is prepared to sell from the unit. In the centrally managed system, and early stages of liberalisation, the cost is the marginal cost.[9] Note however, that if the centrally managed system is not to be subsidised, then the marginal cost issues, described at length throughout this book, are similar in the bilateral and centrally managed models.
(iii) **Capability** – This is primarily the profile of the maximum capacity on the day in question. Whilst the system operator knows the nameplate capacity and the registered transmission entry capacity for the year, the daily capacity changes due to ambient conditions and plant technicalities such as partial outages and fuel diet impact on capacity. The system operator will also require the minimum stable generation that is declared for the day.

The system operator then ranks these in cost order to form a cost stack for each period of the day, commonly halfhourly.

5.1.3.1   The generation stack

The stack will commonly be dominated by three main fuel/technologies, and the individual stacks for each will commonly overlap so that the stack has regions which are dominated by one fuel/technology and some with a mixture. This is shown schematically in Figure 5.5. We shall see later that the stack has more cost components than the marginal cost of fuel.

---

[9] For example in the Argentinean pool, the cost had to be audited.

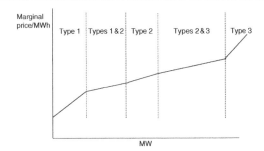

Figure 5.5 The generation stack with three fuels/technologies with overlapping cost structures

Figure 5.6 shows a common representation of a demand profile (in this case the aggregate demand across a winter day) overlaid on the marginal cost stack. Ignoring more complex features such as start costs and variations in demand and generator failure, this gives a rough depiction of likely load factor over a particular period for the various fuel/technology combinations.

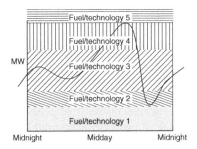

Figure 5.6 Comparison of installed capacity merit order with the demand profile

We can visualise the running of plant of different marginal cost, as seen in Figure 5.7. The assumption of start and stop capability is obvious.

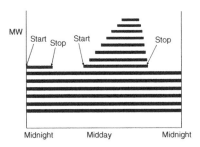

Figure 5.7 Schedules for plant of different marginal costs. The 'double two shift'[10] start-stop cycle for a mid merit plant is shown

---

[10] Double two shift does occur, but not on a regular basis.

We can do the same over a whole year period, by stacking the demand periods regardless of sequence. This is shown in Figure 5.8. Note that in a normal year, fuel/technology 5 does not run at all, but retains sufficient capacity to cover statistical variations in demand and generator failure, provided that there is a method to compensate for it (if it is privately owned), or if it makes overall financial sense to maintain it (if it is centrally owned).

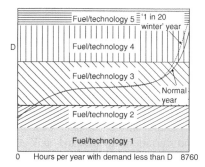

Figure 5.8   Resequencing hours by ranking demand, to form the load duration curve

5.1.3.2   Part loading issues

Whilst the full load merit order is relatively straightforward, the part load merit order is more complicated, since the part load cost/offer is dependent on the likely call off of reserve services as we see at the end of this subsection.

Note that, below full load, the incremental cost of generation decreases with increasing load (see Figure 2.19), whereas the offer ladder submitted to the system operator increases with increasing load. It can be rational for the generator to run at minimum stable generation at a loss, in the hope of balancing[11] offer acceptances, with the plant being hot and ready. Units will commonly offer or bid for incremental generation at incremental prices. For example, suppose that a plant initially only offers an amount equal to minimum stable

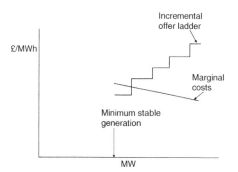

Figure 5.9   Incremental generation from a unit is subject to decreasing marginal costs. The associated offer submissions are subject to increasing marginal price. In this case the generator is prepared to run at an initial loss in the hope of receiving offer acceptances

---

[11] Balancing is covered in section 5.6.

generation for the trial stack, in anticipation of making further income from capacity/reserve. The same plant will offer incremental volume at increasing prices, despite the fact that the marginal cost actually decreases[12] with increasing load.

5.1.4   Construction of the first trial schedule

Centrally managed systems do have large linear programmes[13] which attempt to optimise the whole system, including start costs. In England and Wales, the GOAL (generation order and loading) performed this function, and on privatisation, generators retained copies of it. For our purposes here, the trial schedule method is better because;

(i)   It can be shown that an iterative optimisation from the trial schedules achieves the same final result as a linear programme, with much less exposure to loss of transparency of model behaviour.
(ii)   The compromise of flexibility modelling required to make the linear programme model tractable can cause mis-specification of capacity. In particular, the forms of medium term flexibility described in Chapter 6 cannot be effectively handled in practice.
(iii)   Participants 'trick' the model by gaming their inputs.[14] In particular, plant is incentivised to submit low variable costs and high fixed costs.[15] The testing and sensitivity analysis of this is more easily modelled using a simpler model.
(iv)   The step from linear programme optimisation to market management is a large one. Iterative trial schedules make the steps smaller.
(v)   The model complexity is such that inputs often have to be adjusted from their true values in order for the output to conform to expectations. In other words, in practice, the scheduling question often begins with the answer, or at least the answer for dispatch of certain units.

The first thing that the system operator does is accommodate the 'must run' plant. This will be plant that is inflexible and designed to run baseload (such as nuclear) and plant that has a regulatory status that allows it to run as priority over other plant (that may be cheaper). In the centrally managed system, this will generally be the privately run renewable plant that qualifies for special regulatory status. After adjustment for expected outage rates and transmission losses, this generation is netted against the demand profile.

Then for each halfhour,[16] the system operator compares the generation cost stack to the expected demand (which is assumed to be inelastic unless there are specific interruption agreements), and the first trial schedule will assume a dispatch of each unit that is 'in merit' as shown in Figure 5.10. Units may be 'de-rated' to correct for the average outage rate from declaration to delivery.

Then for each halfhour the system operator will treat interconnector imports and exports as positive and negative generation, struck at the clearing price at the interface. If the markets are cleared simultaneously then (assuming no constraints, or border and wheeling costs)

---

[12] If the efficiency increase for a load change from L to $L + dL$ is from E to $E + dE$, then the marginal efficiency is $(E + dE)/(1 - \frac{L}{E}\frac{dE}{dL})$.

[13] A linear programme is a computer programme that optimises a designated output subject to a set of input coefficients and constraints.

[14] This is caused by Pareto optimality of individual behaviour and is described in more detail in section 10.1.8.

[15] The price adjustment becomes self fulfilling, since by gaining generation from higher merit, the fixed cost per running period reduces.

[16] The halfhour period, that used in Great Britain, is used for convenience here. Balancing periods of 5 and 15 minutes are also used in other countries.

prices are the same on either side of the border, but in practice imports receive the domestic price and exports receive the foreign price. Depending on the system, system operators agree cross border flow, or companies submit offers in one country or other, and secure wheeling and interconnection capacity if necessary. Since the clearing prices at either side of the interface are not known initially, initial assumptions are made.

Then the system is stacked for each halfhour and the unit schedules are formed from the halfhourly sequence.

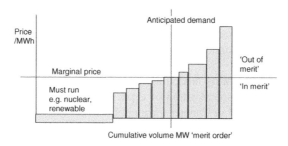

Figure 5.10   The merit order stack, showing must run plant, and the construction of system marginal price

5.1.5   Schedule feasibility and adjustment

There are many reasons why this stack may not be feasible, and if feasible, may not be optimal. The principal reasons are outlined in the subsections below, and each requires a redispatch relative to a trial schedule. The ordering is done differently in different markets.

It should become obvious, that even in the centrally managed system, that the use of market-like mechanisms in constructing the algorithms for optimum plant dispatch, are very effective. Not only does the breaking down of the problem in its elements facilitate multi player market interactions but it is in fact the key rationale for the market opening in the first place.

5.1.5.1   *Schedule adjustment due to transmission constraint*

The principal transmission reason for a dispatch schedule to be unfeasible is due to constraint – the network flow from the generation to the load entails actual or likely power flow through one of more lines in excess of their limits. The respective schedules are called the unconstrained schedule and the constrained schedule.

An example is shown in Figure 5.11. Here the system has seven units of equal size and different marginal offers. The Western demand is equivalent to two units and the Eastern demand is equivalent to two units. The interconnector has a line limit of one unit in either direction. Without the constraint, then the cheapest four units would run, but since they are all in the West, then this would violate the line constraint, and hence one Eastern unit would run ahead of a (cheaper) Western unit. The marginal cost relative to that of an unconstrained system is equal to the marginal cost difference between the most expensive units that run and the cheapest units that do not run.

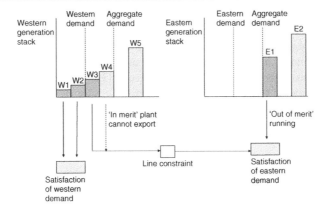

Figure 5.11   Out of merit running due to line constraints

Redispatch changes the aggregate losses, but commonly the first trial schedule does not consider losses (or does so crudely, by assigning a de-rating factor to the unit output). Losses are most important during peak hours, since losses are proportional to the square of the power delivered (see section 2.3.1.5).

5.1.5.2   Schedule adjustments due to transmission redundancy planning

Schedule adjustments to take into account potential line failure is connected to planning for constraints and similar to planning for generator failure. This can be done on a probability basis, or a more simple 'n minus one, n minus two', etc. basis, in which the schedule is designed to contend with one, two or more line failures. The New England ISO provides an excellent example[17] of location marginal pricing differences from single line failure possibilities, which can be used to understand schedule adjustments. After a trial schedule, lines are removed one at a time, and the schedule adjusted until feasible with any single line failure.

5.1.5.3   Schedule adjustments due to requirements for on load generation capacity

This is the second most important driver for alteration of the trial schedule.

We will see in Chapter 6 on capacity that variations in generator and network failure and of demand mean that the system requires short term flexibility of generation, both upwards and downwards.

Each plant dispatch configuration will have a particular capability to deliver capacity. In simple terms, the positive capacity is equal to the total capacity of the dispatched plant minus the amount actually dispatched. The capacity will be compared to the requirement profile (failure profile of dispatched plant, demand variation profile, failure profile of the capacity promised). The grid restrictions (failure profile, redundancy requirement and constraints on delivery of the capacity) are then also taken into account.

---

[17] ISO New England (2005).

This is shown in Figure 5.12, which considers the same physical system as Figure 5.11. For thermal plant to have capacity ready requires plant to be: (i) hot and (ii) running below full capacity. It is not possible to provide capacity from the West to the East since the line is congested and a demand increase in the East could not be fulfilled, and therefore it must be provided from the East to both East and West. The second Eastern unit must be dispatched in order to have hot capacity ready, and the first Eastern unit must deload sufficiently to allow the second Eastern unit to run at minimum stable generation. If minimum stable generation is about 50 % of full load and assuming simply that there is no efficiency loss from running at part load, then the total cost of operation is then equal to $W1 + W2 + W3 + E1/2 + E2/2$. Without the constraint, the cost would have been $W1 + W2 + W3 + W4/2 + E1/2$, and without any constraint or need for hot capacity, then cost would have been $W1 + W2 + W3 + W4$. We can therefore approximately calculate the cost of constraint, of reserve capacity, and of reserve capacity and constraint together.

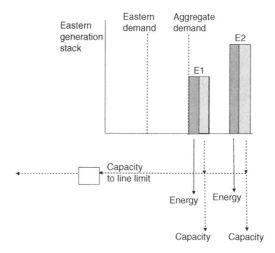

Figure 5.12   Out of merit running due to line constraint and need for capacity

5.1.5.4   Schedule adjustment due to start cost and other time sequence effects

To start up a plant incurs two principal costs, namely energy of start, and plant damage of start. We will also see in Chapter 11 that there are two extra costs of environment and reliability.

In the centrally managed system, the system operator is provided with cost of start and cost of generation. The first trial schedule inherently ignores the cost of starts by sequentially stacking the system 48 times per day and then constructing unit operating schedules. The problem can be solved, at the expense of the addition of much complexity, by including start costs and simultaneously optimising the whole sequence of 48 halfhours.

Start costs can be handled effectively by constructing a trial schedule and then iteratively re-optimising using an algorithm with several steps. For example the first[18] step may say

---

[18] Further steps involve the use of the state of minimum stable generation. For example the loss during a loss making period can be reduced by running at minimum stable generation.

'examine all off periods in the trial schedule and turn them to on periods where the saved cost of start exceeds the loss during the new on period'. Further steps involve iterations of revenue optimisation by alteration between the three states of full load, minimum stable generation and off.

We will see later, that the competitive system requires careful design for commoditising starts since starts are not a useful delivered product.[19] It is certainly possible to have some kind of charging for starts, just as capacity that may not be used is charged for. An example is a rebate that is chargeable on the exercise of a financial option. However, these are impractical in the ESI except for specific instances.[20] It is practical then to 'smear' the cost of start across the assumed running period. This is in fact quite an acceptable method in the centrally managed system and, unlike the linear programme, allows the marginal cost to recognise the quasi-fixed costs that would not be incurred if operation were continuously below initial estimates. See section 6.4.5 and the appendix for more details.

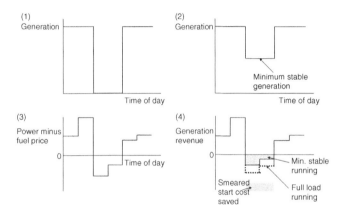

Figure 5.13   Rescheduling from first trial schedule to save start cost. (3) Market prices, (1) First trial schedule, (2) Reschedule, (4) By running at minimum stable generation, the total loss in period of negative margin is below the cost of a start

Start costs are one of the effects for which the operating sequences of plant are important. Bearing in mind that the system operator optimises the whole day in one go, rather than having 48 disconnected optimisations, then we can see that optimising the whole sequence is not trivial. This is further complicated by part loading to maintain reserve and the fact that part loaded plant has an incremental cost that is less than the cost of the part load, and hence does not easily form a stack function. This is discussed further in section 5.4.1.

5.1.5.5   Schedule adjustment due to system stability

System stability is described in section 2.3.1.2. Rescheduling for system stability is closely related to rescheduling for transmission constraint. In essence, there are locational limits over and above those that can be simply described by line constraints.

---

[19] Since a start is necessary for a run, then it is a factor cost that can be treated as a shadow price.

[20] The 'warming contract' in Great Britain between the generator and grid operator, which pays for warm readiness rather than for energy, specifically recognises the cost of start.

The most important kind of system stability is transient stability, and to maintain transient stability there must be enough mechanical inertia in plant, capacitance and line redundancy to contend with surges. Plant supporting physical stability must be electrically near the sources of instability.

System stability is maintained by maintaining nearby plant 'on the bars' that is capable of delivering ancillary services. Different plants have different capabilities for ancillary services (coal plant commonly has the greatest) and to deliver ancillary services, the plant must often be in a particular configuration.

The redispatch can be treated in much the same way as capacity, only it is far less limiting. The simple test is 'does the trial/final dispatch provide sufficient system stability?'.

5.1.5.6 Schedule adjustment due to plant dynamics

The basic information described assumes instantaneous ramping up, flat delivery and instantaneous ramping down of power. In practice, this is not possible for real plant. In addition to ramping rate limits, plant commonly has a minimum on time, minimum off time and other restrictions.

Therefore the first trial schedule must, for each unit, test for compliance with the plant dynamics of each unit. This is generally not an onerous restriction and can be handled by applying algorithms to each unit.

5.1.5.7 Adjustment of annual schedule to recover fixed cost

The reasons described in section 6.4.5 mean that the marginal cost is highly dependent on the running schedule. For this reason, marginal costs should be uplifted by the quasi-fixed[21] costs for the period. This in fact requires an *ex ante* expectation of running schedule for the whole year (and years) ahead, and thereby causes a requirement for medium term re-dispatch. This is true for centrally managed and competitive models, since if the competitive model shows that if a unit is not economic in a competitive market, it should not be economic in a centrally managed market.

The mechanism is as follows;

(i)   Construct the full trial schedule for all units for the year ahead under an initial[22] (lower bound) assumption of uplift of marginal costs above on load fuel cost, for recovery of quasi fixed costs.
(ii) Ensure that all quasi-fixed costs are covered over the year for all units.
(iii) Uplift marginal offer on the lowest merit unit not recovering quasi-fixed costs by an amount equal to shortfall in quasi fixed cost recovery divided by MWh run.
(iv) Iterate from (iii), until quasi fixed cost of unit in question exactly recovered. Then work up the merit order repeating the exercise for all units.

For sustainable equilibrium, all fixed costs should be used instead of just quasi-fixed costs for this exercise.

The plant will either: (i) find an equilibrium, (ii) establish a temporary equilibrium prior to an event such as a planned outage, or (iii) plan to close, thereby eliminating many quasi fixed

---

[21] Here, depending on the regulatory attitude to using market power to ensure a fair return, and regulatory agreement on asset value and fair return, the capital repayment on sunk costs can be regarded as quasi fixed rather than fixed.

[22] Initial assumption can be zero but the iteration takes longer.

costs. This should be the case whether the plant is in the centrally managed or commercial environment.

5.1.5.8 Adjusting schedule for more than one effect

The iterative process to solve one effect will naturally affect the others. This is solved by the application of a sequence of iterations. So for example the first trial schedule may solve for system stability, then do one iteration for start cost saving, then one for quasi fixed cost recovery, then return to the system stability. Optimisation of sequence in each iteration to save computing time is dependent on the physical configuration of the system.

5.1.5.9 The role of hydro power

The special issues relating to electricity are closely connected to the difficulties associated with storage, and hydro energy is the form of electricity that is most closely associated with the solution of storage problems. The characteristics are quite distinct from all other forms of power generation, and the extent of reservoir hydro capability, more than any other generation type, determines the market structure. The key characteristics were described in section 2.2.6.

From a schedule perspective, the interesting fact is that while hydro power has the lowest marginal cost, the need to ration it means that for most systems it must often be treated as if it has the highest marginal cost. To make hydro operate effectively with a daily trial schedule requires a trial marginal offer that is completely unrelated to actual marginal costs and would be effectively described as marginal opportunity cost.

The scheduling of hydro is considered in more detail later and here we cover enough of the basics to make hydro 'fit' into the trial schedule method.

First assume that rainfall, demand and the generation capability of the whole system are deterministic, and that the reservoir is very large and the rainfall very low. We then take the load duration curve and apply hydro power to the highest demand periods. The maximum area that can be covered is equal to the energy equivalent of the total annual rainfall.

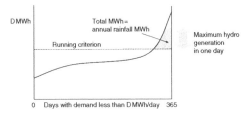

Figure 5.14 First estimate of hydro generation criterion by comparing total annual rainfall with the load duration curve

Using this figure we can see that the initial estimate of the criterion is to run when demand is above the level[23] indicated on the figure. For privately owned generation which is allowed to run using the pool prices without having to submit offers to the pool the same exercise could

---

[23] For ease of illustration, in day profile has been ignored.

be performed with the *ex post* (after day ahead prices are known but in time for dispatch) or *ex ante* price duration curve to obtain a price criterion for running.

This represents the running of the hydro plant if there were no problem of running sequence (i.e. we assume that a known annual quantity of the rain falls on the first day of every year and that there is no capacity limit of the reservoir).

If we take into account the sequencing of output, due to the reservoir limits, then we see from Figure 5.15 that we cannot simply choose all periods with demand above the level indicated on the load duration curve, even if all factors were deterministic.

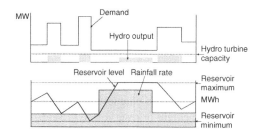

Figure 5.15   Taking into account the time sequence of demand and of rainfall in hydro generation

It is clear that we must schedule not just for the day ahead but for the whole year. There are essentially two alternative methods;

(i)   Optimise the whole system (hydro and everything else) for the whole year, at halfhourly granularity, with a linear programme.
(ii) Choose a price offering algorithm for hydro plant that optimises its expected revenue, subject to a possible regulatory price limit and non usage of market power, and then treat it as normal plant in the generation stack. The key factors of the algorithm are reservoir height, forward price curve, expected rainfall pattern, demand variation and generation failure variation. The same could be done using aggregate demand for the algorithm, but this would not take into account seasonality of capability of the generation mix, or of current plant breakdown status.

The first method is impractical, since even modelling a linear programme for a single day has a number of problems as discussed in section 5.1. In addition, it will not be possible to later on add the effect of uncertainty and capacity.

The second method is practical, allows for the later addition of uncertainty and capacity, and the addition of competition and private ownership. This sets an important precedent and introduces the method for offering other plant types, such as those with annual emission limits.

In practice, real hydro systems are considerably more complicated, more dispersed, with wide variations in size, and different ownerships, than in the simple model shown.

At this point, we recognise that the trial schedule must recognise the stochastic (uncertain) nature of demand (or prices) and of rainfall, the limitations of maximum and minimum dam height, and on rate of change of water level in the reservoir.

This requires, for each hydro plant, a trial schedule, and then iteration of the schedule algorithm until the water level profile is optimal (commonly with the constraint that the level at the end of the year equals the level at the beginning of the year. There are a variety of extra complications. For example our modelling initially requires the plant reservoir level at the end the year to be at the same level as the start of the next year. We can then 'borrow' or 'lend' water between years to improve our optimisation. Further aspects of hydro generation are described in sections 6.4.9 and 6.4.10.

5.1.5.10   Schedule adjustment for environmental factors

Plant that is limited only by a continuous emission limit does not have a schedule limit since it is either allowed to run all the time or not at all.

Plant that has an annual emission limit must have a trial schedule for the whole year, which is iterated until the limit is met. The annual limit has already been introduced for the limit in annual rainfall for a hydro plant. In the deterministic environment, with no 'banking' or 'borrowing' of permits between 'vintage' years, then the modelling is initially simpler than for hydro because the fact that permits can be used at any time means that there is no sequencing problem.

There is a different source of complication in the form of plant breakdown. If the plant breaks, then it cannot produce electricity even if the emission capture equipment is functioning. If the emission capture equipment breaks, the plant can still operate provided that annual limits (and specific limits pertaining to such breakdown) are observed. This modelling is shown in Chapter 11.

Some limits have sequencing effects since the tolerance of environmental load depends on the short term operating history of the plant, such as thermal plume limits for water, as shown schematically in Figure 5.16. The use of translators to handle the algorithm for situations such as these is described in section 8.4.3.

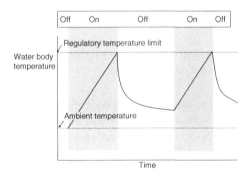

Figure 5.16   Schematic representation of the schedule effect of history dependent impact, in this case the thermal load on water body resulting from operation

It should be noted that environmental limits create contingent capacity on the system. If there is system shortfall that is significant enough for their to be political impact, then the government can elect to temporarily waive or reduce the environmental limits in order to secure more generation. This contingent capacity is an uncompensated public good[24] with probability existence value[25] provided by the generators with environmental limits.

---

[24] See section 10.1.17 for explanation of public goods.
[25] See section 10.1.18 for probability existence value.

5.1.6 Ancillary services

The system requires ancillary services, which are principally reactive power and the family of types of reserve. The requirements for ancillary services depend primarily on (i) location effects such as distance and constraint and (ii) the kind of plant 'on the bars' (for example, hydro plant creates little requirement for ancillary services but wind power commonly creates high requirements).

The need for reactive power can be reduced by alteration of the geography of dispatch, generally by reducing the amount of power travelling long distances, and differs from constraint management in that reactive limits can be overcome by reactive power provision at point sources which are much smaller and cheaper than power generation sources.

The need for reserve can be substantial due to such effects as: (i) sharp load profiles created by the incentives of plant in relation to market commercial mechanisms over the balancing period and (ii) rapid response to the sudden breakdown of large (often nuclear) units.

5.1.7 Profiles within commitment periods

Plants cannot load and deload instantaneously and hence cannot follow the step change profile used in the trial schedules. In addition to this, the demand profile itself does not have a stepped profile but has a finite gradient.

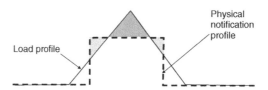

Figure 5.17 Actual plant profiles are not flat across demand periods and the energy delivered during run up and run down may be delivered in low demand periods. To satisfy the physical notification, the sum of the two light areas must equal the darker area

Plant dispatch is reconciled *ex post* not by the MW profile but by the MWh integrated over the granularity of the dispatch period. So, for a unit of maximum capacity Q MW to deliver $\frac{1}{2}$ Q MWh over a single halfhour, it must deliver energy in the preceding and following halfhours (and indeed further preceding halfhours as well).

In commercial market models, two market features are required to ensure smooth operation: (i) economic mechanisms for compensation in adjacent periods and (ii) some incentive for energy profile management within the halfhour. It is common for the system operator to specify 'gates' which the load profile must stay within. Gate violations can either be punished through a points system, or informally, through the system operator not accepting balancing/capacity/other services of plant that has given unreliable gate performance in the past.

Different markets price adjacent periods differently. In the bilateral market, the energy in each period can be sold without difficulty and the effect becomes most relevant in the balancing mechanism. A variety of mechanisms are set up to contend with this. For example, the power outside the halfhour could be compensated at the imbalance spill price (which may be negative), at the same price as the halfhour, or at some other price such as the pre gate closure index price.

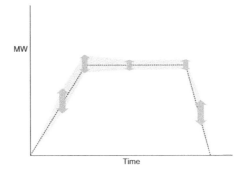

Figure 5.18 To maintain system frequency and stability, system operators require plants not just to deliver agreed energy amounts over contract periods, but to keep the generation profile within 'gates'

The problem of profile within commitment disappears if we use a very short commitment. For example the Australian market clears every five minutes, and the prices of six five minute periods are averaged for the purpose of financial contracts.

5.1.8 Generator failure

Generator failure has the same effect as demand spikes, but differs in probabilistic behaviour and is more localised. In the pool, generator failures and demand spikes are handled in quite different ways. In bilateral markets they are handled in the same way.

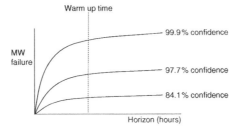

Figure 5.19 The reliability profile of on-load plant according to horizon

When considering failure, we must also consider network failures and interconnector failures. Failures of embedded generation ought to be taken into account but are often grouped with demand variation.

In addition, when modelling the capacity requirements to cover for failures and for demand variation, we must also remember that the capacity is itself imperfectly reliable and indeed the start is commonly the most unreliable period. A failed start is usually recovered, but a critical period may have been lost.

Generator failure is also estimated by the system operator. Most of the reasons are similar to the reasons that the system operator commonly undertakes demand estimation. Different systems require different degrees of information to the system operator. Many systems require no information to be submitted by the generators. In the USA, generators submit

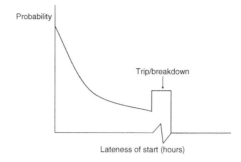

Figure 5.20   Probability distribution of start lateness

historic failure information to be submitted to NERC GADS.[26] Other markets, such as Nordpool, require updated information on likely unit failures in the near term.

The nature of generator failure variation is different to demand variation, since there is, in general less correlation between unit failures.[27]

Probability distributions of total generator failure are considered in the appendix. We note here that the probability of loss of load and the requirement for maintaining short term reserve are closely related to the size of the largest units on the system to the size of the synchronous system. This restricts maximum unit size.

5.2   THE CENTRALLY MANAGED MODEL

In the centrally managed model, all sectors of the ESI are owned and run by the state. As we have seen in dispatch optimisation, even in the complete absence of money flow between sectors, it is still optimal for units to be treated in financial terms for the purposes of optimisation. Here, we examine in more detail how this is done, how competition in generation can be introduced into this model and how consumers are treated.

5.2.1   Information and behaviour in centrally managed systems

5.2.1.1   Information

In the centrally managed model, the system operator knows; (i) fuel costs, (ii) fleet emissions, (iii) annual plant operations and maintenance budgets, (iv) capital costs and (v) historic fail rates. From this she can approximate the marginal operating costs of the plant, although for more accurate modelling, other less tractable cost elements must be taken into account such as capacity, flexibility, future fail rates and discretionary change on any of these.

In this model, it is not necessary for the units to receive income, or even to witness the clearing price. It is quite possible to build the estimated stack and return no information to the generation units other than despatch instructions.

---

[26] Generator Availability Data System.

[27] In the short term, hot weather impacts capacity and efficiency and occasionally forces unit shut down due to insufficient cooling as happened to the nuclear generators in France in 2003. The other connection between units are 'type faults' in which a fault witnessed in one unit causes an increase in the failure probability estimate of that fault in other similar units. Type faults are long term in nature.

However with no information returned to units, then, even if performance can be measured at high level, it cannot be managed, and still less incentivised. High level performance is hard to reconcile to local action and initiative, and low level performance cannot be measured because, in the absence of effective two way communication, then plant operators may articulate measurements, issues and reasons in a sufficiently technical manner for an objective evaluation of these by head office to be ineffective.

5.2.1.2 *Incentive*

For private sector generation, the financial motive is easy to understand, and generation plants can be incentivised to maximise the net of revenue and costs. It is less obvious that this is equally the case in the centrally managed system. In this system, the objective of the unit should be to provide optimum service for a given cost, or (better still) to provide the most cost effective service. This can only be achieved by converting most measures (but not, for example, safety) into financial measures, so that the plant can prioritise and dedicate resource to the priority areas. It is clear that the internal performance measures, incentives, and ultimately personal reward for unit operators dictate that the unit should operate as if it were in a commercial market.

There are two problems:

(i)   The information collected at high level is inherently imperfect. For example, for a coal station, the actual operating efficiency is the electrical energy sent out divided by the coal energy arriving to the station. Within the level of accuracy required to determine a merit order, this efficiency is barely known even over a one year period because of variations of the volume and content on the stockpile, as well as other sources of energy loss through oxidation or 'commercial losses' from purchase contract through transportation and on the stockpile.

(ii) In addition to the potential for misaligned incentives, there is the potential for lack or misalignment of incentive for the provision of information. We will see when examining the pool model that there is strong incentive to give information to the system operator that is not cost reflective, and which 'games' the system to improve the key performance indicator or actual net of revenue and costs. Within a company, if performance incentives are absent of misaligned, then unit operators can fairly easily mislead head office with respect to actual or potential performance, and innovation is stifled. On the other hand, a well set up measurement and incentive system can have a significant effect on 'routinised innovation' from top to bottom of the company.

Figure 5.21   The relationship between innovation, incentive and measurement

Key performance indicators themselves are most effective if they are aligned to the impact on performance, and since there are many performance factors, to assist in the measurement of 'apples and oranges', it is certainly helpful if the performance indicators have a common measure – money.

Figure 5.22   The conversion of unit performance and reconciliation to the corporate statutory accounts

The reconciliation between central/statutory accounts can be problematic because of the central measurement of accrual. While the unit management accounts should capitalise the unit at each year according to its market value, and de-capitalise according to plant life usage, this is quite different to the central methods.

However, because of all the issues noted below, the optimisation problem for the dispatcher becomes intractable because he must calculate all costs for all factors for all units and then optimise the problem which is highly non linear. It is essential for the dispatcher to keep the number of variables small and he must load the effects of all of the factors below into proxy marginal costs.

Many of these costs are understood most effectively and optimised most effectively by the units themselves. The units are most effective at optimisation (i) if they can witness and measure the outcome of optimisation initiatives and (ii) if they are incentivised according to the outcome. This then requires key performance indicators.

5.2.1.3   Behaviour in centrally managed systems

Power generation is a physical process and staff feel a strong identity to the output. To quote Niskanen (1968): '. . . staff, feel that the maintenance of an output of goods which can be touched, seen, counted and weighed constitutes a more obvious justification of their own existence than a problematic reduction of the shareholder's losses'.[28] The issue is greater for plant operating in commercial markets as physical operators have a healthy mistrust of profit that is generated with 'smoke and mirrors' and which due to the intentional or inadvertent loading of assumptions and valuations, and the intentional or unintentional misrepresentation of risks and liabilities on the balance sheet, may never turn to cash. Perceptions of the Enron story only serve to reinforce this view.

Motivated by production, the unit operators will in general try to increase their utilisation, and can do this by understating marginal costs in their submissions. This problem can be exacerbated since it is common for there to be families of units which have very similar design and hence performance, and therefore a minor (and credible) alteration in cost submitted can make a large difference in load factor.

It is clear that even in a fully managed monopoly system, that unit behaviour will ideally tend towards the competitive model. If internal structures are efficient and have a common

---

[28] From Kahn (1988).

measure (money), then the organisation will be efficient. If they are not, then since individuals and departments are driven by private motives rather than public good in the public sector just as they are in the private sector, then the organisation will be inefficient.

Common experience of commercial managers working with power stations is that technical alterations (such as burning new fuels, cycling plant more aggressively, or reducing the level of minimum stable generation), that are technically impossible or infeasible under instruction from head office, can be achieved with interactive dialogue and the provision of commercial measurement and joint incentive.

5.2.2 Introduction of Independent Power Producers (IPP's)

Rather than being just a sudden event at privatisation, state ownership of generation tends to dilute over time. One mechanism for the dilution of state ownership in the ESI is the encouragement of independent power producers (IPP's). IPP's have generally sat fairly comfortably within centrally managed models, since the state owned company gets generation without having to make capital investment, and the IPP's have received a stable return through power purchase agreements (PPA's).

As the ESI unbundled and distribution/supply companies became independent, then they had the need to secure energy. Investment in IPP's represented an alternative source of energy to the non-owned generators, at a known cost. IPP finance from supply companies had an advantage over independent finance in that the security of revenue reduced the required risk premium on capital. In the absence of wholesale markets, IPP generation is regarded as a dedicated source for the supplier. However vertically integrating every supplier's native load to supplier owned generation is not efficient at aggregate level.

5.2.2.1 Power Purchase Agreements – PPA's

PPA's have a spectrum of types, ranging from 'cost plus – best efforts' in which the IPP is to all intents and purposes part of the central system with external finance and subcontracted management, to 'firm with liquidated damages' in which the IPP pays a penalty for each and every shortfall with respect to an agreed generation profile of 'firm' (uninterruptible) power. In modern bilateral markets, firm contracts most efficiently allocate risk (and therefore risk premium) and production incentive to generators.

PPA's can be between the independent power producer (IPP) and the incumbent generator, the system operator, an individual supply company or distribution company, or occasionally direct to a large consumer.[29]

PPA's have had a mixed track record. Largely due to their longevity, they are relatively easy to frustrate[30] as the market mechanisms, while commonly being compatible for continuation of a PPA between willing counterparts, have substantial scope for 're-opening'. This creates a moral hazard for the contracts which increases with market volatility, as with a strong price movement, one party or other will be incentivised to frustrate the contract.

---

[29] In less developed countries, dedicated delivery to a 'host' load is the favoured option because the credit position is relatively secure, and the dependence on the electrical infrastructure is limited.

[30] Contract frustration is the termination of the contract through finding some technicality within it that renders it inoperable.

5.2.2.2   Feed in plant

A common mechanism for supporting renewable generation is the feed-in mechanism. There are variants and the essential mechanism is that the capability of independently owned units is 'fed in' to the fleet of the incumbent monopoly generator or to the supplier. Renewable generation is often treated as must run ahead of fossil/nuclear generation.

As an early move towards industry restructure, some nations have given IPP's protected positions by requiring the incumbent utilities to purchase power from them at the cost of the IPP or the avoided cost of the incumbent (i.e. the cost that the incumbent would have incurred without the IPP). The 1978 (PURPA) law in the USA is the best known example of this. This is described in Chapter 2.

Feed in plant can receive a fixed or variable price according to its nature and scarcity, instead of or as well as the grey power[31] price. It can in addition receive tax benefits from the exchequer or from the industry. The substantial growth of wind power in Germany[32] and Spain and solar power in Spain is supported by the feed in mechanism.

5.2.3   Consumers in the centrally managed system

In the centrally managed model, as we saw in Figure 4.3, it is quite possible for there to be no charge attached to consumption. By the same token, even if the total revenue recovered from consumers equals the total cost of the ESI then there is still no need for consumer prices to reflect the cost to the ESI of the particular consumer segments.

5.2.3.1   Pass through of production costs to consumers

Cost subsidy is common. Whilst in markets undergoing transition, it is common for the residential sector to bear the cost of transitional changes such as stranded assets and legacy fuel arrangements, cross subsidy from industry to the residential sector,[33] or from one industry sector to another,[34] also occurs.

We shall see in Chapter 10 (e.g. Figure 10.31) that cross subsidy reduces aggregate welfare when measured with money and hence mature markets tend to use cross subsidy more as a safety net for a small proportion of consumption than a widespread tool for engineering demand and fiscal management.

5.3   THE SINGLE BUYER

In the single buyer model, all producers must sell to the single buyer, and may not sell direct to consumers or supply companies. The single buyer may be the single supplier or sell to suppliers or vertically integrated regional distributor/suppliers.

---

[31] See section 8.6.

[32] The Electricity Feed-in Act forced suppliers to accept feed in power at 80 % of the historic retail price. The Renewable Energy Act of 2000 changed this to a 20 year fixed price. See Ragwitz and Huber (2004 or 2005).

[33] As a general rule, in maturing markets, it is the residential sector that bears the burden of extra costs such as stranded assets, since it is difficult to pass these costs to the commercial sector after the onset of deregulation. In immature markets, it is industry that bears the burden, since low residential prices are required to maintain votes in parliamentary elections.

[34] For example, in India, the agricultural sector is preferentially subsidised.

There are two extremes of the model:

(i) The single buyer is the same entity (almost always the state) that owns the electricity supply function, and controls prices. If, as is usual for this form, the entity also owns transmission and distribution, then the single buyer controls producer prices, network charges and consumer prices.

(ii) The single buyer is simply a short term co-ordinating intermediary between the generation, transmission and supply companies. Pool markets are of this general form although they can be either voluntary or with limited contracting outside the pool.

All electricity markets have some single buyer involvements. In the bilateral markets, the single buyer (in this case generally owned by the transmission company), takes over at gate closure.[35] Power exchanges, if in control of the market liquidity, have some characteristics of single buyers. The principal difference is that power exchanges operate in all timeframes, not just the very short term.

The monopoly single buyer is naturally the first step of unbundling, and therefore a common phase that is passed through. It is possible for the liberalisation process to stall after the set up of the single buyer, since competition in generation is probably the most important step and economically most material step in liberalisation, and therefore at this stage, the job appears to be half done. However, at this stage, there can be no commercial connection between generator and consumer, and therefore no consumer choice. The model is vulnerable to such forces such as state engineered cross subsidy, and the granting of cheaper tariffs to entities with political power or control.

5.4 THE POOL MODEL

In the pool model all producers submit their offer stacks into the pool, which produces stacks and then sends dispatch instructions. The pool itself is purely an administrative entity and takes no risks. In a mandatory pool, generation is only allowed through the pool. In a voluntary pool, generators can participate in the pool, or the buyer and seller can request dispatch to meet a bilateral contract between them. In a sense, the pool model is the economists' dream, because there is an explicit production function (the generation stack) and consumption function (the system operator's estimate of inelastic demand).

In a modern economy, that energy dispatch, even under central management, is based on marginal economics. The changes from a centrally managed and owned dispatch to a pool system are relatively slight. The key features of pool are:

(i) Dispatch is done by the system operator, independently of the generation and supply functions. The system operator is closely associated with the transmission function.

(ii) Dispatch is optimised on a day ahead basis with no annual information held by the system operator. Where the system operator does dispatch the plant using information other than offer prices, then annual planning is only incorporated either methodologically (e.g. planning hydro on an annual basis and then treating it as must run) or economically (translating the annual planning signals into day ahead offers). Annual effects on schedule, such as rationing of emission permits must be internalised into the unit offer prices.

---

[35] Gate closure is described in section 5.6.

(iii)   Dispatch optimisation is done using a simple set of information provided by generators in 'weight-rate-date' form. Hence extra information such as annual emission limits must be translated by the generators into day ahead offer uplifts.

(iv)   Demand estimation is done top down centrally, rather than bottom up aggregation of supply function estimates.

(v)   The generation units receive money for the energy dispatched, in the form of one or more clearing prices.

(vi)   Ancillary services are provided either as part of the grid code (the signature of which is a licence condition for generators) or by commercial agreements, or both.

(vii) The transmission system operator receive its funding from the single buyer.

(viii) There is some form of behaviour management system to limit the use of market power by generators.

(ix)   There is usually some form of compensation for capacity.

(x)   There is some disincentive for non performance of dispatch instruction.

(xi)   There is an explicit clearing price that is visible to participants.

(xii) Demand is generally drawn from the grid without contract, rather than having to make a commitment in advance.

It is quite possible to operate a pool model even if there is only a monopoly generator. Pools can be compulsory (in which case generation can only be sold through the pool) or voluntary (in which case generators can sell direct to suppliers and then request dispatch to the system operator).

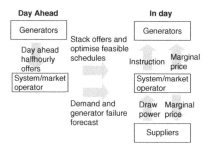

Figure 5.23   The pool mechanism. Arrows denote decision not energy or cash

Pool markets are more prone to abuse than other models, although in practice they have not been abused more than others. The great strength of pool models is the intermediate step from monopoly to competitive markets by the step from monopoly to oligopoly markets.

5.4.1   The trial schedule in the pool

There is in principle no difference between scheduling in the most advanced centrally managed model and the most basic pool model, particularly when the issues of motivation and provision of accurate information are considered. The practical differences are:

(i)   The discretion in many pools to offer at prices above[36] or below marginal price.

(ii) The price regulation that accompanies offer price discretion.

---

[36] In some pool markets, such as Brazil, generators must submit the audited marginal cost.

Commonly, the setup of a pool is coincident with the divestment or break-up of the monopoly incumbent generator. This creates further differences to the centrally managed model, namely:

(i)   The need for each[37] generating company to cover fixed costs (such as repayment of capital) as well as quasi-fixed costs on an *ex ante* expectation basis.

(ii) The associated need for low merit plant to cover fixed costs from market revenues on an *ex ante* expectation basis, when revenue is highly uncertain due to variation in net demand.

(iii) A formal mechanism for the accommodation of feed in and must run plant.

Commonly the first trial schedule has adjustments for plant dynamics and not for capacity and location.

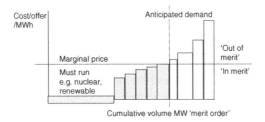

Figure 5.24   Constructing the first system marginal price (SMP) from the first trial schedule (which may be infeasible)

We explained in section 5.1.5.4 that the problem of having to optimise for a whole day with plant for which the incremental cost decreases with load, is problematic. This is further complicated in the pool through the provision by generators of stepped supply functions for tranches of partial load.

The trial schedule does not take emissions into account, although generators can incorporate emission restrictions into their offer prices or schedule submissions. Clearly this requires them to make assumptions on daily and annual load factors.

5.4.2   Subsequent trial schedules and final initial schedule

Usually in pool markets there is just one more schedule after the initial schedule. In the hybrid pool/bilateral markets developed in the 2000's that have developed there can be more. For example, the initial market design for the Italian market had a series of five markets.

The second trial schedule contends principally with the system requirements for capacity (including reserve can be adequately[38] provided for plant that is hot) and for location effects such as thermal constraint. The second trial schedule can be discrete. For example SMP can be formed from the unconstrained schedule, and those plants that have a different dispatch in the constrained schedule have their revenues adjusted without affecting the units with no change to schedule.

---

[37] In equilibrium this is in theory not a constraining condition. However it can make a substantial difference when there is some form of shock to the market structure or prices.

[38] Additional ancillary services requirements can be handled by a raft of bilateral contracts with the system operator, such as hot standby, as well as a series of bilateral agreements or mandatory requirements for on-load plant.

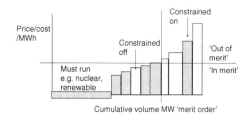

Figure 5.25   Second trial schedule, showing out of merit running due to transmission constraints

5.4.3 Demand

In the pool, suppliers draw power according to requirements, and pay the pool price determined *ex ante* for a volume that is realised *ex post*. They therefore have a volume option, which is passed to suppliers. It is not in the interest of the supplier to commit early by submitting a bid to the pool, although large consumers can be required to do so.

There is no mechanism within the pool for demand management (in the sense here of reduction in demand in response to price signals), except for consumers which are required to submit bids.

5.4.4 Power capacity

Plant that is out of merit in the first trial unconstrained schedule but which runs in the constrained schedule is referred to as 'constrained on'. Constrained on plant usually receives the price it offers at, referred to as 'pay-as-bid', rather than the clearing price of the second schedule, although this does depend on the market.[39] Constrained off plant may, as in the case of the England and Wales pool, receive lost opportunity cost in the form of the difference between SMP and offer price (but incurring an opportunity loss in the difference between shortest run marginal cost and offer price). Alternatively, constrained off plant simply receives nothing, as in the Spanish pool.

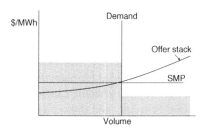

Figure 5.26   Total energy and capacity compensation for in and out of merit plant

---

[39] Generally speaking, the more mature the market, the more that clearing prices rather than bilateral prices are used.

5.4.5 Penalty for failure

Commonly, a pool model will incur no penalty for failure. A generator failing to perform simply loses the revenue from the lost power. Whilst this does provide some incentive to generate, it is apparent that the system operator (who calculates the probabilities of various degrees of failure) must have to instruct lower merit units, and pay their offer prices. There is therefore an incentive for a portfolio generator to fail after instruction if (i) the grid is likely to instruct another unit of its portfolio after the failure declaration and (ii) the offer price minus marginal cost of the replacing unit is greater than the system marginal price minus marginal cost of the replaced unit. Regulators make a technical judgement of the degree to which the failure was avoidable.

Various penalties for failure are possible, for example by buyback of the lost generation at some factor times the system marginal price.

5.4.6 Pool index

Dispatched generators receive system marginal price plus capacity, which totals to pool purchase price (PPP).

The system operator constructs and publishes clearing prices for each halfhour and hence there is a ready made index. The index is a high quality index because there is such a high degree of concentration – all players at day ahead, although it is important to remember that as in all markets, at any one time the price is set by players at the margin and hence it is the concentration near the margin that is important when considering liquidity, price volatility and market power.

5.4.7 Contracts for difference

A contract for difference (CFD) is a financial transaction between two parties who do not necessarily have anything to do with the ESI. There is no explicit connection between the CFD market and the system operator, and there is generally no market operator. With no explicit connection to the market, the system operator is not disincentivised to making changes to the index, and this gives basis risk to CFD participants.

The transaction is in the form of a 'fixed for floating swap' which are common in the financial markets. The transaction is as shown in Figure 5.27. The price F is fixed, whereas the price PPP is 'floating' until the agreed indexation date is reached. This can be understood by regarding the swap as two separate energy contracts. One is the sale of physical energy at a fixed price and the other is a purchase of physical energy at a floating price. The energy flows are equal and opposite and represent the 'exchange of notional'.

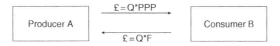

Figure 5.27   The contract for difference. Q is the energy volume in MWh and the index is determined by the pool purchase price (PPP)

The usefulness for generators and consumers/suppliers is shown in Figure 5.28. The generator A, if dispatched, receives the PPP from the system operator, and this serves as an index. Supplier B pays an uplift on PPP to pay for transmission, distribution and other services.

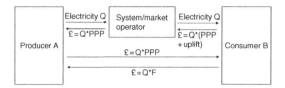

Figure 5.28 The net result of participation in the pool and transaction of a CFD, provided that plant is dispatched

The net result is that B always pays a net price of $Q * (F + uplift)$ and hence retains no risk to PPP. The risk to change in uplift is called basis risk. A, if dispatched, receives a revenue of $Q * F$ and hence is insulated from changes to PPP, provided that PPP exceeds the offer price into the pool.

5.4.7.1 Dispatch risk

It is particularly important to note that the CFD only guarantees the net price if the unit is dispatched. If not dispatched, then the unit makes the CFD price minus PPP, but if PPP is above marginal costs, then the unit makes an opportunity loss. The situation is quite different in the bilateral market in which the contract does secure the revenue.

Dispatch risk is reduced by offering at zero into the pool, but there are other effects such as market influence, and extra revenue from flexible operation. These are considered further in section 10.5 and Chapter 6.

While being constrained on is good for plant economics, being constrained off can be bad. While the system operator may return the apparent lost opportunity of PPP minus offer price to the unit, this will only be sufficient to cover the opportunity loss of being constrained off if the unit had offered at shortest run marginal cost.

5.4.8 Supplier price

The pool purchase price (PPP) is the reference price that generators receive. Suppliers then pay additionally for losses, ancillary services and other system related items in a cost that is called 'uplift'. PPP + uplift = PSP, the pool selling price.

Uplift = Transmission losses + Ancillary services + Other system costs

5.4.8.1 Basis risk

Contracts for difference (CFD's) are exposed to basis risk if the definition of PPP changes. So, if the construction of the index changes, then the CFD will no longer correctly refer to it. For example, suppose that the generation-demand split for charging for transmission losses changes from 50/50 to 100 % by generators. Then PPP would be expected to rise by the amount that generators need to elevate offers to recover the extra cost. A generator who has already locked in a CFD price will incur extra costs but without receiving extra net revenue (as the higher PPP received is offset by a payout to the CFD counterparty). For this reason, CFD contracts and Power Purchase Agreements are highly exposed to changes in the detailed structure of pool arrangements. In addition to this, since the bilateral market is a natural and somewhat inevitable progression from the pool model, the transition in market structure creates both basis risk, and contract frustration risk, since the contract may not be executable or calculable in the new market.

The bilateral market has basis risk in a similar manner. For example if a postage stamp market becomes zonal or nodal, then the notional point for delivery changes in value. Similarly, charges such as losses may change on a regional or sectoral basis.

5.4.9   Fixed cost recovery in the pool

Unlike bilateral markets, pool markets concentrate all the liquidity into the very short term. This emphasises gaming behaviour of participants. The Cournot optimum offer for a multiparticipant pool is shown in section 10.5.9, and it is quite obvious that the more fragmented the generation ownership, the lower the price. A fully fragmented market clears at marginal cost, which will in most instances not cover fixed costs for all players. The gaming and use of market influence in relation to this is described in section 10.5.

5.4.10   Price caps in static schedule

Price caps for halfhour contract periods tend not to be used in pool markets, with the exception of the VOLL price limit, although focal points[40] can acts as *de facto* caps.

Annual price caps for time weighted and volume weighted prices are indeed used however. This makes the implicit assumption that generators in oligopoly have a high degree of price control, and, as described in section 4.6.2, where there are such price caps, the market average tends to the cap price.

5.4.11   Market power in the pool

Figure 5.29 shows how local market power can in principle be used to elevate the clearing price when the highest merit out of merit units are owned by the generator with the lowest merit in merit units. The use of market power and gaming, is described in section 10.5.

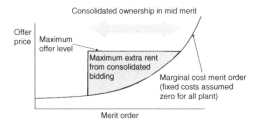

Figure 5.29   Coordinated offers in the mid merit region can alter the generation offer stack

In practice, as described in section 5.4.12 below, in a pool with a small number of players, this tends not to happen for mid merit plant and has no substantial effect for high merit plant.

---

[40] Focal points are explained in section 10.5.18.

5.4.12   Information and communication in the pool

In pool systems, it is common for the system operator to reveal the unit offers[41] after dispatch. This creates the facility for sophisticated communication between participants, including communication for the offering of out of merit units.

In a pool with two mid merit players, the signalling is very well defined since the required vocabulary is small. For example (i) to whom the comment is addressed, (ii) the instruction to the other participants and (iii) the comment on further action if the other participants respond in a favourable and unfavourable manner.

It is quite possible to develop a language with a high level of sophistication. For example, the inconsequential figures in the offer can be used as a language. So, for a crude example, an offer of 23.000734 encloses an actual offer of 23 and a comment with the code 734. This might mean 'if you undercut me again I will retaliate'. Since communicating in this way almost always violates regulations or competition laws and would in any case receive regulatory attention, sophisticated languages do not develop. Nevertheless there is commonly communication through price in pool markets over and above the pure significance of the pure competitive level of the price. The England and Wales pool provides a good example, in which the dominant incumbents, National Power and Powergen, interleaved their offers in order to maintain a high daily stability of market share.

While the pool purchase price is published, different system operators publish different amounts of information with respect to other information such as offers submitted.

5.4.13   Renewable and other generation with special treatment

We have seen that demand does not have to make a bid commitment in the pool, but can simply be drawn from the system. Embedded generation is then treated as negative demand and can therefore supply into the distribution network without pool submission. There are other forms of generation that can be made exempt from the pool rules applicable to large (usually tens of MW) generators.

This plant therefore has a free option on price, and with no market power can extract the full rent from running at any price above marginal cost without fear of collapsing price. The value from the *ex ante* advantage can be calculated using the methods described in section 9.2.

5.4.14   Offering and contracting strategy for generation plant in the pool

There are five pricing levels for generators:

(i)   **Less than short run marginal costs** – To create direct pressure on competitors, to signal a willingness to engage in aggressive pricing.
(ii) **At short run marginal cost levels**.
(iii) **Between short run and medium run (quasi fixed) marginal costs** – If the plant is not in merit when charging medium run marginal costs, then this causes early retirement of the plant. This in turn has the effect of reducing marginal costs (see appendix).

---

[41] For example, in Spain the information is revealed the day after, in Nordpool not at all. In New Zealand before 1999, the information was private and after that became public.

(iv) **At marginal costs plus fixed cost smear** to produce *ex ante* fair rent for fixed costs.

(v) **Above fair rent**.

The challenge in running pool markets is in acknowledging that market influence is inevitable and finding methods to use market influence to ensure that generators get fair rent but not excess rent.

5.4.14.1   *Offering at different costs with and without the contract for difference*

To ignore the issues of gaming and market power, let us consider a very small power plant of marginal cost C that has no CFD contract. Firstly let us assume that the capacity payment is zero, so SMP = PPP.

(i)   If the plant offers into the pool at offer O > C, then if the clearing price PPP is such that that C < PPP < O then the plant will have foregone the opportunity to earn PPP − O.
(ii) If the plant offers into the pool at O < C, then if PPP < O then the plant will lose a marginal value of C − PPP.
(iii) It is therefore optimal for the plant to offer exactly at O = C.

If there is a capacity payment that has no associated strike price, then this is received even if the plant offers at just below the value of lost load. Again, it is optimal for the plant to offer at O = C.

When we consider market power and gaming then it can be quite rational for the plant to offer either below or above C and indeed a many-small-player market will not always find long term equilibrium if all players offer at marginal costs as is shown in section 10.2.3

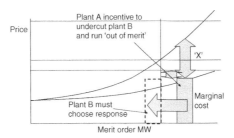

Figure 5.30   The incentive to offer at marginal cost

5.4.14.2   *Contracts for difference, and downward pressure on prices in the pool*

Simple pool markets are highly exposed to the price falling below sustainable levels. The approximate mechanism is as shown in Figure 5.31.

This behaviour, while detrimental to the market, may not be detrimental to the unit if it has hedged all of its generation for the full lifetime of the plant. Since CFD markets are commonly only two or three years then this leaves the generator in practice with high exposure.

Figure 5.31 Unintentional precipitation of price collapse

More sophisticated behaviours can be considered. For example, a generator fearing imminent price collapse can precipitate this collapse. This deters new entrants and hence actually increases the expectation of the forward CFD price once liquidity arrives. This is shown in Figure 5.32.

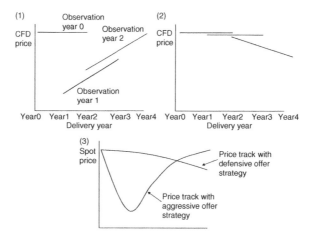

Figure 5.32 Price behaviour has different effects in different timeframes. (1) Aggressive offer collapses short term price and deters new entrants, allowing price recovery, (2) Defensive offer maintains short term price at the expense of causing overcapacity, (3) Spot price tracks under the two strategies

Now consider the same plant that has a CFD struck at price F, where F is greater than marginal cost and F was the prevailing forward price at the time the contract was struck. The plant then makes F − PPP (which may be negative), plus the money made as if the plant were uncontracted. The optimal offer strategy for this plant is unaffected by the holding of the contract.

For a generator, forward CFD sale plus zero[42] offer to the pool is equivalent to a physical forward sale at CFD price, since the zero offer is virtually certain to guarantee dispatch, and even if it does not, in some pool markets (but not others) the unit still receives a net revenue of PPP minus zero if constrained off.

---

[42] Negative offers are not generally allowed in pool markets.

For a generator, forward CFD sale plus offer to the pool at short run marginal costs is equivalent to a guaranteed forward sale at CFD price plus optional revenue for flexibility. If there is no effect of the offer made on subsequent competitor offers (i.e. no market influence), then this is the optimal strategy.

For a supplier, forward CFD purchase of estimated demand plus draw from the grid of actual demand fixes the price at the CFD price[43] for the estimated volume. The imbalance between actual and estimated volume is exposed to PPP.

Ex ante estimation of the offer required to recover fair rent for low merit plant is hard to do, because of the uncertainty of load factor and associated revenue. See section 9.1.20 for the variation of revenue in relation to the value of low merit plant.

5.4.14.3 Gaming equilibrium in the pool

An example of offer behaviour for two dominant mid merit generators is shown in Figure 5.33. In the first instance, both offer each day at some price above short run marginal costs. There are tacit rules of engagement, for example, maintenance of market share, maintenance of merit order, treatment of failed plant. In the second instance, the behaviour is asymmetric and the system may run out of merit. This situation is encountered when new entrants arrive. The incumbent plant may cede load either as a regulatory understanding to accommodate new entrant volume or because it has more to lose in a price war (having higher volume). This is described in section 10.5.13 on the Nash equilibrium. The third is a dynamic version of the first and represents a continual refinement of the rules of engagement for differing circumstances (e.g. for example maintaining market share constancy even if this causes out of merit running after plant failure).

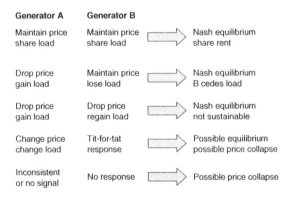

Figure 5.33 Possible equilibria from pool offering strategies

5.4.15 Interpool relationships

In its broadest sense, a pool is a combination of interconnected system, and in this form, pool models of one form or another have been around for a long time. For example the Connecticut Valley Power Exchange was formed in 1925, and the Pennsylvania-New Jersey-Maryland

---

[43] Since the CFD applies to PPP and suppliers pay PSP, then suppliers carry the 'basis' risk of the uplift. This risk is generally small.

(PJM) power pool was formed in 1927. The early models were essentially separate pools, connected by low capacity tie lines, to contend with outages and peak loads.

It is possible for a group of utilities to combine their generating and transmission facilities for more cost-effective management of delivery (economic dispatch). pool revenues and energy acquisition are shared among all members. This is called a 'tight pool'.

5.5 THE BILATERAL MODEL

Just as the technical change from monopoly to single buyer is relatively slight, but is accompanied by more significant changes contractual legislature, regulation infrastructure, participants and participant behaviour, the change from pool to bilateral is similar. The three key technical changes are dispatch, balancing/imbalance and demand side participation.

(i)   **Dispatch** – Units self dispatch by notifying the system operator. If required to redispatch for system reasons, they are compensated at prices determined by them in the balancing mechanism.
(ii) **Demand** – Suppliers must buy energy in advance in the bilateral market. While they can simply draw power, they would pay a high cashout price in the balancing mechanism.
(iii) **Imbalance** – Differences between contracted energy and produced/consumed energy are cashed out in the balancing mechanism.
(iv) **Balancing** – Units provide positive and negative capacity in the balancing mechanism.

Ancillary services are essentially similar in pool and bilateral models, but the physical nature of dispatch and the improved planning and transactional capability of participants that comes with the bilateral markets means that while the system operator still has a monopoly with respect to ancillary services, contracts become more transparent and standardised.

In a multiplayer model, (i) all units must be individually Pareto efficient and (ii) they must be economically viable both *ex ante* and *ex post*, otherwise they withdraw.

5.5.1 Contracting in the bilateral system

When two counterparties have engaged in a transaction, they then notify the system operator. Whilst the system operator will take great notice of the notifications, this is not the sole source of information. The system operator commonly makes his own analysis of aggregate demand, and of the availability of plant and contracts reserve and other contracts accordingly.

Bilateral contracts are commonly called physical contracts. This is more a convenient shorthand to emphasise the difference between pool and bilateral markets, than an accurate description. What is actually changing hands in a forward transaction is an agreement on notification to the system operator.

5.5.2 Physical notification in the bilateral system

The generators and suppliers submit their physical notifications into the system operator. These should equal the contracted positions. In fact there is not always a system to reconcile the contract position (which the market operator is concerned about) and the notification (which the system operator is concerned about). There are various mechanisms to ensure that generators and supplier notifications are consistent. For example, one counterparty could nominate for both.

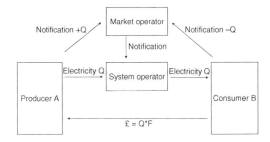

Figure 5.34   Bilateral contracting, and dispatch notification in the bilateral model. System and market operator roles stylised

Note however, that suppliers do not directly control the demand for electricity and hence will always consume an amount slightly different to the physical notification. Since all suppliers are exposed to similar demand volume risks, then the errors do not fully average out across the system.

5.5.3   The market operator in the bilateral market

Consider a bilateral market such as in Great Britain. Suppose that for a particular producer A has sold to supplier B, 500 MWh at a price of £ 30/MWh. While this contract has the 'look and feel' of a physical contract (certainly more so than a contract for difference in the pool), that it is not actually a physical contract, but a valid certificate for physical notification.

B submits a physical notification of withdrawal of 500 MWh to the system operator, and A submits a physical notification of production. Acceptance by the system operator of the physical notification of A will commonly be associated with conditions (such as the load profile in MW over the halfhour). The market operator receives electronic copies of the transaction so that the actual energy flow can be compared to the contracted energy flow for the purpose of calculating balancing payments.

5.5.4   Operational strategy for contracted plant in the bilateral market

In sections 5.4.14.1 and 5.4.14.2 we considered the short term schedule strategy for a very small plant (i.e. with no market influence) in the pool. It was clear that for this plant that the day ahead offer strategy is independent of the contracted position.

The situation is similar for plant in the bilateral market. If the pre gate-closure price in the market exceeds marginal cost, then contracted plant (under the same assumptions about absence of market influence) should wait and then notify the volume to the system operator, and uncontracted plant should sell and then notify. If the pre gate closure price in the market is less than marginal cost, then contracted plant should buy in the market and therefore not notify physical volume, and uncontracted plant should remain uncontracted. The physical operation is therefore unaffected by contract position.

However, this generator can in addition offer electricity in the bilateral market (and subsequently the balancing market) and sell if the price exceeds the marginal cost. Additional income is then gained.

Therefore with no market power, in the risk neutral view world, in the short term offer strategy in the bilateral market is independent of the contract position, just as it was in the pool.

As with the pool the considerations of risk and market power mean that there are perfectly valid reasons for not doing this. A key difference between the bilateral market and the pool here is that in the pool, the buyers do not directly participate and just pay the pool price. In the bilateral market, a buyer must be found, and suppliers will not have short exposed positions so close to prompt because the costs of imbalance are high. Whilst in theory, the prompt bids and offers should not be affected by contractual position, they are in practice. This has the effect of decreasing prompt market volumes and price sensitivities and making the market less vulnerable to collapse.

5.5.5   Hybrid pool/bilateral markets

Pool and bilateral market can be mixed. For example in Spain, generation and supply companies can contract bilaterally and then inform the system operator, although this does not necessarily constitute a self dispatch.

5.6   IMBALANCE AND BALANCING

In the bilateral markets, there is a 'gate closure' after which there is no time for participants to trade with each other and the system operator takes over as monopoly buyer and monopoly seller. This is done in a structured manner through various forms of balancing mechanism. In the England and Wales market for example, gate closure was initially set at 3.5 hours, and it is now 1 hour in the Great Britain market.

After gate closure then participants may only engage with the system operator. All participants have submitted physical notifications but will not deliver or consume exactly what they committed to. Imbalance and balancing mechanisms take care of the commercial element of this.

Whilst balancing mechanisms are particularly associated with bilateral markets, they can also be set up for pool markets.

5.6.1   Market structure for balancing and imbalance

The structure of volume reconciliation for imbalance is as shown in Figure 5.35.

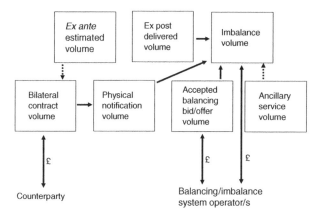

Figure 5.35   Cash flows and calculation of imbalance volume

5.6.2   Imbalance charging

The details of imbalance charging vary greatly, but the basic principles are essentially the same in most instances. The cash flow to/from the providers of balancing is (after various adjustments, for example due to the effect of constraint on balancing requirements) equal to the cash flow to/from the causers of imbalance. The system used in England and Wales is to allow to apply imbalance charge on a gross basis. For example if a company has one unit falling 5 MW short and a unit spilling 5 MW, then both are cashed out at the imbalance price rather than netted.

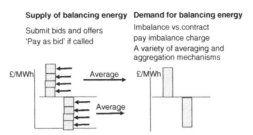

Figure 5.36   Constructing the imbalance charge separately for spill and shortage by taking the average of accepted bids and the average of accepted offers

The effect of imbalance on the effective bid and offer of the market is for there to be a step change at 'gate closure' as shown in Figure 5.37.

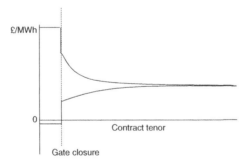

Figure 5.37   Market and imbalance bid/offer in relation to delivery tenor (time between observation time and delivery time)

At the opposite end of the spectrum, excess buyers and sellers get cashed out a single price.
    It is also possible to levy an additional £/MWh information imbalance cost.

5.6.3   Provision of balancing

The Great Britain system represents a good example of the inception and evolution of the balancing mechanism.[44]

---

[44] The balancing mechanism and the settlement of imbalances in the balancing and settlement code are actually quite discrete but in economic terms can be considered together.

Having submitted the Final Physical Notification (FPN) to the System Operator, each Balancing Mechanism (BM) unit,[45] whether it be a producer or consumer, can submit a series of bids and offers that the system operator can call against.

The participants receive nothing if they are not called, and if they are called, then they receive their balancing offer for energy provided, or energy at their balancing bid for energy received. This is called 'pay as bid'.[46]

The balancing offer stack for a single plant is like the whole system in microcosm. Suppose that a plant has bilaterally contracted at minimum stable generation, possibly at a loss, so that the plant is hot to provide balancing. It then submits a stack of balancing offers. Note that the marginal cost of these offers declines due to efficiency gains as shown in section 2.2.18.

To be hot the plant needs to be running and to be able to provide balancing it must be running below full capacity. The system operator gets the balancing service that he needs but it is clear that the offer stack is far more closely related to fixed costs than marginal costs.

Balancing offers can be provided which tie different periods together. Balancing mechanism submissions are accompanied by the limitations of plant dynamics, and the system operator has discretion with respect to call off.

From a medium term perspective, there is some commonality between balancing and LOLP based capacity payments in the pool. In both, the operator the operator decides on (i) offer strategy, (ii) offer payoff and (iii) closure strategy.

A key difference is that with the possible exception of grid related balancing, balancing revenue is a relatively small financial proportion for both generation and demand, since it only applies to a one hour period. Another difference is that there is more of a continuum of information.

5.6.4 Transmission effects in balancing

The balancing mechanism is used to resolve transmission constraints from the bilateral schedules. Even if the bilateral schedules are unconstrained, then imbalance can create constraint and hence balancing acceptances are dependent on electrical location.

5.6.5 Profile effects within the balancing period

The profile effects are described in section 5.1.7. The balancing mechanism aggregates the MWh of electricity delivered/consumed over the balancing period and hence ignores MW profile effects.[47] Generating units providing balancing may provide or be provided with 'gates' within the balancing period to ensure consistency of profile. It is in the generator's interest to stay within the gates to ensure the correct total MWh of the period, but if gates are missed in the early part of the period, then it is in the generators' commercial interests to overshoot the gate in the later part of the period in order to maintain the correct total MWh. Whilst there may be no financial penalty, missing gates on a consistent basis will deter the

---

[45] The definition of a balancing mechanism unit differs. In general, it is plant at least tens of MW.

[46] The term 'pay as bid' is occasionally used for the forward markets, because the contracts are agreed bilaterally. This use of the terminology is not used in this book, and bilateral contracts are regarded as being struck at bilateral clearing prices.

[47] This is not an issue for markets with five minute balancing periods.

system operator from accepting balancing from particular units, since unit selection is at the system operator's discretion.

5.6.6   Transaction strategy

Generator imbalance tends to be low because of the short interval between submission of physical notification and of delivery, and the ability to control load within the period. Since it is easier to drop than raise load, and non intentional variations in load tend to be reducing, then it is optimal for the physical notification to have a small downward bias relative to capability.

Aggregate consumer imbalance would be low if submitted individually, since the diversification is large, and most systemic effects such as temperature do not have impact in balancing timeframes. However, it is the suppliers who submit the physical notifications, and they do not estimate using site by site data but by aggregate. Since the supplier portfolio changes by consumer switching, the suppliers have imperfect knowledge of the aggregate profile. The supplier bias is dependent on the estimation of what the buy and sell cashout prices will be. Risk aversion is not a strong driver here since the balancing period is so short compared to the financial year, although the biases are tempered by; (i) the price limits possible within the balancing mechanism (which can be much higher than the value of lost load, (ii) the maximum negative price and (iii) historic record of very high positive and negative cashout prices.

5.6.7   Transaction cost minimisation

Of the changes from pool to bilateral, the balancing mechanism is one of the main ones. When all participants have learnt to manage their short term generation and demand, and estimation of these, then the balancing mechanism becomes economically less important, but in the learning period, it is business critical. In England and Wales, imbalance costs were deliberately allowed to be high in order to force the behavioural change.

5.6.8   Imbalance revenue distribution

It is clear that if each generation unit and supplier aggregate at grid supply points are cashed out at either the system buy price (SBP) or the system sell price (SSP) that the system operator will be a net receiver of cash. This amount generally has formal definition and colloquial terminology (such as the 'beer fund' and 'black hole money'). It can be 'smeared' back to reduce the system offer price and increase the system bid price, used to fund balancing for constraints and reserve. In Great Britain the imbalance cost for regional balancing aside from aggregate energy imbalance is charged separately in the balancing service use of system charge.

5.6.9   Auction choices

Pay as bid is the most common (e.g. Great Britain, France) but not the only mechanism. Balancing could have clearing prices instead for example.

5.6.10   Issues with balancing mechanisms

Balancing mechanisms have received much attention and controversy. The principal objections are:

(i)   Since in the pool model, the consumers had no requirement to forecast, and had no explicit imbalance cost, then despite the early indications of mechanism, they were ill prepared for the advent of a balancing regime.
(ii)   Imbalance costs were deliberately set to be punitive in the early days, in order to force the proper attention to forecasting and demand management and the cost of imbalance.
(iii)   The aggregation prior to gate closure, and the allowed aggregation after gate closure means that large players received more netting benefits than small players, thereby creating an entry barrier.
(iv)   It is possible for the participants to game the system by information balance (deliberately producing or consuming an amount of energy different to the physical notification[48]). While this can policed by a market abuse licence condition or 'good behaviour' clauses, abuse is in practice hard to differentiate from fair extraction of rent by low merit plant.
(v)   Interaction between balancing, imbalance and constraint allowed gaming.
(vi)   Administrative errors in the submission of notification can be very expensive.[49]
(vii)   If the system operator calls plant on or off at very short notice for system reasons, then the imbalance price can differ greatly from the pre gate closure market price.
(viii) Forms of power with high intermittence, such as wind power, have imbalance costs.
(ix)   Incompatible imbalance regimes and periods between different countries or control areas can be used as a barrier for entry for cross border flow.
(x)   The treatment in some systems of provided reserve as if it were spill/shortfall.

Fundamentally, the questions that drive changes in the balancing and imbalance regimes are:

(i)   Are the financial issues material?
(ii)   If the issues are material then is the cost of imbalance to the perpetrator in excess of the short term cost to the system operator and the long term cost to the ESI and its customers?
(iii)   Does the mechanism signal approximately the right amount of capacity in the short and long term?
(iv)   What are the alternatives?

5.7   RESERVE CONTRACTS

There are three timeframes for reserve; (i) the total duration of the contract, (ii) the temporal delivery resolution of the contract (e.g. five minutes or halfhourly) and (iii) the notice period to load change.

---

[48] For example to gain revenue from acceptance of a balancing offer on volume that is in reality inflexible, a guess that the cash out price is more favourable than the closing price in the bilateral market, deliberate influence of bilateral, cashout or acceptance threshold. In practice deliberate imbalance is risky and only undertaken with respect to a slight bias on positions with high volume uncertainty.

[49] In the early days of the New Electricity Trading Arrangements, there were Notification Errors that caused substantial errors to some participants and which were determined in court.

Reserve contracts have traditionally been bilateral between the system operator and the generators, and under confidential contractual terms. Reserve is increasingly becoming a tradable commodity with a contractual form similar to that of the exchanges (trades are with the system operator but are standardised and the tender is public).

In Chapter 6, we describe examples of the minute contract in Germany, the ICAP capacity contract in PJM and the changes to the reserve contracts in Great Britain.

5.8   WHOLESALE MARKETS

In a mature wholesale markets there are four key elements:

(i)   **Energy** – Forward markets at halfhourly detail, for many years forward, with high deliverability and full firmness.
(ii) **Power capacity** – Option markets which translate directly to the forward markets.
(iii) **Location** – Infrastructure capacity contracts, and physical or financial basis trades between one point, zone, or balancing point or zone to another.
(iv) **Emissions** – Forward markets for many years forward under standardised schemes, at annual resolution.

From a plant perspective, there are four contracts required to deliver/receive physical energy in relation to an energy contract.

(i)   **Energy contract** – The amount of energy notified to be delivered in a short period (e.g. halfhour).
(ii) **Infrastructure capacity contract** – The right to participate physically in the market by delivering/receiving energy at grid supply points.
(iii) **Location contract** – The contract that takes the physical energy produced/consumed to/from the electrical position specified in the energy contract.
(iv) **Emissions certificate** – The certificate generated from the production of electricity.

We can view these as pre-requisites for delivering or receiving energy through a spot (prompt) contract. There is effectively a family of contracts associated with a prompt physical energy contract.

(i)   spot contract;
(ii) forward contract;
(iii) 'vanilla' European Option contract (the simplest part of what we have called 'power capacity');
(iv) 'complex', 'exotic', or 'extra flexibility' contract (the complex part of power capacity);
(v)   financial derivatives of the above.

We consider this family in some detail in the section on pricing. In doing so ignoring for the most part the family associated with the spot contract because even without the family, electricity is an extremely complicated commodity. However, the chapters on location, capacity and environment are intended to provide sufficient building blocks for the two contract families to be combined for practical application. The combination of the families is made explicit in Chapter 11 on financial modelling of power plant.

5.9   POWER EXCHANGES

We have noted that with the exception of the change from bundled centrally managed (effectively a communist model) to unbundled centrally managed, that each structural step in the development of the ESI market is relatively slight. The growth of power exchanges is the slightest of all, but finally bridges the gap between electricity is a intractably complex product for true competitive wholesale trading, to markets tradable by financial counterparties such as commodity traders, funds, investment banks and actively hedging consumers.

In section 5.9.2 we specify some details of power exchanges, and here we present the whole journey from pool to power exchange in a stylised way so that we can track the changes.

5.9.1   The journey to power exchanges

Since not only do definitions of entities vary widely from country to country but from model to model we use stylised definitions for the purpose of these figures:

- **MO** – Market operator. Financial reconciliation only;
- **SB** – Single Buyer. Economic optimiser;
- **SO** – System Operator. Managing the physical system from a starting point of physical notifications;
- **PX** – Power Exchange – Introducing agent, financial clearing house, physical notification agent;
- **PN** – Physical notification – Agreed volume submitted to system operator.

The stylisation is in keeping with the electrical 'details to follow' approach that we have taken overall in order to marry the four building blocks of energy, capacity, location and environment. In doing so we should warn that opinions differ with respect to power exchanges. For example Hogan[50] proposes the 'separation fallacy', and presents the view that the functions of the transmission system operator and of the power exchange cannot be separated, because congestion management, balancing, ancillary services and transmission usage, cannot be effectively handled.

Each model is presented by itself, and as a development from the previous one. It is in fact quite possible for all of the models to exist simultaneously.

In the simplest pool with no demand side participation, Generators submit offer stacks to SB, who constructs a trial schedule using consumption history and submits this to SO, which then manages the imbalance with positive and negative reserve and capacity contracts. A financial power exchange, not integrated with the MO, can operate effectively for contracts for difference in this environment since there is an effective market index. In the absence of the pool index the non integrated PX is vulnerable to index basis, definition, change of definition and illiquidity.

---

[50] Hogan (1995).

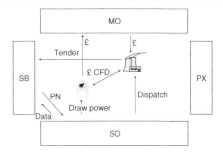

Figure 5.38   Pool. No demand side participation

With the addition of mandatory demand side participation (no bid no energy), SB no longer estimates demand. Commercial mechanisms for demand imbalance are required.

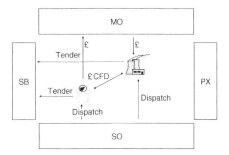

Figure 5.39   Pool model with mandatory demand side participation

In the bilateral model, participants trade with each other instead[51] of the single buyer. Since the bilateral contract is effectively a 'PN promise', then reconciliation is required with the market operator.

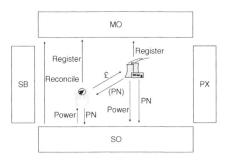

Figure 5.40   Bilateral mechanism

---

[51] Or in addition to. SB trades not shown.

The simplest power exchange is simply an introducing function between participants. This part can be played by brokerage companies which need not have more resource than one person with one telephone.

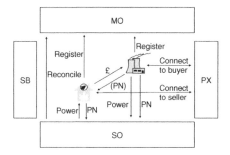

Figure 5.41   Power exchange, just acting as broker

A formal power exchange (the standard interpretation of the term), acts as counterparty, and must therefore reconcile trades.

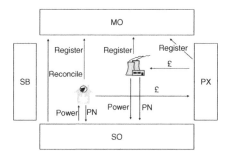

Figure 5.42   Power exchange, acting as financial counterparty

An integrated power exchange (the most advanced model) submits notifications in relation to the net position from trades executed. If bilateral trades (not shown below) are required to be 'posted' or 'crossed' on the exchange, then the exchange is very similar to the single buyer but is driven to reflect market conditions rather than proprietary estimates. In France for example, bilateral trades are submitted directly to SO (RTE, an administrative division of Electricité de France) and trades with Powernext are submitted to SO by Powernext.

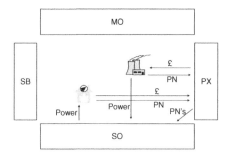

Figure 5.43   Power exchange, integrated with system operation

5.9.2   Specifics of power exchanges

The basic commodity is the same in all cases – a halfhourly (or other period) electricity notification commitment to the system operator. Power exchanges can differ widely in their details:

(i)   **Counterparty visibility** – Whilst it is technically possible for counterparties to identify each other in some exchange models,[52] the standard arrangement is that contracts are anonymous.

(ii)   **Counterparty contract** – In some non electricity exchange models, the contract is bilateral until it is specifically matched by the exchange, and the counterparty becomes the exchange. This mechanism can be used, for example for long term bilateral contracts that, with time, fall within the maximum tenor of the exchange.

(iii)   **Auction mechanism** – The exchanges generally hold an array of bids and offers from participants, that form the production and demand stacks. This can be published in full (with anonymity) or just the most recent trade, the highest bid and the lowest offer. Different offer specifications can/could be accommodated (for example partial completion orders, no partial completion, stop loss orders).

(iv)   **Credit arrangements** – The exchange requires capital to maintain a very high credit rating, which is generally (but need not necessarily be[53]) provided by participants. Trades also require initial margin and variation margin. Margin requires complex algorithms for electricity.

(v)   **System operator notification** – A transaction can be accompanied by a commitment to notify, or notification can be made directly to the exchange, which is then passed to the system operator.

(vi)   **Licence restrictions** – An exchange may be limited by rules beyond the exchange. For example, while a generation or supply license may not be required, registration with a financial regulator may be.

(vii)   **Location** – Liquidity is concentrated by trading at exchange hubs. Clearly, pricing is of postage stamp form within a hub. Exchanges can trade several locations at the same time, including locations in neighbouring markets. Locations can be a single reference location, different zones, or different nodes.

(viii) **Transmission trades** – Within exchange area and across exchange areas.

(ix)   **Cashout mechanism** – The traded contract is a physical notification. Imbalance relative to the physical notification must have the proper financial treatment. This can be done through the exchange, so the system operator sends the prices to the exchange, which pays and collects them on behalf of the system operator. For purely financial index contracts, there is no notification and therefore no cash out.

(x)   **Live trading or day ahead** – Whilst exchanges are best suited for live trading, they can operate in batch mode in a pool-like manner. For example in Belpex in Belgium, the offer profiles for a 24 hour period are submitted at day ahead. This is essentially a pool model with demand side participation. Since pool markets produce high quality indexes (i.e. with high concentration of indices), then the index is amenable for exchange traded financial contracts for difference.

---

[52] For example an off exchange agreement, followed by an 'exchange for physical' posting of both sides of the trade on to the exchange.

[53] For example, EEX in Germany is capitalised by seven clearing banks.

(xi)   **Index construction and publication** – Indexes can be published and could be for example, the closing trade, a weighted average of trades near the close, an average of unaccepted bids and offers, etc.

(xii) **Physical derivative contracts** – For example, European options that deliver as standard physical contracts.

(xiii) **Financial derivative contracts** – For example European options cashed out against the index, average rate options, multi-commodity options, time spread options

(xiv) **Other commodities traded** – For example emissions.

(xv)   **Fungibility with other exchanges** – For example, cross deliverability of emission permits, delivery of electricity in other exchange areas (with transmission entry agreed). For example Belpex in Belgium is 'coupled' with Powernext in France and APX in the Netherlands.

(xvi) **Contract resolution** – In the most mature form, each halfhour (or similar period) can trade individually. In developing form, the contracts are like pool contracts.

5.9.2.1   Virtual power trades

Virtual power is a financial transaction from a power generator to a power supplier that gives the supplier access to a market through access to the power. Virtual power is often presented as partial divestment of power stations, particularly if the contracts are long term or have high degree of optionality. In reality, they are virtually indistinguishable from standard European options, and have very little short term flexibility, although the electricity is 'upstream' (with basis risks akin to power stations) rather than downstream. The buyer pays a capacity (option) fee for the right to a physical notification right at a predetermined marginal (strike) price.

Short term virtual power benefits new entrant suppliers by access to the power. Long term virtual power benefits incumbent generators by giving cash flow stability while retaining short term and detailed flexibility.

The key differences between virtual power and physical power from the perspective of the owner are; (i) the contracts are firm (with the possible exception of *force majeur* clauses) and (ii) the flexibility is highly structured and does not have the extra flexibility described in Chapter 11.

5.9.2.2   Market coupling

We noted in section 2.3 on transmission that it is desirable to plan investment in power generation and in transmission in a coordinated manner. The same applies to the scheduling of power and the booking/paying for transmission capacity within a control area, between control areas and in neighbouring control areas.

To do this requires a coordination of energy and location pricing, and 'coupling' of control areas. Although the concept is not new, and is the idea behind the 'tight pools' in the USA, it is only very recently that there have been concerted efforts to manage price, schedule, capacity and interconnection in a harmonised manner.

The idea behind coupling is simple. A counterparty who buys energy in one region, sells it in another and who undertakes a basis trade (transmission responsibility) can then physically produce it in the latter region and physically consume it in the former.

EuroPEX provides a good example of this in the attempts for flow based market coupling.

5.10   ADVANCED POOL MARKETS

We have seen that the technical changes for each stage of development of the market are relatively slight, and it is the change in practices that is of greater significance. Indeed the generalisation of models into central, single buyer, pool, bilateral and power exchange is more useful in understanding the elements of markets than it is in categorising them. In reality, each market is slightly different and has elements of most models.

The most advanced market of all is the PJM market in the USA, with location marginal pricing, a form of capacity markets and monetisation of ancillary requirements and provision. This has three key elements – a forward financial market, a day ahead market and a real time market.

A key distinction between a day ahead pool-like market and a bilateral market is that whilst the bilateral market simply rolls forward with no particular recognition of the diurnal cycle, the day ahead market treats each calendar day discretely. The bids and offers for a calendar day close at midday on the day before, and the acceptance schedules and location marginal prices are published at 4 pm. The real time market (equivalent to the balancing mechanism) bids and offers close at 6 pm, and are called upon throughout the ensuing day.

The concentration of liquidity creates robust nodal index prices.

Bearing in mind the comments in section 5.4.14.2 and the gaming discussions in section 10.5, this begs the question of why the PJM price does not appear to be susceptible to price manipulation (particularly at nodal level) or price collapse (by all plant offering at marginal cost and fixed costs not being covered by some plant). Some answers could be:

(i)   The maturity of the operator (since 1927) and associated regulatory and participant maturity. The long term stability has meant that equilibrium strategies can be developed, and non equilibrium strategies altered.
(ii)   The commitment of PJM to education (thereby increasing the elasticity of demand response).
(iii) The relatively low vulnerability to transmission constraints and regional market power (for example, with the system being large and round rather than small and long).
(iv)   The cost structure of the generation mix in relation to the demand profile.
(v)   The interplay of the capacity and energy markets.

Locational pricing in PJM is described in section 7.5.1.1.

6

Power Capacity

We have shown that varying demand for electricity cannot simply be satisfied by storing and releasing energy from stock, as it can for other commodities. Power must be generated exactly as it is withdrawn. This creates initial issues for us from the perspective of ESI generation and transportation:

(i) In order we need to maintain sufficient generation to satisfy demand for prospective peak demands in the future, the peak generation capacity must be considerably greater than the average generation. Since power generators have fixed costs, then there must be a way of compensating the generators, and therefore of paying for it by consumers.

(ii) Demand variation and generator failures are both uncertain. Therefore the mechanism of payment and compensation for the provision of capacity must take into account this uncertainty. This adds considerable complexity.

(iii) Since electrical transportation infrastructure is dedicated, and fuel transportation infrastructure is partly or largely dedicated, then transportation has the same issue of having to pay for, and be compensated for the provision of, capacity. The principal difference between the economics of generation and transportation is that transportation has very low marginal costs compared to the fixed costs.

(iv) Transportation infrastructure can fail. This requires a degree of redundancy in the networks. In addition to this, different failure configurations in the generation fleet create different degrees of constraint in the transportation system. For example if all of the generators in the North fail, then Southern generation will be constrained from making up the shortfall by the transmission constraint.

This chapter focuses on power generation, and the physical and commercial provision of amounts of energy that are different from plan, in response to variation in demand. The capacity compensation issues are similar for transporters, although the network issues are more complex and are described in Chapter 7 on location.

6.1 THE DEFINITION OF CAPACITY

A commonly used term for generation readiness is 'capacity', although in practice the term is used rather generally. For planning and analysis we need to be clear about the definition in context.

The term 'capacity' for power generation is used to mean different things to different people at different times. For the purpose of this chapter, we use the following definitions

(i)   **'Capacity'** – the potential to deliver more, or less, electricity than the prior expected[1] for a period in question.
(ii) **'Installed capacity'** – the maximum level of energy produceable or transportable at benchmark conditions of atmospheric temperature, humidity and pressure, and under standard design operating conditions and assuming no capability shortfall.
(iii) **'Maximum capacity'** – the maximum level of energy practically produceable or transportable for the period in question.

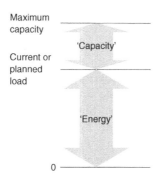

Figure 6.1   Representation of 'Capacity' in relation to maximum capacity for a plant on load or with a planned load

Expressed in this way, power generation capacity has different relevance to different industry actors:

(i)   To the plant operator, capacity represents the operating boundaries for the plant relative to the planned operating schedule, from the next second until the (possibly extended or curtailed) life of the generation unit.
(ii) To the market trader, capacity represents the (positive or negative) energy that is committed to be available relative to a forward schedule or contract, and which can be represented in terms of traded options in a family of increasing complexity. These are formalised in terms of strike price (cost per MWh), delivery period and notice period.
(iii) To the asset financier, the capacity represents the operating boundaries of the plant relative to the financial plan for a 'most likely' or contractually fixed schedule, with particular attention to the revenue attainable from the capacity provision, whether contracted in advance, or realised in real time.
(iv) To the system planner, the capacity represents the total planned, modelled or contractual capability of the system to produce or transport energy at a time period in the future, with particular emphasis on cost of capacity maintenance, cost of capacity delivery in the form of energy, the full probability profile of different levels of calloff and the likelihood of failure to deliver planned or promised capacity into energy.

Capacity can be usefully regarded as energy (positive or negative) times the probability of being called for delivery. A plant with a 50 % probability of running could

---

[1] 'Expected' here means 'most likely'. It is distinct from 'expectation' which is a weighted average of different outcomes.

equivalently be regarded as providing positive energy plus negative capacity with a 50% probability of delivery, or providing positive capacity with a 50% probability of delivery.

From the perspective of demand, we can regard power capacity as the capability and willingness to reduce load relative to contracted or expected requirements. For fixed volume contracts, this is easy to establish. For 'full-requirements' contracts with no volume limit (the standard for residential customers), it is hard to establish a definition and contractual agreement for voluntary demand reduction since there is no volume benchmark to reduce from, but it is more possible to define capacity provision by complete interruption, as then the average consumption for the period in question can be used.

With respect to transmission, the term 'capacity' is generally used to denote the maximum capacity deliverable, and terms such as 'capacity margin', 'reserve margin' and 'redundancy' to describe how much more energy could be transported relative to the prevailing flow. In this chapter, we concentrate on the capacity margin for transmission rather than the installed capacity, which is covered in Chapter 7 on location.

6.2   REQUIREMENTS FOR CAPACITY

Generation, consumption and transportation all create the need for capacity and all provide capacity.

Consider first the single buyer who is the system operator. It is clear that in order to know what to contract, the system operator must evaluate the probability of requirements of the various forms of reserve (notice, sustainability, volume). Let us first consider a single halfhour period.

There are four probability profiles to attend to:

(i)   Generator energy failure (including all failures relative to contract, upstream of the generator, such as energy availability and logistics).
(ii)   Generator capacity failure (the probability of plant contracted for capacity being unable to deliver energy if called).
(iii)   Demand variation.
(iv)   Network failure and constraints (some generator failure and capacity configurations will cause constraints).

6.2.1   Generator failure

For the purposes of modelling and of valuation, we must define failure carefully. For most general purposes the best definition is as follows: Percentage probability of complete failure to deliver the committed service in the period in question, at a particular horizon period, from a particular observation date. This assumes a zero probability of partial failure. At the opposite extreme, it is assumed that plant fails constantly by an amount that is characterised by a constant de-rating. In practice there is of course a spectrum of all failure types in between. This is considered in detail in the appendix. The two extremes of definition give rise to very different distributions of aggregate shortfall in generation due to failure, as seen in Figure 6.3.

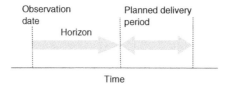

Figure 6.2   The characterisation of power plant failure, in terms of probability of complete failure to deliver at some horizon point in the future

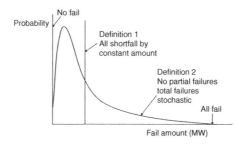

Figure 6.3   The probability densities for aggregate failure, using the two extremes of failure modeling. See text for details

Over and above the difficulty of estimating full probability profiles for a particular period in the near future, there are additional difficulties. These are principally: chronology (sequence), correlation within each profile (weather, type fault) and between profiles (affect of weather on both generation and demand) and discretion to adjust the profiles.

Figure 6.4 shows the discretionary variation of fail rate. In response to the forward price profile, the plant ensures minimum fail rate at the inception of the high price period by configuration, reduction of risk increasing activities prior to the period, and a short term maintenance strategy prior to the high price period that minimises fail rate in the high price period. Then during the high price period, it is frequently possible to delay shutdown after fault diagnosis, albeit at the potential consequence of damage accumulation. This increases the fail rate in the period following the high price period.

Through mechanisms such as these, it is common for fail rates in peak periods to be a fraction of the average fail rate.

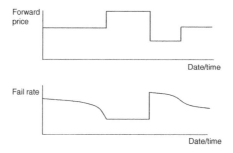

Figure 6.4   Adjustment of *ex ante* plant fail rate profile in response to forward price profile

The time horizon is important in the assessment of fail rate. At a long horizon this is equal to the long run fail rate, which includes major long term outages (but not events that terminate the commercial operation of the plant, and these must be included in the estimates of fail cost). For a short term horizon, whilst the failure percentage of a whole fleet of plant should approximate to the long term average, the only plant considered in planning the short term are those that are not currently in a failed state. The probability profile for failed and operational plant in relation to horizon is shown in Figure 6.5. The day ahead fail rate of on-load plant is less than the long term fail rate. The fail rate of *capacity* however is higher because there is a high fail rate associated with starts, and since plant is not actually on load, the short term horizon fail rate is not nearly 0 % as it is for on load plant.

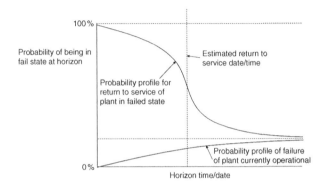

Figure 6.5 Fail rate in relation to horizon, for plant in an on-load operational mode and for plant in a failed state

6.2.1.1 *Power generation from non storable energy*

Renewable energy has different degrees of storability. For example, wind energy, wave energy and tidal energy, are lost if not immediately captured. There is a limited degree of storability of geothermal energy since heat can be stored to a limited degree. Hydro energy, while being the best form of energy storage in the short term, cannot be effectively stored over the long term due to limits on reservoir level.

Since energy from natural sources has a natural variation, then storage limitations restrict the even delivery of power, and the effect on output is then much the same as technical failure.

There are two particular forms of renewable energy for which the variation of the natural flow of energy, combined with the storage limitation, have a significant effect on electricity market design and operation. They are wind power and hydro power.

Wind energy is highly variable over the very short term (seconds), non storable for more than a few seconds, and highly correlated between nearby wind turbines over the short term (hours). The result is a high degree of intermittency of power, which in turn demands a high degree of supporting positive and negative reserve from conventional plant.

Large hydro plant can store energy very effectively for periods of up to months, but not for years, and hence hydro based systems are highly vulnerable to successions of dry years. This has been the case, for example in Brazil and New Zealand.

6.2.2   Demand variation

As the out-turn for a particular halfhour approaches, the absolute uncertainty in demand decreases (for example, due to decreasing uncertainty of weather), but the volatility of uncertainty continues to rise. Eventually, there comes a point where the forward estimation of demand must end, and the demand occurs. No matter how good the model, it cannot perfectly estimate demand even if there are no remaining uncertainties. Within a certain notice period, no more information can be processed and the volatility within that period rises, to a theoretically infinite value as the time to out-turn approaches zero.

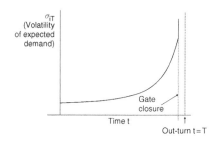

Figure 6.6   Demand uncertainty, expressed as volatility

Fortunately, we have two very useful items of information: (i) what we are consuming now and (ii) what we consumed at this point in the periodic cycle in the past (this time yesterday, this time on the same day of the week last week, this time on this week on this month last year). The variations in historic out-turns gives us good information about the residual uncertainty, particularly if we have regression analysis of, for example, temperature.

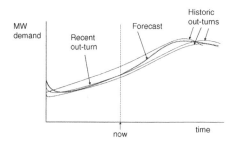

Figure 6.7   Short term demand forecast using current price trend and out-turn history

6.2.3   Network failure

Whereas we tend to do most generation failure and demand variation analysis in aggregate (one MW is treated just like another MW), when we consider networks and network failure we are forced to consider network effects (so 1 MW failure by generation or network in one location is not the same as 1 MW fail in another area). In this chapter, almost all of the analysis is considered in aggregate. Network specific issues are described in Chapter 7 on location.

6.3   THE BASIC ECONOMICS OF PROVISION OF CAPACITY AND RESERVE BY GENERATORS

6.3.1   Representation of generation capacity on the power stack

Whilst it is strictly correct to say that 'electricity cannot be stored', this common statement is a somewhat misleading one. As was demonstrated in Figure 2.1, energy undergoes a series of transformations between different forms on the way to becoming alternating current and after becoming alternating current. Adjustment of the extent and timing of these alterations has the effect of storage.

Capacity has three time factors associated with it: (i) the duration of the capacity contract, (ii) the duration of energy provision under the capacity contract and (iii) the notice period. For example, a generator could receive an annual premium for the provision of energy up to a designated halfhourly profile, provided that the energy were called 24 hours in advance. Here we consider the provision of energy for half an hour, with more than half an hour's notice.

If we ignored for the moment the sequencing of the power generation stacks so that to meet a planned demand profile, the units will be in different states of warmth, then we can regard the plant 'on the bars' to the left of the demand line in Figure 6.8 to be 'hot', and the plant on the right to be 'cold'.

If the system operator needs quick positive response, then the reserve plant must be hot and part loaded. He can instruct one plant to turn down (assuming, for the sake or argument, no change in marginal cost for that plant) and one to run.

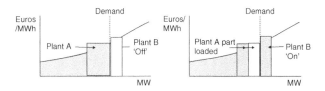

Figure 6.8   Out of merit running to retain 'hot' capacity. (1) without hot capacity, (2) With hot capacity

In the bilateral market mode, the overall on-the-day marginal cost of capacity is equal to the offer[2] price differential between plant A and plant B (ignoring the efficiency cost of part loading, start cost of B, and various other costs). In the centrally managed model, the on-the-day cost differential is equal to the marginal cost differential between the plants, but over a longer period we must consider the fixed costs of plant B.

6.3.2   Provision of capacity by a unit

Consider first a simple system in which all factors such as demand and generator failure are deterministic and there is no storage of any kind.

---

[2] In practice this is slightly problematic due to the way that plants make incremental offers. The incremental offers may increase with the level of offtake, where, due to the efficiency effects described in section 2.2.17, the marginal cost actually decreases with increasing load.

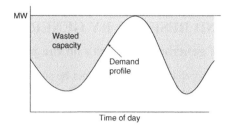

Figure 6.9 Representation of wasted capacity in a deterministic periodic market

In this simple system, the shaded area in Figure 6.9 represents generation that could run but is not required to, and currently performs no useful service. The need to maintain the capacity to run in the peak period does however form part of the unit economics since the fixed costs must be paid.

As we shall see in section 6.4, there are in fact a number of reasons for which the total produceable energy per year may be less than the MW capability times the number of hours per year, and in which the phasing of delivery is discretionary. We can view the plant as one that can run baseload at the adjusted capacity (equal to the total number of MWh deliverable per year, divided by 8,760 hours per year), plus a storage unit that can deliver more power in peak times, up to the actual capacity of the plant, and borrow and lend the energy from off peak periods. This is shown in Figure 6.10.

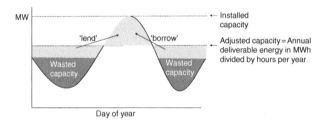

Figure 6.10 Representation of plant with limited load factor in terms of maximum baseload delivery plus storage

If the annual energy delivery limitation is an inherent feature of the plant or its regulatory[3] restrictions, then the capacity is not regarded as 'wasted' in the same sense, since the plant is not valued (and costed) in terms of peak capacity (i.e. $/kw). If the level of storage inherent in the plant equals or exceeds the amount that needs to be rescheduled to meet peak demand, then we can reduce the wasted capacity to zero. If however, the load factor limit from which the storage capability is derived, arrived after purchase of the plant (for example a contraction of environmental limits), then the plant should be revalued at a lower level. This is treated as a one off hit to the plant value.

The description so far assumes a deterministic world. The situation changes when we consider the need for generation to be able to cover for variations due to network and

---

[3] As an aside, it is worth noting that regulatory limits on load factor can add to national security of supply, since in times of shortage, national priorities change, and regulatory limits can be relaxed. This security of supply can be regarded as a public good, which ought to be valued, and the providers compensated.

generator failure and for demand variation. Consider first our demand profile at some particular level of confidence. Figure 6.11 shows the 99 % confidence profile for each hour of the day (i.e. the level that we are 99 % confident will not be exceeded). If we assume that the natural level of energy storage exactly equals the requirement for rescheduling (i.e. the adjusted capacity implies no wasted capacity), then the amount of capacity that must be financed to satisfy the 99 % confidence level for the peak hour is equal to the increase in peak demand at the 99 % confidence level, relative to the expected level of demand.

The 99 % confidence envelope shown applies to each individual hour. The confidence of no shortfall across the day depends on the nature of demand variation and periodicity. Suppose that the periodicity is zero (i.e. the demand profile is flat across the day). If demand variations are completely uncorrelated, then for an hourly demand confidence level of 99 %, the probability of no shortfall at all in a designated day in the future is $99\%^{24} = 79\%$, and the probability of shortfall for every hour of the day is $1\%^{24} = 10^{-46}\%$. If correlation between demand periods across the day is 100 %, then the probability of no failure in the day is 99 %, and the probability of failure all day is 1 %, and the probability of failure for part of the day is 0 %.

The calculations for loss of load due to plant failure are similar in principle. When calculating loss of load probability (LOLP) it is the probability of lost load at any time in the day that is calculated. This is clearly dependent on (i) reserve margin of plant that can respond in time (i.e. is hot for the short notice period, (ii) short horizon fail rate for on-load plant and (iii) short horizon fail-to-start rate for off load plant or fail-to-increase rate for warm plant (synchronised but not on load or at reduced load).

If we are going to retain the capacity such that it can fulfil a demand schedule at the 99 % confidence envelope, then we can represent the requirement for peak and annual adjusted capacity as shown in Figure 6.11.

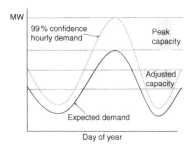

Figure 6.11 The expected demand profile requires a particular level of maximum capacity and of average capacity. If demand is uncertain, then for a particular demand profile, at a particular confidence level, we must calculate a higher peak and average capacity requirement

The generation capability unused (but financed) in the normal year is represented by the change in adjusted capacity (measure in MWh/year) and the peak generation capability (measured in MW) that must be maintained for capacity is shown by the change in peak capacity. The cost is the cost required to fulfil both of these conditions.

We can see that for plant with highly limited load factor, that the cost of maintaining peak capacity above adjusted capacity, in order to meet the winter peak, does not incur a substantial cost of wasted capacity in the summer, because it cannot be used.

We have just considered positive capacity here. We also need to consider negative capacity. Suppose initially that consumers transact only in the spot market and do not enter fixed price fixed volume forward contracts, then if demand falls relative to expected, then the generator will have maintained uncompensated surplus capacity. The economic calculations are very similar to those of the high demand envelope except that there is a greater attention to annual average demand rather than peak demand.

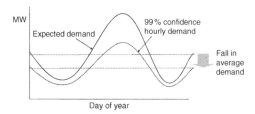

Figure 6.12   Confidence level for net demand less than expected

6.4   MODELLING THE CAPABILITY OF GENERATION CAPACITY

The previous discussion made plain that capacity is expensive to maintain where there is no inherent storage in the plant, but that capacity is cheap or free if there is inherent storage. Since it is so important we examine in some detail some forms of inherent storage. For present purposes, 'medium term' is generally around one year but has granularity of provision to between half an hour and four hours.

6.4.1   Capacity effect of take or pay fuel supply contracts

Gas requires a higher degree of dedicated delivery infrastructure than coal or crude oil, and hence the gas shipper commonly requires some kind of payment commitment. This is manifest in 'take-or-pay' contracts, described in section 2.1.9 in which there is a minimum and maximum 'take' per year. The term 'take or pay' arises from the fact that gas is paid for at minimum take level even if not withdrawn. The minimum take guarantees a minimum income to the gas supplier and the maximum take serves to keep the minimum take at a sufficient level (otherwise buyers would under-declare their likely commitment and negotiate low minimum takes). The maximum take is likely to correspond to the physical maximum capacity of the pipe, because, in the absence of further supply contracts, there is no incentive for the pipeline operator to build more capacity than is paid for.

The minimum take corresponds to the amount of fuel infrastructure that the buyer is prepared to pay for. The maximum take corresponds to the amount of fuel infrastructure that the seller is prepared to commit. For a given take-or-pay price, buyers prefer large differences between minimum and maximum take and sellers prefer small differences.

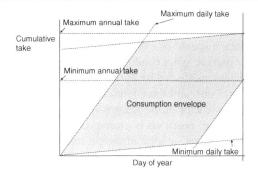

Figure 6.13   Purchase for take or pay supply contract

The effect of the take-or-pay contract is to have a fixed[4] cost and a marginal cost for fuel. The buyer gains by having cheaper gas as can be seen in Figure 6.14.

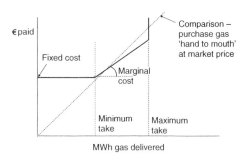

Figure 6.14   Cost of gas to buyer under a take or pay supply contract

In its simple form, the take or pay contract can be regarded in terms of a 'swing' product. Swing is characterised as a commodity derivative contract as described in section 9.4.4. The swing contract can be viewed as 365 daily options per year, with the restriction on a maximum number of exercises.

Suppose that the take or pay contract has a daily minimum of 1 unit, a daily maximum of 2, an annual minimum of 365 and an annual maximum of 450. Then our contract is equivalent to a flat forward purchase contract of 1 unit per day, plus 365 call options of 1 unit each, with an exercise limit of 85 options on separate days.[5]

If instead, the minimum annual take is 400 units, then the contract is equivalent to 365 daily forward purchase contracts, 35 daily forward contracts for the (*ex ante*) highest priced days, plus the option to switch dates on the 35 forward contracts, plus 330 options to be exercised on a maximum of 50 different days which are not the days of the 35 forward contracts.

---

[4] Gas transportation can entail an entry cost to the main transportation system, a carriage cost within the system, and an exit cost from the system, and the same three costs for the local transportation system.

[5] Note that generally speaking, if an option is worth declaring, then it is worth declaring the maximum amount, so we can ignore partial exercises.

If the gas contract has a market location (even if there is a shipping agreement from market location to plant), and there are no contract restrictions, then the contract has no impact on plant storage since it should be exercised 'ruthlessly' (referring only to gas market conditions, and not power market, plant condition or plant economics) and the operation of the plant should be completely unaffected by the contract. If however, the contract is 'burner tip' (the gas may not be sold on), and there is no other source of gas, then the gas supply contract limits the annual load factor of the plant while allowing short term flexibility. The valuation and exercise of 'swing' positions is examined in section 9.4.

Due to the dedicated form of gas supply infrastructure in the form of pipelines, and the low degree of storage,[6] gas prices can be strongly seasonal. For this reason, the expected take of gas commonly has a strong profile, and the time value aspect of the swing optionality principally applies to price effects that change the shape of the forward curve as much as its absolute level.

6.4.2 Capacity effect of annual emission limits

Under some jurisdictions, each power station fleet and/or unit has an annual emission limit or 'bubble' for each emission year, sometimes called a 'vintage' year. If load factor reduction is used as a method for satisfaction of this limit, then the plant operator has an option on schedule. Moreover, the optimal exercise of the option will depend on: (i) the forward volatility of the fuel-power market price spread at the efficiency ratio of the plant, (ii) the forward price profile of the fuel-power market price spread and (iii) the year-to-date consumption of allowances.

By initially ignoring complicating factors such as unit starts, imperfect reliability and the interaction with other plant options, the value of this option, and the optimal exercise plan can be modelled using the swing described in section 9.4. In this sense the emission limit behaves in very much the same way as plant for which the only access to gas is the take-or-pay contract. The difference here is that the marginal cost is zero for the emission limit. The comparison is shown in Figure 6.15.

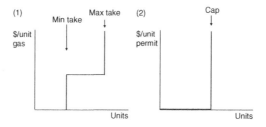

Figure 6.15 Marginal cost of factor for (1) Take-or-pay gas supply contract and (2) Annual emission limit

The value of this option is sensitive to the specifics of the environmental rules, for example: (i) the simultaneous existence of unit limits and a fleet limit that is less than the sum of

---

[6] Gas is stored downstream in the form of underground caverns, although withdrawal and injection rates can be limiting factors. Short term gas storage also exists due to the tolerance for pressure variation in gas pipelines, in the form of 'linepack'. Linepack is the main reason that in-day gas price profile is far less than for electricity and even in the sharpest winter, linepack generally has sufficient gas to run for a few hours.

unit limits, (ii) the banking or borrowing of permits over a vintage period or periods, and the 'interest rate' in terms of non par exchange between allowances in different periods and (iii) emission allowance trading. If there are no limits to trading, then the form of real option owned by the power station changes from a flexicap to a standard European or 'vanilla' option, with a strike price that includes the emission cost into the fuel-power spread.

Figure 6.16 shows the effect of an emission limit constraint on load factor. Since the plant production is rationed then it will not produce in all hours for which revenue exceeds cost but will instead 'store' generation in low margin periods.

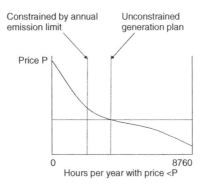

Figure 6.16   Depiction of emission cap on the load duration curve

In fact, the emission cap provides us with a much simpler swing product than does the take or pay contracts, since the difference between annual minimum take and aggregate daily minimum take is problematic, and other standard take or pay contract clauses such as indexation and interruptibility add further complications.

Since emission limits can be relaxed in the event of supply shortage, the presence of an emission limit creates a public good in the form of probability existence value.

6.4.3   Capacity effect of port and other infrastructure contracts

Generators shipping large volumes of coal can secure port capacity and other delivery infrastructure in advance. This capacity can be regarded as a take or pay contract since there is a minimum charge and a maximum volume.

As with all other take or pay contracts, the definition of marginal cost is dependent on the particular circumstance in which the cost is applied. It is somewhere between the marginal cost of transportation and the marginal cost of transportation plus fixed costs smeared over a 'lower likely' throughput.

6.4.4   Capacity effect of coal stocking

There is usually plenty of room on the coal stockyard to store coal. The incremental cost of storing coal rather than delivering straight to the bunker is: (i) double handling cost in taking the coal to the stockyard and back, (ii) loss of calorific value as the coal oxidises in the yard, (iii) stock management costs and (iv) interest costs.

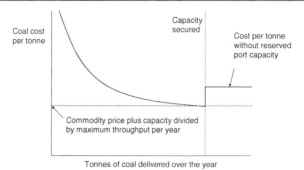

Figure 6.17 The marginal cost of coal delivery with reserved port capacity using a take or pay contract

Offsetting this is: (i) the ability to blend and choose different coals (for example sulphur management at emission 'vintage' year end), (ii) the ability to be opportunist with respect to purchasing and (iii) reduced exposure to logistic failures such as failure of unloading equipment, ships waiting in ports, railway failures and others.

The ability to store coal combined with the international diversity of its supply routes (and hence different phase of seasons) causes coal to have no seasonal price structure, in distinct contrast to gas.

6.4.5 Capacity effect of plant life usage optimisation

In the appendix we see that that all forms of thermal plant[7] can use an 'hours and starts', or 'plant life usage' operating envelope that is determined by the lower bound of the envelopes determined by (i) guarantee and support agreements from original equipment manufacturers, (ii) safety, imposed by internal practice and by licence conditions, (iii) insurers and (iv) internal estimates of plant life usage. The capacity option appears in relation to plant outage dates. Initially, these are fixed due to (i) the choosing of periods of least expected generation margin within the season and (ii) statutory limits on the maximum elapsed time between outages.

This is shown in Figure 6.18. We can see that in the ideal base plan, the operating envelope is reached exactly at the scheduled outage date. If the outage date cannot be moved then the operator has the option to run harder (more hours or more starts) than plan, in which case, some generation must be foregone (this amounts to a reschedule that is equivalent to take or pay). The operator could instead run less hard. If parts will be replaced at the outage then wear cost on parts will not be saved and hence the plant life usage, which forms part of the marginal cost of production, can be considered at this point as 'use it or lose it', or take or pay. This is a long term as well as short term effect and is important in the long term planning of plant condition, since the ideal is for all components to expire at the end of the last day of production.

In addition, the plant operator has the option on plant spend during outages. The greater the spend, the better the condition improvement. The better the condition, the better the

---

[7] This applies to the conventional components of nuclear plant, but the nuclear components are treated differently.

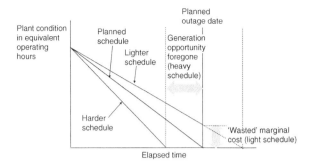

Figure 6.18   The impact of schedule approaching on outage on the marginal cost of production

efficiency and reliability. With respect to ongoing costs, there is commonly an optimum condition. This is discussed in more detail in the appendix.

6.4.6   The role of outage management in capacity

The seasonal nature of gas prices and of power demand causes there to be a concentration of plant requiring outages at particular times. This causes a capacity constraint on contractors in a very similar way to the other capacity constraints described.

Within a power station fleet, this can be mitigated to some degree by flexible labour contracts[8] and by sharing maintenance resource between different plant. For example, if gas plant outages are scheduled in the winter when gas prices are low and coal plant outages are scheduled in the summer when power prices are low, there is some potential to share where the skill required is sufficiently generic to both plant. Although contractors are commonly booked two or three years ahead, there is a limited potential to move outage dates.

6.4.7   Generation above normal maximum capacity

Most plant can generate beyond the normal maximum capacity. The increased fuel flow means that there is usually a plant damage cost, and depending on technology has an efficiency cost or benefit. Some methods of capacity enhancement were described in section 2.2.14.

Figure 6.19 shows that the dependence of fuel prices on the operating load cost profile.

The very high degradation rates of the turbine blades (for CCGT) and pressure parts (for conventional plant) at elevated temperatures offsets the efficiency gain from higher loads. For plant with potential configuration change (such as steam injection for CCGT or reheat bypass for conventional plant), both plant damage and efficiency worsen with increase in load.

Plant is generally designed to operate close to the minimum cost of the figures shown and is clear that there is therefore an assumption made on fuel and power prices in doing so.

It is clear that for higher power prices than in the initial design, that it is optimal for the plant to run at higher loads. In practice, the steepness of the right hand side of the curve

---

[8] Some plants (mainly combined cycle gas turbines) have employment contracts expressed in hours per year, not hours per week.

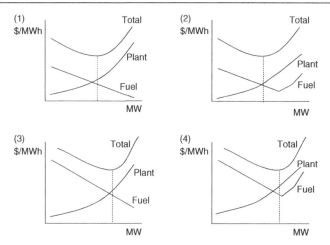

Figure 6.19 The dependence of optimal design load on fuel price. (1) Gas turbine at low fuel prices, (2) Conventional plant at low fuel prices, (3) Gas turbine overfired[9] at high prices, (4) Conventional plant reconfigured at high prices

shown is steep relative to the steepness of the generation stack (not all of which is thermal plant) at design loads and hence the general response mechanism is not for plant to adjust load but for the numbers of plant on the system to adjust. The administration involved in changing maximum operating load is quite substantial, particularly with respect to safety protection, since plant operates outside of its experience envelope.

6.4.8 Long term capacity

To a limited degree, the ratio of fixed to marginal costs can be altered. The cheapest cost for a known rate of production is found by loading marginal costs into fixed costs, but the maximum flexibility for variation is found by converting fixed costs to marginal costs.

Long term capacity is distinct in nature from medium term capacity and involves the increase or decrease of quasi-fixed costs with an associated impact on plant capability or life.

An example of a long term option is the option on the closure date of a power plant. Some decisions now may reduce the optionality of closure. For example cost commitment decisions such as take or pay contracts, major plant investments reduce the option to close early. Similarly cost reduction decisions, such as reduced plant maintenance budget can cause condition loss that is effectively non recoverable and therefore reduce the option to extend life. There are other decisions such as 'opt in' and 'opt out' of directives such as the EU Large Combustion Plant Directive, booking annual transmission entry capacity, and various declarations of plant configuration. Mothballed plant requires a number of costs to maintain the demothball option such as non removal of parts, maintenance of water rights, permits and consents and various other rights and care and maintenance to prevent further degradation.

---

[9] While the fuel price/plant damage trade-off is done at design stage, modes of operation that incur extra plant damage are only done in cooperation with original equipment manufacturers. Steam injection, described in section 2.2.14 is a good example of the practical application of increased load for gas turbines. This is a configurational change that reduces efficiency.

In the longer term, research and development can be regarded as investment in a form of real option.[10] This applies to such measures as carbon sequestration at power plant (which requires a high CO_2 price to be economic), hydrogen power and fuel cells.

Plant options are also connected to upstream options such as build and maintenance of gas pipes and keeping coal mines in readiness.

6.4.9 Hydro

Hydro power from reservoirs has a high ratio of MW capacity to annual MWh energy. The planning of hydro schedules in the presence of volatile power prices and rainfalls is described in section 5.1.5.9.

The annual energy limit for hydro can be treated as a swing problem in much the same way as annual emission limits and take or pay fuel supply contracts. The particular difficulties of stochastic variation in rainfall has some commonality with the stochastic variation in emission abatement cost factors and international emission prices.

6.4.10 Pumped storage

Pumped storage is particularly interesting in consideration of in day capacity, including reserve and balancing, because the source of energy is electricity. Because pumped storage is not 100 % efficient then more energy must be put in than comes out.

There are a range of possible market rules for pumped storage. The plant may be able to draw power at will at a known fixed price (as in most demand in the pool), or be required to contract in advance (as in the bilateral market). It may be able to provide power at will at a known price (as is common for renewable generation in the pool) or be required to contract in advance (as in the bilateral market). Since the different rules represent different degrees of optionality, and it is volatility and price profile rather than absolute price levels that drives the value of pumped storage, then the differences in value and behaviour are substantial. Any optionality granted to pumped storage represents a cross subsidy. This may be inefficient or efficient depending on what marginal generation is consumed, what marginal generation is displaced and what the environmental taxes, permit costs or unrepresented externality costs are associated with the particular kinds of plant.

The balancing mechanism is far more conducive to effective use of pumped storage because the rolling window of balancing tenders and acceptances is short relative to the reservoir capacity and hence the plant can be optimised. The plant will submit both bids and offers each halfhour and, with such closeness to the balancing mechanism, is more conscious than other market participants of system need and therefore has more ability to extract extra rent.

Supposing the pumped storage efficiency is 67 % then it is clear that the minimum price differential of peak price above off peak price is 50 %. To cover fixed costs, the plant needs more than this. This price difference is actually rather substantial and there are few times of year when the forward/*ex ante* daily price cycle exceeds this amount. Hence the plant relies on capacity, and this is a risky form of income that requires a risk adjustment premium.

Let us first consider a short contract period of around half an hour. Immediately after the market has cleared, then for the delivery period in question, all the plant with running

---

[10] The optionality is similar to that in the real options described in this book, but the valuation methods are different. Market instruments cannot be used, and the valuation method uses a probability tree. This method is well documented outside the ESI, but very little within it.

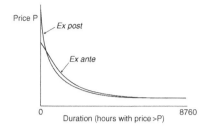

Figure 6.20   The *ex post* load duration curve is much steeper than the *ex ante* curve. Some producers can effectively gain access to the *ex post* curve after day ahead prices have been set

contracts have stored negative energy and all the plant without them will have stored positive energy contracts. As time elapses then the stored positive energy stack depletes and becomes more expensive as the number of plants which could ramp up in time dwindles.

6.5   MODELLING CAPACITY CAPABILITY FROM THE CONSUMER SIDE

Voluntary and involuntary demand reduction can be treated as virtual generation, and indeed has similar issues in terms of notice period, limits, and maximum rates of change. There is an addition a failure-like quality in some contracts, in that some supply companies and consumers could inadvertently sign interruptible contracts that are not interruptible in practice (hospitals, for example). Systems with a designated value of lost load have, in economic terms, infinite generation at the value of lost load.

For convenience, we regard demand in three discrete elements:

(i)   the inelastic and exogenously[11] determined demand;
(ii)   demand reduction relative to requirement/contract, incentivised by contract;
(iii) involuntary interruption.

As discussed in section 2.6.10, price responsive demand management remains underdeveloped in the retail sector. The bulk of demand management is in the industrial and commercial category. Though industrial and commercial demand is dependent on factors such as weather, it is less so than residential, and it is therefore more practical to enter into a contract for a fixed number of MW, with an agreement to reduce by a designated amount if called.

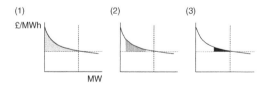

Figure 6.21   Consumer cost of load reduction. (1) Involuntary indiscriminate interruption of some consumers, (2) Structured demand reduction under contract, (3) Real time consumer participation in market

---

[11] Driven by outside forces such as weather.

6.5.1   Modelling value of lost load as a capacity capability

Throughout this chapter, we model lost load, followed by consumer compensation at the value of lost load as a *de facto* voluntary agreement with consumers. In this sense, consumer interruption through lost load is regarded initially as an infinite generator with a marginal cost equal to the value of lost load. By the same token, we could take a more sophisticated approach to the valuation, and then the penalty for lost load in relation to factors that alter it, such as notice period, duration, and period (time of day/week/year).

6.6   COMMERCIAL MECHANISMS – THE GENERATOR PERSPECTIVE

The generators and transporters will only maintain capacity if it is economic to do so, and it is obvious that there is a close connection between energy and capacity and marginal and fixed costs. Put simply, in order to provide capacity, the infrastructure provider must receive either a committed premium for the capacity, or the prospect of sufficient compensation for actual utilisation of the capacity, or a combination. The commercial mechanisms therefore depend on the capability and cost of maintaining capacity, the probability profiles of capacity utilisation and the range of potential commercial instruments for transacting.

Assuming that each unit must be economically viable then each unit must consider its cost of capacity provision and ensure that either: (i) it is being compensated in some way, or (ii) it is free to maintain, or (iii) the capacity is reduced if possible.

There are several methods of rewarding capacity, and the main ones are discussed here. For each we consider what kind of market it can operate in, how it impacts the generator, and how it affects system economics.

In considering the cost and provision of capacity, the following are key factors:

(i)   notice period to begin response;
(ii)   speed of response (e.g. MW/min, or / frequency change) once begun;
(iii)   sustainability of response (see Figure 2.14);
(iv)   contractual period of response delivery (in day, day ahead, month, quarter, year);
(v)   period for providing response (time of day, week, year);
(vi)   sensitivity of response (e.g. to frequency deviation);
(vii)   amount of response in MW;
(viii)   marginal cost of providing response[12];
(ix)   opportunity cost of providing readiness for response.

Capacity is required for the full time spectrum from a few seconds to several decades. From the perspective of electricity markets, it is useful to divide capacity into three periods:

(i)   The period beyond a horizon of about one hour for which market participants can effectively trade with one another.
(ii)   Halfhourly periods with short term contractual horizons (half an hour to a few hours) for which providers of capacity can engage with the system operator in the balancing

---

[12] For example, frequency response not only incurs lost opportunity, but incurs efficiency cost from non optimal plant configuration at the load, and plant damage from raised pressure. In addition, the energy variation may incur costly imbalance charges.

mechanism as monopoly buyer/seller but for which there is not enough time for the bilateral market to operate.

(iii) The provision of short term positive and negative reserve, dispatched at short notice (from seconds) and for short periods (seconds through to minutes) by the system operator or by automatic response to system frequency. The physical provision of reserve was described in section 2.2.14.

Table 6.1 Representation of times for the provision of reserve, capacity and flexibility. Figures indicative and definitions vary by country

	Notice	Delivery	Period	Commitment
Primary response	0–5 sec	5–30 sec	All	1–3 years
Secondary response	5–30 sec	30 sec–5 min	All	1–3 years
Hot standby	5 min–4 hours	30 min–2 hours	All	1–3 years
Balancing and other reserve	1–60 min	1–30 min	All	Day ahead–1 year +
Planned flexibility	1 year +	2–10 hours	Peak or off peak	1–3 years
Vanilla options	4 hours–5 days	2–10 hours	Peak or off peak	3 months–2 years
Extra flexibility	5 mins +	5 mins +	All	All

6.6.1 Day ahead capacity payments in pool markets

In mature bilateral markets, the optimum mechanism is to offer a capacity payment (i.e. an option premium) for firm capacity, that is dependent on the price at which energy is called from the plant. While it is quite possible to design the market so that the system operator can use this mechanism, and it is currently possible for the contract for difference market to include options declarable before generation offer submission to the system operator, pool markets are not mature enough to use this mechanism, and if they were, they would become bilateral markets.

Hence, pool markets use cruder mechanisms. Since there must be some way of valuing the payment, if strike (call off) price is not to be a factor, then the only useful indicators available are the probability and value of lost load. The payment formula could maximise the system operator incentive to minimise the cost of supply, or could be a simpler formula relating to the probability of lost load.

6.6.1.1 Mechanism of loss of load based capacity payments in pool markets

In the England and Wales pool, all plant that bid and was available received a capacity payment, which was the same regardless of offer price.

The capacity payment was calculated using the value of lost load which was set by regulation, the 'disappearance ratio' of failure[13] of the generation fleet declared[14] available, and the variation in demand relative to expectation.

---

[13] Newbery (1998) argues that LOLP calculations underestimated plant reliability. We can understand this from Figure 6.4.

[14] In the England and Wales pool, this was the average of the last eight days declaration, thereby causing a lag.

The price structure was then:

$$PPP = SMP + Capacity$$

$$Capacity = LOLP * (VOLL - SMP)$$

PPP = Pool Purchase Price that producers receive, and which is used as a basis for consumer cost prior to cost uplift.

SMP = System Marginal Price – the clearing price from the generation offer stack and scheduled dispatch (close to, but not necessarily equal to, expected demand).

LOLP = Loss of Load probability

VOLL = Value of Lost Load

Now consider a single buyer pool system. One capacity procedure for an unconstrained system is as follows:

(i)   Receive the cost stack.
(ii)   Estimate demand.
(iii) Construct the System Marginal Price (SMP).
(iv)   Pay all offerors[15] the same capacity payment per MW of capacity declared LOLP * (VOLL - SMP) * plant MW / Total MW.
(v)   If the plant is in merit and dispatched then it receives SMP in addition and hence receives a total of PPP = SMP + LOLP * (VOLL - SMP).
(vi)   If plant is in merit but dispatched at zero or less than full capacity, then on the cancelled load it receives the difference between offer price and SMP. Hence it receives a total of LOLP * (VOLL - SMP) + (SMP-offer).
(vii) If plant is out of merit and dispatched, it receives its offer price. Hence it receives a total off LOLP * (VOLL - SMP) + offer.

If all plant had offered at marginal cost, then each plant is, in theory, indifferent to dispatch or not, and all receive the same capacity payment.

The LOLP based capacity method effectively assumes in economic terms either that there is a generator of infinite capacity and no fixed costs with a marginal cost of VOLL, or that all consumers are willing to accept interruption relative to usual demand, for a compensation equal to VOLL.

6.6.1.2   Economics of loss of load based capacity mechanism

The capacity payment method is clearly oriented to lost load, and we might expect the effect on generators to force them to either end of the fixed/marginal cost spectrum. Mid merit plant might be expected to be incentivised either to: (i) reduce marginal costs to gain more running, or (ii) reduce fixed costs at the expense of marginal costs, since there is no incentive to reduce marginal costs for the provision of pure capacity, and little incentive to reduce marginal costs for infrequent operation at high prices.

---

[15] The terminology used at the time was to 'bid' plant. We have used the term 'offer' throughout this book.

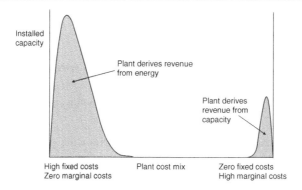

Figure 6.22   Plant profile incentivised by lost-load based capacity payment

In practice, despite the fact that the capacity mechanism is oriented to security of supply as measured by lost load (an event of vanishingly small probability), LOLP in practice is calculated to be sufficiently high during times of medium-to-high demand for the LOLP * VOLL revenue to form a substantial component of the annual revenue of mid merit plant.

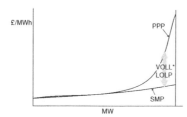

Figure 6.23   Depiction of pool purchase price as the sum of system marginal price and capacity payment

Even so, were it not possible to gain a consolidation benefit by maintaining SMP, mid merit operators would be forced to the ends of the fixed/marginal cost spectrum.

6.6.1.3   Some details of the loss of load based capacity model

Capacity failure – LOLP must be calculated by taking failure of capacity units into account. This can either be done with combinatorial analysis of unit failure. If there is no penalty for failure of capacity units, then there is some incentive to offer poorly maintained 'cardboard units' at very high offer prices (for example VOLL minus £ 1/MWh), with the prospect of never running but always receiving capacity payments. The system operator is therefore obliged to instruct the units occasionally and censure them if they do not function. Note that it is not easy, even for the owner, to test or to know the fail rate of a unit that never runs.

System operator information – The system operator needs information about the prospective failure probability of plant. An obvious partial remedy is for the system operator to insist on the provision of unit specific average fail rates (as happens in the USA under

NERC GADS[16]) and in Nordpool where units must declare expected variations to the norm. It is possible for a called on unit to pay a penalty but there is no obvious price to use. The clearing price or the unit offer prices are too low, but VOLL is too high if load is not actually lost at system level.

Penalties for non delivery – The cost to the consumer of non delivery is related to the amount, notice, duration and flexibility of timing (if any). Fixed penalties will always be too high or too low and will cause inefficient behaviour.

Unit behaviour and incentive – If an in merit plant fails there are a variety of penalties varying from none (e.g. England and Wales pool) to paying double PPP. If a plant declares, is found in merit, receives dispatch instruction and then fails, then the system operator will call on the highest merit plant in the out of merit capacity stack. If this called on plant belongs to the same owner as the failed plant then the owner has made an opportunity loss equal to the offer differential on the two plants on all other in merit plants it owns. If the called on plant belongs to a different owner then the failed plant owner just loses the marginal revenue on the failed plant. So the owner is faced with a choice – if the plant is very unlikely to fail then it should be offered to be 100% sure that this owner gains the revenue rather than a different owner, but if it has a high fail probability then there is some incentive not to offer the plant (or declare it failed). By not offering the plant at all (as distinct from offering it at high price) then LOLP rises and it may be that the total gain made by the owner's fleet exceeds the lost margin from the unit in question. We see that the core problem here is that the system operator has less information on fail probability than the plant owner and must work on long term averages that may not even be unit specific and may be poorly constructed. It would be foolish for the generator not to use information available and yet use of the information is at risk to be regarded as gaming the system.

Constrained off compensation – In the England and Wales market, in merit constrained off units received the difference between SMP and offer, as well as the capacity payment. However, it is quite possible not to give any constrained off payment, such as in Spain.

6.6.1.4 The loss of load based capacity mechanism in practice

Although the capacity mechanism described does in theory not satisfy the system operator's financial incentive to minimise cost of supply, in practice it has worked reasonably well. The reasons include:

(i)   Low load factor plant is commonly old plant reaching obsolescence and unless recently purchased, has low book value.
(ii) High marginal cost plant tends to run for a reasonable number of hours per year due to the provision of reserve and other ancillary services.
(iii) Low load factor plant does not tend to change hands as much as high load factor plant. Whilst a new buyer would drive the plant towards the ends of the fixed/marginal spectrum, the incumbent will be aware that the plant sale may not preserve the market order. Buyers of old plant also often buy them in order to convert them, rather than

---

[16] Generator availability data system. A voluntary participation with the National Electricity Reliability Council in the USA.

run them as they are, since the consenting process is usually much faster than green-field developments, and the various connections, water rights, logistics, labour, local stakeholder support and other factors are substantially in place.

(iv) The price tends to spend more time in the middle regions in an established market. Generators develop market sharing, and the system operator and regulator recognise the benefit of population of middle regions of price.

(v) Incumbent consolidation means that medium high prices (that would be unstable in fragmented markets) are seen in practice.

Objections to the loss of load based capacity mechanism include:

(i) Incentive to withdraw rather than add capacity, due to the effect of withdrawal on capacity price.

(ii) Incentive of mid-to-low merit plant to (suboptimally for the system) drop merit to save fixed costs or increase fixed costs to gain running.

6.6.1.5   Optimisation of installed flexibility

The pool capacity mechanism is a day ahead capacity mechanism. It does not offer medium or long term structured payments to generators (except as an embedded component of PPP in the CFD market). Hence it does not secure optimum capacity in advance.

6.6.2   Fixed cost subsidy, marginal cost energy provision

One way to maintain plant that is required for system security is to subsidise its fixed costs and then pay its marginal costs as incurred for energy. This method is to all intents and purposes the same as the option contracts, but without an economic connection between the volume and type of capacity required and the capacity installed. By paying the fixed costs of installed and new build plant regardless of requirement, there is little economic control of requirements.

An additional issue with the mechanism is the source of the subsidy. If the subsidy is paid for by supply companies to provide a dedicated source of capacity, then the system ends up with too much capacity. If each supply company has a 1 % probability of energy shortfall due to increase in demand, then 1 % represents the upper bound probability of overall system shortfall, in the case of 100 % correlation of shortfall. It is economically inefficient to subsidise the capacity at supply company level. If the subsidy is arranged by the system operator, the subsidy must be collected by a tariff from the supply companies, and similarly the system operator must have a commercial arrangement to sell the energy if required. This arrangement with the supply companies however cannot be firm (a normal prerequisite for contracts). Since the duty of supply companies to provide security of supply is transferred from the supply companies to the system operator, their incentive is to under invest in capacity contracts and 'free ride' on the *ex ante* obligation of the system operator to provide capacity.

6.6.3   Traded options and capacity contracts

In its simplest form, called the European option, a traded call option confers on the buyer, the right, but not the obligation, to buy a fixed amount of commodity, at a fixed price, for delivery on a fixed date, provided that the option is declared by the expiry date. A put option is similar, and confers the right to sell. European options, if declared, become forward contracts.

Traded options do not easily match with pool index prices that contain capacity payments, because for options with very short notice periods, the reference price should be SMP, not PPP. For options with notice periods of a few days, and using a reference price of PPP, then the plant receives a payment for medium term capacity in the form of option premium, and then a payment for short term capacity, in the form of PPP-SMP.

6.6.3.1 Sale of options by producers

Notwithstanding the importance of finding gaming solutions to the position of the producer in the market, options are probably the most important economic and financial tool at the producer's disposal for the purpose of planning.

We show in the section on real options, that in the simplest situation in which the producer can regard his plant as an option to convert fuel to power at a known conversion cost, then we can set up a 'no arbitrage' situation in which the producer sells options at premium C for the right to call fuel-to-power conversion at a strike price K equal to marginal costs. Then, regardless of subsequent operation, the producer cash flow is equal to C minus fixed costs.

Producers have a limited capability to move costs between fixed and marginal, and by observing the prices in the option market, the producer can determine the optimal mix.

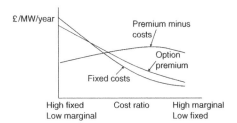

Figure 6.24 Optimum fixed/marginal cost mix as dictated by option premiums available in the market[17]

6.6.3.2 Purchase of options by producers

Producers ideally sell options to secure value for their capacity, but are at risk with respect to plant failure, and hence they have to purchase options as well. For high merit plant, this is fairly straightforward because it can buy from low merit plant. For low merit plant, there is ultimately no more plant to buy from and hence the consumers must (actually or *de facto* by accepting interruption) provide the highest strike capacity options.

6.6.3.3 Use of options by consumers and supply companies

Consumer demand has an expectation value that has trending, periodicity, stochastic variation and uncertainty.

---

[17]This figure shows the line of lowest achievable fixed cost for each level of marginal cost.

Consider the supply company with tariff customers (i.e. customers who pay a flat rate and consume as much as they like at that rate), then in the absence of load shedding, interruption, or other similar agreements, the supply company is contractually committed to deliver the load, and the load is inelastic because there is no incentive for the consumer to reduce load. The supply company then has an inelastic demand profile.

The tariff consumer can be viewed as having a forward contract with volume equal to expected load, plus an 'embedded' volume option. Since load is driven only by outside forces (is exogenously determined) but not by price, then the contract is said to be 'non ruthless'. This limits the supplier risk.

Since the supplier is short of an option to the consumer, he will charge the consumer his option cost. To value the option, the supplier must characterise: (i) the probability distribution of demand, (ii) the probability distribution of prices and (iii) the relationship between them.

The industrial and commercial market is more sensitive to price, less sensitive to weather, more capable of adjusting flexibility, more capable of receiving price signals, more able to settle (since the meters have half hourly price signals), and it is more possible to apply bespoke contracts than with residential customers. Hence it can play a key role in capacity provision, particular in times of high residential demand. The development of demand management option products should decrease the cost of supply to both residential and industrial consumers.

6.6.3.4   Capacity contracts

There are two key generic forms of capacity contract.

In the first form, the seller receives a fixed payment for capacity and then a designated payment for energy if the capacity is called. This is the traded option form described above.

In the second form, there is no specific price for the energy. The capacity contract is simply a commitment to provide a market offer at less than VOLL. The day ahead capacity payment in the England and Wales pool was of this form. We later see in sections 6.10 and 6.11 that the presence of a strike price is essential[18] in making the market 'complete' and thereby giving optimal signals for forward planning.

Other differentiators between contracts are location, firmness, cash out price, withdrawal and non delivery rules and prices.

Whilst options typically operate at high resolution (a few hours), capacity contracts commonly have a lower resolution (one month).

The most developed market in forward capacity is PJM in the USA. The NICAP capacity market deals with the obligation of load serving entities to secure capacity under the Reliability Assurance Agreement for the Mid Atlantic Area Council (MAAC) of NERC, for the purposes of security of supply. The PJM standard is for there to be an expectation of not more than one day per ten years for which available generation capacity falls short of demand.

The installed capacity obligation (which can be satisfied from sources outside the control area) is equal to the peak load (net of firm and formal demand management contracts, called

---

[18] A simple application of option theory indicates that a capacity requirement with no strike price is of no use at all, since an option struck at VOLL can never have more than zero economic value. However, if the option stuck at VOLL has a regulatory value (from satisfying a capacity commitment), then this, along with other factors such as the cost of volatility risk, does engender a partial market for options with strike prices.

mandatory interruptible load, MIL[19]) times the installed reserve margin, that is currently set at 15 %.

Capacity credits apply at monthly resolution. A price cap applies, but this can be raised when the market monitoring unit (MMU) determines that capacity is scarce (defined by the capacity resources falling below 1.01 times the capacity requirement). Consistent with the pool structure of PJM, the capacity auction is closed and has a clearing price.

6.6.3.5 *Non delivery against option or capacity commitments*

VOLL provides a natural limit for non delivery of energy against an option or capacity contract. A limit of VOLL effectively converts the call option into a call spread. So, for example if supplier A calls an option from producer B, then the producer who cannot deliver will either buy the energy in the market to deliver to A, or will buy it back from A at VOLL and therefore pay a net cash amount equal to VOLL minus strike price. This places a high risk on the generator, and if the generating company is small, it may be optimal in terms of cost of risk to place this risk with an insurer or with the supplier (by making the contract non firm or reducing the cashout price from VOLL to some lower number).

Traded capacity obligations commonly have a non delivery penalty.[20] For example in PJM the deficiency penalty was $ 177/MW/day. The producer may elect to delist the capacity, pay the penalty, and sell power in the neighbouring area if the forward baseload price for the day in the neighbouring area exceeds an average of around $ 7.4/MWh more than in PJM. PJM addressed this problem by specifying a minimum period for the offering of capacity and an annual penalty for delisting.

6.6.4   Self insurance for generator shortfall

Within a fleet of power stations, the company can self insure. This is an important mechanism because of the way that consolidated pool markets behave.

Consider unit A3 owned by operator A and suppose that it is about to fail. It is economically most efficient at aggregate level for the system operator to dispatch unit B7 owned by company B. However, it is more economically efficient for company A to dispatch plant A9, rather than buy back the hedge sold energy from B9, provided that there is no negative influence of this strategy on the future behaviour of operator B.

We establish the mutual influence of offer prices in several sections in this book and note that without it, that in some systems, the price is exposed to collapse by falling to marginal cost followed by exit of marginal units. However, here we have a special case. If the gamed arrangement is constancy of market share,[21] then operator A can replace unit A3 with unit A9 without altering the market share. There is therefore out of merit running. The extent to which this occurs in practice depends on the communication method for market sharing and the tolerance period for deviations.

---

[19] MIL has three types. Direct Load Control (DLC) which is controlled directly by the load serving entity (LSE), Firm Service Level (FSL) which involves consumer reduction to a designated level, and Guaranteed Load Drop (GLD) which involves consumer reduction by a designated level.

[20] For a review of capacity obligations in the USA and the changing rules for non delivery, see Shuttleworth *et al.* (2002).

[21] The maintenance of a consistent market share is described in the Stackelberg equilibrium in section 10.5.8.

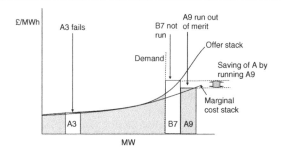

Figure 6.25   Self insurance of operator A by running owned plant A9 out of merit rather than paying the market offer and causing B7 to run

This mechanism can only be done in certain circumstances. For example if unit A3 fails after gate closure in the bilateral market, then operator A may not make the unilateral decision to run plant A9 (pre gate closure A can notify any unit combination to meet contracted load). It is possible prior to gate closure and the economics are identical (A should go to market rather than notify unit A9 to fulfil contracted offers rather than unit A3). In the pool what actually happens is that if at day ahead stage, unit A3 is in a failed state, then unit A9 is offered at marginal cost rather than marginal cost with fixed cost uplift, and therefore the system operator will dispatch A9 ahead of B7. B does not respond because A's market share remains unchanged.

Clearly this is inefficient compared to optimal dispatch. The question is whether the merits of competition outweigh the cost addition from out of merit running.

Internal cover is a mechanism that mainly applies within the mid merit area, but can be relevant in running low merit plant ahead of competitor mid merit plant.

6.6.5   Mutual insurance

Mutual insurance is very similar to internal insurance but is an explicit arrangement between operators. To ensure legality, the arrangement must be agreed with the system operator and possibly the regulator in the pool markets. There is no such explicit restriction in bilateral markets. Generator A and generator B engage in a formal or informal transaction in which each guarantees to provide cover for the other. So if Generator A fails, then generator B sells generator A power at the agreed price and then covers the commitment by running the plant. In the pool model, they cannot actually deliver physical electricity to one another but can agree to submit to the pool at the insurance price rather than VOLL. The 'VCR' contracts in Australia are an example of mutual insurance.

The effect of this is to produce an effective cap to prices in the medium-high price region of the load duration curve.

Consider a four player market in which each has one low merit plant and one high merit plant. The market gaming 'rules' are that A and B share a market share, and that C and D share the other part of the market share. When plant in the A fleet fails, then it is covered by plant from the D fleet.

6.6.6 Value from rare but highly priced energy contracts

If there is no capacity mechanism at all, then the generator internalises the risks, and makes a price offer strategy that is initially optimised on an *ex ante* basis, and revised by *ex post* experience. If this does not provide a fair risk adjusted return on investment, then the generator may plan to withdraw.

This presents two particular problems, one of risk and one of regulation.

Risk – The variance of return for low merit plant receiving income live at out-turn rather than by capacity payments, is higher than for mid merit plant.[22]

Figure 6.26   Profit risk in relation to unit marginal cost

Regulation – Without an option, capacity payment, or similar contract, the unit does not have an obvious way to declare its offer strategy. It could publish it, but in reality this would receive little attention when the unit does not run, and would be forgotten about when the unit runs. Even if the *ex ante* risk position is fair from a capital asset perspective (see section 10.1.24), the unit risks regulatory action to depress the offer price if prices rise and yet can expect no subsidy if returns are less than *ex ante* expectation. The situation has much in common with drug companies. A successful drug must cover not only the marginal cost of production and the research and development costs, but also the research and development costs of all drugs that failed to eventually get to market (the equivalent here of all the hours not generated). The moral hazard from the perspective of the generator is that the capacity of the unit is treated as a public good, but not paid for.[23]

The presence of an absolute price cap in this instance adds clarity, since there is an implicit assumption that pricing at the cap would normally invoke no regulatory action, and the unit can make an *ex ante* decision about whether revenue is sufficient at the cap price to maintain the unit. In this instance, the action of the cap as a focal point concentrates plant and means that there is no merit order at the cap price. This reduces the incentive to reduce marginal costs, so plant moves to the right of the fixed/marginal cost spectrum.

If there is no capacity mechanism and all money is recovered in the spot market, then if the generator must cover its costs in all years (as distinct to covering its costs over a many year period) it would require a greater uplift of costs in a low demand year, as there is less generation over which to smear fixed costs.

Ideally, to maintain constant net revenue in all years, those low merit units that get any running at all will smear their fixed costs over the small running period and therefore charge a higher price in lower demand periods. However, we shall see in section 10.5 on gaming and behaviour, that it is in fact difficult to maintain a higher price when some units get no

---

[22] See section 9.1.20.2 for further details on this.
[23] See section 10.1.17 for explanation of public goods.

running at all. Therefore in the absence of a capacity market, the generator cannot guarantee profit in all years and must therefore: (i) over-recover fixed costs in high demand years by price uplift and under-recover in low demand years and (ii) increase overall recovery to compensate for the cost of risk.

6.6.7   Reserve contracts

6.6.7.1   Minute reserve

The minute reserve contract in Germany is a 15 minute contract that must be fully available within 15 minutes of request. The internet based tender is conducted each day. Acceptance compensation uses pay-as-bid for energy and capacity in all areas except the E.ON one. The capacity price is paid for all accepted offers and the energy is paid/received if scheduled.

6.6.7.2   Warming contracts in Great Britain

We have seen that one reason for plant to contract bilaterally is so that it is hot in order to participate in the balancing mechanism. Since the gate closure period was initially 3.5 hours in the England and Wales system, this was too short a time for cold plant to offer in the balancing mechanism. In order to ensure sufficient reserve, a warming contract was devised to compensate a plant for being warm. This can only be signed with the system operator.

With the shrinking of the gate closure to one hour, a new contract called Pre-Gate Closure Balancing Mechanism Unit Transaction was introduced to allow the system operator to secure sufficient capacity prior to gate closure.

Subsequently the system operator entered consultation[24] to standardise and formalise the reserve contracts to Short Term Operating Reserve Tender (quarterly tender for short term operating reserve), Addition Short Term Operating Reserve Tender (as before but weekly) and Firm Reserve Option (an adaptation of the warming contract for all plant with start up lead times greater than balancing mechanism timescales).

6.6.7.3   Information provided by system operators

Plant making prior commitments to provide capacity at fixed price rather than energy at prompt price is exposed to information asymmetry as the system operator has the most information. System operators accordingly are providing more and more information to plant operators, such as:

(i)   plant outages (planned and breakdown);
(ii) contracted volume of reserve;
(iii) maximum capacity requirement.

6.7   CAPACITY PROVISION – THE SUPPLIER'S PERSPECTIVE

6.7.1   Requirements to secure capacity by load serving entities

This is a particularly important mechanism due to its role in the Standard Market Design described in section 1.6.2. Here we consider requirements to secure capacity in general. We

---

[24] September 2005.

have seen in sections 2.2.24 and 2.6.7 how the medium and long term generator and supplier hedge volume profiles with respect to horizon are lower than the generation hedge profiles, and therefore that in the presence of risk/uncertainty in demand, the forward market does not clear efficiently with respect to optimisation of generation resource. We also saw in section 2.6.7.5 that it is optimal for the supplier's hedge percentage to approximate that of his competitors.

In the short term, the situation is slightly different. The price/volume correlation means that the option hedge is more effective for reducing the risk of volume variation than the forward hedge. However as with the medium term hedge, the volume that the generator wants to sell (100% of capacity) is more than the consumer wants to buy (because the price/volume correlation is less than 100%). The market again does not clear efficiently with respect to optimisation of short term capacity availability (and reliability) planning by generators. Less capacity is booked than is optimal, and in practice, the shortfall is picked up by the system operator through the use of reserve contracts. Whilst units are committed to positive reserve, the capacity dedicated to reserve cannot also be sold for capacity and there is therefore 'spare' capacity on the system.

Consider now the situation of lost load. Those generators that deliver according to contract cannot be blamed. Those generators that fail against contract could be blamed for technical management but not for *ex ante* capacity contracting. Suppliers cannot be blamed directly, with the defence that even if they had hedged the shortfall amount, the generators could not have delivered it. There is therefore no one to point to for short term security of supply.

One answer to this problem (although not necessarily a solution, as it creates other problems), is to require suppliers to secure capacity. We consider this in two parts – the requirement to secure energy and the requirement to secure capacity.

6.7.1.1 Regulatory requirement to secure long term energy

Suppose now that the regulator could force suppliers to buy electricity further forward than initially planned. They might, for example, force an energy purchase to some percentage of current volume as shown in Figure 6.27.

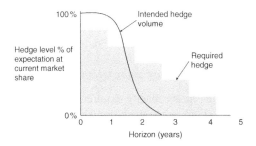

Figure 6.27   Supplier hedge volumes. Intended and mandatory

This has the intended effect of providing the signal to generators in sufficient time for them to turn investment into energy. However, unless the signal exceeds around 80% of expected outturn, then the signal is too weak since it will not attract generation at the margin.

There are numerous practical issues associated with implementing such a policy, including:

(i) **Creation of entry barriers** – New suppliers cannot easily secure long term credit lines.
(ii) **Uncertainty of market share**.
(iii) **Consumer contracts** – For example, a simultaneous indexed supply contract leaves the supply company with no wholesale price risk, so an enforced hedge increases its risk position.
(iv) **Consumer segmentation** – Different consumer segments have different risk profiles.
(v) **Encouragement to consume** – Bursts of high prices serve to increase consumer awareness and drive demand management.
(vi) **Definition of the hedge year** – Calendar year, rolling years, etc.

6.7.1.2 *Regulatory requirement to secure short term energy (prompt to one year)*

The short term in this context differs from the long term in that the optimum short term hedge for a supply company is somewhere around 100 % of expected demand. An enforced hedge at 100 % of expected demand is theoretically possible and would provide advance notice of impending generator shortfall. An additional benefit is in providing creditworthiness of the supplier to the consumer,[25] since the regulator would receive better advance notice of default arising from high wholesale prices as the supplier running out of financial liquidity would not be able to secure hedge contracts.

However, a regulatory requirement to enact what is already in the supplier's interests has the risk of overly crude application (in order to be sufficiently robust, transparent and general) and lead to inefficient capacity management and actually increase the risk of lost load to (some or all) consumers. In addition, detailed regulatory requirements can raise entry barriers to new suppliers due to administration costs.

Here we should note that there can be an incentive for small suppliers to take on a hedge position that is significantly different to other suppliers, by not hedging at all and creating a significant probability of default against supply contract. This is similar to the 'holiday spread'[26] well known for individual traders in the capital markets. If the market rises, the supplier defaults. If the market falls, the supplier gains. This moral hazard increases the incentive of the regulator, supply sector and consumers to mandate a hedge. The situation is much complicated by the erection of entry barriers by this requirement, and the short convexity risk (see Figure 2.51) carried by all suppliers but for which small suppliers have the highest exposure for cash flow reasons.

6.7.1.3 *Regulatory requirement to secure short term capacity*

If suppliers are required to hedge their capacity requirements, then this does provide a strong signal to generators. However, there are several problems:

(i) Capacity requirement is probabilistic in nature, and there is no theoretical limit to demand. Probability is hard enough to establish for each supplier, let alone police by the regulator.

---

[25] In some systems, the energy settlement risk from a supplier default falls not to the consumer but to the supplier community. There have been several defaults of suppliers, for example in Nordpool and Great Britain, and the markets have proved resilient to date.

[26] Put on a large traded position and go on holiday. If the trade becomes in the money, then return to a large bonus. If it becomes out of the money, stay on holiday.

(ii) If each supplier buys the capacity requirement for its own probability distribution, and the regulator disallows capacity provision without 100 % physical cover from generation or demand management, then the total capacity purchased (and financed) is excessive because volume variations between suppliers are not 100 % correlated.

(iii) Generators sell capacity but are not 100 % reliable.

(iv) In the absence of a designated strike price, suppliers could buy capacity struck at VOLL, which is essentially the same as not buying it at all.

6.7.1.4 *Regulatory requirement to secure long term capacity*

This is quite distinct from long term energy and short term capacity. Plant failure rates have very little forward volatility, and supplier's short convex (i.e. concave) delta/volatility position is longer in tenor than the delta position.

If suppliers were required to secure capacity at some level, say 120 % of expected volume, for a period of say three years, then there are potential benefits:

(i)   Even though suppliers could buy any strike price, they may make the effort to buy strike prices low enough to be useful.

(ii) Demand management would be encouraged.

(iii) The short bias from the risk of overhedging relative to the peer group. As described in section 2.6.7, this has the effect of reducing the volatility of retail prices.

6.7.1.5 *Regulatory designation of capacity obligations*

The regulatory requirement is fraught with practical difficulties. The key ones are[27]:

(i)   Formal algorithm for assessment of future load served.

(ii)   Timing – frequency of review and duration of requirement.

(iii) Definition and quantification of reserve margin required.

(iv)   Accounting method.

(v)   Operational rules to ensure that commitments for capacity convert to delivery of energy.

(vi)   Penalties to meet obligations.

6.8 CAPACITY PROVISION – THE NETWORK OPERATOR'S PERSPECTIVE

There is clearly much commonality in the provision of capacity by generators and by the networks. Both are required to serve a load that is periodic and stochastic, and both are exposed to their own failure and failure of the other (i.e. networks to generation and generation to networks). The commonality is the reason that we have been as specific as possible in referring to 'power capacity' as specifically pertaining to energy availability somewhere in the system, and 'network capacity' as the capability to deliver energy. However, the two are so intertwined that it is commonly not possible to be specific.

There are also significant differences between generation and network capacity. From a market perspective, the difference is the different regulatory status. Power generators behave as private entities (even in centrally managed systems) and network operators behave as

---

[27] Adapted from Shuttleworth *et al.* (2002)

public entities (even in highly deregulated systems). This is manifest in their contracts. Generators are not required to sign any contracts, but without contracts they cannot gain revenue, and with contracts, the failure to deliver can be well specified (for example, no penalty, fixed power price penalty or market related liquidated damages). This makes generation capacity slightly easier (although still difficult) to calculate than network capacity. Increments of capacity build or of network reliability cannot be calculated using market contracts, but with shadow prices and estimated willingness to pay by consumers.

6.9   THE SYSTEM OPERATOR'S PERSPECTIVE

In considering the network owner/operator perspective, we attempted to split the role of building and maintenance from the system operator function, in order to highlight the physical aspects of the network. In reality, the roles of the transmission owner are very closely related, and most commonly one company performs all or almost all of the roles. In addition to this, the compensation mechanism described in order to optimise build and maintenance, is not used in practice, and system operator incentives are cruder and except major failures that are deemed to be beyond the system operator's control.[28]

The system operator performs essentially the same calculation as described for the network owner/operator, but this time treats lost load as generation at VOLL at the respective grid supply points, and minimising the total cost of dispatch.

Privately owned system operators commonly have annual incentive schemes, and it is important that these are not misaligned to the optimum described above.

6.9.1   Cost to consumers

We considered the cost to consumers of lost load in section 10.1.5.1 but we have not considered how consumers themselves contribute to lost load and to capacity costs by having consumption that is both periodic and stochastic.

It is theoretically optimal to offer consumers little or no capacity options that are endogenous to consumers (related to internal consumer factors rather than measurable exogenous factors such as temperature). However, this is not the case in practice, because large companies have more resources and data to calculate endogenous risks (i.e. to exogenise them), and the primary motivator to not taking on endogenous risk is moral hazard. Therefore supply companies take on consumer risk and must charge for convexity (demand increase and wholesale price increase go hand in hand), risk (stochastic variation of well defined factors) and uncertainty (uncertainty of risk factors or of relation between risk factors and demand).

The general trend for larger customers is for them to assume a greater degree of the risk and to pay a correspondingly lower premium for convexity, risk and uncertainty. Over time, it is to be expected that lost load may be less of an emotive subject, and more of a purely commercial issue. Generators and transporters are however wary of statements by governments that lost load is a purely commercial issue, with the suspicion that opprobrium and enquiry will follow when lost load actually occurs.

---

[28] For a regulated monopoly, this is reasonable. This is equivalent to a *'force majeur'* clause for generators. However, markets usually operate most efficiently without transfer of endogenous risks (in this case transfer of network failure risk to generators and suppliers), and hence 'firm with liquidated damages' is used to an increasing degree in the wholesale markets for all participants other than network operators.

We can in essence take two approaches, which are closely related.

6.9.1.1   The value of lost load (VOLL) approach

In this approach, the failure to deliver is simply treated as a voluntary sale at VOLL[29] by supply companies at the respective grid supply point. We can see that for a particular generation stack, spread over the network, a demand with deterministic and stochastic elements, and a network with characterised constraints, losses and fail rates on each line, we can, for any element of time, calculate the probability weighted payment of VOLL. By repeating this for all periods of the year, we can calculate the optimum build.

6.9.1.2   The supply/demand of ex ante reliability approach

The *ex ante* confidence of no lost load can be treated as a good (a private good, with public elements[30]). Figure 6.28 shows how this can be represented in terms of fail probability and the supply and demand for *ex ante* confidence of no failure. It is quite clear that 100% confidence is impossible and that high confidence is very expensive.

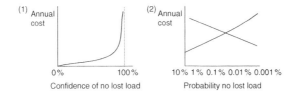

Figure 6.28   Representation of security of supply as a good

6.9.1.3   Consumer payment for system capacity

Supply companies pay for system capacity on behalf of consumers, and this is slightly different to the payment for energy capacity.

For large consumers, what is important for the grid is not their individual peak demand but their demand at the times of the national peak. So the grid company takes a small number of peak halfhours (typically three[31]) and averages them. The periods can be chosen in a number of ways while noting: (i) that they cannot be published to consumers in advance or large consumers will greatly reduce consumption for those specific periods only and these may turn out not to be the actual periods of highest demand and (ii) and *ex post* determination of the periods creates problems of delay in the billing cycle.

For small consumers, real time consumption rates are not known. This problem is handled by grouping customers according to type and assigning a peak-to-average demand ratio for the type. The grid operator knows the aggregate small consumer demand in real time by subtracting large consumer demand from total demand and allowing for losses. For small consumers, the seasonal date of maximum demand in the past is a less useful measure since domestic consumption is much more affected than industrial consumption by weather,

---

[29] also called CENS – cost of energy not supplied.
[30] Probability existence value. See section 10.1.18.
[31] In England and Wales, this is called the Triad.

television schedules and consumer events and hence average winter peak demand is a better proxy for charging than specific peaks, although the ratio of *ex post* peak to *ex post* average is used as an uplift ratio for the charge.

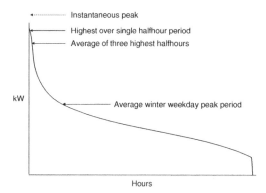

Figure 6.29   Using the load duration curve to calculate infrastructure cost requirements

6.9.2   Placing capacity obligation with the system operator

Just as national government has actual (through ministerial responsibility under an Act of Parliament, directives, etc.) or *de facto* obligation for security of supply, the system operator has a *de facto* obligation that could be formalised by a capacity obligation. The benefit of placing this obligation with the system operator is that the system operator has the greatest knowledge of both aggregate generation capacity in all timeframes and aggregate demand. The drawback is in optimising the incentive. The system operator may be incentivised to cause excessive capacity,[32] or become a *de facto* energy trader with significant market power and conflict of interests.

6.9.3   Placing the capacity obligation with the regulator or ministry

The system operator sits above the generators and the regulator/ministry/energy commission sit above the system operator. It is possible for one of these entities to directly secure capacity from generators to guard against very infrequent events. The capacity can then be released under specific triggers. A similar proposal was made in New Zealand in 2003. Almost by definition, such generation almost never runs, and hence, amongst other issues there are issues with readiness, and the over simplification of the energy stack as being discretely constructed from a constant set of units.

6.10   CAPACITY FACILITATION – CONTRACTUAL INSTRUMENTS

Here we first describe how capacity provision purely by generators is not efficient and that market intermediaries are required to make the market efficient.

---

[32] The system operator with physical transmission activities makes money from new build transmission assets, does not incur costs from generation build or high consumer prices, and has no disincentive to overbuild.

6.10.1   Generator cover

The simplest visualisation is for generator failure to be covered by generators. In Figure 6.30, we see the 'in merit' plant being covered by an equal MW volume from the 'out of merit' stack. Since the insuring plant can fail, then a further stack is required for reinsurance, and so on. It is apparent from this that: (i) it is impossible to ensure 100 % reliability overall without an infinite number of plant, (ii) the probability of call off of each batch of plant declines with the merit of the batch and therefore the revenue derived from the insurance premium must also decline and (iii) to avoid out of merit running, insuring plant that is called to run by the failure of insured plant should buy power from a higher merit plant that is not running, and provide reinsurance for that plant's insurance contract.

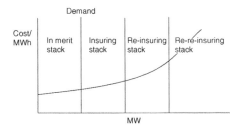

Figure 6.30   Provision of cover for generator failure by a series of low merit plant

It is obvious that we must use probability more effectively to arrange our contracts and that we need to ensure that plant running is always in merit. This can, in theory at least, be managed by insurance contracts from insurance companies. We do this here.

6.10.2   Insurance and reinsurance

Here we consider insurance contracts in some detail. The reason for this will become obvious as we see that the hedge strategy of the insurer drives optimum readiness of installed capacity and that analysis of insurer risks enables us to understand the risks of the generators and suppliers. This is the case even if there is no insurer. This is apparent from the consideration of the plant financial model described in Chapter 11.

We can represent insurance claims in two axes.

Firstly, the claim is only valid if the cause is from a defined list of risks. The division of risks is called facultative.

Secondly the full loss may not be paid, as there is an excess, and the claim may be limited, and if unlimited, passes through a series of reinsurance contracts in a process called retrocession. We can represent all this on the retrocession axis. In the plant financial model, the internal reliability insurance has zero excess, and this passes to an internal insurer (called a 'captive') before being covered in the external market. Since in internal markets, internal contracts are priced at external rates, we need not concern ourselves particularly about the internal/external division when optimising reliability planning.

The facultative/retrocession axes are extremely important when considering optimum reliability management, since the largest claims tend to be caused from systemic exogenous events (such as weather events) thereby causing a very high correlation of risks for extreme events.

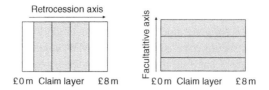

Figure 6.31   Depiction of the two insurance/reinsurance axes

6.10.2.1   The insurance and reinsurance markets for generator failure

Although the liquidity of insurance contracts has decreased substantially since the early part of the century, it is still possible to insure units on an individual basis. Whilst insurance commonly covers material damage[33] and business interruption (lost revenue) together, it is possible to separate them contractually.

The business interruption component of standard insurance contracts, commonly has a long excess period (generally between 30 and 90 days, depending on conditions in the insurance market), and for the insured period covers the whole loss (the difference between market price and marginal cost price). This misses the highly volatile short horizon period. The insurance cover is shown schematically in Figure 6.32, ignoring other conditions such as excess financial amount of claim, and claim limit (where this exists).

Some market participants in the generation, insurance, and re-insurance sectors, addressed the problem of short term market risk by reducing the excess period substantially, but reduced the overall risk level and the moral hazard (generators become less risk averse, or even failing on purpose to uphold price for other units or other reasons) by adding a price trigger. Figure 6.32 shows dual trigger contracts in which the claim is invoked only when (i) the plant fails and (ii) the market price rises above the trigger level.

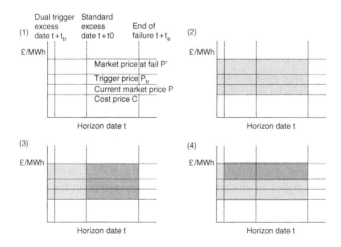

Figure 6.32   Unit failure insurance. (1) Labels for the figures, (2) Uninsured loss, (3) Standard insurance contract[34], (4) Dual trigger insurance contract. In all figures the insurance cover is in dark grey

---

[33] In practice, short term material damage cost is extremely closely related to business interruption cost, because the cost of spare parts on short delivery is closely related to power market conditions.

[34] This is simplified. In practice there is no formal process for determining the market price at fail.

Dual trigger option contracts were developed[35] in the pre-Enron-collapse period at around the year 2000 by generators such as Aquila, and insurers such as Ace. These products have recently declined, due partly due to decrease in the liquidity of the market, and innovative capability of generators, and partly due to raised losses, reduced capital and higher cost of risk in the insurance sector.

6.10.2.2 Payoffs and hedges for the insurer

The dual trigger contracts are of particular interest. The payoff for an insurer who insures a single unit, which then fails, is shown in Figure 6.33. It is immediately obvious that this has the profile of a short call option position.

Figure 6.33 Payoff in relation to market price out-turn for insurer who insures a single unit that then falls

It is the hedge strategy for this insurer that reveals the information to us about market depth. We work through this strategy by gradually addition complications (i.e. relaxing assumptions).

First assume that the trigger price is equal to the prevailing forward price, that forward price changes and failure are uncorrelated, that upward moves in forward prices are as likely as downward prices, and that the probability of failure is F%. The current margin M of the plant is the difference between the market price P and the cost C.[36] Our probabilities and payoff profiles (ignoring the receipt of insurance premium which is the same for all cases) for the unhedged and hedged case are as shown in Table 6.2:

The variance is

$$\left[h^2 \left(\frac{1-F}{2} \right) \right] + \left[(h - \overline{M})^2 \left(\frac{F}{2} \right) \right] + \left[h^2 \left(\frac{1-F}{2} \right) \right] + \left[(-h - \underline{M})^2 \left(\frac{F}{2} \right) \right]$$

$$- \left(\left[h \left(\frac{1-F}{2} \right) \right] + \left[(h - \overline{M}) \frac{F}{2} \right] - \left[h \left(\frac{1-F}{2} \right) \right] - \left[(h + \underline{M}) \frac{F}{2} \right] \right)^2$$

Where $\overline{M} = \max(M + 1, 0)$ and $\underline{M} = \max(M - 1, 0)$

---

[35] For further information on the operation of such contracts, see Eydeland and Wolniec (2002).

[36] We can instead interpret M as the price trigger level below current market. If M = 0, then the insurance will only pay out if the market rises. In this case, the plant is not fully hedged.

Table 6.2 Probability profile of hedged and unhedged insurer payoff for 0 % correlation between client failure and market prices. Insurance premium excluded

	No fail	Fail
Probability		
Market up 1	$(1 - F)/2$	$F/2$
Market down 1	$(1 - F)/2$	$F/2$
Payoff – No hedge		
Market up 1	0	$-\max(M + 1, 0)$
Market down 1	0	$-\max(M - 1, 0)$
Forward hedge h		
Market up 1	$+h$	$h - \max(M + 1, 0)$
Market down 1	$-h$	$-h - \max(M - 1, 0)$

Differentiating the variance with respect to h we find the optimum[37] hedge ratio,

$$2h(1 - F) + F(2h - \overline{M} + \underline{M}) = 0$$

For $M > 1$ this simplifies to $h = F$

For $M = 0$ this simplifies to $h = \frac{1}{2}F$

And of course for $M < 1$ this simplifies to $h = 0$

Note that it is important to use a finite step in market prices rather than an infinitesimal one, since for all correlations above 0 %, failure events cause step changes in prices.

It is obvious from this that the hedge ratio changes with market prices when the market prices are such that plant margin is low. Since we have to buy more electricity when prices rise then we have a negatively 'convex' risk position, which has the general form of the 'short gamma' from a short option position. This will become more obvious when we look at finite correlations between failure and market prices.

It is obvious that while we can adjust[38] our risk profile, that the hedge cannot eliminate the risk. Now it is not just Murphy's law[39] that causes market prices to rise when failures occur, particularly for low merit plant. There is the 'fair' economic effect of requiring a lower merit unit to run, and in addition the potential market behaviour of participants to take the opportunity to gain extra rent. We must therefore attend to the correlation between the price change and the fail status. The example used so far assumes 0 % correlation. If there is 100 % correlation, we can see that we are forced to adjust our price process to make it more skewed. If we now examine the payoff profile, ignoring the payment of option premium, which is the same for all cases, we get a different story.

We can see in Table 6.3 that in the case of 100 % correlation between market price and failure (i.e. failure of this plant is the only cause of price variation) there is only one degree

---

[37] This does not necessarily minimise extreme risk aversion. If correlation between failure and prices is zero, then the optimum hedge ratio is slightly higher than 10 %.

[38] Here we reduce the normal risk and increase the extreme risk. The optimum is therefore dependent on the risk aversion for both.

[39] When toast falls on the floor, it usually lies butter side down.

of freedom for the payoff and therefore that a pure price derivative could fully insure the payoff of the insurer. In this the derivative is a European option, struck at M. The delta of the option close to expiry is 0 when the market price P falls below M, 1/2 at P = M and 1 for P > M, which corresponds to the hedge ratio for the forward contract as shown above.

For M = 0;

Table 6.3 Probability profile of hedged and unhedged insurer payoff for 100 % correlation between client failure and market prices. Insurance premium excluded

	No fail	Fail
Probability		
Market up $1 - F$	0 %	F
Market down F	$1 - F$	0 %
Payoff – No hedge		
Market up $1 - F$	0	$-1 + F$
Market down F	0	0
Payoff – With 1 hedge		
Market up $1 - F$	$h(1 - F)$	$h(1 - F) - 1 + F$
Market down F	$-hF$	$-hF$

For linear disutility of risk with respect to variance, and assuming the price and failure distributions are both normal, we can find the optimum dynamic[40] hedge by differentiating[41] with respect to h:

$$\tfrac{d}{dh}\left[(1 - F)(-hF)^2 + F(h - hF - 1 + F)^2\right] = 0$$

$$h = 1 - F$$

Generalising:

	No fail	Fail
Probability		
Market up $1 + \rho - 2\rho F$	$((1 - F) - \rho(1 - F))/2$	$(F + \rho F)/2$
Market down $1 - \rho + 2\rho F$	$((1 - F) + \rho(1 - F))/2$	$(F - \rho F)/2$
Payoff – No hedge		
Market up $1 + \rho - 2\rho F$	0	$-\max(M + 1 + \rho - 2\rho F, 0)$
Market down $1 - \rho + 2\rho F$	0	$-\max(M - 1 + \rho - 2\rho F, 0)$
Payoff – With hedge		
Market up $1 + \rho - 2\rho F$	$+h(1 + \rho - 2\rho F)$	$+h(1 + \rho - 2\rho F)$ $-\max(M + 1 - \rho + 2\rho F, 0)$
Market down $1 - \rho + 2\rho F$	$-h(1 - \rho + 2\rho F)$	$-h(1 - \rho + 2\rho F)$ $-\max(M - 1 + \rho - 2\rho F, 0)$

---

[40] A dynamic hedge must be adjusted as the market moves.
[41] Here we ignore the differential of expectation of hedge profit in relation to hedge volume, which strictly speaking we may only do in the risk neutral world.

Differentiation and rearrangement gives us:

$$+2h(1-\rho^2-4\rho^2F^2+4F\rho^2)$$
$$-\overline{M}F(1+2\rho+\rho^2-2\rho F-2\rho^2F)$$
$$-\underline{M}F(1-2\rho+\rho^2+2\rho F-2\rho^2F)=0$$

For $M<-1$ we have $h=0$

For $M>1$ h increases to 1

Now consider an insurer who insures ten units. We know from the central limit theory (section 9.1.9) that as the number of units increases, the total failure distribution becomes more normal. With this number of units, we can expect a reasonable correlation between unit failures and price rises. Let us for convenience assume 100 % correlation[42] and consider the payoffs for 0.1 and ten failures. The failures of between two and nine units are not shown and hence the total probability is less than 100 %.

Table 6.4 Probability profile of hedged and unhedged insurer payoff for 100 % correlation between client failure and market prices. Ten units insured. Insurance premium excluded

	No fail	1 Fail	10 Fail
Probability (restore expectation no drift)			
Market down 1	35 %	0 %	0 %
Market up 0.5	0 %	39 %	0 %
Market up 20	0 %	0 %	1E − 10
Payoff – No hedge			
Market down 1	0	n/a	n/a
Market up 0.5	n/a	−0.5	n/a
Market up 20	n/a	n/a	−200

As for a single plant, there is only one degree of freedom here (plant failure is the only cause of price rise) and hence we can hedge with a stack of options (one for each failure combination). In the simple case with identical unit volumes, a stack of ten options at different strike prices from 0.5 to 20 can hedge us perfectly.

Now the question is, who can sell the options to the reinsurer? There are two sources, the out of merit generation units, and the consumers who can shed load.

In competitive equilibrium, units sell options struck at marginal costs, for a premium equal not less than fixed[43] costs. In competitive insurance equilibrium, the insurers pay a

---

[42] Non linear correlation.

[43] Quasi fixed costs must be included in either fixed or marginal costs as appropriate. For the short term, they are loaded into fixed costs.

premium for the options that is equal to the expected payoff after risk adjustments,[44] and the expected payoff can be calculated since the only kind of event driving price changes in this example is plant failure and the insurers calculate the probability of each combination of failures. Here we see how the probability distribution of prices is directly determinable from plant fixed costs, marginal costs and fail rates.

There are now several matters to attend to:

(i)   demand management;
(ii) finite probability of lost load;
(iii) stochastic variation of demand;
(iv) mismatch of options needed and options available;
(v)   failure of plant selling options.

We can treat demand management as a set of perfectly reliable generators with differing fixed and marginal costs. We can treat lost load as demand management, equivalent to a generator of infinite size with a marginal cost of VOLL and zero fixed cost.[45] We can treat stochastic demand as a power disturbance much like plant failure except that the disturbance can be positive as well as negative.

Suppose that demand is deterministic and inelastic, so the only variation in the production/demand balance arises from generator failure.

The in merit plant sell forwards. They then buy insurance from the insurer. The insurer then goes back to market to buy options from the out of merit plant. The aggregate number of options bought broadly equals the in merit volume times the average fail rate. The plant selling options then go to the insurer to buy insurance, who then goes back to the market to buy more options. The total volume of plant committed as a percentage of demand is approximately $\sum_{i=0}^{\infty} F^i$ where F is the fail rate. This is finite[46] but there is a finite probability of lost load.

Finally we realise that we have used the insurer to clear the market through use of information that is endogenous to each unit but exogenous to all other units. Each owner of generation can set up its own insurer for its own units, and provided it has the same information and the same technical capability of the insurer can self insure at the expense of the difference between the internal cost of risk and the external cost of risk.

6.10.2.3 Cost of risk

At first glance it seems odd that a reinsurer[47] can aid the development of the capacity market. However:

(i) Insurers are experienced in handling 'endogenous' risk in which the risk is highly dependent on the specific circumstances of the insured.

---

[44] The insurer is prepared to pay above the expectation value for options, and the plant is prepared to sell for less.

[45] This effectively assumes that there are sufficient consumers who voluntarily reduce demand at VOLL, rather than simply get compensated at VOLL.

[46] For example, if $F = 50\%$ and failures are uncorrelated, then total volume $= 2*$demand. If $F = 10\%$, then total volume $= 1.1111111*$demand.

[47] Insurers and reinsurers have distinct capabilities. Insurers handle well high frequency claims with a high endogenous content. Probability analysis is subservient to claim history and competition. Reinsurers handle well low frequency claims with high exogenous content, and probability analysis is highly sophisticated.

(ii) Reinsurers are experienced in handling the probability impact of high impact low frequency events.

(iii) Reinsurers[48] are well diversified with respect to the specific nature of risks and hence well placed to handle high impact low frequency risks in the ESI.

(iv) Reinsurers have a relatively high cost of 'normal' risk and a relatively low cost of 'extreme' risk.

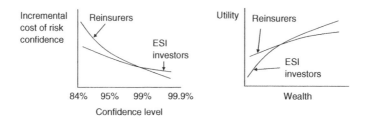

Figure 6.34 Relative cost of risk for reinsurers and ESI investors for different levels of risk, and rationalisation in terms of utility functions

We can assess broadly the cost of insurance risk by combining the utility function with the Generalised Pareto Distribution. Simplifying somewhat, we have for a retrocession band between loss L and loss $L + dL$, using the exponential utility formula, the rate of change of charge for risk with respect to loss band:

$$-\frac{d}{dL} \int_{L}^{L+dL} \exp(-x/\beta)\lambda\exp(x)dx$$

This simplifies to $\lambda\left[\exp(L)\right]^{(1-1/\beta)}$

The exponential formula can be used for unlimited loss.[49] If the reinsurer has limited capital, then the logarithmic utility function is more appropriate:

$$-\frac{d}{dL} \int_{L}^{L+dL} \exp(-x/\beta)\lambda\ln(x_0 - x)dx$$

Which is $\exp(-x/\beta)\lambda\ln(x_0 - x)dx$

Insurance quotes can be calibrated to functions such as these.

The rational behaviour of reinsurers in optimising their risk position entails two specific actions; (i) exogenous contingency arrangements in the power market by purchasing options with low premiums and high strike prices. This in turn finances capacity and (ii) endogenous contingency arrangements such as monitoring plant access to spares, monitoring plant maintenance and reliability performance and actually maintaining direct access to spares.

---

[48] This is quite distinct to the position of insurers, who have far less diversification, and whose premiums are more closely related to recent claims than to complex probability calculations.

[49] Lloyd's of London works in this manner for example.

6.10.3   Traded options

Whilst it is core business for insurers and reinsurers to take endogenous risk, it is not core business for generators to take risk that is specifically endogenous to a counterparty. Generators therefore are better placed to sell options than insurance contracts.

We have already established that the optimum framework is for generators to sell options struck at marginal costs at a premium equal to fixed costs, and that *ex ante* market price distributions can be calculated from failure and demand distributions and the premium/strike price relationships.

We have also established that demand management options are for present purposes 100 % reliable, that there is an option of infinite volume struck at VOLL and with zero premium.

6.11   USE OF OPTIONS TO CONVEY PROBABILITY INFORMATION

We have noted the optimum strategy of selling options struck at marginal costs, established plant failure as a source of volatility, and established the use of option purchases by insurers/reinsurers to hedge risk position. It is then apparent that the option prices are a rich set of information about prospective states of the system.

Let us first assume that insurer cost of risk is zero, that there is no uncertainty (plant can accurately establish *ex ante* fail rates and insurers have direct access to the information) and there is no moral hazard.

Consider first the insurance of the in merit plant. Suppose that there are ten in merit units of equal size and with a 10 % fail rate. The insurer insures all ten and buys option cover initially from one. At equilibrium we know the strike (marginal cost) and the premium (fixed cost). We also know the probability of each failure combination, and how much plant cover is needed for each combination. In this simple case there are 2^{10} failure combinations. The probability of no failures is $(1 - F)^{10}$ and the probability of one failure is $10(1 - F)^9 F$. The payout for no failures is zero, the payout for exactly one[50] failure is equal to marginal cost of the eleventh unit minus the marginal cost of the failed unit, and the payout for more than one failure is equal to weighted average marginal cost of the in merit stack[51] minus the marginal cost of the failed unit. Similarly for exactly n failures the payout is equal to n times the price conditional on failures of n units. The expectation payout must equal insurance premium minus risk adjustment.

Let us now consider the twelfth unit. The risk neutral[52] insurer buys a fraction F = 10 % of the unit capacity in order to hedge the option sold (to the insurer) by the eleventh unit. Now we may not just consider optimum hedges but must consider other payouts. The plant must calculate the probability weighted payout on the $(1 - F)$ of uncommitted capacity and the insurer must calculate the probability weighted payout for greater than on fails.

Finally we must consider the thirteenth and higher units. Each must either (i) sell an option struck at marginal costs with a premium (at least) equal to marginal costs, or (ii) plan

---

[50] Assuming that the insurer compensates the plant at the price visible throughout the failure period, rather than the estimation of what the price would have been without the failure. Note the moral hazard since the unit gains from the price caused by its own failure.

[51] In this simple equilibrium case, all in merit plant receives the same revenue and if the merit order is not periodic then they must all have the same fixed and marginal costs.

[52] Of course the risk neutral argument is hardly valid in this situation, but the argument is easier to develop first in the risk neutral (or very slightly risk averse) case and then consider cost of risk afterwards.

an offer price algorithm that (at least) covers fixed costs on an *ex ante* probability weighted basis.

In this simple example, the only buyer in town is the insurer. The risk neutral (actually slightly risk averse) insurer will buy options from all units on the stack. Note that this should be more efficient than each unit holding back the option and waiting for high prices because: (i) the insurer has better system wide information and (ii) the insurer is better diversified both within and without the ESI and therefore has a lower cost of risk.

So finally we are in the position where the insurer buys options from all plant on the stack. With completely inelastic demand and no VOLL there is no price limit and all available units will secure contracts that cover fixed costs. In the presence of VOLL, then some units will be uneconomic and will withdraw. Demand management and other forms of elasticity cause the further withdrawal of units.

So finally, if unit failures are the only random events we have a self consistent set of:

(i)   the probability of each failure combination;
(ii)   the insurer payout for each unit insurance contract for each failure combination;
(iii) the market price at each failure combination (the marginal cost of the marginal unit);
(iv)   the option premium gained by each unit;
(v)   the insurance premium paid by each unit.

Before moving on we must consider a few details:

(i)   **Demand management and price inelasticity** – Simple demand management contracts (accepting lost load in return for a fixed up front premium and compensation at a predetermined marginal price) can be incorporated very simply as the contracts are treated as perfectly reliable power station units.
(ii)   **Stochastic demand** – Extra demand can be treated as generator failure. Less demand is not as easy to handle, although we can model any demand profile in terms of a discrete combination of generator failure (zero demand being zero failures), although it is easier to model using a continuous distribution.
(iii) **Cost of risk** – The argument was developed in a near risk neutral situation for simplicity. Provided that cost of risk can be established for each unit and insurer, then it is straightforward to incorporate into the calculations.
(iv)   **Granularity** – We have effectively assumed that each unit generates for one period per year. The situation is theoretically similar but practically much more complicated in a many period setting.
(v)   **Periodicity** – Periodicity demand adds some complications. Periodic factor costs (for example rainfall or gas prices) add considerable complexity due to the fact that the merit order becomes periodic.

It is obvious at this point that we have used the insurer as an intermediary to help the market clear in probability terms. We can now add a third agent which is a derivative trader. The insurer buys options from the derivative trader and the derivative trader buys options from the plant. Note that the options that the insurer bought from the units are firm. If a unit fails to physically deliver against its option contract, then it receives energy from the insurer at its marginal cost to enable it to honour the contract.

The issues in the addition in adding a derivative marketplace is that the amount of endogenous information is reduced both because the derivative trader has less information rights than the insurer and because information is more fragmented.

The advantage of using a derivative marketplace is that an open marketplace is more efficient, and option traders are more experienced in creating a liquid market in the spread of option prices between strike prices and tenors.

Now we can see that we have reconciled the economic structure of forward contracts, option contracts and insurance premiums to the *ex ante* probability distribution of prices. By building in uncertainty, we have gone some way into solving the problem of the insufficiency of markets to drive the economic optimum of plant build. We note that whilst the optimum hedge tenor for option contracts exceeds that for forward contracts, we still are only adding completeness over a tenor from two to five years, which is not enough to drive long term plant decisions. However we note that this is not so much a failure of market information but more a problem of how competition in the supply sector and in the competition between non ESI industries with high electricity factor costs, causes a shortening of the tenor of the optimum market hedge.

In this simplified situation, our market is complete because we can efficiently define the probability universe, the optimal hedge strategy and associated physical response. We can in principle develop this simple method to include extra sources of uncertainty. For example, demand variations can be modelled as variations of power plant (more demand than expected is equivalent to more failures than expected).

6.12   EFFECT OF PRICE CAPS ON CAPACITY AND PRICES

The effect of price caps is fairly easy to understand. We can see in Figure 6.35 that if we cap prices then the lowest merit units must either withdraw (thereby causing the possibility of lost load) or increase load factor. This load factor must be at the expense of higher merit plant which must therefore raise its prices. This arrangement causes out of merit running and is therefore economically inefficient in a market with no excess rent. If there is excess rent in the market then the price cap does increase the consumer surplus.

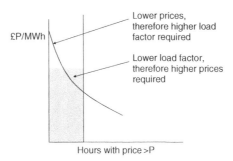

Figure 6.35   Effect of price cap

Prior to the lost load event in California, the price cap had been reduced from $ 1,000/MWh to $ 250/MWh. VOLL in other countries is/was, for example initially £ 2,500/MWh($\sim$ € 4,000) in England and Wales in the pool, 50,000 Kr/MWh ($\sim$ € 6,000) in Norway, 20,000 Kr/MWh ($\sim$ € 2,000) in Sweden, and $ 10,000/MWh ($\sim$ € 6,000) in Australia.

It is sometimes stated that the 'missing revenue' from price capping can be recovered from the option premium that the price capped plant could sell. However, this is only the case if the buyer of the option sees an uncapped revenue or if he benchmarks his option price in relation to the saving of an uncapped loss.

Option prices can, in theory be capped, and capacity prices sometimes are capped.[53] A cap on option prices should have no impact without specific reference to the strike price since the option struck at VOLL has no value. However if option cover is mandatory (equivalent to a capacity requirement), then an option with no economic value (assuming the VOLL is fairly priced) has a regulatory value.

---

[53] For example in PJM.

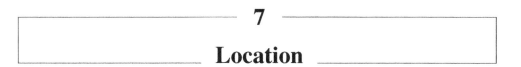

7

Location

At the beginning of this book, we stated that the uniqueness of electricity lies in its time-space characteristics. In this chapter we take a wide view of the issues of energy and emissions moving from one place to another.

Network theory was well developed in the twentieth century and was concerned principally with static optimisation under deterministic conditions. The enhanced responsivity of participants that comes with liberalisation drove extensive theoretical development around the turn of the century on the time element of power – that it is the stochastic evolution of prices. This, and the need to force the market to clear a solution that is approximately the same as the optimised solution for surplus maximisation meant that a lot of new theory had to be developed.

Whilst location has always been part of system design and operation, it has not been a key element of electricity market design until very recently. The increasing importance and profile of location is due to four key factors:

(i)   Increasing commercial complexity of networks due to the interconnection of markets and the wheeling of power across long distances.
(ii)   The increasing importance of barriers and constraints, electrical and otherwise.
(iii)   Increasing geographical widening between fossil fuel sourcing, large scale production, consumption and environmental impact, and the associated impact on security of supply.
(iv)   Increasing extent of small scale renewable generation, embedded in the distribution networks.

Location is a general term, and it is useful to be specific in our interpretation. Each of following changes over geographical and electrical distance, and/or over borders:

(i)   **Geographical** – Distance on the horizontal plane. For example length of wire of pipe.
(ii)   **Topological** – Taking into account height, terrain and water.
(iii)   **Electrical** – Electrical resistance, impedance, voltage, phase, frequency, stability and reactive power.
(iv)   **Political** – Market ideology. Economic boundaries.
(v)   **Legal/regulatory** – Laws on production, consumption, transportation and markets.
(vi)   **Social/cultural** – Attitude to welfare, the environmental and related matters and relative degrees of belief in the internationalisation of environmental flow.
(vii)   **Fiscal** – Taxes on production and consumption. Different fiscal models for direct and indirect taxed. Different macroeconomic models.
(viii)   **Market hubs** – The deviation of power from the economically most efficient route, in order to take advantage of market liquidity.[1]

---

[1] This phenomenom is well known in, for example, the airline industry and the metal markets. However there are extra complications here since power cannot easily be forced to follow the contract path. The economic inefficiency from constraint results from suboptimal dispatch relative to unconstrained dispatch.

(ix) **Security of supply** – The relative impact of border closures for power and primary energy.

(x) **Market structure** – Balancing mechanism, balancing period, market locational model (nodal, zonal, etc.), cost allocation (e.g. between generation and demand), voltage definition of transmission/distribution boundary, etc.

In this chapter we firstly concentrate on electrical location in the form of high voltage transmission, and how this is incorporated into market models. It will become apparent that with increased international energy flow and increased attention on the impact of energy production on the environment, that there must be some way to identify the source of production for consumed electricity. This creates an 'environmental network' for which the transmission network has many useful analogies.

In order to do this, we must first define the various elements of the physical design of the electrical infrastructure, and then construct a combination of mandatory requirements, voluntary bilateral contracts with the system operator and market mechanisms, for participants to engage with. Once defined, our steps are:

(i)   Constructing commercial/market mechanisms for transmission access and usage.
(ii) Creating incentives that can be acted on by generation and demand.
(iii) Modelling participant behaviour under current and prospective market mechanisms to compare market solutions to centrally optimised ones.
(iv) Interlinking the mandatory/commercial/market mechanisms for constraint, losses, stability and redundancy.
(v)   Making the physical and economic modelling transparent[2] enough for generators and consumers to make approximate replicas in order to understand likely costs and hence make appropriate medium and long term decisions.
(vi) Maximising stability of the model from a regulatory perspective so that decisions based on long term signals have reasonably constant economics.
(vii) Maximising the degree to which generators and consumers can lock in infrastructure costs in advance.

Accordingly, we:

(i)   Define the basic elements for modelling and charging.
(ii) Determine the charging mechanisms available to us.
(iii) Determine the classification of electrical location for the purpose of commercial modelling.
(iv) Examine the resulting signalling to transportation, generation and demand for initial siting and ongoing usage.

7.1   INFRASTRUCTURE COSTS TO BE RECOVERED

7.1.1   Build and maintain

Transportation assets have long lives, and indeed the ESI is a sufficiently young industry for much of the installed infrastructure not to have reached its replacement life. Nevertheless,

---

[2] For example DC load flow modelling, which for an AC system is less accurate but more tractable than AC load flow modelling.

substantial maintenance is required for lines, towers, insulators, transformers, breakers, relays, busbars, static var condensers, capacitors and a variety of other equipment.

The need for connection, system reinforcement, construction of lines, towers and ancillary equipment, etc. in relation to new generation or new demand is somewhat different. The true cost incurred by the transportation company is equal to the 'shallow' (nearby) connection cost, plus the long term infrastructure requirements caused by the new load in relation to both current and anticipated loads. This is the 'deep' entry cost. The problem is that with such high cost and long life, allocation of the full cost to the new load that may only be around for a few years, is excessive. Hence the transmission owner must extract the rent from the lines over a longer period of time.

Over and above the build and maintain costs for the transportation owner is the research and development necessary for the application of new equipment for more active management of the system. This is true for distribution as well as transmission companies, since management of distribution networks are becoming more active due to the increase in intermittent embedded generation.

7.1.2 Losses

The treatment of losses is different in the transmission and distribution networks. In transmission, the system operator retains a close identity to losses and has the ability to measure them with real time import and export meters. In distribution, the distribution company commonly has no direct relationship to losses, has a much wider and less certain (underground for example) infrastructure, and exit (i.e. consumer) metering that is commonly late, of low temporal resolution and with varying degrees of correctness.[3] Hence a distribution loss factor is assigned rather than measured and reconciled.

7.1.3 Reactive power

The provision of reactive power by generators is essential to maintain voltage and stability. This provision is costly for the generator, and unless mandatory and uncompensated as part of the statutory grid code (in which case generators load the costs in their prices for real power, which is economically inefficient), requires compensation to the generators. If it is cheaper to do so, the grid can provide reactive power. Since some generation consumes reactive power and different forms of load consume different degrees of reactive power, then it makes sense to charge for metered consumption of reactive power where possible.

7.1.4 Redundancy and security

The general assumption in consumer contracts is that the energy (and capacity) is 'firm'. In an immature market, voluntary demand management and interruptibility is hard to execute and in this situation, system security is a public rather than a private good. This is reinforced by the fact that regardless of private willingness to accept interruption in return for lower prices, lost load has high media and government attention.

---

[3] Apart from the numerous potential data errors, the meter readings record kWh, whilst the actual kW history is important since losses are proportional to the square of the load.

In the absence then of voluntary payment for security of supply, the network operator (and by implication the generators) must levy an involuntary charge for security of supply. Physical features that contribute to security of supply, and which must therefore be compensated somehow are, for example, network redundancy, generator capacity, import arrangements, export reduction arrangements, demand management fee and generator black start.

7.1.5   Cost of constraint

Constraint incurs a cost in real time due to the need to redispatch plant relative to the unconstrained optimum, and the continuation of this causes a long term cost of constraint. This cost is felt by consumers. Constraint cost can be reduced by network build, and hence the system operator must be correctly incentivised to do so.

7.1.6   Commercial losses

'Commercial losses' is a commonly used term for the electricity that is consumed but which is not paid for. Electricity can be dishonestly consumed directly from the distribution network (by wire or transformer), or by a variety of tampering activities with and around the meter.

7.1.7   Wheeling and interconnection

Electricity wheeled the whole way across a country or control area may increase losses or cost of constraint, and in fact would usually do so, since wheeling 'against the flow' is unlikely. This causes an increase in the cost of infrastructure. The effect on system security depends on the interruptibility of the wheeling. If it is interruptible, then security of supply is increased and if it is not then security of supply is usually decreased.

7.2   COUNTERPARTIES FOR PAYMENT AND RECEIPT

A possible ESI design might be to cost transportation on a 'point to point' basis. So, generators sell to the transmission or distribution networks at the respective entry nodes, and consumers pay the networks at the exit nodes, and distribution companies pay transmission companies for electricity at transmission exit/distribution entry and sell to consumers at the distribution exit. This would be enormously complicated for the consumer, and there are numerous complications in relation to reconciliation to the consumer meter.

The common model instead is for the consumer to have a single interface – to the supply company, and for the supply company to pay generators for energy and network operators for transportation. The model could either treat the supply company as collection agent (leading for example, for credit default to incur loss to the network companies) or as retailer (therefore responsible for all costs of getting electricity to the consumer, including the regulated costs). The retailer model is the standard with payment flows as depicted in Figure 4.4.

With increasing deregulation of networks, then there are more network companies to pay, for example, foreign network companies for getting electricity to the border, interconnector companies and independent network operators between the distribution network and the consumer. Different models are possible. For example, the supply company could pay the independent network company and the distribution company, or pay only the independent network company, who then pays the distribution company.

7.3   BASIC CHARGING ELEMENTS FOR LOCATION RELATED CHARGING

The requirements for location related charging are:

(i)   Location signals to generators.
(ii)   Medium term incentive to build network infrastructure for base case require-
       ments – transmission lines, transmission equipment, energy sourcing/capture, generation
       capacity, generation ancillary services.
(iii) Medium term incentive to build network infrastructure for variable requirements
       (capacity and redundancy).
(iv)   Economic treatment of interconnection, and its relationship to energy, capacity, location
       signals and security of supply, wheeling charges.
(v)   Cost recovery and optimisation of spend by the transmission and system operator in
       terms of real estate cost, build, maintain, operate physically, manage energy, losses,
       constraints, ancillary services such as voltage and reserve, and capacity.

We examine below the available charging methods and note at this point that it is very
difficult in practice to recover each cost element exactly once, and absence and double
charging for the same element using different charges, is inevitable.

7.3.1   Connection charges

The connection charge is the charge applied to either generators or consumers when connecting to the network for the first time. We saw in section 2.4.2 that while shallow costs
(infrastructure connecting the load to the grid) are always positive, that deep costs (the
current and future infrastructure reinforcement requirement arising from the new load) could
be positive or negative.

It is quite possible to have no connection charge, and simply amortise the connection
cost and smear across the whole system by collecting just use of system charges. Similarly,
it is possible to charge only generators, only consumers, only generators connected to the
transmission (as distinct from distribution) infrastructure, or only consumers connected only
to the transmission infrastructure.

The standard unit for connection cost is currency per kW installed per year. Since consumption is not known in advance, this must be estimated if charged, and consumption could
be limited to booked capacity provided that the meter data is read and processed at sufficient
(approximately halfhourly) resolution. Similarly, generation would normally be limited to
booked capacity.

As with transmission network use of system charges, it would be ideal to charge in relation
to the kW consumption at the period/s of maximum system demand, but clearly this is not
possible in advance.

Similarly, it would be ideal for connection charges to be reflective of incremental
infrastructure costs. However, there are numerous problems with estimating true deep entry
costs, in establishing an appropriate amortisation period, and with making a transparent
charging mechanism.

7.3.2   Use of system charges

The use of system charge is closely associated with the connection charge, and represents
that part of system build and maintain costs (plus various other costs) that is not captured

by connection charges, plus designated other costs that may include the various forms of frequency response and reserve, reactive power and black start. Ideally, the use of system charges both: (i) respect historic agreements and understandings about future use of system charges when making installation and connection decisions and (ii) correctively incentivise new connections to make system optimal choices (e.g. constraint and loss minimisation) in terms of location and load profile.

The total use of system charge must equal the total system cost, net of other revenues such as connection revenues. Within this constraint, and the basic unit of charging of currency per kW per year, there are numerous dimensions that we examine now.

7.3.2.1   Regional use of system charges

We saw in section 2.3.1.7 how different nodes have different location marginal prices on the day, and in the appendix how we can calculate the node by node marginal cost of new build requirement and how we can create zonal charges from nodal charges. These are the essential ingredients of location based use of system charging. More sophisticated models incorporate losses, security/capacity factors, line redundancy, transfer limits, reactive power and other effects.

7.3.2.2   The generation/demand split for network charging

We see in Chapter 10 on economics that in most situations (those in which all participants have similar knowledge, power, transactional capability and production techniques) that the 'Coase theory' tells us that provided that prices have time to adjust, that it makes no economic difference what the split between generators and demand (suppliers) is. So the total charging base is first divided into the generation percentage and demand percentage, and then collected by zone/node. In principle, provided that the charges are not collared, the generation demand split only makes an absolute difference to charges and not the relative difference between charges between different participants in the same sector.

However, harmonisation between countries/control areas is important. Suppose for example that in country A, generators pay 100 % of charges and country B suppliers pay 100 % of charges, then we can see that power wheeled from A to B may pay 200 %.

In the EU, the standard is for demand (i.e. the supply sector) to pay an aggregate 100 % of the network charge. Whilst the generation sector pays zero in aggregate, some generators could pay and some receive charges.

The lower the demand percentage, the greater the prospect of some consumption areas receiving use of system charges and (if the energy and other costs associated with supply were free) conceivably being paid to consume.

7.3.2.3   Collars for use of system tariffs

In practice system operators prefer not to have negative delivery costs, let alone negative delivered energy costs and can limit the minimum use of system charge to zero. Similarly it is possible to cap charges, for example to satisfy universal service requirements. The financial adjustment from the caps and collars are smeared back into the charges for other participants.

7.3.3   Calculation of capacity cost in relation to system capacity need

In section 10.2.3 we examine in some detail the challenge of calculating capacity costs for periodic or trending capacity for different participants. We can summarise this by saying that the incremental costs for the system operator incurred by one participant are greatest if the period of maximum demand for the participant coincides with the period of maximum system demand.

In the extreme, for consumers with halfhourly meters, the system operator can charge (the supply company, who charges the consumer) retrospectively on the basis of the consumption for the halfhour that proved to have the highest demand. However, since the consumer does not know which period this is, there is no incentive to save system capacity costs by reducing demand in these periods. The use of system charge would also be highly variable, which would be a problem for consumers. The system operator can instead charge on the basis of not the highest system consumption halfhour but the average of the highest n halfhours, where n ranges from about 3 to about 20. Alternatively the system operator can publish his anticipated high demand periods and charge for them. This has the problem that consumers could end up paying near zero capacity charges by substantial consumption reduction in those halfhours without saving the system much money since the peak times may prove *ex post* to be different from those *ex ante*, and because aggregate demand is only a coarse measure of system costs and does not take into account local costs.

For consumers without halfhourly meters, then a profile estimate has to be applied, and the capacity charge is then applied to the energy consumption, on the assumption that the capacity/energy ratio is reasonably constant.

7.3.4   Losses

Loss costs are applied separately to the transmission and distribution sectors, and can have different splits of generator and demand costs, just as for use of system costs.

7.3.4.1   Transmission losses

Electrical losses on the high voltage grid are relatively low compared to distribution losses. Typical losses in the developed economies, which are more densely populated than developing economies, are of the order of 2%–4%. There is still a strong incentive to reduce transmission losses since the total amount of money lost is high as the gross amount of electricity sent out to the grid is high and the carbon dioxide output associated with these losses is high in absolute terms.

Losses can be reduced by:

(i)   Reducing net flow and distance, by dispatching plant nearer the demand.
(ii) Flow routing, for example the path of least resistance. Electricity will do this by itself, but the configuration of breakers in the network for loss minimisation (i.e. all closed) is different to that for least cost of redispatch to resolve constraints.
(iii) Improving physical performance (for example reducing resistance by increasing line redundancy, or reducing line losses by raising voltage or using direct current) and technological performance (for example, resistance, inductance, electrical leaks and transformer losses).
(iv) Physical changes such as raising voltages, using direct current for long lines, and adding lines.

Over the long term, the fleet of generation units can affect losses by altering the choice of which units close and are built in response to the location signal. In the short term, losses act as a netting off of generation submitted to the grid and this can act as an economic signal. However the incremental loss incurred from a unit of generation from any unit is dependent on the flows from all of the other units, and hence (i) this requires *ex ante* iteration to optimise, and (ii) the model is complex.

The incremental losses for each generator could be calculated using the method described in the appendix. However, the sum of true incremental losses does not equal the total loss, because of the variation of redispatch with load. In practice, real time calculation of incremental transmission losses to be used for commercial charging is currently excessively complicated for what is a relatively small cost factor in the total cost of delivered power and hence approximate and average methods are used.

The relative positioning of energy sources, convenient sites for power stations and demand, and the changing[4] of these means that there is commonly a net flow of electricity over a long distance (hundreds/thousands of kilometres).

7.3.4.2   Market models for losses

There is much commonality between loss reduction and constraint reduction. Losses can be handled commercially in a number of ways. For example[5]:

(i)   Marginal losses included in location marginal prices (New York, New Zealand). In this model, the marginal price at each node takes into account both the effect of redispatch to avoid line overload due to a generation/load increment at the node and the financial cost/benefit of the change in marginal total losses from the increment. Here then, losses are recovered at the margin and hence total loss recovery is not equal to total losses. Either payments must be adjusted *pro rata*, or an extra mechanism used for the remaining charge/benefit.

(ii)   Average marginal loss factors applied to generators and loads. In this model, the total losses are calculated as a percentage of all generation input to the system entry points, and this percentage is debited evenly from all generation and load at the same percentage. In Ireland the cost is 100 % to generators. In Argentina and New South Wales it is/was shared. In Victoria the cost was 100 % to loads. In Great Britain it is 45 %/55 %. So, if the loss is 4 %, and the cost is shared equally between generators and load, then generators are credited with 98 MW for every 100 MW delivered to system entry point, and load pays for 102.1 MW for every 100 MW withdrawn. This can be done on an *ex post* actual basis or an *ex ante* basis based on estimates.

(iii) Average losses netted against load at grid supply point. This is specific to the supply points and then generation and load is credited/charged according to electrical distance to the supply point.

(iv)   System administrator buys losses from the market (e.g. in Alberta). In this method, the system operator treats itself as demand in which it consumes an energy amount equal to the losses. Everyone initially gets/pays 100 % of generation/demand but the system operator recovers the cost of losses through other charges.

---

[4] In industrialising economies, energy sourcing, power generation, and demand are commonly relatively close. In the 'post industrial' economies, the separation increases. For example, in the UK there is a demographic movement from North to South and in the USA from the Midwest to the South West. Both away from the long term industrial centres and source of coal.

[5] Drawn largely from Sustman and Brown (2004).

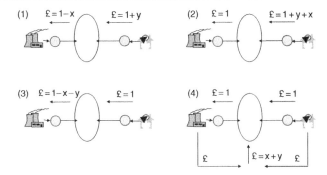

Figure 7.1 Examples of loss charging allocation for 1 MW at the balancing point. (1) Generators and suppliers pay according to the estimate of their incremental losses[6] on getting electricity to/from the balancing point, (2) Suppliers pay for 100 of losses, (3) Generators pay for 100 % of losses, (4) Losses paid for through another mechanism such as use of system charges and imbalance net revenues

7.3.5 Locational element of balancing

In pool markets, the cost of constraint and potentially other regional factors can be calculated from the total generation cost paid between successive[7] trial schedules. Pool prices are of postage stamp (or postage stamp with market split) variety but it is still quite possible to add a regional cost/benefit at nodal or zonal basis on a halfhourly basis to generators prior to dispatch.

In bilateral markets, the cost of constraint and other location factors can be estimated by the generator redispatch done by the system operator using the balancing mechanism, relative to either the physical notification, or the system operator estimate of likely outturn.

With respect to balancing income, units on both sides of the constraint can make extra income from locational balancing. This problem is frequently referred to and gaming effects are closely examined by regulators.

7.3.6 Locational element of reserve and security

The provision of reserve is generally[8] agreed bilaterally between the provider and the system operator. The system operator can apply discriminatory pricing and need not use a clearing price for the various forms of reserve. Therefore reserve is *de facto* priced on a regional basis. Just as with balancing for constraints, the cost of redispatch for reserve and security reasons can be costed on a real time basis.

7.3.7 Regional structure for cross subsidy

The requirement for universal service includes the requirement to provide electricity to rural areas at prices not substantially different to those in urban areas. Since distribution costs

---

[6] The definition used for ease of illustration is that generators must produce $1 + x$ MW to get 1 MW to the balancing point, and that suppliers must buy $1 + y$ MW at the balancing point in order to get 1 MW.

[7] Clearly the ordering of trial schedule is important.

[8] The system operator is the only consumer of reserve. However it is possible to apply a mandatory requirement for reserve which could then be procured rather than produced.

per unit of energy delivered are higher (longer lines to build and maintain and to incur thermal losses over), then this cost must be cross subsidised. The choices are (i) government subsidies, (ii) subsidy from the rest of the regional distribution area ('in area' cross subsidy), (iii) subsidy from other distribution areas ('out of area' cross subsidy) and (iv) subsidy from the transmission system operator via smeared network charges and (v) subsidy from the market operator via smeared energy levies. In Great Britain, out of area cross subsidy is used to subsidise from the whole transmission charging base to the distribution charging base in sparsely populated areas of Scotland. On the generation side, the debate continues as to whether renewable generation should pay a full deep entry charge, or shallow entry accompanied by smearing of infrastructure costs across the whole network charging base.

7.3.7.1   Metering cross subsidies

As is evident from section 2.5, metering costs can be a significant component of the final consumer bill. The sparser the population or consuming asset density of the supplier's customer base, the more expensive the journey time from meter to meter.

7.3.8   Constraints

7.3.8.1   Transmission constraints over the long term

We see in section 5.1.5 how we can handle transmission constraints in the centrally managed system using trial schedules, and in section 2.3.1.7 how transmission constraints can result in location marginal prices that are higher than the most expensive plant on the system. The incremental value of alleviating constraint is the potential congestion rent that is compared to the cost of build and maintaining transmission line (as well as comparing with other things such as the cost of migrating production and demand, and the effect of new build on other factors such as line losses).

For very small increments in transmission infrastructure, we can calculate the congestion rent available from line relief and could in theory pay this through regional connection or use of system charges to the network company. However, transmission investments tend to be both 'lumpy' (large) and long term, and hence the total rent is not equal to the marginal rent times the MW capacity increase, and in addition the transmission company calculates the future as well as current flow patterns in the consideration of infrastructure investments.

7.3.8.2   Transmission constraint on the day

A method of optimising a constrained system is to take a two step approach. This is firstly to 'clear' the stack, ignoring constraints, and then to clear again the stack each side of the transmission constraint. This method is described in more detail for the pool in section 5.4. It has transparency to generating units and hence has advantages (in enabling incentives) and disadvantages (in enabling gaming).

Using location marginal pricing, there is a clearer connection between dispatch and locational prices.

7.3.9   Reactive power

Reactive power has some similarity to constraint as it does create a line limit. Reactive power solution does not incur long term large investment in transmission and distribution lines, but concerns more the behaviour and the installation of point assets (generation units and static var compensators). Reactive power requirement and provision is not coincident with active power requirement and provision since producers can either require or provide reactive power. Hence it is not appropriate to load reactive power costs onto energy prices. The need for reactive power is regional and hence there is a *de facto* regional structure to the prices for reactive power.

Reactive power consumption is metered and charged per kvarh above an agreed limit of power factor.

7.4   MODELS FOR DESIGNATION OF ELECTRICAL LOCATION

Here we describe the alternative methods for designating the electrical location of a point on the network, for the purposes of charging. As with the consideration of electricity across time, the tradeoff is between the high accuracy of high granularity and the tractable management and high liquidity of coarse charging.

It is common in practice to use one form of electrical location designation for one charge and another form for a different charge.

7.4.1   Postage stamp

In postage stamp pricing all points are equivalent in terms of connection and use of system charging. The postage stamp area is generally a country or a control area. Postage stamp is the simplest design, and hence the most common in immature markets. This method has the advantage of concentrating liquidity and therefore allowing higher time granularity. One disadvantage of the method is that it is not suitable for very large areas (more than hundreds of km), particularly if there is a long distance gradient of the prices of primary energy. Such a gradient commonly exists along the pipelines from concentrated sources of gas production, or across land masses from sources of coal production, import or export. This causes a step change in prices across control areas. If the control areas are within one country then this incentivises effective penetration of the distribution network from the cheaper area to the more expensive area. The other obvious disadvantage of the method is that there are no locational signals within the control area and hence it leads to less efficient locational structure of generation and demand, and a smearing of increased transmission costs on well located plant and poorly located plant alike.

Figure 7.2   Zonal pricing – prices are the same at all points within the control area

7.4.2 Zonal

Zones are groupings of nodes. A zone is drawn using the electrical rather than geographical map of the country. Within a zone,[9] all producers are treated equally and all consumers are treated equally. Within each zone, the pricing is postage stamp. Relative to the postage stamp method, this allows locational signals for some elements of connection and use of system without making the model too hard to understand. This significantly reduces the problem of long distance price gradients, but does not handle more local issues such as constraints and redundancy very well. Zonal pricing is commonly used for annual use of system charging.

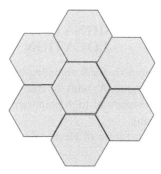

Figure 7.3   Zonal pricing

In Brazil zonal prices are found by designating four fixed zones, and the model assumes no constraints within the zone. The zonal prices are then dependent on the constraints on the tie-lines between zones. The impact of constraining and deconstraining within a zone on the interzone pricing is introduced in the appendix.

7.4.3 Postage stamp with market splitting

The method of market splitting offers a compromise between the purity of location marginal pricing and the liquidity offered by postage stamp pricing. There are several zones (approximately between two and ten), but for short term pricing, they all have the same prices unless there is a constraint between them.

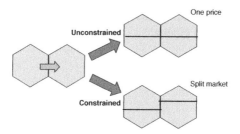

Figure 7.4   Postage stamp with market splitting

---

[9] Commonly the producer zones are mapped differently to the consumer zones.

There are variants, but one method of determining the zonal prices is as follows:

(i)   The system operator first performs an unconstrained trial schedule for the system.
(ii)   If the trial schedule is not infeasible due to constraints then the whole market will clear at one price.
(iii) If the trial schedule is not feasible due to the constraint, then the redispatch to solve the constraint is run.
(iv)   The clearing price is then solved for the group of unconstrained zones either side of the constraint.
(v)   If a zone is a net exporter, then it receives from the neighbouring zone the clearing price of the neighbouring zone.
(vi)   If a zone is a net importer, then it pays the neighbouring zone its own clearing price.

Noting from section 2.3.1.8 and the appendix that the effect of constraints can be long reaching, the solution is not perfect, but in practice captures the main effects of long range constraint

This method is used in Germany and Italy, and Nordpool.

7.4.4 Nodal

The full nodal model is an extension of the zonal model, such that each major bus[10] has its own price. Whilst the zonal model is drawn on a geographical map, the nodal model is far more electrical in emphasis.

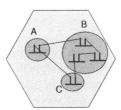

Figure 7.5   The nodal pricing structure. Here, the nodes (buses) in B trade additionally as a hub

From the perspective of an efficient free market in which the problem of market power and gaming is solved, and all participants have perfect knowledge, then nodal pricing is the 'best' mechanism.

It is possible for the market to have a smaller number of nodes than there are buses, in which case there is a 'basis' differential between the bus and the node, which might be simple (distance from bus to fixed node) or complex (cheapest to deliver to different nodes). NEMMCO in Australia charges forward looking losses with respect to the 'swing bus' (equivalent to a balancing point but actual instead of notional) for the delivery period, which therefore is closely related[11] to electrical distance to node.

---

[10] The terms 'bus' and 'node' are generally interchangeable in this context. 'Bus' tends to be used for physical description and 'node' for market and modelling description. In market and modelling terms, it is possible to represent a zone with several buses as a node.

[11] We can see in the appendix that reference to a specific node makes our calculations much easier as if we put 1MW in/out of the system we know where the market model determines that the energy goes out/comes in.

Brazil collects 50 % of transmission system costs each from generation and demand. Of this, 20 % of this is charged nodally, and the balance is charged by the postage stamp method.

In PJM, groups of buses trade as hubs of between three and 237 buses, with the hub price being calculated using equal weights for each.

7.4.4.1   Grouping of nodes

Investment and operational decisions use market prices as signals. When those signals are absent in terms of current active trading for the periods/locations in question, then the market participants require sufficient market transparency for them to estimate the market prices that will eventually be realised. If the number of nodes is equal to the number of transmission entry points, plus the number of transmission exit points plus all other transmission buses, then there is effectively no transparency, and no prospective liquidity.

By grouping the nodes, the complexity reduces significantly. Groups of buses can form a single node and if the number of nodes is large, then they are grouped in zones:

There are various choices for pricing within the zones.

(i)   All buyers and all sellers see the same energy price, although they may be charged different fees for transmission fixed capacity costs, balancing and ancillary services, and losses.

(ii)   Price formulae such as 'cheapest to deliver', in which the generator can deliver to any bus at the nodal price, and the consumer can withdraw from any bus plus/minus a 'basis' relative to the cheapest to deliver price.

7.4.4.2   Hub/virtual node/balancing point

It is common for there to be a point on the system that is a single reference for a larger area. It may be a single node, but more commonly will be a group of nodes which, through a pricing mechanism between them form a hub, or for there to be a 'balancing point' or 'virtual node'. This is a useful concept as it serves to add liquidity to the market, which most trades being at the balancing point, and a smaller number of trades arranging to get power from the balancing point to a specific node or back.

For a system with n nodes, there is a maximum possible $\frac{1}{2} n(n+1)$ 'point to point' nodal connections for trading purposes, which dilutes liquidity. There are only n 'point to hub' connections to the balancing point.[12] The liquidity concentration analogy is very similar to the role of currency outlined in section 10.1.3.

7.4.4.3   Nodal/zonal mixtures

Various mixtures are possible. For example, the Argentinian system has a system load centre, nominally near Buenos Aires which is called the Market Node. There is a market price at this node, and basis prices at other nodes that are calculated according to electrical distance from the node. When there are constraints, then the market splits into local zones with local prices at the nominal local market node, with the split not being according to predetermined zones but according to nodes affected by the congestion.

---

[12] A 'round' system benefits by more than a 'long' system from this effect.

7.4.5 Implicit locational differentials

It is quite possible to have no explicit locational charging structure but for there to be an implicit locational variation in contracts between generators and the system operator and (to a lesser extent) between consumers and the system operator.

There are two types of variation:

(i) **Pricing variation** – Where the system operator can engage bilaterally, and on a monopoly basis, for example for ancillary services, then the price for the service is likely to depend greatly on the extent to what the system operator needs in a particular location. Black start is a good example, for which the system operator requires several geographically dispersed sites.

(ii) **Acceptance variation** – For example, the system operator has discretion on which balancing offers to accept to maximise system security, and is not bound by a merit order. Acceptance likelihood can be affected by electrical position.

7.4.6 Control area

Different control areas have different rules, regional structures, allocations between generation and demand, allocation of imbalance costs and net imbalance revenues and several other aspects. Full harmonisation between control areas takes some time, and hence exporting power must observe the rules of the host control area. Where this creates a *de facto* cross subsidy (for example by exporting or importing synchronous power without supporting system stability,[13] or by not paying use of system charges) a border levy is sometimes applied.[14]

7.4.7 Position in voltage hierarchy

In general, the generators connect the high voltage system and consumers to the low voltage system, and hence we can take a hierarchic view of the flow of energy. However, consumers do connect at different voltages, including direct connection to high voltage transmission, and smaller generators do connect ('embed') at low voltage into the distribution system.

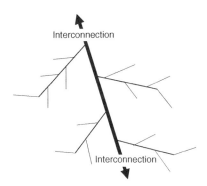

Figure 7.6 Hierarchic representation of high voltage 'radial' grid with no loop flow

---

[13] This happens, for example, from the import from Serbia to Kosovo.
[14] For example in the Czech Republic.

Whilst electrical flow on transmission lines commonly reverses in direction, distribution systems are predominantly unidirectional.

7.5   NODAL ENERGY PRICES, VIRTUAL TRANSMISSION AND NODAL MARKET CONTRACTS

7.5.1   Market models

We have established how nodal prices are formed using generation and demand stacks, but it is not obvious how we can establish nodal prices in a competitive forward energy market with monopoly transportation.

Consider a simple system with a node A being a net importer (source), and node B being a net exporter (sink), and suppose that there is a virtual market node C.

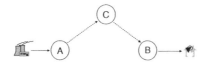

Figure 7.7   Depiction of simple system with balancing point

There are six kinds of 'legs' of trades:

(i)   generators selling at node A;
(ii)   suppliers buying at node A;
(iii)   generators selling at node B;
(iv)   suppliers buying at node B;
(v)   generators selling at C;
(vi)   suppliers buying at node C.

Clearly suppliers at node A and generators at node B have no locational issues to worry about in this context.

Generators at A may sell[15] at A and expect suppliers to transmit[16] the power to their consumers, or may sell at B so that the supplier does not have to transmit the power, or sell at C in which case both parties have to transmit power but location and transmission trades both maximise the use of market liquidity.

To produce day ahead (or any other time when there is a concentration of liquidity) locational marginal prices in the spot or forward market, the system operator needs: (i) generation and demand stacks at each node, (ii) system topology and constraints (including security limits) and (iii) a locational pricing algorithm. This is very possible for the day ahead and still possible in real time (when liquidity is less and the stack is cleared continually rather

---

[15] 'Sell' here means enter into a financial transaction at node A, followed by a dispatch at node A.

[16] Transmission is financial and means pay the difference between the nodal prices.

than in batch mode), but how can the forward nodal market work? Some solutions are set out below:

(i)   Only the balancing point could trade forward, with the participants submitting physical notifications, and finding out *ex post* with no prior indication from the system operator what the transmission cost is.[17] For constrained systems, this includes the redispatch cost from post notification balancing as constraint resolution would not occur in the forward market.

(ii)   All nodes as well as the balancing point could trade. The system operator could indicate location marginal prices from the estimation of prospective day ahead generation and demand stacks, whilst making no commitment.

(iii)   Nodal price indication by the system operator could be from estimates of demands, estimated (from history and present) generator availabilities and offers, and associated location marginal costs.

(iv)   The system operator could support estimation of nodal prices by participants by provision of a/the location marginal price model, with system bus and line information. In a similar vein, the generation incumbents retained the system operator's generation and order loading model in the England and Wales pool.

(v)   The system operator could act as monopoly market maker in node to node (and balancing point, etc.) and engage in transactions in all timeframes. The tender would have to be continuous and open. Prices would be proprietary, and in the absence of discrete tranches the system operator would need to use volume estimates and generator price estimates. The system operator naturally assumes a risk/speculative position through the rational use of information.

(vi)   The system operator, in cooperation with the power exchange could continually clear[18] the market using acceptances from bid and offer stacks lodged at each node. The dilution of concentration of liquidity in this situation would cause high volatility of nodal prices.

(vii)   The system operator could clear the transmission market in auctioned tranches (at low time and space resolution in order to concentrate liquidity). So while nodal trading in the secondary market could happen at any time, nodal swaps with the system operator would happen only in tranches. The first tranche could be years ahead of outturn and would be for a fixed percentage of system capacity. Since generator hedge requirements in the forward market exceed consumer hedge requirements then this can cause forward market distortions, although rational speculative behaviour should reduce this.

For each of the above, losses could be included or treated separately.

7.5.1.1 Nodal pricing in Pennsylvania-New Jersey – Maryland (PJM)

Locational Marginal Pricing (LMP) has been practiced in PJM since 1998, and it is the most advanced LMP market. The System Operator calculates prices over 8,000 nodes every five minutes, to be averaged for each hour, and publishes real time, day ahead and past data.

The primary market, as described in section 5.10, is the day ahead market, and this forms the indices used for the LMP and Financial Transmission Rights/Responsibilities (FTR's) markets.

---

[17] It is quite possible to receive net negative value for generation. See the appendix for explanation of negative node value.

[18] In theory, this is a kind of tâtonnement process as described in section 10.1.8.4.

Participants notify at their local bus (node) but can trade financial transmission rights (i.e. options) and financial transmission responsibilities (i.e. forwards, called obligations in PJM). FTR obligations are financially equivalent to nodal swaps – so the price of A–B plus the price of B–A equals zero. FTR rights have a minimum price equal to the FTR obligation and hence, using standard option terminology, have a zero strike price.

There is therefore a full nodal market, with a good degree of transparency in calculating likely costs for nodal swaps (i.e. 'transmission'). Financial transmission rights and responsibilities have annual and monthly auctions with the system operator, as well as having a secondary market.

The annual FTR auction applies for the whole capacity of the system over a calendar year and is conducted in four tranches of 25 % of volume. Transactions in each round can be netted against transactions in the next round/s. Time resolution is peak and off peak. The annual FTR resolution is limited to hubs, zones, aggregates generators and interface buses. The optimisation engine ensures feasibility of the rights and obligations (obligations net against each other) using a DC load flow model.

The (calendar) monthly FTR auctions are conducted at full nodal level and apply to residual capacity from the annual auctions. Participants can only sell rights that they hold, although since there are indices, then participants can hedge bilaterally in the over the counter market. Since the FTR auctions includes options, then it generates revenue from the option premiums.

In PJM, auction revenue rights (ARR's) precede the FTR auctions. They are allocated to firm transmission service customers. They can be converted to FTRs in the annual FTR auction or converted to revenues from the annual FTR auction revenues.

The PJM website contains a substantial amount of information about the operation of the PJM market.

7.5.1.2 One way financial transmission responsibility, financial basis swaps, and locational contracts for difference

Suppose that the buyer has purchased (in the pool or bilateral market) electricity at node A and requires it at node B (either to satisfy a wholesale sale, a supply base, or for own consumption). He may buy it at A, notify it at B and engage a financial transmission responsibility FTR contract with the system operator or in the secondary market to 'transmit' it from A to B.

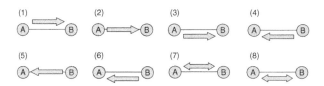

Figure 7.8 Some arrangements for virtual transmission. An arrow above the line denotes the market participant's option to virtually transmit or not, an arrow on the line denotes an obligation on both sides and an arrow below the line denotes non firmness on the part of the system operator

In the short term, the system operator satisfies the FTR by transmitting with available capacity, and by redispatch if the lines are constrained. In the longer term, FTR prices can be used to guide transmission infrastructure investment, and conceivably fund directly from the congestion rent.

If the buyer cannot, for whatever reason, consume the power (for example a downturn in consumer demand), then the surplus energy at B must be resold (or 'spilled' to the real time market or balancing mechanism), and the price could be negative for both locational (see appendix) and balancing (cost to deload inflexible generation) reasons. Similarly, an unanticipated increase in demand at node B must be fulfilled by energy purchase at B or top up power at B in the balancing mechanism.

Suppose that the energy seller defaults on the contract. Again the FTR responsibility remains, and the buyer must source more energy at point A (to consume at B) to fulfil the financial transmission responsibility.

FTR's effectively make a nodal market since the combination of a local price and a transmission price makes prices for all nodes, and provided that there is an index,[19] contracts for differences can be executed for nodal prices and FTR's.

The flow based coupling that is being developed[20] in EuroPEX is very similar to a basis swap. Two coupled markets may have different prices, and a purchase in one area and sale in another will be accompanied by a financial transmission trade. Similarly if two markets have auctions to clear the price in each, then an implicit transmission auction can take place at the same time which will then clear the whole area, and transmit power from one area to the other subject to border capacity.

The addition of liquidity here is much enhanced by the presence of a balancing point.

7.5.1.3   One way financial transmission right – basis option

This is identical to the one way financial responsibility, except that it is a right (option, with a zero strike price) rather than a responsibility.

Generators have a natural exposure to failure variation, and may therefore have some use for the optional element of one way financial transmission rights. So, a generator failure would be accommodated by a purchase of energy at A and financial flow from A to B (netting to a purchase at B).

The New England ISO works in a similar manner. A counterparty buying at one node and selling at another has an uncertain congestion cost. The financial transmission right is an option on the congestion cost, struck at zero. The FTR is financial and is not necessarily accompanied by physical trades.

Transmission system operators cannot easily gauge the probability of exercise of the option and hence have to reserve capacity for full exercise, no exercise, or partial exercise.

7.5.1.4   Two way financial transmission rights – put and call basis option

This is identical to two one way financial rights (options), one in each direction. Suppliers have a natural exposure to demand variation either side of the expectation. The generation that satisfies the demand can almost certainly reduce load to accommodate demand reduction and can commonly increase to accommodate demand increase. So if supply requirement is $Q \pm \Delta$ then the supplier may engage in a one way financial transmission responsibility for Q and a two way financial transmission right (option) for Δ.

---

[19] Whilst pool markets concentrate liquidity to form a high quality index, physical markets have in practice less concentration of liquidity in the prompt market and do not necessarily produce high quality indexes.

[20] There were earlier attempts. For example, the TXU grid in 2001 was an ambitious plan to connect all of the power exchanges and other compatible markets of Europe together with one way financial transmission responsibilities. Unfortunately TXU Europe became bankrupt before this was realised.

Note that this position is identical to the transaction of an FTR obligation of $Q - \Delta$ and a one way FTR right (in the same direction) of 2Δ, or an FTR obligation of $Q + \Delta$ and a one way FTR right (in the opposite direction) of 2Δ. Readers familiar with traded options may recognise this as put-call parity.

7.5.1.5   Non firm financial transmission – non firm basis swap

In theory, transmission trades of all kinds could be 'non firm', meaning that either party can exercise the option not to fulfil their obligation. There is in fact a spectrum of firmness. At one extreme, the non firmness is simply an option, that will be 'ruthlessly' exercised whenever advantageous to the option holder. At the other extreme, only *force majeur* or similar situations would allow invocation of the non firmness. In the middle is a range of possibilities, mainly allowing a degree of protection from liquidated damages and disallowing exercise of the option for purely economic rather than capability reasons. Vaguely defined non firmness is generally an anathema to markets, and non firmness other than fully ruthless is particularly unsuitable for financial transactions.

7.5.1.6   Dedicated physical trades

While financial transmission trades are 'contract path' trades, which are only related to the physical paths by the system marginal cost determined by the system operator, physical or 'flowgate' trades refer to the physical transmission, and would generally only apply in very specific situations such as interconnectors.

7.5.1.7   Marginal and average congestion rent

Location marginal pricing acts, as the name suggests, at the margin. Therefore any congestion rent that can be captured clearly only applies at the margin. If line constraints and generator stacks are discrete rather than continuous, then the congestion rent also has discrete steps, and the potential congestion rent from alleviating a constraint should take into account the volume relieved.

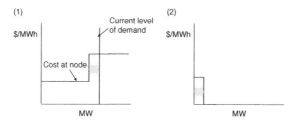

Figure 7.9   (1) Clearing price at the node in relation to demand, (2) Congestion rent available, given the demand level shown in (1)

7.5.2   Transmission allocation at system borders

The pricing mechanisms above refer principally to trades within a system operator control area. Trades between control areas are different because each system operator separately optimises his own area, rather than the whole area.

There are a variety of mechanisms, which can be applied both on a day ahead, or a long term reserved basis:

(i)   **First come first served** – The system operator publishes access prices in advance and sells them to all comers until there is no spare capacity.
(ii) **Pro rata** – On the day capacity is rationed in some way, for example as a ratio to bid capacity.
(iii) **Implicit auction** (market split, e.g. Argentina).
(iv) **Explicit auction** (e.g. Tennet in the Netherlands) – Transmission rights for each period in the future (possibly day ahead) are auctioned.
(v)   **Internal redispatch** (one ISO).
(vi) **Conditional redispatch**.
(vii) **Mixed** – For example, rights may be reserved for a particular period by auction of first come first served, after which time, the capacity becomes use it or lose it, and some or all participants can compete.

Whatever the method, the transmission system operators must be compensated for their costs. Wheeling and net interconnector flow must be paid for and we saw in Figure 2.30 and in the appendix that the joining of two countries both with balanced supply and demand could cause cross border flows. The revenue can either be derived from annual charging across control areas, or by live pricing mechanisms such as live capacity auctions. Charging can be centralised, and in Europe there are moves towards this. A commercial scheme operating across several control areas would require:

(i)   Within the overall costs incurred by a TSO, allocation of costs related to national transmission services and cross-border exchanges.
(ii) Computation of total revenue needed at pan-area level to cover the costs related to cross-border exchanges.
(iii) Computation of the value of the pan-area charges by dividing the required total revenue by the sum of the expected programmed cross-border exchanges.
(iv) Payment of the pan-area charges by market participants who export electricity.
(v)   Collection of the TSO revenues related to exports.
(vi) Redistribution of the collected revenues according to a measurement of the cross-border exchanges based on hourly measurement of energy flow at the tie-lines.

Making consistent charging over large interconnected control areas is a significant challenge. Some of the issues are:

(i)   Physical constraints for interconnector flows.
(ii) Different regulatory regimes, rule details, 'basis' prices vs. headline prices, smearing, balancing, cross subsidy, etc.
(iii) Different tax burdens on generation and supply on either side of border. Border taxation.
(iv) Import restrictions on energy tagged with environmental load.
(v)   Absolute restrictions on cross border permit trades, and general friction to permit trading such as legal risk.
(vi) Use of prices design to provide signals at the margin, giving 'unfair' revenue to under-developed transmission systems and insufficient compensation for prior investments.

7.5.3 Connection allocation

Allocation of connections to transmission grids has much in common with interconnector allocation, with the principal difference being the long term and discrete nature of connections. An additional mechanism that can be used for connection allocation is the interactive method, in which participants pay for or are given options for connection for specific time periods, after which allocation is interactive, and the limited connection availability goes to the first to commit to the full connection charge.

7.5.4 Integration of location based charging elements

Since the signal to site and utilise generation and consumption units can be provided in different ways, it is as easy to double count[21] the signal as it is for the signal to be absent. An example is nodal pricing and location related use of system charges. Whilst the drivers to these charges are not identical, there is an overlap. The general trend is towards nodal pricing, facilitated by the increasing sophistication of ESI participants to understand the system and the increasing memory and computational power of computers. Location dependent annual charges for use of system within a control area is currently relatively uncommon[22] and to some extent is regarded as an alternative to location dependent spot prices. The ideal is to have a full set of location related charges, designed in a complementary manner. It is important in the encouragement of generation build that participants have a reasonable capability to fix their forward charges.

7.6   THE ENERGY COMPLEX

The interaction of all the factors that we have described in this book can create fairly rapid (days to months) changes in flow at continental to intercontinental level. Below are set out some recent examples affecting Europe.

7.6.1 Case examples

7.6.1.1 System interconnectivity

France in 2003. August 2003 provides an excellent example of the long range nature of the energy complex and the relationship between energy sources, technical factors, weather and national differences in environmental policy.

The summer was particularly hot. Whilst water bodies are generally resilient to changes in atmospheric temperature, the heat was sustained enough for them to heat up. This created two problems for nuclear power stations. Firstly, the reduced ability to transport heat away created efficiency loss and increased problems upstream in the plant due to higher temperatures. Secondly, the greater ambient temperature of the water bodies decreased their ecological ability to assimilate and contend with more heat. Since France produces 78 % of its electricity from nuclear power this was a systemic problem, akin to a 'type fault'.[23] France is a

---

[21] Double count can be avoided by payments between the charging methods. For example, if all participants pay non regional use of system charges, they could be rebated part of the excess revenues from on the day regional costs, for example for offsetting losses.

[22] e.g. Great Britain, Greece, Ireland and Italy. For an international survey of transmission charges, see Shuttleworth and Gammons (2004).

[23] A type fault is a systemic fault shared by all plant in a particular family.

substantial net exporter and such a large loss of power generation meant that France needed to import electricity, and with extensive interconnection, had the capability to do so. At that time in the UK, gas prices had recently risen due in part to the increasing role of the Bacton-Zeebrugge[24] interconnector in connecting UK prices to continental gas prices (which were for legacy as much as economic reasons, connected to the price of Brent crude oil). This meant that combined cycle gas turbines (CCGT's) had relatively recently changed from running baseload to running cyclic load and temporary mothballing.[25] Hence there was spare power generation capacity and spare pipeline capacity. The UK CCGT's picked up the load, and reversed the flow of the UK France power interconnector. The gas interconnector reversed flow from Belgium to the UK. The reversal of the gas interconnector drew gas into Europe from Norway, Russia and Algeria. Imports of Uranium from Africa to France reduced over time by an amount equivalent to the lost power generation. So, hot weather in France reduced the net flow of primary energy from West Africa to France, increased it from North Africa to Italy and Russia to Central Europe, and reversed the flows of gas and power between the UK and the continent.

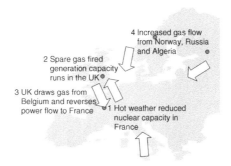

Figure 7.10   Energy flow changes arising from hot weather in France

Great Britain in 2005. In Great Britain, the percentage of power generation that is gas fired is increasing, but the infrastructure build (storage, gas interconnection, pipelines from UK continental shelf, liquefied natural gas infrastructure) has lagged. The system was particularly exposed to unusual coldness in the winter of 2005/6. Since it is undesirable and impractical to curtail[26] residential gas consumption (which is highly sensitive to cold), then amongst the contingency measures was to relax the specification for imported gas, burn non standard fuel at combined cycle gas turbines (CCGT's), to turn off CCGT's, to run coal and oil fired stations beyond normal load, normal hours and normal environmental limits to make up the CCGT shortfall and to drop voltage to reduce power flow.

---

[24] Bacton is on the East of England and Zeebrugge is in Belgium.

[25] Temporary closure.

[26] Whilst electricity can be cut off centrally, gas cannot because of the risk of air ingress through open gas valves, causing an explosive air/gas mix. To curtail gas, the user must close the valve. The potential gas shortages due to high consumption due to extreme weather had high media and political profile in the UK, but at the time of going to print, there had been no centrally administered interruption of gas supplies.

7.6.1.2   Examples of global supply and demand influence

China in 2004. China has enjoyed an economic boom in the early 2000's that is unprecedented in volume in global terms. Being the world's largest steam coal producer and consumer, the swing in volume in steam coal and coking coal for steelmaking had a substantial effect on the international price of coal – and of freight and ships. This had a significant effect on the price of European coal, partly because producers could charge more and partly due to explicit links between domestic and international prices. This temporarily accelerated the shift to gas fired generation and stimulated the liquified natural gas market.

Russia in the 2000's. Western Europe is becoming increasingly dependent on natural gas and with North Sea supplies depleting, Liquified Natural Gas infrastructure being relatively undeveloped and pipeline capacity constraints from North Africa, much of the gas comes from Russia, and ends up going through many countries as far away as Ireland. The gas actually comes from Siberia, which is as far from Moscow as London is, and nearer Japan and China. The Russian economy is growing and it is a common journey to change from commodity export to product export. A change from gas export to electricity export to product export could be envisaged.

Figure 7.11   Migration from primary energy export to product export

7.6.2   Global opinion

Nuclear power in Europe. The social and political climate on nuclear power changes slowly but constantly. In Europe, the most significant effect was the diametrically opposed policies in adjacent France and Italy. France has extensive nuclear power (and very little other power) and substantial exports. Italy curtailed its nuclear power in 1987 after a referendum. British and German policies continue to change around a neutral to slightly negative stance and both have nuclear power but no current nuclear build. Great Britain imports from France and Germany imports from the Czech Republic. At the time of going to print, the possibility of nuclear power in Great Britain was being examined with increasing seriousness.

The carbon dioxide debate is of great significance to the nuclear sector, and since European nations have fixed quotas of CO_2 from the Kyoto protocol, there is increased impetus to procure imports without a CO_2 shadow price.[27] As a result the Italian incumbent, Enel, entered into a cooperation agreement with Electricité de France in 2005 for the joint development of a nuclear power generation programme.

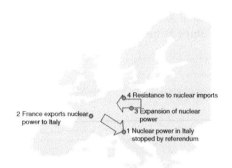

4 Resistance to nuclear imports

3 Expansion of nuclear power

1 Nuclear power in Italy stopped by referendum

2 France exports nuclear power to Italy

Figure 7.12   Nuclear power in Europe

7.7   ENVIRONMENTAL BORDERS

The developed science of transmission management in costly and constrained circumstances is useful in the consideration of emissions. The theory of trade outlined in section 10.1.22 showed that if one country has cheaper factor prices (for example high or absent CO_2 limits or lower CO_2 prices) that: (i) production will gravitate to that country and that (ii) the factor price will tend to equalise.

This is highly significant in the case of CO_2, because CO_2 is a global commodity with no transportation costs to 'market'. The low value of currency in poor countries, means that the 'pure' neoclassical economic solution is for all countries to sign up to limits, and then for rich countries to pay poor countries for CO_2 reduction. This however creates all sorts of problems in benchmarking the initial limits, in proving additionality (that the CO_2 allowance purchase did not simply accompany a CO_2 reduction that was going to occur anyway). These arguments are developed in Chapter 8 on the environment. What is of interest here is the restriction on the free trade of CO_2 and other emission allowances, to contend with the difficulties discussed. The result is that for CO_2 and other allowances we have:

(i)   **Constraints** – Limits on transboundary allowance transfer (country to country, EU/non EU, Annexe 1-2 Kyoto, state to state in USA).
(ii)   **Losses (positive and negative)** – Impact dilution combined with temporal attenuation (a negative loss), or 'harvesting' damage accumulation above a threshold.
(iii) **Rule changes at borders**.
(iv)   **Storage** – Banking and borrowing permits across 'vintage' years at non par rates.
(v)   Political risk/contract frustration/credit on trades done.

---

[27] See section 10.1.26 for an explanation of shadow prices.

(vi)   **Administration and audit costs** – Since schemes have many impacts, moving environmental permits is complicated.

(vii)   **Rule absences at borders** – not all countries have signed up to Kyoto.

(viii) **Moral hazard** – change in schemes, contract frustration.

(ix)   **Kyoto agreements** – Especially Russian, will affect the physical generation map.

(x)   **Pollution havens** – Note that CO2 has global impact and therefore the main mechanism for the environmental Kuznets' curve[28] does not apply.

(xi)   **Change in currency values at borders.**

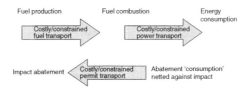

Figure 7.13 Comparison between fuel movement, electricity movement and emission permit movement

We can see in Figure 7.14 that if two countries with different emission schemes form a single scheme that the 'constraint removal' turns the market from a split market to a single market. The impact of trade is also shown in the figure.

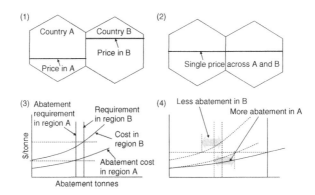

Figure 7.14 Visualisation of emission permit markets in a similar manner to electricity markets

---

[28] See Figure 10.63.

8

Environment, Amenity,
Corporate Responsibility

All activities in our daily lives involve the use of energy, whether by muscle power, mechanical power, or heat and light. The production life cycle and the consumption life cycle of all forms of energy inevitably have an effect on the environment. Per amount of primary energy delivered, the ESI in fact leaves a remarkably light footprint compared to other energy forms, but nevertheless the sheer volume of consumption means that the environmental issues of the ESI are substantial.

Within the ESI life cycle, not including the activities involved in the production of fuel, the main impact is in the generation sector. Because of this and also since it easier for the government to apply pressure to a small number of large generators, rather than a large number of small consumers, this sector has most attention from an environmental perspective. Since the beginning of power generation, there have been continuous improvements in efficiency and environmental impact, driven by commercial considerations and environmental regulation. The increments of performance are now increasingly marginal.

Such is the extent and scale of the issue that the costs of environmental impact could more than double[1] the cost of produced energy, and the industry cannot afford an economically inefficient solution.

In this chapter we define the impacts from the environmental load factors and describe some economic and prescriptive measures for improving the environment. From these factor costs, we can calculate the impact of environmental factors on the price of power.

Not everyone is interested in electricity and economics, but everyone is interested in the environment, and it is through environmental impact that most people perceive the ESI. The literature on environmental impact is enormous and opinions (both informed and uninformed) are widely and freely expressed. Environmental enhancement and environmental economics are an uneasy partnership, because the economics treads on forbidden territory in valuing (and acting on) utility and disutility in monetary terms. Because environmental economic models require simplification and the making of assumptions, they are quite easy to discredit, particularly if another solution (which is equally vulnerable to attack) is not proposed.

8.1 ENVIRONMENTAL PRESSURE

The energy complex creates pressure on the environment in many ways, both from the perspective of resource depletion and of environmental load from the unwanted by-products of the production of electricity. In order to follow the policy principles, outlined in Chapter 3, of prioritisation and costing, we will find it essential to give maximum clarity to the ESI

---

[1] For example in Great Britain in 2001, annual baseload electricity could be bought forward in the wholesale market below £18/MWh. In 2005, the marginal factor cost of CO_2 for coal plant has exceeded £18/MWh.

in terms of economic and prescriptive signals. We will see that definition is particularly difficult for environmental issues but we must nevertheless do the best that we can.

We start with identification of impact factors, and then, for each factor, we try to determine its direct and indirect impact. Then we need to try to attach some form of economic measure to the impact or impact abatement. Some of the uncertainty problems are depicted in Figure 8.1.

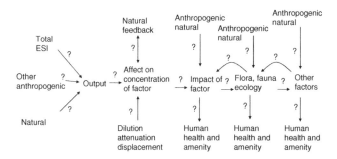

Figure 8.1 Representation of the uncertainties in the relationship between the production of environmental impact factors and of their impacts

It is worth noting that in this multifactor environment with high degrees of uncertainty, there is a high value to diversity, both in generation type and in environmental abatement technology. The diversity prevents us from getting locked in to technologies that later prove to be unsatisfactory. The diversity approach is said[2] to be somewhat at odds with the neoclassical approach, which emphasises 'first past the post' implementation.[3]

8.2 DEFINITIONS

To arrive at a sensible compromise of cost and abatement and a proper prioritisation of measures, it is helpful to define the impact. TEPI[4] identified nine Environmental Pressure Indicators:

(i)   air pollution;
(ii)   climate change;
(iii)   loss of biodiversity;
(iv)   marine environment and coastal zones;
(v)   ozone layer depletion;
(vi)   resource depletion;
(vii)   dispersion of toxic substances;
(viii) urban environmental problems;
(ix)   waste and water pollution.

---

[2] With the inclusion of options in the neoclassical toolkit, this problem is much reduced, since options handle probability rather well. However, options on technology are practically illiquid.

[3] For further description of this, with a worked example for fossil fuel, nuclear and renewable generation, see Stirling (1997).

[4] Towards Environmental Pressure Indicators — A multi year project of Eurostat.

Of these, it identified four priority items for the ESI: resource depletion, waste, climate change and air pollution. For every impact factor, we must define the following:

(i)   Inventory

- Complete list of possible impacts in type and extent, regardless of probability, mapped back to produced factor.

(ii) Lifecycle

- Factor production in the power generation lifecycle for the technology.
- Displacement of other forms of power generation and their impacts.

(iii) Timeline

- Resource renewal rate.
- Resource sustainability without renewal (e.g. coal, nuclear fusion, nuclear fission) at different price levels.
- Attenuation of impact over time, other than by dilution and displacement (e.g. biological or chemical conversion to benign form, or the half life of nucleotides). Does the damage occur once, thereby consuming the pollutant, or does it continue (like the greenhouse effect).
- Damage accumulation. Is lifetime exposure 'harvested' to accumulate damage or do effects attenuate over time.

(iv) Probability

- Probability of production (e.g. nuclear accident, coal mine or power station accident).
- Probability of impact if produced (e.g. CO_2).

(v)   Dilution and displacement

- Displacement of factor from high impact location to low impact location.
- Displacement followed by attenuation (reduction of the substance through chemical, biological or radioactive effects).
- Dilution followed by attenuation to stable concentration below impact threshold.[5]

Whilst environmental load is what holds our attention, we must also be mindful that environmental load is a subset of the total impact of the ESI, and that we must take into account factors such as safety, and amenity (particularly visual amenity of power lines and power installations). It is not customary to take the effect of the ESI on the welfare and the economy (jobs and taxes) into account with environment and amenity, but nevertheless this is important and is described in Chapter 10. Both amenity and economic effects from generation build and closure are commonly highly local in nature.

---

[5] The threshold is the level to which there is no apparent damage. There is little evidence for the existence of thresholds and the World Health Organisation approach here is 'absence of evidence is not evidence of absence'.

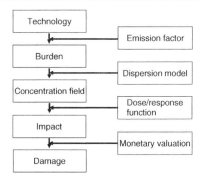

Figure 8.2   Depiction of impact pathways[6]

8.2.1   Definition of production of potential impact factors

Within the ESI, it is power generation that causes most of the pressure, and we can further define the impact:

(i)   **Resource depletion** – consumption of gas, oil, and coal, and gross and net abstraction of water and effect on flow and river level.

(ii)   **Waste** – (Thermal impact, effect on fish, emission to water), landfill and leaching of landfill.

(iii)   **Climate change** – Carbon dioxide production from fossil fuels, methane release from production, methane consumption by combustion of landfill gases, carbon dioxide effects from renewable energy production (crop displacement).

(iv)   **Air pollution** – 'Acid rain' gases (SOx and NOx), Local air quality (smog, particles), Heavy metals to atmosphere, accidental release.

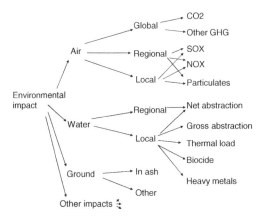

Figure 8.3   High level definition of environmental impact from power stations

---

[6] Source Externe.

The production of many of these was described in detail in section 2.2.10. There we saw that not all impact factors are simply related to the amount of power produced, and that we need to use 'translators' to make the relationship between energy, the amount of impact factor and the regulatory limits. Translators are described in section 8.4.3.

8.2.2 Definition of impact

Once we know what we will produce, or are likely to produce, then we must establish how the factor causes impact. We do this by way of example.

8.2.2.1 Definition of nuclear impact

The debate about nuclear power is characterised by high degrees of uncertainty and the difficulty of evaluating the relative utility discount between current and future generations.

For example,[7] in 1972 a UK report on the Control of Pollution, presented to the Secretary of State for the Environment said 'in effect, we are consciously and deliberately accumulating a toxic substance on the off-chance that it may be possible to get rid of it at a later date. We are committing future generations to tackle a problem which we do not know how to handle' and 'since planned demand for electricity cannot be satisfied without nuclear power, they consider mankind must develop societies which are less extravagant in their use of electricity and other forms of energy. Moreover, they see the need for this change of direction as immediate and urgent'.

We know qualitatively what damage that irradiation does in high dose. What we are very uncertain about is the probability of nuclear events, and the extent of the damage of such events (the data being very limited).

In terms of market design, a very low likelihood of a very high and long lasting damage must be measured against the high likelihood of a low and temporary[8] damage caused by other forms of power.

The potential health and safety risk from nuclear power has always been hotly debated. In 1973 Lave *et al.* used existing data to compare the estimated health effects of the coal and nuclear value chains. They found in mining a cost of 2.4 cents/MWh of thermal energy for nuclear and 32 cents/MWh for coal. In power generation, they arrived at estimates on the effect on public health and safety of between 0.0003c to 0.03c/MWh for nuclear and between 10 and 500c/MWh for coal. The difference is initially striking. However, in doing so, several elements of risk are excluded, such as nuclear accidents, terrorist events, long term health effects, spent fuel disposal, and the relationship between nuclear power and nuclear weapons. The *ex post* measurement of nuclear damage is an unreliable *ex ante* measure of possible impacts.

Thirty years later, the probabilities remain uncertain, largely because they are so low and hence data is limited. There is only one significant data item, the 1986 Chernobyl[9] incident, and while the number of direct deaths is known to be 31, there is little quantitative knowledge of the total health[10] effect from the disaster. Estimates of long term death toll

---

[7] Requoted from Schumacher (1973).

[8] Carbon dioxide is a distinct and important case. The impact is uncertain, but if there is an impact, it is global and relatively long lasting.

[9] In 1986, human error at the Chernobyl reactor in Soviet Ukraine led to an electrical fire and explosions that nearly destroyed one reactor.

[10] It was reported by the British Broadcasting Corporation that a recent study indicated that the psychological impact from the disaster, nearly twenty years on, still has a substantial effect on the economy. Source BBC. 7 Feb 2002.

vary from 14,000 to 475,000 (Savchenko 1995). Some parts of nuclear waste and fallout will last for 24,000 years.

8.2.2.2 Definition of NOx impact

We recall from section 2.2.10 that the nitrogen oxides NOx are produced from the hot flame in power stations. It is considered that there are human health effects of exposure to high doses of NO2 and air quality limits are set to regulate this.

NOx reacts with ultraviolet light to form ozone, which under certain atmospheric conditions, causes a visible smog as a result of photochemical reactions. This is a regional effect with fast attenuation.

NOx in the atmosphere eventually forms nitric acid HNO3 and causes the rain to become more acid. At high concentrations, this is considered to cause changes in soil chemistry and other effects on the ecosystem,[11] crop damage[12] and building damage.[13] This is a long range effect (hundreds to thousands of km) and hence is a 'transboundary' effect from one country to another according to the prevailing wind direction. The condensation of water vapour onto these cloud condensation nuclei to make clouds increases the reflectivity (albedo) of the earth, and thereby reduces the net flux of solar energy.

All NOx that goes up into the air eventually comes back down to earth. However, both dilution to below likely threshold levels and displacement to areas of different ecological assimilative capability can occur.

Different countries feel different impacts. So in the USA, NOx regulation is directed mainly at smog and air quality issues, whereas in Great Britain it is more oriented to human health and ecosystem effects.

8.2.2.3 Definition of impact from transmission lines

The visual amenity effect of transmission lines (and to a lesser extent, distribution lines) makes constant headlines, particularly in local newspapers in relation to renewable generation. Whilst visual amenity has no direct health impact, it cannot be ignored, as many may feel that a good view is as important as small differences in the very small probability of physiological impact.

A recent study[14] indicated an epidemiological association between proximity to high voltage power lines and childhood leukaemia that is apparently statistically significant, and applies at a lower threshold than is suggested by the pooled international study mentioned below. There are possible explanations,[15] such as increased capture[16] and precipitation of aerosol pollutants near power lines and increased capture[17] in the respiratory system due to the charging of the particles, but the lack of information on possible confounders makes interpretation of the study results difficult.

---

[11] e.g. Nilsson (1992).

[12] e.g. Pearce et al. (1992).

[13] e.g. ECOTEC (1992).

[14] Draper et al. (2005).

[15] See also Watts (2005).

[16] National Radiological Protection Board (2004), now part of the Health Protection Agency.

[17] Fews et al. (1999).

This was first examined in 1979.[18] More recently, pooled analysis in nine countries from Europe, North America and New Zealand indicate an overall[19] epidemiological association between exposure to greater[20] than 0.4 micro Teslas magnetic field of power frequency and childhood leukaemia, with little affect on results from adjustment for potentially confounding variables such as socio-economic status. There is no sound scientific explanation for the finding but, if there were a causal association, a very small number of cases would be due to proximity to power lines.

Currently it is not considered that the medical evidence warrants a change in the guidelines on exposure to electric and magnetic fields whether these are from power lines or other sources. It is likely that the visual amenity impact will continue[21] to be the dominant aversion factor.

8.2.2.4   Definition of impact of CO2

The impact of carbon dioxide on global temperatures has a high degree of uncertainty in the manner shown in Figure 8.1. A particular problem in establishing anthropogenic (man made) impact is the fact that the world appears to have cycles for temperature, carbon dioxide concentration, sulphur dioxide concentration and other factors. There are many cycles of different lengths,[22] and currently we are in the midst of a rapid temperature rise with a similar pattern to that of 120,000 years ago. This also coincided with high concentrations of CO2.

For a greater understanding of global cycles, the reader is referred to the large body of literature on the Gaia[23] paradigm. In one interpretation of Gaia, anthropogenic activity is easily absorbed by the ecosystem – although not necessarily in a manner that sustains life for humans![24]

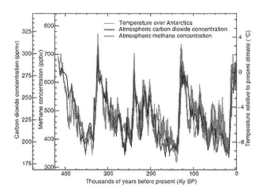

Figure 8.4   CO2 and temperature variation above the arctic for the last 400,000 years. Source Intergovernmental Panel on Climate Change. Reproduced with Permission

---

[18] Wertheimer and Leeper (1979).

[19] Ahlbom *et al.* (2000).

[20] Representing about 0.4 % of the population in the UK.

[21] Ofgem, the Great British regulator recently considered the cost of undergrounding the transmission cables in national parks, and noted that the amenity impact and the expense were very large items that could not be decided at the level of the regulator and needed to be determined directly by government policy or public enquiry. Further information in the UK about health effects can be found from the Health Protection Agency.

[22] See IPCC (2001) for a depiction from four studies showing the carbon dioxide in ice and temperature above Antarctica, showing sharp rises in both about every 110,000 years followed by steady decline. The current position is near the top of a cycle and the question is whether this time that temperature will decline or continue to rise to record heights.

[23] See, for example Schneider (1993).

[24] An alternative view is that we will colonise space when the earth runs out of resource. See Tipler (1995).

The effect of getting CO2 information further and further into the past, in relation to our estimates for the future, is discussed in section 9.5.3.3.

8.2.3   Definition of sensitivity of impact factors once produced

8.2.3.1   Objective definition

Once we know what we have produced, and what it does, we need to understand the capability of the environment to absorb the impact, and of human sensitivity to the impact.

Daly[25] describes the environment as 'an envelope containing, provisioning, and sustaining the entire economy'. The view of the environment as an envelope is a useful one. Inside the envelope, there is not a significant constraint on our activities. Close to the envelope, the constraints are highly limiting.

Our sensitivity to emission production is also much affected by cost and effectiveness of 'end of pipe' solutions, since if they are cheap and effective, it may in some circumstances be simplest to tax the industry for impact and then use the money for impact mitigation. An example is the trading of water rights between farmers and power stations.

We have noted the nine key pressure indicators of international significance. From a local perspective, there are three impact factors that are additionally relevant:

(i) **Habitat** – Conventional power stations are physically large in size and, in common with any change in land use, can cause loss of natural habitat.
(ii) **Amenity** – noise, nuisance, road traffic, visual amenity are often cited.
(iii) Local impact on employment is positive.

8.2.3.2   Subjective evaluation

> 'During Darius' reign, he invited some Greeks who were present to a conference, and asked them to be prepared to eat the corpses of their fathers: they replied that they would not do that for any amount of money. Next, Darius summoned some members of the Indian tribe known as the Callatiae, who eat their parents, and asked them in the presence of the Greeks . . . how much money it would take for them to be willing to cremate their fathers' corpses; they cried out in horror and told him not to say such appalling things. So, these practices have become enshrined as customs just as they are, and I think Pindar was right to have said in his poem that custom is king of all'
> Herodotus – The Histories 3.38[26]

This quote provides an illustration that different people can have very different attitudes to the same effects. Once we have defined impact as best we can, we still encounter substantial variations in sensitivity, for example:

(i) differing values of money in different countries;
(ii) differing tolerance to general environmental impact;
(iii) differing relative preferences to different environmental impacts;
(iv) difficulty in determining the discount rate to apply to future impact in comparison to present impact.

---

[25] Daly (1997).
[26] Original citation by O'Neill (1997). Different translation.

These add to:

(i)   difficulty in isolating individual environmental effects;
(ii)   difficulty in assessing natural vs. anthropogenic output;
(iii) difficulty in assessing and agreeing benchmark outputs;
(iv)   difficulty in assessing dilution and attenuation over time.

These are very hard to separate, benchmark and evaluate, and cultural preferences probably create more uncertainty than either impact factor production, or objective impact of the factor. This creates an enormous barrier to use of economic mechanisms for environmental impact mitigation.

It is naturally common for arguments concerning environmental sensitivities and preferences to be constructed to suit particular economic cases. Given the high degrees of uncertainty, it is commonly possible to find experts in support of either side of most cases.

In general, we expect the environmental preferences of a country to be influenced by the following factors:

(i)   social policy and culture;
(ii)   indigenous fuel mix;
(iii)   topology, weather, coastline;
(iv)   historic generation mix and mode of domestic and industrial heating;
(v)   demand profile;
(vi)   economic priorities;
(vii)   politics;
(viii)   methods of funding infrastructure;
(ix)   wealth and poverty.

8.3   THE POLICY DEBATE

Environmental policy drivers – such as the human health effects of atmospheric pollutants and acidification of sensitive ecosystems – have increased in profile over a long period and have been additionally catalysed by the global warming debate. The environment is now a key element in national and international policy, and is central to the strategy of most major energy companies. For the global political significance, we need look no further than the G8 meeting in 2005 in Edinburgh, Scotland, of the most powerful people in the world, to see the conversion of the agenda of economics and trade, to poverty in Africa and global warming.

Environmental load has always been recognised. As long ago as 1863, a pollution authority was set up in the UK[27] to reduce the smog,[28] called the 'London Particular'. However, the environment only became a mainstream political subject in the 'environmental revolution'[29] of the 1960's. Perhaps the defining moment in policy terms was the UN conference at Stockholm in 1972 when eighteen industrial countries agreed to institutionalise modern environmental policies. At that time, economists were ready and waiting with economic tools for

---

[27] Followed by France, Germany and the Netherlands. The first country to have a comprehensive environmental policy was Japan. Source Skou Andersen (1994).

[28] For an excellent short account of the impact of coal smoke on London from 1257 to the 1950's, see Ackroyd (2001).

[29] Probably the defining moment was the publication of 'Silent Spring' by Rachel Carson in 1962, which in particular alerted the public to the dangers of pesticides.

environmental improvement. In fact, environmental improvement (or at least the limitation of environmental degradation) has substantially followed the 'command and control' method from central government.

The question of 'environmental valuation' is a polar one in the policy debate, with market failure[30] in the neoclassical model[31] being cited as too serious a flaw to apply valuation based environmental economics. Despite this, it is increasingly the case that valuation of environmental goods and bads is used to inform policy decisions on level of ambition in effects reduction.

Environmental policy can have a significant effect on trade. The concept of cheap exports from 'pollution havens' is discussed in section 10.6.2.2, as is the apparent presence of the 'environmental Kuznets curve', for which pollution intensity increases during the early stages of economic growth and then declines. While this curve is encouraging, it may be that in the new global economy, the effect of trade and pollution havens may significantly reduce the environmental improvement arising from the Kuznets effect.

8.4   REGULATION AND INCENTIVE FOR RESTRICTING EMISSIONS AND OTHER IMPACTS

Environmental and amenity impact can be mitigated in a number of ways. The methods can and do work in parallel with each other and local, national and international laws and regulations are applied simultaneously. Main methods are:

(i)   self regulation;
(ii)   annual limits;
(iii)   taxes (fixed price);
(iv)   allowance redemption (variable price);
(v)   continuous limits;
(vi)   non continuous limits;
(vii)   technological prescription (insistence on particular technologies);
(viii) technological benchmarks (insistence on use of best available technique or best available without entailing excessive cost);
(ix)   informal.

8.4.1   Continuous limits

Plant can be fitted with continuous emission monitors, and flue gas sampling can be done for virtually all emissions. Where this is done, if the measurements are sufficiently accurate, it is possible to apply a continuous emission limit.

Continuous emission limits are a half way house between annual limits and technology prescription since, regardless of any benefits that a plant may bring (for example for security of supply) it is disallowed from running if the limit cannot be met. The owner must usually therefore either close the plant (which will then be displaced by compliant technology), or retrofit an abatement technology. Whilst the plant owner can choose the technology, it cannot choose an economic solution (such as adjustment of the load factor mix of its plant of different types), which may be more environmentally beneficial.

---

[30] See section 10.7.
[31] See section 10.1.3.

Instantaneous measurements can be highly variable, and some things (such as dust) are hard to control on an instantaneous basis. In addition, impact is not caused on an instantaneous basis.

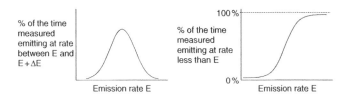

Figure 8.5   Variation in instantaneous measurement of environmental impact factors

From a market perspective, instantaneous limits incur higher fixed costs. In the absence of a load factor limit, plant is not restricted to peak operation.

8.4.2   Non instantaneous limits

Some limits are measured continuously, but some tolerance can be allowed. For example, the limit can be exceeded for x % per month and y % per year, where y < x, or can be exceeded when the plant is operating in a particular[32] mode (usually due to start up or shut down). This form of limit is suitable for emissions that are highest when the plant is changing state and which cannot be readily controlled on an instantaneous basis. Dust is a good example of this, since start ups create relatively high amounts of dust. If the tolerance levels are approached then the plant operator needs to consider measures such as maintaining constancy of load, or using a fuel batch that has low propensity to produce impact factors.

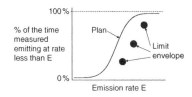

Figure 8.6   Application of tolerance envelope to instantaneous limits

From a market perspective, non instantaneous limits lie between instantaneous limits and annual caps, and drive the plant towards flexible operation with more sensitivity to emission/impact rate than either of the extremes.

---

[32] For example, NOX limits for combined cycle gas turbines can be suspended when the machine is in start up mode.

8.4.3 Environmental tolerance limits and translators

Environmental tolerance limits measure the impact rather than the output. Examples are local air quality limits (particularly in relation to SOx, NOx, dust and particulates), and water temperature and volume limits.

The water temperature effect was shown in Figure 5.16, and we saw how for some plant, the thermal emission to the water body can be adjusted (at an efficiency cost). In addition, there can be limits on river height.

In natural waterbodies, while the environmental load produced by the power station is relatively predictable, the absorptive capability of the environment, at least from a regulatory perspective, has a variation and a degree of randomness to it resulting from the stochastic nature of the hydrological and meteorological inputs.

We can convert the natural measures at the plant and the environment to the regulatory limit by using translators that we construct. An example is shown in Figure 8.7. Readers may recognise this as the construction of shadow prices. This method allows for deterministic and stochastic changes in the assimilative capability of the environment (for example due to changes in river height).

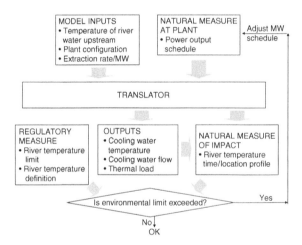

Figure 8.7 Construction of a translator for optimal plant schedule and configuration compliant with regulatory limits

8.4.4 Technology prescription or limits

Emission limits and allowance schemes take many years to implement and can be subject to extended arguments about making special cases for particular participants, agreeing historic or future benchmarks, agreeing measurement techniques and criteria, and others. Partly due to this, governments have commonly taken a more hands on prescriptive approach to mandatory technologies for emission abatement.

A prescriptive solution has both advantages and disadvantages. On the one hand, it creates a level playing field and common standard between producers, and may serve to promote (or protect) a chosen technology that might not otherwise be economically viable, or which might have a first mover disadvantage (the first installation is most expensive as it bears the highest research and development cost and has the least experience in service). On the other hand, competition in technology becomes stifled because the government effectively becomes the monopoly buyer of technology.

At the least prescriptive end of the spectrum, the government will require that the Best Available Technique Not Entailing Excessive Cost (BATNEEC) is installed. Whilst there is clearly room for interpretation of each of the words in the phrase, the range of techniques is usually limited enough for a sensible dialogue and the costs are reasonably definable. This creates the framework for dialogue with government, and government has ultimate control, either directly under primary legislation or through bodies such as regulators under statutory instruments, or by an understanding that a non cooperative generator can expect a high degree of attention, which at minimum incurs high costs.

At the most prescriptive end of the spectrum, the Best Available Technique (BAT) is required. The technology can be prescribed.

The prescriptive method works while the solutions are not excessively costly, but if the solutions are costly, then it is essential to choose the method that maximises benefits in relation to costs.

From a market perspective, prescriptive regulation is much like continuous emission limits, but with less long term flexibility for fuel, plant configuration, retrofits and technological solutions.

8.4.5 Self regulation

Self regulation is increasing, due to employee pressure and the use of ethical filters by investors, such as refusing to invest in companies with designated characteristics, or which do not satisfy designated standards or certification.

From a market perspective, there is an element of moral hazard in self regulation. Plant operators investing in particularly clean technologies are exposed to output prices reflecting the marginal cost of 'pollution haven' producers who spend less on these technologies.

8.4.6 Annual limits (caps)

The use of annual limits to environmental factor production is economically efficient, and provides a viable half way house to the 'pure' solution of environmental taxes, without causing a large shock[33] to the economy.

Unit and/or plant and/or generation fleet belonging to a company are given annual emission limits that may not be exceeded without permission (which might be given for example on a security of supply event). The fleet limit is less than the sum of unit/plant limits.

Emissions can be measured using continuous emission monitors but need not necessarily be so. As described in section 2.2.13, carbon dioxide and sulphur dioxide output can be audited using the heat account and sulphur account of the coal purchased. It is additionally possible to estimate the NOx emissions using an assumed (and agreed) NOx emission factor for the units with the known coals burnt.

Annual quantity limits can also apply to water extraction, dust output and other factors.

From a market perspective, there is the greatest control on total emissions, the greatest flexibility for generators to find the cheapest solution, and the greatest diversity in the generation mix.

---

[33] The effect of shocks is described in section 10.8.

8.4.6.1   Banking and borrowing

Allowances can sometimes be 'banked' (carried over into the next year) or 'borrowed' (from the next year) either at par (one for one) or non par rates.

The scheduled reduction of limits over a number of years (5 to 20) can reduce the economic shock effect and ensuing price rises.

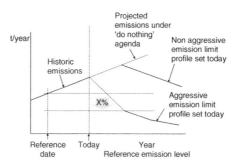

Figure 8.8   Aggressive and non aggressive emission limit profiles

8.4.6.2   Assignation of limits

Allocated emission limits become valuable assets, since zero allocation means a limit of zero, and therefore the assignation rules are important. They vary widely, and some are:

(i)   **'Grandfathering'** – The default limit is a percentage of the historic output rate, either chosen at a particular date or an average. This is generally applied at corporate level rather than at installation level.

(ii)   **Benchmarking** – The limit is applied on a company or installation basis according to the production technology and the output goods. High emission installations are not automatically given higher limits.

(iii)   **Adjustments** – This is a hybrid of the grandfathering and benchmarking methods, in which the grandfathered limit is adjusted on a case by case basis.

(iv)   **Auction** – The national limit is auctioned to all comers.

(v)   Free allocation to new installations.

(vi)   Removal of corporate allocation for closing installations.

8.4.6.3   Buy to retire

Altruistic organisations can buy up emission limits and 'retire'[34] them (return them to the permit market operator with no accompanying emission). They could buy directly in the auction, or pay a company not to use part of its cap. This unequivocally reduces total emission relative to the cap, but increases the marginal cost of generation, and thereby

---

[34] This is sometimes called sequestration. The term 'sequestration' has a variety of uses.

the flowthrough to consumers of the increased market cost of electricity may[35] exceed the environmental gain. This may not be economically optimal, or be the best use of the money used for the permits.

8.4.7   Cap and trade

Under the cap and trade system, different producers of emissions (who may be consumers of electricity) can buy and sell part of their emission allowance. This creates an open market in permits.[36]

From a price development perspective, there are several key dates. For example, the date on which the market structure is decided, the date on which the amount of permits is decided, the date on which permit allocation/auction is conducted, and the date on which the allocation period begins. This is shown schematically in Figure 8.9.

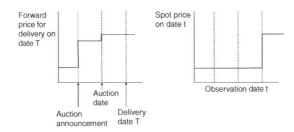

Figure 8.9   Development of forward price of permits with time and development of spot price of permits with time

The rationale of cap and trade is that, for a particular level of environmental spend; it is possible to apply a lower cap if trading is allowed than if it is not.

Suppose that there are five carbon dioxide producers (which come from sectors as diverse as cement making and transport). The government wishes to reduce total emissions. One approach is to take current emissions as benchmark for all sectors, and then apply a blanket percentage reduction to all, allowing no trading. Another approach is for the government to undertake detailed studies, independent of the industries (who naturally take a counter position on the ease of reduction of CO_2), in order to apply different reductions to different sectors. The cap and trade is a compromise between the two, in which the sector by sector reductions have relatively minor variations around the mean, but by allowing trading, there is incentive to all sectors to reduce CO_2 if, and only if, the cost of reduction is less than the CO_2 clearing price.

Suppose that there are five industries, with one participant in each. Each has a single method for CO_2 reduction.

It is obvious from the above diagrams that application of emission caps to different sectors/companies, inevitably moves money between them and therefore effectively causes inadvertent or intended cross subsidies.

---

[35] For a complete market with no market failure, this is definitely the case. For actual markets, the outcome depends on the specific circumstance, but will be most true if the shadow price emission stack is steep.

[36] The proper term in this context is usually 'allowances'.

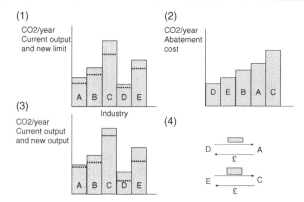

Figure 8.10 Efficient emission reduction using cap and trade. (1) Blanket reduction in limits, (2) Cost of abatement in different sectors, (3) Actual reduction (meeting the total limit), (4) The emission trades

Just as it is efficient for industries to trade amongst themselves (trading from sector to sector, and company to company within sector), it is also efficient for two economic zones, each with a limit to allow trading between each other.[37]

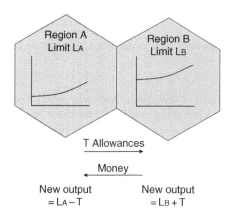

Figure 8.11   Transfer of allowance between economic zones

So, if two countries have different limits, then they can trade allowances at country level and then allocate within their own countries (this is sometimes called 'hot air').

The farther afield the allowances travel, the more potential there is for mistrust and abuse of the system. For example an emission reduction scheme conducted in a country which is currently a pollution haven but which is increasing its environmental awareness may create little or no additionality.

As a result, it is common for cross border trading to be limited, and for scheme registration to operate under very strict conditions.

---

[37] Subject to the welfare optimality of trade – see section 10.1.22.

8.4.7.1 Shadow prices and intracompany trading

Whether or not the cap system allows trading or not, shadow prices[38] for environmental factors develop in the open market,[39] and it is optimal for companies to manage their cap allocations by internal trading. For example, if a company internally allocates the cap the respective units, then internal market trading between units or between units and other parts of the company (for example buyers of low and high sulphur coal) can be set up.[40]

8.4.7.2 The Kyoto Protocol

The Kyoto protocol has a vast and accessible literature, and it is not covered in detail here. For present purposes a summary is sufficient.

The third Conferences of Parties (COP3) of the United Nations Intergovernmental Panel on Climate Change at Kyoto in 1997 determined that ratifying countries would commit to limiting emissions compared with a prior year or period of the six greenhouse gases[41] (GHG's). For the Protocol to come into effect required ratification by 55 parties of the convention responsible for at least 55 % of the annex 1 party emissions in 1990. This was secured with the signature of Russia in 2004.

Definitions followed, for example, which emissions are included (anthropogenic emissions of the basket of six GHG's, from energy production, industrial processes, solvent and other production, agriculture and waste. This includes estimation of GHG emissions resulting from the flatulence of cows, but excludes emissions from international air travel and international shipping), and what counts as carbon reducing (for example forestation). The Kyoto Protocol defines 'flexible mechanisms' to reduce the overall cost of global GHG reduction, such as emission trading and the use of project mechanisms.

Limits are allocated at country level and it is left to governments to develop policy measures to reduce emissions in order to comply with their Kyoto commitments which will in general be a combination of domestic measures and use of the Kyoto flexible mechanisms. The EU has disaggregated its Kyoto target between member states via the 'burden sharing' agreement. Within the EU emission trading scheme for CO2, countries then allocate to the respective sectors. They may allocate less than the cap, leaving the balance of 'hot air' with the government to trade (as is the case in some countries recently acceded to the EU) or more than the cap, leaving the government to purchase the balance (as in the Netherlands). International and domestic schemes can be stricter than the Kyoto protocol, such as the European Trading scheme, but not less strict whilst remaining recognised under the Kyoto protocol.

8.4.7.3 Interscheme trading

In a climate change context, interscheme trading is almost exclusively limited to one of the six greenhouse gases – CO2. Interscheme trading between ratified and non ratified countries is possible. Interscheme trading can also occur with other emissions, principally SOx and NOx and therefore the description below is general.

---

[38] See section 10.1.26.

[39] In the external market, these are manifest as 'basis differentials' in price. See Chapter 9.

[40] The actions for constructing the shadow price stacks are described in section 2.2.12, the inclusion of permits into unit option costs are described in section 11.4, and the environmental economics are described in section 10.6.

[41] CO2, CH4, N2O, SF6, hydrofluorocarbons and perfluorocarbons with global warming potentials expressed as multiples of CO2 equivalent. Since the multiple is dependent on horizon, then 100 years is chosen as the standard.

There are essentially five types of transaction:

(i)   Trading within a country which has an environmental scheme.
(ii) Trading by participants between two countries which are members of an international scheme.
(iii) Trading by participants between two countries which are members of different international schemes.
(iv) Trading by participants between two countries, one which has a scheme and one which does not.
(v)   Trading where there is no scheme or where schemes are incompatible.

The first method is the standard cap and trade.

The second method is easy in principle and can be hard in practice. From a mechanical standpoint, the market mechanism must be harmonised (for example phasing of the emission vintage year). Both regions must recognise one another's certification process. The Joint Implementation of the Kyoto protocol within the European Trading Scheme is an example of this method.

The third method is more complicated still. First and foremost, the environmental market operators must recognise certificates as fungible (valid) for exchange between regimes. To do so, the regions must agree to a sufficient degree on a large number of factors, such as what it in scope (for example whether forestation can generate permits, and which of the six greenhouse gases are included), and what the allocation method is. It is possible and practical for the environmental market operators in the two areas to agree a limit to the net flow of permits from one to the other.

The fourth method is fraught with difficulties in proving additionality. Nevertheless it is an important method of engagement with non aligned countries. In this method, a participant in the area with an environment scheme conducts some kind of emission abatement activity (for example plant efficiency improvement) in a country which is not a member of the scheme. The emission saving is redeemable in the scheme area. Since this increases the emissions physically produced in the scheme area, the process must be recognised in the context of national limits for the Kyoto protocol. This is the basis of the Clean Development Mechanism.

The fifth method involves the payment for virtual certificates by an environmental fund which aims either (i) eventually to redeem the certificates in a scheme, but takes the fungibility risk in the interim, or (ii) to internalise the certificates and retire them, for altruistic reasons (for example for funding research of for greenhouse gas saving activities that fall outside the scope of the Clean Development Mechanism). The fund could be government owned. There is some commonality of this approach with the CO_2 approaches of the USA and Australia in 2005.

In the EU, the Linking Directive connects together the Kyoto Protocol, the European Emissions Trading Scheme, the Joint Implementation and the Clean Development Mechanism. There is no limit to intra-European trading.

There are several environmental funds. Commonly they provide finance for a climate change enhancing scheme and receive the rights to the certificates which they then monetise in the relevant domestic or international market. Examples are the UN prototype carbon fund or the Climate Investment Partnership.

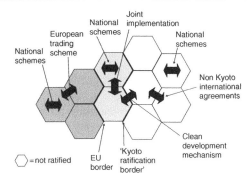

Figure 8.12   Schematic representation of carbon dioxide trading schemes

8.4.8   Emission allowance auctions

In the emission allowance auctions, rather than fixing the price and not restricting emission volume, as occurs with emission taxing, the government can limit the volume, and let the price vary, by holding an auction.

The auctions can operate in a variety of ways, including pay-as-bid or clearing price, sealed or public bids. It should certainly be possible to bid in increments rather than on an all-or-nothing basis.

Auctions can be phased in, by gradually reducing free allocations and auctioning an increasing volume.

8.4.9   Trade no Cap

Ultimately cap and trade systems become taxation systems as the free cap allocation is driven down towards zero and the government or international agency buys and sells allowances at a fixed price (taxation) or variable price for fixed volume. An intermediate solution is for the government to offer permits at what is at any time a fixed price, but at a price that can vary over time. This does involve moral hazard regulatory risk,[42] but allows more explicit control of the government to the management of the combination of price and volume of permits.

For example, a government may make an initial estimate on the price/volume combination of permits that it can procure through Joint Implementation or Clean Development Mechanisms, and issue internal permits accordingly. If the international procurement is easier or harder than the initial estimate, then the government can buy/sell permits within country.

8.4.10   Taxes

Sulphur dioxide taxes were introduced in Japan in 1974. This resulted in Japan leading the flue gas desulphurisation technology at the time and reducing SOx output. The tax varied

---

[42] See section 10.5.16.

by region and the SOx reduction corresponded approximately with the level of tax.[43] CO2 taxes were introduced in Finland in 1990,[44] and Denmark in 1992.

To avoid an economic shock to the system, taxation can be increased incrementally.[45] In addition, if a long notice period is given prior to the application of the tax, then the ESI has time to respond with prices, technologies and plant opening and closure.

Whilst the number of instruments that can be practically and simultaneously applied is limited in the current regime, there has been a tendency for governments to use differentially applied energy taxes to reach overall policy objectives not specifically tied to the taxed emission. For example, it is common not to apply carbon dioxide taxes to carbon dioxide producing plant that uses renewable sources, and to apply climate change taxes indiscriminately regardless of CO2 production.

The advantage of allowance schemes relative to technology prescription schemes is closely related to the disadvantage. The industry is the best place to find economically optimal solutions, but the industry is also in a position to conduct regulatory arbitrage and gaming of the system.

As shown in section 10.4, renewable obligations can take the form of taxes.

8.4.11 Cap and tax

The emission limit system, with allocated limits comes under increasing strain as the years go by, because the precedent for allocation decreases. Eventually the system has to change to a tax or auction system. The tax or auction system can be phased in by gradually decreasing free allocations and charging for them.

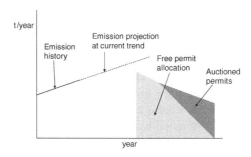

Figure 8.13 Phasing from cap allocation to tax or auction

Taxes and auctions are very similar in nature. Auctions create certain volumes and uncertain prices, and taxes create certain prices and uncertain volumes. In the neoclassical economic model with complete markets and little uncertainty, taxes are better from an optimisation perspective, but with high uncertainty of the actual economic cost, subjective cost[46] and immature markets, auctions are better.

---

[43] See studies by Tsuru and Weidner (1985), Foljanty-Jost (1988), Weidner and Tsuru (1988), Hidefumi (1990).

[44] The first International Energy Agency country to do so. IEA (1994).

[45] Future steps can be accommodated with sufficient notice by the use of leading indices in consumer pricing. Leading indices are described in supply pricing in section 2.6.6.

[46] See section 10.1.12 on contingent valuation.

8.5   OTHER POLICY TOOLS FOR ENVIRONMENTAL ENHANCEMENT

Several other methods of adjusting environmental performance are possible, including:

(i)   Direct subsidy from taxpayer (e.g. tax relief).
(ii)   Direct subsidy from energy sector (e.g. from added supplier tax, supply obligation, or by forced consumption at feed-in tariff).
(iii) Licence restrictions on non 'friendly' generation. This elevates prices by excluding generation from the production stack.
(iv)   Regulatory impositions on non friendly generation. This elevates prices to the extent that this plant sets the clearing price.
(v)   Voluntary consumer premium for tagged friendly energy. This is discussed in section 8.6 below.

8.5.1   Feed in renewable generation

The feed-in method is a common way to sponsor renewable generation. The method is similar to the PURPA method introduced in the USA in 1978.

In this method, the generators or suppliers are required to accept a certain amount of energy into their portfolio, not at market rates, but at some other rate (regulated, avoided cost, actual cost, or other), from privately owned renewable generators.

The electricity cost then becomes a blended rate from incumbent costs and renewable costs. If the incremental system costs from renewable generation (electrical infrastructure, reserve, reactive power and others) are smeared across the participants, then this cost should be added to the blended cost.

The feed-in method is straightforward to operate and lowers the entry barrier to renewable generation.

There is no natural limit to generation build from feed-in tariffs, although there can be a natural limit to the acceptance of the electricity by the generator or supplier.

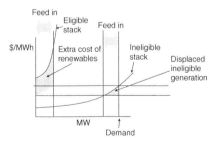

Figure 8.14   Simple economics of the feed-in tariff

8.5.2   Renewable obligation

Renewable obligations on suppliers specify that at least a designated percentage of supply volume must be sourced from renewable sources. The labelling of this power is described in section 8.6, and the economic effect of the obligation is described in section 10.4.

8.6   FUEL LABELLING AND POWER CONTENT LABELLING

Environmental impact is made inevitable by the consumption of electricity, and is produced (amongst other ways) by the generation of electricity. Whilst emission production is relatively easy to find and measure, the nature of electricity flow invisibly through wires and mixing through networks makes it very difficult to assign generation impact to consumption.

Whilst we can in theory assign each increment of demand at the margin to generation units using generation and demand stacks and location marginal pricing, it is common not to do so and in addition the assignation of aggregate[47] demand would be further complicated, Hence we cannot simply assign the power label to the demand. These labels are more like electricity rights, submitted for redemption to the system operator. If, as is usual, electricity is re-traded, then the origin of the electricity is lost. Consider a simple example. Consumer F buys electricity from producer C. Trader T buys electricity from producer A and sells to producer C. Consumer F has no way of knowing how much of his power is physically sourced from producer A and from producer C.

Nevertheless, consumers wish to have some control of the origin of their energy, just as they take an interest in the origin in their food, clothing and other manufactured goods, so that they can make altruistic choices about externality impact. This consumer choice exists over and above the governmental choice in differential taxes/allocations/auction volumes to adjust the generation mix.

The idea behind fuel labelling is that the consumer does gain an element of knowledge (and thereby of control) of the sourcing of the electricity. This can be done by keeping the power and the fuel label together throughout the transaction process from generator to consumer, or by separating them. The key of the separation method is that at the point of production, the electricity good is economically separated from its attendant bads. The bads may not be 'dumped' but must, at minimum, be registered, and, at maximum, paid for. Electricity that is entirely separated from its goods and bads is sometimes termed 'white'[48] electricity. Where electricity is more simply separated into renewable and non renewable, then the non renewable electricity is sometimes termed 'black' electricity (if from fossil fuel) or 'grey' electricity if a fossil/nuclear mix. White electricity with a renewable tag/certificate/label is termed 'green' electricity.

Let us consider an example. Suppose that there are three producers, Nuclearco, Carbonco, Renewco, of equal size. Nuclearco produces a bad H, Carbonco produces a bad I, and Renewco produces no bads (let us assume that the energy is renewable and any bads produced are discounted). Assume that there are three consumers D, E, F, of equal size.

Suppose that there is initially no fuel labelling, and that D buys from Nuclearco, E from Carbonco and F from Renewco. In the absence of re-trading, D has caused H, E has caused I and F has stimulated renewable generation. Many consumers would be prepared to pay a premium for generation from Renewco or for an absence of generation from either Nuclearco and Carbonco.

In the presence of re-trading but the absence of fuel labelling however, then each consumer must assume that it caused an even blend of bads. Consumer F will no longer pay a premium price to producer C for renewable energy because of the 'moral hazard' (Renewco could buy from Nuclearco and re-sell to F) and lack of guarantee of origin.

---

[47] It is correct for unconstrained flow.
[48] Electricity has been referred to as 'white coal' – Hughes (1983).

Now suppose that there is a fuel labelling system. Whilst the fuel labels do not need to follow the white electricity through the wholesale electricity trading system, they must eventually 'find a home'.

This is relatively easy for Renewco. Its generation can be audited and provided with one certificate per MWh of production. When a supplier finally delivers electricity to consumers, then it (in a figurative sense), hands the certificate to the consumers who (under audit), 'retire' certificates as electricity is delivered. In a sense then, the generation characteristics have been recombined with the white power, and the audit trail restored. F will again be prepared to pay a premium for the renewable energy.

Now the central repository can nominally assign the bads to the consumers, assuming an even blend. So the bads as well as the goods are reassembled back with the white energy.

Suppose that consumer D is averse to the production of (carbon) externality I and that E is averse to (nuclear) externality H, but that both are indifferent to other externalities. D and E can then swap the certificates that were handed to them by the system operator as grey labels as seen in Figure 8.16.

Our final situation is this:

(i)   Consumer F has paid a premium rate for renewable generation C.
(ii) Consumer D has paid the white electricity rate for 'yellow'[49] electricity produced in conjunction with H (nominally nuclear in this example).
(iii) Consumer E has paid the white electricity rate for 'black' electricity produced in conjunction with I (nominally coal in this example).

We can see that there is a risk to have a 'pollution haven' – i.e. a consumer who is indifferent to all pollution, and therefore trades with whom do not cause a net decrease in pollution. Whilst this indeed creates the potential for a concentration of 'very bads', the absolute size limitation of the pollution haven (limited by the size of customer base who are ethically indifferent and who can endure the negative publicity) does limit the problem. The situation is similar to that of global CO2. The Kyoto signatories still hope to make an impact even with a potential pollution haven of non signatories.

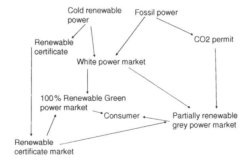

Figure 8.15 Simple fuel labelling with two fuel types

---

[49] The yellow colour code is used for convenience here and is not in general use. Yellow is used as a mnemonic because yellow cake is a stage of Uranium processing.

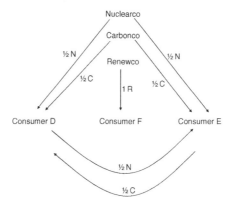

Figure 8.16 Certificate/label trading between consumers

Let us take a simple quantitative approach to the above problem. In example 1 the consumers D, E, F have 100 MW demand each, and each generator has 200 MW capacity. The marginal costs[50] of Nuclearco, Carbonco and Renewco are € 90/MWh, € 100/MWh, and € 150/MWh respectively. We also assume that the generators produce one certificate for yellow, black and green each respectively per MWh of electrical output. We also assume either a competitive market in each sector or a commitment in each to offer at marginal cost into the market stack.

Example 1

	D	E	F	Total
Renewable				0
Carbon				100
Nuclear				200
Grey	100	100	100	300
	(66 %N, 33 %C)	(66 %N, 33 %C)	(66 %N, 33 %C)	
Total	100	100	100	300
Cost	€100	€100	€100	

In example 2 we now assume that consumer F is prepared to pay more, for 10 % green energy. Our output from each generator is then 200 MW, 90 MW and 10 MW respectively. The grey power price is €100/MWh (the marginal cost of the most expensive producer of grey power) and the green certificate price is € 50/MWh. The '10 % green' power price is equal to (90 %*€ 100/MWh + 10 %*€ 150/MWh = € 105/MWh, or 100 %*€ 100/MWh + 10 %*€ 50/MWh = € 105/MWh).

In example 3 we now suppose that consumer F wished to be more specific and requires no nuclear power in the mix. Since grey power cannot be specified in this way, the requirement is expressed as 'all power received must be labelled, none of the labels must be yellow (nuclear), and at least 10 % must be green'. Consumer F then receives 10 green certificates and 90 black certificates for the 100 MWh of consumption. Consumers D and E now consume

---

[50] For simplicity, let us assume that they all have the same fixed costs. It should be stressed that this is not a valid assumption, and that the example is used for illustrative purposes only.

Example 2

	D	E	F	Total
Renewable	0	0	10	10
Carbon				90
Nuclear				200
Grey	100	100	90	290
	(69 %N, 31 %C)	(69 %N, 31 %C)	(69 %N, 31 %C)	
Total	100	100	100	300
Cost	€100	€100	€105	

grey power which is composed of 200 MW from Nuclearco and none from Carbonco. The grey power price is now €90/MWh, the green labels are €60/MWh and the black labels are €10/MWh. Note that consumer F still buys grey power, but this becomes white because F has labels for all of it.

Example 3

	D	E	F	Total
Renewable	0	0	10	10
Carbon	0	0	90	90
Nuclear				200
Grey	100 (100 %N)	100 (100 %N)		200
Total	100	100	100	300
Cost	€90	€90	€105	

In example 4 we suppose that consumer F raises his consumption to 120 MWh. He receives 12 green certificates and 108 black certificates. Consumers D and E continue to consume grey power. Note that a 6.7 % increase in total consumption had a 20 % increase in production from Renewco, an 8 % increase in production from Carbonco, and a 0 % increase in production from Nuclearco.

Example 4

	D	E	F	Total
Renewable	0	0	12	12
Carbon	0	0	108	108
Nuclear				200
Grey	100 (100 %N)	100 (100 %N)		200
Total	100	100	120	320
Cost	€90	€90	€105	

In example 5 we assume that consumer E specifies no nuclear, and as before, this specification is expressed 'buy only labelled power, with none of the labels being nuclear'. This now requires the full capacity of Carbonco and hence causes generation from Renewco without the specific request for green power. As with F before, the grey power bought by E becomes white through the full assignation of labels. Whilst we can see that the power going to D is all from Nuclearco, since the yellow labels do not change hands, then from D's perspective, he has bought grey power.

Example 5

	D	E	F	Total
Renewable	0	8	12	20
Carbon		92	108	200
Nuclear				100
Grey	100 (100 %N)			100
Total	100	100	120	320
Cost	€ 90	€ 104	€ 105	

We can see that even in the presence of an indifferent consumer D (equivalent to the pollution haven described in section 10.6.2.2) that consumers have some influence on preventing as well as encouraging production of certain types. It is also apparent that certificates accompanied by all power types except those associated with the impact of most aversion, have a positive value, even though they are associated with the production of 'bads'. Since all but one power type has a label, then the unlabelled power can be simply calculated by subtraction of total labelled volume from total delivered volume of electricity. This is an important fact when considering the practicalities of fuel labelling, as there is positive incentive to hold all labels but one.

Figure 8.17 shows a system with no grey power (all power is labelled).

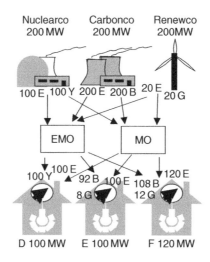

Figure 8.17   Fuel labelling using an (electricity) market operator (MO) and an environmental market operator (EMO). Y = yellow (Nuclearco), B = black (Carbonco) G = Green (Renewco); E = (white) electricity

Figure 8.18 shows how the grey power labels are constructed when certificates are assigned per MWh of production but not all labels change hands. The steps are as follows:

(i)   Collect the total power dispatched from the electricity system operator.
(ii) Administer the certificate flows from producers to consumers (supported by the environmental auditor).
(iii) Assign nominal certificates to all electricity dispatched (assignation of each unit to a category is provided by the environmental auditor).

The environmental market operator now has: (i) full power flow categorised by label, (ii) power flow assigned by certificate flow (and matched to the appropriate labels), (iii) unassigned power flow and (iv) unassigned labels.

The grey mix is found by allocating the unassigned labels evenly to the unassigned power.

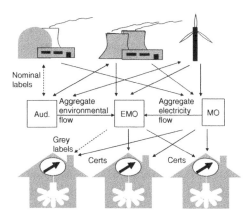

Figure 8.18   Construction of grey power label by deduction from traded labels

Now we must be careful about double counting environmental costs though labelling. For example, that Carbonco paid a tax or a shadow price through a cap and trade system for CO2. It is not then economically efficient to assign a lower value to a carbon label than a green label. In the long term then, consumer action by discriminatory pricing of power labels is not compatible with 'complete' government schemes. However, in the short and medium term, they can be complementary because an immature labelling scheme serves to promote a relatively small percentage of the most environmentally friendly schemes. For example, if the government specifies a renewable obligation of 10 % green, then a consumer may elect to buy 15 % green.

Suppose that a consumer has sight of the externality tax. Whilst it is not economically efficient for the consumer to apply discrimination to a power source if the externality tax has been paid in alignment with the consumer view of the correct tax, the consumer may believe that the tax is too high/low. A consumer who believes that the tax is too low for power type A and too low for power type B can pay a premium for labels from B and refuse power from A. This then acts as a modifying effect over and above the centrally administered taxes. If there is a cap and trade system, then consumers can refer to the trade prices to take a view on the best level of tax. For a cap no trade system, then the shadow prices are invisible to the consumer.

Another issue with source labelling is its coarse nature. Labels are applied to a generic source type per MWh of power production, and therefore the signal for impact mitigation within a production category is lost. It is possible to sub classify. Suppose that we set a benchmark of 1t/MWh, and two standard categories of 0.8t/MWh and 1.2t/MWh then a 100 MW unit producing at 1.1 t/MW would then be said to be producing 25 MW at 0.8t/MWh and 75 MW at 1.2t/MWh. Alternatively we can specifically split production into goods and bads just as is done for cap allocation. The units for the environmental market operator are not MWh of labels but tonnes of emission. However the challenges in making a meaningful statement to the consumer about the sourcing of each kWh of consumption, become significant.

We can conclude that:

(i)   Consumers can stimulate certain kinds of production by purchasing designated certificates.
(ii) Concerted action by consumers can reduce certain kinds of production by the combination of energy labelling and refusal of energy with particular labels.
(iii) If limits on capacity of particular generation types combined with label refusals cause the marginal generation to be of high price, then small changes in demand or label preference can cause large changes in price.
(iv) If labels have monetary value, then all but one label have positive value, even if associated with the production of bads.
(v)   Since all but one label has positive value, the production of the lowest value label can be calculated by subtraction.
(vi) Because all but one label has positive value, and the volume of the last label can be calculated by subtraction, then in the absence of government schemes, the label market would in theory develop self organise over time without government sponsorship.
(vii) In the early stages, source labels and government emission schemes are compatible, but they become incompatible over time.

Green tariffs have been around for some time. For example the Verte tariff in France began in 1956. Source labelling on consumer bills is increasing. In the EU, fuel mix disclosure conditions in the Electricity Directive require that consumer bills must have fuel labels. This is done in practice using the limited number of green labels, plus an estimation of the grey power mix using the method described above.

8.6.1 Physical power labelling

Under a number of jurisdictions, some power is traded with its label all the way through the value chain. This has the advantage of reduced regulatory moral hazard for consumers wanting absolute control on their energy sourcing, and the disadvantage of greatly reduced liquidity.

8.7   THE COST OF ENVIRONMENTAL ENHANCEMENT

If the cost of environmental impact mitigation impacts the marginal cost of production, or the total costs of the marginal producer (as we expect it to), then producer costs flow through to consumers.

Environmental economics are described in section 10.6. Environmental cost shocks are described in section 10.8. The cost of permits is described in section 10.6.2.

8.8   VALUATION OF ENVIRONMENTAL FACTORS

Valuation of environmental factors is fraught with difficulty. These are described in sections 10.1.12 and 10.1.13. It is important to note that even in a fully managed market where there is no explicit pricing, that prices appear in both shadow and hedonic form.[51] Whilst it might seem obvious to make an implicit price explicit (i.e. public), this act becomes explicitly challenged by unsolvable ethical dilemmas.

Let us consider SOx. The assignation of a tax to SOx would be expected to approximately match the compensation or mitigation cost of SOx impact. The application of a SOx limit has a similar effect, differing only in applying certainty to volume instead of price. When the (actual, for cap and trade or shadow) prices have settled down for two emissions, it is sensible to ask whether the cap levels should be adjusted so that the actual or shadow prices more accurately reflect the damage ratio. We note also that in applying ratios rather than absolutes, then we are less exposed to the treading on areas that are ethically 'out of bounds', as discussed above. The prices of NOx and SOx in the USA are a good example of this. While the impacts are different, there is sufficient commonality for us to make a guess as to approximate damage ratios. The NOx/SOx price ratio in the USA has historically been high. Whilst it may be that it is considered that this is justified by the relatively higher health and ecological impact of NOx, it may be that SOx limits are more generous, and/or the cost of SOx abatement lower at the margin.

Note that while the long term price of produced goods gravitates to the cost of production, the long term price of produced bads gravitates to the cost of consumption.

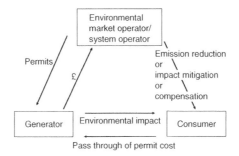

Figure 8.19   Simple model for environmental valuation

8.9   CORPORATE RESPONSIBILITY

Since the ESI is a large scale industry, installations have the potential to affect local areas in air quality, visual amenity, loss of habitat, pressure on roads and infrastructure, as well as the positive effects on jobs, the local economy and an element of control on the production of power.

Corporate Responsibility (CR) is a major issue for the ESI, largely due to the scale on which the industry operates. CR covers the environment, amenity and local issues, but also attends to other issues such as support for vulnerable customers, and the audit trail for the input factors to the industry to the greatest extent possible, for example in terms of safety and working conditions. The CR subject overall is highly complex, due to the relative absence of economic signals for utility, difficulties in measuring welfare and contingent valuation, the uncertainty and debate surrounding many environmental and social issues, the inevitable cost consequence of CR and the interdependence of issues.

---

[51] See section 10.1.26.

Most mechanisms described in this book are neoclassical economic mechanisms in response to policy signals that are themselves connected to public opinion in a manner described in Chapter 3. It is important to recognise that regulation defines the minimum level of environment and social improvement activity. Pressure from investors and employees as well as consumers has a significant effect.

It is established that companies with strong environmental policies tend to have good policies generally. More recently, the 2002 Sarbanes-Oxley Act in the USA significantly strengthened the audit requirements for corporate governance and has placed significant emphasis on the quality of internal systems and processes with respect to supporting the statutory accounts for corporations. Environmental management is closely associated with low as well as high level systems and processes. For example the construction of internal shadow prices for environmental impact factors, as described in section 2.2.12.

Some examples of ethical filters that enable stakeholders to take an objective view of corporate responsibility are:

(i)   Dow Jones Sustainability Indexes;
(ii)   Ethical Investment Research Service;
(iii) FTSE4Good;
(iv)   Transparency International's corruption index for countries;
(v)   Sustainable Asset Management (SAM) group sustainability indices.

Other organisations promoting corporate responsibility are Business in the Community and the Institute of Business Ethics (in the UK). The UN global compact was set up in 2000 to 'bring companies together with UN agencies, labour and civil society to support universal environmental and social principles'.

At national level, interest in environmental balance sheets for the whole country is increasing, and this will increase the alignment of annual corporate statements to national norms, standards and measurements.

8.10   THE ENVIRONMENTAL IMPACT OF CONSUMPTION

'Industrialized societies, so far, have not used power wisely'
Paul Ehrlich – Stamford ecologist/population biologist

If we had limitless cheap resources for the production of power and if this production had no direct environment impact, then excessive activity involving energy consumption would still cause an associated consumption of other resources and other environmental pressures.

As well as there being externalities associated with consumption, it is possible that there are internal effects as well. The epidemiological studies in relation to power frequency magnetic fields in the context of transmission lines have been noted in section 8.2.2.3.

Since electricity is delivered through the low voltage system[52] to the point of use, as well as over long distance, then health impacts directly associated with consumption are possible.[53] Should this be the case, then they are partly an externality and partly an internality (a private bad).

---

[52] Male and Maddock (1990).
[53] McBride *et al.* (1999).

9

Price and Derivatives Modelling

The characteristics of non storage and long distance delivery of electricity, that we might call the space-time characteristic of electricity, is central to the understanding of its price fundamentals. While we can apply standardised techniques from the financial markets, our understanding of the fundamentals is drawn from a wide field of 'commodities' such as bandwidth, airline seats and hotel rooms.

The prices of electricity are more volatile and complicated than any other commodity and often appear to be intractable. However, we can go a long way to modelling prices, by taking a stepwise approach;

(i)   detailed definition of the physical system of generation and transmission;
(ii) establishment of the drivers of demand;
(iii) fundamental interpretation and application of statistical processes;
(iv) application of the various effects of storage (capacity) and non storage;
(v)   adjustment for further effects such as environment, location, cost of risk and transaction costs.

The definition of the physical system has been done in Chapter 2 and the demand variation in sections 2.6.10 and 5.1.1. In this chapter, we introduce the reader to the techniques required for pricing and valuation of wholesale electricity, beginning with the statistical basics, with a focus on features particular to electricity. The mathematics is treated in an informal manner in order to focus on the fundamentals, and to aim for understanding more than purity. We shall also extensively use approximating assumptions between the normal and lognormal distributions, and between local and cumulative correlations, and we shall assume zero or constant interest rates[1] for most of the time. For more formal treatment, the reader is recommended to refer to the textbooks[2] on electricity derivative pricing.

A note is offered at this point to readers familiar with relative pricing of derivatives with replicating portfolios. The approach taken here is one of absolute pricing, using all possible sources of information in the real world, with the use of state variable analysis from derivative pricing to help us with details. This is due to the poor liquidity of electricity derivative markets, but high degree of richness of source of general price information.

The excellent textbooks on energy derivative pricing have been mentioned in the text and listed in the references, and this book is intended to complement these. This chapter introduces the core techniques and develops them in an electricity context. Generic derivative techniques that are well covered in textbooks, and not electricity specific, such as stochastic volatility, are not covered here.

---

[1] This is simply to make the equations shorter and interest costs can easily be adjusted for in all situations except the capital asset pricing model, for which variable interest rates are a known problem.

[2] For financial derivatives see Rebonato, Wilmot *et al.*, Haug, Hull and Hughston (1996), and Baxter and Rennie (1996). For commodities, see Geman (2005). For electricity refer to Eydeland and Wolniec, Clewlow and Strickland (2000), or Bunn (2004). For insurance and weather, see Geman (1999).

9.1   PRICE PROCESSES AND DISTRIBUTIONS

9.1.1   Price processes

A process is the formal statistical definition of the way that a variable moves. We can describe it informally as follows; the change in variable in a small time interval is composed of a *deterministic* change that is either fixed or is precisely determinable from the current state of the system plus a change that is *random* but with a randomness that is precisely defined (this kind of randomness is called *stochastic*).

9.1.2   Random walk

The simplest process is random walk. In this process, in each fixed length time interval, the variable will either increase (up step) or decrease (down step). The probability[3] of up and down steps are both 50 % and they are of equal size. By convention, spot price is commonly noted S so, for a single step

$$\Delta S = \pm \sigma_s \Delta t$$

Here σ_s is the step size.

Now Δt is an infinitesimally small step and we will need to use finite time steps. We need therefore to relate the step height to the step length in finite time.

Consider two steps. As seen in Figure 9.1, after two steps, the average *square* of total step size of the period is equal to $25\,\%^*2^2 + 50\,\%^*0 + 25\,\%^*2^2 = 2$.

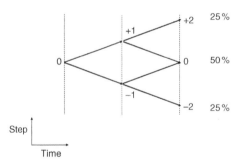

Figure 9.1   Two steps of a random walk process

Similarly, for three steps we have average square total step size $12.5\,\%^*3^2 + 2^*37.5\,\%^*1^2 + 12.5\,\%^*3^2 = 3$.

So we see that the probability weighted square of the total step is proportional to time elapsed. This probability weighted square is termed the variance, and the square root of the variance is termed the standard deviation.

---

[3] Those with experience in derivatives will note that there are two probability measures, the real world and the risk neutral measure. Throughout this chapter we ignore the distinction, and in electricity we can do so legitimately in most applications (see section on cost of risk). When calibrating derivatives, it is the risk neutral measure that is used *de facto*, but in real world probability estimation, such as power station failure, it is the real world measure that we use. For further information see Baxter and Rennie, or Geman (2005).

Over a period of n steps, where n is large, the probability distribution of cumulative step height m (individual steps being of unit height) is given by the binomial distribution;

$$P(m) = \frac{n!}{(n-m)!m!} \cdot \frac{1}{2^n}$$

Where P(m) is the probability of the total step height being m.

For large n, the form of this approximates to the normal distribution.

$$P(x) = \frac{1}{\sqrt{2\pi}} \exp(-(x-\mu)^2/2\sigma^2) \qquad (9.1)$$

Where μ is the mean, σ the standard deviation. x is the distance from the mean μ and $\frac{x-\mu}{\sigma}$ is the number of standard deviations from the mean.

The cumulative probability of a normal distribution of mean μ and standard deviation σ is termed N(μ, σ). $N(\mu, \sigma) = \int_{-\infty}^{\kappa} \frac{1}{\sqrt{2\pi}} \exp(-(x-\mu)^2/2\sigma^2)dx$. N(0,1) represents a standard normal distribution with zero mean and unit standard deviation. The evaluation of the function is available in spreadsheets and software packages, and the polynomial formula is in many textbooks.[4]

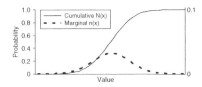

Figure 9.2   Cumulative and marginal probabilities for the normal distribution

The normal distribution is particularly important. We shall see in section 9.1.9 that there is a strong tendency of processes to have terminal distributions that are normal if we have enough steps.

The expectation, denoted by the expectation operator $E[\ ]$, is the probability weighted average. So for discrete events

$$E[S] = \sum_n S * P(S)$$

For continuous interval:

$$E[S] = \int_{-\infty}^{\infty} S * P(S)dS$$

If we depict our process as, in each timeslice, having a step up or down of size $\sqrt{dt}$ then we can see the variance grows linearly with t as before. Since we know also that the terminal distribution of the process has a normal distribution, then we could replace the up or down step with a mini normal distribution in each timestep with the distribution being N(0, $\sqrt{dt}$).

---

[4] e.g. Haug (1998).

If we denote a sampling from the distribution N(0,1) by ε, then we can say that

$$dS = \varepsilon\sqrt{dt} \qquad (9.2)$$

The distribution represented by $N(0, \sqrt{dt})$ is commonly termed dz, so we can instead denote our process:

$$dS = \sigma dz \qquad (9.3)$$

t is measured in years and σ is now the annualised standard deviation.

This is a Wiener process.

9.1.3   Terminal distributions and price returns

We could view the terminal, or cumulative, distribution as the result of a number of paths, each of which is the evolution of the price process.

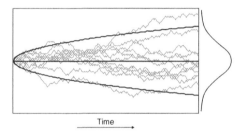

Time

Figure 9.3   Paths generated by random walk, showing mean, one standard deviation either side, as well as the shape of the terminal distribution

We may then superimpose on this process a definite movement in price from one timeslice to another, called a drift. The movement is not probabilistic (i.e. it is deterministic) but could depend on the current status of the system (the current level of the spot price and equilibrium price)

$$dS = \mu(t, S)dt + \sigma(t, S)dz \qquad (9.4)$$

Here the brackets after the terms μ and σ denote the fact that the drift and volatility terms may change in a deterministic manner with time and price.

This process equation, called the Ito process equation in the form represented above, can be extended to include extra features such as jumps, mean reversion and path dependence.

9.1.4   Transformation of process and Ito's Lemma

When doing calculus in the stochastic world we note that the Newtonian 'infinitesimal' calculus that we are learnt at school does not work because the Newtonian assumption that lines appear to be straight if we look at a short enough length, is not true for stochastic processes.

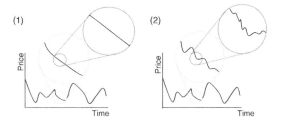

Figure 9.4 Depiction of why standard Newtonian calculus does not work for stochastic processes. (1) In Newtonian calculus all curves look straight when short lengths are looked at at high magnification, (2) In stochastic processes, the path looks granular at all magnifications

Instead, we need to use Ito calculus. Although this can be hard to understand, it is actually fairly straightforward to apply in most situations.

For an Ito process

$$dS = a(t, S)dt + b(t, S)dz \tag{9.5}$$

If we define a function G(S).

Then application of Ito's lemma[5] gives us;

$$dG = \left(\frac{\partial G}{\partial S}a + \frac{\partial G}{\partial t} + \frac{1}{2}\frac{\partial^2 G}{\partial S^2}b^2\right)dt + \frac{\partial G}{\partial S}\sigma dz \tag{9.6}$$

A useful application of Ito's lemma is in the lognormal distribution, as we see next.

9.1.5 Normal and lognormal distributions

The process equation 9.2 shown represents a constant expectation of absolute step size and causes a normal distribution of the power price.

If instead the step size is a constant ratio of price (dS/S – Geometric Brownian Motion), rather than a constant absolute size (dS – Arithmetic Brownian Motion), then our equation looks like

$$dS = \mu(t)Sdt + \sigma(t)Sdz \tag{9.7}$$

If we choose our function G to be the natural logarithm of price, G = ln(S), then we can apply Ito's lemma to equation 9.7. a = μS and b = σS in equation 9.5, and we note that $\partial G/\partial S = 1/S$, $\partial^2 G/\partial S^2 = -1/S^2$ and $\partial G/\partial t = 0$. So

$$d(\ln(S)) = \left(\mu - \frac{\sigma^2}{2}\right)dt + \sigma dz \tag{9.8}$$

This is a very useful result. If the relative returns on price (dS/S) follow random walk then the logarithm of price will also have a random walk, and the terminal distribution of the

---

[5] A lemma is a form of theorem. For further explanation of Ito's lemma see Wilmott *et al.* For proof of Ito's lemma, see Hull (1997).

logarithm of price will be normally distributed (i.e. the terminal distribution of price will be lognormally distributed).

The lognormal distribution (and, by implication the geometric version of Brownian motion) is commonly used in statistical analysis of prices, primarily because the high degree of skewness[6] in relation to the normal distribution represents a good empirical fit to observed distributions and because negative prices are avoided.

It is worth spending a moment considering the intuitive understanding of volatility, which is normally expressed as a percentage.

Suppose that over a unit time period, the price process moves one standard deviation upwards:

$$\ln(S_0) \rightarrow \ln(S_0) + \sigma$$

We can express the term on the right hand side by $\ln(S_0 e^{\sigma})$

$$\text{For small } \sigma, e^{\sigma} \approx 1 + \sigma$$

So, for small σ, our term on the right hand side can be approximated $\ln(S_0(1 + \sigma))$.

So we can interpret σ as the fractional change in price over unit time. This is why, even for the lognormal distribution, that standard deviation is commonly expressed as a percentage. We must beware of using this intuitive measure for volatilities much above about 10 %.

Geometric Brownian Motion (GBM) is used almost universally for the following reasons:

(i)   For prices that grow (forward curve upward sloping and ideally upward curving), GBM is the best distribution.
(ii)   Long term price distributions are skewed due to the volatility of the mean reverting price (section 9.1.11).
(iii) Negative prices are avoided.
(iv)   For high volatilities, the lognormal distributions is essential to ensure no negative prices, and for low volatilities, the normal and lognormal distributions are similar close to the mean, and hence the lognormal distribution is a safer choice for general purposes.

However, we must beware a few things, for example:

(i)   GBM is most naturally suited to growing spot prices, which thereby exhibit an upward sloping and upward curving forward price curve. The upward curve in particular is very rarely seen in practice.
(ii)   Negative prices[7] do occur in the very short term (less than one day horizon) in some actual electricity markets.

The convenience of the high skewness of the distribution of absolute price returns relative to the normal distribution, and strictly positive prices can easily lead us into naïve acceptance of Geometric Brownian Motion, and the associated lognormal distribution. If the high skewness arises for completely different reasons (for example jumps, as we shall see) then it is important that we consider Arithmetic Brownian Motion also. The reason for this is, that

---

[6] Skewness is often described as the extent to which the probability of large movements exceeds that predicted by the normal distribution. In practice the term has a variety of meanings, formal and informal.

[7] Negative prices do occur for electricity, and of the same magnitude as the positive price limit. However, this only occurs post gate closure in the bilateral market, and do not exist in the bilateral forward market. They do not exist in the pool.

as we will see in looking at the central limit theory, over the long term our proper 'state variable' will be normally distributed with no skew. We must be sure whether we believe that this state variable should be price or the logarithm of price.

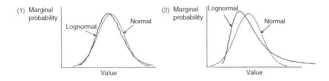

Figure 9.5 Comparison of normal and lognormal probability distributions with the same mean and variance. (1) low volatility, (2) High volatility

9.1.6 Skewness

The term skewness is used in a several ways:

(i)   **For traded options** – the difference in implied volatility between puts and calls of the same magnitude of delta. We shall see this later in section 9.2.2.
(ii) **For general statistical description** – The increase of probability for actual probability distributions relative to the normal distribution, for low probability extremes. A common term meaning the same thing is 'fat tails', since the tail of the distribution is higher than for the normal distribution
(iii) The formal statistical definition is below.

$$skewness = \frac{E\left[X - E(x)\right]^3}{\sigma_X^3}$$

$$kurtosis = \frac{E\left[X - E(x)\right]^4}{\sigma_X^4} - 3$$

9.1.7 The Poisson process

In the simple Poisson process, we advance one time 'slice' at a time, and at each time interval there is either a factor movement of fixed magnitude J, or there is not. The probability of the step is noted q. The appearance or non appearance of the step is called the Bernoulli trial.

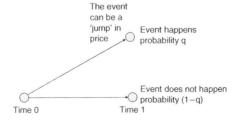

Figure 9.6   A Bernoulli trial – the step of a Poisson process

Note that if $q = 0.5$ and $J = 2$ then this is equivalent to a random walk with $\sigma = 1$ and $\mu = 1$, so we can regard random walk as a special case of a Poisson process, and the normal distribution a special case of the Poisson distribution.

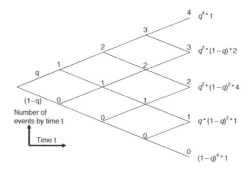

Figure 9.7   Probability tree for the Poisson process

9.1.8   Jump diffusion

We can put the Poisson and the Brownian motions together to make what was called by Merton in 1976 'jump diffusion'.

$$\frac{dS}{S} = \mu(t)dt + Jdq + \sigma dz$$

J can have a distribution which can be normal. We can envisage a process of first throwing the dq die is rolled to see if there is a jump and then the J dispersion to see how big it is. J may also be negative.

Even for infinite[8] jump size and infinitesimally small probability, then the variance still grows linearly with time, as with random walk.

$$Variance = J^2 * q * t$$

The situation is not so simple for the higher moments such as skewness. In fact the odd moments tend to infinity in the short term for the near infinite size jump described.

What this means in practice that for the Poisson distribution, large moves are much more likely than for the normal distribution in the short term, but over the long term, due to the central limit theory that we shall examine, the cumulative distribution is the same as for the normal distribution. This is a very important property for electricity because of the spikiness in short term power prices, and enables us to understand the link between physical events such as power station failure and the modelling of price distributions and the 'smile' structure of traded options.

Jump diffusion is popular for power price modelling because: (i) Geometric Brownian motion in spot or forward price will commonly underestimate the higher moments of commodity price returns, (ii) Jumps can add skewness that attenuates with tenor, which matches observed behaviour and (iii) In the power market, we can understand jumps intuitively in terms of demand spikes and power plant failure.

---

[8] The expectation is unity. The 'Dirac delta' has the equivalent properties.

9.1.9 Central limit theory

The central limit theory is of very high importance[9] in probability theory and in price process modelling. Fortunately, for most purposes we just need to know what it says, rather than how to apply it formally.

Given a sequence of independent identically distributed variates X_i with expectation $E[X_i] = \mu$ and variance $V[X_i] = \sigma^2$, then if the total is defined $S_n = \sum_{i=1}^{n} X_i$, then for increasing n, the composite variate $Y_n = \frac{S_n - n\mu}{\sigma\sqrt{n}}$, converges in distribution to the standard normal distribution N(0,1).

This all looks rather complicated, but the informal version is really rather simple. If we add a number of terminal distributions of the same process together, then if we add enough times, the terminal distribution of the sum will tend to the normal distribution, no matter what the shape of the individual distributions.

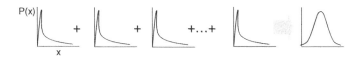

Figure 9.8 Representation of the central limit theory. The summation of most identical distributions tends to the normal distribution

The central limit theorem is very powerful in helping us to understand fundamental processes but must be used with care. For example, if we over summarise by 'all distributions tend to the normal in the long term' we can find ourselves in difficulty. For example, if the near term distribution looks lognormal, then we cannot simply add distributions to get a normal distribution over the long term, because the lognormal distribution is associated with a growing price, which maintains the 'fatness' of the probability tail.

The central limit theory is invoked when constructing distributions that approximate the normal distribution, for example $\varepsilon = -\frac{1}{2}n + \sum_{i=1}^{n} U_i$ where $n \geq \approx 12$ and U is the uniform distribution between 0 and 1.

9.1.10 Extreme value theory

The extreme value theory has much in common with the central limit theory. It is a complicated theory with a useful and simple outcome. In this case, the extreme value theory states that for all 'reasonable' probability distributions, the distribution has the same form at probability extremes, as the generalised Pareto distribution.

The generalised Pareto distribution has the form[10]:

$$G_{\xi,\beta}(x) = 1 - (1 + \xi x/\beta)^{-1/\xi} \text{ for } \xi \neq 0$$

$$G_{\xi,\beta}(x) = 1 - \exp(-x/\beta) \text{ for } \xi = 0$$

(9.9)

Where $\beta > 0$, and where $x \geq 0$ when $\xi \geq 0$, and $0 \leq x \leq -\beta/\xi$ when $\xi < 0$.

---

[9] The first version of what was later called Central Limit Theory (because of its central importance) by Polya, was by Laplace between 1812 and 1820. Later versions were made by Chebyshef, Markov, Lyapunov, Khinchi, Lindeberg, Levy and others.

[10] This form is from McNeill (1999).

If we have a limited sample of extreme events, such as combined plant outages, or price spikes, then we can fit the population that we see to the generalised Pareto distribution, to estimate the probability of even rarer events, such as lost load due to excess demand over generation.

Suppose instead that we are considering the probability/size distribution of the worst event is a particular time period. Define the worst event in a period set of n observations as W, and test to see if there is a sequence of numbers such that the distribution of $(W - b_n)/a_n$ converges to a limiting distribution. If this is so, then the distribution must be of the form $H(x) = H_\xi(x - \mu/\sigma)$ for some ξ, μ and σ.

H(x) is the generalised extreme value distribution:

$$H_\xi(x) = \exp(-(1 + \xi x)^{-1/\xi}) \text{ for } \xi \neq 0$$

$$H_\xi(x) = \exp(-\exp(-x)) \text{ for } \xi = 0$$

This distribution is known as the Fréchet distribution for $\xi > 0$, the Gumbel distribution for $\xi = 0$, and the Weibull distribution for $\xi < 0$.

This is a particularly useful theorem when we are considering high impact low frequency events. This is important for calculating the economic cost failure of low merit plant, for calculating the probability of loss of load, and for modelling of power prices in situations where there is no price cap. It is also extremely useful in various calculations relating to power station failure such as the fair value of strategic spares access transactions and of retrocessive reinsurance contracts relating to plant failure.

9.1.11   Mean reversion

Economic analysis tells us that there is usually some kind of fair or equilibrium price, and that if the prevailing market price differs from that price, then supply and demand will mobilise in such a manner that the market appears to 'try' to revert to the mean price. This is called mean reversion. If the restorative force is proportional to the absolute difference in price from the equilibrium price, then it is represented in equation 9.10.[11] The general proportionality of the force to the distance from the mean is referred to as Hookes Law, in reference to the initial application of this law for the tension of a spring in relation to the amount that it is stretched.

$$dS = \mu(t)dt - k * (S - S_e)dt + \sigma(t)dz \tag{9.10}$$

Where:

k represents the restorative force

S_e is the equilibrium price to which the spot price is 'trying' to revert.

Without the μ term,[12] this is equivalent to the Vasicek process.

We can express the mean reversion in terms of the logarithm of price.

---

[11] Here the price factor is generalised. If n=0, the price distribution is normal (see Vasicek 1998), if n=1 the price distribution is lognormal (see Courtadon, 1982) and if n=0.5, the price distribution is chi-squared (see Cox, Ingersoll and Ross, 1985).

[12] For commodities, Se has a fundamental meaning. For many financial derivatives, this is not the case, and for constant k we can subsume the μ term into K(Se).

$$d(\ln(S)) = \left(\mu - \frac{\sigma^2}{2}\right) dt + k * (\ln(S) - \ln(S_e)) dt + \sigma dz$$

This is an Ornstein-Uhlenbeck process.[13]

We can interpret a non zero long tenor instantaneous volatility ($d > 0$ in our term structure equations described in section 9.2.1) in terms of a constant rate of mean reversion to a stochastic mean.

$$dS_e = \mu_e(t) dt + \sigma_e dz \qquad (9.11)$$

It is certainly possible to make mean reversion more complicated. For example the restorative force need not have a linear relationship with distance of price from its mean (i.e. does not follow Hookes law). However, this linear effect (sometimes called the Samuelson effect) is appealing in terms of fundamental economics and has the additional benefit of having exponential decay, which makes the maths much easier.

Similarly mean reversion rate could have a deterministic and/or stochastic relationship with time and it is intimately bound up with volatility.

$$dk = \mu_k(\sigma_S) dt + \sigma_k dz$$

Where σ_S is the volatility of spot price.

In practice, almost all processes have means that vary. Note that if our price process is Arithmetic Brownian Motion (normal) then we choose (with some economic logic but mainly for modelling convenience) that it is price that mean reverts, and if it is Geometric Brownian Motion (lognormal), then we choose that it is the logarithm of price that mean reverts. Since the logarithm of price has little physical meaning and hence difficult to tie to economic forces, we note that $\ln(S) - \ln(Se) = \ln(S/Se)$. The intuitive meaning then is that the economic restorative force does not respond to absolute price differences $(S - Se)$ but to relative price differences (S/Se). Relative price differential mean reversion is consistent with long term currency fluctuation. If the currency value halved, then, Keynesiasm aside, we should not expect the rate of physical response to change, and would expect the absolute rate of mean reversion to double.

In the short term, currency volatility in G7 economies is low (around 10%) and we do not need to pay attention to it in electricity. In the long term, the currency volatility, which attenuates little with tenor, denominates the fundamental volatility of the commodity. This is considered in section 9.1.21.

If we feel that there is a fundamental,[14] determinable and stable equilibrium Seq:

$$d(\ln(S_e)) = \mu(t, \sigma) dt - k * \left(\ln \frac{S_e}{S_{eq}(t)}\right) dt + \sigma dz$$

In the classical economic model, there are layers of more fundamental denominators, until the most fundamental factors (labour and natural resource) are found. Equations more complicated than 9.10 and 9.11 are little used in practice.

---

[13] Ornstein-Uhlenbeck processes have terminal distributions which are Gaussian (normal) and conditionally Gaussian. See Rebonato (2004).

[14] Here we imply a hierarchy of fundamentalism of economic equilibria, with the most fundamental being utility or welfare. The practical application is that this gives us degree of freedom in modelling the equilibrium price.

In the extreme, the mean reversion rate is infinite and the mean is static. In this case, we do not have a stochastic process since at each time interval we are sampling from a distribution that never changes. The techniques used are then actuarial rather than stochastic. Actuarial techniques are helpful in establishing moments of distributions and correlations, and in the failure analysis of power stations.

9.1.12   Mean reversion with jump diffusion

The jump diffusion model was initially devised by Merton to contend with information shocks to the foreign exchange market. The jump represented a permanent shift to a new price, with no 'memory of old prices'. This is quite suitable for foreign exchange because there is no 'fundamental' rate for foreign exchange rates to revert to.[15]

The problem with application of jump diffusion in the power market, is that empirical evidence is that the jumps are not permanent, and the prices tend to revert back. In other words, they are spikes. Figure 9.9 shows the problem.

In the first instance, with no mean reversion, we see that the market jumps up and stays up. This does not match empirical evidence in the power market.

In the second instance, with random up jumps that are deterministically tied to subsequent down jumps, the down jump must either be immediate, in which case the price is high for an infinitely short time, or it must be delayed, in which case it must be handled by a regime switching model that we shall examine in section 9.1.13.

In the third instance, the jump is brought back down by the mean reversion. This presents no particular theoretical difficulties in modelling, but gives us two particular problems in replicating observed behaviour. Firstly, a Hookes Law mean reversion that is strong enough to restore the deviation from a jump in reasonable time, is so strong that little or no effect persists after the jump. For example, suppose that we start with $S = Se = 1$ and the normal process gets us about 1 above Se and we get a jump of 10, then we want the mean reversion to get us back to within about 100 % of the initial price (i.e. below about Se + 1). So the mean reversion rate would need to be about $(10 - 2)/(10 - 1) = 88\%$ for the time interval of the spike. If we wish to get back to within 10 % of the initial price (still a large change), then the mean reversion rate would need to be $(10 - 1.1)/(10 - 1) = 99\%$, which would overwhelm any stochastic movement apart from the jumps, since the price would revert back to the mean rather than retain a memory of the cumulative effect of random walk.

While the form of the jump, of escarpment shape with a sharp rise and a sloped fall, is intuitively sensible in economic terms, there is a greater degree of asymmetry than observed in practice. There are good economic reasons for a more symmetrical shape. For example, failures and demand spikes are not quite as sudden as they at first appear because of the non-zero warning period and the ability to make limited postponement of power station shutdown.

In Figure 9.9 the first two are clearly not viable for electricity as they stand, and need not be considered further. The third remains problematic, as the jump is so extreme in relation to

---

[15] Purchasing power parity is cited as a short term equilibrium, but in the medium term, inflation effects overwhelm this.

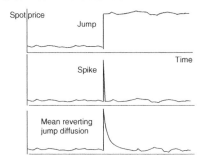

Figure 9.9   Three forms of jump. (1) A permanent shift to price, (2) An up move followed by a deterministic down move of the same size and after a deterministic period, (3) An up move followed by a reversion to the previous price

the normal price process that there is effectively no memory of where the price was before the jump.

What we want is a spike of finite width and a price process that returns to the pre-spike level rather than the equilibrium price?

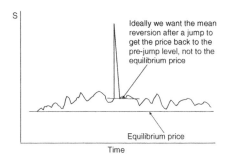

Figure 9.10   Desired properties of price process with spike

9.1.13   Regime switching

We saw in Figure 9.9 that it is very difficult in practice to create a process that causes spikes (i.e. a short term excursion to a very high price) and which can also recover other features of the market such as volatility skewness and volatility attenuation with tenor. Getting the jump is not the problem as such, it is getting the price back down to normal levels. One way of solving this problem is to treat times of peak prices as behaving in a fundamentally different manner. This can be done by regime switching.

In regime switching, we view the market as existing in a number (usually two) of discrete states. For example, the market may exist in a 'normal' state with one process equation, or a 'jump' state, with a different process equation. We have already accepted the principle of two different processes when we introduced jump diffusion, and the only leap that we have made in regime switching is in assuming that only one process at a time is active.

We can represent the probabilities of changing from one state to the other in terms of a transition matrix.

From ↓ to →	normal	jump
normal	$1-q$	q
jump	p	$1-p$

We can see that: (i) we can have a finite residence time in the jump regime and (ii) that in the jump regime we can have a negative drift so that eventually prices get back to normal.

Note that in order to correctly specify the next step of our price movement we need at least two items of information, namely: (i) the current price and (ii) the current state. Our problem is that the market does not directly reveal to us the state. We have to infer it from price history and hence, unless the state is actually revealed by the price (for example if the price exceeds a particular level, then the state must be the jump state), we have a non Markov problem. We deal with Markov and non Markov processes in section 9.1.14.

The process is most amenable for two states, a jump state and a normal state, but several states are possible, or both states could be normal, but with very different process parameters.

We could envisage two continuous processes, with the price continually changing from one to another. In this sense, when a state is returned to, it does not return to the last known price in that state, but to the evolved price. We could instead envisage a single process with two modes, in which case when a state is returned to, the price for that state is the last observed price at that state.

The example below shows two states, both of which are random walks, but which might have very different volatilities, mean reversions and drifts. In this case we consider that the price in one state does not evolve when the state is not active. We need to be careful about specifying the entity of 'spot price', since here we actually need to know the current spot price for both states. For the case in the figure, assuming for convenience that the processes are arithmetic Brownian motion, then the terminal distribution is a normal distribution, composed of the sum of two normal distributions of standard deviation that is derived from the relative proportion of time spent in each state, and the standard deviations of the states.

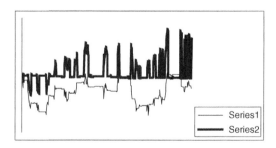

Figure 9.11 Regime switching simulations. In series 1 both regimes are continuous. In series 2, each regime resumes where it left off when it was last active

A high degree of richness can be added by regime switching but this comes with a cost; most applications become path dependent, so trees and closed form solutions cannot be used.

For a very small power system, regime switching has some appeal, since we can imagine the two regimes as 'power station fail' and 'power stations OK'. However in a system of around 200 units, with a high proportion of these not operating at 100% capacity and the variation of lost generation being distributed, it is less applicable. Alternatively, regime switching could potentially be useful for unconstrained and constrained modes of a network.

Regime switching is well suited to two distinct states. This is not a particularly realistic representation of electricity prices, since there is little evidence of distinct bimodality in the market. If the number of regimes increases, then the model becomes somewhat incomprehensible.

9.1.14 Markov processes

In a Markov process, the development of the price process is dependent only on (i) the constant parameters of the process equation (for example the rate of mean reversion is commonly modelled to be constant) and (ii) the current specification of the price process (for example, the price itself). It is entirely independent of further information derived from the path of arrival to the state. A non Markov process can be represented by the following equation:

$$dS = \mu(path)dt + \sigma(path)dz$$

Suppose that we believe that we have a one factor price process, and from regression analysis we find that there is some form of correlation between the price movements and previous price movements, then we have established a path dependence. We can express this is as $dS_i = f(dS_{i-n})$ or $\rho_{dS_i dS_{i-n}} \neq 0$. In this sense, prices appear to have a positive (or negative) momentum. Note that in efficient markets in the risk free world, that forward price processes are always Markov, since if the price history gives us information about a drift of the forward price, then we would have an arbitrage opportunity. The action of traders would swiftly bring the forward price into line with its anticipated value and hence eliminate any drift. While it is economically inefficient for forward prices to have a drift over and above the drift due to cost of risk, there remains a common belief in market momentum. Hence for example, the willingness to buy in a 'rising market'.

In practice there is little autocorrelation in returns in those markets that are traded actively enough to have datasets. There is evidence for autocorrelation of squared returns, which is more pronounced at high sampling frequency. We should view this as autocorrelation of volatility.

Non Markov processes are generally highly undesirable from a modelling perspective, due to the difficulty in modelling and then applying path dependence. Fractional Brownian Motion, described in section 9.5.3.2, is a non Markov process.

9.1.14.1 Making processes Markov by greater level of specification

Suppose that we believe that we have a two factor process, in which both spot price and equilibrium prices are moving.

$$dS = \mu(t)dt - k*(S - S_e)dt + \sigma(t)dz$$
$$dS_e = \mu_e(t)dt + \sigma_e(t)dz$$

To specify the next step of our process, we need to know all of the static parameters, $\mu(t), k, \sigma(t), \mu e(t), \sigma e(t)$, and we need to know the current values of S and Se.

To model our process as a Markov process, we then must carry two items of changing information, S and Se.

Now S, the spot price, is observable. The latent variable[16] Se is not directly observable since it is not traded, but noting that all forward curves must be viable evolutions from price processes (provided that the processes are correctly specified), then we can estimate Se from extrapolation of the forward curve, with sufficient accuracy for our process equation. Hence, with two factors we can model our Markov process.

Now suppose that we have no visibility of the forward curve, and the market reveals to us only the spot price S. Regression analysis will reveal to us that the drift on the spot price has a trend that changes in a stochastic manner arising from the stochastic movement of Se. We will find positive correlation between S_i and S_{i-1}. Since we do not observe Se, then the missing information from the change in Se appears in the autocorrelation of spot prices.

9.1.14.2   *Examples of path dependence*

We see in Chapter 10 on economics, that with stochastic prices, the forward contract market does not give an efficient signal to investors in production and hence over and under investment is not damped. The result is a forward price that lags the investment and which is then path dependent.

Another example is the effect of non tradable emission permits. We showed in section 6.4.2 that we can treat a permit allocation as a swing option, and therefore the amount of permits remaining at a point in time, is dependent both on the prevailing spot and forward price vector, and the price history of the vector. Ongoing production is dependent on remaining permits, and hence forward prices are dependent on the history of the price vector. If the permits are tradable only in the region covered by the electricity price, then the same applies, since there is a high correlation between permit exercise executions by different producers. Forward prices are dependent on the total remaining stock of emission permits that have not been surrendered.

9.1.15   Spot and Forward price processes

Whereas spot prices are like indexes that march through time across periods which might have a very different physical nature (such as peak and off peak), and which are only tradable for a brief period before they turn into physical delivery, forward prices refer to tradable contracts that can be continuously traded until they become spot contracts.

Forward price processes track the progress of individual forward contracts. In the risk neutral world forward contracts have no drift in their stochastic processes. The reason for this is that if we expect a forward price to fall over a time interval, then we would sell forward and then buy at the next time interval and expect to make a profit. Speculators would crowd together and compete away the profit. Since the profit is risky, in the risk averse world the speculators will require a specific level of profit to compensate them for risk.

So the process at observation time t for a forward contract of delivery time T is:

$$dF_{t,T} = \sigma_{T-t}dz + \sigma^n_{i,T,t,T-t}\lambda_i(T, t)dt \qquad (9.12)$$

---

[16] Kalman filters can be useful in the modelling of latent variables.

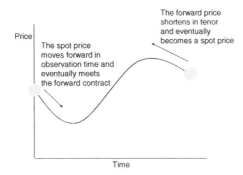

Figure 9.12 Representation of spot price process and forward price process on the forward price curve

Here the drift term arises from cost of risk. Cost of risk is described and the choice between 1 and 2 for n is described in more detail in section 9.1.22.

The attenuation of volatility with tenor for forward contracts is related to the mean reversion of spot contracts. Both assume the action of a restorative force by economic agents whose rate of response is directly proportional to the opportunity (the difference between actual and 'fundamental' price. For spot prices, this is interpreted as a force that is proportional to the opportunity. For forward prices, this is interpreted as a rate of arrival or size of forces that is directly proportional to the opportunity.

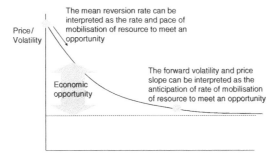

Figure 9.13 Visualisation of forward slope curvature in terms of spot price mean reversion and forward price

If we have information about forward prices and/or about options on forward contracts, then we must calibrate our spot price processes to them. We do this through the mean reversion term (which, for a one factor process, causes an exponential attenuation of volatility with tenor) and the drift term, which we apply after mean reversion in order to recover the forward price and its associated periodicity.

Our first problem is that in stepping through the contracts, we note that, uniquely amongst commodities, we may pass through electricity contracts that are quite different in their qualitative nature. For example, peak contracts follow off peak contracts but may behave in a quite different way.

There are number of ways around this problem. All of them first attend to the periodicity of the market. We now look at periodicity and how we can model the movement of periodic prices.

9.1.15.1 Periodicity

Electricity has three dominant periods – seasonal, weekly and daily. The coarsest periodical representation of price that adequately captures price movements is to have 12 months per year, four–eight time periods per day, and separate weekdays from weekends. If we choose six periods per day, then this gives 144 discrete timeblocks.

We can visualise this by 'wrapping' the continuum of prices, first by month, then by week, then by time of day.

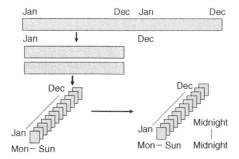

Figure 9.14   Wrapping the continuum of spot prices into three periodic cycles

The result of wrapping with three periodic cycles is a cube of prices, rather than a string.

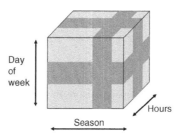

Figure 9.15   The price cube for three periodic cycles

We can view standard contract forms that are traded in the market, and which apply to specific plant. For example, plants that run off peak are interested in off peak contracts, rather than baseload contracts.

The price on any particular forward date is now viewed as a vector of periodic elements, each of which has a volatility for the tenor, and a correlation for the tenor to the other elements. The build up of contract volatility is described in section 9.2.1.3.

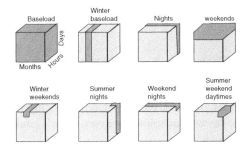

Figure 9.16   Depiction of standard contracts on the pricing cube

9.1.15.2   *Handling periodicity by deseasonalising*

Deseasonalising is the most common approach because it allows the simplest application of standard derivative techniques. To deseasonalise, either the average or the current periodicity is subtracted from the volatility curve and (usually) the forward curve. Then normal spot price processes are applied to the deseasonalised price. Finally the seasonalisation is added back at the end.

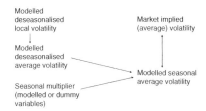

Figure 9.17   Calibration of seasonal volatility

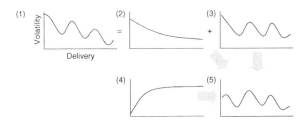

Figure 9.18   Application of seasonal volatility. First decompose the implied volatility curve (1) into a deseasonalised local volatility curve (2) and a seasonality (3). Then apply stochastic process shock (4) and multiply by seasonal factor (3) to get the simulated forward curve shock (5)

We see here that we must make a subjective judgement of how to decompose the curve. We may choose to keep the deseasonalised curve as near an exponential shape as possible and have an uneven seasonal profile, or have a well formed seasonal profile and have a bumpy deseasonalised curve that could not have arisen[17] from the application of the current process to past prices. This technique is very similar to the application of dummy variables in economics.

There are three main problems with the deseasonalisation approach: (i) the adjustment of price by deseasonalisation affects the mean reversion rate and hence causes incorrect drifts, (ii) the seasonalisation is itself stochastic but not independently so, so it is not practical to add a deseasonalised process to stochastic seasonality and (iii) volatility is periodic with respect to observation time t as well as contract delivery time T, and this is generally ignored in the deseasonalisation approach.

Figure 9.19 shows a calibration. In such calibrations, it is important to temper the fit of short term volatilities (less than about six months) to reflect recent history of spot prices. There is little benefit of creating a perfect short tenor fit to a stochastic volatility.

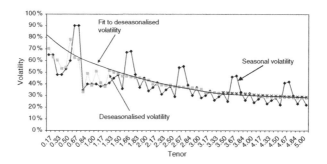

Figure 9.19   Example of the deseasonalisation of volatility. New York over the counter market 2001. Source Innogy

9.1.15.3   Varying the periodicity

If the curve is deseasonalised, then the term structure and the periodic structure can be treated separately. Whilst there are obvious issues in decoupling these, the method is in practice very useful. In order to shock the periodicity, it must first be modelled in order to shock the coefficients.

While trigonometric functions are useful as a basis for periodic structures, they require significant adjustment to fit observed forward curves or spot price histories. For example, the annual seasonal structure tends to have narrow high peaks and long flat troughs. The curves in Figure 9.20 are based on $(\sin \theta)^{\sin \theta}$. While the 'peakiness' can be adjusted to give the high narrow peaks and wide shallow troughs that approximate the actual prices, the problems with the 'shoulder' periods are obvious. Commonly several parameters are required to model the actual market, and the different daily periods have very different seasonal periodicity.

With respect to annual periodicity, from a price perspective, not only is the midwinter peak date not exactly six months away from the midsummer trough date, but the date itself is subject to stochastic shocks. For example from early or late ice melt for hydro based

---

[17] A one factor mean reverting stochastic process applied to a non periodic structure can only create forward curves of exponential form.

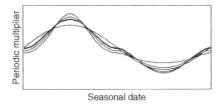

Figure 9.20 Example of simple adjustment to the peakiness of the annual periodicity

systems. This can be represented quite easily by adding a stress term to the midwinter date, as shown in Figure 9.21.
Here

$$Periodic \_ multiplier = \sin(x)$$

$$x = T + stress$$

where T is the delivery date

$$Stress = \chi * \exp(-abs(T - T')) * sign(T' - T)$$

where T' is the date on the forward curve that receives maximum stress. Note that representing a forward curve, the stress does not mean revert.

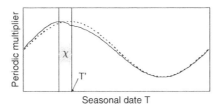

Figure 9.21 Adding deterministic or stochastic adjustment to the mid winter date

We can then add a stochastic variation to χ or add a similar term. For more sophisticated analysis, we can use Fourier series, as shown in section 9.5.3.4, but it is not easy to add a variable stress term due to the instability of Fourier series to small changes in periodicity.

Another example is the change of the amplitude of the periodicity over time. Periodic price structures represent opportunity for exercise of the various kinds of storage described in section 6.4. An increase in storage capability in relation to periodicity results in a decline in the periodic amplitude over the years. From the opposite perspective, a decrease in capacity margin in maturing markets, can result in an increase in periodic amplitude.

We have described periodicity according to contract date. There is additionally periodicity in relation to observation date. For example, if winter is commonly an active period in a particular market, then the volatility of winter prices will be more volatile in the winter than in the summer. This effect, while intuitively known to traders, is difficult to isolate, because it is necessary to 'de-tenorise' (see section 9.3.6.1) the contracts. This can be handled to some degree by applying periodicity to the 'g' in equation 9.25. However this adds to the complications in integrating option volatilities.

9.1.15.4   Handling periodicity by parallel forward processes

The deseasonalisation approach completely separates the stochastic processes that apply to the periodicity of the market and to the deseasonalised market. Alternatively, each period could be treated as a separate commodity, linked by correlation (and possibly an arbitrage relationship leading to co-integration) to the other periods. Instead of there being one spot price process, there are as many processes as there are periods.

Just as we deseasonalised before, to prepare for correlation application, we have to initially 'de-tenorise'[18] – that is to assume initially that all periods are at the same tenor. For example we may initially say that winter and summer contracts both exist at the one year tenor.

The construction of the local volatility of aggregate periods (for example a whole day) from its elements (for example daily peak and off peak) is simply and approximately done using equations in section 9.2.1.3. Then by constructing the local volatilities for a series of tenors, we can fit a volatility function to the series and integrate to get the option volatilities to calibrate to.

This method is particularly useful if we need to know the volatility of one periodic element such as winters, weekdays, or peak hours, or if we want to know the volatility of the spread between prices, whether it be day versus night (for pump storage), winter versus summer (for a variety of options such as conservation of emission permits) or the spread between commodities at different times (for example gas versus off peak power).

The problem with this approach is that the connection between adjacent contracts is lost, and hence 'unreasonable' periodic forms could evolve. This can be solved in part in Monte Carlo modelling since the periods can have the simultaneous application of shared history (e.g. temperature and plant outage) and individual history, and in addition, constraints to the price difference between periods can be applied dynamically. However for other modelling such as stochastic dynamic programming, this method cannot be applied.

This method is similar to the 'string'[19] method of modelling financial derivatives. It is also useful for co-integrated variable (see section 9.1.19). We can view the two connected variables as the walk of a drunken man and his dog. Each has a degree of independence but they are drawn back together when the distance increases (the length of the lead, and the arbitrage relationship between the contracts).

9.1.15.5   Handling periodicity by using a single spot price process

Another way is to attempt to cover the full periodicity in one process. The spot price moves through the full cycle of prices. We can have local volatility, local mean reversion rates and local mean reversion equilibrium prices for each different period.

The problem with this method, is that even if we ignore the volatility of the equilibrium price and assume a one factor process, that the degree to which we need to specify our process is excessive, and we cannot therefore sensibly calibrate, and recalibrate over time.

---

[18] This term is used here for convenience and is not a standard term.
[19] See Santa-Clara and Sornette (1999).

9.1.16   The choice between spot and forward price processes

While spot and forward processes can both be applied to most situations, they do lend themselves better to specific applications, and are alternatives in most instances, and the chosen method depends very much on the nature of the data available and of the background of the modeller. Table 9.1 broadly represents the preference of applicability of the respective approaches.

Table 9.1   Comparison of the use of spot price processes and forward price process for instrument modelling

Feature	Spot price process	Forward price process
Richness of data of spot and forward price history	Best for rich spot price data	Best for rich forward price data. Best if both data are rich
Richness of data of European option price history	Potentially best for high skew/smile short tenor options	Best for rich option price data
Characterisation of asset base economics	Difficult to handle several commodities. Best for swing modelling	Most adaptable to asset modelling. Can handle several commodities (e.g. gas, power, coal). Best for semi-analytic modelling
Data sources	Best for single sources (e.g. spot price history)	Best for multiple fragmented sources (e.g. price histories for market contracts and for asset sales)
Characterisation of demand dynamics	Best for modelling short term in which aggregate demand is volatile	Best for long term demand trends, demand management, customer churn, and capacity modelling
Importance of storage in price dynamics	Best for all but simplest storage, where storage dynamics are constant	Limited to simple modelling but best for assessing impact on market changes
Constancy of market structure, regulation and economics	Best for constant environment. Poor for significant changes	Insufficient fit to rich data set in constant environment. Best handles estimated impact of changes
Auditability and transparency requirements for models	Best mapping both to auditable dataset and to established techniques	Requires extensive documentary support and testing of proprietary data estimation and pricing techniques
Frequency of decision making using modelling	Best for optimal exercise in highly structured environment (e.g. swing)	Best for trading market instruments
Number of factors in price process	Ineffective handling of more than three (spot price volatility, mean reversion rate, equilibrium price volatility)	Empirical handling of multi-factor, but beware of misspecification or pricing other than interpolation
Jumpiness of prices	Best for modelling very spiky processes	Best for modelling very peaky processes
Modeller	Mathematically oriented	Commercially oriented

9.1.17 n factor processes

We have already considered two factor processes in our mean reverting equation 9.10, and the stochastic mean in equation 9.11. We can then, if we wish, allow a positive correlation between the 'dz's' in the process. This may be adequate for modelling in immature markets. In mature markets, which might have high transparency, granularity, and range of traded derivative products, we need to add further sophistication for the following reasons:

(i)   As mentioned in section 9.5, where there is a deep liquid market, for system or asset modelling, we must always use the market and not our private view of fundamentals, for valuation, and differences between our prices and the market prices will quickly cause arbitrage against us.
(ii)   Real markets do not perfectly correspond to our simplified one factor processes and hence we increase the number of degrees of freedom in our models.
(iii) Our single pricing environment must simultaneously and correctly recover the prices of all traded instruments. This decreases our ability to 'fudge' the calibration to market of one instrument by allowing coefficient values that are economically and/or econometrically non sensible. A common example, is the modelling of two factor process with one factor models. A low 'c' in equation 9.23 can compensate for the lack of 'd' in the case of European options, but is unsatisfactory for other options.
(iv)   The very existence of markets alters prices and volatilities over and above the forces due to economic fundamentals. This causes an increase in long tenor volatilities and renders our one factor models insufficient.

Hence we must use more sophisticated models. A common method is to add factors to our forward price process.

$$dF = \sigma_1(\tau)dz_1 + \sigma_2(\tau)dz_2 + \cdots\cdots$$

$$E[dz_1 dz_2] = \rho_{dz_1 dz_2} dt$$

$$z_1 = W_1$$

$$z_2 = \rho W_1 + (1 - \rho^2)W_2$$

Where W1 and W2 are Brownian motions (i.e. like dz).

Each of the volatilities has a different term structure. The formalism behind this process was first expounded by Heath, Jarrow and Morton (HJM) in 1992, and HJM modelling is the mainstay of derivative price modelling in the fixed income markets. There is substantial development and publication in this area, and it is highly technical. For our purposes, we can get away without the formalism because the inaccuracy in ignoring it (that we cannot ignore in the fixed income markets that require high accuracy), is usually acceptable in electricity, and an application of pure HJM without a variety of adjustment such as for skew, is not accurate enough to price electricity derivatives. The principal component method, introduced in section 9.3.6 is generally sufficient.

9.1.18 Correlation

In observing economic events and price processes, we see that certain factors appear to be related to each other, and, if we have data, we can establish this by regression analysis.

In establishing our price processes it is important that we quantify these relationships as best we can. It is rare for there to be anywhere near enough data to have high confidence in our estimates and hence it is very important to develop an intuitive understanding of the likely econometric processes, based on our understanding of the economics of the system. The measurement of correlation is in practice highly problematic, since there is a conflict between the high number of measurements required for a reasonable confidence and the deterministic and stochastic nature of correlation which has a similar term structure to price and volatility. This problem, perhaps more than any other in derivative pricing, causes a need for strong economic analysis to temper the statistical inferences to use for real circumstances.

In handling related variables we need to:

(i)   Establish if possible what the causal relationships are.
(ii) Establish the context dependence of relationships (for example, whether they only apply during peaks).
(iii) Establish the extent to which our chosen correlation method can be used for modelling.

By far the most useful and widely used tool is standard linear correlation that we will examine below. Even when we believe that the calculations are highly deficient, it commonly remains the most practical tool.

Correlation is a highly problematic subject in derivative pricing because:

(i)   Correlation is but one measure of relationships, most useful for standard linear corre-lations of standard normal distributions.
(ii)   Derivative prices can be highly sensitive to correlation.
(iii) Data is highly inadequate in power (due principally to periodicity and low visibility of prices).
(iv)   Distributions are frequently non-normal.
(v)   Even when distributions are normal, correlation is frequently non linear.
(vi)   We generally model local correlation (correlation of short term returns), whereas instru-ments, such as European options are frequently dependent on cumulative (terminal) correlations.
(vii) Effects such as stochastic volatility, and distribution skewness cause a bias to correlation (usually downward).

Our treatment of correlation in this book is of necessity extremely brief, and for brevity and clarity, we use arithmetic Brownian motion rather than geometric Brownian motion more than is warranted in practice. For a more comprehensive introduction to the problems of correlation in an energy context, the reader should refer to Eydeland and Wolniec (2003).

9.1.18.1 Standard linear correlation

With standard linear correlation, we assume that our underlying prices processes are Brownian Motion, and that our correlation is constant for all prices.

If the dispersions of two variables A and B are both normally distributed, and the corre-lation between the variables is standard linear, then the correlation is defined by:

$$\rho_{A,B} = \frac{Cov(A, B)}{\sqrt{Var(A) * Var(B)}}$$

Where:

Var(A) denotes the variance of A
Cov(A,B) is the covariance of A and B.

$$Cov(A, B) = E[(A - E(A))(B - E(B))] = E[AB] - E[A]E[B]$$

In terms of expectation, the formula can be written:

$$\rho_{A,B} = \frac{E[A*B] - E[A]*E[B]}{\sqrt{(E[A^2] - E[A]^2)(E[B^2] - E[B]^2)}}$$

A and B could be prices, logarithms of prices, absolute returns of prices or relative returns of prices depending on the application.

Consider the price process for the spread between the prices of commodity A (e.g. power) and commodity B (e.g. gas) which both follow Arithmetic Brownian Motion.

$$dS_{(A-B)} = \sigma_A dz_A - \sigma_B dz_B$$

where the two dz terms are not independent but are related by:

$$E[dz_A * dz_B] = \rho_{AB} dt$$

If volatility is constant, then the cumulative (also called terminal) correlation of the distributions is the same as the local correlation.

If volatility is varying (stochastic or deterministic) volatilities, the upper bound[20] of the cumulative correlation is the average local correlation

The variance of a composite variable is related to the variance and covariance of the components by the following formula

$$\sigma_{A+B}^2 = \sigma_A^2 + \sigma_B^2 + 2\sigma_A\sigma_B\rho_{AB} \tag{9.13}$$

More generally for a large number of components:

$$\sigma_{\sum_{i=n} Component_i}^2 = \sum_{i=n, j=n} \sigma_i\sigma_j\rho_{ij} \tag{9.14}$$

We can apply this to different (i.e. i'th and j'th) elements in time of a spot price process. If the serial correlation is zero ($\rho_{ij} = 0$), then the variance for constant volatility ($\sigma_i = \sigma_j$) is the sum of variances of the time elements, as seen in equation 9.14. Otherwise the variance has path dependence.

If we are looking at the spread between prices, then we use:

$$\sigma_{A-B}^2 = \sigma_A^2 + \sigma_B^2 - 2\sigma_A\sigma_B\rho_{AB} \tag{9.15}$$

---

[20] See Eydeland and Wolniec (2003).

9.1.19   Co-integration

If we have two correlated random variables, then using the correlation methods described above, it can be shown[21] that for all correlations less than 1 that the variance of the difference between them grows indefinitely over time. This is problematic for the commodity environment where arbitrage relations exist, and is evident in power, particularly in the relation between gas and power, but also in the relation between power contracts of different delivery dates/times.

We need a method that allows the variables to have positive, zero, or negative correlations when price differences are within a range, but for short term correlation of returns to increase as prices differ more, so that the prices are drawn back together.

Suppose that we have a price X that moves according to[22]

$$\Delta X_t = X_t - X_{t-1} = \mu_x + \delta_x Z_{t-1} + \varepsilon_t$$

Where ε_t has mean 0 and variance 1 and Z_{t-1} is a state variable that is stationary and measurable with respect to the information set of variables at time $t - 1$.

Similarly we have a variable Y with

$$\Delta Y_t = Y_t - Y_{t-1} = \mu_y + \delta_y Z_{t-1} + \varepsilon_t$$

Granger (1986) and Engle and Granger (1987) proposed a stationary composite variable

$$Z_t = a + bt + cX_t + Y_t$$

For positive δ terms and negative c we can see that the variables are drawn together.[23]

Whilst the degree of application of co-integration in the ESI is increasing, the current degree is low. This is primarily because (i) it is very difficult to characterise the Z term with market data sets, (ii) For European options, pricing tends to use implied terminal distributions rather than price processes and (iii) for American-type options this adds considerably to the complexity of the tree and Monte Carlo methods.

9.1.20   Conditional expectations

There are many circumstances in power where we need to know our stochastic process mean, contingent on some particular condition being satisfied. Two examples are (i) the situation in which our plant derives its revenue from capacity only, and we need to calculate the cost and therefore required investment in reliability and (ii) the dual fuel fired power station described in section 11.5.

9.1.20.1   Power price expectation, conditional on it exceeding a designated level

We can designate this as $S|S > K$ and we can visualise this as shown in Figure 9.22.

---

[21] See Rebonato (2004).

[22] This representation is from Duan (2001).

[23] Strictly, Granger's representation theorem shows that co-integration can always be represented by an error correction model, and for this to apply for the error correction model shown here $-2 < c\delta_x + \delta_y < 0$.

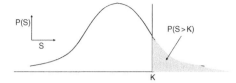

Figure 9.22   The mean spot price, contingent on it exceeding a strike price

The familiar Black-76[24] formula for pricing European options, is:

$$C = F * N(d_1) - K * N(d_2) \tag{9.16}$$

Where C is the call price (prior to interest rate discounting)
K is the strike price
F is the forward price

$$d_1 = \frac{\ln(F/K) + \frac{1}{2}\sigma^2(T-t)}{\sigma\sqrt{T-t}}$$

$$d_2 = \frac{\ln(F/K) - \frac{1}{2}\sigma^2(T-t)}{\sigma\sqrt{T-t}} = d_1 - \sigma\sqrt{T-t}$$

We also note that the forward price is the risk adjusted expectation of the spot price.[25]

$$F_{T,t} = E[S_T] - \lambda_a(T,t)\sigma_a^n(T-t)$$

Where σ_a is the average volatility of the forward contract over the period t to T. $n = 1$ or 2 according to context and is discussed in section 9.1.22.

We note two features of the Black equation.

Firstly that the option delta[26] $\Delta = \dfrac{\partial C}{\partial F} = N(d_1)$

Secondly, that since we definitely pay the strike price if we declare the option and definitely do not pay the strike price if we do not declare the option, then we can see by inspection that $N(d_2)$ in equation 9.16 is a good candidate for the exercise probability, and it can be proved that this is so.

The conditional expectation can be expressed:

$$E(S)\bigg|S > K = K + \frac{\int_{S=K}^{S=\infty} P(S)*(S-K)dS}{\int_{S=K}^{S=\infty} P(S)dS} \tag{9.17}$$

---

[24] Black (1976). The Black Scholes formula was designed for non dividend paying stocks. In the Black-76 formula, no interest rate is applied. The premium is then discounted between the payment date and payoff date. For commodities, it is more suitable than the Black Scholes model.

[25] Strictly speaking, the cost of risk λ is not a simple function of average volatility since the term structures of λ and of volatility are different.

[26] For simple proof, see Haug (1998).

For zero cost of risk ($\lambda = 0$) the term in the numerator is the option premium C, and the term in the denominator is the probability of exercise. So we have, for a perfectly lognormal distribution:

$$E(S)\,|S > K = K + \frac{C}{N(d_2)} \tag{9.18}$$

This ratio gets smaller and smaller with increasing K, and the conditional mean approaches K.

The risk adjusted conditional expectation is more complicated, although it is useful to note that if we use relative pricing, the ratio of the risk adjustments to the option and the forward contracts is equal to the ratio of the standard deviations – see footnote in section 9.1.22.

Note that we have assumed a lognormal distribution. Since electricity price distributions (and electricity-fuel price distributions) are strongly skewed, then we also need to compare the conditional expectation derived from equation 9.18 (the distribution can be inferred from option premiums, if there are any, and a cost of risk adjustment). In addition, we can use the extreme value theory (see section 9.1.10) for very low load factor plant.

The cumulative cost of risk drift is assumed independent[27] of price path and hence the expectation bias of the spot price derived from the option premium is independent of strike.

9.1.20.2 Expectation of distribution variance, conditional on the price exceeding a designated level

For a peaking plant we wish to know the variance of its overall return in relation to the expected return in order to risk adjust the investment value and the variance of the return, conditional on the return exceeding zero in order to assess investment in plant reliability.

This is required for the low merit unit of a risk averse generator that sells options struck at marginal cost and needs to evaluate spend on unit reliability.

We evaluate the variance by using

$$Variance(x) = E\left[x^2\right] - (E\,[x])^2$$

Let us take $x = \max(S - K, 0)$

$E[x] = C = \int_K^\infty SP(S)dS - K\int_K^\infty P(S)dS$ in the risk neutral world[28]

$$Variance(x) = V = \int_K^\infty (S - K)^2 P(S)dS - C^2$$

This can be expressed as[29]:

$$V = F^2\left[\exp\left(\sigma^2 T\right)N(d_3) - N(d_1)^2\right] - N(-d_2)\,K\,[2FN(d_1) - KN(d_2)] \tag{9.19}$$

---

[27] According to convention. In reality the constant cost of risk assumption is dependent on quadratic utility functions. In reality, cost of risk is almost certainly price dependent and probably path dependent. This should add an upward bias to our conditional expectation. Path dependence of the utility function further adds to this bias.

[28] Here we must be very careful not to mix up the risk neutral and real worlds. Obviously, options are priced in the real world so we should apply a risk adjustment to the forward price.

[29] I am indebted to John Putney and Haydyn Brown for this derivation. The reader wishing to verify this may note that the exponential function argument in the integral for call option value is a perfect square.

or

$$V = F\left[F\exp\left(\sigma^2 T\right) N(d_3) - K N(d_1)\right] - C(K + C) \tag{9.20}$$

where

$$d_3 = \frac{\ln\left(\dfrac{F}{K}\right) + \dfrac{3}{2}\sigma^2 T}{\sigma\sqrt{T}}$$

For a given volatility and forward price, the terminal variance of the call payoff decreases with strike price, but the terminal variance or standard deviation of the call payoff divided by the call premium increases monotonically with strike price.

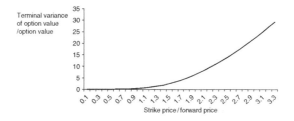

Figure 9.23 Terminal variance of call option divided by strike price, in relation to strike price

For a power plant, we can treat the call premium as a proxy for 'return' and the variance[30] as a proxy for 'risk', and can see that risk/return not only increases with increasing strike (decreasing merit, increasing marginal cost) but increases in a convex manner. This is an extremely important consideration for low merit plant.

Again we must be careful in moving between the risk neutral world and the real world. When we use relative pricing, our ratio of cost of risk drift between call option assets of different moneyness is proportional to the ratio of standard deviations and not variances.

9.1.20.3 Expectation of one commodity price, conditional on a known movement of another commodity price

If we build up our options piece by piece in order to maintain robust calibration, then to calculate our value of the dual fuel option requires us to calculate the coal-gas spread, conditional on the power-coal spread exceeding a particular level.

Suppose that we have two populations of x and y with prior means μ_x, μ_y, standard deviations σ_x, σ_y, and correlation ρ_{xy}. Then if time has lapsed and some exogenous force has occurred, our sampling of the x distribution yields a value X, then our conditional expectation of the sampling of y is now

$$\mu_y\Big|(x = X) = \mu_y + \frac{\rho_{xy}\sigma_y}{\sigma_x}(X - \mu_x) \tag{9.21}$$

---

[30] The same is true if we use standard deviation. For discussion on which to use, see section 9.1.22.

9.1.21 The denominator

We have noted that when considering mean reversion to a stochastic mean, or (almost equivalently) the volatility of long term prices, that the volatility of the currency itself can be a significant contributor to the volatility of the commodity price.

The extreme volatility of near term power price is a direct consequence of storage issues. This issue does not exist in the medium term, and hence medium-to-medium-long (two to about five years) are due to other reasons. Beyond about five years there are three principle drivers: environmental pressure, oil prices, and currency fluctuations. The further into the future we go, the more that elements such as environmental pressure and oil prices can be treated as 'fundamental' but since currency has no fundamental value, its volatility goes on and on and dominates for long tenors.

We can gain an intuitive understanding of this by expressing the commodity and currency price in terms of the numeraire.

$$\frac{C}{\$} = \frac{\frac{C}{N}}{\frac{\$}{N}}$$

Where C is the commodity, $ is the currency, and N the numeraire.

By taking logarithms of both sides and applying our covariance equation 9.14 we get:

$$\sigma^2_{\ln(C/\$)} = \sigma^2_{\ln(\$/N)} - \rho_{\ln(C/N)\ln(\$/N)}\sigma_{\ln(C/N)}\sigma_{\ln(\$/N)} + \sigma^2_{\ln(C/N)}$$

If in the long term, the cumulative (average) volatility of the commodity in the numeraire asset tends to zero, then the volatility of the commodity expressed in currency is equal to the volatility of the currency expressed in the numeraire asset.

9.1.22 Cost of risk

In section 10.1.9 we show why and how risk costs money. We used cost of risk in equation 9.12 for forward price drift. By convention, we say that the cost of risk is positive if, at the margin, the risk aversion of those with long market positions exceeds that of those with short market positions. So the forward price is a downwardly biased indicator of out-turn and therefore the forward price drift is positive.

We have used a fundamental method using physical assets and utility theory to define our cost of risk. This leads us to require a drift that is linear with respect to variance of absolute returns. Amongst other assumptions, our implied assumption is that we have no other risky assets. If we have other assets, then our cost of risk with respect to variation in price of our particular asset is proportional to the increment of the asset to the portfolio covariance, and this increment is proportional to the volatility (i.e. the square root of the variance) of the asset.

The great majority of pricing applications in derivative finance involve relative pricing (the price of one risky asset relative to another) rather than absolute pricing, and hence we usually use linearity of drift in relation to volatility.[31] This is not always the case however. If instead of taking a stock portfolio approach to a long position in a real option, we take

---

[31] Rebonato (2004) shows that by application of Ito's lemma to an Ito process for a derivative of an underlying asset, that the ratio of drifts of the derivative and the underlying asset is the same as the ratio of the volatilities.

the insurance view of a contingent short position in an essentially similar option, we now use a risk free asset (cash) as our benchmark.

The ambiguity about which power to raise σ to in order to estimate cost of risk drift is in practice subsumed by the proprietary nature of risk, the use of cost of risk only for the marginal market buyer and seller, uncertainty of the form of the utility equation, continuous compounding of the risk cost over finite time, volatility of cost of risk, application for geometric rather than arithmetic Brownian motion for high volatilities, problems with the implied assumption[32] that third and higher order derivatives with respect to wealth of the utility function are zero, and problems of using the utility function as the determinant of cost of risk.[33]

Normally in financial modelling we need pay little attention to cost of risk because the risk bias[34] in the calibrating instrument is usually similar to that in the modelled instrument. However in electricity, cost of risk modelling is important for the following reasons:

(i)   If we are making asset, demand, or policy decisions, then to optimise total cost, we must evaluate both our own cost of the risk and the market cost of risk, in order to decide on how to hedge.
(ii) There can be sufficient difference between the calibrating instrument and the required instrument[35] for the costs of risks to be quite different.
(iii) We show in section 10.1.9 that cost of risk is only linear with respect to variance to a limited degree. Electricity exhibits such great ranges in price that we cannot assume an *ex ante* cost of risk that is linear with respect to variance.
(iv) In common with other produced commodities, the absolute cost of risk bias of forward prices (tenor two to five years) with respect to expectation prices can be substantial.
(v)   The market is generally thin for electricity.
(vi) Cost of extreme risk is distinct to cost of normal risk.

There is general consensus that in markets that cannot exhibit negative prices, that cost of risk is positive in the short term (people are more worried about being short than long and consequentially, forward contract price drift is negative[36]). There is more disagreement about the longer term.

On the one hand, electricity is a form of energy that has a positive correlation to the international price for crude oil, and oil price shocks are generally bad for the economy, so electricity stocks may fall when oil prices rise.

On the other hand, while electricity supply companies have uncertain demand, electricity generation companies have invested in plant and therefore have relatively well defined long positions in power (at least relative to fuel). The net pressure from the industry for the long term (more than two years forward) is therefore to sell electricity and buy fuel. The fuel production industry faces the same situation, and needs to sell commodity. Even if cost of

---

[32] Cochrane (2001) considers this in detail, and provides alternative formulae for non quadratic utility functions.

[33] See, for example, Arrow (1971).

[34] The bias is dependent on a probability definition called a probability measure. The forward price is unbiased if we change from the P measure to the Q measure. This level of formality is not necessary for the modelling in this book, but is necessary for formal derivative modelling. For an intuitive explanation of change of measure, see Baxter and Rennie (1996). For application in a commodity context, see Geman (2005).

[35] In particular we cannot construct a riskless hedge replication strategy.

[36] After gate closure in a balancing mechanism in which the maximum negative and maximum positive prices are the same (which they commonly are, as the database field size is the same), then cost of extreme risk for negative prices is significant, although smaller than the cost of extreme risk for positive prices.

oil price risk is positive, there is not a high enough percentage of oil fired generation, or enough impact of oil prices on other fossil fuel prices, to make the cost of electricity price risk positive. Hence the forward price is below the expectation of spot price (i.e. cost of risk is positive).

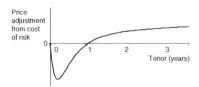

Figure 9.24 Schematic representation of the risk bias of forward prices relative to expectation prices, for different tenors. A positive adjustment means that the spot price expectation is above the forward price

We note here that the average[37] cost of risk λa, and the instantaneous cost of risk λi, are different, and indeed can have opposite signs. We note also that $\lambda(t, T, \tau)$, where $\tau = T - t$, is a function of time (stochastic variation), periodicity (particularly the peaks), and tenor (as seen in the graph above).

9.1.23 Transaction cost

In section 10.1.4.1, we show that we should be able to derive the transaction cost of finite volumes of electricity from the production offer stack. From this, and from the cost of risk, we can roughly establish the term structure of transaction costs. This is shown in Figure 9.25.

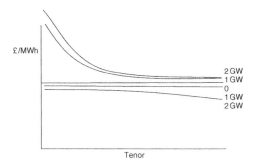

Figure 9.25 The term structure of transaction costs

In a market with higher demand in winter, the power generation stack is steeper in summer due to scheduled plant outages, and hence transaction costs, particularly for high volume offers, are higher than in the winter.

---

[37] Note that when we buy a forward commodity, we apply an *ex ante* cost of risk that is dependent on the expected holding period. Half of maximum contract life is a commonly used period.

9.2 VOLATILITY MODELLING

When we model prices we are modelling the first moment of the price distribution, i.e. $(x - \bar{x})$, where $\bar{x}$ is the mean. When we do volatility modelling, we are initially modelling the second moment of the distribution, $(x - \bar{x})^2$. In fact to model option prices we need to attend to the higher moments of distribution of the form $(x - \bar{x})^n$ where n > 2.

We can conveniently categorise the modelling of volatility into different elements, although there is a high interdependence between them, namely:

(i)   term structure;
(ii) strike structure (higher moments);
(iii) stochastic volatility;
(iv) periodicity;
(v)   path dependence.

Electricity has a highly, and possibly uniquely complex price structure. This is mainly the result of storage difficulties. But for the substantial effects on electricity prices of structural changes, regulatory changes and environmental pressures, the volatility of electricity from the perspective of the consumer would be rather low, particularly in relation to crude oil.

9.2.1 Term structure of volatility – TSOV

The volatility described in the price process equation 9.4 is the instantaneous volatility, also called the local volatility. The payoff of European style options is sensitive to the cumulative, or terminal, distribution of price, which depends on the average volatility.

We know from equation 9.14 that the total variance of an n step process, in which the steps

$$\sigma_a = \left(\frac{\sum_n \sigma_i^2}{n} \right)^{0.5}$$

are uncorrelated, is the sum of the variances of the steps.

Where σ_a is the average volatility.

Over continuous time we integrate

$$\sigma_{a,T,t} = \left(\frac{1}{(T - t)} \int_t^T \sigma^2(s)ds \right)^{0.5}$$

where T is the contract delivery date and t is the observation date.

Note that options do not generally expire at time $= 0$, and since the term structure of electricity prices is very strong, there remains substantial volatility after option expiry.

9.2.1.1 Four factor volatility modelling

The most natural TSOV that fits the one factor mean reverting process is

$$\sigma_{i,\tau} = a * e^{-c\tau} \tag{9.22}$$

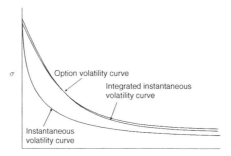

Figure 9.26 The implication of instantaneous volatility by fitting the average volatility to the implied option volatility

where tenor $\tau = T - t$,

'a' can be interpreted as the rate of arrival and the magnitude of exogenous forces on our price system.

'c' can be interpreted as the mean reversion rate, the strength of which is dependent on the force and pace of the restorative force. A change in price might cause this change due to the mode of operation of the rate. For example, if mean reversion applies in economic terms to prices, but in modelling terms to the logarithm of prices, then we may have to increase 'c' when prices rise in order to match the economic force to the modelled rate. Another example of changing 'c' is a non Hooke's law application of mean reversion.

This model makes good sense economically, and the attenuation of volatility with tenor is often called the Samuelson effect.

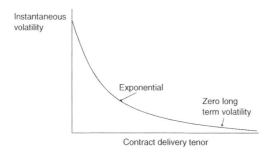

Figure 9.27 The volatility term structure most closely associated with Adam Smith economics and the Samuelson effect

Since forward prices must be feasible evolutions of price processes, then the presence of this equation as the most accurate process equation would be indicated by a forward curve that itself had an exponential shape. Note that arbitrage limits in the slope of the curve cannot be recognised by this process.

If the 'mean reversion price', or 'equilibrium price' is volatile then this will determine the long term volatility, so:

$$\sigma_{i,\tau} = a * e^{-c\tau} + d \tag{9.23}$$

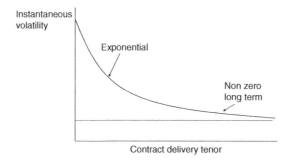

Contract delivery tenor

Figure 9.28   Volatility term structure where the equilibrium price is volatile

A change in 'd' should be associated with current change in long term fundamentals, such as oil prices (which have relatively high long term volatilities due to influence of OPEC[38]), or environmental policy. 'd' is also much affected by the volatility of the currency denominator, as described in section 9.1.21

This is a reasonably satisfactory equation from a modelling perspective. However, it often does not fit empirical evidence of option market prices. Implied volatility curves witnessed in practice are less steep in the short term and more steep in the long term than the exponential form.

Power laws, of the form $\sigma_i(\tau) = \frac{a}{b+c\tau^d}$ can give a better fit.

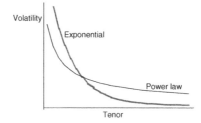

Figure 9.29   The power law function, which in comparison to the exponential function is flatter for short tenors, and steeper for long tenors, often represents a better empirical fit to the prices of traded options for a wide range of tenors

Option traders do use power law functions to get accurate empirical fits for interpolating implied (average) volatilities, but these cannot be tied back to fundamental processes and are not appropriate for most modelling purposes.

Nevertheless, we explain in section 9.5 that it is never correct to use a modelling curve that is inconsistent with the prices of a deep and liquid market, and hence the exponential curve does require adjustment. This can be achieved by adding an extra term to the exponential form.

[38] Organisation of Petroleum Exporting Countries.

In order to keep an approximately exponential form we can modify it to make a better empirical fit by adding a 'b' term as in the following equation.

$$\sigma_{i,\tau} = (a + b\tau)e^{c\tau} + d \qquad (9.24)$$

'b' can be interpreted as a flexing adjustment to the mean reversion rate, associated with the fourth principal component.

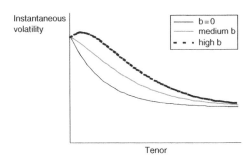

Figure 9.30   Effect of changing 'b' in the four factor volatility equation

This allows a lowering of the 'c' term in fitting observed medium term option volatilities. This equation does not reconcile well to fundamental processes, although it can be rationalised when there are several econometric processes simultaneously applying to the state variables at different granularities (daily and monthly contracts for example).

Since volatility itself is generally volatile, and we wish to keep 'a' constant in order to retain a connection to economic fundamentals and for pricing instruments that are sensitive to it,[39] then we can accommodate volatile volatility by adding a term 'g' which can vary.

A change in 'g' should be associated with short term effects that have little effect on medium and long term fundamentals.[40] Ideally the multiplier term decays away, for example, according to $g = 1 + g_o e^{-ht}$ and then the term could deal with short term effects such as periods of nervousness. 'g0' is then viewed as a perturbation to the traded market. Short term effects that impact our view on long term fundamentals may lead us to change permanently our other coefficients. It can be both stochastic and periodic.[41] A periodic multiplier would have the general form $\sin(jt + l)$ if periodic in relation to observation time and $\sin(mT + n)$ if periodic in relation to delivery time (i.e. the seasonal volatility described in section 9.1.15.2).

Our volatility formula with g is shown below.

$$\sigma_{i,\tau} = ((a + b\tau)e^{-c\tau} + d) * g \qquad (9.25)$$

---

[39] For example, the price of a stochastic strike option, such as a option expiring in ten years with a strike price equal to the spot price outturn in nine years time, should not be affected by a volatile spot market today.

[40] There is a fundamental problem with changing g, and indeed in changing any of the other parameters on a frequent basis. We calibrate the observed market with faith in our econometric characterisation and the stationary nature of our coefficients, and the very next day we change some of them. Rebonato (2004) likens this to the behaviour of an unrepentant sinner. For electricity in particular, the large changes in volatility, and generally poor capture of periodic, regime switch and other effects makes us very sensitive to inefficient pricing.

[41] In the electricity market, the periodicity is seasonal. This effect is well known in the financial markets, for which weekend volatility is less than weekday volatility.

For constant[42] g then, unlike the power law, this equation integrates well. The variance over time t is given by:

$$\sigma_{av,t}^2 = \frac{g^2}{(T-t)}\left[d^2s - \frac{a^2}{2c}e^{-2cs} - \frac{2da}{c}e^{-cs} - \frac{abe^{-2cs}}{c}\left(s + \frac{1}{2c}\right)\right.$$

$$\left. - \frac{b^2e^{-2cs}}{2c}\left(s^2 + \frac{1}{c}\left(s + \frac{1}{2c}\right)\right) - \frac{2dbe^{-cs}}{c}\left(s + \frac{1}{c}\right)\right]_{s=0}^{s=T} \qquad (9.26)$$

If g is periodic or decaying, the formula is a little more complicated, but tractable.

The addition of this term is helpful in dealing with the awkward problem that we are applying a stationary term structure (constant a, c, d) in the real world where volatility is changing. To continuously recalibrate to the market, we must change one of our parameters. Normally there is sufficient dimensionality of the equation and room within the bid/offer envelope to change only one parameter on a frequent (daily) basis and change the other parameters more slowly and in response to our interpretation of what is making volatility change.

For example, holding all parameters constant but g, might represent variations in a market that is nervous rather than changing fundamentally. Ideally, we keep the terms d and a + d as constant as possible. Otherwise, for example a change in today's spot market might cause us to change the long term dynamics of the spot market. The best practice is to take a subjective view of the market, and identify which of a, b, c, d, g (or indeed h, l, m, or n) have been the cause of the change in volatility.

9.2.1.2 Calibration

Widening of a bid/offer spread may produce a bias to the 'fair value' volatility, since the same price difference either side of the mid price is not the same volatility difference. It would be quite possible here not to change the volatility curve if it lies within the bid and offer envelopes of both days.

There is a high degree of discretion in the re-fitting of the volatility equation in a moving market, and the process followed by an individual depends greatly on whether he is more familiar and close to the ebbs and flows of the traded market, or with generation/network/demand events and the impact of macro effects on the microeconomics of the market.

Two cautions should be added here:

(i) complete volatility curves do not exist in practice. If the curve is sourced from a single market maker it does not represent the market at the margin and will instead be shaded towards her interests. The curve is likely to be indicative rather than firm and may change when a quote is requested. If the curve is sourced from a variety of market makers then each individual quote does not represent the market for the tenor in question, since the polling is not simultaneous, it will be biased to the interest of the particular market maker polled rather than the best (unpolled[43]) bid or offer. While this would seem to

---

[42] g is constant for a stationary volatility term structure, in which case there is no need for g. Nevertheless it is common practice to apply stationary formulae to non stationary volatility.
[43] Market makers do not generally give their best prices to the brokers.

be a minor effect, it in fact has a major effect when 'bootstrapping',[44] for example by building instantaneous volatility curves from implied volatility curves.

(ii) The storage issues for electricity cause contracts for the same commodity in different periods to behave quite differently. This greatly reduces the concentration and therefore the liquidity of the market. Therefore while one might be accustomed to be able to trade $ 1 bn in the foreign exchange market with a bid/offer similar to that for $ 10 m, this is not true for electricity. What is observed in the traded market quotations is actually for very small volumes (20 MW say) compared to commonly needed transaction volumes (100 MW say, but up to 500 MW or more for a failed power station unit). It is quite possible for a 100 MW quote to have the same bid as a 20 MW quote but a greatly different offer, or vice versa, and hence great caution should be applied when using the market at the margin to make economic decisions that move the position of the margin.

Our price process must operate at a high enough granularity to capture all power price effects and hence must be at least halfhourly, and yet our calibrating instruments are commonly much coarser, for example monthly or quarterly. We must find a way of connecting these. This we do below.

9.2.1.3   Volatility of aggregated contracts

Let us for the moment ignore periodicity, and consider a one month strip of daily prices. If we know the instantaneous volatilities of each of the individual days (the volatility vector) from the instantaneous volatility term structure, and the instantaneous correlations of each day to each other day from the correlation matrix, then we can calculate the instantaneous volatility of the month contract.

If our process is normal, or lognormal for low volatilities (and therefore approximately normal) we have

$$\sigma_{\sum P_i w_i} = \left(\frac{\sum_{ij} \sigma_i \sigma_j P_i P_j w_i w_j \rho_{ij}}{\sum_{ij} P_i P_j w_i w_j} \right)^{0.5} \tag{9.27}$$

Here σ is absolute (leading to normal distribution) rather than relative (leading to lognormal distribution), but expressed as a percentage of starting price.

The weightings w are required for calculating the volatility of complex shapes (for example baseload plus peak) that are used in the traded market, in which elements appear twice.

The volatility of an aggregate shape is found from the volatilities and correlations of its components. Matrix manipulation is required, which is rather awkward to do manually, but this is generally provided in spreadsheet packages such as Excel.

The steps are:

(i)   populate the correlation matrix and the volatility vectors;
(ii) construct a square matrix A with elements $\rho_{ij}\sigma_i$;
(iii) construct a column matrix (i.e. a vector) B with elements σ_j;

---

[44] Bootstrapping involves fitting equations such as equation 9.25 to families of options of increasing tenor. So, the one month tenor is fitted first, then the two month tenor in a manner that preserves the calibration of the one month tenor, and so on for the third month.

(iv) premultiply B by A to get a row matrix C;
(v)   sum all the elements of C to get the variance of the aggregate shape.

$$\begin{pmatrix} \sigma_1 & \rho_{12}\sigma_1 & \rho_{13}\sigma_1 \\ \rho_{12}\sigma_2 & \sigma_2 & \rho_{23}\sigma_2 \\ \rho_{13}\sigma_3 & \rho_{23}\sigma_3 & \sigma_3 \end{pmatrix} \begin{pmatrix} \sigma_1 \\ \sigma_2 \\ \sigma_3 \end{pmatrix}$$

$$= \begin{pmatrix} \sigma_1^2 + \sigma_1\sigma_2\rho_{12} + \sigma_1\sigma_3\rho_{13} & \sigma_1\sigma_2\rho_{12} + \sigma_2^2 + \sigma_2\sigma_3\rho_{23} & \sigma_1\sigma_3\rho_{13} + \sigma_2\sigma_3\rho_{23} + \sigma_3^2 \end{pmatrix}$$

The covariance matrix should be subjected to a principal component check that reconciles to our understanding of the fundamentals. The method is introduced in section 9.3.6.

9.2.1.4 Relationship between daily 'caplet' volatility and monthly 'swaption' volatility

Once we have constructed our correlation matrix and volatility vector for one level of granularity, then the correlations and volatilities of all elements of lower granularity automatically follow.

Suppose, for example that we have estimated a volatility term structure of the daily baseload contract different tenors. We can construct the volatility of each individual monthly contract using the method described. We can also calculate the correlation between months by noting that we can construct the aggregate volatility of any pair of months either from the daily or the monthly elements. The technique is illustrated in Figure 9.31.

By calculating instantaneous volatilities for monthly contracts at different tenors, we can (for deseasonalised, smile free processes) parametise the monthly volatility term structure using an equation such as equation 9.25, integrate using equation 9.26, and then compare to the volatilities of traded options. We then calibrate by adjusting the term structures of the volatilities and correlations of the daily contracts.

In theory we could begin at the halfhour level and arrive at all volatilities and correlations up to annual. In practice it is more convenient to begin at the daily level, and to conduct a separate calibration exercise for more granular contracts.

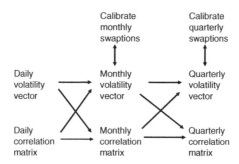

Figure 9.31 Calibration to monthly and quarterly option markets, starting with daily volatilities and correlations

Note that if we choose one particular swap length to be the fundamental process that follows a process equation, and has a 'well behaved' TSOV that can be reconciled to the process equation, that the other swap lengths will in general not be as well behaved (for example they will have positive 'b'). The choice of 'fundamental' swap length to which the process formula is applied is not then a trivial one and it has modelling consequences. Depending on the relationship between market movements and fundamental movement, it should ideally be the most actively traded swap length, or (ideally) the most actively moving fundamental element.

9.2.1.5   Relationship between mean reversion rate and volatility term structure

If the mean reversion rate is of Hooke's law type and the mean is constant, then the volatility term structure and the forward curve will both be of exponential form.

9.2.2   Smile and skew

The terms smile and skew appear most frequently in the pricing of standard European options and represent a convenient language for communication to degree to which the Black Scholes pricing formula, when calibrated to 'at the money' options (strike price = forward price) misprices 'out of the money' options (strike price $\neq$ forward price) relative to the values traded in the market.

The smile and skew are commonly represented as the difference in implied volatility from traded options that are out of the money, relative to the at the money market implied volatility. The moneyness is commonly represented by the option delta (measured using at the money volatility). An equivalent representation is the difference in implied terminal probability distribution relative to the lognormal.

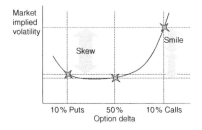

Figure 9.32   Option smile and skew, for 10 % option delta, calculated using at the money volatility

In the language of traders, the smile is the average increase in option volatility above at the money levels for puts and calls for some level of delta (commonly 30 %) and the skew is the difference in volatility between puts and calls of the same delta (commonly 30 % and 10 %).

Smile and skew are much researched in the financial markets, and there are many reasons for the appearance, including:

(i) **Stochastic volatility** – Since the volatility exposure 'kappa' of out of the money options increases with increasing volatility, then the holder of an out of the money option expects to make a gain if the volatility of volatility is non zero. This is called kappa convexity, and traders pay more for out of the money options than is indicated by the Black Scholes equation.

(ii) **Path dependence** – This arises for many reasons. One reason is that if the price enters uncharted territory then uncertainty is higher and the subjective probability of new exogenous forces is higher.

(iii) **Price dependence** – This arises from non Hookes law economic forces (leading also to non Hookes law mean reversion) and from the association of particular prices with low or high volatilities.

(iv) **Process mapping** – If there is an underlying process that is normal, and the price (or log of price) has a deterministic but non linear relationship to the underlying factor, then the volatility of the price will not represent the normal distribution and will therefore have a smile and/or skew in relation to it.

(v) **Cost of volatility risk** – The kappa convexity of out of the money options and the high potential losses of short positions in relation to premium causes option traders to apply a higher risk premium to out of the money options than to at the money options.

(vi) Complex price process, such as regime switching can, and usually do, add to option smile and skew.

The central limit theory tells us smile/skew effects arising from non normal probability distributions disappear for long tenors if our process is correctly mapped. The effects from most other reasons remain.

9.2.2.1 Smile formulae

Since the smile is so large for electricity, it must be modelled. There are a number of arbitrage conditions that must be fulfilled, such as ensuring that call option premium decreases monotonically with strike price. A sin function conveniently observes these conditions. The part of the sin wave that is used is shown in Figure 9.33.

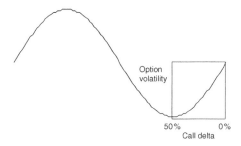

Figure 9.33   Modelling option smile with a sin function

$$CallSmile = \sigma_{a,\Delta} - \sigma_{a,0.5} = 1 + s * \sin(\frac{\Delta'\pi}{2} + \frac{3\pi}{2}) \tag{9.28}$$

Where Δ is the option delta calculated using at the money volatility, $\Delta' = 1 - 2\Delta$ and $0.5 > \Delta > 0$.

This function tends to be too steep near the money and to flat away from the money, and requires some adjustment particular to the market. It is essential to continue to observe the arbitrage conditions.

9.2.2.2   *Term structure of smile*

In theory, the maths associated with the central limit theory can help us determine the attenuation of smile with respect to tenor. In practice this is overly complicated for the electricity market. Smile is established empirically. A simple smile fitting formula such as $s_\tau = s_\infty + s_0 \exp(-k\tau)$ is simple, easy to apply, and has good boundary conditions. Ideally $s_\infty = 0$, although this depends on the mapping of the price process to fundamentals, and the growth of price.

The calibration of smiles is described in section 9.4.2.

9.3   CORRELATION MODELLING

9.3.1   Cross commodity correlation modelling

Since power stations can be regarded as commodity spread options, we need to work with the commodity correlations to evaluate our derivative prices.

If the commodities are uncorrelated, then everything is quite easy. We can simply calculate the probability of conditions, such as the probability that the coal price will be less than the power price but greater than the gas price. Figure 9.34 shows the probability of prices Gas<Coal<Power. Similarly, multivariate trees can be drawn.

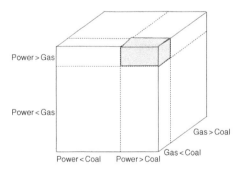

Figure 9.34   Representation of the threefold condition power price exceeds gas price and coal price and coal price exceeds gas price, where all variables are uncorrelated

Unfortunately the situation is much more complicated if the variables are correlated. We must first establish the correlation matrix

$$
\begin{pmatrix}
 & Power & Coal & Gas \\
Power & 1 & \rho_{PC} & \rho_{PG} \\
Coal & \rho_{PC} & 1 & \rho_{CG} \\
Gas & \rho_{PG} & \rho_{CG} & 1
\end{pmatrix}
$$

The correlation matrix must be tested[45] for self consistency. For example, it would not be consistent to enter correlations of 100 % gas price[46] to power price, 100 % for coal price to power price and -100 % for coal price to gas price.

9.3.2   Commodity spread modelling

Power stations can be regarded as commodity spread options and hence we need to model the commodity spreads in order to calculate the option value.

The simplest option is the option to swap one commodity (say gas) for another (say power). This is the option owned by a combined cycle gas turbine. Here we can view the strike price for power as being denominated in gas. So, for zero interest rates we can simply replace the strike price in the Black equation (examined in a little more detail in 9.1.19), by the gas price, So[47]:

$$C = F_P * N(d_1) - F_G * N(d_2)$$

Where F_P is the forward power price and F_G is the forward gas price.

The standard deviation is $\sigma_{P-G} = \left(\sigma_P^2 + \sigma_G^2 - 2\rho_{PG}\sigma_P\sigma_G\right)^{0.5}$

For a small non zero strike and relatively low volatility, we simply transform the commodity, so instead of swapping gas for power, we swap gas for a commodity worth (power plus strike). So if the gas price is F_G and the strike price is K, we simply use an adjusted volatility of $F_G/(F_G + K)$. Note that if F_G is normally distributed, then $F_G + K$ is normally distributed, and before the volatility adjustment, the absolute returns of $F_G + K$ are 100 % correlated to F_G and have the same correlations to other variables as F_G has. The correlation need not be adjusted for low volatilities and low strike prices.

In section 11.5, we consider a power station that could fire on two fuels, coal and gas, and the options that it could sell to capture this value in advance.

We need to know the correlation between the power-gas spread and the power-coal spread.

Referring to equation 9.15, and assuming unit commodity prices for ease of depiction we have:

$$\sigma_{(P-G)-(P-C)} = \sigma_{P-C}^2 + \sigma_{P-G}^2 - 2\sigma_{P-C}\sigma_{P-G}\rho_{P-C,P-G}$$

Here σ is absolute standard deviation, expressed as a percentage of starting price $P_{T,0}$

$$\sigma_{C-G} = \sigma_C^2 + \sigma_G^2 - 2\sigma_C\sigma_G\rho_{CG}$$

Since both equations refer to the aggregate commodity $C - G$, then they must be identical.

Expanding the spread terms, we have:

$$\sigma_P^2 + \sigma_C^2 - 2\sigma_P\sigma_G\rho_{PG} + \sigma_P^2 + \sigma_G^2 - 2\sigma_P\sigma_G\rho_{CG} - 2\sigma_{P-C}\sigma_{P-G}\rho_{P-C,P-G} = \sigma_C^2 + \sigma_G^2 - 2\sigma_C\sigma_G\rho_{CG}$$

---

[45] This can be done crudely by diagonalising the matrix and removing negative eigenvalues (see section 9.3.6). A better, but more difficult approach can be found by the best fit adjustment of the trial matrix to a unit hypersphere. See Jäckel and Rebonato (1999/2000).

[46] Strictly speaking, we mean price returns not prices.

[47] This representation of strike price was first done for a commodity setting by Margrabe (1978) and in a foreign exchange setting by Garman and Kohlhagen (1983).

Eliminating, and expanding further spread terms, we have:

$$\rho_{P-C,P-G} = \frac{\sigma_C\sigma_G\rho_{CG} - \sigma_P\sigma_G\rho_{PG} + \sigma_P^2 + \sigma_P\sigma_C\rho_{PC}}{(\sigma_P^2 + \sigma_C^2 - 2\sigma_P\sigma_C\rho_{PC})^{0.5}(\sigma_P^2 + \sigma_G^2 - 2\sigma_P\sigma_G\rho_{PG})^{0.5}}$$

Putting the commodity prices back in, and expressing σ as percentage volatility, we have

$$\rho_{P-C,P-G} = \frac{\sigma_C P_C\sigma_G P_G\rho_{CG} - \sigma_P P_P\sigma_G P_G\rho_{PG} + \sigma_P^2 P_P^2 + \sigma_P P_P\sigma_C P_C\rho_{PC}}{(\sigma_P^2 P_P^2 + \sigma_C^2 P_C^2 - 2\sigma_P P_P\sigma_C P_C\rho_{PC})^{0.5}(\sigma_P^2 P_P^2 + \sigma_G^2 P_G^2 - 2\sigma_P P_P\sigma_G P_G\rho_{PG})^{0.5}}$$

So we can calculate the correlation between all of the commodity spreads if we know the (small) volatilities and (standard linear) correlations of the commodities. The reader is reminded of the caveat at the beginning of this section; whilst the above expression is quite correct at any instant, the application in practice to the correlation of absolute returns requires the use of assumptions that we may not wish to make, such as that of arithmetic Brownian motion and standard linearity of correlation. We have assumed a perfect mapping between the normal and lognormal distributions and switched from lognormal to normal and back again with impunity. We note also that the correlation is instantaneous and refers to the starting price. If prices change, correlations under this measure will change. Because this mapping is not quite correct for commonly encountered processes, the modelling should be regarded as approximate.

9.3.3 Correlation between long and short duration contracts

In constructing our overall framework for prices, volatilities and correlations, we centre our modelling on one particular contract duration (swap length), usually one day, and construct the volatilities and correlations of longer contract durations (swap lengths) from there. As well as ensuring that the correlation term structure of daily contracts is in keeping with available evidence, the same must be true for monthly contracts. For coarse modelling of some instruments such as swing, it is also common to use monthly contracts for part of the valuation. In addition to this, it is frequently necessary to model the correlation of 'shaped' contracts (i.e. with a volume weighting profile) rather than baseload contracts.

To do this, we can use the same method for commodity spreads. We can model the volatility of a two month contract, which may have a volume profile, either as the sum of daily elements, or the sum of two monthly contracts. This is done in equation 9.29. Note that here as before we assume arithmetic Brownian motion of returns, and volatility σ is absolute rather than relative, but expressed as a percentage of price.

$$(\sigma_{S1+S2})^2 = \frac{\sum\limits_{i,j=2}\sigma_{Si}\sigma_{Sj}W_{si}W_{Sj}F_{Si}F_{Sj}\rho_{SiSj}}{\left(\sum\limits_{i=2}F_{Si}W_{Si}\right)^2} = \sigma_{S1}^2 + \sigma_{S2}^2 + \sigma_{S1}\sigma_{S2}\rho_{S1S2}$$

$$= \frac{\sum\limits_{i,j=60}\sigma_{di}\sigma_{dj}W_{di}W_{dj}F_{di}F_{dj}\rho_{didj}}{\left(\sum\limits_{i=60}F_{di}W_{di}\right)^2} \tag{9.29}$$

Where W represent the weights of the elements of the contracts, F are the forward prices of the contracts, S1 and S2 are the monthly swaps, and di are the daily elements.

$$\rho_{S1S2} = \frac{\sum\limits_{i,j=60} \sigma_{di}\sigma_{dj}W_{di}W_{dj}F_{di}F_{dj}\rho_{didj}}{\sigma_{S1}\sigma_{S2}\left(\sum\limits_{i=60} F_{di}W_{di}\right)^2} - \sigma_{S1}^2 - \sigma_{S2}^2$$

We can represent the volatilities of swap 1 and swap 2 by

$$(\sigma_{S1})^2 = \frac{\sum\limits_{i,j=30} \sigma_{di}\sigma_{dj}W_{di}W_{dj}F_{di}F_{dj}\rho_{didj}}{\left(\sum\limits_{i=30} F_{di}W_{di}\right)^2}$$

$$(\sigma_{S2})^2 = \frac{\sum\limits_{i,j=60}^{i,j=31} \sigma_{di}\sigma_{dj}W_{di}W_{dj}F_{di}F_{dj}\rho_{didj}}{\left(\sum\limits_{i,j=60}^{i,j=31} F_{di}W_{di}\right)^2}$$

As before, we can use matrix algebra, so if A is a square matrix with elements $a_{ij} = \rho_{ij}F_iW_i\sigma_i$ and B is a column matrix with elements $b_j = F_jW_j\sigma_j$, then the sum of the elements of the row matrix AB is equal to the variance of the swap containing the elements specified in matrix A.

This is in fact very useful in estimating the correlation between monthly peak contracts, and hence requires a level of granularity in excess of daily. This makes the matrix very large and hence matrix partitioning is required. We decompose the matrix A into quadrants and the vector B into halves. A1 is the weighted correlation matrix for S1, A3 is the same for S2 and A2 and A4 are the S1 − S2 correlated elements of the covariance matrix. B1 is the price vector for S2 and B2 the price vector for S2.

We can apply the same method to the different periods of the day at a particular tenor. This is useful if, for example, we have estimated the correlations at some medium resolution (fourhourly, say), and we wish either to model something at halfhourly resolution, or at a medium resolution with a different phase (for example, starting at midnight instead of 11 pm). We construct the correlation matrix at halfhourly level and calibrate the ensuing four hourly correlation matrix to our previous estimate.

9.3.4   Correlation measurement using historic data

This correlation can be measured from the examination of time series. The confidence of the correlation estimate is related to the number of observations. There are various methods, including the Fisher z transformation.[48]

---

[48] For more information, see Eydeland and Wolniec (2003).

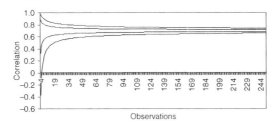

Figure 9.35 Use of the Fisher z transformation to establish confidence for correlation. 70 % and 90 % confidence shown

9.3.5 Correlation models

There are two correlations to model: the deseasonalised correlation between two contracts with different tenors, sometimes called decorrelation and the correlation between two contracts with ostensibly[49] the same tenor but correspond to different elements of the periodic structure.

9.3.5.1 Deseasonalised decorrelation term structure

For the decorrelation term structure, there are certain features that should be observed:

(i)   The correlation between the spot tenor and the infinite tenor should correspond to the correlation between the spot price and the equilibrium price in the process equation.
(ii) Application of the correlation matrix should not cause negative correlations unless specifically required.
(iii) Correlation of a contract to itself must be 100 %.
(iv) Application of the correlation matrix in conjunction with the volatility term structure of its short swaps should cause a volatility term structure of long swaps that declines monotonically with tenor, unless specifically designed not to.
(v)   Correlation should decrease monotonically with contract separation and, for the same contract separation, increase monotonically with the tenor of the shorter tenor contract.
(vi) The 'eigenstructure' of the covariance matrix looks sensible. For example, the first four principal components correspond to shift, tilt, bow and flex, and are of sufficient magnitude (P1 > 80 %, P2 > 50 % of remaining unexplained, P3 > 50 % of remaining unexplained).

One such structure, which is simple and observes the boundary conditions[50] is:

$$\rho_{\tau1,\tau2} = \rho_\infty + (1 - \rho_\infty)\exp(-a * f_1(\tau_1, \tau_2))^\wedge \exp(-b * f_2(\tau_1, \tau_2)) \qquad (9.30)$$

Where the functions are similar to: $f_1 = abs(\tau_1 - \tau_2)$ and $f_2 = \min(\tau_1, \tau_2)$.

For short tenors, the functions f1 and f2 need to be altered slightly. Figure 9.36, with the values used for calibration in Figure 9.19, uses average rather than minimum tenor.

---

[49] Section 9.3.6.1 for 'detenorisation'.
[50] It has good matrix properties. For $\rho_\infty = 0$, and with f1 and f2 as specified in the equation below, all eigenvalues are positive. See Rebonato (2004).

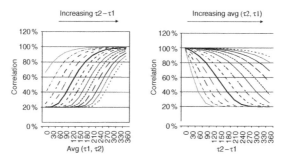

Figure 9.36 Correlation term structures

There are numerous other functions. For example, if the exponential form produces correlations that are too high, then $\rho_{\tau1,\tau2} = \exp(-abs(\tau_1^\alpha - \tau_2^\alpha))$, with $0 < \alpha < 1$, may be more suitable.

9.3.5.2   Detenorised periodic correlation structure

If ρ_{i,τ_1,j,τ_1} is the correlation between the i'th and j'th periods of the day at tenor τ, and $\rho_{\tau_1\tau_2}$ is the correlation between the daily contracts at tenors $\tau1$ and $\tau2$, then we can expect the correlation between element i at $\tau1$ and j at $\tau2$ to be approximately $\rho_{\tau_1\tau_2}\rho_{i,\tau_1,j,\tau_1}$. Note that the correlations of the daily elements must recover the correlations of the daily baseload tenors.

Periodic correlation, for example the correlation to a peak to an adjacent off peak is harder to model, and in practice often has to be calibrated by trial and error. The correlations and volatilities must be such that the volatility of the aggregate 'shape' is observed. For example, if, for a tenor of one week, we specify the instantaneous volatilities and the instantaneous correlation matrix for the six elements of a one day contract, then application of equation 9.14 must give us the instantaneous volatility of the one day contract with a one week tenor.

9.3.5.3   Correlation structure for tenor and period

In the deseasonalising and detenorising process, we 'wrap' the continuous elements of the forward curve into the cube shown in Figure 9.15. In doing this, we are at risk of losing the correlation between adjacent contracts, for example the last period in one day and the first period in the next. The correlation specification must ensure either that this correlation is reasonably high, or that the assignation of a low correlation is done intentionally. Table 9.2 shows this for a tenor sufficiently long for the correlation between adjacent days to be nearly 1.

For low resolutions (peak and off peak for example), the need for adjacent contracts to have high correlation is not important, but it becomes important when we raise the resolution, and essential when we use halfhourly resolution.

9.3.5.4   Non linear integration

We have assumed throughout this chapter that correlations are standard linear. Whilst using more sophisticated models may be more accurate, there are already so many problems with the

Table 9.2 Periodic correlation relationship for a long tenor example. Asterisked fields show adjacent contracts which may have higher orrelations due to arbitrage

	Day 1 Period 1	Day 1 Period 2	Day 1 Period 3	Day 1 Period 4	Day 2 Period 1	Day 2 Period 2	Day 2 Period 3	Day 2 Period 4
Day 1 Period 1	1	a*	b	c	$1\rho_{12}$	$a\rho_{12}$	$b\rho_{12}$	$c\rho_{12}$
Day 1 Period 2		1	d*	e	$a\rho_{12}$	$1\rho_{12}$	$d\rho_{12}$	$e\rho_{12}$
Day 1 Period 3			1	f*	$b\rho_{12}$	$d\rho_{12}$	$1\rho_{12}$	$f\rho_{12}$
Day 1 Period 4				1	$c^{*}\rho_{12}$	$e\rho_{12}$	$f\rho_{12}$	$1\rho_{12}$
Day 2 Period 1					1	$\sim a^{*}$	$\sim b$	$\sim c$
Day 2 Period 2						1	$\sim d^{*}$	$\sim e$
Day 2 Period 3							1	$\sim f^{*}$

measurement, modelling and stability of correlation, that this is worthwhile only in specific applications. However, we should be mindful that correlations are frequently non linear (giving rise to non elliptic bivariate distributions), and that this can be the case even if both distributions are standard normal.

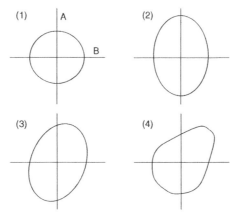

Figure 9.37 Dispersions for A and B with different volatilities and correlations. (1) Same volatility, zero correlation, (2) Different volatility, zero correlation, (3) Nonzero linear correlations, (4) Non linear correlation

There are numerous techniques for handling non linear correlation. However, improved accuracy of correlation handling inevitably reduces the capability to handle the numerous other features for electricity that we have considered, such as smile and jump diffusion. Given the great problem of lack of data for correlation estimation, special handling of non linear correlation is only justified in specific circumstances.

Whilst standard normal correlation is used to the greatest extent possible in ESI problems, other techniques such as rank correlation and copulas are used.

9.3.6   Principal components

Principal components are a relatively simple and powerful method of deconstructing volatility terms structures, and rationalising them in terms of economic fundamentals. The method is not described here, but in essence, involves a manipulation (rotation and sizing) of the covariance matrix to recover the eigenvectors and normalised eigenvalues. It can be proved that the eigenvectors are orthogonal (uncorrelated), and by ranking in order of size, represent the principal movements of the price.[51]

What is important for present purposes is the interpretation of principal components. In the majority of cases, when the analysis is applied, the order of impact (the ranked eigenvalues) can be regarded as 'shift', 'tilt', 'bow' and 'flex'. If the term structure of volatility were relatively flat, then the volatility vectors (the eigenvectors) would look like Figure 9.38.

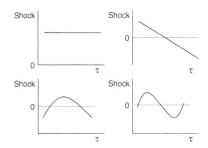

Figure 9.38   Interpretation of the first four prinicipal components. In this figure there is no attenuation with tenor

The figures are somewhat more complicated for attenuating volatility term structures, since the shapes shown must attenuate with tenor. This is quite obvious from Figure 9.38.

The greater the proportion of the highest ranked eigenvectors, the better explained is the market volatility term structure. We would normally hope for the first normalised eigenvector to exceed 0.8 (i.e. explain more than 80 % of the price change), the second, third and fourth to exceed 50 % of the remaining size (so if the first is 0.8, the second should exceed 0.1).

We can also interpret the eigenvectors in terms of our volatility term structure equation 9.24. So 'd' *approximately* represents the first[52] eigenvector, 'a–d' the second, 'c' the third, and 'b' the fourth.

In relation to our term structure of volatility, we can interpret the change to the curve as shown in Figure 9.39.

The reader will recall that 'b' does not map well to process equations and hence we wish for this (and lower ranked) eigenvectors to be small. Figure 9.40 shows the analysis for the volatility curve shown in Figure 9.19. Note that the deseasonalisation process shown for this data in Figure 9.40(1) involves volatility modelling that gives a deceptively good fit to the market, since the deseasonalisation already involved a curve fit. Reasonable boundaries for the parameters of the deseasonalised volatility curve should be explored to test the sensitivity of the analysis to the calibration.

---

[51] The principal components method is well covered in textbooks. For application in a derivatives context, see, for example, London (2005).

[52] It is theoretically possible for the eigenvalues associated with the eigenvectors to appear in a different order than shift, tilt, bow, flex, but this indicates unusual processes.

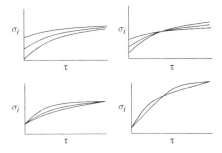

Figure 9.39 Interpretation of the first four prinicipal components in terms of the term structure of volatility

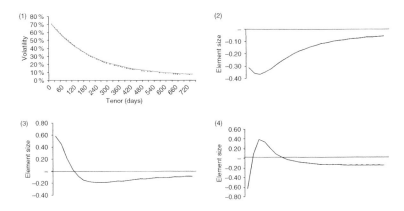

Figure 9.40 Principal component decomposition. (1) Calibration of covariance matrix to market volatility (market and modelled curve indistinguishable at this resolution), (2) First principal component, (3) Second principal component, (4) Third principal component

We can see that the basic features of the first three principal components approximate those in Figure 9.38 when attenuated with tenor. The upturn for short tenors in the first principal component is probably to an excessively steep decorrelation of closely spaced short term elements of the forward curve.

In this analysis, the sizes of the first three eigenvectors were 71 %, 22 %, 6 %. i.e. a total of 99 %.

9.3.6.1 Application of principal component method to periodicity

We can take a similar approach to the periodic structure rather than the term structure of the market. The market will trade a variety of contracts which are daily (for the short term), monthly, seasonal and annual, and for baseload, peaks off peaks and specific profiles. The market bid/offer and the ageing of prices (the brokers do not collect them all at once, so a set of quotes will include recent and old quotes) is such that it is not possible to construct a detailed forward curve from a snapshot of the market. Instead, the market must be modelled in terms of its key elements (peak and off peak for example), and the pricing matrix adjusted according to the receipt of new information. For example, if the residential profile price rises, this could be due to an increase in baseload, peak, or off peak. Some judgement must be used to update the matrix. The price matrix updating can be automated by perturbing the price matrix in a prescriptive manner as new information arrives, not by matching the market 'mid' price but remaining within the bid/offer envelope for all recent quotes. This method creates principal components of sorts. For daily contracts the principal components they are typically: (i) parallel shift of baseload, (ii) parallel shift of peak prices only and (iii) peak/off peak differential. For seasonal profiles they are typically: (i) midwinter date, (ii) amplitude, (iii) peakiness (thinness of the peak and flatness of the trough) and (iv) further adjustments to the parameters of the peaks.

Electricity markets tend to be illiquid, and a relatively large number of different 'shapes' trade throughout the day. It is useful to take a principal component approach, albeit an informal one, to the movement of prices from a periodic standpoint.

For example, our first few principal components within a season might be:

(i)   baseload;
(ii) peak/off peak differential;
(iii) peaks;
(iv) super peaks (a short period within the peak);
(v)   baseload + peaks.

In the absence of recent information, we assume that the granular relationships (for example the price differential between the 42nd and 43rd halfhours of the day) to be unchanged when we see baseload trade. If we see baseload trade at our pricing matrix, then peaks trade at higher than the pricing matrix, and then baseload trades on our matrix again, then we may change the peak/off peak differential rather than raise the peak price. The correlation matrix approach for periodicity is the same for term structure, but we have to 'de-tenorise'. De-tenorisation (not a standard term or process) is the term structure equivalent of deseasonalising periodic structures. All points on the curve are given term structure adjustments and then treated as if they all have the same tenor. Since contract separations must still be taken into account, this is rather awkward and involves more modelling compromises.

9.4   PRICING ELECTRICITY DERIVATIVES

It is often convenient to divide derivative instruments into four categories:

(i)   physical;
(ii) spot, forwards and futures[53];
(iii) European options (often called 'vanilla' or 'plain vanilla' options);
(iv) complex options.

For the purpose of the ESI, we need to add a fifth category

(v)   options exercised 'non ruthlessly'.

Non ruthless exercise means exercise in response to need rather than for exchange.

Other than spot, forwards and futures, the contracts and derivative instruments that we are most interested in in the ESI are:

---

[53] In a forward contract, the cash flow is coincident with the commodity flow, or if not, the interest cost is priced in. A futures contract on a trading exchange is like a future contract. However, if there is a purchase and sale such that commodity flows net, then the cash flows are netted and settled immediately rather than waiting for the initial delivery date.

(i)   average rate contracts;
(ii) European options;
(iii) American options and swing options.

Average rate options (also called Asian options) are also traded. They are not particularly important from a physical perspective, and the electricity specific issues for them are not particularly significant. For pricing methods for average rate options, the reader is referred to the standard textbooks on derivative pricing, listed in footnote 2 at the beginning of this section.

9.4.1   Average rate contracts

The standard average rate contract is a swap, in which a participant pays/receives a fixed price and receives/pays a floating price. The floating price is generally the prompt contract, which is observed and set in the same moment.

It is possible to separate the observation and delivery date, so we might, for example, pay the average price of the baseload contract of 2008, for every single observation day in 2005. Whilst not being a common contract, it is important in relation to retail pricing.

In a physical average rate contract, physical product is delivered at the price determined by the average rate contract.

9.4.2   European options

European call/put options represent the right but not the responsibility to buy/sell commodity at a designated strike price, for a designated delivery date, with a designated notice period. Options have been traded for thousands of years[54] and form part of the fabric of the financial markets. There is an immense literature relating to the prices of European options, and of a wide variety of other forms of options.

They are normally the principal source of volatility information in markets. The ESI is slightly different in that swing options are an important additional source of information. The three essential instruments are: (i) the caplet, (ii) the cap and (iii) the swaption.

A caplet is a standard European option for a short period, This can be as small as a halfhour, but the common minimum is one day. Caplets do not trade on their own.

A cap is a family of caplets with a single strike, purchased in one transaction, but independently exercisable. Structured capacity options that have strike prices are of this form.

A swaption is a European option for a longer period. This can be as small as one day, but would commonly be one month, one quarter, or one year. Cash settled average rate options (on, for example, peak, baseload, or temperature) are of swaption form.

We showed in Figure 9.31 how to calibrate options of different aggregate periods, which for unit weightings we call swaptions for convenience. We now have to consider an additional complication – that of the option smile, which is extreme for electricity.

It is particularly important to note that a cap (for example a monthly cap with daily caplets), even of nominally at the money (the cap strike is equal to the average forward price for the period) has an inherent smile structure, since if there is a forward price profile then the caplets will not be at the money.

---

[54] Aristotle tells us that Thales bought options on olives. It was also Thales who reportedly discovered static electricity.

The cap must then be calibrated with the term structure of smile as well as the term structure of at the money volatility. This is shown (for deseasonalised volatility) in Figure 9.40. Here the short swap represents the prices for the caplet period and the long swap represents the price for the cap and swaption period.

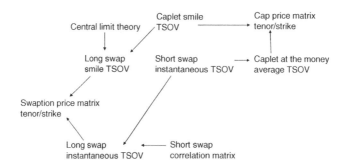

Figure 9.41   Calibration of caps and swaptions, taking smile into account

The above figure assumes a stationary term structure of volatility (e.g. non stochastic) and no seasonal effects. Non stationary effects can be added by the application of adjusting factors to equation 9.25, as shown in section 9.2.1.1.

9.4.3   American options

An American option with a single exercise is identical to a European option, except that instead of the contract delivery date being fixed, it is tied to the exercise date (usually the spot date for the exercise date). It is therefore not certain which contract will be exercised, and this adds complications. American options can be evaluated using either the LSM Monte Carlo method, or the tree, both of which are described below. Single exercise American options are not of particular importance in the ESI, but many-exercise American options, called swing options, are very important.

9.4.3.1   Options with rebate to accommodate start cost

We have noted in several places in the text, that while a plant can be viewed as an option on fuel-to-power conversion, that the plant incurs a start cost. The standard method to incorporate this cost into the European option is to smear the cost over the option period by raising the strike price. An alternative approach is to consider the option as an American option with a rebate (in this case to the option seller). Suppose for example, that the European option is struck over an eight hour run period. The equivalent American option applies to the same run period, but can be exercised for a shorter period. If we suppose that the run period will always end at the same point but could begin at different points, then the strike can be set to the true marginal cost, and a one off rebate applied which is equal to the start cost. There are models to price the rebate, and the principal modelling difference here is to model the balance-of-period price process for valuing the American option.

9.4.4   Swing options

Swing options are American options that allow many exercises. They are variously called take or pay, use it or lose it, or flexicap, depending on the circumstance. A typical annual swing option contract would have 365 daily European options, with a limit to the number of exercises (which is what makes the option an American one). The evaluation of swing options is described below.

9.4.5   Monte Carlo Simulation

Monte Carlo Simulation is often described as the poor man's modelling, since the technique allows us to perform most calculations[55] with limited need to use the complex mathematics of derivatives and stochastic calculus. Since the method allows us to model with only a partial understanding of the econometrics, it allows us to make theoretical errors and oversights, and hence should be used with caution.

A Monte Carlo simulation is the enactment of the process equation, lots of times to create lots of paths. We then apply these paths to situations such as: (i) examining price trajectories and comparing them to actual price paths, (ii) applying processes with high degrees of freedom and calibrating to terminal distributions with a range of tenors and prices, (iii) pricing European options at all strikes, tenors and period lengths and (iv) elementary 'swing' problems (which we shall see later). The process has a considerable richness to simulate features such as price dependent local volatility (i.e. smile), or path dependence.

Practical application is relatively straightforward. The Monte Carlo process simulates the outcome of dz samples, correlated dz samples, jump probabilities and jump sizes.

For example, if a jump probability in a time interval t is q, then Monte Carlo can simply use the uniform distribution[56] to simulate the event probability sampling.

For a one step production of a sampling from the normal distribution (i.e. the term ε) in equation 9.2, there are numerous methods, which are described in textbooks.[57] Remembering the central limit theory, then even summation of uniform distribution, such as is produced by the function rand() in Excel, will work, but this is both inefficient and unreliable.[58]

9.4.5.1   Decision making with Monte Carlo

The Monte Carlo method is not ideally suited for modelling option exercise decisions in which there is a tradeoff between the immediate payoff and the reduced value of the residual option. The reason is that while the tree method shown allows for straightforward backwards induction. Monte Carlo requires correlation analysis, which is awkward and computationally intensive for any number of decisions greater than one.

The method, first described by Carrière, and variously called the Least Squares Method or the Longstaff Schwartz method (LSM is the acronym for both), works as follows:

(i)   Simulate n price trajectories.
(ii) For each timeslice, calculate the exercise value on each trajectory.

---

[55] Monte Carlo is least suitable in circumstances where the optionality is limited as choices have to be made between early and late exercises of options.

[56] The uniform distribution has equal probabilities of all values within the interval between 0 and 1. The rand() term in Excel is a uniform distribution. So we can simulate the probability by if(U < q), where U = rand()

[57] See for example, Clewlow and Strickland (2000) for the production of two variables.

[58] Random numbers created by computers are not really random and have hidden patterns that can cause errors. For details, see Jäckel (2002).

(iii) For the penultimate timeslice, make a table with immediate exercise value X_{n-1} against the hold value Y_{n-1} (the value of exercise at the ultimate timeslice) on each trajectory, and regress to form a quadratic value formula $Y_{n-1} = a_{n-1} + b_{n-1}X_{n-1} + c_{n-1}X_{n-1}^2$.

(iv) For the timeslice before the penultimate timeslice, make a table with the value of immediate exercise X_{n-2} against the hold value Y_{n-2} on the same trajectory, and regress to get the quadratic formula $Y_{n-2} = a_{n-1} + b_{n-2}X_{n-2} + c_{n-2}X_{n-2}^2$.

(v) Repeat back to the first step.

(vi) For each trajectory, we have for each timeslice, both the exercise value and the hold value based on the regression and hence the maximum at each timeslice. We choose the timeslice with the highest maximum to be the stopping time.

(vii) Each trajectory now has a value equal to the exercise value at the stopping time.

(viii) Average the value of the trajectories to arrive at the option value.

Note that whilst for European options, we can ignore interest rate discounting until very late in the valuation process, for American options it must be included at the beginning. In the case of Monte Carlo, we apply discounting to Y at each step.

9.4.6 Modelling with trees

The elementary process modelling in Figure 9.1 used a simple tree. Trees are covered extensively in the literature, for energy, fixed income and general pricing. The particular feature of recombining trees in comparison to Monte Carlo is that by restricting the number of possible states at a particular time, we can force paths to recombine. Instead of focussing on the evolution of paths, we focus on the evolution of probabilities as we move through the tree. The reason that we use trees is in order to calculate values and optimal strategies where there is some form of decision process along the way, which therefore causes a dependence of instrument value on prices along the way and not just the terminal price distribution.

Forcing trees to recombine is not always easy, and it is all too easy to make hidden assumptions. The assumption that we make in a binomial tree with constant timeslices is that the price process is a one factor process (equation 9.22).

Consider first a tree with two timeslices, with different (but deterministically different) volatilities in each time interval. We can see in Figure 9.42(1) that without mean reversion, our paths will not naturally recombine. By adjusting the mean reversion rate we can make[59] the high price nodes experience a stronger downward drift than lower price nodes and for one mean reversion rate, the two nodes B and C meet. If the price process is Geometric Brownian Motion, then the mean reversion rate must be applied to the logarithm of price, otherwise while B and C can be made to meet, the other nodes in the same timeslice will not.

If the process is indeed a one factor mean reverting process, then in fact the connection between the mean reversion rate and the slope of the volatility curve is entirely consistent. Indeed if this were the case, for non stochastic volatility, we could infer the whole forward volatility curve from observation of option premiums at any two tenors. If, however, as is usual, calibration to the observed vector of option prices requires the use of three, four or five parameters (see equations 9.24, 9.25 and adjusting factors described above in equation 9.25),

---

[59] This by itself is not a valid reason to alter a price process. However, mean reversion rate and volatility slope are intimately connected.

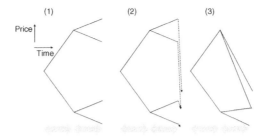

Figure 9.42 (1) Two steps with different volatilities, (2) Adjusting the mean reversion rate such that recombination occurs, (3) The outcome – a recombining tree

then it is clear that in order to replicate the volatility curve, we have to mis-specify the mean reversion rate and thereby the deterministic part of the drift as well.[60]

We can see from the geometry of the tree, that we have to specify our process equation as:[61]

$$d(\ln(S)) = \left[\mu(t) + \frac{\dfrac{d\sigma(t)}{dt}}{\sigma(t)} \ln(S) \right] dt + \sigma(t)\, dz$$

Only for a one factor linearly mean reverting process is $\dfrac{d\sigma(t)/dt}{\sigma(t)}$ constant with respect to t.

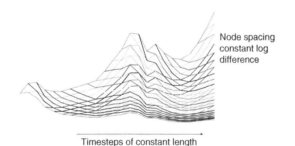

Node spacing
constant log
difference

Timesteps of constant length

Figure 9.43 Recombining tree after Black Derman Toy. For details see text

We must be sure that either (i) our exposure to each modelling effect is the same or similar in the calibrating instrument and our priced instrument,[62] and hence we do not need to worry too much, or (ii) that our fundamental economic analysis supports our econometric assumption and we can isolate the difference between the calibrating instrument and the priced instrument.

---

[60] The restriction of the model was recognised by the main protagonists, Black, Derman and Toy (BDT). For the BDT paper as well as other papers discussing the issue and adding degrees of freedon by altering tree geometry, such as Black and Karaskinski, see Hughston (1996). The book also contains a collection of key papers, such as that by Heath, Jarrow and Morton.

[61] See Hull-White (1993) for further detail, and for an explanation of trinomial trees.

[62] For example, pricing American options using European options to calibrate exposes us to error, but pricing American options by calibrating from American options will be OK.

Some other methods of forcing a recombination without making the explicit connection between volatility slope and mean reversion rate are: (i) varying the timestep[63] with the volatility and (ii) trinomial tree.

The trinomial tree has proved popular in pricing electricity problems and is well documented in the literature.[64] The strong advantage is the ability to independently vary volatility slope and mean reversion rate.

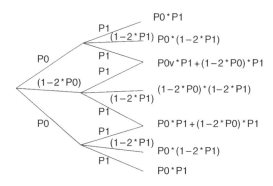

Figure 9.44   Symmetric trinomial tree

There are some simple ways to add skew. For example, we can have a binomial process with probability p of the price rising and (1-p) of it falling, where $p \neq 50\%$.

9.4.6.1   Three dimensional trees

The limited dimensionality of two dimensional trees is shown in Figure 9.45. This shows the evolution of one path, in this case a continued sequence of up steps. At each node, there is only one possible forward price vector (although there remain many possible spot price paths).

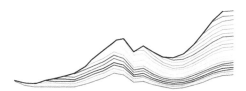

Figure 9.45   Evolution of price path expectation, following one particular price evolution, in this case a continued sequence of up steps. At each node there is only one possible forward price vector expectation

It is quite possible to build a three dimensional tree. Consider a situation in which at time 0 the spot price is 10 and the equilibrium price is 10, and in which the forward curve is

---

[63] This is the Black Karasinski method. Calibration difficulties, and the need to curtail the tree to keep the calculations manageable make application of this model uncommon.

[64] See Hull-White (1996) and Clewlow and Strickland (2000).

completely specified by knowledge of the spot and equilibrium prices. For example[65] for a forward contract, $F_{T,t}$ delivering at time T, and observed at time t, $F_{T,t} = F_e + (F_{t,t} - F_e)^* \exp(-k^*(T - t))$. After one time interval there are four possible states. This can be represented on a two dimensional tree with multiple forward price states per spot price node, by a forest of two dimensional trees or a three dimensional tree. The forest is shown in Figure 9.46. In the first step, the equilibrium price Fe could move from 10 to 9 or 11. The Fe = 11 plane is not shown.

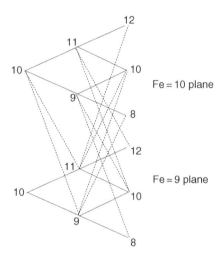

Figure 9.46 Representation of two factors on a forest of trees. Each tree shows the evolution of the spot price for one level of forward equilibrium price. Forward equilibrium price movements are represented by movement between trees. A two step process has three trees, two of which are shown

The spacing between the levels of the tree is constant, since the term structure of the equilibrium price volatility is flat. We can see this from Figure 9.47.

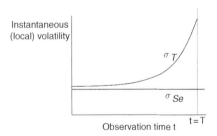

Figure 9.47 Development of the instantaneous volatility of forward contract prices and the equilibrium price

To develop the tree, we must take into account any correlation between spot and equilibrium prices. For slow decay rates it is usually safe to use zero correlation, but if we have

---

[65] This is in fact the only form of forward curve that is consistent with evolution on the tree.

high decay rates (for example to accommodate mean reversion jump diffusion) then the equilibrium price that should ideally have a tenor of at least two years, in practice denotes a fairly short term forward price. Spot and equilibrium prices can have positive correlation due to receiving influence from the same exogenous forces. Correlation can occasionally be negative,[66] but not on a consistent basis.

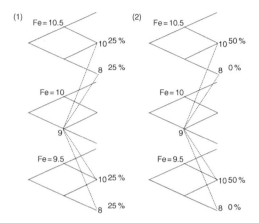

Figure 9.48   (1) 0 % Correlation of spot and equilibrium prices, (2) 100 % Correlation

We can see from equation 9.21 that for general correlation ρ, we can express node probability by $25\%(1+/-\rho)$.

In section 9.2 use the volatility specification (equation 9.24):

$$\sigma_\tau = (a + b\tau)e^{-c\tau} + d$$

Where τ is the contract tenor, the time between the observation time t and the delivery time T.

A two dimensional binomial tree has the restriction that $b = d = 0$. For $d \neq 0$ the two factors are imperfectly correlated, Whilst this cannot easily be captured in a standard three dimensional tree, a partially recombining tree can be constructed.

9.4.6.2 Decision making with trees

Trees are the simplest way to model decision processes in which there are a large number of option decision timeslices, with a number of options that is less than the number of timeslices.

Consider a two period setting in which the holder has a 'swing' option, in which he has the right to buy ('call') electricity at \$ 10.5/MWh in either (or neither) but not both periods.

To do this we construct a tree (assume that a one factor tree is sufficiently representative) and work backwards from the end. This method is called Stochastic Dynamic Programming.

The tree in Figure 9.49 shows the prices and the value of exercise of the option at the node.

---

[66] This is generally due to a cash flow or gaming effect. For example, high spot prices generate high cash returns, which stimulates investment, which lowers forward prices. An incumbent may force down spot prices to deter new entrants, thereby gaining a higher expectation of future spot price. See Figure 5.32.

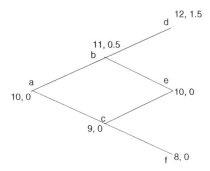

Figure 9.49   Tree showing the evolution of spot price, and the value of exercise at each node of a call option of strikie $ 10.5/MWh

Consider node b. The value of immediate exercise is 0.5. The spot price has 50 % probability of moving to 12 (for which the exercise value is 1.5) and 50 % probability of moving to 10 (for which the exercise value is zero). The 'hold' value of 0.75 at node b therefore exceeds the 'exercise' value of 0.5. On this diagram, node c has a hold and exercise value of 0. The value at node a is therefore 50 % of 0.75 plus 50 % of 0, or 0.375.

   If there are two possible declarations of options, then a forest must be built. One forest shows the instrument value for two remaining declarations, and the second forest shows the value for one remaining declaration. At each node, there is the choice to exercise (and thereby move down to the next tree) or hold (and thereby stay on the same tree).

   The value of nodes on trees with one exercise remaining is as described above. The value of nodes on trees with two exercises remaining is equal to the maximum of (i) (exercise

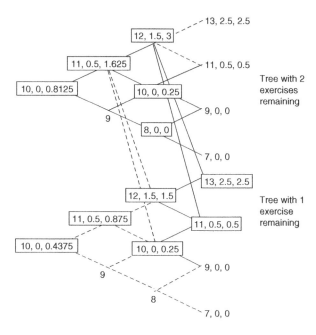

Figure 9.50   A three dimensional forest for a swing option with strike price 10.5. Each node shows the spot price, the incremental value of immediate exercise, and the instrument value

value + 50 %* value of successor node on one exercise remaining tree + 50 %* value of other successor node on one exercise remaining tree) and (ii) (hold value, which is 50 % each times the values of the successor nodes on the two exercise remaining tree).

The valuation of swing options is particularly important for electricity for two reasons: Firstly, as we shall see, much of power station optionality is of the swing variety. Secondly, due to the high presence of swing-like optionality in power stations and in supply contracts for industrial and commercial companies, swing represents a more fundamental valuation product than European options do. Therefore rather than calibrate swing options from the prices of European options and forward prices, in the medium to long term, it is actually the value of swing options that currently drives forward prices and European option volatilities.

9.4.6.3   Some problems with trees

Due to the ease of construction, visibility of process and robustness of calibration, trees are very useful for framing prices when there are decisions to be made, and their use is widespread. However, as with all methods, it is wise to treat them with caution of their limitations.

The main problem is the limitation of specification to the price process. A two dimensional binomial tree requires a zero volatility of equilibrium price. A three dimensional tree enables this price to vary.

The second problem is the unrealistic specification of local volatility. At first sight, the nodes would appear to represent feasible beginnings of trees. This is not the case. We can see this in two ways.

Firstly, the volatility perspective. Each timeslice must calibrate to the European option volatility expiring at that timeslice and hence the node spacing at the final timeslice is related to the *average* volatility over the whole period, and not the spot volatility actually faced on arrival at the node. If either the volatility term structure is flat, gently humped,[67] or the periodic and non periodic drifts are low, this is of little practical significance, but since electricity can easily violate these properties it is more significant. By underestimating the residual volatility, the tree model generally encourages early exercise. Monte Carlo modelling does not have this problem.

Secondly, the price perspective. For extreme movements on the tree, to very high or very low prices, the local drift caused by mean reversion can be very high (in a positive or negative direction), and correspondingly the slope of drift implied by the forward curve can be very high. In practice, arbitrage between prices at extremes[68] can commonly become high for extreme prices, as arbitrage relationships kick in and the economics are determined by natural prices not the logarithm of prices. If the arbitrage relationships force the prices to move in 'lock step'[69] (one for one movement) with each other, then this drives the linear correlation of the logarithm of prices away from 100 %. This is in reality more a limitation of the one factor process than of the two dimensional tree method.

A further problem for trees is the fact that most trees cannot easily model distribution skewness, or option 'smile'. Given the high importance placed on this by the efforts made in modelling jump diffusion, this can be a problem for modelling options with high strike

---

[67] Interest rate volatility curves are often humped due to the impact of central bank rate setting in the short term.

[68] For example, maximum price limits and limits on price slopes due to storage effects.

[69] For a fuller description of this for upward slope (contango) see Harris (2005).

prices. Fortunately, the majority of ESI option applications with trees involve relatively low strike prices.

9.4.7 Modelling swing contracts using semi-analytic methods

Take or pay, or 'swing' contracts, can be regarded in different ways. One way is to view the option as a flexicap, in which (for daily exercise options of one year duration) there are 365 opportunities to exercise, but a limit of total number of exercises. If, as is usual, the annual minimum take exceeds the aggregate daily minimum take, then we are short as well as long of optionality. We can instead view the contract in terms of the most likely forward contract (the exercise pattern that would be engaged if volatility fell to zero and prices became deterministic), plus the option to switch dates, plus the option to put some volume back to the producer. If we are likely to switch dates then we are more interested in the change in slope of the market, rather than the change in absolute level of the market. We are then more interested in the second principal component than the first. Indeed if the second principal component is of significant size, the one factor tree will incorrectly price the swing option.

Semi-analytic methods are very effective in pricing single exercise American options, but run into difficulties with more than a handful of exercises. It is useful to compare the tree and semi-analytic model for single exercise to check the tree model.

9.4.8 Volume options

We have stated that many supply contracts have fixed tariff and no volume restriction. By treating demand as inelastic, deterministically related to exogenous factors which are correlated to price, then we can price these options using standard derivative techniques (at least to the degree that standard assumptions apply).

Suppose that we have a wholesale price P0, a total grid[70] supply point demand D0. Then the payoff of the supplier on his customer portfolio, is $TD - PD = (T - P)D$ where T is the tariff. We can see that if D is positively correlated to P, then the payoff (to the supplier) is concave, as shown in Figure 2.51.

Consider now a derivative contract, in which the payout is $(P - T)$ and is in a 'currency' D. When we convert back to standard currency, we have a payout of $(P - T)D$, which matches our customer contract. The derivative contract is called a 'quanto' contract, which is quite standard in the fixed income markets.

If the correlation between normally distributed absolute returns of D and P were standard linear, then the forward contract is simply priced.

Probability

	$P_0 - dP$	$P_0 + dP$
$D_0 - dD$	$0.25(1 + \rho)$	$0.25(1 - \rho)$
$D_0 + dD$	$0.25(1 - \rho)$	$0.25(1 + \rho)$

---

[70] Using grid demand rather than sectoral demand from the distribution system adds a number of basis risks, for example to embedded generation. However the required demand statistics are not available in the timescale required.

Money payoff relative to base case D_0, P_0

	$P_0 - dP$	$P_0 + dP$
$D_0 - dD$	$dD^*T - (D_0 - dD)(P_0 - dP) + D_0\,P_0$	$dD^*T - (D_0 - dD)(P_0 + dP) + D_0\,P_0$
$D_0 + dD$	$dD^*T - (D_0 + dD)(P_0 - dP) + D_0\,P_0$	$dD^*T - (D_0 + dD)(P_0 + dP) + D_0\,P_0$

The probability weighted expectation is $-\,dPdD\rho$

So we can see that, ignoring non energy costs, the valuation of the contract with non ruthlessly exercised volume option is equal to the expectation volume times tariff minus wholesale price minus (i.e. a cost to the supplier) a convexity bias of approximately[71] $P_0\sigma_P D_0\sigma_D\rho_{P,D}t$. The precise form depends on the term structure of correlations and volatilities, and the proper use of the (possibly non linear) correlation of relative returns. The associated cost of risk, that is charged to the consumer depends on the correlation. For high correlations, then price hedging covers the bulk of the risk and for $\rho = 1$ then the relative (to the forward market) cost of risk is zero. For $\rho = 0$, then demand is a principal component that cannot be hedged at all by price derivatives.

9.4.9   Imbalance pricing

Although the balancing and imbalance mechanisms use different price setting mechanisms to the cleared market, and are with the monopoly operator, there are similarities and arbitrage relationships between the markets.

Consider the following prices

SBP – The price at which short positions get cashed out.

SSP – The price at which long positions get cashed out.

PX0 – The closing price of the market, for small volumes.

PXoff – The offer price for requisite volume in the clearing market just before gate closure.

PXbid – The offer price for requisite volume in the clearing market just before gate closure.

Participants aim to have zero imbalance but this is hard to achieve. Knowing that imbalance is inevitable, they may choose to bias their physical notifications.

Ignoring aspects of balancing and imbalance prices such as smear of the system operator's surplus revenue from imbalance, or locational effects, we can assess rational participant behaviour.

A participant finding himself short will evaluate his expectation of SBP in relation to PXoff to see if it is worth buying in the market or getting cashed out.[72] Similarly, with a long position, he will evaluate his expectation of SSP in relation to PXbid.

Cost of risk would not be expected to be an issue, since with 17,520 balancing events (if halfhourly) per year, the diversification is high. However, risk aversion is commonly

---

[71] Assumes Arithmetic Brownian motions or very low volatility Geometric Brownian motions, standard linear correlations, constant local volatilities and correlations, and flat forward curves.

[72] The prospect of paying transaction costs twice by buying the short position and finding himself actually long is described for longer term management in the appendix (A.2.5).

displayed by participants and balancing/imbalance mechanisms can have sustained periods of consistent biases relative to the closing price of the clearing market.

Cost of loss aversion is more significant, since a lot of money can be gained and lost in imbalance, and cash out prices can be higher than VOLL. The position bias caused by loss aversion is dependent both on the upper and lower (i.e. negative) limits of the cashout prices, and the probabilities of falling long or short (for example power stations are far more likely to lose large amounts of load rather than accidentally producing[73] more). For supply companies, demand spikes can be positive or negative.[74]

9.5 ESTABLISHING FUNDAMENTAL RELATIONSHIPS

'Relying on long-term equilibrium relationships can be quite dangerous and should be only contemplated by entities with deep pockets, and even deeper patience resources'
Eydeland and Wolniec (2003)

This reminds us that if there is a deep and liquid market on both bid and offer side, that we must have a very good reason indeed for using a different price and it is not recommended here.[75] However, fundamental analysis is essential in filling in the information where it is absent or insufficient (instrument, tenor, granularity, volume).

We start by taking an inventory of factors that we believe may influence price, either directly or by influencing factors which directly influence price. Such an inventory is shown schematically in Figure 9.51.

Figure 9.51 Depiction of grouping of factors that can affect price

These are then examined in two complementary ways.

(i) **The non parametric approach** – The historic statistical relationship between the factor and price (starting with the spot index price) is examined, with no preconception about cause or about form of relationship. This approach prioritises the faithful modelling of

---

[73] Large long positions happen by incorrect notification rather than accidental production.

[74] Positive spikes occur from turning on kettles during commercial breaks in popular television programmes. In the UK, there was a large negative spike on the two minute silence commemorating the death of Princess Diana.

[75] see Baxter and Rennie for a fuller description of this.

data which is mainly in the form of time series in the public domain, and uses maximum likelihood estimation to establish the most appropriate parametric form.

(ii) **The fundamental parametric approach** – This begins with a preconception about how the system 'works' according to economic or other analysis, and thereby what econometric form it should follow. This approach prioritises the calibration of model parameters such that they fit a wide universe of data from disparate sources (for example, prices of various kinds of transaction such as market instruments or whole assets).

The different methods have different uses in different situations:

Table 9.3   Circumstances for use of parametric and non parametric methods

	Parametric	Non parametric
spot price history	Best method if absent	Best method if there is a long standing, complete and granular dataset
forward market	Best method if thin market with several different prices (e.g. winter, baseload, peaks, etc.)	Best method if deep and liquid, with granular dataset
option market	Best method if market thin or if options used to calibrate other instruments	Best method for option trading if deep and liquid, with granular dataset
Market stability	Best for modelling changes	Not suitable if significant change
Calibration sources	Best method if wide sources (e.g. bespoke forward contracts, physical transactions)	Best method if single source (e.g. spot price time series)
Requirement	Better suited to forward price processes	Better suited to spot price processes

Consider the situation in which we have collected price returns over a number of sequential timesteps and have counted the number of steps of each size. This is shown in Figure 9.52 and serves as an *ex post* probability histogram. Suppose for example that it is believed from economic analysis that; (i) a factor is the dominant influence on price, (ii) the factor is linearly related to the square of price, and that (iii) the factor moves according to random walk and thereby has a normal terminal distribution. The parametric approach would then model price in terms of the stochastic movement of the factor. The model parameters are adjusted so that the price model is consistent to the observed data within a given level of tolerance, as shown in Figure 9.52. For this particular case, the price would have a chi-squared distribution.

Figure 9.52   Parametric modelling within the historic or implied bid/offer volatility envelope

9.5.1 The exogenous and endogenous worlds

Exogenous forces are forces that lie outside of the modelling system. The forces on temperature are a good example. For our purposes, we model temperature variation simply by actuarial analysis of the past without trying to model what makes it change relative to expectation. Fortunately, temperature is a 'well behaved' normal variable. Another example is plant failure. We model the failure behaviour of plant not owned by us as an exogenous variable. If we owned plant, we could with increasing levels of diagnosis decrease the amount we do not know about plant failure and hence convert an unknown exogenous force to an internal deterministic relationship. (see section 9.1.14.1). It is clear then that there is no clear boundary between endogenous and exogenous forces, and the boundary depends on the resource we have available for diagnostics, analysis and modelling.

We can visualise this as shown in Figure 9.53. Here we assume that the relationships within the endogenous world are deterministic, and that the sole source of uncertainty is in the temperature.

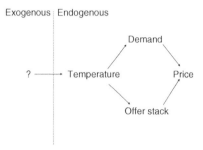

Figure 9.53   Depiction of deterministic relationship in the endogenous world and a single unknown source of exogenous shock to a single factor

We can see that there are other relationships outside our endogenous system. This takes the form of relationships to factors unseen, or unknown facets of relationships to factors seen.

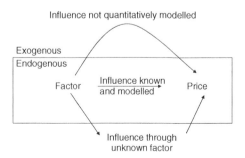

Figure 9.54   Unknown relationships to known factors are treated as exogenous forces

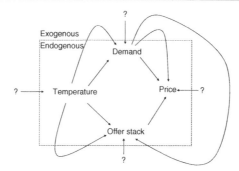

Figure 9.55   Even in a simply modelled system, the exogenous relationships are extensive

For correlation estimation, there are a variety of ways in which variables can influence one another. This is illustrated schematically in Figure 9.56.

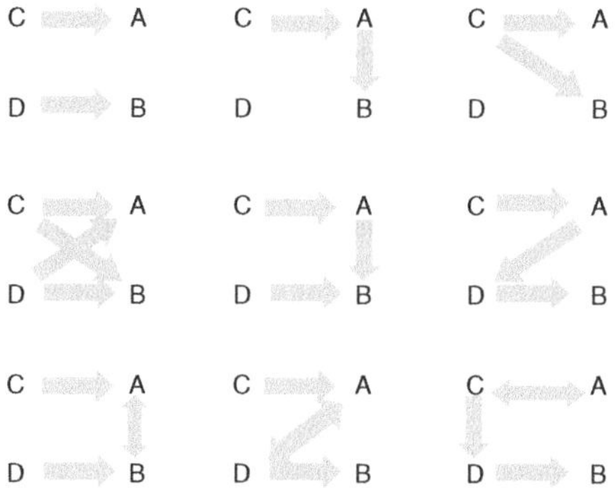

Figure 9.56   Different influence relationships between variables A and B. C and D may be visible or invisible

This may seem as if it will become intractable. Indeed it is not realistically possible to model the whole price universe. Indeed, the neoclassical model suggests that the interactions are probably too complex to model. However for any specific purpose, it is not generally necessary to understand the whole price universe and it is possible to gain insights into parts of it. For example, the long term movement of baseload prices, the effect of peak prices of a particularly cold day, or the effect of a major outage on off peak prices for the next week. In the world of efficient markets a very small piece of information can yield a significant advantage, particularly if the time from decision to realisation is small.

Figures 9.57 and 9.58 exhibit a high level visualisation of the influence of some forces on different elements of the price curve, from the perspective of demand and of generation.

For example, consider the influence of gas prices. In a market where non renewable new build is mainly combined cycle gas turbines (CCGT's), then the medium term baseload price is highly correlated to gas prices and in a market in which CCGT's cycle in the winter in response to very high gas prices, then the off peak power price is correlated to the gas price.

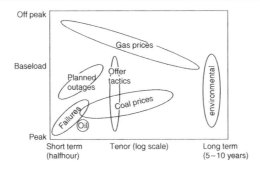

Figure 9.57 Representation of major forces on price from the generation side, mapped by peak/off peak and tenor

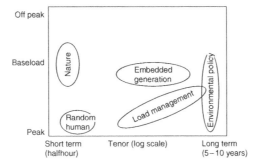

Figure 9.58 Representation of major forces on price from the demand side, mapped by peak/off peak and tenor

As shown in these figures, the interaction of forces is highly dependent on context.

One thing that is frequently, and incorrectly, ignored in asset and market modelling is the mutual impact between price and price factors. Price factors (such as power station build) impacts price and price impacts price factors. The neoclassical framework in which we work most of the time is in fact poorly equipped to handle the circular relationship between prices and price factors, if not coincident. This requires us not just to look at certain aspects of the price universe, but to take a world view of the whole universe to gain an intuitive understanding of the nature of the feedbacks. This is a much more classical interpretation of the economic system.

Finally, we must recognise that the economics of the system as a whole must work so that each element of the ESI makes a fair return and equilibrium can be sustained. Excess return leads to new entrance, and insufficient return leads to early exit. This creates a relationship between power prices and factor prices. Two examples of this are coal prices and emission permit/allowance prices. There are known and unknown components of the relationships.

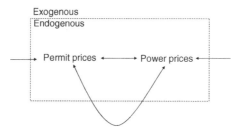

Figure 9.59   Permit prices affect power prices, and the resulting behavioural change then impacts permit prices

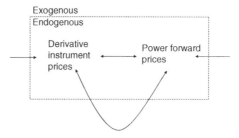

Figure 9.60   The prices of derivative instruments are affected by power prices, but since power plant economics are affected by the instrument prices, then the instrument prices then affect the power prices

9.5.2   Price Growth

The fundamental economic equation for storable[76] commodity price expectation paths is Hotelling's rule,[77] which shows a steady state growth that is bound up with the prevailing interest rate, rather than inflation.

We can understand this intuitively by considering an inflation free world in which we model a produced commodity by a stock of gold which costs a fixed fee, one currency unit, to withdraw. Figure 9.61 shows three possible forward price slopes. The middle slope represents the cash asset profile from selling the gold immediately and investing the money at the risk free rate. For simplicity, simple interest has been used (for compound interest this is called the rolled up money market account). If the forward price slope exceeds the risk free slope, then the highest amount of cash after one year can be realised by selling forward. If the forward slope is less than the risk free slope, then the highest amount of cash after one year can be realised by selling now and investing the money. Competitive pressure then drives down the forward price in the first case (flattening the slope) and down the cash price in the second case (steepening the slope). This continues until the forward slope is equal to the risk free rate slope.

---

[76] The non storability of electricity is a short term effect. In the long term it behaves in much the same way as other commodities that are themselves made from commodities.

[77] Hotelling (1931). For the special case of zero storage costs, zero cost of risk and a few other assumptions, the arbitrage equation in continuous time is $(\partial P_{t,t}/\partial t)/P_{tt} = r$ where Ptt is the spot price and r is the credit free interest rate.

There are a number of reasons why Hotelling's rule has only limited application in practice. For example, if there is no actual storage arbitrage engendered by virtually costless storage then cost of risk depresses the forward price due to the asymmetry in producer and consumer hedge needs, described in sections 2.2.24 and 2.6.7, the maximum forward slope is depressed by the physical cost of storage. If there is virtually costless storage (as there is for gold), then the credit loss expectation and cost of credit risk drives up the leasing rate, which is equivalent to an increase in storage costs.[78]

Figure 9.61 Forward price slopes. $1+r+p$ is the maximum slope with positive storage costs. $1+r$ is the arbitrage free slope for zero storage costs. $1+r-d$ represents zero storage costs and a convenience yield $= d$

Nevertheless, the principle of Hotelling's rule is important, since it establishes that commodities grow in price fundamentally, and that if the forward price curve does not reflect the interest rate curve, then there is something else going on.[79] The other key feature of consideration in long term commodity price trends are depletion of known reserves, reserve discovery, efficiency gains that also increase the viability of reserve extraction, and factor costs in the form of environmental taxes and limits (causing shadow prices).

If we believe that we can establish the fundamental forward price of electricity from (generally baseload) new entrance, and we can estimate the producer price inflation, then we can spline the long and short term curves together. If, ignoring inflation we used a forward curve of the form $F_T = F_\infty + (S - F_\infty)e^{-kT}$, where we have set observation time to 0, F represents the forward price and S the spot price, then if we include inflation, we have $F_T = [F_\infty + (S - F_\infty)e^{-kT}]e^{IT}$. Since we know S, and have a belief in inflation I and F_T for some tenor, then we adjust F_∞ and k to give us the best fit to the observed forward curve.

In general, commodity traders do not apply inflation for periods of less than about five years and so do not use this curve. It is however useful for asset planners who tend to work in 'real' terms and hence include inflation in all years.

9.5.3   Weather, climate, daylight

The ambient atmosphere affects prices in many ways. The principal drivers are:

(i)   cloud cover (effect on temperature and daylight);
(ii) precipitation (short term effect on demand, medium term effect on river height, flow rate and resulting thermal load capacity, and long term effect on major dams).

---

[78] See Harris (2005) for further explanation of this effect.
[79] See Harris (2005) for a description of the effect of inflation on Hotelling's rule.

(iii) pressure (effect of power station efficiency);
(iv) temperature;
(v)   major weather events (storms, hurricanes, lightning strikes);
(vi) times of dawn and dusk;
(vii) solar eclipse (very rare, but causing record demands).

Apart from short term contingency planning for weather events, the atmospheric effects that are commonly modelled are rain, snow and snowmelt, windspeed and temperature. The most amenable to statistical analysis is temperature.

9.5.3.1 Temperature

An example of an established relationship between a factor and power prices is ambient temperature. In temperate countries a common form of relationship between temperature and price is shown in Figure 9.62.

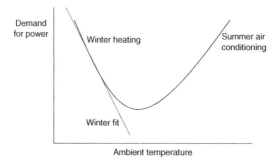

Figure 9.62   Typical relationship between temperature and demand

This is based on regression analysis for the whole year, so in winter, price rises with falling temperature and in summer price rises with rising temperature.

Now supposing that in fact it is considered that the relationship between price and temperatures were in fact not statistical but deterministic.

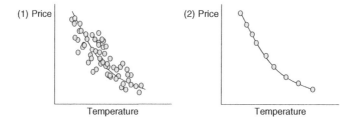

Figure 9.63   Price/temperature relationship. (1) Correlated (non linear), (2) Deterministic

Then we would just model the change in temperature and only convert back to price when we actually need the price for derivative pricing.

We have given attention to the relationship between demand and price by the construction of generation stacks, and have established that this is highly non linear, particularly for high demands. It is immediately obvious that if the demand-temperature relationship is convex, and the price-demand is highly convex for high demands, then even for a perfectly well behaved random walk for temperature, that we can witness very high prices.

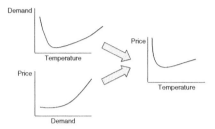

Figure 9.64 The production of a highly skewed price/temperature relationship through two skewed relationships

Figure 9.65 The probability distribution of price can be highly skewed and yet deterministically mapped to normally distributed variable, in this case temperature

We can now take a well behaved stochastic variable (temperature), mapped in a non linear and non monotonic manner to demand, which in turn is mapped in a highly non linear way to price. If this were the end of the story, then we could perfectly rationalise a probability distribution for price that is highly skewed (relative to the normal distribution).

Of course it is not the end of the story. We note next that the relationship between cost and productive capability is itself influenced by temperature, for three main reasons:

(i)   Generators plan their scheduled outages for low demand periods and hence there is less plant on the stack in these periods.
(ii) Plant capacity and plant outage rates are dependent on the ambient temperature (see section 2.2.18).
(iii) The plant offer prices above fuel marginal costs depend on both the run history and the expected run rate of the plant. Both are temperature dependent.

There is a deterministic and stochastic component of each of these.

If temperature is the dominant driver of price, then we can say that we have captured the principal movement in price by capturing temperature changes and that we just need to add some form of noise term to capture the residual movement. In practice, the noise tends to be large relative to the movement explained by temperature.

9.5.3.2 Difference of temperature from the normal distribution

Brownian motion is a special case of a family of processes called fractional Brownian motion.[80] Temperature can be modelled with a generalisation of the process and this successfully models the small difference of temperature from the normal distribution.[81] For most purposes, temperature can be treated as normally distributed with a constant value for mean reversion.

If temperature today differs from the prior estimation of the mean, then the expectation profile of temperature is that of reversion to the mean at an exponential rate. This is a one factor process.

More advanced modelling of temperature is not generally necessary for power price modelling.

9.5.3.3 Temperature trends

We have temperature information in different parts of the world going back 420,000 years.[82] The information derives from information such as dissolved gases in the polar ice caps, and the width of tree rings.

Over a long period, analysis of temperature records indicates that temperature has had a series of cycles of different lengths. Spectral analysis[83] can break these down, and then form the expectation of the temperature path in the future. The path depends on the dataset used and is therefore dependent on the cutoff date of the dataset,[84] so more data from further and further into the past, adjusts our view of the future. If there is a consistent trend between cutoff date and temperature expectation for some date in the future, then this is an indication that there may be a new kind of interaction that has not existed in history, or at least that the interaction has changed.

Whilst the mean temperature over a long period of time displays behaviour that could be random, mean reverting, periodic, or chaotic, historic analysis indicates that temperature in the medium term (a few years) conforms remarkably well to random walk and the normal distribution. For the purpose of price modelling, we can assume a constant forward mean plus a very slight trend.

Temperature trends are modelled, and they are used both for demand modelling and for the thermal efficiency of power stations. In practice, urbanisation has a more significant short term impact than global warming. There are two other effects that are important. The first is the measurement bias that arises from different local trends at measurement stations than global trends – for example if the stations are in towns. The second is the changing pattern of day-night temperatures.

The direct effect on temperature from global warming does not cause a significant effect on demand. However, the greater the belief that anthropogenic CO_2 production causes damage

---

[80] Put simply, fractional Brownian motion has normally distributed increments, with mean zero and variance $(dt)^{2H}$. Brownian motion is a special case with Hurst component H = 0.5. If H > 0.5, the prompt process is non Markovian and has finite covariance between near and long term values. Studies for temperature indicate that H tends to be slightly greater than 0.5. See Brody, Syroka and Zervos (2002) for application in this context.

[81] It has also been shown that principal component analysis can also achieve a similar result to fractional Brownian motion, which makes the stochastic calculus far easier, and this method also makes it far easier to accommodate changes in weather forecasts that use more data than simply the temperature history.

[82] IPCC (2001).

[83] This method is essentially similar to the principal component method described in section 9.3.6.

[84] For example, Transco, the UK gas transporter, in 2005 reduced its statistical demand sampling period from 70 to 17 years, due to an apparent step change in slope.

to the environment, the greater the impact on demand. This belief is increased by increasing annual average temperatures.

When modelling price variations with temperature variations, we must take into account the seasonality of the temperature/demand relationship, and the seasonality of plant availability. Figure 9.66 shows the steepness of the generation stack in Great Britain in the summer, where plant outages are concentrated, due to the lower average prices in the summer.

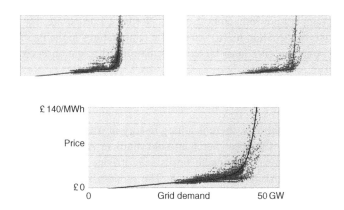

Figure 9.66   Pool price/demand graphs in summer, spring/autumn and winter, England and Wales 1999. Source National Power

9.5.3.4   Temperature periodicity

Temperature has diurnal and annual cycles, as well as a number of possible long range cycles extend from two years to at least 400,000 years. The cycles can be modelled with Fourier series, truncated for maximum stability.

$$T(d) = A + \sum_{n=1}^{3} a_n Cos\left(\frac{2n\pi d}{364}\right) + \sum_{m=1}^{3} b_m Sin\left(\frac{2m\pi d}{364}\right)$$

where T(d) is the temperature for the seasonal date d. We adjust A, a_n and b_n so that the sum of the squares of the errors between the historic data set and the function is minimised.

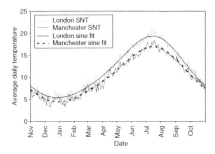

Figure 9.67   Fit of seasonal normal temperature to historic data

9.5.3.5   Forward temperature forecasts

Temperature is not a physically delivered product, and its development cannot be seen easily. We can model temperature as a mean reverting prompt process, with the mean being the standard normal temperature for the time of day and day of year, possibly detrended for longer term effects.

If the mean reversion rate is slow, then today's and recent (if we allow path dependence) temperature are a useful indicator of temperature for the next few weeks.

Other forward temperature indicators used for Northern Europe are, for example (i) sea surface temperatures in the Atlantic, (ii) sea surface temperatures in the Pacific, (iii) northern hemisphere snow cover and (iv) quasi-biennial oscillation. Different observers place different weights on these.

9.5.3.6   Market contracts for temperature

As with most derivative contracts, there is a long history of trading with implied derivatives for weather. In 1298,[85] A Genoese merchant sold alum in Aigues-Mortes in France and committed to buy it in Bruges, contingent on its safe arrival, where he could sell it on. In doing so, he insured his risk to storms at sea. The modern insurance industry has many contracts designed to include and exclude weather and weather event risk.

For normal, rather than extreme, weather events, the most popular weather instrument in the ESI is the heating degree day. The heating degree day has the payoff function $Max(F-T,0)$, where F is an agreed temperature and T is the average temperature of the day in question. This is a cash settled European option, struck at F.

A distinct feature of temperature derivatives[86] is the nature of the cashout. Whereas contracts on deliverable commodities have execution risk, since the exercise of the contract may disturb the market and incur excessive bid/offer costs, the temperature index is unaffected by market trading.

9.5.4   Consumer contracts

Consumer contracts take two principal forms:

(i)   **Tariff agreement** – No ongoing price commitment by the supplier, and no commitment by the consumer to stay with the supplier.
(ii) **Contract** – Price commitment by the supplier, and fixed term commitment on both sides.

There are numerous variations, including:

(i)   No restriction on volumes for tariff customers (this is normal for residential customers and is sometimes called a 'full requirements contract').
(ii)   No variation on volumes for the core element of a contract.
(iii) Limited 'swing' variation for the contract (this is normal for commercial customers).
(iv)   Standing (capacity) charge or no capacity charge.
(v)   Green tariffs of various kinds, for both tariff and contract customers.

---

[85] For a fuller description, see Briys (1999).
[86] For further information on weather derivatives, see Geman (1999).

(vi)   Fully bundled contracts, for which the price is fixed regardless of industry events.

(vii)   Pass through contracts, for which the supplier is contractually entitled to[87] (but may choose not to), raise prices following industry changes such as increase in network charges or renewable obligations. (This is common for commercial customers.)

(viii) Unbundled contracts, in which the contract is fully or partially divided, such that certain elements (such as energy prices or network costs) automatically rise and fall in line with industry changes.

(ix)   Tariffs with price freezes, options, exit fees and other 'contract-like' terms.

From a derivative pricing perspective, the key elements are:

(i)   Green premium.

(ii)   Standing charge (paid by the consumer to the supplier and/or paid by the supplier to its service providers).

(iii)   Wholesale market prices and volatility.

(iv)   Network charges, timing of price control reviews, interim changes to charges, inflation and 'inflation plus X' charges.

(v)   Volumetric options and limitations.

(vi)   Contractual optionality of consumer (for example to terminate the contract/tariff agreement).

(vii)   Practical optionality of supplier (for example to pass through network cost increases where this is allowed under the terms of the agreement, but may result in customer termination).

(viii) Non ruthlessness, consumer stickiness, price leading and following.

(ix)   Mix of fixed and marginal costs of the supplier.

(x)   Wholesale price forwards, options and other derivatives, to allow consumer hedging of unbundled contract risk.

For the short term, over which customer gains and losses are small, then the marginal cost of consumption is tractable using the techniques shown in this chapter, with particular attention to the non linearity of correlation between temperature and demand and the strong variation by consumer sector of the periodicity and size of this correlation.

Over the longer term, there are more issues:

(i)   Recovery of the fixed costs of the supplier, and the fixed costs paid by the supplier (for example to network operators).

(ii)   Competitor positioning and hedge cover.

(iii)   Customer switching, to and from the supplier.

These are not valued using standard derivative techniques. The various aspects of fixed cost recovery are described in several parts of this book, interaction between suppliers is described in section 10.5, and hedge effects on prices are described in sections 5.4.14.2 and 5.5.4.

---

[87] The wording is either explicit or in the form of a material adverse change, or other clauses in the contract.

Customer switching is partly a result of changes in relative price, partly a result of general switching rates in the market, and partly a result of advertising campaigns. Estimating the impact of prices on aggregate consumer volumes and market share is something of a black art. Almost by definition if it is impossible, since if it were possible, then everyone would do it since the stakes are so high, and the next round would be second guessing of participant behaviour.

9.5.5   Valuation of physical assets and risks

The practice of 'real options' seeks to express the valuation of physical assets in terms of financial derivatives. There are essentially two approaches. In the first, the asset is valued in relation to a trajectory of spot (and possibly forward prices), taking into account asset response to prices.[88] In the second, the asset is value in relation to the derivatives that it can sell, and whose contractual responsibilities can be supported by asset response. In the extreme for the perfect asset, the derivative instrument matches the asset capability perfectly, and the asset cash flow is independent of price evolution. This is conceptually the same as the 'no arbitrage' approach on which the Black Scholes theory of European options is founded.

Real options for power generation units are considered in more detail in Chapter 11 and here we focus on the derivative valuation. We first consider the approximate derivative form that the asset corresponds to, and then consider differences to this form.

Here we will consider the situation in which the assets are very small and have no market influence.

9.5.5.1   Power generation capacity

We begin with the most simple situation, in which a power station is a simple fuel-to-power converter with no fixed costs, no start costs, instantaneous changes of loading state, no failure, no emissions, and buying fuel in the spot and forward markets. In addition, we consider the sale of only one kind of option at any time.

We then have a set of European options. The plant is equal to the sum total of options that it can sell. Where fuel must be purchased to fire the power stations, the options are spread options.

In this somewhat contrived circumstance our concerns are: (i) basis risk and (ii) which options to sell. The most important basis risk is the basis between the value of the grid supply point to which the plant exports, and the market index that is used for hedging. This location risk is described in section 7.5.

Ignoring basis risk and the other complications, we can represent high load factor plant valuation as the sum of: (i) baseload valuation, (ii) saving of marginal costs from selling back some energy and adjusting the schedule, (iii) selling European call options to change state and (iv) selling further call options that are dependent on exercise status of European call options. This is shown schematically in Figure 9.68. In this case, the extra flexibility is in the form of short duration options whose exercise is contingent on the exercise status of the European options.

---

[88] This is the form taken by Brennan and Schwartz (1985).

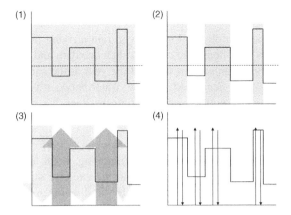

Figure 9.68 Four additive stages of valuation of high load factor plant. (1) Baseload, (2) Planned flexibility, (3) 'Vanilla' optionality, (4) Extra flexibility. Stepped line represents market prices. Grey represents plant operation. Block arrows represent options sold. Line arrows represent contingent options sold. Forward price is shown in each graph

All of the complications have then to be considered one by one.

9.5.5.2   Transmission capacity

From a derivative perspective, the issues in valuing transmission capacity are quite different to those for generation capacity. In particular, we may not make the assumption that we are a small player with no market influence, trading at the margin.

Nevertheless, the handling of state variable behaviour (such as temperature), probability, cost of risk, consumer behaviour and generator behaviour that comes with derivative modelling is very useful in the modelling of the value of incremental build/reinforcement of transmission capacity. With the growth of location marginal pricing, and the variety of 'transmission rights', node-to-node transmission can increasingly be regarded in derivative form.

9.5.5.3   Hydro

The modelling of hydro is quite distinct to the modelling of thermal generation for several reasons:

(i)   Marginal environmental damage from operation is assumed to be minimal.
(ii) Fuel is free but volume is limited and variable.
(iii) Start costs are minimal, and start times and loading rates are fast.
(iv) Marginal cost of plant life usage is small.
(v)   Breakdown rates are very low.

We can treat hydro scheduling and profitability as an optimisation problem with four different degrees of complexity:

(i)   Deterministic prices and deterministic rainfall.
(ii) Stochastic prices and deterministic rainfall.
(iii) Deterministic prices and stochastic rainfall.
(iv) Stochastic prices and stochastic rainfall.

Our modelling issues are:

(i)   We assume a very simple physical model with rain arriving in the form of energy. In reality, dam systems are often more complex than one dam and above-dam water level.
(ii) We treat the dam as if it must start and end the year at the same level. We must then add further optionality to 'lend' and 'borrow' water between years.
(iii) There is a limit on daily withdrawal rate from the dam due to gravity effects on the walls of the lake.

For deterministic rainfall, we can approach the problem as a tree/forest problem as outlined in section 9.4.6, and use stochastic dynamic programming. Each level of the power price tree represents a dam level, which is equivalent to the exercise state in Figure 9.50. The upper and lower height limits are easily handled by disallowing running when the dam is 'empty' and forcing running when the dam is 'full'.

Stochastic rain is harder to handle. In theory it is possible to add a dimension to the tree to allow for weather forecast, so that we have a forest of three dimensional trees, each tree representing a dam height. A two-variable tree is shown in Figure 9.48. However, if we are to retain a sufficiently high resolution of run length, the computation can grow out of control. Whilst, with care, we can use a variety of techniques to save memory and computation time, it does get rather complicated.

9.5.5.4   Storage

The derivative valuation of swing has been fairly well developed in the gas markets, due to the historic practice by producers of selling gas in swing contracts, and in the valuation of underground storage. Power storage (defined as the consumption of power with the express purpose of producing power at a later stage) is less well developed. Nevertheless the swing element of power station contractual capability is significant.

The dominant form of 'power storage' is pumped storage. The key difference between pumped storage and underground gas storage is the relatively low efficiency and high 'injection and withdrawal' rate of pumped storage. This, combined with the limit of dam capacity in relation to turbine capacity, means that we can generally model pumped storage in terms of filling at night and emptying in the day. This is distinct from gas storage which derives most of its value from seasonal variations in price.

We can build up the value of pumped storage as follows:

(i)   Static valuation using deterministic prices.
(ii) Add European option value in relation to deterministic regime.
(iii) Add further options of increasing complexity.

For example, suppose that the deterministic price optimisation arrived at the schedule of cycling every day in the winter, and doing nothing in the summer. The winter options will then be not to cycle, and the summer options will be to cycle. We note here that the 'principal components' here are quite different to the principal components depicted in Figure 9.38 which have a deseasonalised term structure. They are explicitly related to changes in periodicity. The spread option variance is given to us by using a family of correlation matrices of different tenors, and the option is valued by integrating over different tenors. Note that we must be careful to attend to modelling 'details' – for example, we treat periodicity as a multiplier to price rather than an additive to price.

If we cannot fill the dam in a single day, the problem becomes more complicated because there is a serial dependence on exercise.

9.5.5.5 Renewable Obligations Certificates

Suppose that suppliers must either source x % of the electricity from renewable sources, or pay £Y/MWh 'buyout' for shortfalls, and that the buyout revenue is shared by the renewable generators. Suppose also that the market overall can supply z % of power from renewable sources and that the market price for black power is £P/MWh.

If the percentage of generation that is from renewable sources is much less than the target, then the suppliers will simply pay the buyout price and thereby have an expectation of electricity cost of £ $(P + xY)$/MWh. The renewable generators will receive an expectation of £ $(P + xY/z)$/MWh.

For the non renewable generators, as long as $x > z$, then their renewable premium costs are certain and there is no need to hedge. However, the renewable generators face a volatile revenue and will wish to hedge the renewable premium. With no natural buyers the cost of risk will be positive and hence the forward price of renewable obligation certificates is a downward biased expectation of their 'outturn' price. An expected renewable generation percentage calculated from the certificate prices is therefore over-estimated.

Note that the suppliers possess an out of the money put option, since if the certificate value falls below the buyout price then they will buy in the market rather than pay the buyout.

9.5.6 Pricing using world views

It is never correct to plan using proprietary estimates for market values, that fall outside the market bid/offer for the required volume, of the required instrument, at the required granularity, at the required tenor. However, for major asset investments, the traded market is almost always too illiquid, thin in volume, short of term, and with insufficient derivative match and granularity to use. Hence we have to piece together the market using what information that we have. Commonly asset managers and financiers will base the valuation on broad features such as available fuel supply contracts, relative cost relative to general new build cost, and projected supply/demand balance in the country in question. They will then add the finer features such as daily optionality, on the current market, using the techniques in this chapter.

To add information to the relative competitive position of the asset, the kind of generation that will set price, and therefore the broad picture of prices, it is useful to use world views. For example, we may model nuclear and non nuclear scenarios. One way to do this is to consider the relative compatibility of different factors, and assign low probability to, or discount those scenarios involving incompatible factors. A simple example is shown in Table 9.4, and we might consider a number of other features such as:

(i)   Success of carbon sequestration technology.
(ii) Evidence (or otherwise) of anthropogenic CO_2 production on global warming.
(iii) Economic growth of China, India, Russia and other large economies.
(iv) Political climate in the USA.
(v)   Development of opinion and technology in relation to wind power.
(vi) Technology gain in extraction of high cost sources of fossil fuel.

(vii) Development of hydrogen technology.
(viii) Warfare and terrorism.
(ix)   Demand management – technology and culture.
(x)   Population growth, energy intensity, electricity intensity.
(xi)   Changes in financial liquidity.
(xii) Changes in the role of the state.

Table 9.4 Compatible and incompatible factors that form energy scenarios

	Low carbon	Nuclear	International Trade war	Closed borders
Low carbon		✓	?	×
Nuclear			✓	✓
International Trade war				×
Closed borders				

If our view of world prices influences our own actions by isolating some competitive niche, we must consider what our competitors are thinking, and what effects our plan will have on the price.

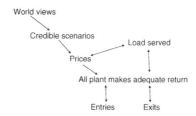

Figure 9.69 Ensuring consistency of prices with equilbrium

Note that this approach has more in common with the classical economic approach than the neoclassical.

9.6 MARKET COMPLETENESS

The methods described in this chapter enable the construction of a complete price/volatility/correlation term structure for all tenors and all granularities and including the three principal periodic cycles of the market. To calibrate this, the problem is that the complete term structure of volatility and correlation of electricity and fuel cannot be established in any one market. It is necessary to construct a single proprietary structure that is recalibrated to as many types of transaction in the ESI that can be captured. Each transaction tells us something different. For example, the build of gas fired power stations gives us information on baseload prices, and the presence of old oil fired power stations gives us information on peak prices. Transactions that can be used for sources of information include:

(i)   sale of operating power stations;
(ii)   sale of pumped storage;
(iii) build of new power stations;

(iv)   contract price of take or pay gas contracts;
(v)   international price of coal and crude oil;
(vi)   schedules of installed plant;
(vii)   forward contracts for baseload, peak and shape;
(viii) option contracts;
(ix)   retail prices;
(x)   power station emission limits;
(xi)   carbon dioxide limits, prices.

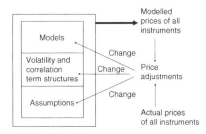

Figure 9.70   Adjustment of a model and calibration universe in relation to all events in the outside world that are relevant to prices

9.6.1   The completeness of markets with options

The lack of market completeness when market factors are stochastic has been an important consideration in the validity of the market approach to drive the optimum economic solution. We showed in section 6.10 that provided that there are option and insurance contracts, that in fact the market can exhibit a high degree of completeness to drive the appropriate level of plant investment in terms of volume, mix of fixed and marginal costs and plant reliability. In fact, the 'option signal' actually has a rather longer tenor than the 'forward signal', although as shown in section 2.6.7, both are shorter than ideal for reasons that are more due to the forces of competition than uncertainty.

Traded options have a number of information benefits:

(i)   They can operate at all timeframes. So, for example the call option for a particular time of a particular day can be written just a few hours before or some years before. The contract form is identical.
(ii)   By tying a well defined and standard financial instrument to the key plant economic parameters of fixed cost and marginal cost, the plant is very effectively defined in market terms.
(iii)   Option prices themselves contain a definition of probabilities of market prices (and, by implication, events).
(iv)   Since the options can be written a long time in advance, the market power associated with short term holding of optionality is greatly reduced.
(v)   The plant can plan its closure strategy in an effective timeframe (e.g. plant to close in a year's time if premiums from one year do not match fixed costs) and the system can respond in an effective timeframe to such decisions as the decision is revealed by the option transactions, or lack of.

(vi) The option strike can contain other risk elements such as fuel price and/or emission permits.

(vii) Options are very closely related to take-or-pay contracts.

The principle problem of trading options are (i) the relatively high degree of expertise required to assess fair value and (ii) the granularity required for them to be effective in the short term.

9.7 EMISSION PERMIT PRICES

9.7.1 Forward price profile

We might expect emission prices to follow broadly the pattern shown in Figure 9.71.

Figure 9.71   Likely evolution of emission permit prices

In the futures markets, the seller generally has the choice of delivery date within the futures contract period. This is also the case for emission permits, except that while in the case of normal commodity futures markets, the seller may elect to deliver early to gain cash flow, there is no advantage in surrendering permits early. Hence there is no forward price profile within any emission vintage year.

Permits can have negative shadow prices, since unused cap allowances cause increased risk of cap reduction.

9.7.2 Banking and borrowing

Banking and borrowing has a significant effect on both prices and volatilities. If the permit scheme allows 1 permit to be banked and used in place of b permits, then the forward price effect is dependent on b. If the market is in contango (rising), at more than 1/b per year then, for zero interest rates, it is economic to bank them. If we consider interest rates r, then this ratio changes to $(1+r)/b$ per year. This will raise the price in earlier year and depress them in the later year. Permit borrowing can be treated in this regard as banking in reverse and may have a different year's 'exchange rate' between the years. We might describe the banking and borrowing rates as at the money if the trading participant is indifferent as to whether to bank/borrow or not.

9.7.3 Volatility of permit prices

If the regime is cap-no-trade, then we commonly treat emission limits as a swing problem and ignore the shadow price of the emission. However, if we have abatement options (other than load factor limitation) which can be engaged in the short term (such as the purchase of lower sulphur coal), this is inefficient since it does not value the abatement option. Instead, we can load the emission onto the power generation strike price as shown in section 11.5. This does present new problems. The shadow price from load factor reduction is dependent on the power price path, since the exercise regime is (or should be) deterministically related to the history of the forward price vector. In practice, this modelling is not frequently undertaken and it is more common to make manual adjustments to the swing valuation, to cater for abatement options other than load factor reduction. In general, the emission price is higher when the spot price has been high and the forward price low (i.e. emission prices are negatively correlated to the level of the price path of the forward slope vector).

In cap and trade, and cap-no-trade, the market price/shadow price volatility of emission permits increases as time marches on in the emission vintage year.

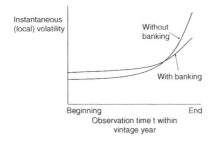

Figure 9.72 Evolution of the volatility of emission permit prices

Banking and borrowing have a significant effect on volatility. Before a vintage year has begun then permits can be borrowed from the previous year or banked into the next year. When the year begins, then only banking is possible.

If permits are banked or borrowed, then this reduces the volatility of the permits in the current vintage year as it approaches closure, at least up to the point at which the banking and borrowing limit is reached. The closer the banking/borrowing rate to 'at the money' the greater the volatility dampening effect. If, as would be expected to be normal, the earlier year is more volatile than the later year, then borrowing would be expected to raise the volatility of the later year because the stock of permits is reduced and the price perturbation greater. Banking could cause the volatility to rise or fall. If the later year is the source of volatility, then banking and borrowing reduce its volatility.

9.8 NETWORK PRICE VOLATILITY

We saw in Figure 2.42 that network costs form a substantial component of delivered energy prices. If network price signals are expressed in the short term market (by location dependent prices) rather than the medium term (by location dependent annual use of system charges) that the true impact of cost volatility due to network issues is felt in the markets.

The practical impact of network effects on the short term cost of delivered energy is dependent on the mix of all of the charges shown in section 7.3 and how these behave.

For example, if system revenues may be set about every five years, then the volatility of the revenues evolves prior to and during the consultation period, and prior to and during the setting of provisional charges. Within the overall volatility of aggregate charges to all suppliers (i.e. revenues) the volatility of charging to the respective supplier segments can be significant. In a sense, the evolution of supplier charges to particular segments is similar to the evolution of wholesale prices, although there are a smaller number of significant price events. Analysis of changes in network charges includes inflation, 'X' (see section 4.6.3), changes to charging methodology, temperature (affects over and under recovery which are passed on to next year's charges), actual and regulatory status of pension deficit pass through.

Short term constraint costs are considerably more complicated and require the simultaneous application of several techniques such as real options, DC load flow, plant failure analysis, demand variation analysis and regime switching.

10

Economic Principles in Relation to the ESI

'Q: How many Conservative economists does it take to change a light bulb?
A: None. Conservative economists just sit in the dark and wait for the Invisible Hand to do it' – Edward. J. Nell. From 'Free Market Conservatism. A Critique of Theory and Practice'

This chapter is not an introduction to the general field of economics, but concentrates on those areas on which an understanding of the economics of the ESI depends, and which are referred to in academic, technical, policy and lobby discussions and literature. Particular attention is paid to neoclassical economics, gaming, equilibrium, welfare and marginal costs.

The reader will notice in this chapter a relatively high degree of attention to economic thought going back to the 19th century. This perhaps reminds us that Keynes famously said that politicians were slaves of defunct economists. There is in fact good reason in economics to make frequent reference to schools of thought. Economists have far less access to data for testing their theories than do practitioners of the physical sciences, and the core element of study – economic man – exhibits less consistent behaviour than inanimate objects. As well as less data and less consistency, the modelling universe has no defined boundaries, and economists are forced to build models of highly simplified economies – for example with two people and two goods. The result of these facts is that each time an economist faces a problem; he must first examine how similar problems have been addressed in the past, what assumptions were made, what the validity of assumptions was, what the sensitivity to assumptions was, what fundamental axioms were relied on, and what analytical tools are available. This due diligence automatically takes virtually every problem back through a trail that traces back to the economists from history, and by choice about assumptions and axioms, the economist finds himself, perhaps unwillingly or unwittingly, in the camp of one economic school or other. By providing specific reference to economic heritage, and by using consistent terminology, new theories are readable and testable by the wider community.

10.1 BASIC ECONOMIC PRINCIPLES IN AN ESI CONTEXT

10.1.1 Microeconomics and macroeconomics

'In microeconomics, we see how and why the Invisible Hand operates (how and why self-interest leads each person toward a spontaneous system of productive cooperation): in macroeconomics we see the consequences of failing to do so' – Hirshleifer (1980)

Microeconomics concerns the behaviour of individuals and organisations in response to specific stimuli. Macroeconomics concerns the behaviour of the economy as a whole, and treats individuals and organisations in aggregate. When considering electricity markets, most analysis uses microeconomics, but when considering high level policy, and particularly the role of the ESI in the fiscal (taxation) system, macroeconomics must be taken into account.

Markets essentially operate in a manner that can be described in terms of marginal neoclassical microeconomics. The markets operate in the context of the macroeconomy. We need to concern ourselves with macroeconomic principles in several ways. For example:

(i)   Corporate and income tax generated by the ESI.
(ii)   The role of the ESI in energy and environmental impact taxation.
(iii) The direct role of the ESI in redistribution of wealth.
(iv)   The need to preserve long term equilibrium of the asset base.

10.1.2   Classical economics

The dominant economic paradigm of the ESI is neoclassical, but there are many features that neoclassical economics handle in an unsatisfactory manner, particularly in the long term. We therefore need to bear in mind the main alternative framework to the neoclassical model, which is the classical model from which it broke away.

Whilst there were forerunners, Adam Smith is regarded as the founder of classical economics, and the theory was developed by Ricardo. The focus of classical economics is on production, supply and costs.[1] The basic classical model has constant costs and constant demand, and producers' surplus from the engagement of natural resources, labour and capital, with particular emphasis on labour. In a competitive environment, competition acts to erode the surplus, so that prices gravitate to the long term cost of production. The classical model is depicted below. In the case of corn, the commodity for production is easy to understand in the form of seeds. Similarly, energy production requires energy. In this model, what is shown in Figure 10.1 as 'commodity for production' is more in the form of raw material, than in the form of equipment, and in the case of corn, is in the form of seed which transforms to corn with the inexhaustible supply of natural energy in the form of sun and rain.

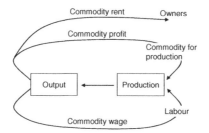

Figure 10.1   The Ricardo classical model[2]

Because classical economics paid no particular attention to activity at the margin, they could not contend effectively with purchase and sale, and neoclassical economics grew

---

[1] This characterisation is from Roll (1938).
[2] Adapted from Sheppard and Barnes (1990).

from this need. Whilst classical economics was superseded by neoclassical economics, more recently, in the 1960's, problems with the neoclassical model led to a resurgence of classical economics, led by Sraffa.

Whilst the neoclassical model is deliberately fragmented in terms of letting the market determine the price of all input and output factors, the classical model is deliberately holistic in terms of grouping them all together and modelling the whole production cycle.

10.1.3   Neoclassical economics

'we may loosely define neoclassical economics as the type of economic theory built on the idea of rational, optimising agents with exogenously determined preference functions, focusing on the equilibrium outcomes and limited types of information problem associated with such optimising behaviour' – Hodgson (1997)

Neoclassical economics became a branch of classical economics with Marshall, Walras and Jevons in the 1870's. The development was very much in connection with the application of the principles of mathematics and the physical sciences to economics. As well as focussing more on the margin than the aggregate, there was, and is, a greater attention on consumption, demand and utility,[3] as well as exchange. Production and consumption are not as distinct as in the classical model – 'Production is the transformation of matter for the purpose of creating things capable of satisfying our wants',[4] and 'capital is nothing but the total of the intermediate products which are generated in the various stages of production'.[5] What is important for our purposes is the end of the classical desire to express value, and price, in terms of the fundamental building blocks of land, labour and capital. Price is driven by preference (for example, labour prices are driven by the relative preferences of leisure and the goods purchasable from income), which has no grounding in absolute value.

The contrast between the classical and neoclassical models is evident from Figure 10.2. The production process is no longer rooted in invariant fundamental cost elements.

Resource endowments

Market exchange

Individual utility-maximisation

Figure 10.2   The neoclassical model[6]

[3] Roll (1992) used this as a description of modern economics.
[4] Schumpeter (1914), commenting on the work of Böhm Bawerk.
[5] Böhm Bawerk, from Schumpeter (1912).
[6] From Sheppard and Barnes (1990).

We can understand the importance of money and the margin in a many-player many-commodity world by considering increasing complexity of exchange. For a many-commodity system, there is an enormously complicated multi-dimensional matrix of indifference curves for each commodity pair for each individual. There will be a clearly defined set of rates[7] since the indifference curves are known to the participants themselves and the price could be calculated with full knowledge of the curves. However, this is not immediately visible to us. If we add a commodity, money, and require all commodities to be traded with money rather than with each other, then the situation gets much simpler. The reader will note that the formation of 'virtual nodes' and 'notional balancing points' in electricity trading, described in section 7.4, has the same effect.

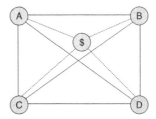

Figure 10.3 The addition of currency as a fifth commodity in a four commodity system reduces the number of necessary exchange rates from six to four

The use of money as the arbiter of value is thereby enshrined in neoclassical economics. Despite the fact that we cannot see the myriad inter-relationships, we can be confident, at least in the world of deterministic demand, that the overall solution is Pareto optimal.

Neoclassical economics require the market to provide the signals for individual and collective action, and without the signals, the market is incomplete and fails. If the only traded instruments are the spot and forward contracts, then the market is incomplete with respect to change. The optimal through-life solution for the ESI is not a static optimisation of the current world, it is an anticipatory optimisation of possible future worlds, in which we sacrifice short term surplus for investment in the flexibility to change production on a probability weighted basis for events in future timeframes.

The neoclassical model goes further than simply explaining the world in terms of production-exchange-consumption. The Austrian School[8] in particular attended to the economics of production by decoupling capital in its two roles of bearer of interest and producer of goods. This further decreased the clear distinction between production and consumption that there is in classical economics.

Externalities such as pollution are not automatically handled by the basic neoclassical model of exchange, and must be either internalised by the addition of taxes, limits or other modifications that alters the behaviour of participants, or their effects must be separately measured when considering total effects and designing policy.

---

[7] Von Neumann proved in 1928 using a mathematical theorem called the Brouwer fixed point theorem that there is always a solution. See Casti (1996). This in fact makes assumptions on the Ricardian forms of the cost functions that are not necessarily valid in all situations. See Figure 10.12 and Varian (1975).

[8] Böhm-Bawerk and Hayek.

10.1.4   The economics of the margin

The birth of neoclassical economics, was also called the 'marginal revolution'. Neoclassical economics concentrate on the economics of the marginal activity (that activity that changes in response to a small upward or downward movement in price paid/received), rather than the aggregate economics of all production and consumption.

The basic and ubiquitous curve is shown in Figure 10.4. The consumption and production curves represent the aggregate amount that participants would consume/produce for each price level. The price elasticity is the percentage amount that demand/production changes for a unit percentage change in price. The flatter the slope, the greater the price elasticity.

For the purposes of this book, the word 'supply' is not used in the context of production, since 'supply business' commonly refers to the downstream retail end of the ESI. For 'demand' in an economics context, we use the terms 'demand', 'consumption' or 'load' according to context, and for 'supply' in the same context we use 'production' or 'generation'. The marginal cost of production curve is constructed from the generation stack described in section 5.1.3.1. Throughout this chapter, we shall be using the term 'price' of electricity. Unless otherwise stated, this refers to the wholesale price of electricity traded in the market. This is downstream of the producer product and upstream of the consumer product.

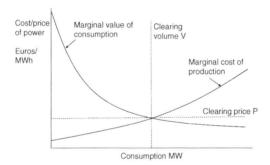

Figure 10.4 Construction of the clearing volume and the market clearing price using the price elasticity of consumption and production

This graph makes a number of assumptions, including for example:

(i) Producers have a clearly defined and known marginal cost and sell if the price exceeds that value.
(ii) Consumers have a clearly defined and known marginal value of consumption and buy if the price is less than that value.

These assumptions in turn suggest other assumptions, such as a fragmented competitive market with no collusion. We shall examine the more important assumptions throughout this chapter.

The marginal producer to the right of the clearing volume in Figure 10.4 (who is not currently producing) could offer more volume to the market, but not only is the prevailing clearing price below his marginal cost for increased production, but to attract additional consumption it would be necessary to reduce the price further. Hence it is not in his interest to increase production. The marginal producer to the left of the clearing volume (who is producing power) would not wish to withdraw volume, since he would lose profit. Hence, under the assumptions stated, the clearing price and clearing volume represent equilibrium conditions in the short term.

10.1.4.1   The marginal price for buying and selling, and for small and large volumes

Whilst the economics are described in terms of smooth continuous curves, the stack function described in section 5.1.3.1 actually has discrete steps in the ESI. This is important in consideration of low merit[9] producers, and in particular the lowest merit producer who actually produces electricity. Where the production function is discontinuous, the relevant marginal cost refers to the participant making the enquiry about the marginal cost. So, the marginal cost for buying (requiring more production) may be less than the marginal cost for selling (requiring less production).

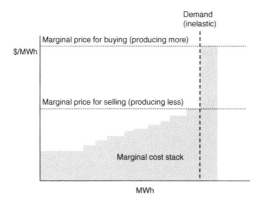

Figure 10.5   Marginal prices for buying and selling for a discrete (i.e. discontinuous) production function

This is made clearer when using market language. Markets are used to a bid price and an offer price, and are accustomed to using the term 'mid' price as a useful reference for calculations, not to be used for actual transaction valuation. In contrast to the old adage 'If you have to ask the price, you can't afford it' we can say here that if you have to go to the energy market to transact, you know which marginal price you need to use, the bid or the offer. It is clear from this figure, that the arithmetic mean of the bid and offer price for a particular volume at the current market is dependent on the volume.

This works well at the margin, and the supply/demand curves help us to build bid/offer curves around the margin, but even if all externalities are captured in the prevailing marginal price, the full curve of the externalities, that we need to know for different prices and volumes, is not. We are only equipped to optimise now for the world 'as is' and with no uncertainty or variation. If for example there is an exogenous shock to a factor cost, such as gas prices, then, while the system will again find an equilibrium optimisation eventually, this will take time for production resources to remobilise and demand to respond, by which

---

[9] Low merit producers are those with highest marginal costs. See section 2.2.

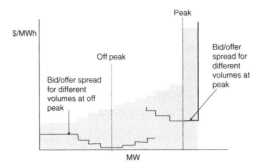

Figure 10.6 Expression of discrete or discontinuous production function in the form of bid/offer functions at different demand volumes

time everything will have changed again. Therefore the application of resource specifically designed to contend with changing drivers is undervalued when considering only static conditions. Due to the rapid variation in factors, the system will always be trying to get to equilibrium optimisation, but always be far from it. In section 10.8 we further examine the effect of shocks and in Chapter 6 how option pricing reveals costs and preferences at the margin, not just for the world as is but for a variety of worlds.

10.1.5   The demand function

In just the same way as the basic production curve assumes that the 'willingness to offer'[10] curve is coincident with the marginal cost curve, we assume that the 'willingness to pay' curve on the demand side is coincident with the curve at which the consumer is indifferent whether he consumes or does not consume. There are a number of reasons why this might *not* be the case. For example:

(i) In multilateral wholesale markets, in which producers and consumers can trade with each other, most electricity is bought in advance in the forward[11] market rather than on a 'hand-to-mouth' basis in the spot[12] market. The spot market therefore represents more of a tidying up[13] of residual positions than a complete view of the demand function. In a fragmented market where there is no market power or influence then contractual position does not affect the spot price, but in the actual market it is commonly the case that it may be worthwhile influencing the spot price in some way by bidding at some price other than the Willingness to Pay price, even if this is to the detriment of the short run economics of the participant.[14]

---

[10] The willingness to offer/pay curves are defined by the price level at which the producer/consumer is indifferent whether he produces/consumes or not.

[11] This is true as much in pool markets as in multilateral markets. In the pool, the contract is explicitly financial rather then physical.

[12] The spot market, also called the prompt market, is the market for immediate or nearly immediate delivery.

[13] In theory, it is optimal for producers and consumers to ignore contractual positions when determining optimal position in the spot market. However, transaction costs, difficulty of mobilising both decision capability and physical resources, and also suboptimal behaviour in the real world, cause the legacy contract position to exert a strong influence on physical volume.

[14] This applies equally to the financial markets and is well known. It may be worth moving the spot price with small volume in a shallow market where a larger position such as a market order, or a derivative position with a price trigger, is advantaged by it.

(ii) Markets rely on speculative activity to maintain efficiency.[15] The activities of speculators, or the speculative activity of physical participants are not defined by utility, welfare
and production functions but rather by cost of risk, and cost of risk is priced into the
forward curve.

For the end consumer, particularly small consumers, purchasing in the retail market, we
have additional problems:

(i)   There is no mechanism for the majority of small consumers to directly reveal their
preferences to the market since they commonly pay a flat tariff rather than having
visibility of real time prices that might invoke a response when prices are high. Only
the larger consumers have sophisticated enough metering and contract arrangements,
to engender a real time response.
(ii) The decision to have the ability to consume electricity (by connecting to the distribution
system), and thereby incur fixed costs, is distinct and over a different timeframe from
the decision of how much to consume at any instant. This is partly explained by the
decreasing marginal utility of consumption (it may be worth connecting just to have
a single light bulb) and partly by the fact that in paying for capacity, longer term
consumption levels must be considered.
(iii) Electricity is bought by supply companies in the anticipation of subsequent sale to
consumers. Industrial and commercial electricity consumers purchase their production
factors such as electricity in anticipation of subsequent sale to product consumers. This
chain of purchasing in anticipation but without actual commitment from consumers
causes an electricity purchasing behaviour in which the aggregate optimal forward volume of electricity purchases is less than the expectation of aggregate spot consumption.
The forward demand curve is therefore to the left (i.e. less demand) than the expected
spot demand curve for the same period. Therefore generators do not see the demand
signal early enough to make the optimal response.

10.1.5.1   The disutility of lost load

In order to optimise the provision of capacity, then we need to quantify the disutility[16] of
lost load. This fact is highly dependent on the mode of load reduction.

If, on a particular day, we find that production capability suddenly falls short of scheduled
demand, then some consumption will have to be reduced. If we could find that consumption
which has least marginal utility (or surplus), then we could reduce load to those particular
consumers. Of course, if we had the individual demand functions, then the next stage of
development would simply be to increase the price, so that those consumers would voluntarily
reduce demand. In reality, even if we could identify each individual demand function at each
moment in time, we cannot generally selectively curtail load but instead have to completely
cut off everyone within a small distribution zone. This gives a far higher disutility, as we
can see in Figure 10.7.

---

[15] The Efficient Market Hypothesis. This includes the speculative activity of physical participants.

[16] Strictly speaking here we describe the lost surplus. Utility and surplus are covered in later sections.

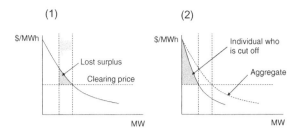

Figure 10.7 Disutility of lost load. (1) Curtailment of least 'valuable' consumption across all consumers, (2) Cutoff of groups of consumers

A regulatory value of lost load of around $ 5,000/MWh would be considered reasonable in most rich countries.[17] At $ 15,000/MWh, a 100 W light bulb costs $ 1.5 per hour. Given the choice between no electricity and the use of one light bulb for $ 1.5/hour, then most consumers in the rich economies would choose to keep the light on. Since they are curtailed from full demand, then if we assume that the consumer surplus in 7(2) is approximately triangle shaped, then the average value of lost load (the light bulb and other devices), is $ 5,000/MWh.[18]

Lost load also causes a loss of producer surplus. The generator, grid, distributor and supply company all have fixed and marginal costs, and the lost load is due to a capacity limit on only one of these. The capacity mismatch causes losses in three of the sectors. The total loss of surplus if curtailed for marginal users rather than cut off for unfortunate users, is shown in Figure 10.8.

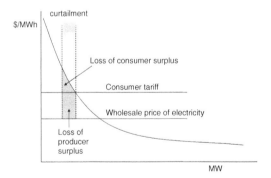

Figure 10.8 Loss of consumer and producer surplus on loss of load of consumers selected according to willingness to lose load

---

[17] The US Congressional budget office documentation on homeland security and the public sector refer to a study (Berkeley 2001) that indicated that consumers would be prepared to pay perhaps 100 times their average bill for periods to avoid interruption. Working back from an average domestic tariff of $ 0.085/kWh (source IEA 2003) then the VOLL price for a period of, say, one week, is around $ 8,500/MWh. From this, a short period VOLL of $ 15,000/MWh seems reasonable.

[18] We have here used the wholesale value for the regulatory value and the retail price for the disutility. At prices this high, the assumptions are valid, because all sectors (generation, transmission, distribution, supply) except the failed sector have marginal costs far less than this.

The disutility is highly dependent on notice period and phase (time of day/week/year), since domestic consumers can adjust their consumption patterns.

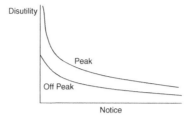

Figure 10.9   Disutility of loss load in relation to notice period for peak and off peak periods

10.1.5.2   Asymmetric or kinked demand functions

In Chapter 2, we saw that different hedge policies created an asymmetry between similar suppliers. This can create asymmetric behaviour. For example, suppose that we have a duopoly with two suppliers A and B, and that if A raises prices that B maintains price to gain market share and if A lowers prices, then B lowers price also to maintain market share. A simplified version of this argument is shown in Figure 10.10.

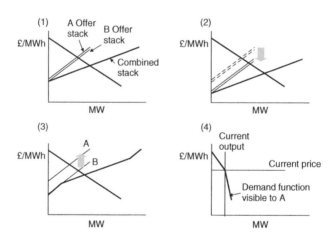

Figure 10.10   Asymmetric demand functions arising from asymmetric competitive response. (1) Duopoly in which pricing structure of A and B is identical, (2) A drops price and B follows, (3) A raises price and B holds price, (4) Resulting demand function visible to A

This theory was initially developed by Paul Sweezey in the 1930's. Note the high significance placed on the prevailing price rather than equilibrium conditions. This can also be understood in terms of reaction curves, as described in section 10.5.7.

10.1.6   The production function

The production curve is derived from the stack function described in section 5.1.3.1. As shown there, producer costs are made up, in approximate descending order, of fuel, capital repayment, environmental, operations and maintenance,[19] reliability losses and management, consumable, central and administration costs, insurance, and licenses, rates, permits, etc.

From the perspective of economics the elements that we must pay special attention to are:

(i)   The definition of fixed costs, quasi fixed costs and marginal costs in different timeframes.
(ii) Capacity factors that blur the distinction between fixed and marginal costs.
(iii) The treatment of sunk costs and particularly of repayment of capital and debt.
(iv) Non traded externality costs, such as emissions.
(v)   Market power, offer behaviour, market interaction and gaming.
(vi) Risk and probability effects.

There are two production curves to which we shall refer to repeatedly. They are the marginal cost stack and the offer stack.

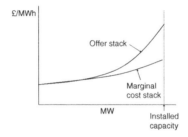

Figure 10.11   Production functions. The marginal cost stack and the offer stack

The large divergence between the two functions is a result of the high periodicity and variability of demand, the high variability of generator failure and the high heterogeneity of plant age, energy source and technology.

It is common in equilibrium modelling to assume constant returns to scale, i.e. a horizontal production function, or decreasing returns to scale (called Ricardian cost curves). This can be correct[20] in the long term (greater than five years) over which period new power stations can be built. In the short term (the day ahead market), for a given installed capacity, both cost and offer functions are upward sloping and upward curving. Examples of decreasing cost functions are shown in Figure 10.12.

We must be careful to treat electricity production and environmental impact abatement separately.[21] Since unabated power stations produce a particular amount of emission, then, no matter what the timeframe, impact abatement is commonly subject to diminishing returns. This is particularly important in the consideration of equilibrium.

---

[19] Operations and maintenance has several subcategories such as core maintenance, operations staff costs and major overhaul.

[20] Correct on a local scale only. A global increase in production would cause an increase in global commodity price.

[21] A common approach is to apportion a part of output to environmental abatement. This approach is not valid in this situation.

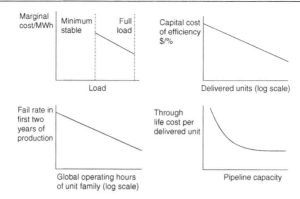

Figure 10.12   Examples of decreasing cost of production with increased volume

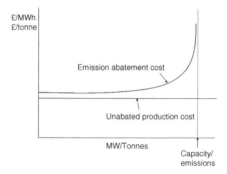

Figure 10.13   Long term producer cost functions

10.1.7   Surplus

The concept of surplus, introduced by Dupuit[22] in 1844 is shown in Figure 10.14. Here we show the aggregate producer surplus – i.e. the total surplus[23] of the producer community without consideration of how this is broken down by producer. Similarly the consumer surplus considers consumers in aggregate without consideration of individual consumers. This is measured in monetary terms.

The marginal function should also contain all externalities (factors not shown on the graph) that affect surplus. For example, if the production produces a useful side benefit (such as flexibility), that a consumer would be prepared to pay for, then this should be included. In addition all effects that are external to the local microeconomics should also be considered, such as the harmful effects of production and consumption. Otherwise the solution will be inefficient in aggregate.

---

[22] As with all such concepts, there were several previous authors, and the author noted was the one who brought recognition to the concept.

[23] The term 'surplus' is not used in corporations. In practice, profit, earnings, interest, tax, depreciation, amortisation and cash flow affect the measure used for corporate optimisation. These distinctions, while being of high importance in corporate planning, can be treated as adjustments to the economics and can usually be ignored.

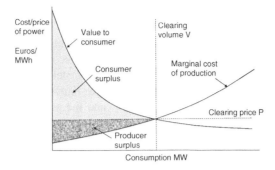

Figure 10.14   Aggregate producer and consumer surpluses at the clearing price, using assumptions noted in the text

Note that in measuring our aggregate surplus, we are effectively assuming that society (i.e. people) receive the whole benefit. Even if, as is usual, a proportion of electricity is sold to industry, the consumer surplus of industry, in a competitive market, flows through to consumers in the form of reduced industry prices due to reduced factor costs.

10.1.8   Pareto optimisation

The Pareto optimal state is the state in which it is not possible to improve the surplus/utility of any player without reducing the surplus/utility of another. In arriving at the Pareto optimal state, all participants must agree to the incremental changes, or at least not disagree them. We can view this as requiring a unanimous rather than a majority vote.

Pareto optimisation is essentially what competitive markets do, when there is no market power, and there is no behavioural influence of one player on another. Consumers will buy up to the point at which the marginal price exceeds the marginal willingness to pay and producers will sell to the point at which the marginal price falls below the willingness to sell (usually marginal cost). Hence at the Pareto optimal point in a fragmented market, the marginal willingness to pay equals the marginal cost of production.

Figure 10.15 shows that if the market price were set by regulation to equal to the intersection of the production marginal cost and demand curves, then Pareto optimisation will automatically clear the market volume at the intersection. If the volume were V3, then the producer could save amount D and the consumer could save amount C by reducing

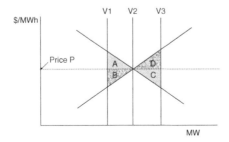

Figure 10.15   Starting with trial volumes V1 or V3, Pareto optimisation drives to the optimal aggregate volume V2

the volume to V2. If the volume were V1, then the producer could gain amount B and the consumer gain amount A by increasing volume to V2.

Now supposing that the price were set by regulation to be different to the intersection value. While price elevation to P2 above the intersection price P1 would initially result in no change in aggregate surplus (since this simply involves transfer of money from one sector to another), but at the price P2, the volume V2 is no longer Pareto optimal since the consumer would prefer to save amount E by consuming less and the producer would prefer to gain amount D by producing more. Pareto optimising behaviour will clear the market at V1 and the aggregate surplus will be less by F than the market solution. We will see later that the setting of a price higher than the intersection value is equivalent to monopolistic behaviour by the producer sector, and that F is termed the 'deadweight' loss.

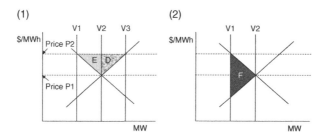

Figure 10.16   (1) Raising the price above the intersection price does not initially change aggregate surplus but makes the volume V2 no longer Pareto optimal, (2) The deadweight loss from regulating the price

We have considered the situation in which tariffs are set by regulation to protect the production sector. Suppose that instead that they are set low. Can Pareto optimisation still arrive at the optimal surplus? If tariffs are reduced, then privately owned producers will reduce volume. The deadweight loss is similar to that caused by high tariffs.

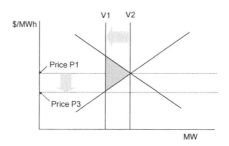

Figure 10.17   Deadweight loss from regulated tariff set lower than supply-demand intersection price

It is obvious from this that if prices are set by regulation, then, at least if fixed costs are zero, any price other than the intersection price, followed by Pareto optimising behaviour, is less efficient, from a surplus perspective, than the market solution. The case for which the producer offer curve is above the marginal cost of production is described in section 10.2.1.

We will see in section 10.1.21 that in the presence of fixed costs that if prices are fixed by the regulator, then they should include fixed costs, otherwise the withdrawal of plant will not optimise aggregate surplus.

10.1.8.1   Pareto optimality, bundling and unbundling

If it is optimal in terms of surplus to set a regulatory price at marginal costs but not reduce production, then Pareto optimisation between the producer and consumer sector will not produce the optimal solution. If we make producers and consumers a single economic unit then we apply Pareto optimisation at a higher level (the ESI to other industries). Whilst this could remain Pareto optimal at producer/consumer level by applying direct taxes to consumers and subsidising fixed cost of producers, it may not be possible to do this efficiently. This is an argument for state ownership, which is generally outweighed by the benefits of improved efficiency, communication and innovation from competition.

We can apply the same argument to fragmentation and unbundling. If we divide our economic unit, by sale or forced divestment, then each new economic unit must behave in a Pareto optimal manner. Whilst it may have been optimal for a firm with two entities to allow one entity to cross subsidise the other in order to maximise group profit, the entities will not behave in this manner when they become independent.

Consider a firm with two related activities, one in which there is a high entry barrier and one with a low entry barrier. It is rational at the level of the firm to cross subsidise from the high entry barrier business to the low entry barrier business, since competition in the low entry barrier business will eventually become competition in the high entry barrier business.

Consider instead a different firm with two producing units. It may be optimal at the level of the firm to withhold production on one unit in order to gain a higher price for the output of the other unit. If the units were sold to two different firms, then this cross subsidy would no longer be Pareto optimal.

10.1.8.2   Pareto optimality and local market power

If a participant has a degree of protection from competition within the firm, then they may use this protection to act to their own personal and private advantage, rather than the entity that they represent, possibly in violation of their civic responsibilities, if the incentive is strong enough. This can explain corporate behaviour that is apparently irrational at the level of the firm but which may be rational (even if not ethical) at the level of the individual. Pareto optimality can be considered at very low level. Where the objectives of the firm and the individual are misaligned, then individual behaviour that optimises the profit of the firm while having some detriment to the individual is not Pareto optimal. This is a significant economic force that pervades corporate life. The alignment of personal to corporate incentives is a strong motivator for opening the ESI to competitive forces. It is particularly important in power stations, because the speed (faster than halfhourly) and complexity of response that is required to optimise corporate profits is far greater than could be handled by a prescription of activities from senior management.

10.1.8.3   Pareto optimality, bads and externalities

At the highest level, aggregate surplus is optimised at international level and includes not just energy, but all externalities in the form of 'goods' such as flexibility or security of supply, 'bads' such as environmental impact, and taxes raised. The Pareto restriction is such that if all participants could vote, then none would vote for a different solution. This is something of a challenge if we internalise the environmental impact and make environmental contract for bads at the same time as we make contracts for electricity goods.

10.1.8.4 Pareto optimality, and optimising of aggregate surplus

No matter how many commodities there are, we can be sure that there is[24] a single solution that represents the optimum, or core, of the economy, in terms of surplus. The process of (eventually) arriving at the optimum, is called the tâtonnement, after Walras. The tâtonnement is particularly important in the consideration of capacity charges for heterogeneous many period demand.

10.1.9 Utility

In a world in which the market cannot deliver the optimal solution because it is incomplete, imperfect, or because social policy requires redistribution of wealth, we need to quantify benefits and disbenefits in some way. Utility is a convenient way to do so.

Utility is the intrinsic value to individuals, the value of satisfying want,[25] or being happy. The very term 'utility' is used to describe the companies forming the ESI, and is evidence of the basic fundamental nature of its offering.

Consider a simple example. Intuitively we know that the more we have of something, then the less the marginal increase in utility. For example, one dollar given to a rich person has less utility benefit than one dollar given to a poor person. We can visualise this with a utility/wealth curve as shown in Figure 10.18.

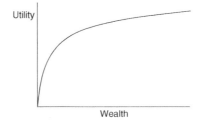

Figure 10.18   An example of a utility curve

In the absence of complete markets for bads, in order to apply economic principles to the cost and benefits of environmental impact abatement, it is necessary to assess some form of utility curve to pollution. Figure 10.19 shows that the different methods of pollution regulation imply quite different utility curves. For example, a pollution cap implies zero utility impact of pollution below the cap level and infinite utility impact above the cap. A pollution tax implies a fairly linear utility function. A cap-and-trade system implies a utility function more in keeping with normal utility functions.

---

[24] For particular production function assumptions, this can be proved with the Brouwer fixed point theorem for a static economy, and von Neumann showed that it can also be proved in a dynamic economy. Sraffa showed that this is not the case for all production functions.

[25] Initial analysis was based on psychology, in which increase of sensory satisfaction decreased with increase in sensory load. The wider interpretation of happiness is more modern.

(i)   In curve 1 we assume that our disutility of pollution is linearly related to the amount, for all levels of pollution.

(ii) In curve 2, we assume that there is some threshold level of pollution below which there is no loss of utility, but above that level, we are increasingly sensitive to unit increases in pollution.

(iii) In curve 3, we assume that initially we follow the form of curve 1, but that as we approach some level of pollution, then there is no further disutility because all of the utility of the environment has been destroyed (for example the fish have died, the lake has dried up, the people that care have moved and other people have arrived, or an area has become uninhabitable due to nuclear fall out).

(iv) Curve 4 is like curve 1, only the disutility of increments of pollution increases with the amount of pollution.

(v)   Curve 5 shows the utility curve that is implied from pollution caps. We effectively assume (or at least signal) that below the cap (threshold) there is no disutility of pollution, but that above the level of the cap, the disutility is infinite per increment of pollution.

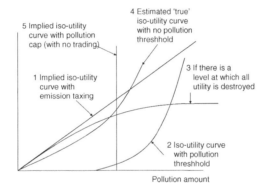

Figure 10.19   Implied iso-utility for a good and a bad for different effects or regulatory regimes for the bad B in relation to the good A

10.1.9.1   Utility functions

Since utility is used in a relative ranked[26] (ordinal) rather than absolute quantified (cardinal) sense, then the point at which utility is zero has no particular significance. What is important in modelling utility is that the behaviour that we model from our utility curve matches observed behaviour. The figures below show simplified forms of some key utility functions.

It is quite obvious that the quadratic form (cubic with no cubic term), that is assumed in most risk valuation problems can act over only a limited range. In the situation of absolute cash constraint but with the absence of contingent liabilities, then the logarithmic form can be very effective. The situation for contingent liabilities, such as that of insurers is better matched by the exponential distribution.[27]

---

[26] Ranking all outcomes for one individual, but not allowing ranking of outcomes for different individuals.

[27] In the experience of the author, implied cost of risk from the variation of premium with excess, does indeed fit the exponential utility function. The extreme value theory is used for loss distributions at the extremes.

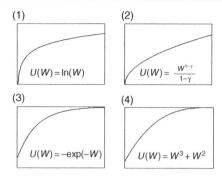

Figure 10.20 Example of utility functions. (1) logarithmic, (2) power law, (3) exponential, (4) cubic. Additional constants can move the curves up and down and to the left and right

10.1.9.2   Use of utility functions to determine cost of risk

Cost of risk has an important influence on electricity prices. In the first instance, cost of 'normal' risk determines the cost-of-risk drift on forward prices. In the second instance, cost of 'extreme' risk determines the higher moments of price distribution and the structure of implied volatility. Utility can help us with both an intuitive understanding and a quantitative estimation of cost of risk.

Consider a utility function as in Figure 10.18 and suppose that due to variations in commodity price, that the wealth becomes variable over time. A holding in a commodity that is intended for exchange rather than use, or a holding of cash for the purchase of a commodity to be used both satisfy this condition.

We can see in Figure 10.21 that if wealth has 50% chance of rising by a particular amount over a time interval and 50% chance of falling by the same amount, then the average utility is expected to fall over the period. If the rising and falling can be prevented by a commodity hedge transaction, then the fall in utility can be avoided. The more volatile the commodity and the more concave the curve, the greater the utility loss. This is called cost of risk. While utility is hard to establish directly, aspects of it can be inferred. For example, stock market portfolios have historically produced returns greater than government bonds since investors have required the extra return to compensate for the extra risk. Since historic market volatilities and returns can be measured, then the cost of risk can be calculated,[28] and in turn the utility curve concavity inferred.

Figure 10.21 shows what happens to utility if wealth changes. If wealth follows Brownian motion with standard deviation ΔW, then the Taylor's expansion for the probability weighted upward and downward price movements tells us that the expected change in utility ΔU is given by:

$$E\left[U\right] - U_0 = \frac{1}{2}\frac{\partial U}{\partial W}\Delta W - \frac{1}{2}\frac{\partial U}{\partial W}\Delta W - \frac{1}{2}\frac{\partial^2 U}{\partial W^2}\left(\Delta W\right)^2 - \frac{1}{2}\frac{\partial^2 U}{\partial W^2}\left(\Delta W\right)^2$$

$$-\cdots\frac{1}{2}\left(1 + (-1)^n\right)\frac{\partial^n U}{\partial U^n}\left(\Delta W\right)^n$$

---

[28] A large number of assumptions must be made to do so, so the answer should be regarded as indicative. However the 'equity risk premium' is calculated and used in calculating the fair return for privately owned regulated utilities.

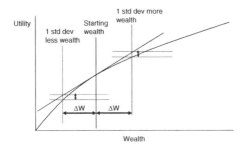

Figure 10.21   Risk of variation in wealth, for example by commodity price variation, incurs an expectation of loss of utility

It is apparent from this that for relatively small changes or for quadratic utility functions of the form $U = a + bW + cW^2$, where c < 0, that

$$E[U] - U_0 = c\frac{\partial^2 U}{\partial W^2}(\Delta W)^2$$

So we see[29] that the absolute cost of risk over a period is proportional to the curvature of the utility curve and the variance of wealth. This is a useful property, since, because for Brownian motion variance grows linearly with time, so wealth must grow linearly[30] with time to maintain *ex ante*[31] utility at a constant level. This is the cost of risk drift described in equation 9.12 and section 9.1.22.

It is also worth noting at this point that utility functions do not tend to be quadratic in form,[32] and hence: (i) the cost of risk drift is only constant over short time intervals, (ii) the cost of risk drift for low frequency high impact events does not have a simple relationship with time and (iii) cost of risk is only linear with respect to variance for small variances.

The second use of utility functions for risk calculations refers to extreme risk. By estimating a utility function, then it is possible to infer the relative aversion to risks at different levels of confidence. This is particularly useful in calculating the insurance[33] premium for low frequency high impact events, and the volatility that relates to these events. Section 6.10.2 showed the effect that insurance and insurance premiums can have on capacity. For insurers, loss aversion, rather than risk aversion, is the most appropriate description.

In the ESI, major power station failures constitute low frequency high impact events associated in the extreme with loss of load and hence there is direct relevance to the price distribution at very high prices. The risk premium (which is a factor cost for power stations and hence adds to the power price) in relation to probability (and inversely related to load factor) is shown schematically below.

Cost of extreme risk is also useful in the valuation of 'far out the money' options.

---

[29] Use of utility to rationalise cost of risk does not meet universal agreement. Theory (see Arrow 1971) suggests that cost of risk is less than suggested by utility for small risks, and that loss aversion (see Kahneman and Tversky 1979) may better explain cost of extreme risk. However for practical purposes the utility approach is practical, robust and can be calibrated to observed behaviour.

[30] Note quite linear, since increasing wealth decreases absolute risk aversion.

[31] We assume here a fixed relationship between utility and wealth. In reality, utility is almost certainly path dependent, so two people with the same wealth will have different utilities if one has become richer and the other poorer.

[32] For further details, as well as evaluation for non quadratic forms, see Cochrane.

[33] In practice it is the reinsurance premium, since insurers go to reinsurers, who go to more reinsurers.

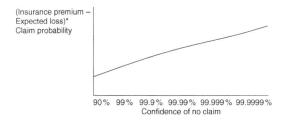

Figure 10.22   Calibration of cost of extreme risk from insurance premiums

10.1.9.3   Use of utility functions to determine the redistribution of wealth

We can see from Figure 10.23, that in the absence of all other considerations, then it is socially beneficial to redistribute wealth from rich to poor. However, participants, knowing that this redistribution will occur will behave differently in terms of the submission to the market of the functions of production and demand, and we must take this into account.

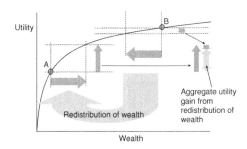

Figure 10.23   Aggregate utility gain from the redistribution of wealth

We can estimate the deadweight loss of wealth redistribution and therefore need to calculate the social benefit. Clearly this is no easy matter, particularly since 'wealth' must use some proxy measure such as income, assets, energy endowment, or other measure. We then need to apply the utility curve to the wealth measure to arrive at, for example the marginal social value of income transfer. Note that Figure 10.23 assumes that we can in this instance make direct interpersonal comparisons of utility. Whilst Pigou in the earlier part of the twentieth century said[34] 'transference of income from a relatively rich man to a relatively poor man . . . since it enables more intense wants to be satisfied at the expense of less intense wants, must increase the aggregate sum of satisfaction', Arrow[35] in 1951 said 'the viewpoint that will be taken here that interpersonal comparison of utilities has no meaning' and 'the only meaning the concepts of utility have is their indications of actual behaviour'.

10.1.9.4   Utility in economics

Marginal utility was first used in an economics context by the Austrian Wieser, but it was Alfred Marshall in around 1890 who was responsible for developing its use in mainstream

[34] 'The Economics of Welfare', fourth edition 1932.
[35] Social choice and individual values.

marginal economics. The real attention then was to rationalise the decreasing marginal utility of increasing consumption. Rich and poor can then be characterised simply by endowment of commodity, and the marginal aggregate utility of redistribution of wealth explained. Marshall also introduced substitutability and complementarity and thereby the difficulty of multicommodity exchange rates.

The neoclassical application of marginal economics optimises aggregate surplus (subject to Pareto constraints), where surplus is quantified in terms of money. The problem is that at policy level, the true optimisation objective is (or ought to be) not money, but utility. We will see that our problems are compounded by the fact that policy makers seek to optimise aggregate welfare, and the aggregate welfare of groups of individuals is not necessarily equal to the aggregate utility.

Wherever possible nowadays, testable indifference curves are used instead of estimated utility functions. This is described in section 10.1.11 on preference.

10.1.10   Welfare

Policy makers want to optimise utility for all society. We have already noted that since utility can not be exchanged, then we cannot fully rely on markets to optimise utility. There is a further problem, which is that the aggregate welfare of society is not necessarily equal to the linear sum of the utilities. As a result, regulatory adjustments such as discriminatory pricing, that optimise aggregate utility, will not necessarily optimise overall welfare. Hence we must take the welfare functions into account.

10.1.10.1   Welfare functions

There are various welfare functions, for example:

(i)   The unweighted greatest good of the greatest number. (The Benthamite function) $W = \sum_n U_i$.

(ii) The weighted greatest good of the greatest number. (Classical utilitarian) $W = \sum_n w_i U_i$.

(iii) The minimum utility of any individual (Rawlsian minimax utility) $W = \min(u_1 \ldots u_i)$.

(iv) Combinations – for example the Benthamite function subject to no individual utility falling below a set threshold. $W = \left(\sum_n U_i \right) | \min(U_1 \ldots U_n) > k$.

For the ESI, the combination function is of particular interest because this is closest to the actual welfare function used (albeit somewhat crudely) for the recognition of the fuel poor.[36]

The Bergson Samuelson utility function is commonly quoted. This specifically connects the welfare to the endowment of goods $W = f(U(G))$, where Utility U is a function of goods endowment G. This can apply to any of the above functions.

10.1.10.2   Welfare economics

The economic world is fundamentally unequal and hence there are problems of welfare. However the fact that individuals are endowed with a number of different commodities does not particularly add to the welfare problem, since we can be confident that Pareto

---

[36] Fuel poverty is defined by a set percentage of expendable income being on fuel (including electricity) bills.

optimisation will cause us to arrive at the optimum, or core of the economy, if we adjust the endowment of a single good (e.g. money).

10.1.11 Preference

Economics has always drawn heavily from physics, mathematics, philosophy and the social sciences. Never more so than in the 1930's, when mechanistic application of axioms that contained universal truths, were called into question. In Europe, the 'logical positivist' school,[37] led by Karl Popper, devalued the use of statements that could not be disproved by experiment. Specifically, this disallowed the interpersonal comparison of utility curves,[38] since they could not be directly observed. Economists swam with the tide, for developments at the time in, for example, mathematics,[39] and linguistic philosophy[40] were broadly consistent. In addition, the use of utility in economics was associated with utilitarian philosophy, which was itself associated with 19th century Victorian England and before, and of less relevance for the 20th century.

The result in economics was the 'Hicksian revolution'[41] in which utility curves were replaced by indifference curves, in which one commodity is swapped for another, and the declining marginal utility of consumption of a commodity is reflected by the slope (i.e. exchange rate) of the indifference curve.

Wherever possible then, rather than use subjective utility, we try to quantify value by establishing indifference curves.

In terms of economics, preference has a similar meaning to that in everyday life, only more formal. Preference is initially qualitative – 'I prefer x to y', but wherever possible a quantification is applied. For example, 'At my current state, I am indifferent to whether I receive 1 (small) unit of x or R units of y'. Here the rate R is called the marginal rate of substitution, and is effectively an exchange rate at the limit,[42] at the margin, for the particular individual, at the current state, with a particular endowment of goods.

There are two[43] principal axioms of preference that we rely on. For analytic purposes we can generally forget about them, but when it comes to challenging the results, we should revisit them to consider their impacts. The axioms are that preferences are:

(i) **Complete** – We can actually make a comparison between two 'bundles'. This effectively implies an exchange rate at the margin, at which the individual is indifferent to exchange.

(ii) **Transitive** – If we prefer x to y and y to z, then we prefer x to z. This implies that we can formulate the x/z exchange rate if we know the x/y and y/z exchange rates.

In constructing indifference curves, there are essentially two kinds of relationship between goods – substitution (margarine is a substitute for butter) and complements (left shoes

---

[37] In America, the related school was the 'operationalists'.

[38] Ordinal utility curves, which were simply ranking rather than quantification of preferences. Interpersonal comparison of utility curves effectively had to be quantitative to make the comparison meaningful, and thereby forced the ordinal utility curves to become cardinal utility curves, albeit with no specific relevance to the zero point.

[39] Gödel.

[40] Ayer.

[41] Hick's most important book was 'Value and Capital' (1939). For further reading on the Hicksian revolution, see Walsh (1970).

[42] I am indifferent to give 1 unit of z for R of y, but would prefer to receive more than R units of y.

[43] The third axiom is reflexivity – that a bundle is at least as good as itself. This is not important for our present purposes.

complement right shoes). Perfect complements can be regarded as parts of a single commodity – so a left shoe only has value if it is accompanied by a right shoe. In section 8.6 we examine green labelling for fuel. In presence of a specification on the minimum number of green labels delivered per MWh, then the label and the power are complementary goods.

Combined with the axioms of preference, and noting the complementarity or substitutability of the goods (and bads) we can envisage iso-utility curves for the relative consumption by a particular consumer of two goods A and B.

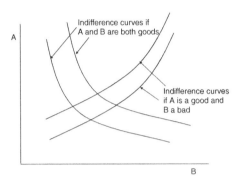

Figure 10.24   Iso-utility curves for two different goods, and a good and a bad

Note that in constructing the individual exchange rate, we have not needed to know the absolute utility of the individual good, only the relative marginal utility and complementarity/substitutability. We may, either by direct observation of exchange, or enquiry have some points to which we can calibrate our curves.

10.1.11.1   Finding exchange rate limits and Pareto optimal endowments with the Edgeworth box

The Edgeworth box is a useful method of finding the Pareto optimal endowments. We imagine a two person, two good economy, in which the amount of both goods (one of which might be money) is fixed. We start with initial endowments. These are shown in Figure 10.25(1), where, for example, G_{A1} is the endowment of good 1 to participant A. The position in the box shows the endowments of both goods to both participants. Figure 10.25(2) shows the family of indifference curves for participant A, including the indifference curve which includes the current endowment. Participant B's indifference curves are represented with the lowest utility starting at the top right corner. The curve that includes the current endowment is shown in Figure 10.25(3). We can see that if the endowments change to anywhere in the shaded area that both participants will gain in utility. One exchange is shown in Figure 10.25(4). We can see that there is not a unique exchange rate, but that it is bounded by the indifference curves. The final Pareto optimal position is on the line from bottom left to top right of the diagram that follows the loci of points for which the indifference curves are tangent to each other.

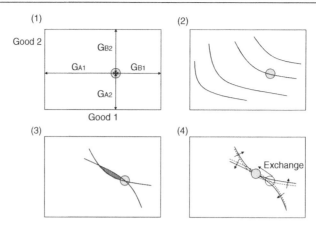

Figure 10.25 The Edgeworth box. (1) Showing the relative endowments of the limited amounts of goods 1 and 2 to participants A and B, (2) Showing the indifference curves of A, (3) Showing the initial endowment on the indifference curves of A and B, (4) Exchange increases the utility of both A and B

10.1.11.2   Some issues with preference

Preference is a very useful concept in estimating a marginal rate of substitution, and indeed to make real choices, some quantification must be done, but in practice it is fraught with difficulty. The difficulties are principally:

(i)   Estimating a marginal rate of substitution between very different things, for example loss of visual amenity versus increases in a particular health risk.
(ii) Estimating substitutability and complementarity, for example whether heating can be done with either gas or power, and whether both gas and power are required for a particular function (such as cooking).
(iii) Estimating the initial endowments.
(iv) Commonly a benefit is conferred on one individual or set of individuals as a private good and cost conferred on another as a public bad.

To make a judgement on preference that is informed by expressed opinion or guessed opinion, rather than actual choice, then we need to consider how choice is formulated and expressed, and in what context it is made. For example, Sen, in 'Choice, Welfare and Measurement'[44] lists several definitions of preference for an individual with respect to two goods/bads/outcomes.

(i)   The person gets more satisfaction in state x than in state y.
(ii) The person thinks that he is better off in state x than state y.
(iii) The person is better off with x than with y.
(iv) The person prefers that x rather than y occurs.
(v)   The person would like to so choose that x rather than y occurs.
(vi) The person believes that it would be right to so choose that x rather than y occurs.

---

[44] Sen (1982).

(vii)   The person believes that it would be better if x were to occur rather than y.

(viii)   The person so chooses that x rather than y occurs.

So, for one individual with an initial private and public endowment of x and y, to make a decision about resource allocation, there are eight possible marginal rates of substitution. The directly expressed preference of the individual will depend on rationality of behaviour, ethical position, knowledge, perceptions and other features. The government expressed preference will depend on social policy, scientific and other knowledge, popular opinion and other policy drivers shown in section 3.2.

Such are the difficulties, that the very idea of quantifying preferences is often called into question.[45] In applying marginal microeconomic principles to utility and disutility, it is important to remember (and easy to forget) the assumptions that we make along the way.

In disallowing subjective and only allowing objectively determined preference, we do often find that lack of data makes us less able to make value judgements. By removing the tool of interpersonal comparison of utility, we find that it is indeterminate whether a particular outcome is good for society of not, if it is good for one section and bad for another and we may not make a quantitative comparison. We are then forced to declare ourselves indifferent when we are really indeterminate.[46] From a policy perspective, the question is whether the value judgement that we need to make enables us to improve society, or indeed whether the best outcome is truly indeterminate with facts available, and we therefore have to declare ourselves indifferent.

From the perspective of our needs for the ESI, particularly in understanding the economics and movement of prices, and in making policy decisions based on extensive valuations of the total impact of production, this leaves us rather stranded. The use of quantifiable utility curves is an essential piece of economic apparatus that we are denied, and, in an incomplete market, in which preferences are not revealed to us, even at the margin, by prices, we cannot effectively plan using standard neoclassical economics as a basis. Therefore we must in practice recognise utility concepts for (i) valuing goods and bads for which we have no price information, (ii) risk aversion and (iii) welfare and redistribution of wealth.

10.1.11.3   Two factor preference

When considering preferences, we are primarily concerned not with the good itself, but with the want that is satisfied by the good. Virtually all goods have different aspects to them. Where this gives particular problems is in the consideration of bads. For example, the emissions of SOx and NOx are grouped together due to their estimated common ecological impacts from 'acid rain'. However, whilst the effect of acidity can be broadly compared for SOx and NOx, they have different effects also. The problem here comes in applying preference. In a tradable neoclassical setting, the marginal aggregate surplus arising from benefits and disbenefits of goods and bads is automatically optimised if all elements are measurable and tradable. However, particularly in the case of bads, we have to make rather complex comparisons. For example the effect of SOx and NOx in reducing global warming (see section 8.2.2.2) or the effect of NOx in combination with sunlight and regional air circulation conditions in relation to urban smog.

---

[45] See Foster (1997).

[46] This is formalised in the Arrow's Impossibility Theorem, which shows that in a plural society where everyone gets a say, that there is no way to make an effective choice.

So while we may be able to compare 'bundles' of SOx with bundles of NOx in terms of a simplified ecological effect, it may be impractical to compare the bundles in terms of aggregate outcome. Therefore in welfare economics, we cannot necessarily rely on the axiom of completeness of preference.

10.1.12   Contingent valuation

The contingent valuation method is used extensively in environmental economics, with much controversy. The essence of contingent valuation is that we discover a willingness to pay not by actual transaction but by polling, or 'eliciting' participants as to how much they would pay to avoid or would need to receive in order to accept a particular bad.

The approach is used, rather than for valuing compensation, to incorporate the value of public bads into investment, production, technology and abatement decisions.

If participants answer honestly,[47] rationally, and with full knowledge, then we can construct the demand/production function.

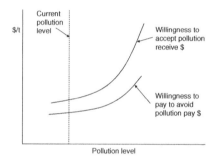

Figure 10.26   Estimating pollution consumption curve by eliciting responses

There are significant difficulties with this approach, including:

(i)   The difference between willingness to pay and willingness to accept is commonly substantial and thereby the valuation is ambiguous.
(ii) The level and curvature of the lines is affected by the marginal utility of wealth. So a poor person may have significant disutility from pollution but no ability to pay. Also, the more one pays/receives, the more/less the money is worth in utility terms.
(iii) If the provision of information can influence an action or a cost, then the potential for gaming and misinformation is obvious.
(iv) This implies widespread knowledge of complex factors outside of common experience. The divorce rate in the West is indication that even in generally familiar circumstances, that knowledge of the future is insufficient to make optimal decisions.

---

[47] If the provision of information can influence an action or a cost, then the potential for gaming is obvious. While there are mechanisms, such as the Clark tax, to ensure honesty for small transactions with small number of participants, they are not applicable to the general public.

10.1.13   Valuation approaches to mortality and morbidity

The rendering implicit of latent valuation is a central problem in the neoclassical model and is starkest in the valuation of life and health. Whilst emphatically not being dismissive about this problem, but noting that discussion is out of scope for this book, and that a brief description is inevitably oversimplified, we look briefly at some valuation issues.

Whilst each logical step taken in valuing a statistical life is consistent with the neoclassical paradigm, the logical conclusion of the monetary valuation of life itself both has ethically unacceptable consequences and is ultimately illogical.

To place a value on statistical life is relatively straightforward in neoclassical terms[48] in macroeconomic situations in autarkies (closed economies), since with a budget constraint of £ W, the state can save X statistical lives, or taking the concept further, Y statistical life years, or Z statistical quality life years. The money can be allocated to road safety, train safety, healthcare, etc. It would, for example, appear to be sensible to spend less money on railway safety and save tens or hundreds of lives on the roads by assigning the saving to road safety measures. The explicit comparison of increased cost per statistical life saved (and by implication saving per statistical life lost) then makes the 'shadow price' value of a statistical life explicit. It is the translation from cost of statistical lives saved to value of statistical lives lost and the application below macroeconomic level to value of life (as distinct from statistical life) that causes ethical and logical difficulties.

The neoclassical model, optimising as it does money surplus, leads straight to the differential value of life according to the wealth of the individual. Indeed this can be explained in terms of budget constraint. Assuming that one would (i.e. could) spend a remaining lifetimes' expendable earnings to save one's own life then the differential value of life under this model becomes obvious. Whilst the money surplus maximising and Pareto optimal solution is to preferentially save the lives of rich people, it is obvious that if we instead choose a life to be the fundamental numeraire asset (which is consistent with the principles of classical economics) that we have simply revealed the weakness of the role of money as store of value in the neoclassical model in maximising utility.

Understanding the problem does not make it go away, and the real practical question is whether it is appropriate to assign a value to (statistical or otherwise) life and health at any level, and if so, how far down in application from global to local and from macro to micro is it appropriate to apply.

Where this problem is most evident in the ESI is in the consideration of emissions – for example how much to spend on abating, what tax to charge, whether to allow trading, and whether damage cost is differentiated by country.

10.1.14   Policy

Welfare has more relevance to policy makers than surplus or utility. The policy maker effectively has choices:

(i) **Central management** – Attempt to formally quantify welfare and optimise by centralised ownership, management and pricing.

(ii) **Constrained market** – Allow the market to operate but apply some form of utility constraint, for example in regulating discriminatory prices to the fuel poor.

---

[48] For analysis using this approach, see, for example, Pearce (1995).

(iii) **Active market intervention** – Allow the market to operate but apply more widespread regulated discriminatory pricing, levies, and cross subsidies to redistribute wealth by operations within the ESI.

(iv) **Compensation** – Ignore all welfare issues within the ESI and expect that these will be achieved by the taxation and welfare system.

(v) **Prescription** – Restriction on permissions, and licensing of a limited range of technology.

10.1.15 Discriminatory pricing

In Figure 10.4, we saw that for a uniform product in a free market with unrestricted access, that everyone pays the same price, the clearing price, since there is no reason for anyone to pay a higher price when they can access the clearing price, and producers would reduce output if prices fell.

At the opposite extreme, we have first degree price discrimination, in which the supplier knows exactly the demand functions of the consumers, can restrict access to the open market, and can practically engage in a pricing policy that extracts the full consumer surplus. So, for example, the producer would charge a high price (the willingness to pay price) for the first element of good, and a decreasing price for increasing amounts, in line with the demand function.

Real markets lie in between the two extremes, although due to the need for dedicated infrastructure, and that fact that a consumer can only be supplied by one supplier and that changing supplier is a time consuming process, means that there is more scope for discriminatory pricing in electricity than in most other markets.

In second degree price discrimination, the supplier creates price discrimination by product discrimination. Electricity is a highly homogenous product, particularly from the consumer perspective, and apart from very specialised uses, the only real capability to differentiate by product is to offer different degrees of interruptibility (differentiation by source labelling is somewhat different). Even so, this is barely product differentiation, because the interruptibility can be fairly easily unbundled from the delivered product.

In third degree price discrimination, the supplier charges different customers different amounts for the same product, and manages to do so by providing different tariffs for different customer types. So customers will be charged differently according to area, type of house, or other criterion available to the supplier and allowed by the regulator. Third degree price discrimination can also have a volume dependence of tariff.

Whilst discriminatory pricing by the supplier for reasons of their own advantage is outlawed in energy regulations, discriminatory pricing for the fuel poor is commonly mandated.

It should be noted that whilst the term 'discriminatory pricing' is clear in economics, it is commonly used in a different sense in regulation. Regulators commonly enforce discriminatory pricing in an economic sense while prohibiting discriminatory pricing in a regulatory sense (meaning by pricing in such a manner that entry barriers are maintained).

10.1.15.1 Non uniform pricing

A form of discriminatory pricing is nonuniform pricing, in which the price for the product is dependent on the volume consumed.

We assume here that producers sell to supply companies at the clearing price, and supply companies sell on at discriminatory prices.

Ideally, we would like to charge for the first kW at a cheap price, and then charge an increasing amount for more consumption. This is the most socially equitable, and incentivises energy conservation. If a monopoly producer sold direct to consumers and the sales price curve is coincident with the producer cost curve, then the producer surplus is transferred to the consumer sector. If producers sell to suppliers at the wholesale clearing price then the supply company would make a loss, and so would have to elevate the sales price curve and thereby cause a deadweight loss. If competitive producers sold direct to customers, they would not voluntarily sell at less than the clearing price.

Suppose instead that we charge decreasing amounts for increasing consumption. This is consistent with the capture of fixed costs. We may expect some arbitrage, as buyers aggregate where they can. This is consistent with the inverse elasticity rule but charges the smallest consumers (commonly the fuel poor), the highest tariff. If the sales price curve is coincident with the willingness to pay curve, then the full consumer surplus is captured by producers.

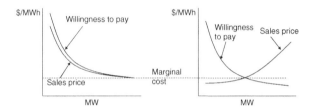

Figure 10.27   Non uniform pricing, showing decreasing or increasing marginal price with consumption volume

So, in the presence of fixed costs, decreasing price with increasing volume may make economic sense, but is problematic from an ecological and welfare perspective.

10.1.15.2   Discriminatory pricing and Ramsey pricing

Throughout this chapter and in later chapters, we encounter the problem of ensuring that Pareto optimising behaviour at the margin maintains the optimal surplus in aggregate. This has been a limiting problem.

The obvious place to look is in discriminatory pricing, in which we leave the market to its own devices at the margin, whilst choosing some targeted interventions away from the margin that will not impact behaviour.

The general method of applying price discrimination to the most inelastic market sectors is called the Inverse Elasticity Rule, and optimising consumer welfare subject to the constraint that producer surplus (including producer fixed[49] costs) is not less than zero, is called the Ramsey[50] optimum. This method of pricing is well known in regulatory economics and public policy. Most research is in the area of the postal system, but there are many examples in electricity, with perhaps the best known being the application by Boiteux for the pricing of Electricité de France in the 1950's and 1960's.

---

[49] 'Fair' return can be included in the fixed costs.
[50] Ramsey (1927) who first recommended the method for optimal excise taxation.

Figure 10.28 shows that in this simple case that the total surplus can be preserved even with the constraint that producer surplus must equal producer fixed costs. The price discrimination merely moves profit from one sector to another.

In the extreme, we can envisage a circumstance in which we apply discriminatory pricing to all producers and production and all consumers and production at the margin, while ensuring that the price discrimination is always zero at the margin. Here we have a centrally managed system that apparently delivers us a market solution. Whether it is actually efficient for the market to clear at the marginal price, is discussed in section 10.1.8.

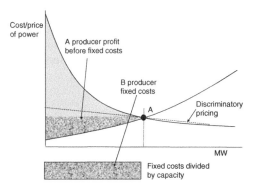

Figure 10.28   Ramsey pricing. The least elastic consumers pay discriminatory higher prices. In this figure, the price line is found by rotating about point A until the textured areas are equal. Since the clearing volume does not change then there is no deadweight loss

There are practical difficulties with application of Ramsey pricing, for example:

(i)   The clearing price and volume must be known *ex ante* in all periods in order to know how much uplift to apply to prices, and the production/demand intersection point in order not to adjust prices there.

(ii) For a product such as electricity that is homogenous with little or no quality differentiation, it is hard to establish a criterion that applies to that part of consumption that is most inelastic, and harder to establish a pricing regime that applies in a monotonic manner to price elasticity.

(iii) Demand is heterogeneous with respect to time and hence the diagram is much more complicated when considering more than one price setting.

(iv) Relative consumer preferences are heterogeneous (periodic, trending, and stochastic) with respect to time. As a result, the most price inelastic consumer in one period is not the most price inelastic in another period.

(v)   Even if demand is homogenous across time, then a pricing regime is problematic. Ideally we identify the whole demand curve for each participant and charge discriminatory rates according to the individual slopes. Since the demand functions are not visible, the best that we can do is to charge different consumers different flat tariffs.

(vi) Ramsey pricing adds most cost to the first unit of consumption (ranking by utility rather than chronology) rather than the last (marginal) unit. So an individual tariff would have a decreasing marginal cost with increasing consumption. This is the opposite of what we would choose from a welfare or ecological perspective.

(vii) It is only practically possible to apply different price uplifts to different consumers rather than different consumption. Since consumption curves tend to be convex, one consumer does not have greater price elasticity of demand over all consumption levels than another, and hence the uplift is not efficiently applied to consumption.

For more formal treatment of Ramsey pricing, see Baumol and Bradford (1970) or Crew and Kleindorfer (1992).

10.1.15.3   Product differentiation

In electricity the core physical product is essentially homogenous. Differences are (i) wholesale energy interruptibility, (ii) local network interruptibility, (iii) energy source and (iv) reactive power. Difference between systems are: (i) technical effects such as transience, (ii) voltage and voltage stability and (iii) frequency and frequency stability.

However, the uses of electricity are less homogenous. The uses effectively divide into heat and light, motors and electromagnetic uses such as television and radio. By understanding these uses we can better understand how differentiation can affect prices. The delivered product can then be non homogenous in terms of periodicity of volume, absolute flexibility of consumption and notice period required for requested consumption changes.

10.1.16 Problems with cross subsidy and redistribution of wealth

The simple economists' solution to pollution and resource depletion is to allow the market prices to rise and thereby reduce demand. The social problem with this approach is that the effect on the fuel poor is disproportionate. Figures 10.29 and 10.30 show that not only is the fuel poor consumption impacted harder than non fuel poor consumption by price rises, but for the same level of consumption reduction, the utility effect is greater for the fuel poor.

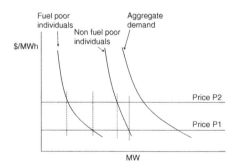

Figure 10.29 Increase in tariff has a disproportionate effect on consumption of the fuel poor

As a result of this, it is hard to create a price signal strong enough to reduce consumption of the non fuel poor without excessive utility impact on the fuel poor.

Redistribution of wealth by discriminatory pricing is one method. However, even apart from the practical problems, there are two particular problems that arise, the deadweight loss (since efficient Ramsey pricing is impossible in practice) and the destruction of competition.

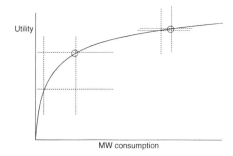

Figure 10.30   Disproportionate decrease in consumption of the fuel poor has an exacerbated effect on utility

If regulatory pricing structures cause the market to clear at any price other than the natural clearing price then there is a deadweight loss. If the redistribution of wealth is handled not by discriminatory pricing but by government subsidy to consumers per kWh of consumption, the effect is exactly the same as discriminatory pricing, since the subsidy (conditional on consumption) increases the willingness to pay and distorts the clearing price.

Subsidy within the consumption sector (as opposed to subsidy from production sector to consumption sector) also causes a deadweight loss, as is shown in Figure 10.31.

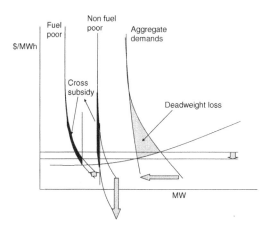

Figure 10.31   Deadweight loss from cross subsidy within the consumer sector

Destruction of competition – If a market participant is forced by regulation to cross subsidise internally (i.e. within the ESI rather than through taxes) from one consumer sector to another, by discriminatory pricing rather than by a centrally administered levy and subsidy system, then this creates incentive for participants to increase activity in the subsidising sector (with high prices) and decrease in the subsidised sector (with low prices). New entrants will prefer to act only in the subsidising sector and thereby undercut the incumbents, since they do not need to charge extra for the cross subsidy. The incumbents in turn claim protection either in the subsidised sector (and raise prices by at least the cross subsidy, thereby negating or reversing the cross subsidy) or in the subsidising sector, thereby denying competition in the subsidising sector. In fact, the mere threat of discriminatory pricing by an incumbent can be sufficient to deter a new entrant. This is described in more detail in the pre-emption tactics in the game theory section 10.5.15.

10.1.17 Public goods and private goods

A purely private good is one in which one individual engages in a private contract with another individual and all of the benefit of the good is conferred on the buyer, and there are no externalities anywhere.

A purely public good is one in which the benefit is conferred generally and cannot be excluded to those contractually engaged. The production of a rainbow, if this could be done, could be regarded as a purely public good. Since the good cannot be excluded, it cannot be re-traded once produced since there is no incentive to pay for it.

Another feature of public goods is non rivalry. Since the purely public good cannot be excluded, there is little or no incentive for a small participant to pay for it if he can free ride, and little incentive for additional producers to make it since they may not get paid. The good is then financed by enforced collection through taxes or similar mechanisms, and the taxes given to the service provider.

In reality, there are no purely public goods, because access or consumption is always excluded in some way. For example, a rainbow confers no benefit to blind people or shift workers. Nevertheless the public element of the good is important.

Where the concept of public goods and bads is particularly important is in environmental impact. This is felt by the general public. There are several ways in which the financial element of this public bad from productive activity can be handled:

(i)   **Specific producer taxation** – Producers pay an involuntary tax for the specific impact.
(ii) **Specific consumer taxation** – Consumers pay an involuntary tax for electricity sourced from production with a particular impact.
(iii) **Voluntary consumer payments** – Consumers voluntarily pay a premium in the form of an environmental levy, in return for some form of environmental benefit such as guarantee of origin from green sources. The individual receives the benefit of the change, and so do the general public. We might regard this as the purchase of a public good, since the individual benefit is in most cases infinitesimal in comparison to the public benefit.
(iv) **Voluntary producer change** – Producers voluntarily spend more on impact reduction than required by generation and/or spend on more expensive but greener technologies and/or greener primary energy sources.
(v)   **Levies and rebates and subsidies** – Imposition of levies on all production or consumption combined with rebates to production or consumption of registered green sources and/or subsidies funded by the levies.

The general literature about public goods considers for example lighthouses, hospitals, museums, public parks, network television and others. Each sheds a slightly different light on the problem of public goods. Particular problems, from a theoretical perspective are the nature of curtailment, as shown in section 10.1.5.1, and voluntary payment for green sourcing that can be treated as public good donations.

10.1.18   Existence value

Existence value refers to the value of goods that confer no direct benefit to the individual but instead confers the benefit of 'knowing that it is there'. The existence of a national park that is not visited by the individual is a commonly quoted example of existence value to that individual.

For the purpose of the ESI, existence value should be strictly separated into altruistic[51] value (paid specifically for the benefit of others) and probability value (a service that may[52] be used by the individual in the future).

Some[53] aspects of security of supply could be regarded as a public good with probability value.

Voluntary payment of green premium for guarantee that energy received is ultimately derived from renewable sources should be regarded as altruistic[54] value.

10.1.19   Goods and bads

As is obvious from the name, goods confer utility on the (public or private) consumer. By the same token, bads confer disutility.

Bads are highly problematic from the perspective of economics because:

(i)   They tend to be public rather than private.
(ii) Even where damage is limited to an individual contracting entity, it is hard to define the property rights (see section 10.6.3) with sufficient robustness to prevent one party conferring a bad without engaging into a contract, or if the rights are robust, from preventing monopolistic behaviour from the recipient of the bads.
(iii) Benefits and disbenefits are complex, and hard to define and measure.
(iv) Utility of disbenefit is hard to define and measure.

Where bads are tradable and with clear property rights, they can be treated in the same manner as goods, but with negative sign, and with marginal utility that may be convex or concave (see Figure 10.19). Economically speaking, demand for permits for the right to emit is treated as demand for emissions.

10.1.20   Externalities

Externalities are the economic impacts of an activity that are felt outside of the associated transactions. So, for example, local pollution is an externality if, and only if, there is no voluntary bilateral engagement between producer and local citizens to accept the pollution or engage in an end of pipe solution.

---

[51] This usage was first described by Krutilla (1967).

[52] This argument was first advanced by Weisbrod (1964), giving rise to a 'Weisbrodian public good'.

[53] Some, but not all. For example preferential non-interruptibility is a private good, but reduced interruptibility through a higher general capacity payment is a public good.

[54] From the perspective of the firm, apparently altruistic behaviour can be justified by ethical investors accepting a lower rate of return on the condition that certain ethical conditions are satisfied.

Lack of capture of externalities results in market failure because the full economics are not taken into account and policy makers are forced to add patches to the system to partially replicate the forces of the market.

Externalities abound and tend to be public bads,[55] which, as we have seen are the most difficult. There is a positive incentive for both parties of a transaction to ignore the externalities that are market bads. This must be addressed by policy makers.

A particularly problematic externality for the ESI is the fact that energy consumption commonly has a deleterious ecological impact over and above any externalities of production. This makes the concept of surplus more difficult to manage.

To add to the difficulties, externalities can have a variety of different utility/volume functions. We have already noted that for planning under uncertainty, that we must quantify all market factors, not just at the margin.

10.1.21   Equilibrium

In this book there is significant attention to the distinct recovery of fixed and marginal costs, with the specific argument that even if it is optimal on any particular day for the market to clear at marginal costs, this does not represent equilibrium because rational producers will change offer tactics or withdraw.

In equilibrium, we do not pay attention to fixed and marginal costs but consider instead the recovery of total costs. So, for power generators, we smear the fixed costs over the expected load factor. In equilibrium, prices adjust so that all generators make zero[56] annual profit in a competitive environment.

By equilibrium modelling we can assess producer and consumer behaviour and welfare maximisation in sustainable circumstances. This helps us, for example, in long term environmental regulation, since we can estimate what the factor costs are for different environmental regimes and limits/prices, and formulate what the price/duration curve must look like in the medium and long term, taking into account new build, planned closure, life extension and early closure.

It is common in equilibrium modelling to assume constant returns to scale (cost not rising with volume), although as we saw in Figure 10.12, we must be very wary of this in ESI problems and in particular when considering the marginal cost of part loaded plant, and environmental impact abatement.[57]

We saw in section 10.1.8 that it might be optimal in terms of surplus for the regulator to set prices equal to the marginal cost of the marginal generator, and to refund the producers an amount that compensates fixed costs from direct (i.e. income, inheritance) taxes raised from consumers. The equilibrium argument, shown in Figure 10.32, shows that there is a deadweight loss equal to the subsidy, and therefore that if prices are regulated, that at least in this simple example in which all plant has the same load factor, they should be at fully loaded and not marginal costs.

---

[55] Public goods tend not to be produced by private trade, and for externalities produced that are private goods, the vendor will look for clients who are prepared to pay extra for them.

[56] We could more usefully say that they make zero alpha. See section 10.1.24.1.

[57] A common method in equilibrium modelling is to assign a fixed proportion of output to impact abatement. For our purposes in the ESI, it is essential not to assume that we have constant returns to scale in this regard.

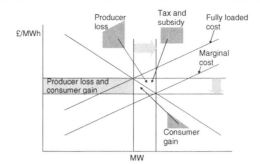

Figure 10.32 Loss of equilibrium surplus from regulating prices at marginal costs and refunding loss of fixed costs through direct taxation

10.1.22   Trade

We saw in our examination of the Edgeworth box how trade between two consumers with different initial endowment can arrive at the Pareto optimum position (but not necessarily the maximum welfare – this requires involuntary reallocation). We now must consider the effect of trade on production, export and prices.

10.1.22.1   Trade and production efficiency

Suppose that country A produces coffee at A $c/tonne and bananas also at A $c/tonne, and that country B produces coffee at B $c/tonne and bananas at 0.5B $c/tonne. Here A $ is the currency of country A and B $ is the currency of country B. We also assume that the single productive resource can be applied to either good. Assuming that we are in competitive equilibrium and therefore that goods are produced at cost price, we can see that it would be rational for country A to sell coffee in return for bananas at any rate better than one tonne of bananas for one tonne of coffee, and it would be rational for country B to sell bananas in return for bananas at any rate better than one tonne of bananas for half a tonne of coffee. The trade will cause a reallocation of resource, so country A will increase coffee production and decrease banana production, and country B will do the opposite. Trade is Pareto optimal, and in terms of aggregate surplus (but not necessarily welfare), trade is beneficial to both countries.[58]

   This is the core of the theory of trade advanced by David Ricardo. He considered the difference in productivity to be a result of efficiency rather than natural endowment, and in this sense, the theory traces straight back to Adam Smith. An additional feature of the model is that Ricardo specifically excluded the consideration of capital movement between countries.

   If returns to scale are constant, and marginal utility is independent of wealth, then countries will in this model divert all resource to production of one of the two goods. Normally however, the production curve is upward sloping and the consumption curve is downward sloping.

   The Ricardo model is too limited for most uses and the Ricardo theory was extended to the Ricardo-Viner theory which allowed for two goods and three production factors, two of which were dedicated to a particular good and one which could be applied to either.

---

[58] This is subject to a variety of hidden assumptions. It would not be true for example if one country had high fixed costs and the other country has high market or other power.

10.1.22.2 Trade and natural endowment

Instead of production efficiency differentials, trade could be driven by differential factor endowments in different countries. Natural resource and pollution tolerance are the most important endowments for present purposes.

The Heckscher-Ohlin model shows that for a two good, two factor economy, in which good 1 is most intensive of factor[59] 1, that a country with a higher endowment (and therefore[60] a lower cost) of factor 1 will have a higher output of good 1. The Rybczinski theorem shows that an increase in the supply (and decrease in price) of factor 1, with a limited productive capability, will lead to an increase in output of good 1 and reduction of output of good 2. The Stolper Samuelson theorem shows that an increase in price of good 1 will lead to an increase in cost (and increase in volume) of good 1. The factor-price equalisation theorem states that factor prices converge in the same way as goods prices and is a direct result of the Heckscher-Ohlin model. We can see this easily in the form of a highly mobile factor, such as the requirement for an internationally certified permit to produce carbon dioxide. The evidence for immobile factors such as labour is less compelling.

We saw in Figure 10.19 that in the case of pollution tolerance as a factor endowment, there is a wide range of shape of 'production functions', from constant returns for scale and unlimited output (pollution tax) to zero cost but limited output (in the case of cap with no trading). The equilibrium algebra of trade must be applied with some care.

10.1.22.3 Trade and movement of capital

Consider two countries with similar technologies, factor endowments and preferences, but which have different currency exchange rate to some international benchmark currency. If we allow the countries to trade, then we can express the consumption and production functions in international currency, and then aggregate them, as shown in Figure 10.33. This shows that the aggregate surplus is increased.

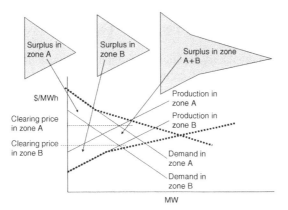

Figure 10.33 Increase in surplus arising from allowing trading between two previously closed economic zones

---

[59] One factor could be labour.

[60] All of these theories assume that the marginal cost of resource increases with increasing use of the resource, i.e. returns to scale are not constant.

10.1.22.4   Trade and welfare

Figure 10.34 shows that in the expensive country, consumption increases, production decreases, commodity is imported, and money (capital) leaves the country. Prices are lowered. The opposite happens in the other country.

It is obvious from the above that while trade may be beneficial in aggregate surplus, that it may be welfare destroying, both in terms of loss of labour and in terms of increase in prices.

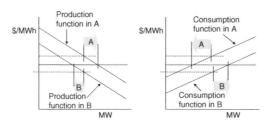

Figure 10.34   Effect of trade with movement of capital. (1) Consumption increases for A (the country with high currency value) and reduces for B, (2) Production increases in B and reduces in A

We can reach the optimum, or core, of the economy by adjustment of the initial endowment of one factor (money is the easiest), and then allow Pareto optimisation through trading to reach the core. However, without the adjustment of factor endowment, then trade can be welfare destroying. Suppose that B buys from A a quantity of good. The purchase (which is Pareto optimal for A and B) drives up the price of the good for C. Even if another good falls in price at the same time (possibly the good that B sells to A), then this does not help C if this is not a good that C consumes.

10.1.22.5   Pollution tolerance and trade

A country may be more pollution tolerant because the environment has more assimilative capability for reasons described in section 8.2, or because the monetary cost assigned by regulation to pollution is lower.

For all environmental regulatory regimes, environmental impact abatement can be treated as a production factor cost. We can then treat pollution tolerance as a resource endowment, but because the economic value is determined by regulation, we must treat the resource as a virtual one.

Suppose that there are two countries, in which everything is identical (for example wealth, factor endowments, industries) except for environmental policies, and in which industry pollution is purely local (i.e. there is no transboundary pollution). The tighter environmental policy, whether applied by taxes, purchasable permits, limits, technology prescription, or other means, results in higher factor costs. This drives industrial production to the region with weaker limits. This region then becomes a 'pollution haven'.[61] It is as economically inefficient in aggregate to have two different strengths of environmental regulation as it is to have different prices.

It could be that the weak environmental regulation is intentional, designed to stimulate economic growth. There is then a state determined trade-off between ecological damage and

---

[61] For a fuller description of these, together with an equilibrium model for fixed production and abatement costs, see Copeland and Scott Taylor (2003).

economic development. This creates a challenge for importers (for example, of electricity or primary energy). Knowing that the production is more damaging to workers and/or the local environment, ethical procurement policy may prevent import. This argument is well known in the purchase of clothes made in 'sweat shops' in countries with cheap labour. In the ESI, the main imports are fossil and partly processed nuclear fuel, and the issues include mine health and safety, mineral rights and indigenous populations, ecological impact at source, labour conditions and child labour. However, at the same time, this creates the opportunity for protectionism in the form of non tariff barriers. It may be that a weak environmental policy with respect to a particular pollutant is a result of a lower damage in a particular country. It is then efficient in terms of welfare either to migrate the industry to the more assimilative country, or to export unwanted by-products that can be shipped.

The situation is slightly different if there is transboundary pollution. Then, from a local perspective, it is economically efficient for countries to have weak environmental policies, since they only receive part of the disutility from the production of public bads. From a global perspective, it is not efficient.

We can see more the ethical considerations from the development of trade arise. Items such as environmental sensitivity are hard to measure, and if we measure them in money terms (which is exactly what the neoclassical model does), then we immediately head into issues relating to the strong difference in the purchasing power of money (purchasing power parity), between different countries. The marginal willingness to pay to reduce pollution is low in poor countries is low because the currency value is low, and hence while money surplus may be increased by trade with pollution havens, aggregate utility may not be.

10.1.22.6   Summary of issues with trade

It is apparent that trade, and particularly global trade involving the movement of capital, whilst being part of the dominant paradigm of neoclassical economics, is not without its problems. We can briefly summarise them here:

(i)   **Incompleteness** – The traded market does not include all signals.
(ii) **Market power** – Market power can be used to the detriment of aggregate surplus.
(iii) **Welfare** – Trade optimises money surplus and can reduce welfare.
(iv) **Valuation of externalities** – Valuation to internalise them is complicated and highly unreliable.
(v)   **Capital** – Movement of capital can exacerbate welfare destruction.

10.1.23   Fixed and marginal costs

We can usefully divide costs into truly fixed, quasi fixed, long run marginal and short run marginal.

Truly fixed costs are those costs that are incurred regardless of any change in the fortunes of the plant, the market, the regulatory circumstances, or anything else. The only truly fixed costs are the fixed liabilities of the plant owner. In a competitive market, we should also regard the cost of equity at a 'fair' *ex ante* risk adjusted rate as a form of debt. If the plant owner fails financially, then these costs may not be paid and to the degree to which the firm can alter the likely repayment of equity relative to debt, then there is a non fixed element to debt costs. While this is particularly important in asset financing, it is not particularly important in the consideration of optimum pricing.

Short run marginal costs are those costs that are inevitably incurred as a result of a small increment of generation, where here the increment is not measured as MW in relation to a plan or contract, but MWh over the next hour in time and without which the next hour of generation is impossible. Virtually all costs are excluded from this definition. For example, coal is not necessarily included because an hour of generation is not impossible without committing to coal spend, since coal can be drawn from stock. Gas is included but only at the marginal cost, rather than including the capacity cost. Plant life utilisation and other plant costs are not included, but short term reliability[62] costs should be.

Long run marginal costs are those costs that are incurred over a long period from increments of running at equilibrium. These should include fuel and consumable costs, capacity costs smeared, plant life usage costs, labour costs, cost of environmental permits and costs of reliability losses.

Quasi-fixed costs are those fixed and long run marginal costs which can be avoided with sufficient planning, and which involve a reduced capability or life of plant. In practice we should view quasi fixed costs as those can be avoided over a horizon from between one and four years, usually by planning to mothball or close.

The relationship between all of the different costs is important in regulation and in gaming.

10.1.24   Cost of capital

The cost of debt can be regarded as a truly fixed cost since its repayment is not related to the operation of the plant. We can regard the plant as having a fixed payment stream due to the creditors and a floating payment stream due to the shareholders, where the payment is indexed to the earnings of the plant.

The cost of capital repayment is clearly related to the cost of the plant, whether it is built or purchased. For built plant, the repayment is derived from the build cost, which is not closely[63] related to current[64] market conditions. For bought plant, the plant cost is not derived from its build cost but its current market value as a fuel-to-power converter since sellers would not sell at much less than this, and buyers would not pay much more. The truly fixed cost is therefore closely related to market conditions at the time of purchase. So, if a low merit plant historically offered at a particular premium above short run marginal costs and was dispatched, then the market value of the plant reflects this.

We can immediately see a problem here. Fixed costs are dependent on a blend of current and past market prices, particularly if the plant is purchased. We are aware of a circular argument. If offering at marginal costs will not cover the fixed cost of the plant in a normal year, then the plant must uplift its offer to cover fixed costs. But the fixed costs are themselves dependent on the uplift that market power and market gaming solutions allow. We can then apply this argument to all plant on the stack and find then that all plant exactly makes a zero excess return over the risk adjusted cost of capital. We encounter a similar situation when considering the energy costs of supply companies.

This presents a problem to the regulator. New purchasers of old plant will naturally expect to make a fair return on capital and hence will use purchase cost as the arbiter of capital

---

[62] In simple terms, this is the net marginal revenue at full capability, multiplied by the probability of failure.

[63] In practice a number of cost elements are highly correlated to market conditions, such as queuing time for build slots, commissioning costs, etc.

[64] It is however very closely related to past market conditions, since new entrant equilibrium determines that forward market prices are close to new entrant costs for plant of the particular load factors.

amount and therefore of the fixed cost that must be recovered. If repayment of capital cost is not recognised as a *bona fide* fixed cost to be recovered, then sale of plant is effectively precluded, thereby denying competition in generation. If it is recognised, then the circular relationship between fixed costs and price uplifts above market costs can be increased, and moreover this creates the capability for low merit plant to elevate prices in order to improve the operating margin of higher merit plant in the same fleet.

There is also a moral hazard problem with cost of capital. A firm has liabilities and contingent liabilities to a number of counterparties, including creditors, shareholders, trading counterparties and obligees (participants to whom the firm has contracted commitments). These liabilities have very different forms. For example, shareholders derive all of the upside from improved profits, but are the first to lose money if the company fails. Apart from the employees themselves, shareholders have the strongest voice, followed by creditors.[65] The other obligations of the firm may not feature as highly as they should, for example, the commitment to decommission nuclear power stations. Unless there is ring fenced cash set aside for such obligations, or if they are underwritten by a third party, then they are at risk. This is one reason why governments have commonly retained the nuclear sector, or found it hard to sell with the liabilities included.

10.1.24.1   The Capital Asset Pricing Model

The Capital Asset Pricing Model (CAPM) is a standard method of calculating the fair *ex ante* cost of capital in relation to the risks faced by the firm. It is implicitly and explicitly used by regulators in the setting of tariffs and revenues.

CAPM is well documented in corporate finance textbooks. It was formulated in 1964–5 from work by Sharpe and Lintner and Treynor, and grew from a number of component theories and elements from Modigliani, Miller, Mossin, Tobin, Lucas and Markovitz.

In essence, there are two elements to CAPM:

(i)   Investors are risk averse in a linear manner with terminal variance (see sections 10.1.9.2 and 9.1.22).
(ii) Investors own stock market portfolios and hence are most risk averse to assets with high correlation to the stock market (i.e. low diversifiability). The covariance between the asset and the stock market is called the beta.

In calculating the fair revenues for a natural monopoly, the regulator considers the following:

(i)   The value to assign to the asset base.
(ii)   The 'risk free' rate – chosen by convention to be the government bond rate
(iii) The beta of the stock.
(iv)   The gearing (ratio of debt to equity) of the stock. The gearing affects the equity risk and the equity return. In addition, there is a 'tax shield' effect since debt payments do not attract tax, whereas dividends paid from corporate profits do attract tax on the profits.
(v)   The equity risk premium, i.e. the increase in *ex ante* annual return over and above the risk free rate that is required for the stock to be fairly valued in the market place. This is assessed by historic analysis.

---

[65] The recent increase in the power of creditors is partly a result of the Enron disaster and increasing scrutiny of contingent liabilities in the form of off balance sheet instruments.

In practice, regulated monopolies commonly enjoy a high allowance for beta. This is for two principal reasons. Firstly, beta is a stock valuation measure rather than a revenues measure, and portfolio behaviour causes short term market volatility for stocks with regulated revenues which is commonly higher than is indicated by the cost and revenue volatility. Secondly, many of the revenue elements are self regulating, thereby reducing their volatility. For example, revenues are commonly indexed to inflation, thereby reducing a source of risk relative to cost, and over and under recovery of revenues is commonly allowed by regulation to be recaptured in the following year. In addition, some aspects of regulated prices are passed straight through the consumers, thereby reducing the risk to the differential to revenues and factor costs.

An interpretation of CAPM is very relevant to the ESI. Instead of viewing our *ex ante* cash flow as a risky return on capital, we can view[66] it in three parts: (i) a risk free return at the risk free rate, plus (ii) a risky outcome with an expectation equal to the market value of the cost of the particular risk, plus (iii) a residual amount which we may call the 'alpha'. Now let us consider what we mean by profit. Risk free investors gain the 'real interest rate', which is the difference between inflation and the actual (called 'nominal') interest rate. In a sense this can be called profit. Risk takers gain the difference between the insurance annuity and the disutility of risk. This also can be called profit. There is a market value for this risk, sometimes called the equity risk premium. If the *ex ante* expectation value of the difference is less than the equity risk premium, then investors will sell the stock. The stock price reduction with a constant net revenue thereby restores the equity risk premium. Therefore, in an efficient market with rational expectations, the stock is always expected to deliver the market equity risk premium. However, the downward stock price correction resulting from lower regulated prices, causes a one off reduction to the asset base of the shareholders. If this is a result of a decrease in regulated revenue, then this is regarded as a moral hazard on the part of the regulator, betraying an implied promise to allow 'fair' returns. If the *ex ante* expectation value of the difference, discovered by deep study by one individual, is more than the market expectation, then the individual expects a positive 'alpha'.

10.1.25 Fundamental measures

The neoclassical approach places money at the centre of the system, and explicitly recognises that money has a different purchasing power for utility to different people in different places. In intercommodity exchange, Pareto optimisation in the neoclassical model optimises financial surplus. Whilst money acts as a good medium of exchange at the margin as it is tangible, measurable and mobile, it is highly imperfect in its role of store of value over the medium and long term when 'value' is interpreted fundamentally in terms of utility.

Ideally we want a universal asset that is not only more closely related to utility than money, but is actually tradable. Such an asset is a numeraire asset. While the concept of the numeraire was first formally introduced by Walras, it was effectively recognised by Adam Smith, who stated that an hour of labour was the most universal and fundamental asset. However, the search for a numeraire asset has been elusive and all candidates have proved to have prices that are sufficiently volatile relative to other goods for us to believe that their fundamental 'values' are themselves volatile.

---

[66] See Treynor (1999).

For the long term, currency is a particularly unreliable numeraire asset for a number of reasons, including:

(i)   The currency refers to a particular country or set of countries and the purchasing power of that currency is only stable in that country. It is therefore unsuitable for long term international considerations.
(ii) Having no direct use, money has no fundamental value and in the long term is more volatile than physical assets. As we saw in section 9.1.21, this creates issues for us in volatility modelling.
(iii) Money assets incorporate a moral hazard since a nation with debt denominated in its own currency can simply print notes to discharge the debt. The ensuing inflation reduces the purchasing power of the debt.

The problems are well known, and there have been attempts to create numeraire assets,[67] or to make money into a more effective numeraire asset.[68] No satisfactory candidate for numeraire asset has emerged. A tonne of carbon dioxide permits has some candidate qualities since it is: (i) tradable, (ii) international, (iii) fundamental in its own right and (iv) whilst global warming does not cause homogenous disutility to all people, the disutility is universal and broadly irrespective of wealth. In fact, a cap and trade system for CO_2, in which all countries sign, and with limits fixed and known over the long term (50 years), does create an international asset in the form of permits, that is a good a candidate for numeraire as many, although there is a significant moral hazard risk from change in contractual terms, or abrogation of commitments.

10.1.26   Hedonic and shadow prices

Hedonic and shadow prices are prices that are not directly revealed. Hedonic prices are the prices implied for products that can only be delivered as part of other products. So, for example, in a market in which there are no pollution permits or renewable certificates, consumers may pay more for power from green sources. The difference between the 'black' power price and the 'green' power price is the hedonic price for the 'renewable-ness' of the energy.

Shadow prices are the implied prices of constraints. For example, if the SOx limit for a generation unit were relieved by one tonne, then it could produce more power and therefore receive more revenue. By calculating the extra revenue, we can calculate the shadow price. Similar, if we increase transmission line capacity by 1 MW, we can increase total surplus between produces and consumers.

10.1.27   Price growth

The prices of all things grow naturally as the value of money deflates, but there are other impacts, in terms of productive efficiency which depresses prices, and commodity scarcity, which increases them. The debate about the net effect has been going on for a long time for all produced commodities. The economist Simon famously bet the ecologist Ehrlich in 1980 to name five commodities that would rise in price over ten years. Ehrlich chose copper, chrome, nickel, tin and tungsten and the basket fell relative to the inflation index.[69]

---

[67] Special Drawing Rights are an international currency basket and gold. This reduces the risk to specific currencies.

[68] The gold standard tied money to gold at a fixed exchange rate. Gold is more fundamental than money in the long term, but in the short term is more volatile in value.

[69] Actually, the basket only fell 2 % short of the 58 % inflation over the period.

10.2   OPTIMAL PRICING BY ASSET OWNERS

10.2.1   The privately owned monopoly operator

Whilst it is not to the interest of the monopoly producer to produce more than the clearing volume, it is potentially in his interest to produce less. This situation is illustrated in the situation where the producer is a privately owned monopoly. By withholding production, the producer can make more profits. This is shown in Figure 10.35. The consumer surplus is reduced by a greater degree than the producer gain and hence the solution is welfare inefficient. This is called the 'dead weight loss' of the monopoly, and is a useful concept in the consideration of localised monopoly in the form of market power.

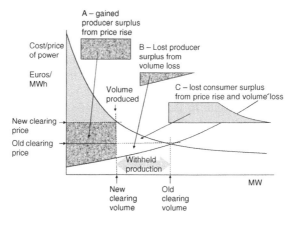

Figure 10.35   Withdrawal of production by monopoly seller increases producer surplus but aggregate surplus falls by the 'deadweight' cost $B + C - A$

From this we can construct an optimum output for the monopolist as shown in Figure 10.36. This curve applies not just to complete monopolists but to all participants over the regions in which they have market power.

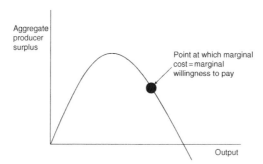

Figure 10.36   Optimisation of volume output for a monopolist

Note that the optimum producer surplus for a fragmented producer community, if the producers could agree to volume restraint, is for the total output to equal the optimum monopoly output, and for the producers to agree a method of sharing this output.

10.2.2 Forward hedging – timing effects

The nature of producer and consumer/supplier hedging was discussed in sections 2.2.24 and 2.6.7 respectively. Supply companies and large consumers hedge a fraction of anticipated demand. If the market cost of risk is small, then producers will hedge as much as possible if[70] the forward price exceeds marginal plus quasi-fixed costs.

Consider a fragmented market that clears at marginal costs. We can see from Figure 10.37 that the forward market will clear at lower volume than the future spot market for the same delivery date will, and that although producers offer at higher prices, the reduced volume means that the forward price could be higher or lower than the expected spot clearing price. The volume however is always less than the expectation of final demand. The market therefore gives an insufficient signal to producers to optimise production levels. To make production decisions with a lead time of more than two or three years, producers need to examine the volume fundamentals of the market as well as the prevailing prices. So, they anticipate demand, and observe the total impending capacity of competing production.

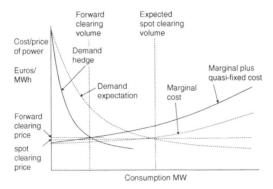

Figure 10.37   Clearing volumes and prices in the spot and forward market

In a market with no power or influence, the final contractual position in the spot market is independent of forward contract position. In other words, producers should in theory ignore their hedge positions when considering dispatch. However in practice, market influence factors (see section 5.4.14) and irrational behaviour both cause hedge position to influence dispatch.

10.2.3 Fixed cost recovery

Fixed cost recovery is one of the central problems of electricity pricing. If all producers in a fragmented market offer at marginal cost at all times, a variety of fixed cost outcomes are possible including:

(i) **All producers except one recover fixed costs** – This happens when there is a high degree of temporal inhomogeneity of demand and of the production stack (i.e. demand is highly periodic, and the low merit units in the winter are mid merit in the summer).

---

[70] There is a conflict of interests between creditors and shareholders. Shareholders will not lock in a loss and prefer to maintain the option of higher revenues. Creditors would prefer to lock in certainty of payment and have no interest in shareholder upside. In solvent companies, the shareholder wish tends to prevail.

(ii) **No producers recover fixed costs** – This happens when there demand variation is low and the fixed to marginal cost ratio of the producers is high.
(iii) **One or more sectors do not recover fixed costs** – These might be all low, mid or high merit plant, or all of one type of technology.

Solutions, which are described at various points in the book are:

(i)   consolidate (see section 10.5.3);
(ii)   central management;
(iii) discriminatory pricing (see section 10.1.15);
(iv)   subsidise production through direct taxation, rather than value added tax (see section 10.2.3.1);
(v)   uplift offers above marginal prices by pursuing a gaming solution (see section 10.5);
(vi)   capacity payments.

10.2.3.1 Conversion of indirect to direct taxes

The gaming solution is exposed to 'cheating', in which a producer free rides on the rise in price caused by price uplift from competitor plant. A way to avoid this is to prevent cheating by centralising the price markup, for example by *ad valorem*[71] energy tax or levy collected centrally and then redistributed to generators. If redistribution were according to credited energy production, then the tax is effectively a form of cartel, or regulated price.

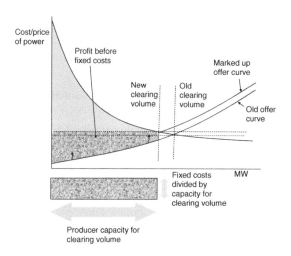

Figure 10.38 Recovery of fixed cost by uniform markup of all prices. Prices marked up such that two textured areas are equal

One problem is that since low marginal cost producers have the highest fixed costs, an *ad valorem* tax will either not compensate fixed costs for low merit plant, or will give a windfall to high merit plant.

---

[71] An *ad valorem* tax is one that is applied at a fixed rate rather than a percentage of the output price.

10.2.3.2 Two part tariffs, energy and entry/capacity

Various mechanisms are possible, such as a flat capacity fee that is unrelated to anticipated or maximum usable capacity. While such schemes are common for the pricing of public goods, fee structures that do not relate directly to capacity rights are not of particular interest here. We will assume here that the entry fee is equal to capacity booked (known *ex ante* in the deterministic world) times clearing price.

In 1946 Coase[72] suggested a two part tariff, in which consumers pay a fixed entry fee that covers the fixed costs of the producers[73] and a variable fee for actual consumption that is set at the marginal cost of production. We will see later that this is very similar to paying an option premium and an option strike price, or a capacity fee and a marginal price.

Capacity charging exists throughout the ESI for charging for fuel, networks, metering, generation, and supply. The heterogeneity of electricity demand with respect to time presents particular problems that are greater than with other commodities, and hence we walk through this in some detail. For convenience, we assume that the system operator owns or controls the capacity.

To do so, it is necessary to make some modelling simplifications. For the purposes of this example, we envisage a temporary power station unit[74] with no costs other than fuel, and with an efficiency that declines linearly with output and a maximum output equal to unit capacity. The fixed cost here is the amortised[75] repayment on the capital cost of the unit, spent in advance and not changeable. The lifetime of the unit is directly proportional to the capital amount spent, and the incremental cost of capacity increases linearly with increasing unit size. We consider a marketplace with three consumers and one privately owned generator that for regulatory reasons is required to (and does) honestly report its marginal costs for energy and capacity, and offers to the clearing market at these marginal costs.

For all examples here, the consumers (and producers, in the case of transmission) must book capacity in advance, initially at a single price for all periods. They know their demand functions, and all have the same slope of demand curve at all times, although the absolute levels of demand (and prices) may differ by consumer and by period. At this point, we are initially treating capacity as a private good (capacity booked by C may not be used by A unless by agreement).

The arguments described refer to power generation, but can be applied to transmission.

Single period setting. Deterministic demand. Single producer

For the single period deterministic setting, the amount of energy purchased is the same as the amount of capacity booked and hence in this simple example in which capacity is treated as a marginal cost, there is no qualitative difference in the charging of energy and capacity since energy cannot be bought without capacity and there is no reason to buy capacity without energy.

---

[72] Coase (1946). The tariff is also called the Hopkinson tariff after the engineer who supposedly first suggested it. See Kahn (1988).

[73] This is common in the ESI. For example consumer tariffs and contracts, network charges and take or pay fuel supply.

[74] This example uses power stations. We could equally well have used network assets.

[75] Amortisation spreads the capital repayment over the period of debt rather than paying it all back at the end. It is simplest here to imagine an interest rate of zero and even amortisation of capital repayment.

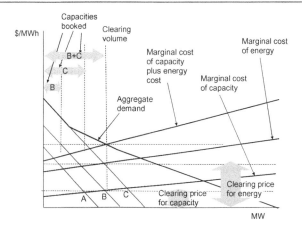

Figure 10.39   Constructing the clearing price in a single period setting. For details see text

Two period setting. Deterministic demand. Constant consumer ranking. Single producer

First consider the situation in which the ranking order of dominance[76] of consumers is the same in both periods. For the same amount of capacity as used in period 1 they would pay the same rate (in $/MW/period) in period 2, but for the increase in capacity they must effectively pay double since the extra capacity was not paid for or used in period 1. It must be paid for in period 1 to use in period 2. This is shown in Figure 10.40.

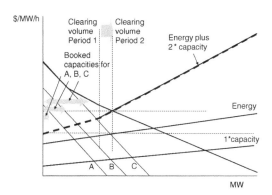

Figure 10.40   Constructing the clearing price in a two period setting. For details see text

Having paid for some extra capacity in period 2, the marginal cost of consumption in period 1 changes for that extra capacity. This is shown in Figure 10.41. C always dominates A and so no participant finds himself consuming more in period 1 than he booked in period 2.

---

[76] Dominance means that one consumer will pay a higher price than another for all consumption levels, i.e. the demand lines do not cross.

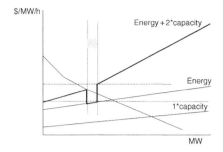

Figure 10.41 Revisiting consumption in period 1 with extra capacity booked in period 2 regarded as free

While concentrating on capacity, let us make the simplifying assumption that energy has constant returns to scale in any time period. We can then net the cost of energy from the demand function to assess our demand for capacity.

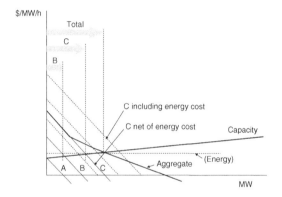

Figure 10.42 Adjusting the demand curves for energy cost to create a pure demand for capacity

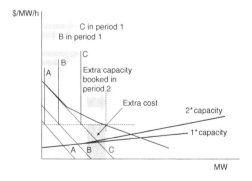

Figure 10.43 Prices and costs for capacity in the second period

Then we go back to the first period as before to book some more energy using the free extra capacity booked for period 2.

For a three period setting we follow the same process, beginning with the lowest demand period and moving through to the highest demand period for capacity booking and back again for energy.

Since C always dominates A in this example, then the distinction between a public and private good is not important. To consider its general importance, let us reverse the order of demand in period 2.

Two period setting. Deterministic demand. Changing consumer ranking. Single producer

By reversing the order of demands in period 2, A now consumes the most and C the least.

First consider the current situation in which capacity is a private good that cannot be exchanged between participants, and which, once reserved by a participant may not be used by the capacity provider for another participant even if unused.

If each participant trades bilaterally with the system operator and books the optimal level of capacity, then the total capacity purchased over the two periods will exceed that for a set of consumers that (i) could trade capacity with each other, (ii) had consistent order of dominance in all periods, or (iii) were actually just one consumer. This has three effects: (i) transfer of 'too much' money to the provider of capacity if (as is common) the provider has more knowledge in aggregate than the sum of consumer knowledge, (ii) loss of aggregate surplus since more capacity is purchased than is needed and (iii) increase in the marginal cost of capacity above the cost for the required amount of capacity.

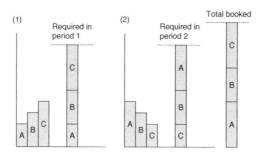

Figure 10.44   If each consumer books capacity as an untradable private good, then too much capacity is booked

There are various solutions to this:

(i)   Repeated polling of participants for higher and higher capacity combinations (vectors), followed by a single transaction at the clearing price (a single clearing price or one for each period). This would result in the market solution. This is a tâtonnement process.
(ii)   Book the full amount of capacity required, and then immediately retrade in each period before excess capacity is built. This will eventually result in the market solution for capacity allocation, but excessive gaming by participants might result in net prices paid that are 'unfair'. This is effectively a tâtonnement process.
(iii)   Book the amount of capacity required in the lowest period, and then immediately retrade in each period before excess capacity is built. Comments as above.
(iv)   Allow the booking of excess capacity as shown in Figure 10.44. Whilst this is inefficient for deterministic demand, it is less so for stochastic demand.

(v)   Consumers submit their demand functions for all periods to the system operator. The system operator then performs the calculations on behalf of the consumers, and charges them the same price as the market solution for tradable private capacity would have (eventually) found.

(vi) System operator estimates demand functions. He then does the same calculations as above. In the ESI, demand is considered to be fairly inelastic in the short term, and the system operator will commonly have better information than the participants themselves (since a change of supplier results in no loss of information to the system operator but it does to the suppliers). Demand must then be allocated in some way in order to collect the capacity charges, but is in reality non-firm, since there is uncertainty in the forecast. Methods of charging are described in Chapter 6 on capacity.

So we can see that we have implicitly or explicitly created a capacity vector. At this point in time, electricity markets are not mature enough to trade capacity vectors in transmission (i.e. a high resolution forward market, including periodicity), although some forward markets in energy have traded at the requisite resolution.

Single period setting. Stochastic demand. Monotonic consumer ranking. Single producer

This introduces a new level of complexity that is a real problem. We have already noted that there is a high uncertainty[77] associated with capacity booking. The nature of electricity is such that it is largely sold at a flat tariff with volume that is estimated from historic consumption but not actually limited. Industrial and commercial contracts also generally allow load variation between the minimum and maximum.

With stochastic demand, then no matter how much capacity gets booked, there is always a finite probability of loss of load. To optimise the capacity booked, we need to make an assessment of the disutility of loss of load. This is not easy, as is shown in section 10.1.5.1.

The i'th consumer could buy capacity q_i from the system operator with the conditions that (i) even if the capacity is available then the consumer may not use more capacity than booked without entering into further contracts, and (ii) if total demand on capacity exceeds total booked (and financed and built) capacity then capacity will be rationed (i.e. be non firm).

If the system operator decides to build more capacity than the aggregate booking, then, if called, this should be priced at the total extra cost divided by what the *ex ante* call off rate was expected to be, plus the risk premium. The risk premium represents extreme risk in the sense described in section 10.1.9.2 and is likely to significantly exceed the risk neutral cost or the cost with risk adjusted for quadratic risk aversion. For the system operator to do this requires guessing of demand variation. The total knowledge required is (i) the probability profile of individual and aggregate demand, and (ii) the disutility (or contractual compensation) of lost load. If both consumers and system operator make decisions (consumers on how much to book and the system operator on how much to build), then all participants need the same information.

---

[77] Distinct from high risk. Uncertainty means that with enough time and resource we could establish the knowledge. Risk means that even with more investigation, that exogenous factors prevent us from knowing.

10.2.3.3   Relation between two part tariffs and non uniform pricing

We can see that two (or multi) part tariffs have a similarity to non uniform pricing.

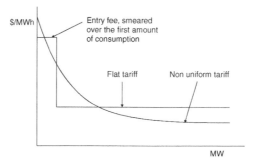

Figure 10.45   Comparison of two part tariffs with non uniform pricing

The application is dependent on how the capacity charge is constructed. If it is on a per capita basis, then not only does it discriminate against small users, but it will cause withdrawal of consumers. If on an energy consumption basis, then it is, to all intents and purposes, not a fixed charge but a flat tariff, best related to peak consumption.

For further information on optimal pricing of two part tariffs, see Brown and Sibley (1986).

10.2.3.4   Cost allocation to producers

In examples for the pricing of capacity, we assumed that the system operator does not restrict capacity in order to raise price and gain the monopoly rent. We continue to make the same assumption for two or more producers.

In the case of generating capacity, the contract between the consumer and the producer can be a bilateral private contract, and there is therefore no issue of cost allocation. In the case of transmission capacity, it is a public good because open access requires that access cannot be denied to one part of the network.

The specifics of some models are described in Chapter 7 on location, and we can summarise the main models at high level:

(i)   **Relative Output Method (ROM)** – sharing according to the volumetric share of service provided.
(ii) **Gross Revenue Method (GRM)** – sharing according to financial contribution to total revenue.
(iii) **Attributable Cost Method (ACM)** – sharing according to the contribution to total cost.

Each has its difficulties. The attributable cost method is the easiest to measure, but creates no disincentive to save costs, or even not to build unnecessary assets. Hence to make the system operate, some form of central management of consents would be required. The system is therefore effectively a centrally managed system with: (i) regulated private subcontracting of plant build, operation, and maintenance with closely regulated revenues, and (ii) the requirement for the system operator to be omniscient of all present and future costs and capabilities, and to have an economic model to prescribe the schedule of plant opening and closure.

10.2.3.5   Further considerations

One problem that we have is the moral hazard for interruptibility. If a consumer books uninterruptible capacity, then still, regardless of contractual position, the state is likely to prioritise interruption according to national or social need. There is commonly a hierarchy of interruptibility. For example, hospitals have high priority. If consumers feel that security of supply changes from being a private to a public good at the moment that it is required, then there is no incentive to pay for it bilaterally.

10.3   REGULATED PRICES

In 301 AD, the Roman emperor Diocletian, noticing, amongst general price increases, that the local price of food rose as his armies approached, commanded that prices should be fixed. We note that the price rose for two reasons. Firstly, that the marginal cost of getting food to the army increased with total volume consumed (because it was attracted from a wider radius with correspondingly higher transport costs). Secondly that traders may have raised their prices in a consolidated manner when confronted with a price insensitive buyer. If consolidation was sufficient to raise the clearing price above the marginal cost for the last increment of volume, then Diocletian would have been correct, since the sellers would behave rationally and sell at a lower clearing price. If, on the other hand, the clearing price was competitive, then a reduction in price would result in a reduction of available food at the clearing price. As it happened, the price fixing led to shortages and black markets.

Since the market must clear above the marginal price, some form of market power or gaming must be exercised. If market power or gaming is exercised to gain a fair return, then it can be exercised to gain an excess return. The regulator therefore takes an interest in prices.

The regulator/system operator has a number of choices for price control. For example:

(i)   Detailed central prescription of hourly wholesale prices and/or retail charges.
(ii)   Absolute cap on the wholesale price in any trading period.
(iii)   Cap on the time weighted average wholesale price over a longer period (usually a year).
(iv)   Cap on the demand weighted average wholesale price over a longer period.
(v)   *Ad hoc* review of *ex post* returns after periods of high wholesale prices, followed by fines or impositions for future prices.
(vi)   Prices based on costs (estimated *ex ante*, audited *ex post* with next year adjustments for over and under recovery).
(vii)   Cap on the annual revenue based on the *ex ante* fair risk adjusted return on capital, but without prescription on the breakdown of prices.

Caps applied to average prices or average revenues represent the level above which the regulator allows formally or above which regulatory scrutiny becomes onerous. They therefore also represent the level below which regulatory action is not onerous and hence to some degree, they represent price setting rather than price capping. The gravitation of prices to the regulatory price caps is strongly assisted by the action of the price as a focal point.[78] We will see this later in the section on gaming.

---

[78] The London Metal Exchange provided a good example of the effect of focal points. Limits on backwardation (borrowing rates) were occasionally imposed, and prices commonly remained at the limit. This was to the advantage of the commodity holder (who improved certainty of loan income) and the offtaker or short position, whose worst case costs/losses were limited.

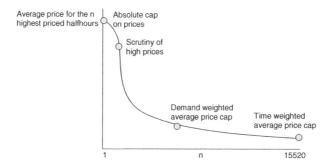

Figure 10.46   Depiction of the regulatory price envelope

One challenge that the regulators have is that they have a particular interest in the domestic sector, and within that sector, they have particular interest in the fuel poor. This creates two particular problems:

(i) **Difference between wholesale and retail prices** – The market that is easiest to measure and directly influence is the wholesale market, and yet neither producer nor consumer have direct access to this price.
(ii) **Cross subsidy** – Cross subsidy may be welfare efficient but causes a deadweight loss, and destroys competition. While energy law commonly proscribes cross subsidy, regulators commonly require cross subsidy to be applied to the fuel poor.

10.4   TAXES AND SUBSIDIES

There are different reasons for applying taxes in the ESI:

(i)   to compensate for the damage caused directly or indirectly by production or consumption;
(ii) to fund public services, in or out of the ESI;
(iii) to redistribute wealth;
(iv) to convert indirect taxes to direct taxes.

Each has a different effect on the economy and their effects are mixed. For example a public service may be applied specifically to a section of society, thereby causing redistribution of wealth.

Taxes and subsidies can be applied in a number of ways:

(i)   Value added tax applied at the point of consumption. Collected by the supply companies on behalf of the government as a 'hard pass through' (the collection revenue amount appears on the bill, is paid to the government if collected by supply companies, and not paid if not collected).
(ii) Consumer levies termed as environmental levies, explicit on the consumer bill.
(iii) Forced acceptance of a product or service at above market prices (the feed in mechanism).
(iv) Producer levies that are treated as environmental levies.
(v)   Supplier levies termed as environmental levies.

(vi)   Cross subsidies from consumer sector to other sectors (such as stranded costs, specific consumers, fuel producers).
(vii)   Supplier obligations that are practically treated as levies.
(viii) Ad hoc taxes to ESI sectors, such as windfall taxes.
(ix)   Corporation tax and corporate windfall tax.
(x)   Direct grants.
(xi)   Tax breaks (mainly on VAT).
(xii)   Levy exemptions.
(xiii) Emission taxing.
(xiv)   Targeted taxes on producer sectors.
(xv)   Subsidies from government.
(xvi)   Government driven cross subsidies within the industry.

Consider, for example, the obligation of suppliers to ensure that x % of their consumption is ultimately sourced from renewable energy (as defined and registered by regulation), or pay a buyout fine of £ y/MWh. Suppose also that the fines are recycled within the ESI by giving the money evenly per MWh to renewable energy producers. Provided that £ y/MWh is greater than the marginal net (net of receipts for energy) cost of renewable energy production, then this obligation is effectively a levy of x * y £/MWh of demand.

10.4.1   Deadweight loss of taxes

We saw in section 10.2.1 that monopolistic behaviour causes a deadweight loss. Taxes also cause a deadweight loss as is shown in Figure 10.47.

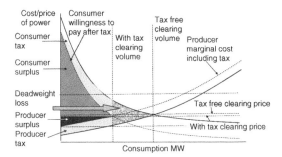

Figure 10.47   The deadweight loss of a tax

10.4.2   The role of the ESI in the fiscal structure of the macroeconomy

Welfare – The neoclassical viewpoint is that welfare optimisation is ideally a problem external to the microeconomic market structure problem, and is part of a macroeconomic problem handled by government. If there is an efficient fiscal or other mechanism outside the ESI to redistribute wealth in a manner that is socially optimal, then policy makers need not (and indeed should not) apply utility to microeconomic problems.

However, the difficulties in measuring utility and applying a wealth based (as distinct from income or expenditure based) fiscal regime, are immediately obvious, and in some circumstances, such as fuel poverty, the discovery and discrimination can be more effectively applied directly within the ESI rather than by government, and the necessary services and cross subsidies applied directly rather than from government determined grant allocations. Hence, the ESI becomes *de facto* part of the macroeconomic fiscal management of the economy.

There are practical as well as economic reasons why this is the case, although the practical reasons are not necessarily ideal. If the welfare gain from redistribution more than offsets the utility cost of deadweight losses from taxes then redistribution of wealth is considered. The effect of redistribution of wealth on incentive must also be considered. The question is whether it is more efficient to allow the ESI to clear according to marginal neoclassical economics and then apply taxes and subsidies at government level, or if the industry should effectively hypothecate by collecting direct taxes from one set of consumers and pay subsidies to another.

Tax revenue – The second role of the ESI in the fiscal structure of the macroeconomy is in revenue generation for the government in the form of taxes, and in the reduction of welfare costs by the provision of employment.

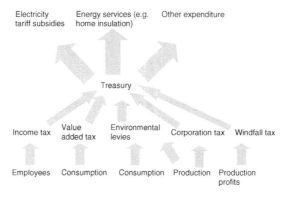

Figure 10.48 Use of taxes from the ESI for ESI and other purposes

Since the ESI generates tax revenue, then the government takes this into account when making decisions with respect to subsidising the industry. Subsidies are commonly limited by international regulations on state aid.

Harmonisation – For international exchange, tax harmonisation is important. Differential rates of value added tax in different countries do not significantly affect the international wholesale market, but different environmental tax regimes can do. For example if one country taxes at the point of production and one at the point of consumption, then this may cause excess electricity flow from the latter to the former.

10.5   GAMES, INTERACTION AND BEHAVIOUR

Throughout this book, we have frequently begun analysis with a particular set of characteristics and assumptions:

(i)   A very large number of very small producers in which no units in sequence in the merit order belong to a single producer.

(ii) The market behaviour of one participant has no effect on the behaviour of other participants.
(iii) The merit order of the producer stack is consistent across the year.
(iv) Demand and plant outages are deterministic and known.

In this situation, it is optimal for producers to offer at marginal costs. However, as we saw, this behaviour leads to the situation in which one or more producers do not cover fixed and quasi fixed costs and may withdraw from the system. The result must either be that the system operates with occasional lost load or that a different behaviour set emerges in which at least one producer offers above marginal costs.

If we are to accept the prospect of offering above fixed costs, how this can be managed (i.e. how we keep the price up above marginal costs, but how we limit it to 'fair' value) in a multi-participant market. To do so we first examine the general interaction and behaviour of participants and then consider more formal 'gaming' solutions. It should be noted that 'gaming' is commonly used in a pejorative sense in the ESI. The study of gaming is highly formal, and gaming behaviour is an essential component of transaction behaviour, without which there would be no equilibrium.

10.5.1   Use of information without interaction

Suppose that each producer is fully aware of the cost structure of all other producers. For all of the hours for which the lowest merit unit is required to run, then it is optimal under the assumptions described to offer not at marginal costs, but at just below the marginal cost of the unit next down the merit order. This is shown in Figure 10.49.

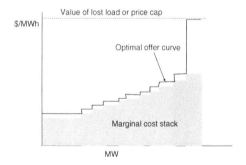

Figure 10.49 Optimal offer behaviour for a discretised production stack in the hours of highest demand. For assumptions see text

The effect on the lowest merit producer is quite obvious. His output volume in those periods is not limited by his competitive position but only by the price elasticity of demand, or a regulatory price cap, or regulatory intervention.

In this circumstance, it is quite possible, that if the lowest merit producer actually runs, then he will uplift the clearing price sufficiently for a small number of periods to improve the average price attained by lower merit producers, and so increase their potential to cover fixed costs. Hence, with no offer interaction, the system can (but not definitely will – it depends on the fixed/marginal cost mix of the generation stack) attain equilibrium.

However, the situation is rather more complicated in real life where demand and plant outages are uncertain. If the lowest merit producer has a finite expected load factor, then the probability of lost load must be reasonably high. In reality, there is no clearly defined lowest merit producer since there are many ways to get more load. Hence, looking at the very lowest merit producer is only useful from a theoretical perspective, and we must consider units with a reasonable load factor.

10.5.2   Local consolidation

With knowledge of the cost structure of the generation stack, one way to increase revenue with invoking the need for participant interaction is to consolidate plant in particular areas of the merit order.

We have already seen in Figure 10.49 how it is optimal[79] for each producer to offer not at marginal costs, but at least as high as the lowest marginal cost of lower merit competitor plant. We can extend this further by adjusting ownership of plant so that local consolidation is increased. This is shown in Figure 10.50.

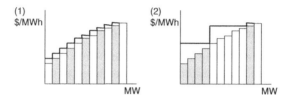

Figure 10.50   Local consolidation with no change in overall market share of capacity, as a means to maintain price to recover fixed costs. Two producers, one shaded and one unshaded. The bold lines represent the offer submissions

Note that units within the fleet do not act as free agents and the offers submitted on their behalf, even though improving their revenues, are not necessarily the offers that they would have submitted on their own.

10.5.3   Collaboration

If the generation stack remains fragmented, then another way for generators to offer at above marginal costs. In order not to lose volume, they must all agree to this. One way to do this of course is to collaborate by explicit verbal agreement.

However, we cannot necessarily infer that there has been collaboration if we observe an offer stack above the marginal cost stack. Two other alternatives are possible:

Firstly, the offers may be a result of a repeated game (we will see these later), in which participants communicate to a greater or lesser degree with their price offers but do not explicitly collaborate.

Secondly, since marginal cost offering by all participants may result in some or all losing money overall, then since they are heading for bankruptcy, any new offer strategy may be better and cannot be worse. Hence a strategy of offering above marginal costs may occur

---

[79] In the absence of an equilibrium 'supergame' with interleaved offers, as described in section 5.4.12.

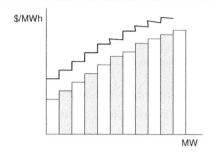

Figure 10.51 Gaming solution to fixed cost recovery. Agree uplift to marginal costs. Units of producer A are in grey and producer B are in white

not in response to competitor offers, but in response to the need to change offer strategy to survive.

10.5.4   Repeated games

Suppose that there are two alternative offers – MC = marginal cost, EQ = marginal cost plus fixed cost, smeared over the running period.

If producer A offers one day at MC, and B offers at EQ, then A will gain load with no loss of price. Producer B may 'retaliate' the next day to 'punish' A for 'stealing' load. Since the deadlock is not to the interest of either party, some other response strategy must appear.

It may be that A is in a stronger position (for example by having a dominant strategy that we will see later), so we may see an offer pattern of:

$$MC \ EQ \ MC \ EQ \ MC \ EQ \ MC \ EQ \ \text{(with A leading)}$$

if B is better off with this strategy than for

$$MC \ MC \ MC \ MC \ MC \ MC$$

Alternatively, if A is not in a strong position, he may share the load, so the pattern is:

$$MC \ EQ \ EQ \ EQ \ EQ \ EQ \ EQ \ EQ$$

We will examine the formality of these games later.

10.5.5   Interactive behaviour of mid merit plant

Let us consider how participants might arrive at a stable, equilibrium, offer pattern. Firstly we consider mid merit units. The situation for mid merit plant is quite different to low merit plant because mid merit sets price for the majority of the time and hence in the pool there is a daily experience of the close connection between offer prices, accepted volumes, declined volumes and the clearing price

Each day, the participants alter their offer structure in the light of the previous day's results, which include a participant's own offers, competitor offers, own volume accepted, competitor volume accepted and gross (before fixed costs) and net (after fixed costs) profit.

While we will see later that in a one-shot game (a producer that produced for only one day), that it might be optimal for producers to offer at marginal costs, that since all producers might do the same, the strategy is not sustainable in a 'game' of many sittings.

There can be then, particularly in pool markets, a rather complex 'dialogue', since the offer stack contains many units.

10.5.6   Interactive behaviour of low merit plant

This depends on the information revealed by the system/market operator in the pool. If no information is revealed about offer stacks, then the game is played like a 'one shot' game when demand is low (and plant has a low probability of being called) and a repeated game when demand is high (and plant may get called for part of every day). If the full offer stack is revealed, then even when the low merit units are not being called, there can be a constant interchange of information, with gaming responses such as collusion and punishment.

10.5.7   Reaction curves

We have described above an informal approach to one aspect of interaction in the electricity markets – the day ahead offer to the pool. We must now look at approaches that can be applied more formally.

Consider a two producer market in which a particular participant is established as the 'leader', meaning that he makes his price or volume decisions first. Figure 10.52 shows the situation in which the market leader decides to maintain a particular market share[80] and prices to maintain that share. He is called a quantity leader. His plant is regarded by the other participants as 'must run'. The follower then compares the residual generation stack to the residual demand curve, determines the monopoly rent on the residual market, and arrives at the clearing price as shown in Figure 10.52.

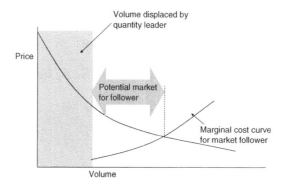

Figure 10.52   Optimisation potential of the output volume of the market follower once the market quantity leader has determined his output level

It is clear that the more that the leader sells, that the less it will be optimal for the follower to sell.

---

[80] Here the demand is depicted as inelastic and therefore a market share requirement is the same as a volume requirement.

For each level of output from the market leader there are two levels of output for the market follower which give the same surplus to the follower, and one optimum, the reaction curve, for the market follower. This is shown in Figure 10.53.

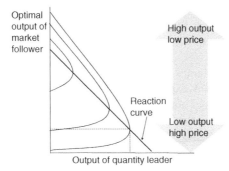

Figure 10.53 Isoprofit lines for the market follower and the reaction curve of the market follower to the market leader

The lines are isoprofit lines (i.e. profit is the same at any point on an isoprofit line). We can see that the higher profit lines are on the left since for any given level of output of the firm 2 (the follower) profit reduces as firm 1 (the leader) increases output since this depresses the clearing price.

10.5.8   Sequential quantity response – Stackelberg game

Continuing the above example, the offer behaviour of player 2 (follower) affects the surplus of player 1 (leader) since it affects the clearing price that both players receive. Player 1 will then respond.

So, in the knowledge of the reaction curve of firm 2, firm 1 will choose the output that touches its lowest isoprofit curve. We can see by inspection that lower isoprofit curves have higher profit since for any level of output of firm 1, profit decreases with increasing output of firm 2 due to the depressing effect on clearing price. We can represent this graphically as shown in Figure 10.54. This is known as the Stackelberg equilibrium.

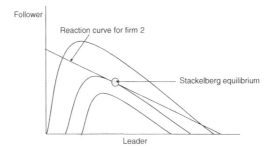

Figure 10.54 Isoprofit lines for the market leader, and the optimal volume for the market leader

We can apply the same approach to an n player game, in which case the reaction curves are considered in aggregate (e.g. for a three player game, firm 1 considers what firms 2 plus 3 will do in aggregate).

10.5.9 Simultaneous volume response – Cournot game

In a Cournot equilibrium, each firm maximises its output choice subject to the belief of output choice of the other firm. Once the choices are revealed, it is not optimal for either firm to alter its output choice.

Let us consider pairs of volumes for players 1 and 2 in relation to the point at which the reaction curves cross. If firm 1 expects firm 2 to produce volume g, then it will plan to produce volume h, but if firm 2 thinks firm 1 will produce volume h, then it will plan to produce volume i. We can see that the solution ends up at the reaction curve intersection. At the intersection, neither wishes to change their volume.

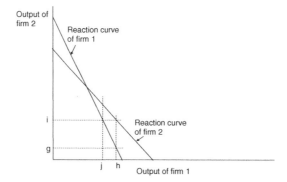

Figure 10.55   Cournot equilibrium

We can extend this to a three player market. Players 2 and 3 will have reaction curves to each other that depend on the expected output of 1. The family of Cournot equilibria for the combined volumes of 2 and 3 in relation to the expected output of 1 is the reaction curve of $2+3$ to 1. Similarly we can draw the reaction curve of 1 to $2+3$ and hence we can find the Cournot equilibrium. We can extend this to a many player market.

Since the Cournot is such an important game, it is worth looking at the mathematics for a simple case.[81]

Suppose that the industry has N firms who all have the same cost c. For a cleared demand volume q, the demand price p is denoted by D(q).

Each will optimise his output to maximise profit.

The profit of the i'th firm is the clearing price minus the cost price c, times the volume q_i.

$$\pi_i = p^* q_i - c^* q_i = (D(q) - c) q_i$$

The optimal volume output is found by:

$$\frac{\partial \pi_i}{\partial q_i} = \frac{\partial D(q)}{\partial q_i} q_i + D(q) - c = 0$$

---

[81] This representation is from Binmore (1992).

The firms are identical. Each firm assumes that each other firm will produce $\frac{q}{N}$, and that knowing this, it is not optimal to produce more, or less.

Now let us take the special case for constant price elasticity of demand, we have:

$$p = D(q) = k^* q^* \exp(-\varepsilon)$$

So we have:

$$\frac{p}{c} = (1 - \frac{\varepsilon}{N})^{-1}$$

This gives us the price/cost ratio for a monopolist ($N = 1$), and for a perfectly competitive market ($N \to \infty$), then $p \to c$, i.e. the price tends to the marginal cost.

10.5.10   Comparison of Stackelberg and Cournot outcomes

The maximum surplus that can be derived for the producer sector is that derived if it were a monopoly, and hence running at the levels indicated by monopoly and sharing the monopoly rent is optimal in aggregate. The Cournot and the Stackelberg outcomes both give producers less surplus than they would have from sharing the monopoly rent and more than they would have if they had to offer their units in competition to each other. Neither optimises the resource allocation between them (i.e. units run out of merit).

The volume comparison can be shown graphically:

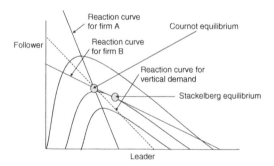

Figure 10.56   Comparison of the Cournot and Stackelberg equilibrium

10.5.11   Price leadership – Bertrand game

Instead of deciding on volume output and letting the market determine the price, the price leader could decide on a price offering and let the market determine the volume. Whereas in quantity leadership, the follower can influence the price by adjusting volume, in price leadership he cannot. If he prices above the price leader then (provided that the product has no differentiation), he will not sell any product. If he prices below, then he will simply earn less. Therefore the optimal strategy for the follower is to sell all the volume that he can produce at less than the clearing price.

In pool markets, difficulty in understanding and auditing unit costs drives participants to communicate through market share, which is much easier to identify. This means that volume games are more relevant.

10.5.12   Gaming and payoff matrices

When considering offer strategies, the payoff matrix is a convenient method of identifying the outcomes associated with offers of the participants. We begin by looking at dominant strategies.

10.5.12.1   Dominant strategies

Consider the situation in which the system has an inelastic demand of 10 GW and there are two producers. Producer A has nine 1 GW units of very low marginal cost (nominally zero in this example) and one unit of high marginal cost (0.5/MWh). Producer B has one unit identical to the high marginal cost unit of producer A. They both offer simultaneously in to the pool. Let us suppose that the system operator accepts offers of prices of 0, 0.8 or 1 and shares load equally between equal offers. Suppose that the nine low marginal cost units offer at 0. For the marginal unit the producers can therefore offer at 0.8 or 1. In this example, we assume that the market demand is very slightly higher than 10 GW $(10 + \delta\,GW)$ and hence clears at the offer price of the unit that runs at $\delta\,GW$. For convenience, this volume is not shown in the table.

We can summarise the payoffs as follows:

Game 1

	B offer at 0.8	B offer at 1
A offer at 0.8	A sells 9.5 B sells 0.5 Price = 0.8 A payoff = 9.5*0.8 − 0.5*0.5 = 7.35 B payoff = 0.5*0.8 − 0.5*0.5 = 0.15	A sells 10 B sells 0 Price = 1 A payoff = 10*1−1*0.5 = 9.5 B payoff = 0
A offer at 1	A sells 9 B sells 1 Price = 1 A payoff = 9*1 = 9 B payoff = 1*1−1*0.5 = 0.5	A sells 9.5 B sells 0.5 Price = 1 A payoff = 9.5*1− 0.5*0.5 = 9.25 B payoff = 0.5*1− 0.5*0.5 = 0.25

We can summarise the payoffs as follows, with the payoff of A preceding that of B in each box.

Game 1 payoff summary

A B	B Offer at 0.8	B Offer at 1
A Offer at 0.8	7.35, 0.15	9.5, 0
A Offer at 1	9, 0.5	9.25, 0.25

We note that regardless of what B thinks that A will offer at, he should offer at 0.8, since 0.15 is better than 0 and 0.5 is better than 0.25. This is then a dominant strategy for B.

The offer for A depends on the offer of B. If A thinks that B will offer at 0.8, then A should offer at 1, and if A thinks that B will offer at 1, then A should offer at 0.8. However since B has a dominant strategy, then A is destined to offer at 1. The outcome is therefore 9 for A and 0.5 for B.

This situation is similar to one in which there is a dominant incumbent generator, and a new entrant Independent Power Producer. The incumbent has more to lose in a price war and therefore accommodates the new entrant with a market share greater than it would enjoy if its unit were part of the incumbent fleet. The only reason to cede volume at the margin is to protect the price for the high merit/low marginal cost plant.

10.5.13 Nash equilibria

It is not always the case that there is a dominant strategy. However it may not be necessary for equilibrium for the choice of A to be optimal for *all* choices of B, but only optimal for the *optimal* choice of B. If A chooses a strategy that is a Nash equilibrium, then he will not regret his choice when B reveals his choice, provided that B also chose a Nash equilibrium.

Suppose in the above example, the offer choices are 1 and 0.6, rather than 1 and 0.8. This time the demand is very slightly less than 10 GW. Our payoff matrix is then:

Game 2 payoff summary

A B	B Offer at 0.6	B Offer at 1
A Offer at 0.6	5.45, 0.05	5.5, 0
A Offer at 1	5.4, 0.1	9.25, 0.25

Now:

If A thinks B will offer at 0.6, A will offer at 0.6

If A thinks B will offer at 1, A will offer at 1

If B thinks A will offer at 0.6, B will offer at 0.6

If B thinks A will offer at 1, B will offer at 1

It is never optimal for A and B to offer at 0.6, 1 or 1, 0.6 respectively, and there are two viable equilibria: 0.6, 0.6 and 1, 1. These are called Nash equilibria, after Nash who invented them in around 1950.

We are particularly interested in games of similar players. Consider two producers with two units each, all of which have cost = 1. Acceptable offers are 1.5 and 2.5. Demand is slightly less than two units.

Our outcomes can be depicted as follows:

Game 3 Volume output

A B	B Offer at 1.5	B Offer at 2.5
A Offer at 1.5	1, 1	2, 0
A Offer at 2.5	0, 2	1, 1

Game 3 Price result

A B	B Offer at 1.5	B Offer at 2.5
A Offer at 1.5	1.5	1.5
A Offer at 2.5	1.5	2.5

Game 3 Net payoff result

A B	B Offer at 1.5	B Offer at 2.5
A Offer at 1.5	$1.5 - 1 = 0.5, 1.5 - 1 = 0.5$	$(2^*1.5) - (2^*1) = 1, 0$
A Offer at 2.5	$0, (2^*1.5) - (2^*1) = 1$	$2.5 - 1 = 1.5, 2.5 - 1 = 1.5$

Game 3 Net payoff summary

A B	B Offer at 1.5	B Offer at 2.5
A Offer at 1.5	0.5, 0.5	1,0
A Offer at 2.5	0, 1	1.5, 1.5

The Nash equilibrium is the same as before. Any equilibrium for which either participant does not cover fixed costs may be a Nash equilibrium for a one shot game, but is not an economic equilibrium and cannot necessarily be a viable equilibrium for a repeated game. Suppose, for example, the fixed costs are 0.75, then an offer strategy for A and B of (1,1) is not a sustainable offer strategy.

We can represent the payoff diagram graphically:

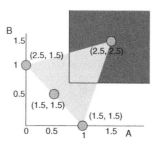

Figure 10.57 Payoff diagram for game 3 (see text). The dark grey area shows the feasible area in equilibrium

We will see later that when we consider repeated games that the higher priced state with offers for A and B of (2, 2) can be stable provided that there is a focal point – i.e. there is an obvious number to offer at.

In reality of course, participants can offer at a whole range of prices. Consider the situations in which participants might offer slightly above 1.5 by an amount x, or below by an amount y.

Whilst $(0.5 - y, 0.5 - y)$ is only marginally less than $(0.5, 0.5)$ for small y, it is far less risky for each player, since if each offers at $1.5 - y$, then the worst case outcome is $0.5 - y$,

Game 4 payoffs

A B	B Offer at $1.5 - y$	B Offer at 1.5
A Offer at $1.5 - y$	$1.5 - y - 1 = 0.5 - y, 1.5 - y - 1 = 0.5 - y$	$(2^*(1.5 - y)) - (2^*1) = 1 - 2y, 0$
A Offer at 1.5	$0, (2^*(1.5 - y)) - (2^*1) = 1 - 2y$	$1.5 - 1 = 0.5, 1.5 - 1 = 0.5$

Game 4 payoff summary

A B	B Offer at $1.5 - y$	B Offer at 1.5
A Offer at $1.5 - y$	$0.5 - y, 0.5 - y$	$1 - 2y, 0$
A Offer at 1.5	$0, 1 - 2y$	$0.5, 0.5$

whereas if they offer at 1.5, then the worst case is 0. $(1.5 - y, 1.5 - y)$ may be the 'risk dominant' strategy.[82]

We can draw this on a diagram. For ease of illustration, y is chosen to be near zero.

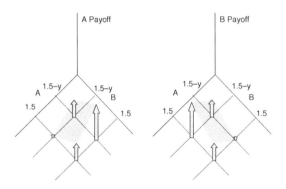

Figure 10.58   Payoffs for A and B in game 3

10.5.13.1   Strategy in the presence of risk aversion

If A and B are risk averse, then they may wish to choose the strategy which has the highest minimum payoff (called the minimax). We can see from the figure, that in this case the only Nash equilibrium is $(1.5 - y, 1.5 - y)$. So we see that with risk aversion undercutting price is the only equilibrium, and maintaining price is not one.

It appears then that we might spiral down to marginal cost offering on both sides. However, consider the situation at marginal costs.

Game 5 payoffs

A B	B Offer at 1	B Offer at $1 + x$
A Offer at 1	$1 - 1 = 0, 1 - 1 = 0$	$(2^*1) - (2^*1) = 0, 0$
A Offer at $1 + x$	$0, (2^*1) - (2^*1) = 0$	$1 + x - 1 = x, 1 + x - 1 = x,$

[82] See Harsanyi and Selten for a formal examination of risk in game theory.

Game 5 payoff summary

A	B	B Offer at 1	B Offer at $1 + x$
A Offer at 1		0, 0	0, 0
A Offer at $1 + x$		0, 0	x, x

Here, in the situation of a limited range of offers, both players have a dominant strategy of offering at the higher price.

In games 2 to 5 we have to this point assumed that the market demand is slightly less than two units and therefore if one player offers low and the other high, then the market will clear at the lower price. In game 1 we considered a demand slightly above ten units and so the market will clear at the high price. Consider game 3, and assume that the demand is $2 + 2v$, where v is a small volume. We now have;

Game 6 Payoffs

A B	B Offer at 1.5	B Offer at 2.5
A Offer at 1.5	$(1.5 - 1)^*(1 + v),$ $(1.5 - 1)^*(1 + v) = 0.5^*(1 + v),$ $0.5^*(1 + v)$	$((2^*2.5) - (2^*1))^*(1 + v),$ $0 = 3^*(1 + v), 0$
A Offer at 2.5	$0, ((2^*2.5) - (2^*1))^*(1 + v) =$ $3^*(1 + v)$	$(2.5 - 1)^*(1 + v), (2.5 - 1)^*$ $(1 + v)$

For very small v, this gives us:

Game 6 payoff summary

A	B	B Offer at 1.5	B Offer at 2.5
A Offer at 1.5		0.5, 0.5	3, 0
A Offer at 2.5		0, 3	1.5, 1.5

Now both have a dominant strategy to offer at 1.5, since 3 is better than 1.5, and 0.5 is better than 0.

10.5.14   Repeated games and cooperative games

Whilst there are one shot games, such as the application of windfall taxes, or the building of new plant, the majority of the games are repeated games, or 'supergames'. We have seen that repeated games can occur through communication (reward and punishment) or simply in response to the impact of current game price status on expected annual profits.

The most important case of repeated games in the context of the ESI is the pool, since plant can only be dispatched by offering into the pool. While theory initially suggests that the bilateral market would be identical, because participants should ignore hedge position when trading in the day ahead market, this is not the case, because: (i) hedge position does in practice affect day ahead behaviour, (ii) the 'tâtonnement' process of repeated bids and offers cannot occur quickly enough to efficiently clear in the day ahead market and (iii) communication is only at the margin whereas in the pool a whole offer stack can be seen.

We have seen that in the presence of risk aversion, that a two player game is under constant pressure to drive costs down to marginal costs. In the repeated game, the most stable strategy that sustains equilibrium is the 'tit for tat' game in which the first offer is high, and then each participants follows the other by offering at high or low prices. Although in 'laboratory' circumstances, the tit for tat strategy with no modification is optimal, in practice the level of offer complication of a whole offer stack (with a stack that changes due to unit failure), in the presence of stochastic demand and no simple focal point, requires participant to frequently re-start the game with a high offer, rather than pursue retaliation indefinitely.

In the presence of variable costs and prices, it is difficult to agree on focal points to offer on. In the case of the pool, the regulatory envelope shown in Figure 4.9 can act as a focal path (each of which must be simultaneously found). Extra information such as own and competitors' cost structure, unit failures, and last year's volumes and prices can enable participants to find the focal path.

The situation with three participants becomes more complicated because bilateral communication is not possible without the evolution of a reasonably sophisticated language using the whole offer stack. The pressure for the market to clear at marginal cost is high. Without either explicit collaboration, or very clear focal points, the pool market becomes untenable if the unit stacks are such that fixed costs cannot be recovered. Such a unit stack might be for example one with very similar units, all of which have low marginal and high fixed costs, such as brown coal units.

10.5.15 New entrance – pre-emption and optionality

In Chapter 11 we see the real option value in delaying commitment to run. The same applies to delay to spend on capability in order to respond to market conditions. The assumption here is that decisions made by one firm do not affect prices or competitor behaviour. We must now examine the degree to which decisions made by a firm do affect competitors, and we will see how pre-emptive decisions are commonly advantageous to the firm.

In the discussion of Stackelberg equilibrium, we saw that if one participant pre-empts the market and claims a market share, then the follower, even if he has the potential to build and run plant with identical cost structure, makes less money because he has to accept a smaller share.

The question of course is whether the market follower can affect the situation. Suppose for example, that participant A (nominally the leader) has merely declared an intention to produce a particular volume but has not actually committed to the capacity investment. It would make sense then for participant B to irrevocably commit to capacity investment and inform A of this fact. A then becomes *de facto* the market follower, since it is too late to deter B from investment.

The key here, in stark contrast to the Real Option method of management, is that B achieves dominance and increases his surplus by reducing[83] his choices and ensuring that his competitors know this.

We saw something similar in game 1. If one player has a dominant strategy, then the other player has to accept the situation.

Real options are most applicable when the participant has little market power or influence, and in situations where market risks are high due to strong exogenous forces.

---

[83] Actually reducing his apparent choices. He may secretly keep options open, and competitors will expect him to do this.

Pre-emption is most applicable when the participant has a substantial market influence, and in situations where demand volumes are relatively deterministic and inelastic. Recent work has developed the relationship between these two areas.[84]

10.5.15.1 New entrance

Consider two potential new entrants, both of whom have no other plant, and both with plant designed for baseload operation. One has a plant design with low fixed costs and high marginal costs, and the other has high fixed costs and low marginal costs. For most cost structures, the dominant strategy for the low marginal cost producer is to undercut the high marginal cost producer. This encourages the build of new plant, that normally has low marginal costs and high fixed costs, but discourages the build of baseload plant design with low fixed costs and high marginal costs, even if the through life costs are less than those with lower marginal costs.

As a general rule, new plant has high fixed costs (due to repayment of capital and also due to the common accounting treatment of depreciation) and low marginal costs (being more efficient than old plant), and even if the total cost is higher, it has a dominant strategy to run ahead of old plant. We also saw in game 1 that a large player will cede load to a small player in order to maintain price.

It is clear then that new entrant plant has a merit order advantage, even if total costs are the same as existing plant. This is further increased if it is owned by an independent power producer rather than a large incumbent.

Build can increase and increase, forcing incumbent baseload plant to lower load factors, until the forward baseload price is less than the total cost of the new entrant. Note that it is quite possible for the forward price to fall below new entrant costs since an aggressive producer can build, not sell forward initially, and gradually sell as the forward price drifts up. The cost of risk drift is shown in equation 9.12.

10.5.16 Gaming by institutions

Institutions such as government bodies and the regulator are in a difficult position. They are in a position at any time to adjust rules, taxes or prices to move surplus from the producer to consumer sector, but there is an implied commitment to fairness to the producer sector in allowing it to recover fixed costs, and an ongoing requirement to encourage investment in production by providing commitment and precedent.

10.5.16.1 Gaming by the regulator

Investors in the ESI do so in anticipation of returns that equal or exceed the risk adjusted cost of capital. If the same information is available to all investors, then competition will drive the stock price to the level at which the alpha to zero, so the stock exactly earns the 'fair' market rate. Since the regulator can implicitly or explicitly control prices, and in the short term is more aligned to consumers than producers, there is the moral hazard that the regulator can cause prices to be lower than might have reasonably been expected. The regulatory uncertainty adds to the cost of capital, and thereby the energy price. If the regulatory risk is not realised (regulation is as expected) then the *ex post* surplus is delivered to ESI investors.

---

[84] See, for example, Sparla (2001).

Therefore regulatory uncertainty is bad for consumers. While uncertainty can be reduced by fixed term price controls, these are short relative to investment timeframes. If the regulatory price regime lasts five years, then for an investment decision that has a random phase relative to the regulatory cycle, then it only lasts for two and a half years. This has no effect on the return on any investment that does not yield returns within that period.

However, the regulator has to make many judgements, and so there is effectively a repeated game, and in this game, investors will adjust their bid price for stock to reflect the regulatory risk.

10.5.16.2   Gaming by government

The government situation is similar to that of the regulator, but applies more in laws and taxes than in price regulation. The government can adjust ESI profits by application of specific taxes and subsidies, such as environmental taxes (that do not necessarily reflect environmental cost), and windfall taxes.

10.5.16.3   Gaming by the single buyer

The single buyer can save energy purchase costs by clearing the market in stages. He can intentionally underestimate demand and pay one set of generators the clearing price, and then increase the demand estimate and call on the other generators. Depending on the market structure, this could be a second tranche at a second clearing price, or paying the plant its offer price (pay as bid). The saving is shown in Figure 10.59.

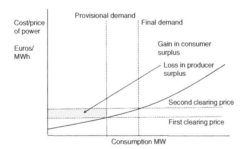

Figure 10.59   System operator saving cost by clearing the market in two stages

In common with other games by the government and regulator, the behaviour for a one-shot game will be quite different to that of a repeated game. If the system operator does clear the market in stages, then generators will respond by adjusting their offer prices in the first or second stage.

10.5.17   Auctions

Electricity contracting is often described in the form of auctions. The most important is the clearing price. This is like an auction in which all offerors who offer (sealed or unsealed[85])

---

[85] A good example of a clearing market with a specific auction with open bids, run by an auctioneer, is the gold fix, in which the gold fixing members submit bids and offers on behalf of their clients. Until 1998 the silver fix used closed bids.

above the clearing price, which is known *ex ante*, sell at the clearing price, which is the price of the highest accepted offer. We saw in Figure 10.49 that in a market in which participants know one anothers' offers, that the market in fact can clear at the price of the lowest offer not accepted rather than at the price of the highest accepted offer.

The balancing mechanism in Great Britain uses a sealed bid pay as bid auction. In this auction, generators submit irrevocable sealed offers. Then all offers below a particular level are accepted, and each participant receives what they offer. This is described in section 5.6.3.

Other auction types are possible. For example, a balancing mechanism could operate by acceptance of all offers below a particular level, followed by sale of electricity by accepted participants at the price at the next higher offer.[86] This encourages generators to offer at lower prices.

Policy makers and regulators design auctions that are most effective in making participants bid at the level of their indifference curves. Note that in the case of balancing, this is impossible.

10.5.18   Focal points

Focal points represent points that participants are attracted to for no other reason than that they are easy to find. The figure below shows the example of a map which is given to two participants who cannot communicate but are asked to meet at a particular point on the map.

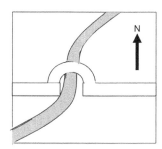

Figure 10.60   Example of a focal point on a map

Focal points are important in pool offering. As we saw, it is difficult for players to play a cooperative game unless they can find a focal point.

10.5.19   Supply function equilibria

We have established five key features in electricity pricing, namely: (i) marginal cost stacks of the generators, (ii) the demand function and demand management (iii) gaming and behaviour, (iv) the need to recover fixed costs and (v) stochastic variations. We have dealt with the cost stacks in detail, and treated demand as essentially inelastic, with demand management and lost load being treated as virtual generation. We have also described the generator offer stacks both in terms of the (constant) equilibrium offer stacks that ensure the

---

[86] This is the principle of the Vickrey auction, popularised by the internet auction site EBay (although in EBay, the winner takes all).

recovery of fixed costs and the approach of using options and insurance to deal with fixed costs and uncertainty. Finally we have considered mutual influences of prices and volumes (i.e. gaming).

At this point, while we have introduced the concepts of gaming, reaction curves, and residual demand, we have not made a firm connection between generator offer stacks, and the demand function of the day, and therefore have not attended to simulations of real market behaviour in the short term market. The Supply Function Equilibrium (SFE) approach endeavours to do this.

Suppose that our microeconomic universe (demand function, producer cost structure, participant behaviour) is such that for the participants' cost structures and the demand function at any halfhour, that there is a single clearing price/volume equilibrium. For all participant units not offering close to the clearing price, then it makes little difference exactly what the offer price is, since it is not operating at the margin. Therefore, for any participant for any halfhour, there is a potentially infinite set of offer stacks, provided that they are the same at and near the margin. For a particular gaming behaviour, according to which the clearing price is determined, this is shown in Figure 10.61.

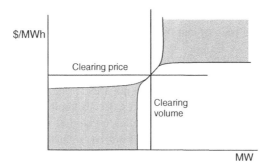

Figure 10.61   The range (in grey) of supply function equilibria for a firm in a symmetrical two firm setting in which there is a single solution for clearing price/volume

Now suppose that we do one (or both) of two things. In the first, we require a single offer stack for the generator to apply for the whole day, rather than allowing 48 different stacks. In the second, we allow demand uncertainty by applying a one dimensional shock (the simplest being a simple movement to the left or right) to the demand function. Note that the offer stacks must be submitted before the volume (i.e. demand function) uncertainty is resolved. Now the marginal unit changes, and hence the offer of each unit that has either an uncertain or a varying run schedule becomes important. The range of equilibrium solutions is now much narrowed.

This application of uncertainty in this regard was examined by Klemperer and Meyer. They took the firm's profit function of clearing price minus average marginal cost times volume output by the firm, and differentiated this with respect to price to arrive at a differential equation that the supply function must observe to be optimal for the firm. For symmetrical firms (i.e. with the same cost functions and exhibiting the same behaviour), this greatly limited the range of supply function equilibria. Figure 10.62 shows the extremes of the SFE for two symmetric firms, with the Bertrand equilibrium intersecting the 'half-demand' (equally sharing the demand) function (with no uncertainty) with a horizontal slope, and the Cournot equilibrium intersecting it with a vertical slope.

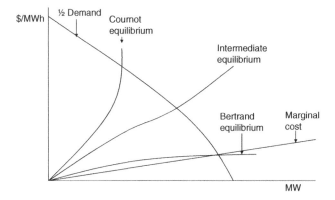

Figure 10.62 Supply function equilibria, showing a general intermediate function for uncertain demand, and the Cournot and Bertrand for a known demand function.

SFE's for electricity have been or can be developed to incorporate a number of features:

(i) **Price caps** – The existence of price caps does not change the differential equation, but the demand function price is capped and strategic behaviour is altered since above a certain level of demand, the volume does not affect price. The strategic offer behaviour is dependent on the offer acceptance rules (for example, if all generation offers are dispatched at the same pro rata level of offered volume).

(ii) **Capacity limits** – In practice, each generator has a capacity limit, and therefore lost load is a possibility. Capacity limits and price limits are closely connected because capacity limits create market power and because price limits affect generation volume maintained.

(iii) **The effect of contracts** – We have noted in several places in this book that where there is market influence, that contract position affects the optimal offer stack. The contract profit and loss can be easily added into the profit function of the firm, which is again differentiated with respect to price to derive the SFE. In doing this we see that the greater the contract position, the lower the SFE and hence the lower the clearing price. It should be noted that hedge volume affects forward price in a similar way to offer volume affecting spot price.

(iv) **Non symmetric** – Non symmetric behaviour by firms is not easily handled by the SFE approach, since there can be a potentially large number of SFE pairs (for a two player market). However, we saw in game 1 in section 10.5.12.1 that we need to model asymmetric behaviour at the margin.

(v) **Greater range of demand functions** – The demand function shown in the graph[87] is concave (downward curving). Whilst this is a reasonable representation of the short term electricity demand function in the high price region, we may need to relax the restriction of concavity.

---

[87] This is the form used in Klemperer and Meyer (1989). The assumption is relaxed in Anderson and Xu (2005).

(vi) **Non simultaneous reaction curves** – The main way to assess a competitors behaviour in advance is to analyse past behaviour. So, for example, participant A may assume that participant B will submit the same stack today that he did yesterday, and hence A submits a stack that is optimal with respect to this. B does the same. It is clear that A and B are always one or more steps behind in their assessments. This can mean that the stacks cycle[88] over time rather than settling on a stable equilibrium.

(vii) **Long term equilibria** – The SFE approach generally ignores fixed costs, and fixed cost recovery in this context has been little studied. We noted in section 10.1.21 that it is essential to include fixed costs when considering the deadweight loss from inefficient pricing. Whilst it is hard to incorporate fixed costs into the SFE approach, we can examine solutions or simulations with respect to each unit (i.e. not just each firm but each unit within the firm) to test for fixed cost recovery. If fixed costs are not recovered, the solution is not feasible in the long term and some pricing adjustment must be made.

(viii) **More sophisticated shocks to the demand function** – The SFE approach generally considers a simple shock/error term to the demand function, moving it to the left or right. In practice of course, the shocks are more complicated than this. We expect height and slope of the demand function to change. For any one dimensional shock, then we can construct an SFE, but we cannot do so for higher dimensional shocks.

10.6 ENVIRONMENTAL ECONOMICS

Environmental impact is an externality of high importance, and indeed environmental considerations are currently the most dominant force in the ESI. The problem is that the neoclassical model does not cater well for externalities, environmental externalities are very difficult to consistently internalise in a global economy, the uncertainties relating to environmental impact and impact tolerance are very high, and there is a high degree of controversy with respect to the politics, economics, ethics, science and practicalities relating to the methods of reducing impact.

Here we focus on the key features, which are valuation, environmental taxation, property rights and harmonisation.

10.6.1 Valuation

We described in section 8.1 the enormous uncertainty with respect to assessment of environmental impact, and in section 10.1.11 the difficulty associated with subjective monetisation of preference. Such is the uncertainty that it is commonly stated that conversion of preference or even remediation cost to a monetary measure is either so inaccurate or so inefficient in terms of welfare that it is actively misleading to use the results. The literature on this subject is vast, and no attempt is made here to adjudicate. We can make some general points, and demonstrate the core methods, should we choose to use monetary valuation.

According to the environmental Kuznets curve, *per capita* pollution increases up to a (low for developed countries) level and then decreases. We can rationalise this in terms of decreasing marginal utility of goods and increasing marginal disutility of pollution with increasing wealth. We can also rationalise it in terms of increasing efficiency and decreasing cost of

---

[88] See Day and Bunn (2001) for further discussion on this.

environmental impact abatement through increasing experience borne of the necessity of working with tighter and tighter regulations.

Figure 10.63   Shapes of utility functions that lead to a rise and then fall in per capita pollution as economies develop – the environmental Kuznets curve

10.6.2   Environmental taxes

10.6.2.1   Pigou tax

Environmental taxes are often called Pigou taxes after Pigou,[89] who was one of the key early influences in welfare economics. The Pigou tax is charged on a per unit basis.

By charging a tax, environmental impact ceases to be an externality. As with all taxes that affect production levels at the margin, environmental taxes cause a deadweight loss in terms of surplus ignoring the externality. This is shown in Figure 10.64. Here we assume: (i) that environment taxes are the same as environmental damage costs at the margin and (ii) assuming linearity of environmental costs in relation to environmental output and linearity of environmental damage costs in relation to plant output.

The tax raised is represented by rectangular area B. The deadweight loss from reduced volume is represented by the triangular area A. The saved externality cost is represented by the rectangular area C.

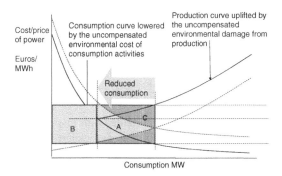

Figure 10.64   The effect of applying environmental tax to producers and consumers according to the damage done in the act of producing and consuming electricity

The lost consumer surplus is shown as the difference in shaded areas in Figure 10.65.

The tax raised compensates for the damage, but there are distribution issues since it is difficult to allocate the tax spend on services precisely in line with receipt of pollution, and

---

[89] Pigou 1877 to 1959. His original work specified tax as a compensation for farmers whose land was damaged by a neighbour's rabbits. See Pigou (1932).

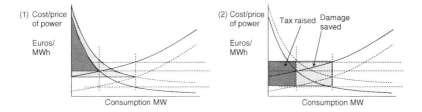

Figure 10.65   Loss of consumer surplus from taxation

the tax cannot efficiently be refunded in cash per unit of consumption for reasons described in section 10.1.16.

10.6.2.2   Tax harmonisation and pollution havens

Suppose that we tax electricity per MWh produced at the point of production in country A and at the point of consumption in country B. Then producers in B will wish to sell to consumers in A, since country A has higher electricity prices. We can see that even if both countries apply environmental taxes, that the regimes are incompatible and trade is inefficient. However it is by no means easy to adjust the fiscal structure of the economy to suit environmental taxation.

Suppose now that pollution has transboundary impact but that country C applies no tax at all. We saw in section 10.1.22.5 that we can treat environmental assimilative capability and local tolerance as a virtual resource, so effectively country C has lower factor costs. Country C will then wish to export to country A, and will be indifferent with respect to imports from and exports to country B.

Country C is said to be a pollution haven with respect to country A. The pollution haven theory states that dirty industries will move from developed countries with tight environmental regulation to less developed countries with laxer environmental regulation, and that clean industries will move in the opposite direction. There is some anecdotal evidence for this, but there are several reasons for the reverse to be true.[90]

10.6.2.3   Inefficiency effects from environmental taxation

At this point, we have assumed that all producers produce the same amount of environmental damage per MWh of production. This is not the case in practice. Let us first consider as above, the case in which all producers produce the same damage per MWh. In this case we assume inelastic demand for convenience.

Supposing that every MWh of generation creates exactly the same environmental damage, and that tax is charged to generators per MWh produced. The elevation of the production curve is shown below. We have here assumed inelastic demand in the short term. The tax is an increase to marginal rather than fixed costs and hence the producers uplift their prices by the tax amount, and the tax increase is passed straight through to consumers. They pay higher prices. However, the tax raised goes to the government, which finds its way back to consumers in the end.

---

[90] See Copeland and Scott Taylor (2003).

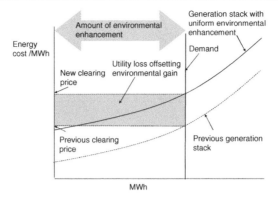

Figure 10.66   Taxation and surplus for uniform environmental impact production and tax per MWh production

Now let us assume that only the low merit sector causes damage. Our situation is now as shown in Figure 10.67. In the limit, at which the level of demand is such that the amount of low merit production is near zero, then the only result is an elevation of the clearing price, with a corresponding detriment to aggregate consumer surplus.

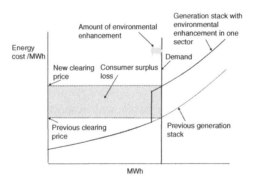

Figure 10.67   Taxation and surplus when only the low merit sector produces environmental impact and is taxed

The situation is slightly more complicated for high merit plant. First consider the stack in terms of through life (i.e. fixed plus marginal) rather than fixed costs. If the plant is making a surplus, and the tax cost elevation is not sufficient to bring the plant out of merit, then there is no consumer change and simply a loss to consumer surplus. This is shown in Figure 10.68, prior to re-ordering the stack.

However, if we represent the stack as a marginal cost stack and assume that all plant is at through life equilibrium (marginal surplus equals fixed cost for all plant), then the plant will automatically become out of merit. An example of high merit plant that would be affected is nuclear plant.

It is apparent from this analysis that it is extremely difficult to tax efficiently, and that an inefficient tax that is rapidly applied can have a significant shock effect. We should also note that a shock in shadow prices due to a rapidly applied environmental constraint has a similar effect, although of course raises no tax.

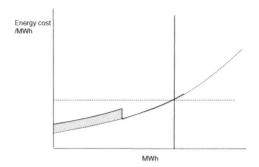

Figure 10.68   Taxation and surplus when only the high merit sector produces environmental impact and is taxed. Figure shows stack before merit re-ordering

10.6.3   Property rights

Consider a simple case in which there are two participants.[91] One who wishes to produce a commodity but who cannot do so without polluting, and one who is the recipient of the pollution but not of the commodity. There are two alternatives for property rights:

(i)   The producer may have the right to pollute.
(ii) The recipient may have a right not to receive pollution, and therefore have a *de facto* right to prevent production.

We can depict these on the Edgeworth box that we described in section 10.1.11.1. Applying this method to environmental impact abatement shows that regardless of the property right (e.g. initial endowment of permits), the level of pollution will be the same. The pollution level is shown in Figure 10.69.[92]

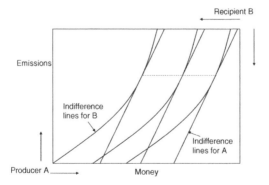

Figure 10.69   Edgeworth box for producer and recipient of pollution

The Pareto optimisation by trading actions for both extremes of property right endowment is shown in Figure 10.70.

---

[91] Assume all pollution goes to recipient.
[92] We have a made a number of assumptions for the purpose of illustration including quasilinear (parallel) preference lines, constant returns to scale, and convex emission/money preference curve.

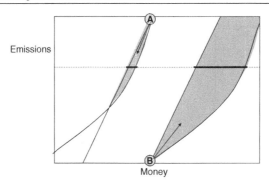

Figure 10.70 Pareto optimisation of pollution from initial endowments at both extremes (all to producer A or all to recipient B)

This theory is associated with the work of Coase and is often called the Coase theory.

We can apply the same argument to the purchaser of the good.

Consider the situation in which the production of electricity, to be sold by Producer 1 to Consumer 2, incidentally impacts Non Consumer 3, in the form of pollution.

The theory states that provided that the property rights are well defined, then it does not matter whether 1 or 2 compensates 3.

Suppose that electricity costs \$C/MWh for all amounts, that the willingness to pay is \$P/MWh, and that the cost of pollution to 3 for all amounts is \$E/MWh.

If there are no property rights, then 1 can sell electricity to 2 without any requirement to compensate 3. If however 3 has well defined property rights, then he can halt production until he has forged an agreement to be compensated. Suppose that the economics of production are just satisfied, then:

If 1 pays 3 \$E/MWh, then 1 will offer at \$(C + E)/MWh $(C + E = P)$

If 2 pays 3 \$E/MWh then 2 will bid at \$(P − E)/MWh $(C = P − E)$

Suppose now that 1 can decrease environmental impact at cost F, and that 2 can pay a contractor for an end of pipe capture at cost G. If F and G are greater than C, then it is optimal to pollute and compensate. If, for example, F < C, then the economy has a surplus. However this could be captured by any one of 1, 2 or 3.

We note also, that if cost C is applied as a shock (a tax or shadow price) then 1 or 2 or both make a shock loss and 3 makes a shock relative gain. Over time, electricity prices adjust to pass the cost into the consumer sector.

10.6.3.1 Problems with compensation for pollution

We have already introduced some efficiency problems, including:

(i)   inefficient impact on consumer surplus resulting from wholesale price effects (see section 10.6.2.3);
(ii) deadweight loss of taxes (see section 10.4.1.1);
(iii) uncertainty of valuation, and gaming with consumers.

Here we look at inefficient consumer allocation, and the impact on behaviour.

Suppose that the tax benefit to consumers does not appear through the fiscal system in a manner that is unconnected to consumption but instead is awarded per unit of consumption. This increases their willingness to pay.

Our situation is then this:

(i)   Producer is taxed $ T/MWh.
(ii) Producer raises price to consumers by $ T/MWh.
(iii) Consumers are awarded $ T/MWh.

If the system works efficiently, then there is no net effect. If the system works inefficiently, then there are windfalls and deficits to different producers and consumers.

Consider a simplified example in which there is a pollution source with damage that reduces with distance. First assume that all recipients are compensated at the same rate, and this is set such that no recipient is worse off as a result of pollution. This is shown in Figure 10.71. We can see that the aggregate tax exceeds the aggregate damage. If property rights are set such that anyone moving into the pollution area can receive compensation, then migration will increase the problem.

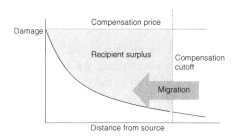

Figure 10.71   The economic problems of compensation of affected parties

This argument applies for all levels of pollution compensation level above the level of the least affected person within the zone, only this time some recipients are made worse off by pollution.

Baumol shows that it is not economically efficient to compensate the recipients of pollution, since this reduces their motivation to avoid or mitigate it. Suppose that the cost of the pollution is PP and the person has access to an end of pipe solution costing C, then if C < PP, he will engage the solution. If however, the person is compensated by PC, then the end of pipe solution will only be engaged if C < PP − PC. Meanwhile the producer costs have risen by PC.

10.7   MARKET FAILURE

Markets can fail for all kinds of reasons. The following list is presented by Hawken *et al.* to illustrate the unfeasible 'fantasy' of a completely free market: They represent challenges that must be faced.

(i)   All participants have perfect information about the future.
(ii) There is perfect competition.

(iii)   Prices are absolutely accurate and up-to-date.

(iv)   Price signals completely reflect every cost to society: There are no externalities.

(v)   There is no monopoly.

(vi)   There is no monopsony.

(vii)   No individual transaction can move the market, affecting wider price patterns.

(viii) No resource in unemployed or underemployed.

(ix)   There's absolutely nothing that can't readily be bought and sold.

(x)   Any deal can be done without friction.

(xi)   All deals are instantaneous.

(xii)   No subsidies or other distortions exist.

(xiii) No barriers to market entry or exit exist.

(xiv)   There is no regulation.

(xv)   There is no taxation (or, if there is, it does not distort resource allocations in any way).

(xvi)   All investments are completely divisible and fungible – they can be traded and exchanged in sufficiently uniform and standardised chunks.

(xvii) At the appropriate risk-adjusted interest rate, unlimited capital is available to everyone.

(xviii) Everyone is motivated solely by maximising personal 'utility', often measured by wealth or income.

There are other failings, particularly in relation to risk and uncertainty. The free market defence is that, for most or possibly all of these, the free market can contend with them without too much inefficiency. Alternatively free marketers say that the world has to go round somehow and the free market is the least worst economic solution. The big questions are which of these or other problems are real 'showstoppers' that undermine the fundamental operation of the free market, either in its entirety or in a specific instance.

Perhaps the two greatest issues to attend to with respect to solving market failure are: (i) environmental valuation, and regulatory methods of causing optimal response and (ii) optimisation in the face of risk and uncertainty.[93]

10.8 SHOCKS

Consider the situation in which there is a sudden (shock) increase in demand. This can result in the demand function suddenly moving right, up, or both. For convenience, we show only an upward shock in Figure 10.72. In this figure, we assume due to demand being either periodic or stochastic, that all producers on the stack are in equilibrium (those that appear out of merit on the diagram that represents an instant in time are in merit at other times).

The production stack is optimised for the demand, and if there is a demand shock (which we assume to apply *ex ante* to all future demands at a consistent uplift), then less efficient production will be rapidly mobilised.

---

[93] e.g. Dasgupta and Heal (1979) and particularly Chapter 2 'The impossibility of fully informative price systems'. In 1982 David Newbery and Joseph Stiglitz of Princeton proved that in an uncertain world that competitive equilibrium is not a Pareto optimum.

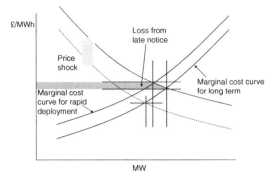

Figure 10.72 Surplus loss from lack of notice for mobilisation of production resource

We can also view the cost of shocks in market terms. Note that the mean reversion assumption in section 9.1.11 is fundamentally related to the pace and volume of resource mobilisation in response to price shocks.

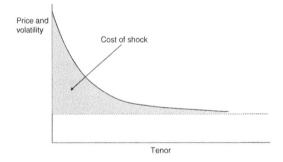

Figure 10.73 The economic inefficiency of a shock, as observed from the market

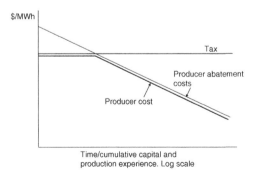

Figure 10.74 Shock taxation, and possible gradual increase in taxation in line with production possibility

10.9   THE POLITICAL ECONOMICS OF LIBERALISATION

'Liberty, the mother, not the daughter, of order' – Proudhon

Electricity is a relatively new service, and the derivative markets in currencies, interest rates, crude oil and metals are also new. At the same time, the policy challenges such as global warming are new and the competitive capitalist model is new too. Electricity is a very difficult commodity. The result of all this, is that electricity markets are designed rather than just evolving around market policy events (such as the ending of the Bretton Woods agreement in 1971, which then allowed the opening of currency and interest rate markets, and the ending of the Gold Standard in 1933, which allowed the opening of bullion trading).

As a result of this, the academic world has had a very close association with the ESI, and particularly the structure of the markets. Regulators are commonly drawn from universities, and academics commonly reside in particular camps. Certain political and philosophical views have had a great influence on the development of the market structure of the industry.

A strong influence on European liberalisation in general, and the evolution of the Great Britain electricity market in particular, has been the 'Austrian School' of economics. Academic and other literature on the ESI makes frequent reference to the Austrian School. For example: 'The market would then spontaneously, in true Austrian form, find ways of trading, and futures and contract frameworks would emerge form the competitive process. Institutions would develop naturally' – from Helm (2003).

The Austrian school was founded in the 1870's[94] by Menger, Böhm-Bawerk and Wieser, and the foremost thinkers of the school in the 20th century were von Mises and Hayek. The work of Hayek in particular has had a strong influence on the ESI.

The early Austrian school was neoclassical in nature. The 20th century Austrian model takes the neoclassical model and uses it to roll back the role of the state from planning the economy. The general release of control of the state and allowance of the markets to determine prices and volumes is liberalisation.

By coincidence, the philosopher most relevant to the development as the ESI, Karl Popper, was also from Austria. Popper essentially took the view that economic systems evolved in the same way that nature evolved through the survival of the fittest. We cannot expect to design the 'right' model of the markets, but by experimenting with various designs in different countries will reveal the models that are most fit for purpose. Sometimes a poor design can survive in a benign environment and sometimes a good design with minor flaws may fail due to its incapability to handle some particular event. As shown in Figure 4.1, Popper would regard a crisis such as that in California as an inevitable consequence of rapid and sweeping change, and would recommend incremental changes and diverse solutions.

Recent attention to the political economics of the ESI has concentrated on the political, social and economic factors that drive change. For example, Rufín, in 'The Political Economy of Institutional Change in Electricity Supply Industry', concentrates on the degree of public and private ownership and the degree of competition in the ESI and by modelling

---

[94] Gossen, though not Austrian, presaged the marginalist revolution, and was acknowledged by Jevons. Though disparaged by Walras for the utilitarian approach, he must have had some influence on the German speaking economists. The roots of the Austrian School go back to Thomas Aquinas

the correlation between factors and ESI changes arrived at key three factors for the ESI, namely;

(i)   **Institutional constraints** – Principally the independence of the judiciary.
(ii)   **Ideology**.
(iii) **Distributional conflict** – The fight for relative share of the economic rent available in the market.

11
Financial Modelling of Power Plant

Power stations are at the heart of electricity price modelling. In this section we show how the building blocks of energy, power capacity and environment come together in power plant, how they relate to the configuration and operation of plant and how items such as cost of risk and low probability modelling are included.

To do this, we briefly demonstrate a financial model for a power generation organisation. The core techniques used are standard in 'real option'[1] methodology, although there is little literature on 'endogenous' aspects of shadow prices and failure insurance in this context. We use the No Arbitrage philosophy, in making option exercise cash flow neutral and thereby valuing the plant by the difference between premium received and fixed costs due. In doing so, we must be particularly careful in moving between 'real world pricing' that we have used throughout this book, and 'risk neutral pricing' which is standard for derivative pricing and the no arbitrage approach in particular. This is discussed in section 9.1.22.

The efficient market hypothesis requires that if there is a deep and liquid market in options, and that if we do not have a different cost of risk bias to that of the market at the margin, then we *must* value our asset in this way, since to value in any other way incurs an implied inefficient speculative position in the market. Note that it is not the speculation *per se* that is the problem, it is the inefficiency of the speculation. If we wish to speculate then we should optimise the asset according to the market dictate, and then speculate as an independent activity.

11.1 POWER PLANT FINANCIAL MODEL

If a power plant financial model contains all of the cash flows of the business and therefore all of the risks of the business, then the model must be complete. Here we introduce an internal market to capture all flows. There are three key areas – (i) 'firm' fuel to power conversion, (ii) environmental costs and (iii) reliability costs. Underpinning these is the operating cost model of the plant. The three secondary areas are credit management, capital provision and costing and insurance. These are shown in Figure 11.1.[2]

Since these components capture the full cost of running the plant, it is best for each to be modelled as a profit centre. Then they act as risk centres. Every contract, for every period (ideally at hourly or halfhourly resolution), has a contract for each of these boxes. The value of the plant is equal to the sum of the cash flows, discounted at the risk free rate, minus the cost of risk, applied individually to each profit centre, with a centralised aggregation of the risk diversity benefit, handled by capital management. For brevity, the cost of risk

---

[1] The practice of real options treats physical assets in terms of financial options. In a power station context, see Ronn (2002).
[2] For further details of this model, see Harris (2002).

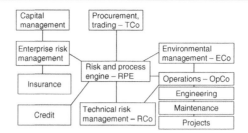

Figure 11.1   A representation of the cost structure of power plant

calculations are not covered here, but the relevant cost of risk disciplines are covered in other parts of the book.

High merit plant derives value by four tranches of internal and external contracts:

(i)   **Baseload** – Forward contracts for the conversion of fuel to power (i.e. purchase of fuel and sale of power) at a capacity that has a seasonal profile, and excluding planned outages.

(ii) **Planned flexibility** – The planned deloads or stops relative to baseload, to avoid losses during low conversion margin periods.

(iii) **Vanilla options** – Unplanned but highly structured loads and deloads at relatively short notice. These are European option contracts. Note that these contracts are very different to planned flexibility contracts from a derivative perspective as they are option and not forward contracts. To the physical power plant they differ only in notice period.

(iv) **Extra flexibility** – This is a family of extra contracts layered on top of each other for more and more options. For example, fuel switches and the provision of reserve after the vanilla options have expired or exercised. The valuation of these requires the calculation of the conditional properties of distributions, as described in section 9.1.20.

When these are added, and remembering that we are initially ignoring cost of risk, we can show the build up of the value of the plant.

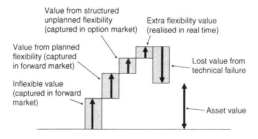

Figure 11.2   The build up of plant value using the real option methodology

The reader may note that this building block approach differs from the fairly common approach of capturing the whole plant value in a single derivative. The building block approach is favoured by the author because it places a strict priority in order of total value for:

(i) **Liquidity** – Baseload is more liquid than 'shape' (price profile), which is more liquid than European options. Extra flexibility options barely trade at all with the exception of swing.

(ii) **Cost of risk** – This is relatively tractable for baseload, and slightly less so for shape. Cost of volatility risk is just about tractable (see section 9.2.2) and cost of more complex risks is not.

(iii) **Robustness** – Derivative valuation models are full of hidden assumptions. These are most visible using this approach.

(iv) **Operational risk** – Complex valuations are extremely difficult to audit. In this approach, the majority of the value can be explained and tested with a high degree of auditability.

(v) **Familiarity** – Complex options (also called 'exotics') are a specialist area. European options require less specialist knowledge. Forward contracts are more readily accessible.

The plant value then forms the major component of fixed costs through the debt and equity[3] repayments.

We will here examine the four major entities – TCo the internal market operator for power and fuel, ECo the internal market operator in environmental effects, RCo the internal 'zero excess' insurer for plant failure, OpCo the internal profit centre for plant operations, maintenance and stewardship. We place the Risk and Process Engine (RPE) at the centre.

11.2   THE BASELOAD CONTRACT

We will for the moment assume that there are no planned outages in the year and that seasonal and diurnal ambient conditions do not affect plant performance. The contracts for each power plant unit for the year ahead are as follows:

(i) TCo sells fuel at halfhourly profile to RPE and buys power at the same profile.[4]

(ii) Eco sells the internal environmental permits for the year. These include internal auction of corporate allocation and internal contract of traded[5] emission permits, struck at market prices. It also includes input factors that can be handled by Translators, such as described[6] in section 8.4.3.

(iii) RCo sells a zero excess insurance policy to RPE for the business interruption[7] cost of plant failure.

(iv) RPE pays OpCo on an 'hours and starts' basis, as described in the appendix. Note that this cost is committed in advance on a 'take or pay' basis. Saved internal cost from saved running is dependent on actual saving as described in Chapter 6 on capacity.

---

[3] Equity costs are treated as risk free repayment plus fair reward for risk taking, as described in section 10.1.24. In the purest modelling form, supranormal 'alpha' return is not a fixed cost. In practice, this is commonly implicit in the use of internal corporate hurdles for rate of return.

[4] Note that while the contracts are expressed to plant operators as conversion contracts, they must be separate power and fuel contracts to cater for imbalance, failure, efficiency and other changes.

[5] If the market is liquid, then the contract is most appropriately placed with TCo rather than ECo.

[6] More detailed discussion is beyond the scope of this book. In brief, the shadow cost associated with a limit on the assimilative capability of the environment is treated as an internally tradable limit.

[7] The material damage aspect is part of the different contract with another internal insurer in the 'insurance' box on Figure 11.1, with additional contracts with internal providers of actual or virtual strategic spares.

11.2.1 Contracts on failure

(i) RCo sells power to RPE at C, the non fuel marginal cost (itself equal to the OpCo rebate from reduction in running), and receives from RPE the saved fuel and environmental permit.

(ii) RCo buys power from TCo at P' (the prevailing market offer price for the appropriate volume for the appropriate tenor). Since the market prices might have changed between insurance and failure, we can see that RCo takes market as well as reliability risk. If prices are not periodic or failure not price responsive, and P' uncorrelated with failure of the unit, then the hedge is straightforward, as described in section 6.10 and the risk neutral valuation of the premium[8] is also straightforward.

(iii) RCo sells the fuel to TCo at the prevailing market price

(iv) RCo sells the permit to ECo at the prevailing external or internal (shadow) price. As with energy prices, RCo takes the price exposure.

11.3   THE PLANNED FLEXIBILITY CONTRACT

The mechanics of this contract are similar to that of the baseload contract, and in practice for plants other than those for which baseload is the normal mode of operation, they are optimised together. Since the planned flexibility contract involves deloads, it involves a general decrease of environmental costs with ECo, a general decrease of plant costs with OpCo and a general decrease of reliability costs with RCo. The item of most significance is the introduction of unit starts, which have costs in all three categories.

11.4   THE VANILLA OPTION CONTRACT

The first two contracts above are a formalised version of the way that many generation companies run in the modern markets. The vanilla option contracts are considerably harder to formalise and of great interest in the understanding of the pricing and economics of the ESI overall. For brevity, we will consider only the call options from minimum stable generation to full load. The inherent storage in market-like contracts (fuel and emissions) and other costs, are described in section 6.4 and there are alternative treatments. For simplicity here we strike the internal option as a 'vanilla' European option with several factors in the strike price and note that this becomes a swing option from a TCo perspective. Contractual specifications of European options are described in section 9.4.2.

The strike price of the option is:

$$\text{Power strike} = \text{Fuel} + \text{Permits} + \text{PLU} + \text{NFMC} + \text{Rel}$$

Where PLU is the marginal operations cost as described in the appendix and measured here per MWh,[9] and NFMC is the non fuel non PLU marginal cost (e.g. consumables). Rel is the incremental cost of the reliability contract, discussed below.

---

[8] Risk adjustment is cost of loss aversion, but should be adjusted downwards for internal diversification of all risks and therefore to avoid double counting of risks.

[9] Start costs can in theory be applied as standard option formulae for a 'rebate' but in practice are best smeared over the option period and expressed per MWh.

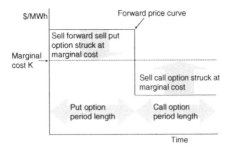

Figure 11.3   Sale of options on top of the planned flexibility forward contracts

11.4.1   Cost of the reliability contract on the option contract

This is rather complicated for the following reasons:

(i)   Price and price events are correlated with reliability and failure events.
(ii) Power price (and spread prices) conditional on option exercise is rather complicated (see section 9.1.20).
(iii) Price variation conditional on option exercise is rather complicated (see section 9.1.20).
(iv) Permit price is closely related to power price and has path dependence (see section 9.7).
(v)   For low merit plant, valuation is complicated because it relies on demand reduction to act as virtual power plant.

11.5   EXTRA FLEXIBILITY

Power plant commonly has many forms of overlapping flexibility, and the challenge is to remove the overlaps for contractual and valuation purposes. Two[10] examples of extra flexibilities are:

(i) fuel switch capability;
(ii) sale of reserve after vanilla option expiry or exercise.

The fuel switch capability is a very good example of a derivative that can be handled as a single three commodity derivative which is not transparent, or a dominant two commodity derivative (power-coal) which is robust, transparent and tradable plus two commodity derivatives (power-gas and coal-gas contingent on power-coal prices) which are less robust and which use analytics which are approximate, as described in section 9.3.

The three derivatives are:

(i)   Sell power-coal option at strike price Kpc.
(ii) Sell power-gas option, exercisable contingent on $Pp - Pc < Kpc$.
(iii) Sell coal-gas option, exercisable contingent on $Pp - Pc > Kpc$.

These can be calculated using the methods described in section 9.1.20.

---

[10] For more examples, see Harris (2002).

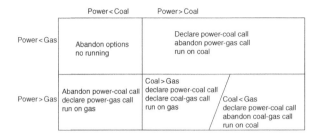

Figure 11.4   Action on exercise of the three options sold by a dual fired power station

11.6   FINANCE AND HEDGING

For plant that never fails and with costs that are steady or hedgeable, the hedge decisions are fairly simple – hedging is transacted if the loss expectation on the hedge is less than the cost of risk saving from the hedge. There are two key elements to consider here – volatile costs with a correlation to input or output prices (principally the traded or shadow prices of environmental permits) and the impact of failure.

11.6.1   Plant failure as a limiting factor in growth and return

Risk adjusted return on equity capital can be maximised by hedging, borrowing and expanding. The expansion cycle is shown below. Without expansion, the simple act of borrowing (i.e. increasing gearing) increases the expectation of investor return for reasons described in section 10.1.24.1.

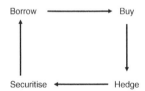

Figure 11.5   The expansion cycle to maximise risk adjusted return on equity capital

If we could cover all risks (for example, if the only risks were market risks, and they could be covered by hedging), then provided that the cost of risk transference (in this, hedging) at the margin, is less than the cost of debt, then the company can gear up and expand indefinitely to achieve a return on equity capital that is limited only by investment opportunities.

The problem is that for power plant that can fail, that whilst the expansion cycle increases risk adjusted return on equity capital (which is sensitive to the 'normal' variance of return), that this represents a moral hazard to the creditors, since 'extreme' risk (low probability large events) increases. This arises because as total plant size for the same capital increases, the total possible loss from covering a short hedge position after plant failures increases, while the 'equity buffer'[11] that takes the loss before the creditors start to lose money remains the same size.

This conflict of interest is apparent when we show that each entity only cares about one slice along the risk diagram shown below, and is completely indifferent to the terminal performance outside the slice. Figure 11.6 shows this, including the contingent liabilities of the firm (for example to claims against it), that are partially insured. Here the term 'externality' is used to cover all liabilities that are not honoured directly or covered by insurance.

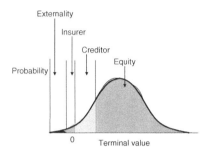

Figure 11.6 Depiction of the risk positions of the stakeholders in the firm

Let us now ignore for a moment the externalities and consider just the position of shareholders and creditors. Figure 11.7 shows the initial position with an unhedged single asset, followed by the effect of the hedge. Note that while the normal risk is decreased, the extreme risk is increased because of the unlimited risk of buying back a short hedge position on failure. An expanded asset base then increases the expectation of return, but then there is a conflict between the needs of the creditor and the shareholder.

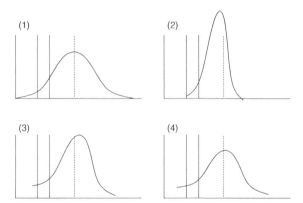

Figure 11.7 Hedging an expanding asset base. (1) unhedged single asset (2) hedged single asset (3) optimal hedge position for shareholder with expanded asset base (4) optimal hedge position for creditor with expanded asset base

---

[11] This is readily understood from the KMV model, now used by KMV Moody's. In brief the expectation value of the core asset, the probability distribution of the core asset value, the stock value, the stock volatility, the debt and the default probability are related. Any one of these can be inferred if all of the others are known.

By externally insuring failure events, then both creditor and shareholder risks are reduced, at the cost of loss of expectation profit.

The debt and equity relationships are shown schematically in Figure 11.8. We can infer from this that even for an infinite opportunity set of investments with the same costs, that the increasing cost of debt leads to diminishing increase in stock alpha with increased investment and there is an optimum investment, gearing and hedge level. The gearing and hedge level and thereby the stock alpha can in principle be significantly increased by insurance.

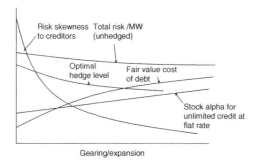

Figure 11.8 Schematic representation of generation stakeholder factors in relation to debt gearing and asset expansion

11.6.2 Cost of risk

There are a number of difficulties arising when trying to apply cost of risk as a practical cost factor to a firm. We have already come across the question of the underlying portfolio of the risk taking stakeholders when considering whether variance of the square root of variance is the best denominator. This depends on the implicit and assumed correlation between the risk of the stakeholder portfolio and the risk profile provided by the firm. So, for example, we assume that our shareholders have share portfolios and that our reinsurers have cash portfolios. The cost of risk according to the probability slice is then not only dependent on all of the complications of distribution skewness, implied utility functions and the mix of risk and loss aversion, but we have significant correlation issues to attend to as well. The same issues apply to the other two stakeholders shown in Figure 11.6, the creditors and all of those who may be affected by, but not compensated by, the firm if bankrupt. For example, the same events that may cause a firm to go bankrupt may cause similar stakeholder impact directly or through the impact on other stakeholdings. This correlation was depicted in Figure 6.31.

It is obvious then that applying a cost of risk at enterprise level to the mix of stakeholders is a process that requires compromises and assumptions. There are essentially two approaches to this. The first is to take the risk profiles of all of the elements shown in Figure 11.1, and apply broad correlations between the profit centres and between the stakeholders, or particular events can be chosen to establish systemic relationships between the risks of the elements and the risks faced by the stakeholders.

11.6.3   Value at Risk – VAR

Value at risk is a very common method of expressing risk. If we are X % confident of losing not more than £ Y over a particular period, then £ Y is said to be our value at risk, or VAR. The 95 % confidence level is most commonly used, and represents a good compromise between the needs of the shareholders, and other stakeholders who are concerned with higher confidence levels. VAR estimates are tested by measuring the daily profits (or other measure) and viewing in retrospect whether the percentage of observations outside the VAR level approximates the VAR percentage. So for 95 % VAR, one day in twenty should exhibit movement beyond the VAR level. We often need to know the expectation of losses, conditional on exceedance of VAR levels, and can use the extreme value theory to estimate this at high confidence levels.

When we refer to VAR we must specify:

(i)   **Scope** – The thing that we are measuring (an asset, a trading book, a corporation, a contract, etc.).
(ii) **Tenor** – How much of the thing we are looking at (year 1 of a project, the next 7 years, all years, etc.).
(iii) **Horizon** – The period over which we are observing change.
(iv) **Accounting rule** – cash, profit, net present value, etc.
(v)   **Dimensions** – what risk factors we are modelling, and the restrictions of our risk factors, such as n factors, volatility, etc.
(vi) **Assumptions** – e.g. corporate response such as rehedging, real options actions, risk factors ignored.

Without these, VAR results are unreliable at best and meaningless at worst, although unfortunately a lack of proper specification of these factors is very common. To avoid despondency on this, it is worth noting that the practices involved in production of a VAR that may be unreliable, are themselves extremely useful, in formalising control and measurement, in developing analytic techniques, and in the reporting by-products that are useful in their own right.

11.6.4   Corporate financial measures

The concepts used here clearly separate the future value discounting at the 'risk free' rate and the absolute adjustment to future value in relation to 'normal and extreme' risk incurred by the stakeholders. Whilst this is the most correct way to evaluate risk and financial decisions, it is not readily communicable and the calculations are complex and opaque. Corporations commonly use more primitive measures for assessing the hurdle rates for activities that consume cash, risk, or both. It is therefore a common requirement to convert technical measures into the common currencies of corporate finance, such as net present value (NPV – cash flows discounted at the internal corporate hurdle rate), weighted average cost of capital (WACC – the cost of corporate debt at market rates, the mark to market of fixed interest rate transactions, the mark to market of the differential between current credit spreads and of existing transactions, the cost of equity and corporate gearing). For good housekeeping, expansion decisions should satisfy both technical measures and corporate measures. The different measures can cause different optimum levels of risk transfer. This, and the question of identifying stakeholder portfolios, correlation of risks to their portfolios and assessing risk preferences, remain substantially unsolved in general application of corporate finance, in and outside the ESI.

11.7 ACCOUNTING

In the perfect world, corporate financial decisions are motivated by the optimisation of net present value. However, standard accrual accounting does not recognise value that is expected in the future. Mark to market accounting does recognise this value but since the demise of Enron, has been much mistrusted by investors. The reality is that there is less difference between the methods than is commonly realised, due to the use of discretion in items such as exceptional items, provisions, conservative valuations and others. It is the greater capability to include illiquid[12] assets with uncertain values on the balance sheet that has led to unease and scope for abuse. In general, the International Accounting Standards follow the Federal Accounting Standards in moving increasingly to recognising liquid forward value by mark to market accounting.

For present purposes what is important is our treatment of 'cash' in our 'no arbitrage' real option model. We have implicitly used mark to market conventions, for example by treating plant life usage as cash flow, spend on plant as capitalised and then depreciated with PLU rather than evenly over time. The full implementation of the model requires that each entity has zero balance sheet value, so for example, the assets, hedges and internal insurance contracts are revalued each year, and have a 'virtual cash account' on which interest is paid/received, that is equal and opposite to the mark to market value.[13]

---

[12] Prudent mark to market accounting assesses values at 'fair value' but includes a liquidity provision that effectively marks the asset value down to its liquidation value.

[13] A few moments consideration reveal that this arrangement ensures that profit is accounted correctly. For example a long one year forward contract struck at $110/MWh when the forward market is at $100/MWh when the interest rate is 5% should be accompanied by a virtual overdraft of $9.5.

12

Security of Supply

'Member states may propose on undertakings operating in the electricity (gas) sector, in the general economics interest, public service obligations which may relate to security ... including energy efficiency and climate protection. Such obligations shall be clearly defined, transparent, non-discriminatory, verifiable and shall guarantee access for EU electricity (gas) companies to national consumers. Member States may introduce the implementation of long-term planning ... ' – EU Article 3(2) electricity and gas

It is common for there to be regulation at international, national, ministerial and industry sector level with respect to security of supply. In a competitive industry, it is hard to pin down actual and accountable responsibility.

Security of supply, to the extent to which it is defined at all, has a wide variety of definitions. Whilst at high level it is obvious what the general subject is, for actions that enhance security of supply to be costed and prioritised with other measures, it must be defined.

For present purposes, we define concern over security of supply into two distinct areas: (i) the risk or likelihood of *cessation* of provision of electricity, for whatever reason, of power to a party who currently uses and needs it and (ii) the current or prospective *absence* of provision, for whatever reason, of electricity to a party whose welfare or effectiveness would be enhanced by it.

Expressed in this way, the two parts of the definition split expectation and uncertainty, and in doing so, it is immediately apparent that the issue is quite different for those able to pay in developed economies, and those unable to pay or who live in areas that are not electrified. In keeping with the focus of this book on maturing wholesale markets, greater attention here is made to the first part of the definition.

12.1 SUPPLY CHAIN

To deliver electricity to a paying consumer requires each stage of the value chain to be functional, or for there to be sufficient redundancy and capacity in the chain to contend with shortfalls in individual links of the chain.

We can conveniently divide the links in accordance with our definitions of tiers of the ESI in Chapter 1:

(i)   energy source (presence, accessibility);
(ii) capture primary energy at source;
(iii) delivery of primary energy from source;
(iv) processing of primary energy;
(v)   delivery of processed primary energy;

(vi)   power generation capability from primary energy (processed or otherwise);
(vii)   transmission of electric power through the high voltage system;
(viii) distribution of electric power from the transmission network to consumers;
(ix)   management of demand in times of shortage;
(x)   ability of suppliers to pay;
(xi)   ability of consumers to pay (particularly universal service).

Each of these has several dimensions:

(i)   time horizon (now, this year, this decade, this lifetime, next generations);
(ii)   probability profile;
(iii)   dependence on common external factors;
(iv)   notice to fail;
(v)   MW amount of loss and MW amount remaining secure.

We also noted in Chapter 3 that security of finance for the ESI (and therefore security of supply) is dependent on effective operation of the supply process downstream of the distribution network. This includes prevention of theft, effective meter reading, bill calculation, production and delivery, payment infrastructure (banks, collecting stations, etc.) enforcement and (ultimately) disconnection.

Loss of load probability (LOLP) clearly admits the non zero probability of system failure to meet demand, so we ought to see this event at some time, at some part of the world. For example, if all countries used the PJM standard of not more than one day per ten years then over ten countries we would expect about one day per year.

12.1.1 Sources

We identified the sources of energy in section 2.1. There is a substantial variation in the endowments of these sources in different countries, and the social and technological limitations in harnessing the energy also varies very strongly. We have seen that the presence of one form of power generation on the system, such as wind or nuclear, places requirements for another kind of generation (principally hydro, coal and oil) and there is therefore a volume limit of any plant type at any point in time. Security of supply places further limits.

Access to energy sources is limited, or potentially limited, by external issues (such as political instability, infrastructure breakdown, production interruption), political or regulatory limits to technology installation (e.g. nuclear), social limits to technology installation (e.g. siting where amenity is affected), environmental limits to technology installation or continuation and by natural variations (e.g. rainfall).

What every nation seeks to avoid is a concentration of risk to any one exposure, and thereby seeks a mix of source and technology. There is a high alignment of the strategic objectives of renewable energy and security of supply.

Exposure to energy sources varies in timescale. For example (global weather changes aside), hydro power is highly sustainable over the long term, but the aggregate rainfall in one country from one year to the next is highly variable, and in fact the general volume of water in rainfall, lakes and water tables moves over a period of years. A dry year causes electricity shortages not just for a period of hours, but for a whole season. This has been a significant problem in, for example, New Zealand and Brazil.

Geopolitical risk is quite different to that of weather risk, and we are reminded of the famous quote by Thomas Mackinder as early as 1919 and echoed frequently ever since: 'Who rules East Europe commands the Heartland; Who rules the Heartland commands the World-Island; Who rules the World-Island commands the World'.

The high exposure of Europe to gas supplies from Russia can be classed as a geopolitical risk but could be better represented as the risk to depletion of, and competition for, a concentrated source a long way away, with many buyers along the pipe. Gas leaving Siberia for Ireland may pass through Northern Ireland, Scotland, England, Belgium, Germany, the Czech Republic, Slovakia, the Ukraine and across Russia. One way to mitigate such risk is to limit the percentage of any particular primary energy as a percentage of total energy imports, from a particular country, or through a particular supply route. The problem here is in the competition barriers that such policies erect.

The transportation of fossil fuel is intimately bound up with the extraction (and upstream activities such as exploration). In a sense, the production asset and transportation assets are complementary goods. Due to the high capital cost of production and transportation, where fuel requires dedicated transportation infrastructure, then the sale of the fuel is accompanied by long term take or pay contracts that ensure at least a minimum cash flow for the asset owner. One of the challenges in the opening of energy markets is to unbundle production transportation and sale in such a manner that entry barriers are lowered while at the same time securing income for a long enough term to secure the capital repayment on the asset development.

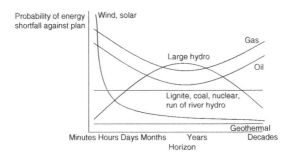

Figure 12.1 Schematic representation of the security of supply to power stations of the various forms of energy

The most apparent shortages due to energy insufficiency have been due to low rainfall in hydro dominated systems (e.g. Brazil in 2001 and New Zealand in 2003). These events point to the need to rely on diverse energy sources rather than specifically the unreliability of hydro energy in the form of rain.

12.1.2 Power generation capacity

The more uniform the power generation base, the greater the exposure to systemic risks and the less able to contend with the wide degree of services required to manage the electrical system. So the system must contend for example, with lack of wind on a particular day, a dry year, problems with gas infrastructure, type faults in all types of thermal plant, transient instability and support, reactive power, black start, reserve and other factors and changing relative importance of plant impacts such as nuclear fears, carbon dioxide and visual impacts.

Lost load due to aggregate insufficiency of generation capacity has been extremely rare in the industrial nations, although with power station lives over 30 years and a relatively new regime of high competition, it is too early to tell if investment signals are strong enough and regulatory risk low enough for the optimal amount and mix of capacity to be built in the future.

There are few opportunities to observe lost load as a result of generator insufficiency. The best known example of generator insufficiency is in California[1] in 2000.

12.1.3   Transmission

While a transmission network failure is a great nuisance, there have been few instances in industrial countries in which transmission failures cause outages for more than a day and for more than a few percent of the control area. There have been a number of well publicised transmission failure events over the last few years in the USA, most countries in Europe and other places.[2] The loss from transmission failure is considerably less than that of distribution failure in terms of average hours lost, but transmission failures have high media, political and international profile. When such failures occur, it is partly due to insufficiency (since greater line redundancy and switching capability would reduce the incidence) they are commonly due to temporary instability arising from local events. Transmission sufficiency is generally more related to the economic cost of redispatch to resolve transmission constraints than aggregate insufficiency to deliver energy.

Different approaches can be taken to transmission reliability. One way is to estimate the fail rates per component and work to a MW failure threshold. Another is the 'n minus one' approach, in which the system is designed and dispatched to operate without loss for one failure.[3]

12.1.4   Distribution

The distribution network tends to be more hierarchic (radial rather than looped) than the transmission network and for this reason there is less system wide interdependency.

In terms of hours lost per year, the distribution sector accounts for the greatest losses,[4] but there is the least long term risk, since distribution can be constructed relatively quickly, and because the incentive for connection is local, then the opposition to loss of visual amenity is reduced.

The challenge that is emerging for this sector is in renewable generation and other embedded generation. This makes the network less hierarchic and unidirectional and system wide dependencies increase.

12.1.5   Suppliers

It is normally impossible (in the short term) or very difficult (in the medium term) to disconnect customers. Therefore, if a supplier defaults on his commitment to purchase energy

---

[1] CAISO (2000).

[2] See, for example, JESS (2003) for international events in 2003, or Hyman (2005) for major events over 40 years in the USA, and PSERC website for international events.

[3] See, for example, ISO New England (2005) for an example of this approach.

[4] For example in Great Britain, the average number of interruptions per 100 customers was 78.4, and the average customer minutes lost was 94.3. Source Ofgem (2005).

to satisfy consumer requirements, the energy will still flow according to the consumer demand. Even if this were not the case, the various regulations and licence conditions involving security of supply, supply obligations and protection for vulnerable customers commonly prevent this. Therefore it is common for the unpaid for energy from a supplier default not to be paid for by the consumer, in the form of a contract surcharge, but for the costs to be borne by the supply sector, and socialised within it, in the interim between supplier default and signature of new consumer contracts.

12.1.6   Consumers

The supply sector is not commonly mentioned in discussions of security of supply because in industrial countries, the issues tend to be economic rather than technical, and in developing and transition countries the priorities have been (i) generation capacity and availability and (ii) electrification.

However, the supply business is an essential element of security of supply in all economies. In the developed economies, the challenge is in the way that marginal economics drive the demand reduction that must be achieved for sustainable electricity supply. As any economist will say, elevating the price is a sure and efficient (in a neoclassical sense for financial surplus) way to reduce demand, particularly if the good cannot be rationed (thereby is public good). At this same time as this puts upward pressure on prices, the costs of environmental improvement put significantly more pressure. Price elasticity of demand is low for the rich households, and so achieving demand reduction through the price signal can have a disproportionate effect on those with lower incomes.

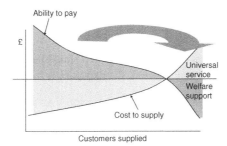

Figure 12.2   Schematic representation of the use of producer surplus and discriminatory pricing to fund universal service and welfare support

12.2   RESERVE MARGIN

Reserve margin is a commonly used term for high level communication. It is in reality a very approximate way of describing the system.

12.2.1   Scenario approach concept of reserve margin

The reserve margin for current demand, and currently available generation is shown in Figure 12.3.

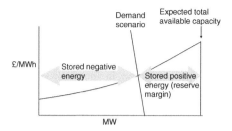

Figure 12.3 Representation of capacity and simple reserve margin on the daily stack

Commonly, the demand for the purposes of calculation of estimated margin is chosen to correspond to some scenario, for example, a one-in-twenty cold winter. Prospective generation capability is also assumed to correspond to a conservative estimate. The reserve margin is then the amount of capacity available over and above the 'reasonable worst case'.

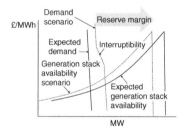

Figure 12.4 Depiction of reserve margin, taking into account demand variation generator availability variation and structured interruptibility of demand

For thermal generation, greatest attention is paid to a short spell (peak hours for a few days) of very high demand. For hydro generation, the exposure is to a longer period (season/year) of high demand and/or low rainfall.

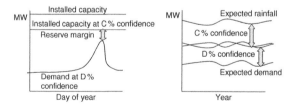

Figure 12.5 Scenario approaches to in-year security of supply for thermal and hydro systems

12.2.2 Probability approach to reserve margin

The scenario approach arrives at a MW figure for reserve margin. The probability approach arrives at a probability of lost load. If we ignore locational issues for a moment, then we can see how to do this for thermal generation by lumping together generator failure and demand variation, (remembering that their distribution types are quite different). Then we can apply a bivariate distribution to the net. The probability is represented in two dimensions in Figure 12.6.

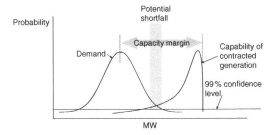

Figure 12.6 Two dimensional schematic representation of the probability of lost load

Although represented here in one plane, the bivariate distribution should be properly represented in three dimensions. An uncorrelated bivariate distribution does not present complications if the univariate distributions are well characterised. Correlated bivariate distributions must be solved numerically. This is not particularly simple even if both distributions are standard normal and the correlation is standard linear.[5]

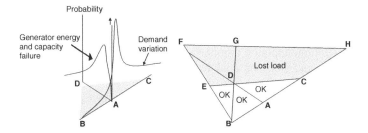

Figure 12.7 Three dimensional representation of the probability of lost load, given no correlation between failure of committed energy, failure of capacity and of variation in demand

(i)   On ADC (AD = capacity = AC), the increase in demand plus the failure of energy and capacity is less than the capacity and hence there is no lost load.
(ii) On ABED the lower demand allows a greater capacity and energy failure without losing load.
(iii) On plane CDEFGH there is lost load.

12.2.3   The effect of import, export and transit

Limitation or expansion of imports and exports of primary energy and of electricity can have different effects in different timeframes. For example, a country that consistently exports domestic primary energy or secondary energy from domestic sources, may simultaneously improve short term security of supply (since exports could be cut in times of shortage) and worsen long term security of supply (by domestic depletion). For example, the UK has now

---

[5] See, for example, Vasicek (1998) for a solution for normally distributed variables.

increased its dependence on gas from Norway, Libya and Russia through the depletion of reserves on the UK continental shelf. Similarly, France has a surplus of generation capacity for domestic use but high dependency on a single type of imported fuel.

12.3   THE RESPONSIBILITY FOR SECURITY OF SUPPLY

Responsibility for security of supply is in practice highly fragmented. For example, while a ministry may have responsibility for it, it can have little impact on the short term (for example, mandatory demand reduction, restriction of environmental limits), and the long term impact must be measured in order to enhance and not prevent the operation of the market.

We have seen that the hedge requirements for generators and suppliers/consumers are very different beyond the build time horizon for power stations, and this greatly reduces the ability of the market to assist in the build decision and in supporting the financing. Instead, generators commonly take a long term supply/demand view of the macro energy/political/environmental picture as described in section 9.5.6. Whilst the fuel source and generation industries are most directly connected to security of supply, it is not always effective to place requirements upon them because the fuel market is international and there is no obvious mechanism to order generators to build without abandoning the market.

In practice, the stewardship of security of supply commonly falls to the transmission operators. They conduct long term energy flow and supply studies and estimate the total exposure to different scenarios. These then become signals to government to influence at the margin (for example allowing the build of nuclear power stations, providing incentives for renewable generation, applying moratoria to gas fired power stations, and adjusting the environmental limits and rules on coal fired power stations to make them economic or uneconomic).

Placing requirements on the supply sector has been described in section 6.7, along with the issues associated with these. In this respect, governments have a degree of choice, particularly in the industrial and commercial sector as to whether to treat short term security of supply as a purely commercial issue (taking cheaper power while accepting occasional interruptions) or whether electricity is too important an international measure of national efficiency to allow this. Long term security of supply (the probability of sustained shortage due principally to shortage of energy source or insufficiency of conversion capability) is a different issue. This form of security of supply could be regarded as a public good, since even if a small number of suppliers, consumers, generators and fuel producers invest in it, national emergency conditions would commonly convert the private good to a public one. We have already seen that the volatility of income of power plant with low load factor (i.e. that required for security of supply) is very high, and the regulatory hazard of price control during a security of supply event is sufficient to deter private build for this purpose without capacity payment. The situation is different if the capacity payment market is developed. We have already shown that suppliers would ideally hedge capacity further forward than they would secure energy, and that suppliers and consumers are incentivised to hedge in a similar manner to their competitors. It may be that option/capacity markets can solve the issue of long term security of supply, but these infants are currently growing at a slower rate than may be required.

Appendix

A.1 PLANT LIFE USAGE

Throughout this book we have represented the cost of operating and maintaining the plant as a marginal rather than a fixed cost. Intuitively we can understand this, because just as with driving a car, the more we use the plant and the more we ask of it (for example in load changes), the quicker it will degrade, and the more we must spend to maintain it.

We can formalise plant life usage using a simple technique that is well known (if not entirely well established) in combined cycle gas turbines, and which we here apply to whole plant. This is the 'equivalent operating hour' (EOH) approach. In this approach, there are two plant states, 'full load' and 'off', and we incur damage each time we start, and for every hour that we operate.

From an engineering perspective, it is by no means obvious that we are justified in using this approach, because 'hours' and 'starts' incur different kinds of damage, and as we can see in Figure A.1 (1) and (2), under some damage modes, the EOH[1] approach would not be valid. In practice, the damage rate is close enough to Figure A.1 (3) for us to define it as:

$$\text{Cumulative damage} = S*\text{number of starts} + H*\text{number of operating hours}$$

which is as depicted in Figure A.1 (4)

In practice, it is useful to add some extra terms so:

$$\text{Plant Life Usage} = S*\text{starts} + H*\text{operating hours} + M*\text{megawatt hours} + C*\text{on load cycles} + T*\text{calendar time}$$

A complicating factor is that plant life usage essentially takes two forms:

(i) The reduction in residual life of the plant without significant impact on current performance. An example might be a slowly growing crack in a thick section such as a boiler header that does not affect performance but requires replacement after a critical amount of growth, before fracture probability exceeds a particular level.

---

[1] Limits to hours, starts, or EOH are used by original equipment manufacturers to limit the warranty on components, particularly gas turbine blades. In contractual limits to EOH, commercial considerations are as important as engineering principles.

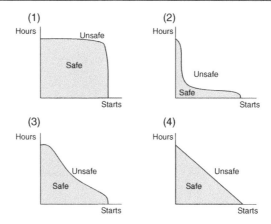

Figure A.1   Plant damage and operating envelope. (1) Limited damage interaction between hours on load and starts, (2) High damage interaction between hours and starts, (3) Medium interaction, (4) The equivalent operating hour approximation

(ii) The effect on current performance. The greatest impact is generally in reliability, but it is also felt in efficiency, maintenance cost, flexibility and occasionally in environmental performance. An example of short term impact is a boiler tube leak.

Ignoring the residual life effect for the moment, then we can approximately depict plant performance in relation to plant condition, plant condition to plant life usage and plant maintenance and repair spend to plant condition improvement. These are broadly represented in Figure A.2.

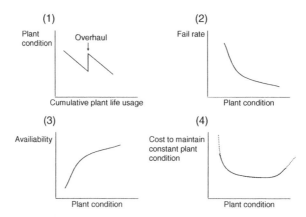

Figure A.2   Schematic relationships between plant life usage, plant condition, availability, fail rate and maintenance cost

These graphs, with specific calibration and adaptation for the plant in question and for the intensity[2] of the prospective operating regime, can be used to optimise the phase, frequency

---

[2] The fail rate is dependent on various factors such as run length, due to Markov effects, interval between runs, due to effect on opportunity maintenance and starts pattern, due to imperfect modelling of the EOH formula, and warmth of plant.

and level of plant maintenance and overhaul in relation to the prevailing conditions in forward market prices and volatilities.

We can relate fail rate to plant condition. In practice, the fail rate is additionally dependent on the operating regime of the plant. Some regimes incur higher fail rate because, for example: (i) the interval between runs is insufficient to conduct 'opportunity maintenance' and (ii) they fall outside the 'experience envelope' of hours/starts profile of the plant.

It should be noted that the 'true' value (the value if sold in the market) of the plant should be used for this optimisation, and not the accounting value, which is commonly written down in a straight line manner over a time that is less than actual plant life.

Note that the PLU for optimisation purposes is dependent on damage done and the future operation. A plant just about to close has virtually zero PLU for example. It is also clear then that PLU varies with time, prices, and other factors. It is therefore, in theory at least, a stochastic nature.

A.2 POWER PLANT FAILURE AND PHYSICAL RISK

A.2.1 Causes of failure

Power plant failure is a complicated subject, and great care must be taken in modelling fail rate (and failure type) in relation to plant condition, particularly when running plant with new load profiles outside the experience envelope.[3] Failure can arise from all kinds of sources, including:

(i)   Functioning normally in all respects except compliance with environmental limits.
(ii)   Inability to contend with a new environmental limit.
(iii) Short term change in assimilative capability of the environment (e.g. water bodies warm or at low level).
(iv) Logistics outside the plant (roads, railways, ports, etc.).
(v)   Rare events (hurricanes, epidemics, etc.).

A.2.2 Combinatorial analysis

In planning unit portfolio hedging in the short and medium term, a useful method is combinatorial analysis, in which the prospective failure condition using Figure A.2 is estimated for each unit, and the probability of each combination of possible failures is calculated.

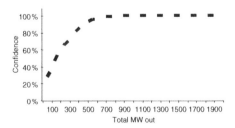

Figure A.3 Combinatorial analysis of aggregate failure of plant portfolio of 20 units

---

[3] The experience envelope can be envisaged on Figure A.1 as the range of hours/starts ratios for historic operation, and the limit of PLU total consumed.

A.2.3   Monte Carlo modelling

An effective way to model plant failure is by Monte Carlo modelling. This enables a greater degree of scenario analysis than combinatorial analysis.

One process is as follows:

(i)   Determine the starting position of the plant (on or off load, failed or not failed). Let us assume that we are not failed and on load.
(ii)   Simulate the time to the next failure. If failure is a non Markov process (see section A.2.6.1), then this can be done simply by sampling from a distribution (lognormal is usually adequate). If failure is a Markov process, then small steps must be used, in which the instantaneous fail rate changes over time.
(iii)   At the point of failure, simulate the failure extent of the plant. For example, slight loss of load, half of load due to failure of one turbine, or all load.
(iv)   If the plant has failed partially, continue the Poisson process.
(v)   If the plant has failed completely, simulate the time to return to service using an appropriate distribution (normal is generally adequate).

At the same time, the development of prices and of liquidity (manifest as the difference between 'mid' price and offer price for the volume in question) can be simulated using methods described in Chapter 9.

A.2.4   Cost of failure

Modelling plant failure is central to the pricing of peak electricity and to the financing of power and hedging of power stations.

Some failures are worse than others. The worst failures, per MWh lost are:

(i)   with little or no notice, since this incurs higher transaction costs;
(ii)   of short duration, since this implies low average notice period;
(iii)   partial, since this additionally incurs efficiency loss, although this effect is offset by the increase in transaction cost/MWh for short large failures;
(iv)   with unpredictable return to service, since this increases the extent of double transaction costs (buying power and then not needing it on early return);
(v)   uninfluenceable, since influenceability of fail time for a particular fail rate can save on peak energy costs and transaction costs.

A.2.5   Hedging return to service

When a unit fails, the power that was hedge sold must be bought back in the market for the failure period. However, the failure period is not known. Suppose that the hedge is bought back to the estimated return to service date. If the plant returns to service early, then the power must be resold, thereby incurring a 'round trip' cost of selling, buying and then reselling the power. If the plant returns to service late, then power must be bought 'hand to mouth' to cover the initial hedge in the short term market (that lacks depth). The optimum hedge can be modelled in relation to the particular market profile of increasing bid-to-offer costs with shrinking tenors.

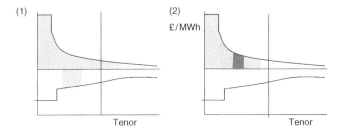

Figure A.4   Cost of incorrect estimation of return to service date after sudden failure. (1) hedge too long and sell back power on a round trip, (2) hedge too short and pay a higher offer price for the second hedge tranch

A.2.6   State space modelling of power plant

Medium term fail rates are heavily dependent on the access to spare equipment. For example, if a generator rotor is on site, then installation of a spare rotor can begin straight away. If a suitable rotor can be bought or borrowed from another plant (perhaps in another company), then the delay for a repair or replacement is much reduced, but the cost of the purchase/lease of equipment will be closely related to market conditions and may cost a multiple of the cost of a new item that is ordered a long time ahead. Plant owners holding spares calculate the economics in terms of the potential saving in their own financial shortfall on failure and on the rental/sale income. As a rule of thumb guideline, the cost premium for short term delivery of a spare item generally costs about half the amount of money it saves by early return to service.

Power plant reliability can be modelled using RAM (which stands for reliability, availability, maintainability) analysis. Using this model, the plant is viewed as a set of components, in series or parallel, each of which has a probability of failure. Whilst RAM analysis is rarely used for whole plant in actual operation, it is a useful technique in relation to major items for which spares can be held or accessed, such as generator transformers, and gas turbine blades.

Figure A.5 refers to a plant with three units. Two of the units have new rotors, one has an old one and there is on site a spare which, due to its age could only be used temporarily and would need to be replaced within six months (the delivery time for a new rotor). The decision is whether to buy a spare rotor now.

The figure shows a state space model with the three rotors in place and the spare rotor, which is replaced with another spare if the spare is used. The model shows the possible evolutions each six months according to the different possible failure permutations. As we can see, there are five possible states of the plant, not including the low probability state in which there is no spare, or in which there are insufficient rotors to run all units. By running a monthly resolution Monte Carlo simulation we can calculate the expected total cost with the temporary spare, or with the addition of a new spare.

In this simple model we have assumed no degradation in service. If we take degradation into account then the number of possible overall states is much larger since we need to include a range of component states from new to old.

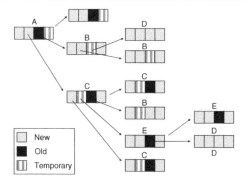

Figure A.5   State space configurations for a three unit station with one spare generator rotor (shown on the right of each representation). Each time interval represents different failure combinations, with 'no fail' being uppermost in each case

A.2.6.1   Markov and non-Markov fail rates

A plant fail rate profile is represented as Markov if the fail rate is dependent only on the current represented state of the plant, and not on history. The practical reality is that with sufficient information and modelling capability, we could always represent plant failure as Markov, but that these are commonly insufficient, and therefore the accumulated change on one aspect of plant status is not effectively captured and hence gives us a non-Markov process in our modelling regime.

In general, fail rates increase with component age. They also increase with time on load, after the initial fail rate of start. It is very common in failure modelling to use a 'bath tub curve' profile, in which fail rate falls after initial defects fail and then increases as condition worsens. Such a curve is shown in Figure A.6. However, the bath tub curve contains a number of hidden assumptions, and in commercial modelling in electricity markets, it is essential to use the correct profile for the particular circumstance.[4]

Figure A.6   Common fail rate profile of unit after scheduled start

A.2.6.2   Technical value at risk

We showed in Chapter 11 that it is best to model technical failure in conjunction with market price variation, and the Monte Carlo analysis was done with this in mind. It is then possible to construct a probability versus annual loss profile for individual units and fleets

---

[4] The classic paper on failure profiles is Nowlan and Heap (1978).

of units. From this we can construct our 'technical value at risk' (TVAR) in conjunction with our other value-at-risk measures. This influences: (i) our market hedging policy, since forward sales of power decrease first order market risk but increase worst case risk realised by simultaneous price rises and plant failures, (ii) our insurance policy in terms of premium and excess and (iii) our reliability and spares strategy in relation to our insurance policy and our cost of capital.

Technical value at risk depends on the definition – for example the degree to which changes in market prices and environmental limits are included (see Chapter 11). In addition it depends on the insurance position.

A.3   REACTIVE POWER

Suppose that the load voltage at a device is:[5]

$$v(t) = V_{max} \cos(\omega t + \delta)$$

Here ω nominally denotes the phase at the voltage source and δ the relative phase of the device and the source.

For a purely resistive load:

$$i_R(t) = I_{R,max} \cos(\omega t + \delta)$$

where;

$$I_{R,max} = V_{max}/R$$

Using a little trigonometry, we can see that the instantaneous power drawn by the load is:

$$P_R(t) = v(t)i_R(t) = \tfrac{1}{2}V_{max}I_{R,max}\left(1 + \cos(2(\omega t + \delta))\right) = VI_R\left(1 + \cos(2(\omega t + \delta))\right)$$

We can see that this has an average value of VI_R.

For a purely inductive load, the current lags the voltage:

$$i_L(t) = I_{L,max} \cos(\omega t + \delta - \tfrac{\pi}{2})$$

where:

$$I_{L,max} = V_{max}/X_L$$

and $X_L = \omega L$ is the inductive reactance.

The instantaneous power drawn is:

$$P_L(t) = v(t)i_L(t) = V_{max}I_{L,max}\cos(\omega t + \delta)\cos(\omega t + \delta - \tfrac{\pi}{2})$$
$$= \tfrac{1}{2}V_{max}I_{L,max}\cos(2(\omega t + \delta) - \tfrac{\pi}{2}) = VI_L\sin(2(\omega t + \delta))$$

This has an average value of zero but flows to and fro.

---

[5] The ensuing representation of reactive power is drawn from Glover and Sarma (2002).

For a purely capacitive load, the current leads the voltage:

$$i_L(t) = I_{C,max} \cos(\omega t + \delta + \tfrac{\pi}{2})$$

where:

$$I_{L,max} = V_{max}/X_C$$

and $X_C = 1/\omega C$ is the capacitive reactance.

The instantaneous power drawn is

$$P_L(t) = v(t) i_C(t) = V_{max} I_{C,max} \cos(\omega t + \delta) \cos(\omega t + \delta + \tfrac{\pi}{2})$$
$$= \tfrac{1}{2} V_{max} I_{C,max} \cos(2(\omega t + \delta) + \tfrac{\pi}{2}) = VI_C \sin(2(\omega t + \delta))$$

This has an average value of zero.

For a general load with all three components then:

$$i(t) = I_{max} \cos(\omega t + \beta)$$

Letting $I \cos(\delta - \beta) = I_R$ and $I \sin(\delta - \beta) = I_X$ then some tedious algebra gives us

$$P(t) = VI_R(1 + \cos(2(\omega t + \delta))) + VI_X \sin(2(\omega t + \delta))$$

We can see that the term on the left corresponds to the resistive part of the load and the term on the right to the inductive part of the load.

The average power delivered to the resistive part of the load is:

$$P = VI_R = VI \cos(\delta - \beta)$$

The term $\cos(\delta - \beta)$ is termed the power factor and $(\delta - \beta)$ is termed the power angle. We can see that the delivery of real power is at its maximum when $(\delta = \beta)$.

We can see that whilst reactive power does not directly cause efficiency losses, that the backwards and forwards flow of power due to the inductive load, compromises the ability to draw real power.

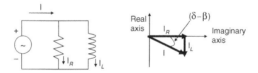

Figure A.7   Circuit and phasor diagram

In a simple sense, we can regard the need for reactive power to be caused by voltage and current deviating from their optimal phase difference and cause instability (as the current might 'catch up' the next voltage cycle). Reactive power requirement is created by inductive load and by line impedance,[6] and hence a long line requires more reactive power support than a short one. By increasing the generator voltage for the same power, the current is lower and thereby the reactive power consumption is reduced. That is all we currently really need to know for market design in DC mode, although AC load flow modelling is becoming increasingly important, especially for distribution networks.

---

[6] Transmission lines can have capacitance at low load and impedance at high load.

A.4   DIRECT CURRENT LOAD FLOW MODELLING

In Chapter 7 on location, we encountered some results that appear to be counter-intuitive. Here, we examine direct current load flow modelling in sufficient depth to understand three features of constrained networks:

(i)   The potential for the location marginal price to be higher than the most expensive plant on the system.
(ii) The potential for the location marginal price to be negative.
(iii) The potential for constraints in one system to create constraints in another system connected to it by an unconstrained line.

We begin by taking a relatively simple circuit with five nodes, as shown in Figure A.8.

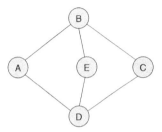

Figure A.8   Simple loop system

Each node has power (i.e. current) flowing into or out of the node from generation or demand. We need to establish the six unknown currents and can do this by applying Kirchhoff's Current Law (KCL) four times and Kirchhoff's Voltage Law (KVL) once.

The first line of Table A.1 is an application of KCL for the node A. So the equation is $I_a = I_{ab} - I_{da}$, where here the sign convention is positive for current flowing into the node and positive for current flowing in order of the letters in the subscript, so I_{ab} flows from a to b.

The fifth line is an application of KVL. So the equation is $0 = -I_{ab}R_{ab} - I_{da}R_{da} + I_{de}R_{de} + I_{eb}R_{eb}$.

Table A.1   Matrix used for solving currents in Figure A.8

	Iab	Ibc	Icd	Ida	Ide	Ieb
Ia	1	0	0	−1	0	0
Ib	−1	1	0	0	0	−1
Ic	0	−1	1	0	0	0
Id	0	0	−1	1	1	0
0	−Rab	0	0	−Rda	Rde	Reb
0	−Rab	−Rbc	−Rcd	−Rda	0	0

If we represent the column on the left by a column vector A, the table by a 6×6 matrix B, and the row vector of currents I_{ab} to I_{eb} by C, then we note from matrix algebra that $A = BC$ and hence $\overline{B}A = C$, where $\overline{B}$ is the inverse of B. This gives us our currents.

Constructing the inverse of a matrix is rather involved, but fortunately this operation, and the matrix multiplication is rendered simple by standard spreadsheet packages such as Microsoft Excel.

Now we can examine the situation in which we may wish to pay to dump load. The network below has two generators and two loads. The line DE is constrained to 25 MW. Generator A costs £60/MWh and generator B costs £30/MWh. Each line has a resistance of one Ohm (set very small so that there are no losses to account for).

Figure A.9 (1) shows the least cost dispatch. The load from B is limited by the constraint.

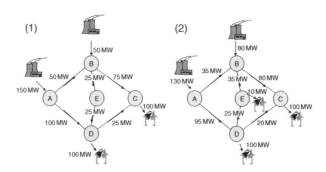

Figure A.9   Reduction of total cost to serve by dumping load at node E to relieve constraint on DE

Now suppose that there is a potential consumer at E, who offers to draw 10 MW of power for a negative price of £ 10/MWh. Figure A.10 (2) shows the least cost dispatch. The draw of power from E enables us to send out more power from B and reduce dispatch from A.

In Figure A.10 (1), our total cost for the 200 MW of load is 150 MW*£ 60/MWh + 50MW*£ 30MWh = £10,500.

In Figure A.10 (2), our total cost for the 200 MW of load is 130 MW*£ 60/MWh + 80 MW*£ 30MWh + 10 MW*£ 10/MWh = £10,300.

Hence it is economic in this situation to pay to dump load.

We also noted the mutual impact between constraint in systems. We can visualise this by the connection of two small systems, depicted ABC and DEF in Figure A.10. The currents are calculated in exactly the same way as before, solving for net currents in five nodes (KCL for A, B, C, D, E) and three circuits (KVL for BCEF, ABF, and CDE). Now suppose that line AB is constrained at less than 30 MW.

By decreasing generation at A by 1 MW and decreasing generation at F by 1 MW we reduce flow over AB by 0.1 MW. This alleviates the constraint on AB but if generation from F is more expensive than for A then this increases the cost of the system overall and the AEF system in particular.

Suppose instead that line BC is constrained to below 110 MW, the load that it would bear if the systems were not interconnected, and suppose also that for flexibility or security reasons we cannot solve the constraint by redispatch of units B and D. The same 1 MW redispatch of units A and F causes a 0.03 MW relief on the line. It is obvious from this that if the number of flexible units is small, then an extensive redispatch may be required to give substantive line relief.

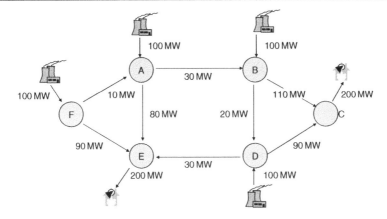

Figure A.10   Interconnection of two balanced systems, FAE and BCD

To model constraint in larger systems, we reduce the network by using Thevenin's theorem,[7] which states that if network A, with sources and resistances, is connected by two lines to network B, then we can model the effect of A on B as if it were a single source in series with a single resistance.[8]

We can easily calculate the cost of constraint from an increment in point to point flow. It is less obvious how we calculate the increase on constraint from 1 MW increase in generation/demand at a node without assignation of the associated demand/generation.

A.4.1   Calculating transmission charges from DC load flow

One method for calculating transmission network use of system charges is very similar to the calculation of constraint costs. The essential difference is that the marginal cost of generation is ignored and hence all generation capacity is included, whether dispatched or not, and the cost of physical line build is included.

The system is balanced by pro-rating the generation capacity to the expected peak demand with a security factor added. Using the solved current flows, the nodal transmission network use of system (TNUoS) price is calculated by calculating the cost of line reinforcement for a 1 MW increase in load at the node, maintaining the current level of constraint. If lines have very small resistance, then this is driven entirely by constraint relief.

If charging application is to be zonal, then the aggregate nodal charge is smeared (also called socialised) across all nodes in the zone so that all nodes in a zone pay the same price.

A.4.2   Calculation of losses

Losses can be handled in a simple system by treating them as load as shown in Figure A.11. Since the loss is not a fixed load but dependent on the current, then it can not be immediately

---

[7] See textbooks on electrical systems, e.g. Eaton and Cohen (1972).
[8] For further information, see, for example, Cathey and Nasar (1984).

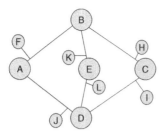

Figure A.11   Handling of line losses by treatment as load

solved in the method shown above. However, we can solve by trial and error, first by setting losses to zero, then by iteration, each time adjusting the loss to the current on the line times the resistance.

References

SOURCES

Ackroyd, P. (2001) *London – The Biography*. Vintage. Random House.

Ahlbom, A. Day, N. Feychting, M. *et al.* (2000) 'A Pooled Analysis of Magnetic Fields and Childhood Leukaemia'. *British Journal of Cancer*, **83**, 692–698.

Alexander (2001 ed.) *Mastering Risk. Volume 2: Applications*. Financial Times, Prentice Hall.

Anderson, E.J. and Xu, H. (2005) 'Supply Function Equilibrium in Electricity Spot Markets with Contracts and Price Caps'. *Journal of Optimization Theory and Applications*, **124(2)**, 257–283.

Arrow, K. (second edition 1963, first published 1951) *Social Choice and Individual Values*. Yale University Press.

Arrow, K. (1971) *Essays in the Theory of Risk Aversion*. Markham Publishing Company.

Ayala, U. and Millán, J. (2003) 'Colombia: Coping with Reform Crisis' in Millán, J. and von der Fehr.

Baldick, R., Grant, R. and Kahn, E. (2004) 'Theory and Application of Linear Supply Function Equilibrium in Electricity Markets'. *Journal of Regulatory Economics*, **25(2)**, 143–167.

Barle, S. and Cakici, N. (1998), 'Growing a Smiling Tree' from Broadie, M. and Glasserman, P. in *Hedging with Trees*. Risk Books, London.

Baumol. W.J. (2002) *The Free Market Innovation Machine*. Princeton University Press.

Baumol, W.J. and Bradford, D.F. (1970) 'Optimal Departures from Marginal Cost'. *American Economic Review*, **60**, 265–283.

Baxter, M. and Rennie, A. (1996) *Financial Calculus*. Cambridge University Press.

Berkeley (2001) 'Lawrence Berkeley Laboratory, Scoping Study on trends in the Economic Value of Electricity Reliability in the U.S. Economy'. Berkeley California. Lawrence Berkeley Laboratory, June.

Binmore, K. (1992) *Fun and Games – A Text on Game Theory*. D.C. Heath.

Black, F. (1976) 'The Pricing of Commodity Contracts'. *Journal of Financial Economics*, **3**, 167–179.

Black, F. and Scholes, M. (1973) 'The Pricing of Options and Corporate Liabilities' *Journal of Political Economy*, **81**, 637–659.

Black, F., Derman, E. and Toy, W. (1990) 'A One-Factor Model of Interest Rates and its Application to Treasury Bond Options' *Financial Analysts Journal*, January–February, 33–39.

Boiteux, M. (1949) 'La Tarification des Demandes en Point:Application de la Théorie de la Vente au Coût Marginal'. *Révue Génerale de l'Electricité*, **59** (August), 22–40.

Boiteux, M. (1956) 'Sur la Gestion des Monopolies Public Astrients à l'Equilibre Budgétaire'. *Econometrica*, **24** (January), 22–40, translated by W.J. Baumol as 'On the Management of Public Monopolies Subject to Budgetary Constraints'. *Journal of Economic Theory*, **3** (September), 219–240.

Bolle, F. (1992) 'Supply Function Equilibria and the Danger of Tacit Collusion: The Case of Spot Markets for Electricity'. *Energy Economics*, **14**, 94–102.

Bower, J. (2003) 'Why Ofgem?'. On Oxford Institute of Energy Studies website.

Brennan, M.J. and Schwartz, E.S. (1985) 'Evaluating Natural Resource Investments'. *Journal of Business*, **58(2)**, 135–157.

Brennan, T.J., Palmer, K. and Martinez, S.A. (2002) 'Alternating Currents – Electricity Markets and Public Policy'. Resources for the Future. Washington DC.

Briys, E. (1999) 'Pricing Mother Nature', in Geman.

Broadie, M. and Glasserman, P. (eds.) (1998) *Hedging with Trees*. Risk Books.

Brody, D.C., Syroka, J. and Zervos, M. (2002) 'Dynamical Pricing of Weather Derivatives'. *Quantitative Finance*, **2**, 189–198.

Brown, S.J. and Sibley, D.S. (1986. reprinted 2003) *The Theory of Public Utility Pricing*. Cambridge University Press.

Brzezniak, Z. and Zastawniak, T. (2000) *Basic Stochastic Processes*. Springer.

Buchanan, R.A. (1991) *The Power of the Machine*. Penguin.

Bunn, D.W. (ed.) (2004) *Modelling Prices in Competitive Electricity Markets*. Wiley Finance, John Wiley and Sons, Ltd.

Burke, J. (1985) *The Day the Universe Changed*. Back Bay Books. Little, Brown and Company, USA.

CAISO (2000) 'Report on California Energy Market Issues and Performance: May–June 2000 Special report' on website.

California ISO (2000) 'Report on California Energy Market Issues and Performance: May–June 2000. Special Report'. by the Department of Market Analysis. California Independent System Operator.

Carrière, J. (1996) 'Valuation of Early Exercise of Options using Simulations and Nonparametric Regression'. *Insurance, Mathematics and Economics*, **19**, 12–30.

Carson, R. (first published 1962, reprinted 2000) 'Silent Spring'. Penguin.

Casti, J.L. (1996) *Five Golden Rules – Great Theories of 20th Century Mathematics – and Why They Matter*. John Wiley & Sons, Inc.

Cathey, J.J. and Nasar, S.A. (second edition 1984) *Basic Electrical Engineering*. Schaum's Outline Series. McGraw Hill.

Caves, R.E. and Jonson, H.G. (eds.) (1968) *Readings in International Economics*. Allen and Unwin.

Çengel, Y.A, and Boles, M.A. (third edition 1998) *Thermodynamics – An Engineering Approach*. McGraw-Hill.

CERA (2004) 'European Power Country Profiles'. On website.

Chao, Hung-po, and Huntington, H.G. (1998) *Designing Competitive Electricity Markets*. Kluwer Academic Publishers.

Chesshire, J. (1996) 'UK Electricity Supply Under Public Ownership'. from 'the British Electricity Experiment', Surrey.

CIGRE (2001) 'Review of Industry Structure and Reform Status'. Study Committee 37 – Power System Planning and Development. Working Group 37.32.

Clewlow, L. and Strickland, C. (2000) *Energy Derivatives: Pricing and Risk Management*. Lacima Publications.

Coase, R.H. (1946) 'The Marginal Cost Controversy'. *Economica*, **13**, 169–189.

Coase, R.H. (1974) 'The Lighthouse in Economics'. *Journal of Law of Economics*, **17(2)**, 357–376.

Cochrane, J.H (2001) *Asset Pricing*. Princeton University Press.

Codognet, M.-K., Glachant, J.-M., Lévêque, F. and Plagnet, M.-A. (2002) 'Mergers and Acquisitions in the European Electricity Sector: Cases and Patterns'. On CERNA website.

Copeland, B.R. and Scott Taylor, M. (2003) *Trade and the Environment – Theory and Evidence*. Princeton University Press.

Courtadon, G. (1982). 'The Pricing of Options on Default Free Bonds'. *Journal of Financial and Quantitative Analysis*, **17**, 75–100.

Cox, J.C., Ingersoll, J.E. and Ross, S.A. (1985) 'A Theory of Term Structure of Interest Rates'. *Econometrica*, **53**, 385–407.

Craig, J.R, Vaughan, D.J and Skinner, B.J (1996) *Resources of the Herat: Origin, Use and Environmental Impact*. Upper Saddle River. NJ, Prentice Hall.

Crew, M.A. and Kleindorfer, P.R. (1992) *The Economics of the Postal Service*. Kluwer Academic Publishers.

Daly, H.E. (1997) 'Uneconomic growth; From Empty World to Full-World Economics'. Rice University. De-Lange Woodlands Conference Sustainable Development. Managing the Transition. Houston Texas, Columbia University Press Conference Volume.

Dasgupta, P.S. and Heal, G.M. (1974) 'The Optimal Depletion of Exhaustible Resources'. *Review of Economic Studies, Symposium on the Economics of Exhaustible Resources*, 3–28.

Dasgupta, P.S. and Heal, G.M. (1979) Economic Theory and Exhaustible Resources. Cambridge University Press.

Day, C.J. and Bunn, D.W. (2001) 'Divestiture of Generation Assets in the Electricity Pool of England and Wales: A Computational Approach to Analyzing Market Power'. *Journal of Electricity Economics*, **19(2)**, 123–141.

Debreu, G. (1970) 'Economies with a Finite Set of Equilibria'. *Econometrica*, **38(3)**, 387–392.

Dixit, A.K. and Norman, V. (1980. reprinted 2002) *Theory of International Trade – a Dual, General Equilibrium Approach*. Cambridge University Press.

Draper, G., Kroll, V.T. and Swanson, J. (2005) 'Childhood cancer in relation to distance from high voltage power lines in England and Wales: a case control study'. *British Medical Journal*, **75**, 1505–1521.

Duan, J.-C. (2001) 'Cointegration: the New Risk Relationship' in Alexander.

Eaton, J.R. and Cohen, E. (1972) *Electric Power Transmission Systems*. Prentice Hall.

ECOTEC (1992) 'A Cost Benefit Analysis of Reduced Acid Deposition: A Revised Approach for Evaluating Buildings and Building Materials' ECOTEC Birmingham.

El Agraa, A.M. (ed.) (third edition 1990) *The Economics of the European Community*. Philip Allan.

Engle, R.F. and Granger, C.W.J. (1987) 'Cointegration and error correction: representation, estimation and testing'. *Econometrica*, **55**, 251–276.

Ensor, R.C.K. (1936) *England 1870–1914 – The Oxford History of England*. Oxford University Press.

Eydeland, A. and Wolniec, K. (2002) 'Operating and Risk Managing Power Plants' in Ronn.

Eydeland, A. and Wolniec, K. (2003) *Energy and Power Risk Management: New Developments in Modeling, Pricing and Hedging*. Wiley Finance, John Wiley & Sons, Inc.

Fews, A.P., Henshaw, D.I., Keitch, P.A., Close J.J., and Wilding, R.J. (1999) 'Increased exposure to pollutant aerosols under high voltage power lines'. *International Journal of Radiation Biology*, **75**, 1505–1521.

Fitzgibbons, A. (1995) *Adam Smith's System of Liberty, Wealth and Virtue – The Moral and Political Foundation of The Wealth of Nations*. Clarendon Press.

Foley, G. (1976) *The Energy Question*. Penguin.

Foljanty-Jost, G. (1988) 'Emissionabgage in Japan – Ruckblick auf ein unweltpolitisches Modell'. Berlin. Forschtungstelle fur Umweltpolitik.

Foster, J. (1997) *Valuing Nature? – Economics, Ethics and the Environment*. Routledge.

Fox, L. (2002) *Enron – The rise and fall*. John Wiley and Sons, Inc.

Galbraith, J.K. (first published 1973, 1974 edition) *Economics and the Public Purpose*. André Deutsch, Thetford, Norfolk.

Garman, M. and Kohlhagen, S. (1983) 'Foreign Currency Option Values'. *Journal of International Money and Finance*, **2** (December), 231–237.

Geman, H. (1999) *Insurance and Weather Derivatives*. Risk Books, Risk Publications.

Geman, H. (2005) *Commodities and Commodity Derivatives*. Wiley Finance, John Wiley and Sons, Ltd.

Glover, J.D. and Sarma, M.S. (2002 – third edition) *Power System Analysis and Design*. Brooks/Cole.

Granger, C. (1986) 'Developments in the Study of Cointegrated Variables' *Oxford Bulletin of Economics and Statistics*, **3**, 213–228.

Green, R.J. (1996) 'Increasing Competition in the British Electricity Spot Market'. *The Journal of Industrial Economics* **XLIV**, 2.

Green, R.J. and Newbery, D.M. (1992) 'Competition in the British Electricity Spot Market'. *Journal of Political Economy*, **100(5)**, 929–953.

Grossman, G.M. and Krueger, A.B. (1993) 'Environmental Impacts of a North American Free Trade Agreement' in Garber, P. (ed.) *The Mexico-US Free Trade Agreement*. Cambridge MIT Press.

Hall, P.A. (ed.) (1989) *The Political Power of Economic Ideas*. Princeton University Press.

Hall, P. (1998) *Cities in Civilisation*. Weidenfield and Nicholson.

Harris, C. (2002) 'Real Options for Real Assets – A No Arbitrage Approach', in Ronn.

Harris, C. (2004) 'Forecasting Higher Moments of the Power Price Using Medium Term Equilibrium Economics and the Value of Security of Supply', in Bunn.

Harris, C. (2005) 'The Structure of Metal Markets and Metal Prices', in Geman.

Harsanyi, J.C. and Selten, R. (1988) *A General Theory of Equilibrium Selection in Games*. MIT Press.

Haug, E.G. (1998) *The Complete Guide to Option Pricing Formulas*. McGraw-Hill.

Hawken, P., Lovins, A.B. and Lovins, L.H. (1999) *Natural Capitalism*. Earthscan Publications.

Hayek, F. (1945). *The Road to Serfdom*. Routledge Classics (2001).

Heath, D., Jarrow, R. and Morton, A. (1992) 'Bond Pricing and the Term Structure of Interest Rates: A New Methodology'. *Econometrica*, **60**, 77–105.

Helm, D. (2003) *Energy, the State, and the Market – British Energy Policy since 1979*. Oxford University Press.

Helm, D. and Jenkinson, T. (eds) (1998) *Competition in Regulated Industries*. Oxford University Press.

Henney, A. (1994) 'A Study of the Privatisation of the Electricity Supply Industry in England and Wales'. London, EEE Ltd.

HERA (2002) Hemispheric Energy Regulatory Assistance Project of the IIE 'Best Practices Guide – Electricity Regulation in Latin America' on IIE website.

Herodotus. *Histories* (c.425 BCE) 3.38. Translation by Waterfield, R., Oxford University Press.

Hicks, J.R. (1939) *Value and Capital*. Oxford University Press.

Hidefumi, I. (1990) 'Economic Incentives as a Means of Environmental Policy: Interactive Effects of Standards and Economic Incentives in Air Pollution Control in Japan', pp. 57–91 in Binswanger, H.-C. and Janicke, M. *Environmental Charges*, Berlin: Forschungsstelle fur Umweltpolitik.

Hirshleifer, J. (second edition 1980) '*Price Theory and Applications*'. Prentice Hall.

Hodgson (1997) 'Economics, Environmental Policy and the Transcendence of Utilitarianism', in Foster.

Hogan, W. (1995) 'A Wholesale Pool Spot Market Must be Administered by the Independent System operator: Avoiding the Separation Fallacy'. *The Electricity Journal*, December, 26–37.

Hogan, W. (2005) 'Electricity Market Restructuring: Successful Market Design' Electricity Committee NARUC Summer Meetings. On Hogan website.

Hogwood, B.W. and Gunn, L.A. (1984) *Policy analysis for the Real World*. Oxford University Press.

Hotelling, H. (1931) 'The Economics of Exhaustible Resources'. *Journal of Political Economy* **39**, April, 137–175.

Hughes, T.P. (1993 edition, first published 1983) *Networks of Power*. Johns Hopkins.

Hughston, L. (ed.) (1996) *Vasicek and Beyond: Approaches to Building and Applying Interest Rate Models*. Risk Books, London.

Hull, J.C. (Third edition 1997) *Option, Futures and Other Derivatives*. Prentice-Hall.

Hull, J. and White, A. (1993) 'Single Factor Interest Rate Models and the Valuation of Interest Rate Derivative securities'. *Journal of Financial and Quantitative Analysis*, **28**, 235–254. Reprinted in *Hull-White on Derivatives* (1996) Risk Publications.

Hunt, S. (2002) *Making Competition Work in Electricity* Wiley Finance. John Wiley & Sons, Ltd.

Hunt, S. and Shuttleworth, G. (1996, reprinted 2001) *Competition and Choice in Electricity*. John Wiley & Sons, Ltd.

Hyman, L.S. (Eighth edition 2005) 'America's Electric Utilities: Past, Present and Future'. Public Utilities Reports, Inc. Vienna, Virginia.

IEA International Energy Agency (1994) 'Electricity Supply Industry – Structure, Ownership and Regulation in OECD countries'.

IEA International Energy Agency (2005) 'Key World Energy Statistics'. On website.

IEA International Energy Agency (June 2005) 'Monthly Electricity Survey'. On website.

IPPC (International Panel on Climate Change) (2001). Working Group 1 – The Scientific Basis. 1. The Climate System: an Overview. On website.

ISO New England (2005) ISO New England Manual for Financial Transmission Rights. Manual M-06. Revision 5. August. On website.

Jäckel, P. (2002) *Monte Carlo Methods in Finance*. John Wiley & Sons, Ltd.

Jäckel, P. and Rebonato, R. (1999/2000) 'The Most General Methodology for Creating a Valid Correlation Matrix for Risk Management and Option Pricing Purposes'. *Journal of Risk*, **2(2)**, Winter.

Jamasb, T. (2002) 'Reform and Regulation of the Electricity Sectors in Developing Countries'. DAE working paper WP 0226, CMI working paper 08.

Jamasb, T., Mota, R., Newbery, D. and Pollit, M. (2004) 'Electricity Sector Reform in Developing Countries: A Survey of Empirical Evidence on Determinants and Performance'. Cambridge Working Papers in Economics CWPE 0439, CME working paper 47.

Jamasb, T., Newbery, D. and Pollit, M. (2004) 'Core Indicators for Determinants and Performance of Electricity Sector in Developing Countries'. Cambridge Working Papers in Economics CWPE 0438, CME working paper 46.

Jehl, F. (1937) *Menlo Park Reminiscences, Volume One*. Edison Institute.

JESS (2003) International Blackouts in August & September 2003. On website.

Jones, C.W. (2004) *EU Energy Law Volume I*. Claeys and Casteels.

Joskow (2003) 'The Difficult Transition to Competitive Electricity Markets in the U.S.' from the conference 'Electricity Deregulation: Where From Here?' at the Bush Presidential Conference Center. Texas A&M University, April 4, 2003. On Joskow website at MIT.

Kahn, A. *The Economics of Regulation* (second edition 1988. First Published 1970–1971). John Wiley and Sons, Inc, New York.

Kahn, R. (1989 First written in 1930) *The Economics of the Short Period*. Macmillan.

Kahneman, D. and Tversky, A. (1979) 'Prospect Theory: An Analysis of Decision under Risk'. *Econometrica*, **47**, March, 263–291.

Kirkwood, R.C. and Longley, A.J. (1995) *Clean Technology and the Environment*. Blackie Academia and Professional.

Klemperer, P.D. and Meyer, M.A. (1989) 'Supply Function Equilibria in Oligopoly under Uncertainty'. *Econometrica*, **57(6)**, 1243–1277.

Krutilla (1967) 'Conservation Reconsidered'. *American Economic Review*, **57**, 777–786.

Kuhn, T.S. (Third edition 1962) *The Structure of Scientific Revolutions*. University of Chicago Press.

Landes, D.S. (1965) 'Technological Change and Development in Western Europe, 1750–1914' from *The Cambridge Economic History of Europe*. Cambridge University Press.

Lave, L.B and Freeburg, L.C. (1973) 'Health Effects of Electricity Generation from Coal, Oil and Nuclear Fuels'. *Nuclear Safety*, **14** (Sep/Oct).

Lenin, V.I. (1920) 'Our Foreign and Domestic Position and the Tasks of the Party'. *Works*, vol. 31, p. 419.

Lintner, J. (1965) 'The Valuation of Risk Assets and the Selection of Risky Investments in Stock Portfolios and Capital Budgets'. *Review of Economics and Statistics*, **47** (February), 13–37.

Littlechild, S. (2005 I) 'Smaller Suppliers in The UK Domestic Electricity Market: Experience, Concerns and Policy Recommendations'. University of Cambridge Electricity Policy Research Group. On CMI website.

Littlechild, S. (2005 II) 'Beyond Regulation' IEA/LBS Beesley Lectures on Regulation series XV. Institute of Economic Affairs. On CMI website.

Loi Lei Lai (ed.) (2001) *Power System Restructuring and Deregulation – Trading, Performance and Information Technology*. John Wiley & Sons, Ltd.

Lomborg, B. (1998) *The Skeptical Environmentalist – measuring the real state of the world*. Cambridge University Press.

Lomborg, B. (English Edition 2001. First written in 1998 in Danish). *The Skeptical Environmentalist – Measuring the Real State of the World*. Cambridge University Press.

London, J. (2005) *Modelling Derivatives in C++*. Wiley Finance., John Wiley & Sons, Inc.

Longstaff, F. and Schwartz, E. (2001) 'Valuing American Options by Simulation – A least squares approach'. *Review of Financial Studies*, **14**, 113–147.

Male, D.C. and Maddock, B.J. (1990) 'Power-Frequency Magnetic Field: Measurement and Exposure Assessment', pp. 36–105 CIGRE Session. Paris.

Margrabe, W. (1978) 'The Value of an Option to Exchange One Asset for Another'. *Journal of Finance*, **33**, 177–196.

Marshall, A. (eighth Edition. first published 1890) *Principles of Economics*. Macmillan.

McBride, M.L. *et al.* (1999) 'Power-Frequency Electric and Magnetic Fields and Risk of Childhood Leukaemia in Canada'. *American Journal of Epidemiology*, **149**, 831–842.

McGowan, F. (1990) *EC Energy Policy*, in El Agraa.

McNeil, A.J. (1999) 'Extreme value theory for risk managers' in *Internal Modelling and CAD II: Qualifying and Quantifying Risk Within a Financial Institution*. RISK Books.

McQuail, D. and Windahl, S. (1993) *Communication Models for the Study of Mass Communications*. Longman.

Millán, J. and von der Fer, N.-H.M. (eds 2003) *Keeping the Lights On – Power Sector Reform in Latin America*. Published by Inter.-American Development Bank. Distributed by Johns Hopkins University Press.

Munson, R. (1985) *The Power Makers*. Rodale Press.

National Radiological Protection Board. (2004) 'Particle deposition in the vicinity of power lines and possible effects on health' Documents of the NRPB **15(1)**.

Nell, J.E. (1984) *Free Market Conservatism. A Critique of Theory and Practice*. George Allen and Unwin.

Newbery, D.M. (1998) *The Regulator's View of the English Electricity Pool*. Utilities Policy, **7(3)**, 129–141.

Newbery D.M. (1999) *Privatization, Restructuring and Regulation of Network Utilities*. MIT Press.

Newbery, D.M. and Stiglitz, J.E. (1981) *The Theory of Commodity Price Stabilization: A Study in the Economics of Risk*. Oxford University Press.

Nilsson, S. (1992) 'Economic Impacts of Forest Decline Caused by Air Pollutants in Europe', In 'The Economic Impact of Air Pollution in Timber Markets'. US Department of Agricultura, Asheville, North Carolina.

Niskanen (1971) *Bureaucracy and Representative Government*. Aldine-Atherton.

Nowlan, F.S. and Heap, H.F. (1978) 'Reliability-Centred Maintenance'. United Airlines/Office of the Assistant Secretary of Defense. Reproduced by National Technical Information Service.

Ofgem (2005) '2004/5 Electricity Distribution Quality of Service Report'. On website.

O'Neill, J. (1997) 'Value Pluralism, Incommensurability and Institutions', in Foster, J. (ed.) Valuing Nature, Routeledge.

Ormerod, P. (1994) *The Death of Economics*. Faber and Faber.

Parsons (1995) *Public Policy*. Edward Elgar.

Pearce, D.W. (1995) 'The Economics of Pollution', in Kirkwood and Longley.

Pearce, D.W., Bann, C. and Georgiou, S. (1992) *The Social Cost of Fuel Cycles*. HMSO.

Pigou, A.C. (third edition 1932, reprinted 2002) *The Economics of Welfare*. Transaction Publishers.

Platt, H.L. (1991) *The Electric City: Energy and the Growth of the Chicago Area*. The University of Chicago Press.

Popper (First published 1945, Reprinted 2003) *The Open Society and its Enemies*. Routledge Classics.

Ragwitz, M. and Huber, C. (2004 or 2005) 'Feed-In Systems in Germany and Spain – a Comparison'. Energy Economics Group. http://www.erneuerbare-energien.de/files/english/renewable_energy/downloads/application/pdf/langfassung_einspeisesysteme_en.pdf.

Ramsey, F.P. (1927) 'A Contribution to the Theory of Taxation'. *Economic Journal*, **37**, 46–61.

Rebonato, R. (Second edition 1998) *Interest Rate Option Models*, John Wiley & Sons, Ltd.

Rebonato, R, (Second edition 2004) *Volatility and Correlation – The Perfect Hedger and the Fox.* John Wiley & Sons, Ltd.

Regulatory Assistance Project (2000) 'Best Practices Guide: Implementing Power Sector Reform'. Prepared for USAID and others. Implemented by IEE and prepared by the Regulatory Assistance Project.

Roll, E. (Fifth edition 1992. first published 1938) *A history of economic thought.* Faber and Faber.

Ronn, E.I. (ed.) (2002) *Real Options and Energy Management.* Risk Books, London.

Rufín, C. (2003) *The Political Economy of Institutional Change in the Electricity Supply Industry.* Edward Elgar.

Rustebakke, H.M. *et al.* (Fourth edition 1983) *Electric Utility Systems Practice.* New York, John Wiley & Sons, Inc.

Rybczynski, T.M. (1955) 'Factor Endowments and Relative Commodity Prices', reprinted in Caves and Johnson (1968).

Santa-Clara, P. and Sornette, D. (1999. First version 1997) 'The Dynamics of the Forward Interest Rate Curve with Stochastic String Shocks'. Anderson Graduate School of Management, and Institute of Geophysics and Planetary Physics, and Department of Earth and Space Sciences, University of California. Finance Working Paper sponsored by Capital Management Sciences.

Savchenko, V.K. (1995) 'The Ecology of the Chernobyl Catastrophe: Scientific Outlines of an International Programme of Collaborative Research'. Man and the Biosphere Series. Volume 16. UNESCO, Paris, and Parthenon Publishing, Carnforth.

Scammell, W.M. (1975) *International Monetary Policy – Bretton Woods and After.* Macmillan Press.

Schama, S. (1995) *Landscape and Memory.* Vintage Books. Random House.

Schneider, S.H. (ed.) (1993) *Scientists on Gaia.* MIT Press.

Schumacher, E.E. (Abacus edition 1974. First published 1973) *Small is Beautiful. A study of economics as if people mattered.*

Schumpeter (1914) 'Das Wissenschaftliche Lebenswerk Eugen von Böhm-Bawerks'. *Zeitschrift fur Volkwirtschaft Sozialpolitik und Verwaltung.* Vol. xxiii, pp. 454–528. Translated by Herbert Zassenhaus. Reprinted in Schumpeter 1997.

Schumpeter (1997) *Ten Great Economists – From Marx to Keynes.* Routledge.

Sen, A. (1982, second printing 1998) *Choice, Welfare and Measurement.* Harvard University Press.

Sharpe, W.F. (1964) 'Capital Asset Prices: A Theory of Market Equilibrium under Conditions of Risk'. *Journal of Finance,* **19** (September), 425–442.

Sheppard, E. and Barnes, T.J. (1990) *The Capitalist Space Economy.* Unwin Hyman.

Shuttleworth, G., Falk, J., Meehan, E. Rosenzweig, M. and Fraser, H. (2002) 'Electricity Markets and Capacity Obligations'. On NERA website.

Shuttleworth, G. and Gammons, S. (2004) 'Review of GB-Wide Transmission Pricing'. On NERA website.

Skou Andersen, M. (1994) *Governance by Green Taxes.* Manchester University Press.

Smith, A. (1776, Reprinted in 1986) *The Wealth of Nations.* Penguin Classics.

Sparla, T. (2001) 'Strategic Real Options with the German Power Market in View'. PhD thesis. Dortmund University.

Sraffa, P. (1972, First published 1960) *The Production of Commodities by Means of Commodities.* Cambridge University Press.

Stirling, A. (1997) 'Multi-Criteria Mapping'. From Foster (ed.) (1997).

Stoft, S. (2002) *Power System Economics – Designing Markets for Electricity.* IEEE – Wiley Interscience, John Wiley & Sons, Inc.

Stolper, W. and Samuelson, P.A. (1941) 'Protection and Real Wages'. *Review of Economics Studies,* **9**(1), 58–83.

Sustman, J. and Brown VI, J.P.W 'The hidden cost of LMP: Marginal Losses'. New Energy Associates. Presented at Power-Gen 2004.

Sweeney, J.L. (2002) *The California Electricity Crisis.* Hoover Press.

Thatcher, M. (1993) *The Downing Street Years.* Harper Collins.

Tipler, F. (1995, 1996 edition) *The Physics of Immortality.* Pan.

Tirole, J. (1988, Seventh printing 1994) *Industrial Economics.* MIT Press.

Treynor, J. (1999) 'Towards a Theory of Market Value of Risky Assets'. In Hughston.

Tsuru, S. and Weidner, H. (1985) *Ein modell fur uns: Die Ervolger der japanischen Unweltpolitik.* Köln, Kiepenheuer and Witsch.

Twidell, J.W. (1995) 'Clean Energy Supply and Use' in Kirkwood and Longley.

Uhlenbeck, G.E. and Ornstein, L.S. (1930) 'On the Theory of Brownian Motion'. *Physical Review,* **36**, 823–841.

Varian, H.R. (1975) 'A Third Remark on the Number of Equilibria in an Economy'. *Econometrica,* **43**(5/6), 985–986.

Varian, H. R. (Sixth edition 2003) *Intermediate Microeconomics.* Norton.

Vasicek, O.A. (1998) 'A series expansion for the bivariate normal integral'. *Journal of Computational Finance.* Summer.

Vogelsgang, I. (2002) 'Incentive Regulation and Competition in Public Utility Markets: A 20-Year Perspective'. *Journal of Regulatory Economics*, **22(1)**, 5–27.

Walsh, V.C. (1970) *Introduction to Contemporary Microeconomics*. McGraw-Hill.

Watts. G. (2005) 'Scientific Commentary: Power to Confuse'. *British Medical Journal*. June, 1293.

WEC (1998) 'The Benefits and Deficiencies of Energy Sector Liberalisation – Electricity'.

WEC (2001) 'Electricity Market Design and Creation in Asia Pacific', London.

WEC (2005) 'WEC Statement 2005 – Delivering Sustainability: Challenges and Opportunities for the Energy Industry'.

Weedy, B.M. and Cory, B.J. (fourth edition 2001) 'Electric Power Systems' John Wiley & Sons, Ltd.

Weidner, H. and Tsuru, S. (eds 1988) *Environmental Policy in Japan*. Sigma.

Weir Committee (1925) 'Report of the committee to review the National Problem of the Supply of Electricity'. HMSO.

Weisbrod, B.A. (1964) 'Collective-Consumption Services of Individual-Consumption Goods' *Quarterly Journal of Economics*, **78**, 471–477.

Wertheimer, N. and Leeper, E. (1979) 'Electrical wiring configurations and childhood cancer'. *American Journal of Epidemiology*, **109(3)**, 273–284.

Wilmott, P., Howison, S. and Dewynne, J. (third edition 1997) *The Mathematics of Financial Derivatives*. Cambridge University Press.

Wilson, A.J. (1994) *The Living Rock*. Woodhead.

Wood, A.J. and Wollenberg, B.F. (1996) *Power Generation Operation and Control*. Wiley Interscience. John Wiley & Sons, Inc.

SELECTION OF USEFUL WEBSITES AND REFERENCES FROM THE TEXT

Instititutions

International

APEx The Association of Power Exchanges www.theapex.org This website contains a member list and a number of useful links.

CIGRE Conseil Internationale des Grands Réseaux Électriques (International Council on Large Electric Systems) www.cigre.org.

IAEA – International Atomic Energy Authority www.iaea.org.

IEA – International Energy Agency www.iea.org.

IPCC – Intergovernmental Panel on Climate Change www.ipcc.ch.

ITDG Intermediate Technology Development Group. Now renamed Practical Action. www.itdg.org.

Sustainable Asset Management www.sam-group.com.

TEPI – Towards Environmental Pressure Indicators www.e-m-a-i-l.nu/tepi/.

Transparency International www.transparency.org.

UCTE Union for the Coordination of the Transmission of Electricity www.ucte.org.

United Nations Statistics Division unstats.un.org/unsd/.

United Nations Prototype Carbon Fund.

WANO – World Association of Nuclear Operators www.wano.org.uk.

WEC – World Energy Council www.worldenergy.org.

World Nuclear Association www.world-nuclear.org.

European Region

CEER – Council of European Energy Regulators www.ceer-eu.org.

CERNA Centre d'économie industrielle. Ecole Nationale Supérieure des Mines de Paris www.cerna.ensmp.fr.

Cogen Europe – The European Association for the Promotion of Cogeneration www.cogen.org.

ERRA – Energy Regulators Regional Association www.erranet.org (this website contains links to the individual regulators).

ETSO – European Transmission System Operators www.etso-net.org.

Eurelectric – Union of the Electricity Industry www.eurelectric.org.

EuroPEX – Association of European Power Exchanges (APX Netherlands, Borzen Slovenia, OMEL Spain, EEX Germany, GME Italy, Powernext France, Nord Pool Scandinavia) EXAA, Belpex www.europex.org.

Eurostat – Statistical Office of the European Union www. europa.eu.int/comm/eurostat.
EWEA – European Wind Energy Association www.ewea.org.
Externe – A research project of the European Commission www.externe.info.
TEPI – Towards Environmental Pressure Indicators.
UCTE Union for the Co-ordination of the Transmission of Electricity www.ucte.org (this website contains links to transmission system operators in member countries).

United States

CAEM – Center for the Advancement of Energy Markets www.caem.org.
CAISO – California Independent System Operator www.caiso.com.
CIA factbook www.cia.gov/cia/publications/factbook.
Congressional Budget Office www.cbo.gov.
Dow Jones Sustainability Indexes www.sustainability-indexes.com.
EERE Energy Efficiency and Renewable Energy (US Department of Energy) www.energy.eere.gov.
EIA US Energy Information Administration www.eia.doe.gov.
FERC Federal Electricity Regulatory Commission. www.ferc.gov.
IIE Institute of International Education (the Energy Group therin) www.iie.org.
MAAC – Mid Atlantic Area Council (of NERC) www.maac-rc.org.
National Hydrogen Association www.hydrogenus.com.
NERC North American Electric Reliability Council www.nerc.com.
PJM Pennsylvania New Jersey Maryland Interconnection www.pjm.com.
PSERC Power Systems Engineering Research Center www.pserc.wisc.edu.
Regulatory Assistance Project www.rapmaine.com.
USAID U.S. Agency for International Development www.info.usaid.gov.

Great Britain

AEP – Association of Electricity Producers www.aepuk.com.
BBC British Broadcasting Corporation www.bbc.co.uk.
BOPCRIS British Official Publications Collaborative Reader Information Service www.bopcris.ac.uk.
Business in the Community www.bitc.org.uk.
Carbon Trust www.thecarbontrust.co.uk.
Elexon (the GB market operator) www.elexon.co.uk.
Energywatch (consumer protection body) www.energywatch.org.uk.
ERA – Energy Retail Association www.energy-retail.org.uk.
ENA – Energy Networks Association www.energynetworks.org.
FTSE4good www.ftse.com/ftse4good.
Fuel Poverty Advisory Group www.defra.gov.uk/environment/energy/fuelpov/fpag.
Health Protection Agency www.hpa.org.uk.
HSE – Health and Safety Executive www.hse.gov.uk.
Institute of Business Ethics www.ibe.org.uk.
JESS – Department of Trade and Industry Joint Energy Security of Supply Working Group www.dti.gov.uk/energy/jess/index.
National Grid (the GB system operator) www.nationalgrid.com/uk.
Office of National Statistics www.statistics.gov.uk.
Ofgem – (The regulator for gas and power) www.ofgem.gov.uk.

Other countries

NEMMCO National Electricity Market Management Company www.nemmco.com.au.

Academic and related information

University of Cambridge Electricity Policy Research Group www.electricitypolicy.org.
CMI (Cambridge-MIT Institute, Cambridge University Department of Applied Economics UK and Massachusetts Institute of Technology Center for Energy and Environmental Policy Research) www.cambridge-mit.org.

Harvard Electricity Policy Group www.ksg.harvard.edu/hepg/.
London Business School www.london.edu/facultyresearch6243.
Oxford Institute for Energy Studies www.oxfordenergy.org.
Paul Joskow http://econ.www.mit.edu/faculty/pjoskow/papers.
William Hogan (JFK School of Government) www.whogan.com.

Consulting and other organisations referred to in text

CERA Cambridge Energy Research Associates www.cera.com.
Lacima (Clewlow and Strickland) www.lacimagroup.com.
Moody's|KMV www.moodyskmv.com.
NERA National Economic Research Associates www.nera.com.
Natural Capital (Hawken, Lovins and Lovins) info@naturalcapital.org.
New Energy Associates www.newenergyassoc.com.
OXERA www.oxera.com.
PSI Energy Economics Group eem.web.psi.ch/Teaching/Teaching.

Index

Index compiled by Indexing Specialists (UK) Ltd

Printed and bound by CPI Group (UK) Ltd, Croydon, CR0 4YY

23/04/2025

14660969-0004